BLACK HISTORY: A REAPPRAISAL

BLACK HISTORY
A Reappraisal

Edited with Commentary
by Melvin Drimmer

Doubleday & Company, Inc.
Garden City, New York
1968

Grateful acknowledgment is made for the use of the following material:
Lines from "Harlem" from *The Panther and the Lash* by Langston
Hughes. Copyright © 1967 by Langston Hughes. Reprinted by permission
of Alfred A. Knopf, Inc.

"Of Our Spiritual Strivings" from *The Souls of Black Folk* by W. E. B.
Du Bois. Published by Fawcett Publications, Inc.

African History by Philip D. Curtin. Reprinted by permission of the author
and the Service Center for Teachers of History.

"Kingdoms of the Old Sudan" from *The Lost Cities of Africa* by Basil
Davidson. Copyright © 1959 by Basil Davidson. Reprinted by permission of
Atlantic-Little, Brown and Company.

"The Negro in the Americas" from *Slave and Citizen* by Frank Tannenbaum. Copyright 1946 by Alfred A. Knopf, Inc. Reprinted by permission of
Alfred A. Knopf, Inc.

"Slavery and the Genesis of American Race Prejudice" by Carl Degler
from *Comparative Studies in Society and History*, Volume II (October
1959). Reprinted by permission of the Society for the Comparative Study of
Society and History.

"Was Slavery Dying Before the Cotton Gin?" by Melvin Drimmer.
Published by permission of the author.

"Slavery and the Founding Fathers" by Staughton Lynd. Published by
permission of the author.

"Evacuation with the British" from *The Negro in the American Revolution* by Benjamin Quarles. Reprinted by permission of The University of
North Carolina Press.

"The Historian and Southern Negro Slavery" by Kenneth M. Stampp from
the *American Historical Review*, Volume LVII (April 1952). Reprinted by
permission of the author and the American Historical Association.

"Motherhood in Bondage" from *The Negro Family in the United States*
by E. Franklin Frazier. Copyright © 1966 by The University of Chicago.
Reprinted by permission of The University of Chicago Press.

"Slavery and Personality" from *Slavery: A Problem in American In-
stitutional and Intellectual Life* by Stanley Elkins. Copyright © 1959 by
The University of Chicago. Reprinted by permission of The University of
Chicago Press.

"The Black Abolitionist" from *North of Slavery, the Negro in the Free
States, 1790–1860* by Leon F. Litwack. Copyright © 1961 by The University
of Chicago. Reprinted by permission of The University of Chicago Press.

"The Causes of the Civil War: A Note on Historical Sentimentalism"
by Arthur M. Schlesinger, Jr. from the *Partisan Review*, Volume XVI
(October 1949). Reprinted by permission of the author.

"The Negro: Innately Inferior or Equal" from *The Struggle for Equality:
Abolitionists and the Negro in the Civil War and Reconstruction* by James
M. McPherson. Copyright © 1964 by Princeton University Press. Reprinted
by permission of Princeton University Press.

". . . even the slave becomes a man . . ." from *The Sable Arm: Negro
Troops in the Union Army, 1861–1865* by Dudley Taylor Cornish. Copy-

vi

ACKNOWLEDGMENTS

A debt of gratitude is due those friends who encouraged me to do this book; Herbert Hill, National Labor Secretary of the N.A.A.C.P.. Lawrence Stessin of Hofstra University, and Armin Rappaport of the University of California (Berkeley). Sincere thanks are owed to those historians who generously shared their knowledge and research with me: Clarence Bacote, Samuel Du Bois Cook, Vincent Harding, C. Eric Lincoln, Staughton Lynd, Edward Sweatt, and Howard Zinn, all, at one time, colleagues at Spelman and the colleges of the Atlanta University Center; to John Hope Franklin of the University of Chicago; August Meier of Kent State University, and George Shepperson of Edinburgh University. Through the generosity of the non-Western Studies program of the Atlanta University Center and the Ford Foundation, I was able to spend the academic year 1966–67 in England as a post-doctoral student at the School of Oriental and African Studies, University of London, studying African history. The year of study has greatly deepened my understanding of the Negro American past. Dr. Albert E. Manley, President of Spelman College, kindly granted my request for a leave of absence.

Most important, both reader and I are indebted to the scholars who have allowed us to share their works, and to their publishers for permission to reprint the articles and selections. I wish, in addition, to thank Loretta Barrett, my editor at Doubleday, for the advice and support she gave this project.

London
June, 1967

CONTENTS

For my students at Spelman and the colleges of the Atlanta University Center who taught me the meaning of what it was to be a Negro in white America.

Your country? How came it yours? Before the Pilgrims landed we were here. Here we have brought our three gifts and mingled them with yours: a gift of story and song—soft, stirring melody in an ill-harmonized and unmelodious land; the gift of sweat and brawn to beat back the wilderness, conquer the soil and lay the foundations of this vast economic empire two hundred years earlier than your weak hands could have done it; the third, a gift of the Spirit. Around us the history of the land has centered for thrice a hundred years; out of the nation's heart we have called all that was best to throttle and subdue all that was worst; fire and blood, prayer and sacrifice, have billowed over this people, and they have found peace only in the altars of the God of Right. Nor has our gift of the Spirit been merely passive. Actively we have woven ourselves with the very warp and woof of this nation,—we have fought their battles, shared their sorrow, mingled our blood with theirs, and generation after generation have pleaded with a headstrong, careless people to despise not Justice, Mercy, and Truth, lest the nation be smitten with a curse. Our song, our toil, our cheer, and warning have been given to this nation in blood-brotherhood. Are not these gifts worth the giving? Is not this work and striving? Would America have been America without her Negro people?

W. E. B. DU BOIS, The Souls of Black Folk

What happens to a dream deferred?

> Does it dry up
> like a raisin in the sun?
> Or fester like a sore—
> And then run?
> Does it stink like rotten meat?
> Or crust and sugar over—
> like a syrupy sweet?

> Maybe it just sags
> like a heavy load.
> *Or does it explode?*

LANGSTON HUGHES, Harlem

INTRODUCTION

I

Literature on the Negro has increased so greatly in volume and quality in the last decade that it has been difficult for even experts to keep abreast of the latest monographs, essays, and reviews. This collection of essays in Negro American history is intended to make available works of recent historical scholarship on the Negro, a subject that has become the biggest single domestic issue in the United States. All but three of the essays in this volume were written after 1945, with the majority appearing in the 1960s. The history of the Negro and of American history has been enriched by this recent scholarship, but as yet, little new material has been incorporated into history textbooks or filtered into popular thought. So in a sense these essays will appear to many readers as "revisionist" and so they should be taken. It is hoped that they will provide new perspectives in Negro history.

II

Until recent years, it was not easy to get a clear or accurate picture of Negro life and history. Not only was there a small audience for Negro history, outside of Negroes and specialized groups of scholars, but a large body of American historical writing was written with an anti-Negro bias. When Negroes were not portrayed in distorted images, they were simply left out of the historical picture. A pioneer Negro historian, E. A. Johnson in his *A School History of the Negro Race in America,* noted in 1891 that "white authors . . . studiously left out many of the creditable deeds of the Negro. . . . How must the little colored child feel when he has completed the assigned course of U. S. History and in it found not one word of credit, not one word of favorable comment for even one among the millions of his foreparents, who have lived through nearly three centuries of his country's history!" Instead, Negro and white children were fed with pictures of the barbaric African, the happy slave, the irresponsible and ignorant freedman, the carefree song-and-dance man. The Negro case was ignored by historians. Staughton Lynd in *The Journal of Negro History* has shown that the two most influential historians of modern American history, Frederick Jackson Turner and Charles Beard, were indifferent to the Negro and when in need of some information on the Negro they turned to the very biased accounts of U. B. Phillips, John W. Burgess, and William A. Dunning. The only protest against Phillips' racist *American Negro Slavery* (1918) came from the Negro historian, Carter G. Woodson, who charged Phillips with falsifying history by so arranging the facts as to make the reader believe "that the Negroes were satisfied with it [slavery]." Phillips only viewed the slaves as chattel, never as men, and he failed to find it a "system of exploiting one man for the benefit of another."[1] Negro history students were often discouraged from doing graduate work. A. A. Taylor, author of three important studies on Reconstruction and later Dean at Fisk University, was driven from the University of Michigan by U. B. Phillips and had to take his Ph.D. at Harvard. Like the Negro himself, the Negro historian and Negro history remained segregated.

White historians could not claim ignorance as a cause of their neglect and distortion of Negro history. Negroes had a keen interest in their past. The first history of the Negro was written as early as 1841 by James Pennington, and there soon appeared historical studies written by William C. Nell, Martin R. Delany, Joseph T. Wilson, William Still, and William T. Alexander.[2] George Washington Williams' impressive and well-researched, two-volumed *History of the Negro Race in America* (1883) ran to nearly one thousand pages.

By the early twentieth century, W. E. B. Du Bois and Carter

[1] Carter G. Woodson, *Mississippi Valley Historical Review,* 5 (March, 1919), pp. 480–481.
[2] John Hope Franklin, "Pioneer Negro Historians," *Negro Digest* (February, 1966), pp. 4–9.

G. Woodson, editor of the *Journal of Negro History*, represented a new vanguard of university-trained historians and social scientists, and these two Harvard Ph.D.s were followed by a number of scholars who have distinguished American social science: Horace Mann Bond, Horace R. Cayton, Allison Davis, St. Clair Drake, John Hope Franklin, E. Franklin Frazier, Lorenzo J. Green, Abram L. Harris, Charles S. Johnson, Alain Locke, Rayford Logan, Benjamin Quarles, J. Saunders Redding, Ira Reid, A. A. Taylor, Charles H. Wesley, and Monroe Work. Still, Negro history did not penetrate into American historical literature or educational programs.

With the 1940s, however, three works appeared, which made dramatic impacts upon the American reading public: Richard Wright's *Native Son* (1940), Gunnar Myrdal and associates' *An American Dilemma* (1944), and John Hope Franklin's *From Slavery to Freedom* (1947). Their successes owed much to the changing attitudes of Americans under the impact of the New Deal, the resistence to the Nazi's racial policy, and to the democratic and egalitarian ideals fostered by the Allies in World War II.

The pace of historical research on the Negro quickened in the fifties although American graduate schools still remained inadequately staffed and with uneven library resources for the training of students in Negro history. Outside of the Negro colleges and universities, there were few schools in America that taught Negro history; yet in many colleges new or little-explored areas were opened up or re-examined: African history, slavery and race relations in the Americas, patterns of Negro antebellum life in the North and South, slavery and its effects on personality, Reconstruction, the origins and development of segregation. Du Bois was the subject of two biographies, and studies appeared on Marcus Garvey, and Booker T. Washington. New journals such as the *Journal of African History, Comparative Studies in Society and History*, and *Freedomways* joined the older *Journals of Negro History, Phylon*, and *Journal of Southern History* in publishing important new material in Negro history.

By the mid-sixties Negro history was *au courant*. It was attracting many of the brightest and most able scholars in

American history. Books for high school students appeared, while civil rights groups pressed to have Negro history appear in the school curriculum.[3] The U. S. Office of Education underwrote the cost of summer institutes in Negro history for high school teachers. The academic and commercial publishing houses responded to the discovery of Negro history by republishing a number of works that had remained unavailable for some time, and we have seen the recent reprinting of works by Tannenbaum, Du Bois, Frazier, Donnan, Herskovits, Myrdal, Aptheker, Drake and Cayton, Redding, Logan, Foner, and others (See Bibliography).

III

Why has Negro history taken on such importance? Obviously the most important reason is that the civil rights revolution, and with it the dramatic change in the status of Negroes, has made the Negro visible for white America. Across the nation the Negro's presence is being felt for the first time. Negro athletes now dominate all major professional sports, and Negro artists continue to excel in popular music and entertainment. The critic, Leslie Fiedler, has suggested that the life style of American teen-agers is patterned on Negro models. Politically the Negro has made his appearance in the highest echelons of government, and the coming years will see a dramatic shift in the balance of power in dozens of major northern cities as Negro officeholders replace whites. But it is in the massive slums of American cities that the real news is taking place. For here, the Negro masses are in revolt against poverty and their own helplessness in the face of white-controlled economic forces. Every uprising, every *jacquerie,* is a call for help directed to an indifferent and smug middle class, now living for the most part in suburbs that ring the lifeless core of America's major cities. We may see, as there are already indications, the cities of America under martial law and in a state of perpetual siege. Violence, as the Martinique born, French-speaking Negro psychiatrist and revolutionary Frantz Fanon has suggested in *The Wretched of*

[3] The New York *Times,* August 31, 1966.

the Earth, may be the only recourse left to the exploited and humiliated masses.

For the middle-class white American who grew up thinking of the Negro as a passive figure in the shadows of American life, Negro militancy and violence is seen as a threat to his own security, and more so, to his own feeling that he is in no way guilty for the present happenings. Americans are unable to understand why the Negroes are not satisfied with their lot, or why they do not use middle-class methods to redress their grievances. On looking for an answer to the problem, the white American finds that intellectuals and the leadership class are incapable of providing him with an answer. Negro history is then turned to as a way of understanding the Negro problem and as a guide in helping public authorities make policy.

Negroes, on the other hand, see their history as a way of building self-pride and breaking the negative image of themselves, which society has imposed and which their poverty reinforces. However, some Negroes want their history sugar-coated with tales exclusively of heroic "freedom fighters." It does little good to hide from the brutality and horror of slavery or the tragedy of human history. We know from our own times how people can be victimized, enslaved, and destroyed without putting up effective resistance. Slavery was too strong a system to be easily broken by unarmed and unorganized people. Under the conditions of American slavery, it was fortunate that the Negro was even able to survive. The history of the Negro needs no embellishment or the doctoring of mythmakers. Negroes need not be ashamed of their past. One of the reasons why white society has had to falsify or ignore Negro history was not only to discredit the Negro, but also to protect itself from the awful truth of what it has inflicted on millions of innocent people.

Negro history has become important for scholars of American intellectual and social history as a way of testing the beliefs and ideals Americans profess to believe in. Why has America, which was able to digest and integrate so many millions of diverse nationalities, religions, and cultures been unable to accept the Negro? What has happened to the American dream, or is it only for white men? Historians have realized that the Negro and the white man's response to him may form one of the major motifs running through American history. Negro history, far from being tangential, has become central to an understanding of America. David B. Davis, Carl Degler, Milton Cantor, Staughton Lynd, Stuart Bruchey, Douglass C. North, Arthur M. Schlesinger, Jr., Kenneth Stampp, and C. Vann Woodward have already shown how central the Negro was to American economic development and political history.[4] Any new study of American history must take the importance of the Negro into account.

The final factor that has changed the course of Negro history has been the rise of the Third World since World War II. These ex-colonial areas, now holding the majority of the peoples of the world, have brought about an entirely new relationship between the colored and white nations.[5]

We have moved into a new phase of world history, prophesied by Du Bois in 1900 when he wrote: "The problem of the twentieth century is the problem of the color line—the relation of the darker to the lighter races of men in Asia and Africa, in America and the islands of the sea."[6] The colored peoples have a new sense of historical destiny and intend to attain the self-respect and economic development that was denied them by circumstances of their own earlier history and the later exploitation by the European powers.

The greatest liability in America's dealings with the former colonial people has been our pattern of race relations. Dean Rusk admitted in 1961 that "the biggest single burden that we

[4] See the following: David B. Davis, *The Problem of Slavery in Western Culture* (1966); Carl Degler, "Slavery and the Genesis of American Race Prejudice," *Comparative Studies in Society and History,* II (October, 1959), pp. 49–66; Milton Cantor, "The Image of the Negro in Colonial Literature," *New England Quarterly,* 36 (1963), pp. 452–477; Staughton Lynd, "Slavery and the Founding Fathers" [pp. 117–131 in this volume]; Stuart Bruchey, *Cotton and the Growth of the American Economy, 1790–1860* (1967); Douglass C. North, *The Economic Growth of the United States* (1966 edition); Arthur M. Schlesinger, Jr., "The Causes of the Civil War: A Note on Historical Sentimentalism," *Partisan Review,* XVI (October, 1949) [pp. 223–236 in this volume]; Kenneth M. Stampp, *The Era of Reconstruction* (1965); C. Vann Woodward, *Origins of the New South* (1951), and *The Strange Career of Jim Crow* (1955) [pp. 326–336 in this volume].

[5] A good introduction is provided by Geoffrey Barraclough in *An Introduction to Contemporary History* (1966, revised edition).

[6] W. E. B. Du Bois, *The Souls of Black Folk* (1961 edition), p. 23.

carry on our backs in our foreign relations in the 1960s is the problem of racial discrimination at home. There is just no question about it." And Robert Kennedy, while Attorney General, argued that America must prove to the world "that we really mean it when we say all men are created free and are equal before the law.[7] For even if the nations of Africa and Asia do not as yet have great economic or military power, they still control the vast quantities of the world's raw materials and potential wealth. The United States now finds itself vying with Moscow and Peking for their support.

The American race problem has in the process become internationalized. For the first time in their history, Negro Americans are no longer without friends in the councils of the world. When the colored peoples of the world had no power and meant little in world affairs, there were few reasons for American leaders to take notice of Du Bois, Garvey, or Negro grievances. This has all changed. Malcolm X was one of the first Negro leaders to understand this point. "The *first thing* the American power structure doesn't want any Negroes to start is thinking internationally."[8] Cassius Clay-Muhammad Ali is the most successful exponent of this idea. The Negro American finds himself a figure of international concern. As anyone who has been abroad can verify, news of American racial incidents make the front pages, acting to reinforce the view held by many that America is not only insincere about its new racial attitudes, but that as a nation it is unstable, irrational, and as the Gaullists argue, not fitted to lead the Western alliance.

IV

These essays do not pretend to answer the questions or solve the problems of white-Negro relations. Certainly, anyone familiar with the history of race relations in this nation could not be optimistic about the peaceful or short-term resolution of the conflict. They can, however, clear away some of the prevailing myths about the Negro and, hopefully, provide the historical

[7] Both the statements of Dean Rusk and Robert Kennedy come from Harold R. Isaacs, *The New World of Negro Americans* (1963), p. 19.
[8] Malcolm X, *Autobiography* (1966), p. 347.

perspective for an understanding of what has been going on and why. An understanding of the past does not ensure that the future can be predicted, but as yet there is nothing else that will serve as a substitute.

A short introduction has been written for each selection in the hope of placing the article or essay in its historical framework. The bibliographical notes in my introductions and at the end of the book can be used to follow up some of the questions raised by the essays. It has been impossible in a volume of this size to reprint all the significant pieces that have caused historians to rethink the Negro past and American history, but I hope a start has been made.

If nothing else, we may learn that the Negro too has a history, and he sees American history quite differently and from a far different perspective than that presented in traditionally written textbooks and held by most white Americans. We need a history that will be broad enough to encompass the Negro, and when that is done, white America will then understand the meaning of Langston Hughes' lines:

> "I, too, sing America.
> I am the darker brother."

EDITOR'S NOTE: Many of the books and articles discussed in the editor's introductions are referred to by the authors' names only. Full details are given at the back of the book in the bibliography. Because of the length of some essays we have had to shorten them and renumber the footnotes. It is hoped that the major theme has been kept intact.

I. PROLOGUE

*Some day the Awakening will come, when the pent-up vigor
of ten million souls shall sweep irresistibly toward the Goal,
out of the Valley of the Shadow of Death, where all that
makes life worth living—Liberty, Justice, and Right—is marked
"For White People Only."*

W. E. B. DU BOIS, *The Souls of Black Folk,* 1903

William Edward Burghardt Du Bois

The essays in this book were chosen because each in its own
way leads to a reassessment of the history of the Negro American, and in a larger sense, American history as a whole. But
before these essays could be written, Negroes first had to
create a new understanding of who they were and what their
relationship was to American society and history.

For many years Negroes accepted the values of the larger
white society and the picture which that society drew of their
past and prospects for the future. Whether the teacher was
the "Miss Ann" of the Big House, or the New Englander,
General Samuel Armstrong of Hampton Institute—and Armstrong's most famous disciple, Booker T. Washington—Negroes were taught to consider themselves and their past with
shame. The historical education of Negro youths consisted in
a denigration of their past, whether it be as African, bondsman, or newly freed citizen. The classic statement of this philosophy was found in Washington's *Up From Slavery.*

Every American seemed to have a glorious past, except the
Negro. The Negro and American Indian students at Hampton
Institute in 1900 were taught something about the history of
the American Indian. A surviving photograph of the time
shows an Indian student in front of a history class magnifi-
cently outfitted in the costume of an Indian chief. One can
only wonder what mirror was held up to the Negro students.

Were they shown as naked savages or Moslem scholars of Timbuktu, Denné, and Katsina; the faithful slave or Toussaint L'Ouverture; the minstrel man or the Negro Civil War volunteer?

When did Negroes reject this negative vision of themselves, and begin to reassess their own history? I would like to suggest that the starting point began with the publication of W. E. B. Du Bois' *The Souls of Black Folk*. Du Bois' book had a great impact upon young Negro intellectuals. James Weldon Johnson, himself one of the important figures in the creation of this new Negro image, recalled in his autobiography, *Along This Way* (1935), that Du Bois' book "had a greater effect upon and within the Negro race in America than any other single book published in this country since *Uncle Tom's Cabin*." Since its publication *The Souls of Black Folk* has passed through more than thirty editions. It proved to be, as the *Nashville Banner* predicted, "dangerous for the Negro to read, for it will only excite discontent and fill his imagination with things that do not exist, or things that should not bear upon his mind."

Here was a voice, blending scholarship with militancy, poetry with prophecy. Du Bois called upon Negroes to create a new image out of their own history and experiences, merging Africa and America, "into a better and truer self." Du Bois saw Negro regeneration coming from within. A close reading of *The Souls of Black Folk* shows it to be a fervent black nationalist document. Not only does Du Bois consciously identify with Africa, "blackness," and the rural Negro, but the whole tone of the book is a dialogue between Du Bois and the Negro people, intimate, direct, and highly personal, in which whites may listen but are not of principal concern. As *Up From Slavery* was directed toward the good will of white people, *The Souls of Black Folk* is directed to the black consciousness of the Negro masses. What unites Du Bois and his readers is not the American cult of material well-being or social uplift, but what contemporaries term "soul" or negritude.

Before the Negro could break the mental shackles of a white-imposed inferiority complex, he had to identify the schizophrenia that was a symptom of his plight in an overwhelming white—and hostile—America, namely, the problem of identity. Who am I, and what role should I play in American society? In *The Souls of Black Folk*, Du Bois saw the problem in these terms:

"The history of the American Negro is the history of this strife,—this longing to attain self-conscious manhood, to merge his double self into a better and truer self. In this merging he wishes neither of the older selves to be lost. He would not Africanize America, for America has too much to teach the world and Africa. He would not bleach his Negro soul in a flood of white Americanism, for he knows that Negro blood has a message for the world. He simply wishes to make it possible for a man to be both a Negro and an American, without being cursed and spit upon by his fellows, without having the doors of Opportunity closed roughly in his face."

Only in coming to terms with this double self, with Africa and America, could the Negro renaissance begin. With it he could create a new self image based on his unique heritage and historical experience. Historians are just beginning to understand the profound implications of the question with which Du Bois ended the book: "Would America have been America without her Negro people?" When that question is answered by white Americans, only then will they be able to come to terms with the Negro, with American ideals, and with themselves.

The essay that set the tone for *The Souls of Black Folk*, and for that matter, an understanding of Negro history in the twentieth century, "Of Our Spiritual Strivings," appeared in 1897 when Du Bois was twenty-nine, fresh with a Doctorate in History from Harvard University. All those working in the field, whether we agree or disagree with all of his assumptions, owe an immense debt to this man for the direction he gave to the study and understanding of American history. The following essays are, in their own ways, extensions of the work Du Bois began.

OF OUR SPIRITUAL STRIVINGS

SOURCE: W. E. B. Du Bois, "Of Our Spiritual Strivings," *The Souls of Black Folk* (New York: Fawcett Publications, Premier Americana edition, 1961), 15–22.

Between me and the other world there is ever an unasked question: unasked by some through feelings of delicacy; by others through the difficulty of rightly framing it. All, nevertheless, flutter round it. They approach me in a half-hesitant sort of way, eye me curiously or compassionately, and then, instead of saying directly, How does it feel to be a problem? they say, I know an excellent colored man in my town; or, I fought at Mechanicsville; or, Do not these Southern outrages make your blood boil? At these I smile, or am interested, or reduce the boiling to a simmer, as the occasion may require. To the real question, How does it feel to be a problem? I answer seldom a word.

And yet, being a problem is a strange experience,—peculiar even for one who has never been anything else, save perhaps in babyhood and in Europe. It is in the early days of rollicking boyhood that the revelation first bursts upon one, all in a day, as it were. I remember well when the shadow swept across me. I was a little thing, away up in the hills of New England, where the dark Housatonic winds between Hoosac and Taghkanic to the sea. In a wee wooden schoolhouse, something put it into the boys' and girls' heads to buy gorgeous visiting-cards—ten cents a package—and exchange. The exchange was merry, till one girl, a tall newcomer, refused my card,—refused it peremptorily, with a glance. Then it dawned upon me with a certain suddenness that I was different from the others; or like, mayhap, in heart and life and belonging, but shut out from their world by a vast veil. I had thereafter no desire to tear down that veil, to creep through; I held all beyond it in common contempt, and lived above it in a region of blue sky and great wandering shadows. That sky was bluest when I could beat my mates at examination-time, or beat them at a foot-race, or even beat their stringy heads. Alas, with the years all this fine contempt began to fade; for the worlds I longed for, and all their dazzling opportunities, were theirs, not mine. But they should not keep these prizes, I said; some, all, I would wrest from them. Just how I would do it I could never decide: by reading law, by healing the sick, by telling the wonderful tales that swam in my head,—some way. With other black boys the strife was not so fiercely sunny: their youth shrunk into tasteless sycophancy, or into silent hatred of the pale world about them and mocking distrust of everything white; or wasted itself in a bitter cry, Why did God make me an outcast and a stranger in mine own house? The shades of the prison-house closed round about us all: walls straight and stubborn to the whitest, but relentlessly narrow, tall, and unscalable to sons of night who must plod darkly on in resignation, or beat unavailing palms against the stone, or steadily, half hopelessly, watch the streak of blue above.

After the Egyptian and Indian, the Greek and Roman, the Teuton and Mongolian, the Negro is a sort of seventh son, born with a veil, and gifted with second-sight in this American world, —a world which yields him no true self-consciousness, but only lets him see himself through the revelation of the other world. It is a peculiar sensation, this double-consciousness, this sense of always looking at one's self through the eyes of others, of measuring one's soul by the tape of a world that looks on in amused contempt and pity. One ever feels his twoness,—an American, a Negro; two souls, two thoughts, two unreconciled strivings; two warring ideals in one dark body, whose dogged strength alone keeps it from being torn asunder.

The history of the American Negro is the history of this strife,—this longing to attain self-conscious manhood, to merge his double self into a better and truer self. In this merging he wishes neither of the older selves to be lost. He would not Africanize America, for America has too much to teach the world and Africa. He would not bleach his Negro soul in a flood of white Americanism, for he knows that Negro blood has a message for the world. He simply wishes to make it possible for a man to be both a Negro and an American, without being cursed and spit upon by his fellows, without having the doors of Opportunity closed roughly in his face.

This, then, is the end of his striving: to be a co-worker in the kingdom of culture, to escape both death and isolation, to husband and use his best powers and his latent genius. These powers of body and mind have in the past been strangely wasted, dispersed, or forgotten. The shadow of a mighty Negro past flits through the tale of Ethiopia the Shadowy and of Egypt the Sphinx. Throughout history, the powers of single black men flash here and there like falling stars, and die sometimes before the world has rightly gauged their brightness. Here in America, in the few days since Emancipation, the black man's turning hither and thither in hesitant and doubtful striving has often made his very strength to lose effectiveness, to seem like absence of power, like weakness. And yet it is not weakness,—it is the contradiction of double aims. The double-aimed struggle of the black artisan—on the one hand to escape white contempt for a nation of mere hewers of wood and drawers of water, and on the other hand to plough and nail and dig for a poverty-stricken horde—could only result in making him a poor craftsman, for he had but half a heart in either cause. By the poverty and ignorance of his people, the Negro minister or doctor was tempted toward quackery and demagogy; and by the criticism of the other world, toward ideals that made him ashamed of his lowly tasks. The would-be black *savant* was confronted by the paradox that the knowledge his people needed was a twice-told tale to his white neighbors, while the knowledge which would teach the white world was Greek to his own flesh and blood. The innate love of harmony and beauty that set the ruder souls of his people a-dancing and a-singing raised but confusion and doubt in the soul of the black artist; for the beauty revealed to him was the soul-beauty of a race which his larger audience despised, and he could not articulate the message of another people. This waste of double aims, this seeking to satisfy two unreconciled ideals, has wrought sad havoc with the courage and faith and deeds of ten thousand people—has sent them often wooing false gods and invoking false means of salvation, and at times has even seemed about to make them ashamed of themselves.

Away back in the days of bondage they thought to see in one divine event the end of all doubt and disappointment; few men ever worshipped Freedom with half such unquestioning faith as did the American Negro for two centuries. To him, so far as he thought and dreamed, slavery was indeed the sum of all villainies, the cause of all sorrow, the root of all prejudice; Emancipation was the key to a promised land of sweeter beauty than ever stretched before the eyes of wearied Israelites. In song and exhortation swelled one refrain—Liberty; in his tears and curses the God he implored had Freedom in his right hand. At last it came,—suddenly, fearfully, like a dream. With one wild carnival of blood and passion came the message in his own plantive cadences:—

> "Shout, O children!
> Shout, you're free!
> For God has bought your liberty!"

Years have passed away since then,—ten, twenty, forty; forty years of national life, forty years of renewal and development, and yet the swarthy spectre sits in its accustomed seat at the Nation's feast. In vain do we cry to this our vastest social problem:—

> "Take any shape but that, and my firm nerves
> Shall never tremble!"

The Nation has not yet found peace from its sins; the freedman has not yet found in freedom his promised land. Whatever of good may have come in these years of change, the shadow of a deep disappointment rests upon the Negro people,—a disappointment all the more bitter because the unattained ideal was unbounded save by the simple ignorance of a lowly people.

The first decade was merely a prolongation of the vain search for freedom, the boon that seemed ever barely to elude their grasp,—like a tantalizing will-o'-the-wisp, maddening and misleading the headless host. The holocaust of war, the terrors of the Ku-Klux Klan, the lies of carpet-baggers, the disorganization of industry, and the contradictory advice of friends and foes, left the bewildered serf with no new watchword beyond the old cry for freedom. As the time flew, however, he began to grasp a new idea. The ideal of liberty demanded for its attainment powerful means, and these the Fifteenth Amendment gave him. The ballot, which before he had looked upon as a visible sign of freedom, he now regarded as the chief means of gaining and perfecting the liberty with which war had partially endowed him.

And why not? Had not votes made war and emancipated millions? Had not votes enfranchised the freedmen? Was anything
impossible to a power that had done all this? A million black
men started with renewed zeal to vote themselves into the kingdom. So the decade flew away, the revolution of 1876 came, and
left the half-free serf weary, wondering, but still inspired. Slowly
but steadily, in the following years, a new vision began gradually
to replace the dream of political power,—a powerful movement,
the rise of another ideal to guide the unguided, another pillar of
fire by night after a clouded day. It was the ideal of "book-
learning"; the curiosity, born of compulsory ignorance, to know
and test the power of the cabalistic letters of the white man,
the longing to know. Here at last seemed to have been discovered
the mountain path to Canaan; longer than the highway of Emancipation and law, steep and rugged, but straight, leading to
heights high enough to overlook life.

Up the new path the advance guard toiled, slowly, heavily,
doggedly; only those who have watched and guided the falter-
ing feet, the misty minds, the dull understandings, of the dark
pupils of these schools know how faithfully, how piteously, this
people strove to learn. It was weary work. The cold statistician
wrote down the inches of progress here and there, noted also
where here and there a foot had slipped or some one had fallen.
To the tired climbers, the horizon was ever dark, the mists were
often cold, the Canaan was always dim and far away. If, however,
the vistas disclosed as yet no goal, no resting-place, little but
flattery and criticism, the journey at least gave leisure for reflec-
tion and self-examination; it changed the child of Emancipation
to the youth with dawning self-consciousness, self-realization,
self-respect. In those sombre forests of his striving his own soul
rose before him, and he saw himself,—darkly as through a veil;
and yet he saw in himself some faint revelation of his power, of
his mission. He began to have a dim feeling that, to attain his
place in the world, he must be himself, and not another. For the
first time he sought to analyze the burden he bore upon his back,
that dead-weight of social degradation partially masked behind a
half-named Negro problem. He felt his poverty; without a cent,
without a home, without land, tools, or savings, he had entered
into competition with rich, landed, skilled neighbors. To be a

poor man is hard, but to be a poor race in a land of dollars is the very bottom of hardships. He felt the weight of his ignorance,— not simply of letters, but of life, of business, of the humanities; the accumulated sloth and shirking and awkwardness of decades and centuries shackled his hands and feet. Nor was his burden all poverty and ignorance. The red stain of bastardy, which two centuries of systematic legal defilement of Negro women had stamped upon his race, meant not only the loss of ancient African chastity, but also the hereditary weight of a mass of corruption from white adulterers, threatening almost the obliteration of the Negro home.

A people thus handicapped ought not to be asked to race with the world, but rather allowed to give all its time and thought to its own social problems. But alas! while sociologists gleefully count his bastards and his prostitutes, the very soul of the toiling, sweating black man is darkened by the shadow of a vast despair. Men call the shadow prejudice, and learnedly explain it as the natural defence of culture against barbarism, learning against ignorance, purity against crime, the "higher" against the "lower" races. To which the Negro cries Amen! and swears that to so much of this strange prejudice as is founded on just homage to civilization, culture, righteousness, and progress, he humbly bows and meekly does obeisance. But before that nameless prejudice that leaps beyond all this he stands helpless, dismayed, and well-nigh speechless; before that personal disrespect and mockery, the ridicule and systematic humiliation, the distortion of fact and wanton license of fancy, the cynical ignoring of the better and the boisterous welcoming of the worse, the all-pervading desire to inculcate disdain for everything black, from Toussaint to the devil,—before this there rises a sickening despair that would disarm and discourage any nation save that black host to whom "discouragement" is an unwritten word.

But the facing of so vast a prejudice could not but bring the inevitable self-questioning, self-disparagement, and lowering of ideals which ever accompany repression and breed in an atmosphere of contempt and hate. Whisperings and portents came borne upon the four winds: Lo! we are diseased and dying, cried the dark hosts; we cannot write, our voting is vain; what need of education, since we must always cook and serve? And the Nation echoed and enforced this self-criticism, saying: Be content to be servants, and nothing more; what need of higher culture for half-men? Away with the black man's ballot, by force or fraud,—and behold the suicide of a race! Nevertheless, out of the evil came something of good,—the more careful adjustment of education to real life, the clearer perception of the Negroes' social responsibilities, and the sobering realization of the meaning of progress.

So dawned the time of *Sturm und Drang:* storm and stress to-day rocks our little boat on the mad waters of the world-sea; there is within and without the sound of conflict, the burning of body and rending of soul; inspiration strives with doubt, and faith with vain questionings. The bright ideals of the past,— physical freedom, political power, the training of brains and the training of hands,—all these in turn have waxed and waned, until even the last grows dim and overcast. Are they all wrong,— all false? No, not that, but each alone was oversimple and incom-plete,—the dreams of a credulous race-childhood, or the fond imaginings of the other world which does not know and does not want to know our power. To be really true, all these ideals must be melted and welded into one. The training of the schools we need to-day more than ever,—the training of deft hands, quick eyes and ears, and above all the broader, deeper, higher culture of gifted minds and pure hearts. The power of the ballot we need in sheer self-defence,—else what shall save us from a sec-ond slavery? Freedom, too, the long-sought, we still seek,—the freedom of life and limb, the freedom to work and think, the freedom to love and aspire. Work, culture, liberty,—all these we need, not singly but together, not successively but together, each growing and aiding each, and all striving toward that vaster ideal that swims before the Negro people, the ideal of human brother-hood, gained through the unifying ideal of Race; the ideal of fostering and developing the traits and talents of the Negro, not in opposition to or contempt for other races, but rather in large conformity to the greater ideals of the American Republic, in or-der that some day on American soil two world-races may give each to each those characteristics both so sadly lack. We the darker ones come even now not altogether empty-handed: there are to-day no truer exponents of the pure human spirit of the Declaration of Independence than the American Negroes; there is no true American music but the wild sweet melodies of the Negro slave; the American fairy tales and folk-lore are Indian and African; and, all in all, we black men seem the sole oasis of simple faith and reverence in a dusty desert of dollars and smartness. Will America be poorer if she replaces her brutal dyspeptic blundering with light-hearted but determined Negro humility, or her coarse and cruel wit with loving jovial good-humor, or her vulgar music with the soul of the Sorrow Songs?

Merely a concrete test of the underlying principles of the great republic is the Negro Problem, and the spiritual striving of the freedmen's sons is the travail of souls whose burden is almost beyond the measure of their strength, but who bear it in the name of an historic race, in the name of this the land of their fathers' fathers, and in the name of human opportunity.

II. AFRICA AND THE BEGINNINGS

I call Gold,
Gold is mute.
I call Cloth,
Cloth is mute.
It is Mankind that matters.
AKAN SAYING

Philip D. Curtin

One of the most important developments in post-1945 historical scholarship has been the systematic and professional exploration of the African past. Despite such skeptics as Professor Hugh Trevor-Roper of Oxford who wrote in *The Listener* that African history consisted mainly of "the unrewarding gyrations of barbarous tribes in picturesque but irrelevant corners of the globe," by the 1960s African history was distinctly in vogue in the leading universities of Europe and the United States. Of equal importance is the fact that in Africa itself a younger generation of university-trained historians had developed, and Ibadan, Lagos, Dakar, Ghana, and East Africa have become important centers for the study of the African past.

The history of Africa is one of the most challenging modern historical studies. Conventional documents are scarce, and early written records are in Arabic, or as in the case of the writings inscribed on the monuments of Meroë, undeciphered. Archival material is still overwhelmingly from European sources, colonial-office records, missionary societies, trading companies, and various travelers. Historians using African sources have to rely on oral traditions, which require an intimate knowledge of West African or Bantu languages, anthropology, archaeology, and linguistics. At present we are still on the threshold of African history. As Roland Oliver has written in *The Dawn of African History,* we can at this time "only walk around the perimeter-wall of African history, peering in wherever there is a window. As we get to know the perimeter better, we keep on finding more windows." But already the results can be read in the numerous theses, published monographs, and journals of African history (*See* Bibliography).

There is also a marked change of emphasis in writing African history, which for the first time is being written from the African's point of view. Historians are aware that Africa has a history of its own, independent of European discovery and intervention. African institutions and society were not primitive, and until the advent of the industrial revolution in Europe, Africans were able to meet the European powers on terms of equality. Africa was the dark continent only to the Europeans, who were restricted to coastal areas by powerful African nations. In art, agriculture, social and political organization, religion, trade and commerce, African society had made considerable strides. The high level of culture made the Africans attractive to Europeans as a source of skilled labor after the failure of Indian enslavement on New World plantations. Studies by Basil Davidson, J. D. Omer-Cooper, K. O. Dike, Robert I. Rotberg, Jan Vansina, J. F. A. Ajayi, Monica Wilson, George Shepperson, and J. C. Anene, to mention a few, have succeeded in portraying the African side of events. Their studies sweep aside the myths that Africans either docilely accepted European control or were incapable of responding creatively to the invaders. In fact, a well developed state structure prevented Europeans from being able to control Africa until the last quarter of the nineteenth century.

The reasons for the increasing interest in Africa are not hard to find. The rise of African nationalism, the end of colonialism, the establishment of over thirty new nations, the African presence in world affairs and at the United Nations, and the recognition of the vast economic potential of the African continent has brought Africa, as never before, to the attention of scholars, cold war statesmen, and economic planners.

Africans have themselves fostered the study of their history in the fight against colonialism, and now use it as an important tool in binding together their multilingual and tribal nations. Moreover, Africans and the Negroes of the Americas look upon African history as a way of countering the traditional European view that Africa had nothing before the com-

ing of the white man. History so written was a way of making
the Negro accept an inferior place in society, but Africans and
Negro Americans now see African history as a liberating force,
giving them pride in their past and self-confidence for the
present and future.

So much has happened within a relatively short period that
historians have needed a survey of recent research that would
allow them to keep abreast of developing trends, as well as
give them some introduction into a field for which few were
trained in graduate school or university. This need has been
fulfilled by Philip D. Curtin in his short work *African History*
written for the American Historical Association. In addition
to summarizing new material, he has proposed some answers
to the crucial question of why Africa developed along different lines than Europe. Professor Curtin teaches African history at the University of Wisconsin (Madison), and is on the
editorial board of the *Journal of African History*. His most recent book is *The Image of Africa, British Ideas and Action,
1780–1850* (1964).

AFRICAN HISTORY

SOURCE: Philip D. Curtin, *African History* (New York: Macmillan, 1964),
1–6, 23–29, 38–39, 40–45.

The Emergence of African History

America's new position in the world after 1945 called for a new
perspective. Before the Second World War, we could think in
terms of a sea-based view of the world. Maps showed a Western
Hemisphere, conveniently isolated behind a moat of oceans. In
terms of the air age, these maps were seriously distorted. They
were not even centered on the United States, but on a point in
the Pacific Ocean near the Galapagos Islands. After the war, a
new look at the globe showed that the bulge of Africa and the
bulge of Brazil were about equally far away. Viewed from New
York, Buenos Aires was farther away from Timbuktu, that
ancient symbol of inaccessibility.

Our earlier view of world history was equally distorted. It too needed a change of perspective that would show more accurately how the modern world came to be as it is. Like the hemispheric map of an isolated America, the older history showed only part of the truth. Many human societies remained beyond the horizon. Instead of trying to explain the modern world in terms of its past, or even tracing the rise of human civilizations, the older history began with the United States. It then searched for the roots of American civilization. It was, in effect, "history taught backward"—back to the colonial period on this continent, then back to Europe, and still further back to the Western Middle Ages, Rome, Greece, and the ancient civilizations of the Near East.

This pattern of "world history" not only moved through time, it moved through space as well, hopping a quarter of the way around the earth from Mesopotamia to America. It was not even the history of our ancestors. (Some of them came from Europe, and some from Africa; but very few came from Mesopotamia.) This "world history" was really the history of those peoples from whom we borrowed most of the technology and culture that later developed into American civilization. By any objective standard, it was a very distorted view of world history, but it served a purpose. It *did* help to explain the origins of the modern American way of life. It was therefore distorted for a sufficient reason. The danger of misunderstanding enters only when we forget that it *was* distorted and come to believe that it really is the history of the modern world. One of the failures of history teaching in past decades has been the failure to make this point clear. Most students exposed to "world history" courses thought they were really learning world history. In fact, we were not even trying to teach world history—only American history pushed back through time.

There are historical reasons for this error. No further back than the eighteenth century, Western historians made a serious effort to ask: "How did the modern world come to be as it is?" In eighteenth-century England, for example, the great standard compendium of world history was the *Universal History,* published between 1736 and 1765 in sixty-five volumes. It served students of history at that time in much the same way the *Cambridge Modern History* served students in the early twentieth century. The *Cambridge Modern History*, however, was really only a history of modern Europe, while the *Universal History* devoted about half of its volumes to the non-Western world. One-eighth of the section on modern history was given over to Africa.[1]

The change that took place between about 1750 and about 1900 was, of course, the industrial revolution. Before the marvels of steam and steel, Europeans and Americans were likely to think of their own civilization as one among many. They thought, perhaps naturally, that it was the best civilization in the world, but they could not ignore the others altogether. European overseas expansion before 1750 was largely commercial, and the time when Europe would conquer the world was still to come. With industrial technology, however, and economic growth at unprecedented rates, the Western self-image began to change. Europeans and Americans began to place a much higher value on their accomplishments. When they thought of progress, they thought of their own rapid progress over recent decades. By contrast, the pace of historical change in other societies seemed slow, and Europeans began to talk about the "changeless East." In fact, "the East" was far from changeless; only the very rapid European changes of the nineteenth century made it seem slow. But the new rate of European change altered the Western concept of history—if history is the study of change, then societies thought to be static had no history worth speaking of. The new pattern of historical thought began in Europe and concentrated on the achievements of Europe. Americans easily took it over and extended it to their own country.

The rise of this attitude, which can be labelled "cultural arrogance," had other side-effects that helped bring about the neglect of African history. Of these, the rise of pseudo-scientific racism was crucial. Racism was not especially new in the nineteenth century: most people in most societies have distrusted others who looked different or had different customs. This ordinary or xenophobic racial distrust can be removed by further acquaintance, or by education. Nineteenth-century racism was another

---

[1] By contrast, a modern standard reference work, W. L. Langer (Ed.), *An Encyclopedia of World History* (Boston, Houghton Mifflin, 1948) spends only one-twentieth of its section on Modern History with Africa.

matter. It arose partly from the fact that Negroes were often slaves in the United States or tropical America, but it was made much worse by a serious mistake on the part of European and American scientists. When they first began to study human societies, they looked for factors that seemed to have caused the rise of civilization. One obvious and superficial fact was racial difference: Europeans were white. Non-Europeans, by and large, were not. Furthermore, in tune with the common cultural arrogance of the period, Europeans thought they had "civilization." Other peoples were considered to have only a static "barbarism." When these two points were added, it seemed obvious that light-colored peoples were somehow superior to dark-colored peoples. This view was, of course, quite unhistoric. Dropping back five or six millennia, it would have appeared that only relatively dark people had civilization, and the ancestors of the modern Europeans were merely barbarians on the northern fringes of the civilized world.

The feeling of belonging to a superior race was, nevertheless, satisfying. It grew gradually in importance during the first half of the nineteenth century, both in the United States and in Europe.[2] About 1850, a number of scientists carried this racism further still and tried to prove that Europeans were anatomically very different from other peoples. Detailed studies developed the hypothesis that race was the major determining cause of all historical change. . . . In the second half of the century, pseudo-scientific racism gained still more strength from the misapplication of the Darwinian theory. By 1900, its acceptance in scientific circles was virtually universal throughout the West.

Then from the first decade of the twentieth century, better scientific investigation began to make itself felt. It was found that race and culture were completely independent of one another. Not only did race have nothing to do with the course of history, there was no significant difference between the innate abilities or propensities of different races. After the First World War, pseudo-scientific racism began to decline rapidly in all respectable scientific circles. Today it continues only as a popular myth, or in societies where it is politically useful. (In modern

[2] For the early development of pseudo-scientific racism, see P. D. Curtin, *The Image of Africa* (Madison, University of Wisconsin Press, 1964).

Africa, for example, it is still encouraged by the governments of Southern Rhodesia and the Republic of South Africa as an argument for white domination over the non-white majority.)

The importance of pseudo-scientific racism for the study of African history lies in the fact that racism was most prominent at precisely the period when Europeans conquered and colonized Africa. The colonizers, who had the best opportunity to investigate the African past, assumed (as a by-product of their racial attitudes) that Africa could have no history worth investigating. When European historians wrote about Africa, they usually confined their study to the activity of their own people. Thus, what passed for African history was really only the history of Europeans in Africa. Some of it was good history, and some bad, but it left the impression that no other history of Africa was known—or could be discovered.[3]

Before the Second World War, most of the important contributions to African history were made by non-historians. Some authors wrote about current events, and the passage of time turned their work into history. Among the works of political scientists R. L. Buell's *The Native Problem in Africa*[4] is still valuable, since he was among the first to look for the impact of Europe on African societies. The intensive infiltration of tropical Africa by the political scientists, however, came only in the 1950's.

Two other groups of non-historians were responsible for most investigations of African history. One was the administrative officers in the colonial service of the European powers. They lived in Africa, and they often had enough leisure to collect data, including oral traditions. Even though their methods were not up to the best of recent professional standards, their work has turned out to be invaluable. The second group was the anthropologists, the first scholars to take up serious research in Africa itself. Like the administrators, they were in a position to collect traditional histories, and at times they did so. On the other hand, they sometimes passed over valuable data that is now lost. One reason for this (aside from the fact that they were not historians) was the nature of anthropology itself in the early

[3] As an example of this historical tradition at its best, see Harry R. Rudin, *Germans in the Cameroons, 1884–1914: A Case Study of Modern Imperalism* (New Haven, Yale University Press, 1938).

[4] 2 vols. (New York, Macmillan, 1928).

part of this century. Anthropology was then concerned to study people as "primitive" and untouched by civilization as possible. Anthropologists therefore sought out the most isolated "tribes" they could find. The larger and more complex African societies were neglected. Emphasis was also placed on the more static characteristics of any African people. One result of this attitude is still present among modern anthropologists, who occasionally write in the "anthropological present," using the present tense for past as well as present.[5] This search for the static past had two important results. On one hand it made anthropologists' work less valuable as data for historians. On the other, it furthered the popular impression that Africa was still a "primitive" place "just out of the stone age."

Another problem for American history comes from the fact that physical anthropologists were and are professionally concerned with the description of physical types—that is, of human races. As a result of their professional concern, they were often led to overemphasize the importance of race, even in the inter-war period when pseudo-scientific racism as a whole was dying out. Some of their racism spread over to other members of the discipline, and anthropologists have been among the principal authors of racist interpretations of African history—as well as the principal enemies of pseudo-scientific racism.

The prevalence of racial interpretations in otherwise-respectable books of the recent past poses a special problem for all teachers of African history. It may be easy for the trained historian, conscious of the probable racial bias of these works, to make adjustments accordingly. Students, however, cannot be counted on to read so critically, and a strong presumption exists that any work of African history published before 1935 will be racist to some degree, if only in ways of which the author was unconscious. This warning applies even to "revised" versions of many of the old standard works.[6]

[5] The careful reader of recent journalism will occasionally catch an echo from the distant past, when a reporter tries to do his homework with the anthropologists and ends by giving the "news" of kingdoms that disappeared a century or more ago.

[6] A striking example is the re-publication of C. G. Seligman's *The Races of Africa* in 1957 by Oxford University Press as a volume in the "Home University Library of Modern Knowledge." Seligman's book was first

AFRICAN CIVILIZATION AND WORLD CIVILIZATION:
THE PROBLEM OF "LAG"

It should be clear from what has been said that African history over the past two millennia shows a pattern of change equivalent to the pace of change in other parts of the world. The older view that African societies were "primitive" or static has been completely discredited, but serious problems of interpretation still remain. Western cultural arrogance is still prevalent, and racism lingers. In reaction, some modern African intellectuals have tried to show great civilizations in the past, grander than anything that actually existed. The underlying fact is one of differing cultures, just emerging from a colonial era in which Europeans were dominant and Africans were subordinated to alien rule. It is clear that colonial rule resulted from a situation in which African societies somehow lagged behind the pace of development in the West. The crucial problem for the historian is to explain the nature of the lag and to assess its causes. The task is far from easy. The political and emotional implications stretch out in every direction, involving such disparate matters as American race relations and international politics.

At base the problem is one of making rational value judgments about "levels" of human culture. Scholars once talked about "higher" and "lower" cultures with far more confidence than they do today. It is now clear that such judgments were based on Western values. They were neither universally acceptable, nor subject to rational proof. Cultural judgments are, indeed, extremely difficult to defend. Estheticians can formulate a rational basis for judging the relative merits of two symphonic works in the Western musical style, or two pieces of African music. Within a given stylistic framework, a consensus (if not complete agreement) is often possible. Without a stylistic form, there is no

published in 1930, and its interpretation of African history was thoroughly racist. Since then, it has been just as thoroughly discredited. But the "revision" for the new edition, though carried out by respectable scholars, was done with respect for Seligman's memory rather than for the best modern knowledge. The work remains an important document of a certain stage in the progress of anthropological knowledge, but it should not be accepted as either modern or authoritative.

standard for measuring whether, for example, African music is "better" than Western music. A symphony orchestra may have more players and a more complex score, but this is merely a matter of technique without any necessary bearing on the beauty of the sound produced.

In some matters, such as ethical judgments, all cultures share certain ideas about right and wrong. Needless killing of human beings is generally considered to be wrong, but the key word is "needless." Some African societies, only a century ago, practiced human sacrifice as a regular part of their religion. Western observers condemned this practice as evil, because it was unnecessary. During the First World War, the nations of Europe sent millions of soldiers against the enemy machine guns. An outside observer might well believe that this sacrifice of human life was equally evil, and for the same reasons. Thus, while the ethical judgment may be universal, the judgment of need is culture-bound.

Technology, however, is an aspect of culture where rational judgment is possible. If technology is broadly defined as the body of knowledge and skill about the *means* of producing goods and services, then each technique can be measured by its effectiveness in serving the desired end. For efficiency in written communication, a phonetic alphabet is better than a syllabary, which, in turn, is better than pictographs. A Chinese may prefer, for sentimental or other reasons, to use his thousands of individual characters, but he must still admit that, compared with a phonetic alphabet, they are inefficient for written communication. What is true of linguistic techniques is broadly true of agricultural, political, or industrial technology as well. In the field of technology—and, one is tempted to add, in that field alone—it is possible to make rough estimates of the degree of advancement achieved by differing cultures.

Limiting our judgment to technology alone, it is clear that African culture lagged behind that of Western Europe in the nineteenth century. The question, however, remains: how great was this lag, and how may it be explained historically?

There is no serious problem in understanding why progress might be slow in the far south, toward the tip of the African continent. That part of the world was obviously the end of the road, and any invention or discovery made elsewhere could only be received after a long process of diffusion down the whole length of the African continent. The Bushmen of southern Africa therefore remained relatively "primitive," for the same reason that other isolated peoples of Australia and Patagonia also lagged behind.

The more difficult problem lies farther north particularly in the region just south of the Sahara. There, the northern savanna, an open country of grassland and scattered trees, stretches from Cape Verde in the west to the Red Sea in the east. This is the Sudan, the country of the Negroes. If, in the earliest periods before sea transportation, this region fell behind the civilization of North Africa and the Near East, then automatically every region farther south fell behind as well. The crucial lag in African development is hence to be found in the changing relations between the Sudan and the rest of Afro-Eurasia.

The origin of agriculture is a convenient touchstone, since agriculture (as opposed to hunting and gathering) was an essential step toward civilization of any kind. Most historians now agree that agriculture was invented only a very few times—perhaps only once—and the earliest agricultural society existed in southwest Asia about the eighth millennium B.C. This earliest agriculture was accompanied by an assemblage of stone tools of an improved type, called neolithic. The archaeological evidence for the spread of neolithic tools and agriculture in Afro-Eurasia suggests that both diffused from the ancient Near East. In the early stages of this movement, therefore, all the world lagged behind the few agricultural communities. By about 4000 B.C., neolithic tools, but possibly not agriculture, had already reached the Negro peoples to the south of the present Sahara desert. The commencement of the neolithic age in sub-Saharan Africa was thus roughly simultaneous with the earliest neolithic in India or China, and about a thousand years ahead of the arrival of the neolithic in northwest Europe. At that point, it would seem that Europe lagged behind, while parts of Africa were among the leading areas of the world.

At this point, however, an element of uncertainty appears. One view, recently summarized by Oliver and Fage, holds that neolithic tools and the skills for making them were present south of the Sahara about 4000 B.C.; but they were not accompanied by agriculture, since the food crops used in the Levant and Egypt were not suitable for cultivation in the tropical savanna conditions.[7] Only the knowledge that agriculture was possible seems to have been received. Two to three thousand years were to pass before wild species locally available could be ennobled and made to serve as the basis for savanna agriculture. According to this view, developed agriculture south of the desert began only in the second millennium B.C. If this is correct, the Sudan had to accept a delay for reasons of climate. Thus sub-Saharan Africa acquired a two-thousand year lag behind Egypt, and a thousand-year lag behind western Europe.

A second view, however, suggests that the lag in African development came from a different source altogether—that Africa, indeed, may have begun as a world leader in agriculture and only fell behind later. According to this hypothesis, food crops were cultivated south of the Sahara at least as early as 3000 B.C. and perhaps a good deal earlier. The evidence is skimpy, but it rests on two points. First, on botanical grounds it seems likely that cotton was cultivated in sub-Saharan Africa at least as early as 3000 B.C. If this were so, food crops were probably cultivated even earlier. Furthermore, certain pottery found in Kenya can be dated to about 5000 B.C., and it is linked stylistically with the pottery of Jericho, where agriculture appears to have been practiced as early as 8000 B.C.

This view threatens some of the usual assumptions about the civilization of ancient Egypt. It is known that many cultural traits found in Negro Africa are similar to those of ancient Egypt. Most authorities have assumed that these traits came from Egypt, having diffused southward along the Nile and thus reached the open savanna country south of the desert. But there is no proof that Egypt always gave, and Negro Africa always received. If agriculture south of the desert can be confirmed at a date as early as 5000 B.C., Egypt and sub-Saharan Africa would have been very much on a par at that period. The Nile valley as a route of cultural interchange could easily have been a two-way street, and Egyptian civilization might well have borrowed cultural

[7] Oliver and Fage, *Short History*, 27–28.

forms *from* Negro Africa, rather than acting solely as a center of diffusion *into* Negro Africa.[8]

In any event, this hypothesis would hold that the lag in African development came at a later stage—not from slow development of agriculture, but from the failure to move on to the urban civilization of the bronze age, as Egypt and Mesopotamia did. In fact, the ease of communication across the present-day Sahara, following the Nile valley route, appears to have changed abruptly in the fourth millennium B.C. Sub-Saharan Africa almost certainly received domestic animals by this route, but it failed to adopt the use of bronze or writing which developed in Egypt a little later. Instead, bronze came into Negro Africa only shortly before the assimilation of iron technology in the first millennium B.C. Thus, sub-Saharan Africa for all practical purposes skipped the bronze age altogether, and it appears to have done so because of broken contact with North Africa over a period lasting from sometime in the fourth millennium to sometime in the first. This period of time corresponds to a climatic change, the post-Makalian dry phase which created the present Sahara desert. In time, improved transportation made it possible again to cross the desiccated Sahara, but only after three thousand years of isolation for sub-Saharan Africa. These millennia set tropical Africa so far behind the rest of the Afro-Eurasian land mass, it required several thousand years before the gap could begin to narrow.[9]

Whichever interpretation may be most accurate, authorities agree that special problems, either of isolation or of adapting agriculture to new environments, produced a lag of two or three millennia behind the pace of development in the Near East. If the comparison is made between the Sudan and northwest Europe, however, they were nearly at the same level during the first millennium B.C. Both had by then received iron and agriculture. Neither had yet created an urban civilization. But in the future, Europe was to shoot ahead, while Africa remained in her position of relative backwardness. The remaining problem is to explain the cause of Europe's greater success.

[8] C. Wrigley, "Speculations on the Economic Prehistory of Africa," *Journal of African History*, I, 189–203 (1960).
[9] Wrigley, "Economic Prehistory of Africa," pp. 200–201.

A part of the answer lies in the way civilization grew. The new complex of technological development, which we call the first civilizations, did not simply spread outward from a central point of origin. The combination of metallurgy, writing, developed agriculture, and cities was not possible in all environments. But it was possible in certain places, often thousands of miles apart—lower Egypt and the eastern Mediterranean, Mesopotamia, the Indus Valley, and the north Chinese river valleys. The technological base of all these was similar, but their early development in isolation led them down divergent paths. In all, however, the pace of historical change was quicker than it had been in the period before agriculture, just as it was to become quicker still after the industrial revolution. By 1000 B.C., all of these small foci of civilization were in communication with one another, at least frequently enough to assure that an invention or new technique in one could sooner or later be borrowed by the others. As they came into an area of intercommunication, their progress was even faster. Each of them could then spread out and take in surrounding regions, which may have been unsuited to civilization in its earlier stages.[10]

In the west, the expanding frontiers of civilization reached out along the shores of the Mediterranean. Sea trade made possible the foundation of trading towns, the frontier posts of civilization among the barbarians. These were established both in northwestern Africa and in southern Europe. By about 500 B.C., Egyptian civilization had also been carried south, across the desert to the Nilotic Sudan, where the kingdom of Kush represented an outlier of civilization among the African barbarians, much as the Greek city of Marseille did among the European barbarians. A second outpost of civilization was established about the same time in the Ethiopian highlands and the Red Sea coast near the southern exit from the sea. This was the kingdom of Axum.

In the last years before the beginning of the Christian era, Europe was partly civilized south of the Alps and largely barbar-

---

[10] Thoughtful recent interpretations of early history, revising the Western-centered "world history" approach, are found in Marshall G. S. Hodgson, "Interrelations of Societies in History," *Comparative Studies in Society and History*, V, 227–250 (January 1963) and William H. McNeill, *The Rise of the West. A History of the Human Community* (Chicago, University of Chicago Press, 1963).

ian north of the Alps. The Sudan was civilized in the east (in Axum and Kush) but barbarian in the west (toward Lake Chad and beyond to the Atlantic). Northwest Europe and the Sudan were still level; but northern Europe was just across the Alps from the growing Roman Empire, and the Sudan was hundreds of miles away across the desert. As Rome absorbed elements from all the civilizations of the Mediterranean basin and developed them into a new synthesis, they were carried across the Alps into northern Europe during the few centuries of Roman control in Gaul and Britain. They were not carried south of the Sahara: even Christianity penetrated to Nubia and Axum only after the western Roman Empire had fallen. Though barbarism had then returned to the countries north of the Alps, they remained on the fringes of civilization, still preserved by Byzantium and a few remaining urban centers in southern Europe.

Thus the level of Sudanic and north European technology may have remained about equal from the fifth century A.D. to about the tenth. The revival of Carolingian Europe could be balanced against an equivalent attainment in the new empire of Ghana in the Western Sudan. The precise measurement of European against African civilization at this time, however, was already beside the point. Ghana was cut off from easy contact with any other civilized area, subject to nomadic attacks on the homeland and on the caravan routes to the north. Europe was free of barbarian invasions after the tenth century. It was also able to rebuild its civilization through the mediation of Byzantium and Islam. By the time of the crusades, northwest Europe was fully within the zone of intercommunication with other world civilizations. Overland trade linked the Baltic and North Seas with the Mediterranean. Seaborne trade soon ventured regularly into the Atlantic. The Sudan, on the other hand, remained cut off behind the barrier of the Sahara.

There is no need here to trace the rising technical prowess of the Europeans, or the way they borrowed and assimilated techniques of other civilizations, added their own discoveries, and finally produced modern science and the industrial revolution.[11]

[11] For authoritative and readable recent summaries see: McNeill, *The Rise of the West* and Robert L. Reynolds, *Europe Emerges. Transition toward an Industrial World-Wide Society 600–1750* (Madison, University of Wisconsin Press, 1961).

The point, for present purposes, is simply this: The lag in African development, as seen at the nineteenth-century confrontation with Europe, had two components. One was the ancient lag behind the Near Eastern civilization, which was shared for a time by northwest Europe. The second was the European advance, which carried the West further ahead technologically than either the Sudan or the Near East. This second component has no direct relation to African history. It was produced by unusual achievements in Europe, not unusual failures outside Europe. The Sudan has progressed steadily during the past millennium. There is no cause to ask why it did not progress as fast as Europe: it moved ahead at about the same rate as most other human societies in the period between the first civilizations and the industrial revolution. Only Europe's unusual dynamic break-through into industrialism made Africa and other civilizations of the world appear static.

TRIBES, CULTURES, AND STATES

Still another left-over from the belief in a static and primitive Africa is the problem of terminology. "Tribes" and "tribalism" are frequently used, even today, but they create enormous confusion. In fact, the term "tribe" came into use in the nineteenth century, replacing the earlier European custom of talking about African "nations" or "kingdoms." It was consciously pejorative, designed to suggest a savage society. Then anthropologists took up the term and used it with more neutrality—merely to mean any group of people with a common and relatively homogeneous way of life.[12] In this sense, the term can be used without being insulting, but this kind of "tribe" cannot be a focus of group action. The individual may not even know to which "tribe" the anthropologists have assigned him. The best modern historical practice is to avoid the term altogether, or else to define it precisely when it is used. . . .

The framework of most African history, however, is not the "tribe" or culture area, but the state. Our knowledge of stateless people is so vague and general, they are necessarily covered

[12] Some anthropologists, however, dislike the term and refuse to use it. See M. J. Herskovits, *The Human Factor in Changing Africa* (New York, Knopf, 1962), pp. 69–70.

rapidly in broad strokes. Detailed history makes its appearance with the state, and this means that detailed African history appears first in the north. North Africa and its outliers in Axum and Kush occupy the center of the stage until about the tenth century. Then, through the remainder of the European Middle Ages, Ghana, Mali, Songhai, Kanem-Bornu, Wadai, and Darfur begin to make their appearance.[13] Just before the arrival of the Portuguese in the fifteenth century, the states south of the Congo forest begin to have a consecutive known history,[14] while those states south of the Limpopo only begin to appear at the end of the eighteenth century.[15] Meanwhile, Europeans on the coasts brought new problems, both for the Africans of that time and for later historians of Africa.

THE SLAVE TRADE

The earliest important impact of Europe on sub-Saharan Africa was the slave trade, and the period of its dominance lasted about two centuries, from 1650 to 1850. During this era, the frontiers of European influence in the New World tropics were established on the base of African manpower. Many more Africans than Europeans moved overseas as settlers, though

[13] Summary histories in English are available for all but the states of the central Sudan. For the Western Sudan, see E. W. Bovill, *The Golden Trade of the Moors* (London, Oxford, 1958). For the Nilotic Sudan, see A. J. Arkell, *A History of the Sudan to A.D. 1821* (London, Athlone Press, 1955). For the East African coast, see R. Oliver and G. Mathew, *History of East Africa*. The best summary of the central Sudan is Y. Urvoy, *Histoire de l'empire du Bornou* (Paris, Larose, 1949).

[14] No good summary has yet been published, but J. Vansina's forthcoming *Kings of the Southern Savanna* (due in 1964), should help to fill that gap, while the lake region of East Africa is already covered by Oliver and Mathew, *History of East Africa*.

[15] The foundation of the southern African states is not well summarized anywhere. M. Gluckmann, "The Kingdom of the Zulu in South Africa," in M. Fortes and E. E. Evans-Pritchard (eds.), *African Political Systems* (London, Oxford Press, 1940), pp. 25–35, is helpful for the Zulu alone. D. F. Ellenberger, *History of the Basuto* (London, Caxton, 1912) is older, but useful for the foundation of the Sotho state. The standard histories of South Africa also deal with these events, but only as a part of the story of the European invasions, and from the European point of view. See C. W. de Kiewiet, *A History of South Africa: Social and Economic* (London, Oxford Press, 1941) and E. A. Walker, *A History of Southern Africa*, 3rd ed. (London, Longmans, 1957).

their migrations were involuntary. By 1850, a third of the people of African descent lived outside of Africa.

The slave trade has been studied intensively from the American side. We know a good deal about West Indian plantations and the cotton kingdom of the ante-bellum South. We know something about the organization of the slave trade at sea and in the principal ports on the African coast.[16] But we know very little about the organization of the trade from the interior down to these ports. This part was managed by African merchants and political authorities. Before the full impact of the trade can be accurately assessed, we will need to know more about the sources of supply and the ways in which those regions met the demand for slaves. It seems clear, however, that the trade shifted from region to region, depending on African political conditions. Its effects were consequently different at different times and places.

Western historians have nevertheless tried to estimate the over-all influence of the slave trade on Africa. This line of investigation began with the first campaigns to abolish the slave trade, and many different views have been set forth. One extreme position holds that the slave trade was infinitely destructive to the social well-being of Africa—that it was, indeed, the principal cause of African backwardness. Basil Davidson's *Black Mother* represents this point of view. At the other extreme, some historians have argued that African backwardness came from a lack of commerce with the outside world. The slave trade might not be the most beneficial commerce, but it was better than no commerce at all: it may even have furthered the course of African development. Rigorous versions of this thesis have no support among modern historians of Africa, but Oliver and Fage, in their *Short History of Africa*, feel that the slave trade may have brought limited benefits, at least to certain parts of West Africa.[17] The East African slave trade is usually considered separately, and no one argues that it was beneficial

[16] Among recent studies have been: K. G. Davies, *The Royal African Company* (London, Longmans, 1957); André Delcourt, *La France et les établissements français au Sénégal entre 1713 et 1763* (Dakar, I.F.A.N., 1952); and Abdoulaye Ly, *La Compagnie du Sénégal* ([Paris], Présence Africaine, 1958).

[17] See esp. pp. 121–124.

to any but the slave traders. Too many accounts of the devastation of the interior were reported by nineteenth-century European travelers in Africa.

One of the principal problems that remains to be solved is the precise relation between European guns and political power within Africa. It is often suggested that the introduction of guns, rather than simply the European willingness to buy slaves, was the real cause of dislocation in Africa. According to this view, the gun trade began a vicious circle. African states that sold slaves for guns gained the power to capture more slaves. Those that did not sell slaves for guns became the hunted, rather than the hunters. Thus, African states were forced into the slave trade as the price of survival. This vicious circle certainly operated in the last few decades of the slave trade, especially after the introduction of breach-loaders in the second half of the nineteenth century. Muzzle-loaders may not have been an important military factor in wooded country and in the absence of artillery. Bowmen could let off several arrows while musketeers were reloading, and, in the savanna country of the Western Sudan, cavalry remained dominant long after firearms were known and used.

Recent research has also tended to revise certain older views about the slave trade. Historians in the era of racism often explained the use of African labor in tropical America as a result of the "primitive" condition of Africa and the natural docility of the Africans. It is now clear that Africa was not primitive and Africans were far from docile. Slave revolts were a standard feature of tropical America until the middle of the nineteenth century. Not only were the Afro-Americans of Saint Domingue (now the Republic of Haiti) the first non-Europeans to overthrow colonial rule, several other revolts were at least temporarily successful. Between 1630 and 1694, Africans from the Congo set up an independent African state in northeast Brazil and maintained themselves against European attack. When they were finally defeated by the Portuguese, it required a force of some three thousand men, equipped with artillery.[18]

[18] Edison Carneiro, *Guerras de los palmares* (México, D. F., Fondo de la Cultura Económica, 1946). Translated from Portuguese by Tomás Munõz Molina.

On Jamaica and elsewhere, escaped slaves managed to organize themselves in the mountains and to maintain their freedom until the end of plantation slavery.

Another revision helps to explain why Africans came to make up the great bulk of slaves in the Western world, replacing the Slavs who had been the typical slaves of classical antiquity. New research on medieval slavery in Mediterranean Europe has served to underline the fact that slavery did not disappear there after the fall of Rome. It continued throughout the Middle Ages and, in some places, as late as the eighteenth century. Furthermore, Mediterranean slavery had nothing to do with race. It was mainly a matter of religion: Christians enslaved Muslims and Muslims enslaved Christians.[19] Negro Africans were present among the Mediterranean slaves, even before the Portuguese voyages down the African coast, but they were only one group among many.

As the institution of slavery was carried to America by the first Hispanic settlers and conquerors, American Indians were enslaved, Europeans were sent out as forced workers under various legal devices, and African slaves were imported. The Hispanic powers discovered at an early date that, of these three groups, the Africans made the most efficient labor force. They could survive in the environment of the American tropics better than either of the other two. At the time, no one knew why this was so, but it was usually attributed to some special qualities of the Negro race. Recent work on medical history, however, makes it clear that early environment, rather than race, is the true explanation.

Endemic disease may cause a high rate of infant mortality, but it produces a population relatively well adjusted to survive later attacks of diseases common in that environment. Smallpox, measles, and other diseases of Europe were endemic throughout most of the Afro-Eurasian land mass. Adult Africans, like adult Europeans, were unlikely to die in great numbers from this cause. But American Indians were not accustomed to the Afro-Eurasian diseases. When Europeans and Africans first went to

[19] See Charles Verlinden's monumental study of slavery in Europe, the first volume of which appeared as *L'esclavage dans l'Europe médiévale. Peninsule Ibérique-France* (Bruges, De Tempel, 1955).

America, the Indian populations were swept by a series of disastrous epidemics. Those in the tropical lowlands fared especially badly, since they encountered both the general range of Afro-Eurasian endemic disease and those peculiar to tropical Africa. Europeans also sustained higher mortality rates in the West Indies than in Europe, and even Africans had a higher mortality rate on arrival in America than they would have had in Africa.

The pattern that emerged, however, was one of very high European mortality in tropical Africa, but a lower rate in tropical America. This was one factor that made America, rather than Africa, the most desirable place to grow tropical staples under European management. But America was rapidly becoming depopulated. The alternative was to import either Europeans or Africans, and the Africans were best fitted to survive. In time, a later generation of tropical Americans of any race would have become equally resistant to the diseases of the new West Indian environment, but, before this could take place, social patterns and European ideas had become fired. The myth arose that Africans and only Africans could work successfully in hot climates, and the only way to obtain an African working class was through the slave trade.[20]

An African labor force had still another advantage: workers could be purchased on the African coast. Africa already had its own systems of domestic slavery, and a slave trade within Africa existed before Europeans appeared. African society was also accustomed to trade, and African merchants merely had to adapt themselves to the new economic demand. Unlike most Asian countries in the sixteenth or seventeenth centuries, African states were anxious to buy the European manufactures and Indian textiles offered on the coasts. As the demand for slaves increased, the African ability to supply the demand increased as well. Trade routes penetrated far into the interior,

[20] There is no convenient summary of this interpretation, but elements of it may be found in Eric Williams, *Capitalism and Slavery* (Chapel Hill, University of North Carolina Press, 1944); P. M. Ashburn, *The Ranks of Death: A Medical History of the Conquest of America* (New York, Coward-McCann, 1947); McNeill, *The Rise of the West*, pp. 571–574; and P. D. Curtin, " 'The White Man's Grave:' Image and Reality, 1780–1850," *Journal of British Studies*, I, 94–110 (November 1961).

supplying alien goods in return for captives. In a very real sense, it was African commercial organization, not the alleged primitiveness of African society, that made the slave trade possible. A genuine primitive society could not possibly have reorganized itself to supply up to 100,000 captives a year.

NEW INTERPRETATIONS OF THE "PRE-COLONIAL CENTURY," 1780–1880

Shortly after 1780, the older set of relations between Africa and the outside world began to change, and the change originated in the West. The beginning of the industrial revolution was one factor. The American and French Revolutions brought a new concern about the rights of man and the inhumanity of the slave trade. By 1808, Britain, the United States, and certain other countries made the slave trade illegal for their own nationals, largely for humanitarian reasons. Nevertheless, the actual number of slaves taken across the Atlantic increased greatly during the first half of the nineteenth century, as Cuba and Brazil increased the output of their slave plantations in an effort to meet the demand for tropical staples by an industrializing Europe. In time, the slave trade stopped, but only after a long transition from commercial relations based on the slave trade (up to 1808) to those based mainly on trade in other commodities (after about 1850). From then onward until the 1880's, African readjustment moved rapidly on the West African coast, but readjustment was cut off abruptly in the 1880's by the establishment of wholesale European control.

Historians have recently taken a new look at this period in West African history, often on a state-by-state basis.[21] They

21 The pioneer work in this field was K. O. Dike, *Trade and Politics in the Niger Delta 1830–1885* (Oxford, Clarendon Press, 1956). Other recent work includes Saburi O. Biobaku, *The Egba and their Neighbours 1842–1872* (Oxford, Clarendon Press, 1957); C. W. Newbury, *The Western Slave Coast and Its Rulers* (Oxford, Clarendon Press, 1961); Christopher Fyfe, *A History of Sierra Leone* (London, Oxford Press, 1962); G. I. Jones, *The Trading States of the Oil Rivers* (London, Oxford Press, 1963); Ivor Wilks, *The Northern Factor in Ashanti History* [Legon], University College of Ghana, 1961); B. Schnapper, *La Politique et le commerce français dans le golfe de Guinée de 1838 à 1871* (Paris, Mouton, 1961); John D. Hargreaves, *Prelude to the Partition of West Africa* (London, Macmillan, 1963).

have especially concentrated on the African side of the commercial revolution. The result is a brand new picture of great complexity, as African rulers and merchants tried frantically to meet the modern world on something like equal terms. The older view, that African societies waited patiently for the dynamic leadership of colonial tutelage, has been drastically revised.

Simultaneous with the commercial revolution on the coast, a very important series of religious revolutions took place in the Western Sudan. They were apparently unconnected with the coastal changes, taking their lead instead from the new reforming movements within world-wide Islam. The result in West Africa was a period of intense intellectual and religious ferment, accompanied by the rise of a new series of Sudanese empires.[22] All the results of present research-in-progress have not yet been published, but a revised picture of African affairs in the interior is emerging to parallel the new view of coastal history. Together, they show some of the directions in which West Africa was heading on the eve of the European invasions.

Basil Davidson

Although archaeological discoveries have given us some knowledge of early African peoples and neolithic civilization, the history of early Africa remains to be written. Our most accurate and extensive knowledge of ancient African states and societies comes from West Africa. The three most famous African kingdoms flourished from the ninth to the sixteenth centuries in the Western Sudan, the land Muslims called Biled es Sudan, Land of the Black People. These kingdoms, Ghana, Mali, and Songhay, all bordering the upper Niger river, as well as the Hausa states of what is now northern Nigeria, and Kanem-Bornu further northeast, played an important part in the history of Africa. Having connections with North Africa and the Near East, these states served as a con-

[22] The most convenient summary to date is H. F. C. Smith, "A Neglected Theme of West African History: The Islamic Revolutions of the 19th Century," *Journal of the Historical Society of Nigeria*, II, 169–185 (1961).

duit whereby goods and ideas passed between West Africans and the Arabs and Europeans to the North.

The power of Ghana, Mali, and Songhay lay in their ability to control the gold trade from West Africa to the Muslim and Christian countries of the North. Before the gold of the American mines flowed into Europe, Africa was the main source of this metal so needed for European coinage and trade. In addition to gold, West Africa supplied ivory, skins, pepper, foodstuffs, and slaves to the Maghreb (the Arab term for present-day Morocco and Algeria) and to Egypt. By the eighth century, the trade routes across the Sahara brought Islamic merchants and religious teachers. Under their influence many West Africans were converted to Islam. The Sudan became ideologically linked to the great Muslim civilizations in Morocco, Spain, Egypt, Turkey, and Persia.

Reports about these black African kingdoms circulated throughout the Muslim world. "The king of Ghana is a great king," wrote a Muslim traveler in A.D. 891. "In his territory are mines, of gold, and under him a number of kingdoms. . . . In all this country there is gold." Descriptions of the Sudan were related by the Arab travelers al-Bakri (1067), al-Omari (1336), ibn-Batuta (1364), al-Maghili (1495), ibn-Khaldun (c. 1380), Leo Africanus (c. 1520), and by the Negro scholars, Mahoud Kati in *Tarikh al-Fettash* (c. 1593), Abderrahman es-Sadi in *Tarikh al-Sudan* (c. 1665), and the unknown authors of *The Kano Chronicle*. Muslim scholars from the North filtered into West Africa as did technical and military aid from Islamic Spain and Turkey. The constant pilgrimages to Mecca brought African rulers and their courts into contact with the latest developments in the Islamic world. The ruling classes of Western Sudan showed themselves to be highly cultured and sophisticated. When the British explorer, Hugh Clapperton met the great Muhammad Bello, Sultan of Sokoto (now northern Nigeria) in 1826, he found him reading an Arabic copy of Euclid's *Elements*. The Sultan, Clapperton wrote in his journal, "said that his family had a copy of Euclid brought by one of their relations, who had procured it in Mecca. . . ."

But knowledge of these African kingdoms was not limited to Muslims alone. In 1375 the Jewish cartographer, Abraham Creques, living in Majorca, produced his "Catalan Map" with the location of Timbuktu, Mali, Gao, and other Sudanic cities.

Near the bottom of the map is a picture of Mansa Kankan Musa, Emperor of Mali, sitting on his throne holding gold in his outstretched right hand. Europeans soon learned how to go "to the land of the Negroes in Guinea," but it was to be by sea because the land route lay in the hands of the Muslims of the Maghreb. By 1482 King John II of Portugal had built *Sâo Jorge da Mina* in the center of the richest region of Guinea, the Gold Coast, or as the Portuguese called it, *Costa da Mina.*

However, for a period of over four hundred years, the Europeans remained ignorant of the interior of Africa. The ancient states of the Sudan were relegated to mythology—the Timbuktu of storytellers. But these kingdoms and others did exist, and an introduction to them told from African and Islamic sources has been written by Basil Davidson, Thomas Hodgkin, Freda Wolfson, E. W. Bovill, and H. R. Palmer.

The British historian and journalist, Basil Davidson, has retold the history of the three most famous medieval African kingdoms in *The Lost Cities of Africa* (1959), from which the following piece is extracted.

KINGDOMS OF THE OLD SUDAN

SOURCE: Basil Davidson, "Kingdoms of the Old Sudan," from *The Lost Cities of Africa* (Boston: Little, Brown, 1959), 81–103.

Ghana

Everywhere in the ancient world, iron proved a revolutionary equipment that enabled men to build new and more complex societies; and it was no different in Africa. Once its metallurgy was understood, iron was much more easily obtained than copper or bronze, and was much more efficient. Those who had it could exercise, over those who did not have it, something of the same order of superiority as musketeers would later exercise over spearmen. Thus the peoples of Ghana, remarks El Zouhri some time before A.D. 1150, make expeditions against neighbors "who know not iron and fight with bars of ebony." The Ghanaians "can defeat them because they fight with swords and lances."

The early kingdoms of the old Sudan were thus the product of an iron-using superiority. This means that while the beginnings of organized statehood in the Western Sudan cannot be traced beyond the eighth century—though oral tradition takes them vaguely some way further back—their earliest origins can be safely attached to the period of installation of iron extractive industries and of social changes associated with that development. This period begins around 300 B.C.

Both for work and warfare, the trans-Saharan trade had shown by then the superiority of iron over other metals. Whether by individual skill or native invention, by the capture of prisoners or the purchase of secrets, by the migration of groups or of whole peoples from the north and northeast, iron was beginning to be mined and worked south of the Sahara. Thenceforth iron gave a new mastery over soil and forest, but also—as El Zouhri remarked in his illuminating comment—over stone and bone and wood-using neighbors. It gave, that is, an impulse to conquest and centralized government. It shook the foundations of Stone Age tribalism. It promoted new forms of social organization. It accompanied the creation of an African feudalism; and this feudalism, though always modified and molded by tribal law and custom, would have many parallels with feudalism in medieval Europe.

To this formative influence another, not much less disturbing and creative, was added. Emerging from the revolutionary growth of an ironworking industry and the changes it implied, these new states grew strong and prospered from their conquests but even more, as it would seem, from their international trade. Peoples of the Western Sudan might not control the sources of West African gold: for these lay mostly in the forest belt, and none of the states of the Sudan would succeed in any lasting penetration there. But they controlled the passage of this gold to the northward. Their cities flourished on its trade. They sold it to the intermediaries of the Sahara, who sold it again to the Mediterranean world and Europe; and they bought from these intermediaries the goods of Europe and the Mediterranean. In El Bekri's words, they or their agents carried gold "into every country." There is no exaggeration, Mauny argues, "in saying that the Sudan was one of the principal providers of gold to

the Mediterranean world right through the Middle Ages, up to
the discovery of America. It was this gold which had built the
power of Ghana, and that of the Mandingo empire."

Behind the obscurities of early West African history, therefore,
one may reasonably detect iron smelting and international trade
as underlying factors which had decisive influence in the hands
of men who practiced them. Political and military concentration became possible and, at least for those who could rule, desirable. Alliances of interest emerged, became fused into centers
of power, acquired geographical identity, reappeared as territorial states; even when, as was surely the case, the people of
the riverside villages and the nomads following their herds
continued to live in much the same way as they had lived before.

Among these emergent states of the Western Sudan the
earliest that rose to fame and fortune was Ghana. Its territory
lay to the north and northwest of the upper Niger: significantly
enough, on the gold routes to the north. El Fazari, soon after
A.D. 800, named it "the land of gold." Shortly before 833 Kwarizmi
marked it on a map that was otherwise a copy of one which
Ptolemy had drawn long centuries before. But it was not for
another two hundred years that a North African would write
of Ghana in any detail. Then comes the vivid account of Abdallah
ibn Abdel Aziz, known as Abu Ubaid, or better still as El
Bekri. And although it is a work of compilation, written by a
man who never visited Africa (or at any rate never visited
the Sudan), this description of El Bekri's has the illuminating
touch of full and good material. Writing at Córdoba in southern
Spain, where he had at his disposal the official records of the
Ummayad rulers and the gossip of contemporary pioneers, El
Bekri sets forth in careful and discriminating detail what well-
informed Mediterranean opinion, based on many firsthand reports and much military intelligence, believed to be the truth
about Ghana and the lands beyond the desert. His work was
finished in 1067, some thirteen years after Ibn Yasin, the Almoravid ruler of North Africa, had marched southward to invade
those lands and had captured Aoudaghast, a tributary city of
Ghana. This invasion had brought the Western Sudan much
closer to the Mediterranean and Spain; and it was this that
gave El Bekri his wide choice of material.

"The king of Ghana," El Bekri is writing in the year after William of Normandy crossed the English Channel, "can put two hundred thousand warriors in the field, more than forty thousand of them being armed with bow and arrow." It would be interesting to know what the Normans might have thought of Ghana. Anglo-Saxon England could easily have seemed a poor and lowly place beside it. "Ghana," says El Bekri in 1067, "is the title of the king of this people," and "the name of their country is Aoukar. The king who governs them at the moment . . . is called Tenkamenin, who came to the throne in 455 [that is, A.D. 1062] . . . Tenkamenin is master of a great empire and of a power which is formidable."

That this was more than travelers' embroidery may be seen from the fact that it took the Almoravid armies—rapidly victorious elsewhere—no fewer than fourteen years to subdue Ghana and seize its capital city. Ibn Yasin, fervent promoter of Islam, had marched southward from the Maghreb in 1054. In the following year he took Aoudaghast, a city that is entirely vanished today but was situated, according to El Bekri, two months' southward from Sijilmassa and fifteen days from the capital of Ghana. El Bekri says that Aoudaghast was "a very large city with several markets, many date palms and henna trees as big as olives," and "filled with fine houses and solid buildings." This city—a Sudanese city with many Moorish traders, for it lay at the southern terminal of the trans-Saharan caravan trail from Sijilmassa—the Almoravids "took by storm, violating women and carrying off all they found there, saying it was legal booty." But it was not until 1076 that another Almoravid leader, Abu Bakr, could take the capital of Ghana itself.

This capital had two cities six miles apart, while the space between was also covered with dwellings. In the first of these cities was the king's residence, "a fortress and several huts with rounded roofs, all being enclosed by a wall." The second, which also had a dozen mosques, was a merchant city of the Muslims: a city, that is, of those who had come southward to settle or tarry and trade—much, indeed, like the *sabun gari* outside the walls of modern Kano; although there in Kano it is from the south that men have come for trade and settlement. Of manners at the court of this pagan king, El Bekri provides a celebrated description.

"When he gives audience to his people, to listen to their complaints and set them to rights, he sits in a pavilion around which stand his horses caparisoned in cloth of gold; behind him stand ten pages holding shields and gold-mounted swords; and on his right hand are the sons of the princes of his empire, splendidly clad and with gold plaited into their hair. The governor of the city is seated on the ground in front of the king, and all around him are his viziers in the same position. The gate of the chamber is guarded by dogs of an excellent breed, who never leave the king's seat, they wear collars of gold and silver. . . . The beginning of an audience is announced by the beating of a kind of drum which they call *deba*, made of a long piece of hollowed wood . . ."

Where was this capital city? As long ago as 1914 a French district officer, Bonnel de Mezières, dug into a site that was suggested by tradition (although not by any visible projection above the flat savannah) at a remote spot in the Sahel, a scrub and sand country north of the upper Niger. De Mezières found enough to make him believe that this had probably been the capital of Ghana in El Bekri's day; and later excavation has gone far to vindicate him.

Renewed work at this site of Kumbi Saleh, lying two hundred and five miles north of the modern city of Bamako on the Niger, began in 1939; only to be stopped, almost at once, by the war. Ten years later Thomassey and Mauny were at last able to undertake a systematic examination of these promising ruins in the light of a modern understanding of the matter. By 1951 they had tracked the remains of a large and elaborate Muslim city which had covered a square mile and may have had a population of about thirty thousand people, very numerous for the world of eight or nine hundred years ago when this city had evidently flourished.

Reasons for believing that this was the merchant city of Ghana reported by El Bekri, and that the king's city may yet be identified nearby—that Kumbi Saleh, in short, was Ghana's capital through the last period of its life as an organized state— are not yet conclusive, but they are strong. Thus the *Tarikh el Fettach* says that Kumbi had been the capital of the empire of the Kayamaga, while the *Tarikh es Sudan* explains that Kayamaga had been the name of the first king of Ghana (who had, according to tradition, no fewer than forty-three successors). And while there are other "Kumbis" in the region of Kumbi Saleh, there is none which offers archeological evidence of having once existed as a city of the first importance.

That Kumbi Saleh had been this, though, admits of no argument at all. Level with its dusty sub-Saharan plain though it is today, Kumbi Saleh had once been great. Among many large dwellings and a mosque, two mansions excavated by Thomassey suggest something of its scale and comfort. One of these was about sixty-six feet long and forty-two feet wide, and had seven rooms opening out of one another on two stories connected by an efficient staircase. The other was still larger, and had nine rooms. Built mainly in blocks of slatelike schist cemented with banco, their interior walls had been decorated with a yellow plaster of which a little is still preserved. No objects in silver or gold were found, but a large store of objects in iron, indicating, as Mauny has commented, "an already advanced civilization, both urban and agricultural." Among these iron objects were lances, knives, arrowheads, nails, a varied collection of farming tools, and one of the finest pairs of scissors of early medieval date ever to be found in any country. A large quantity of glass weights, evidently for weighing gold, were recovered; many fragments of pottery of Mediterranean provenance; and seventy-seven pieces of painted stone, of which fifty-three bore verses of the Koran in an Arabic script, while twenty-four others had decorated motifs.

Trade and tribute were the sources of its wealth. Ghana lay between the salt deposits of the north and the gold deposits of the south, and profited mightily from exchange between the two. Such was the southern need of salt that a gold-producing people called the Ferawi, according to El Bekri, would buy it for an equal weight of gold. But gold was also the commodity that the north wanted most. Thus the imperial ambition of successive states in the Sudan, drawing their wealth from this international trade, would be to monopolize the southern sources of gold—the "mysterious" land of Wangara and its gold-bearing soil that lay in fact somewhere near the sources of the Senegal River—and, secondly, to capture the principal salt deposits of the north, notably those at Taghaza in the northern desert, as well as to dominate the caravan roads. Ghana managed the first but not the second. Mali, after Ghana, would go far toward succeeding in both.

The rulers of Ghana not only knew the supreme trading value of gold, they also understood the need and the means of upholding it. El Bekri makes this clear. "The best gold in the country," he says, "is found at Ghiarou, a town that is eighteen days' journey from the capital, lying in a country filled with Negro peoples" and covered with their villages. "All nuggets of gold that are found in the mines of this empire belong to the king; but he leaves to his people the gold dust that everyone knows. Without this precaution gold would become so plentiful that it would practically lose its value."

They equally understood the value of trading tribute. The king of Ghana "exacts the right of one dinar of gold on each donkey-load of salt that enters the country, and two dinars of gold on each load of salt that goes out." Salt and gold would always be stable commodities; but others were important. "A load of copper"—entering Ghana from the copper mines of the southern Sahara—"pays him five mithcals, and each load of merchandise ten mithcals."[1] Here one glimpses the familiar picture of a centralized government which has discovered the art and exercise of taxation, another witness of stability and statehood.

In 1054 the Almoravid rulers came south to make converts to Islam and to chastise pagans, but they also came for loot. They had the salt deposits under their control; they sought now to capture the gold deposits as well. Their coming was brief but disastrous. Three hundred years after El Bekri, Ibn Khaldun would summarize the experience. The Almoravids "spread their dominion over the Negroes [of Ghana], devastated their territory and plundered their property. Having submitted them to poll tax they imposed on them a tribute, and compelled a great number of them to become Moslems. The authority of the kings of Ghana being destroyed, their neighbors, the Sosso, took

[1] The *mithcal* was about one-eighth of an ounce of gold.

their country and reduced its inhabitants to slavery." By the thirteenth century the state and cities of Ghana, or such as survived, were far gone in decay.

But the pattern of trade and tribute which had made Ghana strong over many centuries was not destroyed. If anything, it was strengthened. With Ghana and after Ghana, other states appeared. Conquest from the north, never more than spasmodic, repeatedly gave way to prolonged periods of peaceful trading; and it was the desert intermediaries in this trade, marauding Tuaregs and their kind, who regularly threatened this peace rather than the Arabs or Berbers of the north.

By 1213, according to a more or less respectable tradition, Allakoi Keita had founded the Mandingo state that would pass into history as the empire of Mali, or Melle; and twenty-five years later his successor, Sundiata, overthrew the Sosso rulers who had established themselves in Ghana not long before. Sundiata took the then capital of Ghana from the Sosso in 1240, destroyed it, and established his own capital (or the first of his capitals) in the south, perhaps at Niani or Jeriba on the upper Niger. He and his successors would dominate much of the Western Sudan for another hundred years.

They would dominate weaker rivals and enfeoffed subjects. For by this time the whole country of the Niger bend and its hinterland—more than half a million square miles of high and often well-watered grasslands—was drawn into the control of more or less centralized states. Some of these have achieved a place in history, through slender surviving records; others have left behind them no more than the curious echo of their names. Meanwhile far to the eastward, and at about the same time, another great savannah region was undergoing the same de-tribalizing and centralizing process; and would throw up, then and later, the states and empires of the Hausa and Fulani, of Kanem and Bornu and Darfur.

In this crystallizing process one strong power and ruling people, or federation of peoples, would rival or succeed or coexist with another, sometimes overlapping in time and place, sometimes continuing its life under different names and dynasties. In a limited sense the Mandingo empire of Mali may be said to have followed Ghana; and Songhay may be said to have followed Mali just as Bornu would follow Kanem. But any picture of one empire simply ousting another in mechanical succession would be false; the development across the whole region was rather a continuous growth of governing institutions interrupted by dynastic rivalries, foreign invasion, and the individual changes and chances of history.

And in all this there were parallels with contemporary Europe. The peoples of Europe and the Sudan might be as different from each other as the latitudes they lived in: the fundamental patterns of their social growth were often surprisingly alike. In both there was the steady organization of central power and tribute against an economic background of peasant agriculture, pastoralism, and an expanding use of metals. Trade, in both, was a great driving motor.

Timbuktu and Djenné, Walata, Gao, Agadès—these were the Milans and Nurembergs of the medieval Sudan: much less magnificent, indeed, yet rich and powerful and imposing in their time and place. Trading cities first and foremost, they welcomed the caravans which came in stumbling thirst out of the northern desert with loads of copper and salt, Venetian beads, the sword blades of Europe and Damascus. They assembled and dispatched the caravans which embarked again northward on that fearful journey, often with slaves, and the merchants with their ever more precious purseloads of gold. Their reputation spread across the world.

Mali

Timbuktu and Djenné, both to become famous throughout the Islamic world for their commerce and learning, seem to have grown into cities by the twelfth century. But their eminence dates from Mandingo supremacy and its empire of Mali. Then it was, in 1307, that the most renowned of all the monarchs of the old Sudan, *Mansa* (sultan or emperor) Kankan Musa, inherited power over Mali and began to extend its dominion. After much success in conquest and diplomacy, this remarkable man followed others from the Western Sudan on pilgrimage to Mecca, and gave the world a proof of the widespread loyalties of Islam as well as a chance of measuring the wealth of Sudanese civilization.

His going through Cairo in 1324, his camel trains and servants and his wives and gifts and arrogant horsemen, all the trappings of a king whose realm would soon comprise a land as large as western Europe and as civilized as most of its kind in Europe, still lingered as familiar gossip in North Africa a hundred years later; for Kankan Musa went with a pleasantly memorable supply of gold as well as pomp and circumstance. An interesting contemporary estimate of Cairo's opinion was later recorded by a senior official of that city. Although El Omari's *Africa Without Egypt* was written some time later, the writer was in a position to found his chapter on Mali from information gathered by men who had seen the Mandingo monarch on his way to Mecca.

He quotes a jurist of Cairo, who had talked with Kankan Musa, as having heard from the emperor that the length of his realm was "about one year." El Omari adds that he heard the same from another source, "but El Dukkali considers that it is four months long and as much wide; and this opinion of El Dukkali is preferable, since Kankan Musa may very well have swollen the real size of his realm." We know in fact that Mali at the time of Kankan Musa's journey, or soon after, had enclosed within its governing system the approaches to the salt deposits of Taghaza on the northern fringes of the Sahara, as well as the approaches to the gold country in the far south on the southern fringes of the savannah; while to the west it reached as far as the Atlantic, and eastward held the copper mines and caravan center of Takedda and probably the lands beyond.

This realm had grown during Kankan Musa's pilgrimage. In 1325 his army commander, Sagaman-dir, took the Songhay capital of Gao on the middle Niger; and with Gao there fell to the dominion of Mali the whole wide trading area which the Songhay had already captured to the north of them. Thus for size and wealth if not for the number of its people, who were comparatively few when compared with the empires of the East, Mali was one of the greatest states in the world of its time. Kankan Musa returned home by way of Gao, enjoying his general's conquest and receiving the submission of the Songhay king and notables, and went on upstream to Timbuktu.

There in Timbuktu he caused new mosques to be raised, mosques that would long be famous in the whole Sudan. They are said to have followed the design of a poet of Granada in southern Spain, Abu Ishaq es Saheli, whom the emperor had come to know in Mecca and persuaded to return with him. Ibn Battuta, visiting Timbuktu some twenty years later, says that he saw the grave of this "meritorious poet," while the mosque of Timbuktu attached to Abu Ishaq's name would long be famous. And soon after Kankan Musa's visit, according to tradition, the earliest flat-roofed houses were built in Gao and Timbuktu. In any case the wealth of these cities must greatly have expanded from this time, for Mali had succeeded better than Ghana and now controlled the country to the north as well as the country to the south—many sources of copper, salt, and gold, as well as the caravan trails between.

Centers of commerce and religion, these cities became centers of learning. Scholars sheltered in their relative ease and security. The literate culture of the Western Sudan, already in existence for several hundred years, flowered in Timbuktu during years that saw, in Europe, the ravage of the Hundred Years' War. No one now can say how much it flowered, nor what fruits it bore, for the books that men read or wrote there are lost or not yet found; but Leo Africanus, two centuries later, gives some measure of the city's intellectual life. "In Timbuktu," he says, "there are numerous judges, doctors and clerics, all receiving good salaries from the king. He pays great respect to men of learning. There is a big demand for books in manuscript, imported from Barbary. More profit is made from the book trade than from any other line of business." The king in question was Mohammed Askia of Songhay; but conditions would not have greatly differed in the years of plenitude that came in the wake of Kankan Musa's conquest.

This was a civilization in its own right, standing to North Africa in much the same relationship of influence as Kush had stood to Egypt, and achieving, as Kush had achieved, its own original and independent growth. Peace reigned over the long caravan trails. Men were free to travel and trade and prosper as they could. There would be interruptions in this security, true enough—Mossi raiders would pillage Timbuktu only eight years after Kankan Musa's visit—but they would remain interruptions, disturbing rarely the everyday peace that Ibn Battuta found. And they must have disturbed even less the peasants and pastoralists who dwelt and throve on the banks of the Niger and out across the plains beyond. Many of these remained pagan even at the height of Islamic fame in the cities and gave, with their stolid clinging to the ancient ways, another native and authentic accent to this Sudanese civilization.

The excellent Ibn Battuta has left some pleasant travel notes of Mali. Always interested in women, he found those of Walata of "surpassing beauty"—no mean compliment, perhaps, from a man who had seen so many nations; moreover (and this he found upsetting as well as remarkable) they were "shown more respect than the men." The state of affairs at Walata, which he calls "the northernmost province of the Negroes," was "indeed extraordinary. Their men show no signs of jealousy whatever. No one claims descent from his father, but on the contrary from his mother's brother. A person's heirs are his sister's sons, not his own sons. This is a thing which I have seen nowhere in the world except among the Indians of Malabar. But *those* are heathens; *these* people are Muslims, punctilious in observing the hour of prayer, studying books of law, and memorizing the Koran. Yet their women show no bashfulness before men and do not veil themselves, though they are assiduous in attending prayer . . ." Even Islam had not succeeded in overthrowing matrilineal succession in the Sudan. Though strictly orthodox, Islam here would develop a distinctively Sudanese outlook in ethical and social matters.

These women, Ibn Battuta found to his surprise (and, one may think, to his delight), had "friends" or "companions" amongst men outside their own families, and the men in the same way had "companions" amongst the women of other families. "A man may go into his house and find his wife entertaining her 'companion,' but he takes no objection to it. One day at Walata I went into the qadi's house, after asking his permission to enter, and found him with a young woman of remarkable beauty. When I saw her I was shocked and turned to go out, but she laughed at me, instead of being overcome with shame, and the qadi said to me 'Why are you going out? She is my companion.'" And yet this qadi, says Ibn Battuta, "was a theologian and a pilgrim to boot."

With the conquests of Kankan Musa the rulers grew wealthier; and the cities, profiting from their control of the caravan terminals and their increasing monopoly of the more important products, followed suit. Perhaps Djenné was the greatest of them. "It is because of this hallowed town," the author of the *Tarikh es Sudan* would write some three hundred years later, but the comment will apply to the dominion of Mali as well as to the later dominion of Songhay, "that caravans come to Timbuktu from all points of the horizon." Crossing southward over the Sahara in the mid-nineteenth century, Heinrich Barth could still find potent evidence of the extent and wealth of this far-flung trading system. Though reduced by then to proportions that might be insignificant when compared with the carrying trade of nineteenth century Europe, it made a still convincing witness to the commercial machinery which had helped to build and maintain states and long-enduring dynasties in this savannah country of the Middle Ages.

Even through the eyes of this late observer, the scene grows wonderfully clear and vivid. Precise and intelligent, Barth was never content with general observations; he had the good reporter's attachment to fact. He always went to the heart of the matter and wanted to know the scale of trading profit, not only for his own day, but also for the past. "The importance of the trade of Agadès, and the wealth of the place in general," he comments in one of his typically factual observations, "appear very clearly from the large tribute, of 150,000 ducats, which the king of Agadès was able to pay to that of Songhay"—some 250 years, that is, before Barth himself would visit the place.

In the same thoughtful probing manner he looked into the value and the nature of the salt trade, a trans-Saharan staple whose handling would not have greatly changed over the centuries, and has left an admirably detailed account of the means whereby bold and enterprising men could profit from it. During the dominion of Songhay, he found, the second-in-authority at Agadès—one of the south Saharan caravan stations—had had to levy tax on all merchandise imported into the town. (It would not have been much different under the earlier dominion of Mali; and the king of Ghana, long before that, had done the same on his narrower frontiers.) This office had been of great importance in providing royal revenue, but also in the means of individual enrichment.

For the chief duty of this official, Barth found, was "to accompany annually the salt caravan of the Kel-Gerès, which supplies the western part of the Middle Sudan with the salt of Bilma, from Agadès to Sokoto; and to protect it on the road as well as to secure it against exorbitant exactions on the part of the Fulbe [Fulani] of Sokoto. For this trouble he receives one *kantu*, that is to say the eighth part of a middle-sized camel load . . . a contribution which forms a considerable income in this country, probably of from eight to ten thousand Spanish dollars; the caravan consisting generally of some thousand camels, not all equally laden, and the *kantu* of salt fetching in Sudan from five thousand to seven or eight thousand *kurdi*, or shells, which are worth from two to three dollars. Under such circumstances those officers, who at the same time trade on their own account, cannot but amass considerable wealth."

Tales of fabulous kingly wealth had always been common. El Bekri had long before reported the king of Ghana as having a nugget of gold so large and heavy that he could safely tether his horse to it. But with the growth of Mali and its trading network the fables acquired a more statistical shape, and ceased perhaps to be fables after all. Kankan Musa was said to have taken five hundred slaves on the Mecca pilgrimage, each carrying a staff of gold that weighed about six pounds. On his baggage camels there were said to be eighty to one hundred loads of gold, each weighing about three hundred pounds. And anyone who has chanced to see a modern durbar of chiefs and traditional rulers in West Africa, a parade flashing with scores and hundreds of golden staffs—wooden staffs, no doubt, yet covered with beaten gold—will not find this so hard to credit.

Accumulation of wealth promoted trade, but it also promoted industry. "The great advantage of Kano," Barth wrote of that north Nigerian town, but medieval Timbuktu and Gao and Djenné would have reproduced something of the same pattern, "is that commerce and manufactures go hand in hand, and almost every family has its share in them. There is really something grand in this kind of industry, which spreads to the north as far as Murzuk, Ghat, and even Tripoli; to the west, not only to Timbuktu, but in some degree as far as the shores of the Atlantic, the very inhabitants of Arguin [on the Atlantic coast] dressing in the cloth woven and dyed in Kano; to the east, all over Bornu, although there it comes into contact with the native industry of the country; while to the south it maintains a rivalry with the native industry . . ."

Trading links multiplied. By 1400, according to Ibu Khaldun, annual caravans across the Sahara by way of the Hoggar Mountains counted no fewer than twelve thousand camels; and this was only one of half a dozen well-used routes. But the caravans went in many directions as well as to and from the northward and the Mediterranean; the whole Sudan was crisscrossed by their patient profit-seeking trails. Thus Bornu—in what is now northeastern Nigeria—bought copper from Wadai, its neighbor to the eastward; and Wadai had this copper in turn from Darfur, again to the eastward. Mali imported vastly from the Mediterranean as well as from Egypt, whether by way of the eastern or the northern routes—silks and damascened blades and horses in quantity. Schoolmen of the Muslim seats of learning traveled back and forth. Pilgrims walked to Mecca. Currencies evolved in gold or copper or shells or weight of stuffs, or in salt or metal pieces. Only to the southward could these savannah kingdoms seldom penetrate, but even there, beyond the forest barrier, they had their trading interest; and cola nuts from southern Nigeria were much in demand.

Against this restless enterprising background of conquest and centralizing government and continental trade, the kingdoms and empires rose and fell across a thousand years and more; yet only now perhaps, while the Western Sudan stands on the threshold of a regained independence, can their achievement win its full perspective and importance. This achievement was large and memorable, and is relevant to the re-emergence of an independent Sudan. When Kankan Musa died in 1332 he left behind him, in Bovill's words, "an empire which in the history of purely African states was as remarkable for its size as for its wealth; and which provided a striking example of the capacity of the Negro for political organisation."

Songhay

The Songhay empire of the middle Niger came to power after Mali had passed its apogee, and carried the civilization of the Western Sudan some further steps toward maturity.

Today the Songhay, a Negro people who may number some six hundred and fifty thousand, live along the Niger in their ancient home between the region of Timbuktu and the frontiers of modern Nigeria. They till the soil and raise cattle, and essentially are the same as they have always been: a people whose destinies and habits are inseparable from the river on whose wide banks they live. For much more than a thousand years they have occupied this middle reach of the Niger as it flows and broadens through rolling sun-scorched grasslands; and usually they have had dominion over it.

Their literate culture, at least in Arabic, goes back some nine hundred years; while it was a man of this nation, though writing in Timbuktu, who composed the *Tarikh el Fettach* in the last years of the sixteenth century. Thus the city of Gao was to the Songhay, for learning and for trade and government, what Timbuktu and Djenné were to others: and Gao, indeed, has yielded some of the most interesting inscriptions in the whole of Africa. Found in 1939 at Sané, some four miles from the center of modern Gao, these appear in Arabic on a number of royal tombstones dating to the first part of the twelfth century. "Here lies the tomb of the king who defended God's religion, and who rests in God, Abu Abdallah Mohammed," declares one of them, adding that the king died in the year 494 after the Hegira, which is 1100: proof both of the early establishment of Islam in Gao, and of early regard for letters and for learning.

The origin of this Negro people is obscure, and that of their kings confused with many stories of eastern or northern provenance. At some remote time the whole of this river region is said to have been populated by a people divided traditionally into "masters of the soil" and "masters of the water"; and these

are said to have belonged in turn to an ancient family of West
African peoples. To these early inhabitants, migrants were added.
Tradition says that these migrants included the Sorko, a fisher-
folk coming from the east (perhaps from Lake Chad by way
of the Benue River), and the Gow, who were hunters; and these
two appear among the founders of the Songhay nation. Their
most important settlement was at Koukya, or Gounguia; almost
certainly this was near the falls of Labbezenga in the Dendi
country, lying on the northwestern frontiers of what is now
Nigeria.

Another tradition says that a group of Berber migrants arrived
at Koukya, perhaps in the seventh century A.D., being connected
with the Lemta of Libya; and established themselves as chiefs
of the Songhay people. Disturbed by this, the Sorko people
are said to have migrated upstream and founded the settlement
and later city of Gao, and even to have pushed on westward
as far as Mopti in the lake region above Timbuktu. The "Berber"
kings of Koukya later followed them: in A.D. 1010 Dia (or Za)
Kossoi took Gao from the Sorko and established the Songhay
capital there, and it is from then that the state and later empire
of Gao may be said to have begun. One need take neither
the dates nor the traditions too seriously. All that comes out
as relatively sure is that the Songhay empire of Gao had its
organized beginnings in the region of Dendi; that its civilization
was the product of native initiative stimulated by migrant in-
cursion; and that, with others, it took its rise in early centuries
after the western Sudan had fully entered its Iron Age.

King Kossoi of Gao is said to have accepted Islam in 1009;
and here, perhaps, tradition is well founded. This was the period
that came before the Almoravid ravages and conquests, and no
doubt those Almoravid armies would have had zealous men,
whether merchants or scholars, to go before them. There is also
another and persuasive light on this. According to the *Tarikh
el Fettach*—written by a man well placed to know the traditions
of his own people—this early Songhay monarch was converted
by argument of the merchants of Gao, whose position at the
southern end of one of the great caravan trails (the same,
indeed, as the Garamantes may have used a thousand years
earlier) had already made them rich and commercially persua-

sive. Their neighbors to the north—Lemtuna Berbers of the Adrar region—were energetic Muslims in their time; and commerce and religion had evidently moved together into Gao. And then conquest—as it generally would in Africa—easily followed commerce and religion: Dia Kossoi made himself master of Gao and accepted Islam.

This is what tradition says; and tradition, in this case, may be taken as largely in the right. The names and dates and details are no doubt subject to correction; thus the twelfth-century tombstones of Gao, made of marble brought piously from Spain, give royal names that are different from those of the *Tarikhs*. Here, in any case, the substantial point is that Islam, like Christianity elsewhere, would prove a great solvent of peoples and founder of states. It cut across tribal gods and ancestor beliefs as Christianity had done in Europe, and gave new scope for the building of many-peopled kingdoms and constellations of power. Long afterward, in the nineteenth century, European missionaries would see in "Christianity and commerce" a sovereign combination for civilizing and unifying tribal Africa; and it may not be unreasonable to imagine that Dia Kossoi and men like Kankan Musa, who governed on a much grander scale than he did, must have seen "Islam and commerce" in something of the same light.

These river people grew strong, at all events, from the stability of their mixed economy of farming and fishing and cattle-raising, from the importance of their trading cities, and from the success they had in uniting themselves against rivals. In growing strong they moved from merely tribal loyalties and forms of organization into the many-peopled empire of Gao. Their tribute-paying submission to Mali, imposed in 1325, lasted little more than fifty years. Thereafter their infant state survived invasion by another Sudanese people, the Mossi, as well as repeated attacks by desert Tuareg during the century that followed. And in course of time, through this tough compacting process, they aspired to greatness. The eighteenth ruler of the line of kings founded by Kossoi in A.D. 1010, Sonni Ali, came to power in 1464 and made Songhay the most powerful state in the Sudan of his time, except perhaps for Bornu to the eastward.

Like Kankan Musa of Mali, Sonni Ali established a single

hegemony over much of the river and its hinterland, and accumulated, through a now familiar process of tribute and trade, wealth and power that were no less brilliant in the eyes of the men of his day. His predecessors had built on strong foundations; Sonni Ali, extending them, seized Timbuktu and Djenné from their Mandingo rulers and made these cities part of his dominion.

Of the motives that inspired him, or the shape they may have taken in his mind, the meager record says little. Sonni Ali has come down through tradition as a man of unusual courage and strength of purpose who, though probably not himself a pagan, had more than a little sympathy for the pagan traditions of the Songhay people. Muslim biographers invariably regard him as an enemy of their faith, or at least of orthodoxy[2]; and his descendants, by way of seeming to confirm this, are popularly invested with a reputation for skill and power in the magic arts. More probably, Sonni Ali cared little for the principles of other people's religion but much for the tactics of his own ambition. He recalls, faintly though the records murmur, the kings of the Europe of his day—bold in the field and cunning in council, playing off one enemy against another, superstitious in the manner of his fathers, given to fits of furious impatience with the logic-chopping of religious schoolmen; but loyal always to the cause of a strong central power which he, and he alone, should dominate.

One approaches nearer to the reality of those days of empire-building with his successor, Mohammed Askia, who comes luminously from the record. This man, whose name was Mohammed Touré but who took the title of Askia, and became Askia the Great, mounted the Songhay throne in 1493 and reigned for thirty-five momentous years. He pushed the frontiers of the Songhay empire as far as Segu in the west and the sub-Saharan region of Aïr in the northeast, realizing once again something of the unified control of far north and far south that Kankan Musa had achieved. Yet his real triumph was to endow Songhay with an administrative system which marked a new and long advance towards a truly centralized state.

Sonni Ali and his predecessors had established and maintained a state power that was still, essentially, a tribal power obliged

[2] The orthodoxy, here, of the Malekite rites of Islam.

to take account of tribal boundaries and rivalries. Mohammed Askia seems to have gone much beyond that. Muslim biographers are loud in their praises of him; and there is little doubt that the Askia saw in "Islam and commerce" a powerful and dependable ally for this centralizing work. And just as Timbuktu and Djenné had owed much of their importance to the unifying power of Kankan Musa, so now did these and other cities of the Western Sudan expand again and flourish after a difficult interregnum. It is characteristic of this expansion that the men who wrote the *Tarikh es Sudan* and the *Tarikh el Fettach* (and other men, among them the renowned Ahmed Baba, of whose undoubtedly copious writings only six works of importance are known to have survived, though others may still be found) should have lived in Timbuktu during and immediately after Mohammed Askia's reign.

This Songhay empire which Sonni Ali and Mohammed Askia forged and founded in the years, crucial to Europe, which saw the first maritime travels to West Africa and the rise of England as a naval power, lasted in the flower of its independence for little more than a century.

The Western Sudan in the time of its institutional growth was less fortunate, if one may contemplate the parallel for a moment, than Western Europe. For Europe suffered its last destructive invasions from without during the Magyar raids of the ninth and tenth centuries—the period of Almoravid penetration and conquest in the Western Sudan. But in 1591 the Moroccan armies of El Mansur emerged from the Sahara, captured Gao and Timbuktu, scattered the armies of the Songhay ruler, Askia Ishak, and ruined the state. Though as brief as the Almoravid invasion of five centuries earlier, this Moroccan experience was hardly less destructive. Decline set in. Timbuktu and Djenné retained their tradition and practice of scholarship, but within narrower limits: even Gao, a little more fortunate, could not afterward claim more than a small provincial fame. By 1600 the great days of the Western Sudan are over.

III. SLAVERY TAKES ROOT
IN THE AMERICAS

How is it that we hear the loudest yelps for liberty among the drivers of negroes?   DR. SAMUEL JOHNSON

I advance it, therefore, as a suspicion only, that the blacks, whether originally a distinct race, or made distinct by time and circumstance, are inferior to the whites in the endowment both of body and of mind.

THOMAS JEFFERSON, *Notes on Virginia*, 1784

Frank Tannenbaum

The growing trend among historians of Negro slavery has been away from the question of its profitability and toward a comparative analysis of it in the Americas. The institution of slavery and the problem of color have not been exclusively a North American dilemma. Negro slavery existed in the West Indies and the Caribbean, in Central and South America. Through comparative studies, historians have discovered that Latin countries showed less rigidity and more humanity in the treatment of their slaves than did Anglo-Saxon countries. In Latin America, racism, while not eradicated, was blunted by customs and institutions. The Negro found that upon freedom, which came without the havoc of civil wars, society did not erect obstacles to prevent him from enjoying his civil and social rights. Why was slavery and the treatment of Negroes milder, if only by degrees, in Latin American countries?

The men who have redirected our study to this question are Gilberto Freyre, Frank Tannenbaum, Stanley Elkins. They have argued that slavery was far milder in feudal Latin Catholic cultures than in capitalistic Anglo-Saxon Protestant areas because the basic humanity, "the moral personality," of the slave managed to be preserved. Customs and institutions, unknown to British and American slave societies, protected the

Negro. Tannenbaum has written: "The acceptance of the idea of the spiritual equality of all men made for a friendly, an elastic milieu within which social change could occur in peace." In a society where the Negro slave was recognized as a person, however low his present station, that society could also envision him as being a citizen, a free man. In North America and the British West Indies, slaves were reduced to the state of *things*, completely outside the protection of the church, the courts and law, and the state. It was to be more than a question of actual treatment, although Freyre does make much of the humanized paternalism between master and slave in Northeastern Brazil. The problem hinged on whether a culture would accept the basic humanity of the slave. In America, the established body of opinion, expressed in the words of Chief Justice Taney of the Supreme Court, declared that "a Negro has no rights which a white man need respect." In Latin America, institutions and customs acted to protect the slave and lead to his manumission. For example, Professor Herbert S. Klein found that in 1860 Cuba and Virginia had nearly the same number of Negroes, about 550,000, yet in Cuba 213,167 or 39% were already free while in Virginia the figure was only 58,042 or 11%. Also, in Brazil, by 1872 over half its colored population had been freed by voluntary manumission, and it required no destructive war to bring about the final end of slavery in 1889.

Since Tannenbaum's seminal work, Stanley Elkins has projected Tannenbaum's hypothesis into more controversial territory, charging that under American slavery a system analogous to the Nazi concentration camp developed, destroying the normal personality of the slave and reducing him to the infantile "Sambo" of slave folklore (*See* p. 183). Herbert Klein's study of the role of the churches in Cuba and Virginia concluded that the Catholic church in Cuba acted as a break upon the plantation system, a fact not evident in the Anglican church in Virginia. A recent study by J. G. Taylor of slavery in Louisiana would seem to support the contention that slavery was harsher under American than Spanish-French rule.

However, no sooner had the Freyre-Tannenbaum-Elkins theses begun to make an impact than serious objections were raised. While admitting that there were differences in slave systems, the critics rejected the ideological causations put forth. The differences were not due to institutions or customs modifying slavery, but rather as Professor Elsa Goveia has written, it was "the state of slavery which set limits to what the Catholics, Anglicans, or any of the other varieties of Christian could hope to achieve." Other commentators have argued that the planters in Brazil and elsewhere disregarded the admonitions of the Catholic church, while the Spanish and Portuguese crowns seldom enforced their statutes protecting the slaves. They conclude that in both cultures slavery was inhuman. Professor Marvin Harris totally rejects the view that slaves were treated better in Latin America because of some commitment to religious ideals. Slaves were treated as they were—harshly—because they were "the most defenseless of all immigrant groups." The Virginia planters showed little regard for their white indentured servants and would have enslaved "their fellow Englishmen . . . had they been able to get away with it. But such a policy was out of the question as long as there was a King and a Parliament in England." David B. Davis believes that there is not enough statistical evidence "to assume that the treatment of slaves was substantially better in Latin America than in the British Colonies, taken as a whole." Charles R. Boxer, the foremost authority on the Portuguese overseas empire has written: "The treatment of African slaves in Brazil, if not worse than that which was meted out to their brethren in the Spanish, French, English and Dutch colonies in the Western hemisphere, was at any rate nothing to be proud of." Colonial Brazil, Boxer reminds us, was characterized as being "a hell for Blacks, a purgatory for Whites, and a paradise for Mulattoes."

We can be certain that the debate will continue. The present findings suggest that the comparative approach will become the most fruitful new method of approaching the subject of slavery. The following selection is taken from Professor Tannenbaum's *Slave and Citizen*. A leading American authority on Mexico and Latin America, Frank Tannenbaum is Professor Emeritus of Latin American History, Columbia University.

THE NEGRO IN THE AMERICAS

SOURCE: Frank Tannenbaum, "The Negro in the Americas," from *Slave and Citizen* (New York, Knopf, 1946), vii–ix, 42–44, 45, 48–59, 60, 61–65, 68–70, 71–74, 76–80, 81–82.

Introduction

As I look at this little book upon a great subject I find that I am more unhappy now that it is finished than I was when writing it. It raises more questions, by implication at least, than it answers. And the questions it raises are those that trouble our own day. They are questions of freedom, liberty, justice, law, and morality. All of them revolve about the place of man in the world and the relation of men to each other. Slavery was not merely a legal relation; it was also a moral one. It implied an ethical bias and a system of human values, and illustrated more succinctly, perhaps, than any other human experience the significance of an ethical philosophy. For if one thing stands out clearly from the study of slavery, it is that the definition of man as a moral being proved the most important influence both in the treatment of the slave and in the final abolition of slavery. Once it was believed that all men are free by nature and equal in the sight of God, once the doctrine of the spiritual identity of all men, slave or free, came to rule men's minds and condition their legal system, then the very nature of slavery came to reflect the accepted doctrine.

The idea of the moral value of the individual outlasted slavery and became the chief source of its undoing. This belief has persisted throughout the last two thousand years. It is the chief heritage of the Western, the European world, and the very survival of European culture—perhaps of the European man—depends upon the survival of this doctrine. If it were to be lost, the European scheme of values would be lost with it.

There is in the history of slavery an important contribution to the theory of social change. Wherever the law accepted the doctrine of the moral personality of the slave and made possible the gradual achievement of freedom implicit in such a doctrine, the slave system was abolished peacefully. Where the slave was denied recognition as a moral person and was therefore considered incapable of freedom, the abolition of slavery was accomplished by force—that is, by revolution. The acceptance of the idea of the spiritual equality of all men made for a friendly, an elastic milieu within which social change could occur in peace. On the other hand, where the slave was denied a moral status, the law and the *mores* hardened and became stratified, and their historical outcome proved to be violence and revolution.

The adventure of the Negro in the New World has been structured differently in the United States than in the other parts of this hemisphere. In spite of his adaptability, his willingness, and his competence, in spite of his complete identification with the *mores* of the United States, he is excluded and denied. A barrier has been drawn against the Negro. This barrier has never been completely effective, but it has served to deny to him the very things that are of greatest value among us—equality of opportunity for growth and development as a man among men. The shadow of slavery is still cast ahead of us, and we behave toward the Negro as if the imputation of slavery had something of a slave by nature in it. The Emancipation may have legally freed the Negro, but it failed morally to free the white man, and by that failure it denied to the Negro the moral status requisite for effective legal freedom.

But this did not occur in the other parts of this world we call new and free. It did not occur because the very nature of the institution of slavery was developed in a different moral and legal setting, and in turn shaped the political and ethical biases that have manifestly separated the United States from the other parts of the New World in this respect. The separation is a moral one. We have denied ourselves the acceptance of the Negro as a man because we have denied him the moral competence to become one, and in that have challenged the religious, political, and scientific bases upon which our civilization and our scheme of values rest. This separation has a historical basis, and in turn it has molded the varied historical outcome.

The Negro slave arriving in the Iberian Peninsula in the

middle of the fifteenth century found a propitious environment.[1] The setting, legal as well as moral, that made this easy transition possible was due to the fact that the people of the Iberian Peninsula were not strangers to slavery. The institution of slavery, which had long since died out in the rest of western Europe, had here survived for a number of reasons, especially because of the continuing wars with the Moors, which lasted until the very year of the discovery of America. At the end of the fifteenth century there were numerous slaves in Portugal and Spain, and especially in Andalusia, among them not only Negroes, but Moors, Jews, and apparently Spaniards as well. . . .

But the mere survival of slavery in itself is perhaps less important than the persistence of a long tradition of slave law that had come down through the Justinian Code. The great codification of Spanish traditional law, which in itself summarizes the Mediterranean legal *mores* of many centuries, was elaborated by Alfonso the Wise between the years 1263 and 1265. In this code there is inherent belief in the equality of men under the law of nature, and slavery therefore is something against both nature and reason. . . .

This belief that equality among men is natural and reasonable is, therefore, both pagan and Christian, and stems from the Stoics and from the Christian fathers. The conception that man is free and equal, especially equal in the sight of God, made slavery as such a mundane and somewhat immaterial matter.

[1] Elizabeth Donnan, *Documents Illustrative of the History of the Slave Trade to America* (Washington, D.C., Carnegie Institution; 1930), Vol. I ("1441–1700,"), p. 29: "For as our people did not find them hardened in the belief of the other Moors, and saw how they came in unto the law of Christ with a good will, they made no difference between them and their free servants, born in our own country. But those whom they saw fitted for managing property, they set free and married to women who were natives of the land, making with them a division of their property, as if they had been bestowed on those who married them by the will of their own fathers, and for the merits of their service they were bound to act in a like manner. Yea, and some widows of good family who bought some of these female slaves, either adopted them or left them a portion of their estate by will, so that in the future they married right well, treating them as entirely free. Suffice it that I never saw one of these slaves put in irons like other captives, and scarcely any one who did not turn Christian and was not very gently treated." Quoted from *The Chronicle of the Discovery and Conquest of Guinea*, by Gomes Eannes de Azurara.

The master had, in fact, no greater moral status than the slave, and spiritually the slave might be a better man than his master. *Las Siete Partidas* was framed within this Christian doctrine, and the slave had a body of law, protective of him as a human being, which was already there when the Negro arrived and had been elaborated long before he came upon the scene. And when he did come, the Spaniard may not have known him as a Negro, but the Spanish law and *mores* knew him as a slave and made him the beneficiary of the ancient legal heritage. This law provided, among other matters, for the following:

The slave might marry a free person if the slave status was known to the other party. Slaves could marry against the will of their master if they continued serving him as before. Once married, they could not be sold apart, except under conditions permitting them to live as man and wife. If the slave married a free person with the knowledge of his master, and the master did not announce the fact of the existing slave status, then the slave by that mere fact became free. If married slaves owned by separate masters could not live together because of distance, the church should persuade one or the other to sell his slave. If neither of the masters could be persuaded, the church was to buy one of them so that the married slaves could live together. The children followed the status of their mother, and the child of a free mother remained free even if she later became a slave. In spite of his full powers over his slave, the master might neither kill nor injure him unless authorized by the judge, nor abuse him against reason or nature, nor starve him to death. But if the master did any of these things, the slave could complain to the judge, and if the complaint were verified, the judge must sell him, giving the price to the owner, and the slave might never be returned to the original master. Any Jewish or Moorish slave became free upon turning Christian, and even if the master himself later became a Christian, he recovered no rights over his former slave.

Las Siete Partidas goes into considerable detail in defining the conditions under which manumission could occur. A master might manumit his slave in the church or outside of it, before a judge or other person, by testament or by letter; but he must do this by himself, in person. If one of the owners of a slave wished to free him, then the other must accept a just price fixed by the local judge. A slave became free against his master's will by denouncing a forced rape against a virgin, by denouncing a maker of false money, by discovering disloyalty against the King, by denouncing the murderer of his master. The slave could become free if he became a cleric with the consent of his master, or in certain cases without his consent, providing another slave in his place. And if the former slave became a bishop, he had to put up two slaves, each valued at the price that he himself was worth, while still a slave. A Christian slave living among the Moors might return to live among the Christians as a free man.

The slave could appeal to the courts (1) if he had been freed by will and testament, and the document maliciously hidden; under these circumstances he could appeal against anyone holding him; (2) if the slave had money from another and entrusted it to someone for the purpose of being bought from his master and given his liberty, and if then this person refused to carry out the trust, by refusing either to buy him or to free him if he had bought him; and (3) if he had been bought with the understanding that he would be freed on the receipt of the purchase price from the slave, and refused either to accept the money or to release him after accepting it. He could appeal to the courts for defense of the property of his master in his master's absence, and the King's slaves could appeal to the courts in defense of the King's property, or of their own persons—a special privilege permitted the King's slaves in honor of their master. A man considering himself free, but demanded for a slave, might have a representative to defend him; a man held a slave, but claiming to be free, might argue his own case, but not have a representative, and he must be permitted to argue and reason his case; the slave's relatives might plead for him, and even a stranger could do so, for "all the laws of the world aid toward freedom." Slaves could be witnesses, even against their masters, in accusations for treason against the King; in cases of murder of either master or mistress by either spouse; or in cases against the mistress for adultery; when one of the two owners of a slave was accused of killing the other; or in case of suspicion that the prospective heirs have killed the master of another slave. A slave who became the heir of his master, in part or in totality, automatically became free. If a father appointed a slave as the guardian of his children, the slave by that fact became free; and if he was the slave of more than one person and became an heir of one of his masters, the other must accept a price in reason for that part of the slave which belonged to him. He who killed his slave intentionally must suffer the penalty for homicide, and if the slave died as a result of punishment without intention to kill, then the master must suffer five years' exile.

Spanish law, custom, and tradition were transferred to America and came to govern the position of the Negro slave. It is interesting to note that a large body of new law was developed for the treatment of the Indians in America, whereas the Negro's position was covered by isolated *cedulas* dealing with special problems. It was not until 1789 that a formal code dealing with the Negro slave was promulgated. But this new code, as recognized by the preamble itself, is merely a summary of the ancient and traditional law. Saco says of it that it merely repeats in amplified form "our ancient laws," and the practice recommended is "very usual in our dominions of the Indies."

This body of law, containing the legal tradition of the Spanish people and also influenced by the Catholic doctrine of the equality of all men in the sight of God, was biased in favor of freedom and opened the gates to manumission when slavery was transferred to the New World. The law in Spanish and Portuguese America facilitated manumission, the tax-gatherer did not oppose it,[2] and the church ranked it among the works singularly agreeable to God. A hundred social devices narrowed the gap between bondage and liberty, encouraged the master to release his slave, and the bondsman to achieve freedom on his own account. From the sixteenth to the nineteenth century, slaves in Brazil, by reimbursing the original purchase price, could compel their masters to free them.[3] In Cuba and in Mexico the price might be fixed at the request of the Negro, and the slave was

---

[2] "In the Cuban market freedom was the only commodity which could be bought untaxed; every negro against whom no one had proved a claim of servitude was deemed free. . . ." William Law Mathieson, *British Slavery and Its Abolition* (London: Longmans, Green & Co., 1926), pp. 37–38.

[3] Sir Harry Johnston, op. cit., p. 89. D. P. Kidder and J. C. Fletcher: *Brazil and the Brazilians* (New York: Childs and Peterson; 1857), p. 133.

freed even if he cost "triple of the sum."[4] The right to have his price declared aided the Negro in seeking a new master, and the owner was required to transfer him to another.[5]

The law further permitted the slave to free himself by installments, and this became a widely spread custom, especially in Cuba.[6] A slave worth six hundred dollars could buy himself out in twenty-four installments of twenty-five dollars each, and with every payment he acquired one twenty-fourth of his own freedom. Thus, when he had paid fifty dollars, he owned one twelfth of himself.[7] On delivering his first installment, he could move from his master's house,[8] and thereafter pay interest on the remaining sum, thus acquiring a position not materially different in effect from that of a man in debt who had specific monetary obligations. There seem to have been many instances of slaves paying out all of the installments due on their purchase price except the last fifty or one hundred dollars, and on these paying one half a real per day for every fifty pesos. The advantage in this arrangement apparently lay in the fact that a Negro, thus partially a slave, could escape the payment of taxes on his property and be free from military service.[9]

In effect, slavery under both law and custom had, for all practical purposes, become a contractual arrangement between the master and his bondsman. There may have been no written contract between the two parties, but the state behaved, in effect, as if such a contract did exist, and used its powers to enforce it. This presumed contract was of a strictly limited liability on the part of the slave, and the state, by employing the officially provided protector of slaves, could and did define the financial obligation of the slave to his master in each specific instance as it arose. Slavery had thus from a very early date, at least in so far as the practice was concerned, moved from a "status," or "caste," "by law of nature," or because of "innate inferiority," or because of the "just judgment and provision

[4] Alexander Humboldt: *Political Essay on the Kingdom of New Spain,* translated by John Black (New York: I. Riley; 1811), Vol. I, p. 181.
[5] Richard Henry Dana, Jr.: *To Cuba and Back* (Boston: Tichnor and Fields; 1859), p. 249.
[6] Fernando Ortiz: *Los Negros Esclavos* (Havana, 1916), p. 313.
[7] Alexander Humboldt: *The Island of Cuba,* op. cit., p. 211.
[8] Fernando Ortiz, op. cit., p. 317.
[9] Ibid., p. 315.

of holy script," to become a mere matter of an available sum of money for redemption. Slavery had become a matter of financial competence on the part of the slave, and by that fact lost a great part of the degrading imputation that attached to slavery where it was looked upon as evidence of moral or biological inferiority. Slavery could be wiped out by a fixed purchase price, and therefore the taint of slavery proved neither very deep nor indelible.

In addition to making freedom something obtainable for money, which the slave had the right to acquire and possess, the state made manumission possible for a number of other reasons. A Negro could be freed if unduly punished by his master.[10] He was at liberty to marry a free non-slave (and the master could not legally interfere), and as under the law the children followed the mother, a slave's children born of a free mother were also free.[11] Slaves in Brazil who joined the army to fight in the Paraguayan war were freed by decree on November 6, 1866, and some twenty thousand Negroes were thus liberated.[12]

In the wars of independence many thousands of slaves in Venezuela and Colombia were freed by Bolívar and enlisted in the army of liberation. In Argentina perhaps as many as a third of San Martín's host that crossed the Andes was composed of freed Negroes. And, finally, as early as 1733, by a special *cedula* repeated twice later, slaves escaping to Cuba from other West Indian islands because they wished to embrace the Catholic religion could be neither returned to their masters, nor sold, nor given in slavery to any other person.[13]

But significant and varied as were these provisions of the law in the Spanish and Portuguese colonies, they were less important in the long run than the social arrangements and expectancies that prevailed. It was permissible for a slave child in Brazil to be freed at the baptismal font by an offer of twenty milreis,[14] and in Cuba for twenty-five dollars.[15] A female slave could seek a godfather for her baby in some respectable person, hoping that

[10] Alexander Humboldt: *Political Essay*, op. cit., p. 181.
[11] Henry Koster: *Travels in Brazil* (Philadelphia: M. Carey & Son; 1817), Vol. II, p. 202. Fernando Ortiz, op. cit., p. 337.
[12] Percy Alvin Martin, "Slavery and Abolition in Brazil," *Hispanic American Historical Review*, XIII (May, 1933), p. 174.
[13] Fernando Ortiz, op. cit., p. 351.
[14] Robert Southey: *History of Brazil* (London, 1819), Part III, p. 784.
[15] William Law Mathieson, op. cit., p. 37.

the moral obligation imposed upon the godfather would lead to freeing the child. It was both a meritorious and a pious deed to accept such a responsibility and to fulfill its implicit commitments, and it bestowed distinction upon him who accepted them.[16] In the mining regions of Minas Geraes a slave who found a seventeen and a half carat diamond was crowned with a floral wreath, dressed in a white suit, carried on the shoulders of fellow slaves to the presence of his master, and freed and allowed to work for himself.[17] A parent having ten children could claim freedom, whether male or female.

The freeing of one's slaves was an honorific tradition, and men fulfilled it on numerous occasions. Favorite wet nurses were often freed; slaves were manumitted on happy occasions in the family—a birth of a first son, or the marriage of one of the master's children. In fact, the excuses and the occasions were numerous —the passing of an examination in school by the young master, a family festival, a national holiday, and, of course, by will upon the death of the master.[18] A cataloguing of the occasions for manumission in such a country as Brazil might almost lead to wonder at the persistence of slavery; but as I have pointed out above, the importations of slaves were large and continuous in Brazil all through the colonial period and late into the nineteenth century.

Opportunities for escape from slavery were further facilitated by the system of labor that prevailed in many places, particularly in cities. Slaves were often encouraged to hire themselves out and bring their masters a fixed part of their wages, keeping the rest. Skilled artisans, masons, carpenters, blacksmiths, wheelwrights, tailors, and musicians were special gainers from the arrangement.[19] . . . Women often hired themselves out as wet nurses, and both male and female slaves peddled a thousand wares through the streets.[20] . . .

With all its cruelty, abuse, hardship, and inhumanity, the atmosphere in Brazil and in the Spanish-American countries

[16] Henry Koster, op. cit., p. 195.
[17] John Mawe: *Travels in the Interior of Brazil* (London: Longman, Hurst, Rees, Orme & Brown; 1812), p. 318.
[18] Percy Alvin Martin, op. cit., p. 170.
[19] Fernando Ortiz, op. cit., p. 318.
[20] Thomas Ewbank, op. cit., pp. 92–3.

made for manumission. Even in the rural regions individuals were allowed to sell the products from their own plots, given them to work for themselves, and to save their money toward the day of freedom. In Cuba, one writer notes, the raising of pigs by slaves provided a ready source of the sums accumulated for such a purpose.[21] It should be further noticed that, in addition to their Sundays, the Negroes in Brazil had many holidays, amounting all together to eighty-four days a year, which they could use for their own purposes, and for garnering such funds as their immediate skill and opportunities made possible. The purchase of one's freedom was so accepted a tradition among the Negroes that many a Negro bought the freedom of his wife and children while he himself continued laboring as a slave, and among the freed Negroes societies were organized for pooling resources and collecting funds for the freeing of the brethren still in bondage.[22]

These many provisions favoring manumission were strongly influenced by the church. Without interfering with the institution of slavery where the domestic law accepted it, the church early condemned the slave trade and prohibited Catholics from taking part in it. The prohibition was not effective, though it in some measure may have influenced the Spaniards to a rather limited participation in the trade as such. The slave trade had been condemned by Pius II on October 7, 1462, by Paul III on May 29, 1537, by Urban VIII on April 2, 1639, by Benedict XIV on December 20, 1741, and finally by Gregory XVI on December 3, 1839. The grounds of the condemnation were that innocent and free persons were illegally and by force captured and sold into slavery, that rapine, cruelty, and war were stimulated in the search for human beings to be sold at a profit. The Franciscan Father Thomas Mercado had condemned the slave trade in the strongest terms in the year 1587, on the grounds that it fostered two thousand falsehoods, a thousand robberies, and a thousand deceptions. But the church did not interfere with the customary institution where it derived from known practices in a given community, such as born slaves, slaves taken in a just

[21] Rev. Abiel Abbot: *Letters Written in the Interior of Cuba* (Boston: Bowles and Dearborn; 1829), p. 97.
[22] Arthur Ramos: *The Negro in Brazil*, translated from the Portuguese by Richard Pattee (Washington, D.C., 1939), p. 70.

war, or those who had sold themselves or had been condemned by a legitimate court.

The presumption against the slave trade was that it forced people into slavery outside the law and against their will. More important in the long run than the condemnation of the slave trade proved the church's insistence that slave and master were equal in the sight of God. Whatever the formal relations between slave and master, they must both recognize their relationship to each other as moral human beings and as brothers in Christ. The master had an obligation to protect the spiritual integrity of the slave, to teach him the Christian religion, to help him achieve the privileges of the sacraments, to guide him into living a good life, and to protect him from mortal sin. The slave had a right to become a Christian, to be baptized, and to be considered a member of the Christian community. Baptism was considered his entrance into the community, and until he was sufficiently instructed to be able to receive it, he was looked upon as out of the community and as something less than human.

From the very beginning the Catholic churches in America insisted that masters bring their slaves to church to learn the doctrine and participate in the communion. The assembled bishops in Mexico in the year 1555 urged all Spaniards to send the Indians, and especially the Negroes, to church[23]; similarly in Cuba in 1680.

In fact, Negroes were baptized in Angola[24] before leaving for their Atlantic journey to Brazil. Upon arrival they were instructed in the doctrine, and as evidence of their baptism carried about their necks a mark of the royal crown. As a Catholic the slave was married in the church, and the banns were regularly published.[25] It gave the slave's family a moral and religious character unknown in other American slave systems. It became part of the ordinary routine on the slave plantations for the master and slaves to attend church on Sundays, and regularly before retiring at night the slaves gathered before the master's house to receive his blessings.[26] If married by the church, they

[23] Concilios Provinciales, Primero y Segundo, Mexico, En los Años de 1555 y 1565 (Mexico, 1769), Concilio primero, Cap. III, p. 44.

[24] Henry Koster, op. cit., p. 198.

[25] Ibid., p. 202.

[26] Alfred R. Wallace: A Narrative of Travels on the Amazon and Rio Negro (London: Reeve & Co.; 1853), p. 92.

could not be separated by the master. Religious fraternities sprang up among the slaves. These were often influential and honorific institutions, with regularly elected officers, and funds for the celebration of religious holidays subscribed to by the slaves out of their own meager savings. In Brazil the slaves adopted the Lady of the Rosary as their own special patroness, sometimes painting her black. In a measure these religious fraternities emulated those of the whites, if they did not compete with them, and the slaves found a source of pride in becoming members, and honor in serving one of these religious fraternities as an official.[27]

If the Latin-American environment was favorable to freedom, the British and American were hostile.[28] Legal obstacles were placed in the way of manumission, and it was discouraged in every other manner. The presumption was in favor of slavery.[29] . . .

In the southern part of the United States the position of the slave was closely similar to that in the British West Indies. What is important to note is the tendency to identify the Negro with the slave. The mere fact of being a Negro was presumptive of a slave status. . . .

Under the British West Indian and United States laws the Negro slave could not hope for self-redemption by purchase, and as slavery was assumed to be perpetual, there was only one route to freedom—manumission. But this route, if not entirely blocked, was made difficult by numerous impediments. The bias in favor of keeping the Negro in servitude contrasts with the other slave systems here under consideration, describes the explicit and the implicit test of the two systems, and foreshadows

[27] Robert Southey, op. cit., p. 784.
[28] There were, briefly speaking, three slave systems in the Western Hemisphere. The British, American, Dutch, and Danish were at one extreme, and the Spanish and Portuguese at the other. In between these two fell the French. The first of these groups is characterized by the fact that they had no effective slave tradition, no slave law, and that their religious institutions were little concerned about the Negro. At the other extreme there were both a slave law and a belief that the spiritual personality of the slave transcended his slave status. In between them the French suffered from the lack of a slave tradition and slave law, but did have the same religious principles as the Spaniards and Portuguese. If one were forced to arrange these systems of slavery in order of severity, the Dutch would seem to stand as the hardest, the Portuguese as the mildest, and the French, in between, as having elements of both.
[29] William Law Mathieson, op. cit., pp. 38–40.

their ultimate outcome. For the attitude toward manumission is the crucial element in slavery; it implies the judgment of the moral status of the slave, and foreshadows his role in case of freedom.

Just as the favoring of manumission is perhaps the most characteristic and significant feature of the Latin-American slave system, so opposition to manumission and denial of opportunities for it are the primary aspect of slavery in the British West Indies and in the United States. The frequency and ease of manumission, more than any other factor, influence the character and ultimate outcome of the two slave systems in this hemisphere. For the ease of manumission bespeaks, even if only implicitly, a friendly attitude toward the person whose freedom is thus made possible and encouraged, just as the systematic obstruction of manumission implies a complete, if unconscious, attitude of hostility to those whose freedom is opposed or denied. And these contrasting attitudes toward manumission work themselves out in a hundred small, perhaps unnoticed, but significant details in the treatment of the Negro, both as a slave and when freed. Either policy reveals the bent of the system, and casts ahead of itself the long-run consequence of immediate practice and attitude.

In the United States, "in every slaveholding state . . . restrictions . . . have been placed upon the manumission of Negro slaves. . . . In several of the states domestic manumission, that is, manumission to take effect within the state is prohibited." . . .

The slave had no protector to appeal to, and the master had, in some instances, exceeding power over him. An early Jamaican statute provided: "If any slave by punishment from his owner for running away, or other offence, suffer in life or limb, none shall be liable to the law for the same; but whoever shall kill a slave out of willfulness, wantonness, or bloody-mindedness, shall suffer three months' imprisonment and pay £50 to the owner of the slave." Thus willful murder had been reduced to a misdemeanor if committed on a slave. But it is more surprising that if the murder was committed by an indentured servant, he too could expiate the murder by thirty-nine lashes and four years' service. Tennessee provided that the law defining the killing of a slave as murder should not apply "to any person killing a slave . . . in the act of resistance . . . or dying under

moderate correction." The Georgia constitution safeguards against
the charge of murder if the "death should happen by accident
in giving such slave moderate correction." In South Carolina
the act of 1740 provided that willful murder of a slave should
cost the perpetrator "seven hundred pounds current money," and
this law, which remained on the statute books till 1821, further
provided that if the murder occurred "on sudden heat and
passion," it should cost him only £350. But such minor punishments as willfully cutting out the tongue, putting out the eye,
castrating, scalding, and similar offenses would, according to
the above law, involve the culprit in a cost of merely "one
hundred pounds of current money."

Where laws existed protecting the slave against unusual
punishment, they were difficult to enforce because he was
denied the right to testify in the courts. In the United States,
according to Cobb, the rule that slaves could not testify for
or against free white persons was enforced without exception;
most of the states prohibited such testimony by express statute,
others by custom and decision of the courts. In Illinois and
Iowa this prohibition extended to free persons of color or emancipated slaves. The testimony of any Negro or mulatto, free
or bond, was accepted in Virginia only in cases where free
Negroes and mulattoes were parties, and in no other case whatsoever. Similar laws were enacted in most of the Southern
states.

The slave had no protector to appeal to, and he could not
have his price specified for purposes of redemption and was
not allowed to accumulate property to buy his freedom. The
slave could acquire no property, and if any property came to
him, it would belong to his master; and, being incapable of
acquiring property, he could not convey it or give it away. . . .

In 1779 North Carolina prohibited the ownership of animals
by slaves. Mississippi prohibited a master from allowing his
slave to trade like a freeman, and Maryland from permitting
him to keep "stock of any description," nor could he acquire
money beyond his wages for the purchase of the freedom of his
children.

There was no custom of freeing the children at the baptismal
font for a nominal price, there was nothing known of the moral

role of the godfather for the slave child, and the slave family had no status either in law or in public recognition.

The law recognized no marriage relation between slaves. There followed no inheritance of blood even after emancipation, and spouses might be witnesses against each other. It was part of the record that "A slave never has maintained an action against the violator of his bed. A slave is not admonished for incontinence, or punished for fornication or adultery; never prosecuted for bigamy, or petty treason, for killing a husband being a slave, any more than admitted to an appeal for murder."[30]

Under the law of most of the Southern states, there was no regard for the Negro family, no question of the right of the owner to sell his slaves separately, and no limitation upon separating husband and wife, or child from its mother. That this was so may be seen from the following advertisements:

NEGROES FOR SALE.—A negro woman, 24 years of age, and her two children, one eight and the other three years old. Said negroes will be sold SEPARATELY or together, *as desired.* The woman is a good seamstress. She will be sold low for cash, or EXCHANGED FOR GROCERIES.

For terms, apply to MATTHEW BLISS & Co., 1 *Front Levee*
[*New Orleans Bee*]

I WILL GIVE THE HIGHEST CASH PRICE for likely Negroes, from 10 to 25 years of age.

GEORGE KEPHART
[*Alexandria* (D.C.) *Gazette*]

ONE HUNDRED AND TWENTY NEGROES FOR SALE.—The subscriber has *just arrived from Petersburg, Virginia,* with one hundred and twenty *likely young negroes* of both sexes and every description, which he offers for sale on the most reasonable terms. The lot now on hand consists of ploughboys, several likely and well-qualified house servants of both sexes, *several women with children, small girls* suitable for nurses, and SEVERAL SMALL BOYS WITHOUT THEIR MOTHERS. Planters and *traders* are earnestly requested to give the subscriber a call previously to making purchases *elsewhere,* as he is enabled to sell as cheap or cheaper than can be sold by *any other person in the trade.*

BENJAMIN DAVIS
(Hamburg, S.C., September 28, 1838)[31]

---

[30] "Opinion of Daniel Dulany, Esq., Attorney General of Maryland," Maryland Reports, 561, 563; quoted in George M. Stroud, *A Sketch of the Laws Relating to Slavery in the United States of America* (2nd edition, Philadelphia: H. Longstreth: 1856), pp. 60–61.

[31] William Goodell, *The American Slave Code* (New York, 1853), pp. 54–55.

But even more convincing than the advertisements is the following record compiled by Frederic C. Bancroft from four cargoes of Negroes shipped to New Orleans in 1834 and 1835:

Of the four cargoes making a total of 646 slaves, 396 were apparently owned by Franklin & Armfield. Among these there were only two full families: the fathers were 21 and 22 years of age, the mothers 19 and 20, and the children 1 and 1½. There were 20 husbandless mothers with 33 children, of whom one was 2 weeks old, 4 others were less than 1 year old, 19 were from 1 to 4 years old, and 9 were from 5 to 12 years of age. The remaining 337 were single and may be grouped thus:

```
  5 were from  6 to  9 years old, both inclusive
 68    "    "  10  "  15   "    "    "    "
145    "    "  16  "  21   "    "    "    "
101    "    "  22  "  30   "    "    "    "
  9    "    "  31  "  39   "    "    "    "
  8    "    "  40  "  50   "    "    "    "
  1 above      50,  a man of 60.
```

93 per cent of these 337 were from 10 to 30 years of age.[32]

Under the law a slave could not acquire property by earning it, by gift, or by inheritance. Not having any property, he could make no will, and could not take by descent, "there being in him no inheritable blood." In South Carolina slaves were described as "chattels personal . . . to all intents, constructions and purposes whatsoever." In Louisiana the slave ". . . can do nothing, possess nothing, nor acquire anything but what must belong to his master." In 1806, slaves were defined as real estate. The same principle ruled in Kentucky, but except for purposes of sale and execution of debts they were considered chattel. Most of the states defined slaves as chattel, and the laws of Maryland (1791) declared that "In case the personal property of a ward shall consist of specific articles such as slaves, working beasts, animals of any kind, stock furniture, plate, books, and so forth, the court . . . may at any time pass an order for the sale thereof."

In fact, the issue of female slaves in Maryland was considered part of the use, like that of other female animals. Court decisions are cited to the effect: "Suppose a brood mare is hired for

---

[32] Frederic C. Bancroft: *Slave-Trading in the Old South* (Baltimore: J. H. Furst Co.; 1931), p. 63.

five years, the foals belong to him who has a part of the use of the dam. The slave in Maryland, in this respect, is placed on no higher or different grounds." . . .

This business had its implications and consequences. The Negro female was reduced to a breeding animal. "She [a girl about twenty years of age] . . . is very prolific in her generating qualities, and affords a rare opportunity for any person who wishes to raise a family of strong, healthy servants for . . . [his] own use. . . ." The emphasis was upon raising children, for they could be sold at high prices. The records show that a child of four was worth $200, and another of six $150, while there are indications of even higher prices. In 1857 children of four, five, and eight years were sold for $376, $400, and $785, respectively.[33] The thing to do was to breed the Negro girls young. "A girl of seventeen that had borne two children was called a 'rattlin' good breeder' and commanded an extraordinary price."[34] The demise of the sanctity of marriage had become absolute, and the Negro had lost his moral personality. Legally he was a chattel under the law, and in practice an animal to be bred for the market. The logic of the situation worked itself out in time, but in the process the moral personality of the slave as a human being became completely obscured. It is no wonder that the right of redemption was seemingly nonexistent and the opportunity for manumission greatly restricted.

Carl Degler

"Amerika, du hast es besser," wrote the aged Goethe, and Americans have agreed. America was created as a paradise, a garden supposedly free of the problems that afflicted the Old World. Yet we have been unable to reconcile America's original sin, Negro racism, with the image of the paradise. Instead, we have repressed the problem by refusing to see it as central to understanding American history. Historians from Frederick Jackson Turner to Daniel Boorstin have told us that

[33] Quoted in Frederic C. Bancroft, op. cit., p. 79.
[34] Frederic C. Bancroft, op. cit., p. 82.

the American experience and environment transformed older European institutions. The New World should make the new man, yet the problem of racism persists, and continues to grow.

By the end of the first century of American settlement the belief in Negro inferiority was deeply imbedded into the Colonial psyche. In 1731, the English philosopher and clergyman George Berkeley reported after spending three years in Rhode Island that American slaveholders had "an irrational contempt of the blacks, as creatures of another species, who had no right to be instructed or admitted to the sacrement" (Thomas F. Gossett, *Race: The History of An Idea in America*). In *Notes on Virginia,* written a half century after Berkeley's sermon, Thomas Jefferson concluded "that the blacks are inferior to the whites in the endowments both of body and of mind." Slavery became interwoven into the fabric of American society, giving justification to John C. Calhoun's words that "slavery has grown with our growth, and strengthened with our strength. . . ." How did it all begin?

Oscar and Mary Handlin attempted to explain the origins of Negro slavery in their essay "Origins of the Southern Labor System." Their main point was that "slavery was not there from the start. . . . It emerged rather from the adjustment to American condition of traditional European institutions." According to Professor Handlin, Negroes were originally regarded as servants. After the 1660s the pressure of attracting white servants led to making their conditions more favorable than those of Negroes. In the process the status of Negroes deteriorated into slavery. With the development of a large scale plantation economy in the 1690s and the importation of numerous slaves, the economic necessity for the keeping of slaves became paramount. While other lower-class immigrants made their way into a higher social class, leaving their social origins behind, the Negroes' color remained their badge of inferiority and slavery. "Color," the Handlins have written, "then emerged as the token of slave status; the trace of color became the trace of slavery." And while the "American environment broke down the traditional European conception of servitude," it left the Negro with the defined status of chattel.

The Handlin's case has not been supported by recent research. The colonists who came to North America did not have to learn or devise a place for the blacks. By the time of

American settlement, slavery flourished in Latin America and the Caribbean, and English people used Negro slaves on Bermuda, Barbados, and New Providence. The prejudice against blacks was already established, and the American colonists accepted the racial attitudes of their compatriots as Winthrop D. Jordan has already shown in "The Influence of the West Indies on the Origins of New England Slavery." The slave trade was hemispheric and all the European powers had their hands in the slave trade. It was not by chance that a Dutch ship brought the first slaves to Virginia. Many of the early Negroes in Virginia had Spanish and Portuguese names, and there can be little doubt that the settlers in Virginia and elsewhere knew that Negroes were being held as slaves in the West Indies and Latin America. The legal definition was a formality that came later. Milton Cantor has found from a study of colonial literature that "the earliest settlers viewed him [the Negro] as different and inferior." It is highly debatable, concluded Professor Cantor, that the "Negro servant was the equal of the white."

In the following article, Carl Degler, Professor of American History at Vassar College, opens again the question of the origins of American slavery. For Professor Degler, "it would seem, then, that instead of slavery being the root of the discrimination visited upon the Negro in America, slavery was itself molded by the early colonists' discrimination against the outsider." The roots of American racism can be found in our earliest history. Two recent studies investigating the problem raised by Professor Degler were written by Winthrop D. Jordan and Arnold A. Sio. Degler further elaborates his argument in *Out of Our Past* (1959).

SLAVERY AND THE GENESIS OF AMERICAN RACE PREJUDICE

SOURCE: Carl Degler, "Slavery and the Genesis of American Race Prejudice," *Comparative Studies in Society and History*, II (October, 1959), 49–62, 65–66.

Over a century ago, Tocqueville named slavery as the source of the American prejudice against the Negro. Contrary to the situation in antiquity, he remarked: "Among the moderns the abstract and transient fact of slavery is fatally united with the physical and permanent fact of color." Furthermore, he wrote, though "slavery recedes" in some portions of the United States, "the prejudice to which it has given birth is immovable"[1] More modern observers of the American past have also stressed this causal connection between the institution of slavery and the color prejudice of Americans.[2] Moreover, it is patent to anyone conversant with the nature of American slavery, particularly as it functioned in the nineteenth century, that the impress of bondage upon the character and future of the Negro in the United States has been both deep and enduring.

But if one examines other societies which the Negro entered as a slave, it is apparent that the consequences of slavery have not always been those attributed to the American form. Ten years ago, for example, Frank Tannenbaum demonstrated that in the Spanish and Portuguese colonies in South America, slavery did not leave upon the freed Negro anything like the prejudicial mark which it did in the United States.[3] He and others[4] have shown that once the status of slavery was left behind, the Negro in the lands south of the Rio Grande was accorded a remarkable degree of social equality with the whites. In the light of such differing consequences, the role of slavery in the development of the American prejudice against the Negro needs to be re-examined, with particular attention paid to the historical details of origins.

I

Tannenbaum showed that in the Portuguese and Spanish colonies there were at least three historical forces or traditions which tended to prevent the attribution of inferiority to the Negro aside from the legal one of slavery. One was the continuance of the Roman law of slavery in the Iberian countries, another was the influence of the Roman Catholic Church, and the third was the long history—by Anglo-American standards—

[1] Democracy in America (New York, 1948), I, 358–60.
[2] Most recently, Oscar and Mary Handlin, "The Origins of the Southern Labor System," William and Mary Quarterly, 3rd Series, VII (April, 1950), 199–222.
[3] Slave and Citizen; The Negro in the Americas (New York, 1946).
[4] Gilberto Freyre, Brazil: An Interpretation (New York, 1945), pp. 96–101; Donald Pierson, Negroes in Brazil (Chicago, 1942), pp. 330–6.

of contacts with darker-skinned peoples in the course of the Reconquest and the African explorations of the fifteenth and sixteenth centuries. Roman law, at least in its later forms, viewed slavery as a mere accident, of which anyone could be the victim. As such it tended to forestall the identification of the black man with slavery, thus permitting the Negro to escape from the stigma of his degraded status once he ceased to be a slave. The same end, Tannenbaum showed, was served by the Roman Church's insistence upon the equality of all Christians and by the long familiarity of the Iberians with Negroes and Moors.

In North America, of course, none of these forces was operative —a fact which partly explains the differing type of slavery and status for Negroes in the two places. But this cannot be the whole explanation since it is only negative. We know, in effect, what were the forces which permitted the slave and the Negro in South America to be treated as a human being, but other than the negative fact that these forces did not obtain in the North American colonies, we know little as to why the Negro as slave or freedman, occupied a degraded position compared with that of any white man. A more positive explanation is to be found in an examination of the early history of the Negro in North America.

It has long been recognized that the appearance of legal slavery in the laws of the English colonies was remarkably slow. The first mention does not occur until after 1660—some forty years after the arrival of the first Negroes. Lest we think that slavery existed in fact before it did in law, two historians have assured us recently that such was not the case. "The status of Negroes was that of servants", Oscar and Mary Handlin have written, "and so they were identified and treated down to the 1660's."[5] This late, or at least, slow development of slavery[6]

---

[5] Handlin, "Origins of Southern Labor," p. 203.

[6] Virtually all historians of the institution agree on this. See U. B. Phillips, *American Negro Slavery* (New York, 1933), pp. 74–77; J. C. Ballagh, *History of Slavery in Virginia* (Baltimore, 1902), pp. 28–35. More recently, however, Susie Ames, *Studies of the Virginia Eastern Shore in the Seventeenth Century* (Richmond, 1940), pp. 101–10 and W. F. Craven, *Southern Colonies in the Seventeenth Century, 1607–1689* (Baton Rouge, 1949), pp. 217–9 have more than suggested that it is possible that slavery existed in Virginia almost from the very beginning of the Negro's history in America.

complicates our problem. For if there was no slavery in the
beginning, then we must account for its coming into being some
forty years after the introduction of the Negro. There was no
such problem in the history of slavery in the Iberian colonies,
where the legal institution of slavery came in the ships with
the first settlers.

The Handlins' attempt to answer the question as to why
slavery was slow in appearing in the statutes is, to me, not
convincing. Essentially their explanation is that by the 1660's,
for a number of reasons which do not have to be discussed
here, the position of the white servant was improving, while
that of the Negroes was sinking to slavery. In this manner, the
Handlins contend, Negro and white servants, heretofore treated
alike, attained different status. There are at least two major
objections to this argument. First of all, their explanation, by
depending upon the improving position of white servants as
it does, cannot apply to New England, where servants were
of minor importance. Yet the New England colonies, like the
Southern, developed a system of slavery for the Negro that
fixed him in a position of permanent inferiority. The greatest
weakness of the Handlins' case is the difficulty in showing
that the white servant's position was improving during and immediately after the 1660's.

Without attempting to go into any great detail on the matter,
several acts of the Maryland and Virginia legislatures during
the 1660's and 1670's can be cited to indicate that an improving
status for white servants was at best doubtful. In 1662, Maryland
restricted a servant's travel without a pass to two miles beyond
his master's house[7]; in 1671 the same colony lengthened the
time of servants who arrived without indenture from four to
five years.[8] Virginia in 1668 provided that a runaway could
be corporally punished and also have additional time exacted
from him.[9] If, as these instances suggest, the white servant's
status was not improving, then we are left without an explanation for the differing status accorded white and Negro servants
after 1660.

[7] *Maryland Archives*, I, 451.
[8] *Ibid.*, II, 335.
[9] W. W. Hening, *Statutes at Large; being a Collection of all the Laws of
Virginia* . . . (Richmond, 1809), II, 266.

Actually, by asking why slavery developed late in the English colonies we are setting ourselves a problem which obscures rather than clarifies the primary question of why slavery in North America seemed to leave a different mark on the Negro than it did in South America. To ask why slavery in the English colonies produced discrimination against Negroes after 1660 is to make the tacit assumption that prior to the establishment of slavery there was none. If, instead, the question is put, "Which appeared first, slavery or discrimination?" then no prejudgment is made. Indeed, it now opens a possibility for answering the question as to why the slavery in the English colonies, unlike that in the Spanish and Portuguese, led to a caste position for Negroes, whether free or slave. In short, the recent work of the Handlins and the fact that slavery first appeared in the statutes of the English colonies forty years after the Negro's arrival, have tended to obscure the real possibility that the Negro was actually *never* treated as an equal of the white man, servant or free.

It is true that when Negroes were first imported into the English colonies there was no law of slavery and therefore whatever status they were to have would be the work of the future. This absence of a status for black men, which, it will be remembered was not true for the Spanish and Portuguese colonies, made it possible for almost any kind of status to be worked out. It was conceivable that they would be accorded the same status as white servants, as the Handlins have argued; it was also possible that they would not. It all depended upon the reactions of the people who received the Negroes.

It is the argument of this paper that the status of the Negro in the English colonies was worked out within a framework of discrimination; that from the outset, as far as the available evidence tells us, the Negro was treated as an inferior to the white man, servant or free. If this be true, then it would follow that as slavery evolved as a legal status, it reflected and included as a part of its essence, this same discrimination which white men had practised against the Negro all along and before any statutes decreed it. It was in its evolution, then, that American colonial slavery differed from Iberian, since in the colonies of Spain and Portugal, the legal status of the slave was fixed before the Negro came to the Americas. Moreover, in South America there were at least three major traditional safeguards which tended to protect the free Negro against being treated as an inferior. In summary, the peculiar character of slavery in the English colonies as compared with that in the Iberian, was the result of two circumstances. One, that there was no law of slavery at all in the beginning, and two, that discrimination against the Negro antedated the legal status of slavery. As a result, slavery, when it developed in the English colonies, could not help but be infused with the social attitude which had prevailed from the beginning, namely, that Negroes were inferior.

II

It is indeed true as the Handlins in their article have emphasized that before the seventeenth century the Negro was rarely called a slave. But this fact should not overshadow the historical evidence which points to the institution without employing the name. Because no discriminatory title is placed upon the Negro we must not think that he was being treated like a white servant; for there is too much evidence to the contrary. Although the growth of a fully developed slave law was slow, unsteady and often unarticulated in surviving records, this is what one would expect when an institution is first being worked out.[10] It is not the same, however, as saying that no slavery or discrimination against the Negro existed in the first decades of the Negro's history in America.

As will appear from the evidence which follows, the kinds of discrimination visited upon Negroes varied immensely. In the early 1640's it sometimes stopped short of lifetime servitude or inheritable status—the two attributes of true slavery—in other

[10] John C. Hurd, *Law of Freedom and Bondage in the United States* (Boston, 1858–61), I, 163, points out that the trade "in negroes as merchandise was . . . recognized as legitimate by European governments, without any direct sanction from positive legislation, but rested on the general customs among nations, known both in municipal and international private law." Furthermore, he reported that none of the colonies ever found it necessary to pass laws legalizing slavery. He quotes from the Connecticut Code of 1821: "Slavery was never directly established by statute; but has been indirectly sanctioned by various statutes and frequently recognized by courts, so that it may be said to have been established by law." I, 212 n.

instances it included both. But regardless of the form of discrimination, the important point is that from the 1630's up until slavery clearly appeared in the statutes in the 1660's, the Negroes were being set apart and discriminated against as compared with the treatment accorded Englishmen, whether servants or free.

The colonists of the early seventeenth century were well aware of a distinction between indentured servitude and slavery.[11] This is quite clear from the evidence in the very early years of the century. The most obvious means the English colonists had for learning of a different treatment for Negroes from that for white servants was the slave trade[12] and the slave system of the Spanish and Portuguese colonies. As early as 1623, a voyager's book published in London indicated that Englishmen knew of the Negro as a slave in the South American colonies of Spain. The book told of the trade in "blacke people" who were "sold unto the Spaniard for him to carry into the West Indies, to remaine as slaves, either in their Mines or in any other servile uses, they in those countries put them to".[13] In the phrase "remaine as slaves" is the element of unlimited service.

The Englishmen's treatment of another dark-skinned, non-Christian people—the Indians—further supports the argument

[11] The Handlins, "Origins of Southern Labor", pp. 203–4, have argued that in the early years slavery meant nothing more than a low form of labor and that it had no basis in law. This is true insofar as statute law is concerned, but, as will appear later, in practice quite a different situation obtained.

[12] The Handlins, "Origins of Southern Labor", pp. 203–4, argue that the continental colonies could not have learned about a different status for Negroes from that of white servants from the slave trade because, they say, "the company of Royal Adventurers referred to their cargo as 'Negers', 'Negro-servants', 'Servants . . . from Africa', or 'Negro Persons' but rarely as slaves." They overlook, however, abundant references to Negro slaves in the correspondence of the contemporary Royal African Company. Thus in 1663 a warrant for that company refers to "negro slaves" as a part of its monopoly. *Calendar of State Papers, Colonial*, V, 121; see also p. 204. In that same year the Privy Council wrote that the Spanish were "seeking to trade with our island of Barbada for a supply of Negro Slaves . . .". And then the letter referred to a "supply of Negro Servants", and later still "for every Negro Person a Slave" and then "all such Negro Slaves". E. Donnan, *Documents Illustrative of the History of the Slave Trade*, (Washington, 1930), I, 161–2.

[13] Quoted in Donnan, *Slave Trade*, I, 125.

that a special and inferior status was accorded the Negro virtually from the first arrival. Indian slavery was practised in all of the English settlements almost from the beginning[14] and, though it received its impetus from the perennial wars between the races, the fact that an inferior and onerous service was established for the Indian makes it plausible to suppose that a similar status would be reserved for the equally different and pagan Negro.

The continental English could also draw upon other models of a differentiated status for Negroes. The earliest English colony to experiment with large numbers of Negroes in its midst was the shortlived settlement of Providence island, situated in the western Caribbean, just off the Mosquito Coast. By 1637, long before Barbados and the other British sugar islands utilized great numbers of Negroes, almost half of the population of this Puritan venture was black. Such a disproportion of races caused great alarm among the directors of the Company in London and repeated efforts were made to restrict the influx of blacks.[15] Partly because of its large numbers of Negroes, Old Providence became well known to the mainland colonies of Virginia and New England.[16] A. P. Newton has said that Old Providence

forms the connecting link between almost every English colonising enterprise in the first half of the seventeenth century from Virginia and Bermuda to New England and Jamaica, and thus it is of much greater importance than its actual accomplishments would justify.[17]

Under such circumstances, it was to be expected that knowledge of the status accorded Negroes by these Englishmen would be transmitted to those on the mainland with whom they had such close and frequent contact.

Though the word "slave" is never applied to the Negroes on Providence, and only rarely the word "Servant", "Negroes", which was the term used, were obviously *sui generis;* they were people

---

[14] See particularly, Almon Lauber, *Indian Slavery in Colonial Times Within the Present Limits of the United States* (New York, 1913), Chap. IV.

[15] A. P. Newton, *The Colonising Activities of the English Puritans* (New Haven, 1914), p. 258.

[16] *Ibid.,* p. 260.

[17] A. P. Newton, *The European Nations in the West Indies, 1493–1688* (London, 1933), pp. 173–4.

apart from the English. The Company, for example, distrusted them. "Association [Tortuga island] was deserted thro' their mutinous conduct", the Company told the Governor of Old Providence in 1637. "Further trade for them prohibited, with exceptions, until Providence be furnished with English."[18] In another communication the Company again alluded to the dangers of "too great a number" of Negroes on the island and promised to send 200 English servants over to be exchanged for as many Negroes.[19] A clearer suggestion of the difference in status between an English servant and a Negro is contained in the Company's letter announcing the forwarding of the 200 servants. As a further precaution against being overwhelmed by Negroes, it was ordered that a "family of fourteen"—which would include servants—was not to have more than six Negroes. "The surplusage may be sold to the poor men who have served their apprenticeship".[20] But the Negroes, apparently, were serving for life.

Other British island colonies in the seventeenth century also provide evidence which is suggestive of this same development of a differing status for Negroes, even though the word "slave" was not always employed. Though apparently the first Negroes were only brought to Bermuda in 1617,[21] as early as 1623 the Assembly passed an "Act to restrayne the insolencies of Negroes". The blacks were accused of stealing and of carrying "secretly cudgels, and other weapons and working tools". Such weapons, it was said, were "very dangerous and not meete to be suffered to be carried by such Vassals . . .", Already, in other words, Negroes were treated as a class apart. To reinforce this, Negroes were forbidden to "weare any weapon in the daytyme" and they were not to be outside or off their master's land during "any undue hours in the night tyme . . . ".[22]

During the 1630's there were other indications that Negroes were treated as inferiors. As early as 1630 some Negroes' servitude was already slavery in that it was for life and in-

[18] Calendar of State Papers, Colonial, I, 249.
[19] Ibid., pp. 277–8.
[20] Ibid., pp. 278–9.
[21] J. H. Lefroy, Memorials of the Discovery and Early Settlement of the Bermudas or Somers Islands, 1515–1685 (London, 1877), I, 127.
[22] Ibid., I, 308–9.

heritable. One Lew Forde possessed a Negro man, while the Company owned his wife; the couple had two children. Forde desired "to know which of the said children properly belong to himself and which to the Company". The Council gave him the older child and the Company received the other.[23] A letter of Roger Wood in 1634 suggests that Negroes were already serving for life, for he asked to have a Negro, named Sambo, given to him, so that through the Negro "I or myne may *ever* be able" to carry on an old feud with an enemy who owned Sambo's wife.[24]

There is further evidence of discrimination against Negroes in later years. A grand jury in 1652 cited one Henry Gaunt as being "suspected of being unnecessarily conversant with negro women"—he had been giving them presents. The presentment added that "if he hath not left his familiarity with such creatures, it is desired that such abominations be inquired into, least the land mourne for them".[25] The discrimination reached a high point in 1656 when the Governor proclaimed that "any Englishman" who discovered a Negro walking about at night without a pass, was empowered to "kill him then and theire without mercye". The proclamation further ordered that all free Negroes "shall be banished from these Islands, never to return eyther by purchase of any man, or otherwise . . .".[26] When some Negroes asked the Governor for their freedom in 1669, he denied they had any such claim, saying that they had been "purchased by" their masters "without condition or limitation. It being likewise soe practised in these American plantations and other parts of the world."[27]

In Barbados Negroes were already slaves when Richard Ligon lived there in 1647–50. "The Iland", he later wrote, "is divided

[23] *Ibid.*, I, 505. Cases in 1676 and 1685 indicate that this practice of dividing the children became the standard practice under slavery in a colony where the parcels of slaves were so small that few masters could have a spouse on their plantations for each of his adult Negroes. *Ibid.*, II, 427, 547–8.
[24] *Ibid.*, I, 539. Emphasis added.
[25] *Ibid.*, II, 30.
[26] *Ibid.*, II, 95–6.
[27] *Ibid.*, II, 293. As late as 1662 the perpetual character of slavery for Negroes was being obscured by their serving for ninety-nine years. See *Ibid.*, II, 166, 184.

into three sorts of men, viz: Masters, servants, and slaves. The slaves and their posterity, being subject to their masters for ever," in contrast to the servants who are owned "but for five years . . .".[28] On that island as at Bermuda it was reported that Negroes were not permitted "to touch or handle any weapons".[29]

On Jamaica, as on the other two islands, a clear distinction was made between the status of the Negro and that of the English servant. In 1656 one resident of the island wrote the Protector in England urging the importation of African Negroes because then, he said, "the planters would have to pay for them" and therefore "they would have an interest in preserving their lives, *which was* wanting in the case of bond servants . . .".[30]

It is apparent, then, that the colonists on the mainland had ample opportunity before 1660 to learn of a different status for black men from that for Englishmen, whether servants or free.

III

From the evidence available it would seem that the Englishmen in Virginia and Maryland learned their lesson well. This is true even though the sources available on the Negro's position in these colonies in the early years are not as abundant as we would like. It seems quite evident that the black man was set apart from the white on the continent just as he was being set apart in the island colonies. For example, in Virginia in 1630, one Hugh Davis was "soundly whipped before an Assembly of Negroes and others for abusing himself to the dishonor of God and the shame of Christians, by defiling his body in lying with a negro".[31] The unChristian-like character of such behavior

[28] Richard Ligon, *A True and Exact History of the Island of Barbados* (London, 1657), p. 43.

[29] *Ibid.*, p. 46.

[30] Quoted in Richard B. Morris, *Government and Labor in Early America* (New York, 1946), p. 499. As early as 1633, on the island of Tortuga, the separation of whites, servants or no, from Negroes was in evidence. At a time of anarchy on the island, "The eighty-odd Englishmen in the island had formed a council among themselves for the government of the colony and to keep in subjection the one hundred and fifty negroes, twenty-seven of whom were the company's property". Newton, *Colonising Activities*, p. 214.

[31] Hening, *Statutes*, I, 146.

was emphasized ten years later when Robert Sweet was ordered to do penance in Church for "getting a negro woman with child".[32] An act passed in the Maryland legislature in 1639 indicated that at that early date the word "slave" was being applied to non-Englishmen. The act was an enumeration of the rights of "all Christian inhabitants (slaves excepted)".[33] The slaves referred to could have been only Indians or Negroes,[34] since all white servants were Christians. It is also significant of the differing treatment of the two races that though Maryland and Virginia very early in their history enacted laws fixing limits to the terms for servants who entered without written contracts, Negroes were never included in such protective provisions.[35] The first of such laws were placed upon the books in 1639 in Maryland and 1643 in Virginia; in the Maryland statute, it was explicitly stated: "Slaves excepted".[36]

In yet another way, Negroes and slaves were singled out for special status in the years before 1650. A Virginia law of 1640 provided that "all masters" should try to furnish arms to themselves and "all those of their families which shall be capable of arms"—which would include servants—"(excepting negros)".[37] Not until 1648 did Maryland get around to such a prohibition, when it was provided that no guns should be given to "any Pagan for killing meate or to any other use", upon pain of a heavy fine.[38] At no time were white servants denied the right

[32] *Ibid.*, I, 552.

[33] *Maryland Archives*, I, 80.

[34] It is not known whether there were any Negroes in Maryland at that date. J. R. Brackett, *The Negro in Maryland* (Baltimore, 1889), p. 26 found no evidence of Negroes before 1642.

[35] Handlin, "Origins of Southern Labor", p. 210; Hening, *Statutes*, I, 411, 539. This is not to say that some Negroes were not indentured servants, for there is evidence to show that limited service was enjoyed by some black men. This was true even during the period after the recognition of slavery in the statutes. In October, 1673, for instance, the Council and General Court of Virginia ordered that "Andrew Moore A Servant Negro", who asserted he was to serve only five years, and who had the support of several "oathes", was declared free. Moreover, his erstwhile master was compelled to "pay him Corne and Clothes According to the custome of the country" and 400 pounds of tobacco and cask for the Negro's service since his time expired and to "pay costs". *Minutes of the Council and General Court of Colonial Virginia*, edited by H. R. McIlwaine (Richmond, 1924), p. 354.

[36] Hening, *Statutes*, I, 257; *Maryland Archives*, I, 80.

[37] *William and Mary Quarterly*, Second Series, IV (July, 1924), 147.

[38] *Maryland Archives*, I, 233.

to bear arms; indeed, as these statutes inform us, they were
enjoined to possess weapons.[39]

One other class of discriminatory acts against Negroes in
Virginia and Maryland before 1660 also deserves to be noticed.
Three different times before 1660–in 1643, 1644 and 1658–
the Virginia assembly (and in 1654, the Maryland legislature)
included Negro and Indian women among the "tithables". But
white servant women were never placed in such a category,[40]
inasmuch as they were not expected to work in the fields. From
the beginning, it would seem, Negro women, whether free or
bond, were treated by the law differently from white women
servants.[41]

It is not until the 1640's that evidence of a status for Negroes
akin to slavery, and, therefore, something more than mere
discrimination begins to appear in the sources. Two cases of
punishment for runaway servants in 1640 throw some light on
the working out of a differentiated status for Negroes. The first
case concerned three runaways, of whom two were white men
and the third a Negro. All three were given thirty lashes, with

[39] Handlin, "Origins of Southern Labor", p. 209, implies that these early
restrictions were later repealed. "Until the 1660's", the Handlins write,
"the statutes on the Negroes were not at all unique. Nor did they add up to
a decided trend." In substantiation of this point they instance the "fluctuations" in the Negro's right to bear arms. Their cited evidence, however, does
not sustain his generalization. Four references to the statutes of Virginia
are made; of these four, only two deal with arms bearing. The first one,
that referred to in the text above, indicates that Negroes were not to be
armed. The other reference is at best an ambiguous statement about who
is taxable and which of the taxables are to serve in the militia. It in no
wise constitutes either a repeal or even a contradiction of the earlier statute,
which, therefore, must be presumed to be controlling. Their evidence for
"fluctuations" in the right of Indians to bear arms suffers from the same
weakness of sources. The two statutes they cite merely confirm the right
of certain Indians to possess guns and deny them to other Indians. No
"fluctuation" in rights is involved.
[40] Hening, *Statutes*, I, 242, 292, 455; *Maryland Archives*, I, 342. The
statement in Handlin, "Origins of Southern Labor", p. 217n, that the "first
sign of discrimination was in 1668 when white but not Negro women were
exempt", is therefore erroneous.
[41] In his well-known emigrant pamphlet, *Leah and Rachel* (London,
1656), p. 12, John Hammond casts some interesting light on contemporary
opinion regarding women who worked in the fields in Virginia. "The Women
are not (as is reported) put into the ground to work, but occupie such
domestique imployments and housewifery as in England . . . yet some
wenches that are nasty, beastly and not fit to be so imployed are put into
the ground . . ."

the white men having the terms owed their masters extended a year, at the completion of which they were to work for the colony for three more years. The other, "being a Negro named John Punch shall serve his said master or his assigns for the time of his natural Life here or elsewhere".[42] Not only was the Negro's punishment the most severe, and for no apparent reason, but he was, in effect, reduced to slavery. It is also clear, however, that up until the issuing of the sentence, he must have had the status of a servant.

The second case, also of 1640, suggests that by that date some Negroes were already slaves. Six white men and a Negro were implicated in a plot to run away. The punishments meted out varied, but Christopher Miller "a dutchman" (a prime agent in the business) "was given the harshest treatment of all: thirty stripes, burning with an "R" on the cheek, a shackle placed on his leg for a year "and longer if said master shall see cause" and seven years of service for the colony upon completion of his time due his master. The only other one of the seven plotters to receive the stripes, the shackle and the "R" was the Negro Emanuel, but, significantly, he did not receive any sentence of work for the colony. Presumably he was already serving his master for a life-time—i.e., he was a slave.[43] About this time in Maryland it does not seem to have been unusual to speak of Negroes as slaves, for in 1642 one "John Skinner mariner" agreed "to deliver unto . . . Leonard Calvert, fourteen negro-men-slaves and three women-slaves".[44]

From a proceeding before the House of Burgesses in 1666 it appears that as early as 1644 that body was being called upon to determine who was a slave. The Journal of the House for 1666 reports that in 1644 a certain "mulata" bought "as a slave for Ever" was adjudged by the Assembly "no slave and but to serve as other Christian servants do and was freed in September 1665".[45] Though no reason was given for the verdict,

[42] Minutes of the Council, p. 466.
[43] Ibid., p. 467.
[44] Catterall, Judicial Cases, I, 57 n. Mrs. Catterall does not think any Negroes came under this agreement, but the language itself testifies to an accepted special status for Negroes at that time.
[45] Journals of the House of Burgesses of Virginia, edited by H. R. McIlwaine (Richmond, 1914), II, 34.

from the words "other Christian servants" it is possible that he was a Christian, for it was believed in the early years of the English colonies that baptism rendered a slave free. In any case, the Assembly uttered no prohibition of slavery as such and the owner was sufficiently surprised and aggrieved by the decision to appeal for recompense from the Assembly, even though the Negro's service was twenty-one years, an unheard of term for a "Christian servant".[46]

In early seventeenth century inventories of estates, there are two distinctions which appear in the reckoning of the value of servants and Negroes. Uniformly, the Negroes were more valuable, even as children, than any white servant. Secondly, the naming of a servant is usually followed by the number of years yet remaining to his service; for the Negroes no such notation appears. Thus in an inventory in Virginia in 1643, a 22-year old white servant, with eight years still to serve, was valued at 1,000 pounds of tobacco, while a "negro boy" was rated at 3,000 pounds and a white boy with seven years to serve was listed as worth 700 pounds. An eight-year old Negro girl was calculated to be worth 2,000 pounds. On another inventory in 1655, two good men servants with four years to serve were rated at 1,300 pounds of tobacco, and a woman servant with only two years to go was valued at 800 pounds. Two Negro boys, however, who had no limit set to their terms, were evaluated at 4,100 pounds apiece, and a Negro girl was said to be worth 5,500 pounds.[47]

These great differences in valuation of Negro and white "servants" strongly suggest, as does the failure to indicate term of service for the Negroes, that the latter were slaves at least in regard to life-time service. Beyond a question, there was some

[46] Ibid., II, 34-5. His plea, however, was turned down, the Assembly not knowing "any Reason why the Publick should be answerable for the inadvertency of the Buyer . . ."

[47] John H. Russell, The Free Negro in Virginia, 1619-1865 (Baltimore, 1913), p. 36. Russell concludes from his survey of inventories of estates for this early period that Negroes were valued from 20 to 30 pounds sterling, "while white servants of the longest term . . . receive a valuation of not more than £15 sterling". Ibid., p. 35. Catterall, Judicial Cases, I, 58 n, upon concluding her investigation of inventories of estates, picked 1644 as the date at which " 'servant' standing alone, had generally become synonomous with 'white servant' and 'negro' with 'negro slave', . . ."

service which these blacks were rendering which enhanced their value—a service, moreover, which was not or could not be exacted from the whites. Furthermore, a Maryland deed of 1649 adumbrated slave status not only of life-time term, but of inheritance of status. Three Negroes "and all their issue both male and female" were deeded.[48]

Russell and Ames culled from the Virginia court records of the 1640's and 1650's several instances of Negroes held in a status that can be called true slavery. For example, in 1646 a Negro woman and a Negro boy were sold to Stephen Charlton to be of use to him and his "heyers etc. for ever." A Negro girl was sold in 1652 "with her Issue and produce . . . and their services forever." Two years later a Negro girl was sold to one Arm-steadinger "and his heyers . . . forever with all her increase both male and female."[49] For March 12, 1655 the minutes of the Council and General Court of Virginia contain the entry, "Mulatto held to be a slave and appeal taken".[50] Yet this is five years before Negro slavery is even implied in the statutes and fifteen before it is declared. An early case of what appears to be true slavery was found by Miss Ames on the Virginia eastern shore. In 1635 two Negroes were brought to the area; over twenty years later, in 1656, the widow of the master was bequeathing the child of one of the original Negroes and the other Negro and her children.[51] This was much more than mere servitude—the term was longer than twenty years and apparently the status was inheritable.

Wesley Frank Craven, in his study of the seventeenth-century Southern colonies, has concluded that in the treatment of the

[48] Catterall, *Judicial Cases*, IV, 9.

[49] Russell, *Free Negro in Virginia*, pp. 34–5. He also reports the instance of a Negro by the name of John Casor who was claimed, in 1655, as a "Negro for his life", but he was rescued from such a status by two witnesses testifying that he had an indenture. *Ibid.*, pp. 32–3.

[50] *Minutes of the Council*, p. 504. Handlin, "Origins of Southern Labor", p. 216, in arguing the late development of a different status for Negroes as compared with whites in Virginia, says: "As late as the 1660's the law had not even a word to describe the children of mixed marriages. But two decades later, the term mulatto is used . . ." Such a statement is obviously misleading, for though the Handlins presumably mean statute law, the decisions of the General Court were also "law". The *Oxford English Dictionary* cites references for the word "mulatto" for 1595, 1613 and 1657.

[51] Ames, *Eastern Shore*, p. 105.

Negro "the trend from the first was toward a sharp distinction between him and the white servant".[52] In view of the evidence presented here, this seems a reasonable conclusion.

Concurrently with these examples of onerous service or actual slavery of Negroes, there were of course other members of the race who did gain their freedom.[53] But the presence of Negroes rising out of servitude to freedom[54] does not destroy the evidence that others were sinking into slavery; it merely underscores the unsteady evolution of a slave status. The supposition that the practice of slavery long antedated the law is strengthened by the tangential manner in which recognition of Negro slavery first appeared in the Virginia statutes.[55] It occurred in 1660 in a law dealing with punishments for runaway servants, where casual references was made to those "negroes who are incapable of making satisfaction by addition of time",[56] since they were already serving for life.

Soon thereafter, as various legal questions regarding the status of Negroes came to the fore, the institution was further defined by statute law. In 1662 Virginia provided that the status of the offspring of a white man and a Negro would follow that of the mother—an interesting and unexplained departure from the common law and a reversion to Roman law. The same law stated that "any christian" fornicating "with a negro man or woman . . . shall pay double the fines imposed by the former act". Two years later Maryland prescribed service for Negroes "durante vita" and provided for hereditary status to

[52] Craven, *Southern Colonies,* p. 219.

[53] See especially Russell, *Free Negro in Virginia,* pp. 36–9. See also Brackett, *Negro in Maryland,* p. 37.

[54] An indication that even freedom for the Negro carried certain disabilities is afforded by an instance reported by Ames, *Eastern Shore,* p. 107 from the Northampton County court records of 1654. For contempt of authority and abuse of certain persons, Anthony Longoe, a Negro, was ordered, almost twenty years after his release from service, to receive "thirty lashes now applied, and tomorrow morning thirty lashes more".

[55] A year earlier, 1659/60, a statute dealing with trade with the Dutch promised remission of a ten shilling tax if "the said Dutch or other forreiners shall import any negro slaves . . .". This is the first reference in the Virginia statutes to Negroes as slaves. Hening, *Statutes,* I, 540.

[56] Hening, *Statutes,* II, 26. The equivalent Maryland statute (1663) referred to "Negroes and other Slaves, who are incapeable of makeing Stisfaction [sic] by Addition of Tyme . . ." *Maryland Archives,* I, 489.

descend through the father. Any free white woman who married
a slave was to serve her husband's master for the duration of
the slave's life, and her children would serve the master until
they were thirty years of age. Presumably, no penalty was to
be exacted of a free white man who married a Negro slave.[57]

As early as 1669 the Virginia law virtually washed its hands
of protecting the Negro held as a slave. It allowed punishment
of refractory slaves up to and including accidental death, relieving the master, explicitly, of any fear of prosecution, on the
assumption that no man would "destroy of his owne estate".[58]

In fact by 1680 the law of Virginia had erected a high wall
around the Negro. One discerns in the phrase "any negro or
other slave" how the word "negro" had taken on the meaning of
slave. Moreover, in the act of 1680 one begins to see the
lineaments of the later slave codes. No Negro may carry any
weapon of any kind, nor leave his master's grounds without a
pass, nor shall "any negroe or other slave . . . presume to lift
his hand in opposition against any christian", and if a Negro
runs away and resists recapture it "shall be lawful for such
person or persons to kill said negroe or slave . . .".[59]

Yet it would be a quarter of a century before Negroes would
comprise even a fifth of the population of Virginia. Thus long
before slavery or black labor became an important part of the
Southern economy, a special and inferior status had been worked

[57] Hening, *Statutes*, II, 170: *Maryland Archives*, I, 533-4. Handlin,
"Origins of Southern Labor", p. 215 sees the genesis of these prohibitions
in concern over status rather than in objection to racial intermarriage. This
seems to be true for Maryland. But in speaking of the Virginia circumstances
they write: "It was to guard against the complications of status that the
laws after 1691 forbade 'spurious' or illegitimate mixed marriages of the
slave and the free . . ." Actually, however, the Virginia statute of 1691
(Hening, *Statutes*, III, 87) clearly aimed at the prevention of "abominable
mixture and spurious issue" by forbidding marriage of "English or other
white man or woman being free" with "a negro, mulatto or Indian man
or woman *bond or free*". (Emphasis added.)

[58] Hening, *Statutes*, II, 270. The working out of the exact legal status
of slave property, however, was a slow one. A Virginia law of 1705
(Hening, *Statutes*, III, 333-4), declared "Negro, Mulatto and Indian
Slaves . . . to be real estate", but there were a number of exceptions which
suggest the later chattel nature of property in slaves. In South Carolina
slaves were decreed to be real estate in 1690 and not until 1740 were
they said to be legally chattels. Hurd, *Law of Freedom*, I, 297, 303.

[59] Hening, *Statutes*, II, 481-2.

out for the Negroes who came to the English colonies. Unquestionably it was a demand for labor which dragged the Negro to American shores, but the status which he acquired here cannot be explained by reference to that economic motive. Long before black labor was as economically important as unfree white labor, the Negro had been consigned to a special discriminatory status which mirrored the social discrimination Englishmen practised against him.[60]

IV

In the course of the seventeenth century New Englanders, like Southerners, developed a system of slavery which seemed permanently to fasten its stigma upon the Negro race. But because of the small number of Negroes in the northern provinces, the development of a form of slavery, which left a caste in its wake, cannot be attributed to pressure from increasing numbers of blacks, or even from an insistent demand for cheap labor. Rather it seems clearly to be the consequence of the general social discrimination against the Negro. For in the northern region, as in the southern, discrimination against the Negro preceded the evolution of a slave status and by that fact helped to shape the form that institution would assume. . . .

Thus, like the colonists to the South, the New Englanders enacted into law, in the absence of any prior English law of slavery, their recognition of the Negroes as different and inferior. This was the way of the seventeenth century; only with a later conception of the brotherhood of all men would such legal discrimination begin to recede; but by then, generations of close association between the degraded status of slavery and black color would leave the same prejudice against the Negro in the North that it did in the South.

[60] Like Virginia, Maryland developed its slave law and status long before the Negroes had become an important aspect of the labor force. As late as 1712, Negroes made up only slightly more than 20 per cent of the population. Brackett, *Negro in Maryland,* pp. 38–9. If Virginia was slow in bringing her slave practices out into the open air of the statute books, the same could not be said of Carolina. In the Fundamental Constitutions, drawn up in 1669, it is stated in article CX that "Every freeman of Carolina shall have absolute power and authority over his negro slaves, of what opinion or religion so ever".

It would seem, then, that instead of slavery being the root of the discrimination visited upon the Negro in America, slavery was itself molded by the early colonists' discrimination against the outlander. In the absence of any law of slavery or commandments of the Church to the contrary—as was true of Brazil and Spanish-America—the institution of slavery into which the African was placed in the English colonies inevitably mirrored that discrimination and, in so doing, perpetuated it.

Once the English embodied their discrimination against the Negro in slave law, the logic of the law took over. Through the early eighteenth century, judges and legislatures in all the colonies elaborated the law along the discriminatory lines laid down in the amorphous beginnings. In doing so, of course, especially in the South, they had the added incentive of perpetuating and securing a labor system which by then had become indispensable to the economy. The cleavage between the races was in that manner deepened and hardened into the shape which became quite familiar by the nineteenth century. In due time, particularly in the South, the correspondence between the black man and slavery would appear so perfect that it would be difficult to believe that the Negro was fitted for anything other than the degraded status in which he was almost always found. It would also be forgotten that the discrimination had begun long before slavery had come upon the scene.

Melvin Drimmer

There has been a growing uneasiness over the answers given by historians for the failure of the Revolutionary generation to deal decisively with slavery. If slavery was unprofitable, as has been long contested, why did the slave states do so little to free their slaves? If it was contrary to the liberal sentiments of the Revolution, why was the institution that Jefferson saw fit to describe as "an assemblage of horrors," written permanently into the Constitution and permitted to expand into the southwestern territories?

The traditional answers hold that the spirit of the Revolu-

tion combined with the economic stagnation and decline
forced the planters to take the necessary steps to end the slave
trade and that these same factors would have eventually
forced them to end slavery itself. But in 1793, Eli Whitney
invented the cotton gin and saved the agricultural economy
of the South. This in turn created a demand for slaves,
brought prosperity to the region, and destroyed any thought
of freeing the six hundred thousand slaves. The implication
in this argument is that had not the cotton gin made slavery
profitable, America might have rid itself of slavery without
the terrible bloodshed that was to follow.

Like other myths, the "myth of the cotton gin" contained
some truth. Cotton certainly did bring great prosperity to the
lower South, and even provided an expanding market for Virginia's excess slaves. By the turn of the century, in response
to English demand and high prices, cotton was on the way to
becoming king.

It is part of the myth, however, that the success of cotton
restored prosperity to a dying region. Studies by L. C. Gray
and Merrill Jensen cite evidence to show that Southern agriculture and the economy had strongly recovered from the
devastation of the war, and the loss of markets following the
peace of 1783. By the late 1780s Southern agriculture had
diversified, with Virginia being the largest producer of wheat
and South Carolina *exporting* corn and timber in record
amounts. In addition, the large numbers of slaves employed
in skilled positions on and off plantations indicate that a pool
of manpower was available that would have allowed the
South to enter industrial production sooner than it did. The
success of cotton rather than restoring prosperity to a dying
region redirected the South's energies and resources to even
more profitable undertakings.

Moreover, a recent study of Virginia during the period
1776–1815 by Robert McColley has found little evidence
to show that the slaveowners were willing to abandon or modify the institution, nor did they consider it a detriment to
their economic prosperity. Prices for slaves remained high,
and far from abandoning the institution, the number of slaveowners continued to increase. Virginians, with the exceptions
of Jefferson, George Wythe, and St. George Tucker, showed
little sentiment for abolishing slavery. Slavery was so inter-

woven into the domestic and social order of the state that no planters seriously considered emancipation unless it was in the presence of foreign or Northern visitors. Virginia liberalism was for white men only.

Finally, to argue that slavery would have been abolished once the planters were convinced that slavery was unprofitable overlooks an even more important factor: the inability of white Americans to view Negroes as free men. Few Americans had an answer of what to do with the Negroes once free. It was the general American view that the races could not live together side by side in peace. Even Jefferson, who advocated abolition, advocated that Negroes, once free, be resettled on Western lands. As long as white men held that Negroes were inferior abolition was out of the question.

Dr. Drimmer re-examines the evidence that supports the traditional view that slavery was in decline before the introduction of the cotton gin. He suggests that the question be reopened and the period reappraised in the light of these findings.

WAS SLAVERY DYING
BEFORE THE COTTON GIN?*

SOURCE: Melvin Drimmer, "Was Slavery Dying Before the Cotton Gin?" Copyright in possession of the author.

During the great Senate debates of 1850 Daniel Webster asked: "What, then, have been the causes which have created so new a feeling in favor of slavery in the South—which have changed the whole nomenclature of the South on the subject. . . . It [Slavery] has now become an institution, a cherished institution there; no evil, no scourge, but a great religious, social and moral blessing. . . . I suppose this sin, is owing to the sudden uprising and rapid growth of the cotton plantation in the South." Salmon P. Chase seconded Webster's remarks. "Doubtless, sir,

---

* A version of this paper was read at the meeting of the American Historical Association in Washington, D.C., December 30, 1964. An expanded version with complementary documents will be published by Prentice-Hall in its *American Historical Studies* Series under the editorship of Dr. Lorman Ratner.

this was a leading cause. The production of cotton, in consequence of the invention of the cotton-gin."[1]

The currently held view is that the cotton gin revolutionized the South and saved slavery. For slavery the cotton-gin came at the right moment. A biographer of Eli Whitney asserted: "The cotton gin, finding the plantation in decline, revitalized it. . . . The cotton plantation gave the Negro a new value; slavery which had been dying out, was resuscitated; suddenly it possessed a vigorous and aggressive life."[2] Revolutionary idealism and economic necessity were acting as pincers to contain and ultimately crush the institution. The leading statesmen of the Revolution had condemned slavery and worked for its extinction. In 1787 slavery was prohibited in the territory north of the Ohio, and in the Convention, the slave trade, in the words of a delegate to the Massachusetts Ratifying Convention, "although . . . not smitten by an apoplexy . . . has received a mortal wound, and will die of consumption."[3]

What I term the "myth of the cotton gin" was best summed up by the Marxist literary and social historian V. F. Calverton. Calverton wrote:

It was at this time [c. 1775] that black slaves began to lose their appeal in the South and antislavery societies were organized. With the decline of [the] rice, indigo, and tobacco industries, Negro slaves were no longer a great necessity. If it had not been for Whitney's invention of the cotton gin in 1794, there would never have been a Civil War in the country. Whitney's invention revolutionized Southern industry, made cotton the South's major crop, and revived slavery as the *sine qua non* of their economic life, and when put to the test, they were willing to fight to preserve it.[4]

[1] Daniel Webster, March 7, 1850 and Salmon P. Chase, March 26, 1850, quoted in William Goddell, *Slavery and Anti-Slavery* (New York, 1855), 133–134.

[2] Jeannette Mirsky and Allan Nevins, *The World of Eli Whitney* (Collier Books edition, New York, 1962), 79.

[3] Jonathan Elliot, editor, *The Debates in the Several State Conventions on the Adoption of the Federal Constitution,* 4 Volumes (Washington, 1854), II, 41. Hereafter cited as Elliot.

[4] V. F. Calverton, *The Awakening of America* (New York, 1939), 303. Another statement along this line was made by Thomas Gray, Jr., "The South Still Gropes in Eli Whitney's Shadow," *Georgia Historical Quarterly,* XX (March, 1936), 352. Gray wrote: "When Whitney turned his face towards the South in 1793, slavery was a dying institution. The work of slaves was confined largely to the cultivation of rice, an industry which in

Doubts as to the validity of this interpretation were raised when I had occasion to refer to John Hope Franklin's text, *From Slavery to Freedom*, and came across the following passage which opened up the question. Franklin wrote: "In eleven years from 1783 to 1793, Liverpool traders alone were responsible for the importation of 303,757, while in the following eleven years they were certainly responsible for as many. . . . The closing years of the eighteenth century represented the peak in the slave trade."[5] How many of these reached North America Franklin did not state, but the figures in themselves were impressive and added to the slaves brought in by ships of other ports one could imagine the tremendous scope of "this assemblage of horrors." Upon tracing down the sources for Franklin's figures, they proved to be correct.[6]

The immediate question was why would slaves be imported into any area if they were not profitable, if the planters feared emancipation in the near future, or if the crops which the slaves produced were losing their markets. I began to re-examine some of the assumptions regarding the status of slavery in the post-Revolutionary years. What was the condition of Southern agriculture? How many slaves were imported, and how did the growth rate of the slave population compare with that of the white? Why did the planters fight so hard to keep open the

---

the natural course of events, was destined to pass from the American scene. Many Southern masters had already liberated their slaves and many of those who retained theirs offered apologies. A few years more and slavery in America would have been no more. Whitney's hand changed all this." This interpretation is standard text-book fare. For a similar statement see Samuel Eliot Morison and Henry Steele Commager, *The Growth of the American Republic*, 2 Volumes (New York, 1956), I, 317. J. W. Schulte Nordholt, *The People That Walk in Darkness* (New York, 1961), 48.

[5] John Hope Franklin, *From Slavery to Freedom* (New York, 1952), 57–58.

[6] Frank Tannenbaum also uses these figures in *Slave and Citizen* (New York, 1963), 18. He based his figures on "Dickey Sam," *Liverpool and Slavery* (Liverpool, 1884). The original source, however, is *A General and Descriptive History of the Ancient and Present State of the Town of Liverpool. . . . Together with a circumstan-Account of the True Causes of its extensive African Trade. The whole carefully compiled from Original Manuscripts, Authentic Records, and other Warranted Authorities* (Liverpool, 1795). A copy of this work can be found in the Slaughter Collection, Trevor Arnett Library, Atlanta University.

slave trade, making this a price for joining in the new government? Why, if slavery was on the road to ultimate extinction, was it written indelibly into the Constitution in the form of the three-fifths formula and the fugitive slave law? Why was there no national prohibition against slavery into the territories, or means or plans for the gradual emancipation of the slaves? In fact, what real evidence do we have that slavery was declining?

The Revolutionary generation, far from dealing head on with the question of slavery, failed to come to grips with the problem. Time and again efforts for containing or emancipating the slaves were side-stepped and lost. Actions taken in the North to halt the slave trade and free their chattel, while having symbolic value, were basically tangential and, as W. E. B. Du Bois noted, only blinded the nation "to the strong hold which slavery had on the country."[7]

If slavery was dying why did the slave states fail to act? An examination of the record shows that the slaveowners had little intention of freeing their slaves, which far from viewing as a liability they viewed as a distinct asset. "Without negroes," Rawlins Lowndes of South Carolina claimed, "this state would degenerate into one of the most contemptible in the Union. . . . Negroes are our wealth, our only natural resource."[8] At every turn the South worked to insure its peculiar property, a property which Samuel Chase of Maryland declared, "should not be considered . . . more than cattle."[9] U. B. Phillips, more than half-a-century ago, cautioned historians against taking the "expressions

[7] For the legislative action of the Northern states see W. E. B. Du Bois, *The Suppression of the African Slave-Trade to the United States of America, 1638–1870* (New York, 1954), 52, 222–242. The Northern states with few slaves looked at the matter of manumission quite differently from the South. Vermont with 50 slaves and New Hampshire with 456 were in quite a different position than Virginia with nearly 300,000, and Maryland, North and South Carolina, with over 100,000 each. There was a certain mockery in Jefferson's letter of 1785 to Dr. Richard Price when he told the Englishman that north of the Chesapeake one may find an opponent of slavery "as you may find here and there a robber and a murderer. . . . In that part of America, there being few slaves, they easily disencumber themselves." Thomas Jefferson to Dr. Richard Price, August 7, 1785, *The Papers of Thomas Jefferson,* edited by Julian Boyd (Princeton, 1953), VIII, 356–357.
[8] Elliot, *Debates,* IV, 272.
[9] *Ibid.,* I, 71.

of the metaphysical statesmen of the period" as gauging Southern sentiment. "In a word," Phillips wrote, "as soon as the excitement of the Revolutionary times was over and the body politic began to set its house in order for everyday life, even the theorists stopped questioning the infinite, and the people in the Negro districts proceeded much as they had done in colonial times."[10]

The American Revolution began with the deletion of Jefferson's bitter condemnation of the slave trade in the Declaration of Independence, and ended with a clause written into the Treaty of Paris for the return of stolen or escaped slaves. At the time of Jay's Treaty the planters were still demanding compensation for their "negroes and other property."[11] The Articles of Confederation were completely silent on the matter of slavery. Jefferson's draft for a revised Virginia constitution which included a clause for the gradual emancipation of slaves was not submitted to the legislature, Jefferson realizing that "the public mind would not yet bear the proposition."[12] At the same time North Carolina, South Carolina, and Georgia remained adamant and rejected various attempts to ameliorate the condition of their slaves.[13]

[10] U. B. Phillips, "The Slavery Issue in Federal Politics," in *The South in the Building of the Nation*, 12 Vols., (Richmond, 1909), V, 391–392.
[11] Samuel Flagg Bemis, *Jay's Treaty* (New York, 1924), 46, 50, 196.
[12] For Jefferson's emancipation proposal see *The Papers of Thomas Jefferson*, VI, 278 ff. Jefferson's reaction is quoted in L. C. Gray, *History of Agriculture in the Southern United States to 1860*, 2 Volumes (Washington, 1933), II, 618. Hereafter cited as Gray.
[13] North Carolina in 1777 tightened its manumission laws and all Negroes emancipated without the consent of the County Court were ordered to be resold into slavery, a move aimed at the Quakers who had recently freed their slaves. See Richard Hildreth, *The History of the United States*, 6 Volumes (New York, 1849), III, 394.
South Carolina remained inflexible regarding the question of abolition. Under no circumstances would it hear of it. In 1779 with the state under attack by the British, the legislature refused Colonel John Laurens' request to raise three regiments of slaves to defend the state. Three years later with the state virtually under British control and the legislature practically in hiding, the South Carolina lawmakers again turned down Laurens' suggestion. When Washington heard of the failure of the legislature to approve the project he lamented that the spirit of freedom which had so strongly marked the early stages of the war had subsided. The South Carolina legislature offered its own plan. Rather than arm slaves they would give to each man who enlisted a slave, and for each year of service an additional slave would be added, the slaves conveniently coming from the property of confiscated Tory estates. For the history of this project see

The only bright spots were the Virginia and Maryland enactments of 1778 and 1783, respectively, forbidding the importation of slaves, and Virginia's repeal of an old colonial statute which severely limited manumission. Neither state went further. Maryland's House of Delegates continually rejected petitions for gradual emancipation in 1785, 1787, 1789, each time by a larger vote. Virginia's House of Burgesses unanimously rejected a petition for emancipation, and within a decade had tightened its manumission laws. Washington wrote Lafayette in 1785 that petitions for the abolition of slavery could scarcely obtain a hearing in the Virginia legislature.[14]

Two years after the close of the Revolution Jefferson surveyed the situation for the Englishman, Dr. Richard Price. He found the area south of the Chesapeake strongly holding to its slave interests while "from the mouth to the head of the Chesapeake," the bulk of the population would theoretically approve of emancipation, but only a small minority would put it into practice. In 1786 the situation had changed little. "The disposition to emancipate them," Jefferson wrote, "is strongest in Virginia. Those who desire it, form as yet, the minority of the whole state. . . . In Maryland and North Carolina a very few are disposed to emancipate. In South Carolina and Georgia, not the smallest symptom of it."[15]

Historians have generally overlooked the failure of the Confederation and the new government to keep slavery out of the territories. Jefferson had in the original draft for the Ordinance of 1784 prohibited slavery in all the Western territory acquired

---

David Duncan Wallace, *The Life of Henry Laurens* (New York, 1915), 449–452. See John Richard Alden, *The South in the Revolution, 1763–1789* (Baton Rouge, Louisiana, 1957), 225–226. Jeffrey R. Brackett, "The Status of the Slave, 1775–1789," in *Essays in the Constitutional History of the United States in the Formative Period,* edited by J. Franklin Jameson (Boston and New York, 1889), 310.

Georgia showed the lengths to which the states went to preserve slavery. In 1782 the legislature sent emissaries into the British lines to negotiate with them for the purchase of their own slaves who had escaped and were about to be evacuated with the British. See Gray, *op. cit.,* II, 596, and Brackett, *op. cit.,* 310.

[14] Brackett, *op. cit.,* 302. Allan Nevins, *The American States During and After the Revolution, 1775–1789* (New York, 1927), 449.

[15] Jefferson to Price, August 7, 1785, *Papers of Thomas Jefferson, op. cit.,* VIII, 356–357. Gray, *op. cit.,* II, 618.

by the Peace Treaty. This provision was eliminated from the draft by the vote of the Southern states.[16] It is mistaken, therefore, to regard the Northwest Ordinance of 1787 as the highwater mark of the post-war antislavery movement.[17] The Northwest Ordinance was a poorly watered-down version of Jefferson's much more complete plan. The area south of the Ohio was left open to slavery. George Mason told the Constitutional Convention that the "Western people are already calling out for slaves for their new lands," and by the time of the first census, slavery was firmly entrenched in Kentucky and Tennessee.[18]

The debates in the Constitutional and Ratifying conventions made it clear that the slaveowners had no intention of modifying their position. They presented no indications that slavery was unprofitable or dying. Interest, not idealism, was the guiding force behind the Convention. John Rutledge of South Carolina told the delegates regarding the question of the slave trade that "religion and humanity had nothing to do with the question. Interest alone is the governing principle with nations. . . . The people of those States [North Carolina, South Carolina, and Georgia] will never be such fools as to give up so important an interest."[19] Slavery, he insisted, would benefit the entire nation. Virginia's slaves would rise in value, and New England would profit from carrying slaves and the products which the slaves produced. Even George Mason's denunciation of slavery was interpreted as cloaking self-interest. Oliver Ellsworth of Connecticut sharply answered Mason by saying that if the Virginian felt so concerned about slavery, he might begin by freeing those he

[16] See the essay by Julian Boyd under the title "Editor's Note" in *The Papers of Thomas Jefferson*, VI, 581-600. Boyd goes into the details of the Ordinance of 1784, and how it came about that the antislavery clause was eliminated.

[17] John Hope Franklin so regards the Northwest Ordinance. Franklin, *op. cit.*, 140. Richard Hildreth attributed the South's acceptance of the Ordinance of 1787, which was passed with the approval of the Southern states, to "the idea, afterward acted upon, of securing, under future terms of cession, the continuation of slavery in the territory south of the Ohio." Hildreth, *op. cit.*, III, 528-529.

[18] James Madison, *The Debates in the Federal Convention of 1787. . . .*, edited by Gaillard Hunt and James Brown Scott (New York, 1920), 443. Hereafter cited as Madison. The first census showed Kentucky to have 12,000 slaves and Tennessee 3,000. By 1800 Kentucky had 40,000 slaves, Tennessee, 13,500.

[19] *Ibid.*, 442, 446.

already possessed. Virginia opposed the importation of slaves, so
Ellsworth reasoned, because "as slaves multiply so fast in Virginia
and Maryland . . . it is cheaper to raise than import them."[20]

The slaveowners not only received what they could reasonably
hope from the Convention, but they demanded and received
more. A bargain between New England and Carolina extended
the free period for slave importations from 1800 to 1808. Madison
protested at once. He had been outflanked by the carriers and the
receivers. "Twenty years will produce all the mischief that can be
apprehended from the liberty to import slaves," he warned.[21]
Time was on the side of the slaveowners. The West would demand slaves, and like a cancer, slavery would spread until it
completely infested the body politic. The Convention disregarded
Madison's words. With New England joining Maryland, the
Carolinas, and Georgia, the slave trade was given eight more
years of life. Even this did not satisfy the South Carolinians, for
no sooner were they home when they predicted that come 1808
Congress would take no action to halt the trade.[22]

The debates in the state ratifying conventions presented conflicting opinions regarding slavery. In the North with few
slaves, delegates predicted the eventual disappearance of slavery
throughout the country. In the South, with nearly all the 700,000
slaves, the delegates were assured and reassured by the supporters of the Constitution that their slave interests would be
protected by the new government. This was the theme in Virginia
where Madison and Randolph, the latter having just switched to
the side of the Constitution, continually impressed upon the delegates the benefits the slaveholders would derive from Federal
government. They would be protected by a fugitive slave law,
by adequate representation, by higher prices for their slaves once
the slave trade came to an end, and by national military aid in
case of domestic insurrection. Madison denied that the Constitution gave the government the power to "interpose with respect to
the property in slaves now held by these states."[23] Randolph

<hr />

[20] *Ibid.*, 444.
[21] *Ibid.*, 467.
[22] David Ramsey, "An Address to the Freemen of South Carolina on the
subject of the Federal Constitution," in *The Federalist and Other Constitutional Papers*, edited by E. H. Scott (Chicago, 1898), 923.
[23] Elliot, *op. cit.*, III, 197, 262–263, 417, 541.

challenged his opponents to cite the passage "that has a tendency to the *abolition of slavery?* . . . . I believe, whatever we may think here, that there was not a member of the Virginia delegation who had the *smallest suspicion of the abolition of slavery.*"[24]

The traditional champions of Negro emancipation, George Mason and Patrick Henry, presented no such arguments to the Virginia delegates. Mason attacked the Constitution because it contained "no clause . . . that will prevent the northern and eastern states from meddling with our whole property of that kind." On the one hand Mason came out against the extension of the slave trade, and on the other hand he complained that "there is no provision for securing to the southern states those [slaves] they now possess." Henry supported Mason. He demanded to know why the Constitution did not contain specific safeguards for slavery. This omission, he charged, was by design. Congress would lay heavy duties on slaves which would "amount to emancipation. . . . This might compel the southern states to liberate their negroes."[25]

A similar picture emerged from the debates in the North and South Carolina conventions. James Iredell quieted antifederalist criticism by demanding to know where in the Constitution did it give Congress the "power to abolish [the] slavery of those slaves who are now in the country."[26] In South Carolina, the antifederalist spokesman, Rawlins Lowndes, attacked the Constitution for putting an end to the slave trade after twenty years. He spoke for the farmers and smaller planters of the up-country who hoped to possess more slaves at cheaper prices. "Why confine us to twenty years, or rather why limit us at all?" Lowndes presented no moral qualms about slavery. It was a positive good, he argued, which "could be justified on the principles of religion, humanity and justice." General C. C. Pinckney tried to reassure Lowndes by affirming that as long as there was one acre of swamp land left in the state, he would oppose restricting the slave trade. Pinckney pointed to the fact that South Carolina

---

[24] *Ibid.,* 541. For statements in Northern conventions predicting the eradication of slavery see Elliot, I, 107, 452–453.
[25] *Ibid.,* III, 417, 420.
[26] *Ibid.,* IV, 102.

would be free to import an unlimited number of negroes for twenty years, "nor is it declared that the importation shall be then stopped; it may be continued."[27]

II

One reason why the planters were disinclined to consider emancipation was on account of the favorable economic developments which emerged in the Southern states after the war and prior to the cotton gin. This is another aspect of the question which has been overlooked. The Southern planter following the Revolution in no way resembled Chekhov's spiritless aristocrats and intellectuals patiently waiting for the end. The years following the American Revolution found the Southern states making remarkable strides after the devastation of war and the readjustment necessitated by the need of finding new markets. The leading authorities on the region during this period, L. C. Gray and Merrill Jensen, concur in the opinion that the South was flourishing. By 1790 Southern agriculture, far from being in the doldrums, had surpassed all pre-Revolutionary records, and the South was well on the way towards developing a diversified agricultural economy. To the staples of tobacco, rice, and indigo were added wheat, corn, lumber products, and livestock raising. The land was cleared and drained, canals were begun, the interior was opened up, slaves were moved into the backcountry and into the West. There were considerable technical innovations. L. C. Gray found "the period immediately following the close of the Revolutionary war was one of considerable technical progress in Southern agriculture." Planters were experimenting with new crops such as wheat, wool, and hemp, and in Northern Virginia with new techniques such as deep plowing, the use of animal fertilizers, and the iron plow. In South Carolina an Agricultural Society was formed in 1785 for the purpose of improving methods and crops. Southern representatives were busy finding new markets—in France, the West Indies—and smuggling goods into markets that were technically closed to them. Slave labor was particularly flexible. For example, in South Carolina slaves were being used as coopers and in the production of corn and in Virginia slaves constituted the bulk of the workers in the iron

[27] *Ibid.*, IV, 272, 286.

foundaries and in wheat production in the tidewater region.[28]
We should let the figures speak for themselves.

Rice production increased from 280 million pounds in the
period 1770–1773 to 320 million pounds in the period 1791–
1794, a rise of 14% over the colonial period.[29]

Tobacco exports in 1792 were 36% above the 1770 figure and
the average price was higher in the decade following the Revolution than the decade prior to it.[30]

Indigo which is supposed to have died out due to a loss of
the British subsidy reached its all time high in both pounds
produced and market value in 1792.[31]

Often left out of the economic picture is the diversity of
Southern agriculture. As both Gray and Jensen show, the South

[28] Rather than having a footnote after each fact, I will combine them
under one number. For an estimate of the agricultural situation see Gray, II,
605, 607, 612, 614, 618. Merrill Jensen, *The New Nation* (New York, 1950),
192, 195, 216, 217, 235, 237. Curtis P. Nettels, *The Emergence of a National Economy, 1775–1815* (New York, 1962), chapters IV, VII., also
tables 6, 13, 14, 16. For new techniques in agricultural production see
Richard Beale Davis, *Intellectual Life in Jefferson's Virginia, 1790–1830*
(Chapel Hill, 1964), 152–153. For developments in South Carolina see
Charles Gregg Singer, *South Carolina in the Confederation* (Philadelphia,
1941), 22–26; also John Drayton, *A View of South Carolina* (Charleston,
1802), 166–168, 173. On new markets for Southern products see "Letters
of Morris Brailsford to Thomas Jefferson," edited by Richard Walsh, *South
Carolina Historical and Genealogical Magazine*, 58 (1957), 133. For the use
of Negroes in the production of corn see Elizabeth Donnan, editor, *Documents Illustrative of the History of the Slave Trade in America*, 4 Volumes
(Washington, 1935), IV, 478. On the use of slaves as coopers see Richard
Walsh, "The Charleston Mechanics," *South Carolina Historical Magazine*,
60 (1959), 124. On the use of slaves in the Virginia foundries see Kathleen
Bruce, "Slave Labor in the Virginia Iron Industry," *William and Mary
Historical Magazine*, 2nd Series, VI (October, 1926), 291–292. On the use
of slaves in tidewater wheat production see George C. Rogers, Jr., *Evolution
of a Federalist: William Loughton Smith of Charleston (1758–1812)* (Columbia, South Carolina, 1962), 230.

[29] For South Carolina's recovery in rice production see Drayton, *op. cit.*,
166–168, 173; Gray, *op. cit.*, II, 609; Nettels, *op. cit.*, table 16. For the
figures for South Carolina's pre-Revolutionary rice production see Singer,
op. cit., 18.

[30] For tobacco production see Jensen, *op. cit.*, 235. Also *The South
in the Building of a Nation*, 12 Volumes (Richmond, 1909), V, 159, 162–
163. In 1774 colonial production reached 100 million pounds; in 1790 it
was 130 million pounds. In 1790 tobacco was the second most valuable
export commodity, in 1791 it was first. See Gray, *op. cit.*, II, 606.

[31] For indigo see Gray, *op. cit.*, II, 610. He also includes comparative
figures for 1771 and 1792.

during the period 1783–1793 was the great American bread-basket. In 1792 the South produced 60% of the American corn, 63% of the American wheat and 38% of the flour. In 1791 Virginia, not Pennsylvania, was the largest producer of wheat and corn, and in that same year Virginia ranked first among states in the value of its domestic produce. But Virginia was not alone. In 1792 Maryland, North Carolina, and South Carolina produced nearly half-a-million bushels of corn for export. South Carolina presents an interesting note regarding the diversity and growth of foodstuffs in the South. In 1770 the state *exported* 13,598 bushels of corn, in 1792 it *exported* 99,986 bushels. Lumber is another forgotten industry. In 1770, the best pre-Revolutionary year for the production of lumber, some 700,000 feet were exported. By 1786 South Carolina alone exported nearly two million feet, and in the following year, lumber products, not rice, became the most important export article from that state.[32]

Prices also remained high. Tobacco prices were up and Madison reported in 1784 that the price of the last crop sold from 36–42 shillings a hundred and "brought more specie to the country than it ever contained at one time." By 1792 corn was double the price it had been in 1774–1775; wheat was six shillings a bushel or twice that of the pre-war price, and by 1800 it was selling for twice the price it had been in 1786. The market in the early 1790's was bullish. William L. Smith, the Federalist congressman from Charleston who was also one of the leading merchants of the city, predicted in June, 1792, that the approaching war between France and Britain would add to the prosperity of the area, and his hopes were born out as the price of slaves rose and the demand for American agricultural produce increased.[33]

[32] On the South as being the American breadbasket see Jensen, *op. cit.*, 237. Also Arthur B. Peterson, "Commerce of Virginia, 1789–1791," *William and Mary Historical Magazine,* 2nd Series, X (October, 1930), 302–309. On Southern production of grain and corn see Gray, *op. cit.*, II, 607–609. On lumber production for 1770 see *Historical Statistics of the United States, Colonial Times to 1957* (Washington, 1957), 771. For South Carolina lumber production see Singer, *op. cit.*, 24.

[33] For prices of agricultural commodities see Jensen, *op. cit.*, 235–236. Rogers, *op. cit.*, 234. For the rise in slave and agricultural prices see Richard Hildreth, *Despotism in America; or An Inquiry into the Nature and Results of the Slave-Holding System in the United States* (4th edition, Boston, 1849), 172.

Another major index to measure the state of Southern agriculture is to compare the tons of shipping clearing Southern ports in the late 80's and early 90's with pre-Revolutionary days. Merrill Jensen found that Maryland and North Carolina doubled its volume, and South Carolina and Virginia fell just short of this.[34]

III

The close of the Revolution saw the reopening of the African slave trade on a scale never before reached. Elizabeth Donnan estimated that between 1787–1790 alone over eighty thousand Negroes were taken out of Africa each year. The Liverpool slavers carried 303,000 slaves from 1783–1793 and 323,000 from 1795–1804, making the figure before the cotton gin comparable to the post cotton gin years. In her study of the New England slave trade after the Revolution Professor Donnan found that the trade "was revived as soon as peace made possible a general restoration of commerce," and this view has been supported by other authorities. From testimony taken before Parliament in 1789 it was reported that American ships were plying the coast of Africa in record numbers, and by 1796 the governor of Sierre Leone wrote that "the number of American slave traders on the coast has increased to an unprecedented degree."[35]

Du Bois, while unable to give a specific figure for the number of slaves imported after the Revolution, stated that in the period 1783–1787 "many thousands of Negroes came into the United States." Dr. Samuel Hopkins of Rhode Island deplored the reopening of the trade. He reported in 1785 of the "thousands of slaves brought into these United States, and sold at extraordinary prices . . . in some of the Southern States, and especially South Carolina." Despite prohibitions against the trade in New England and prohibitions against the importation of slaves in almost all the Southern states, especially after the Haitian rebellion of 1791, the trade went on continually. William Ellery, a leading Rhode Island opponent of slavery, wrote in 1791: "An Ethiopian could as soon change his skin as a Newport merchant

[34] On the volume of shipping see Jensen, *op. cit.*, 216–217.
[35] Donnan, *op. cit.*, II, 567. Elizabeth Donnan, "The New England Slave Trade After the Revolution," *New England Quarterly*, II (1930), 252, 263.

could be induced to change so lucrative a trade as that in slaves for the slow profits of any manufactory."[36]

In South Carolina within the first two years after the peace nearly 12,000 slaves were brought into the state and according to a contemporary account, "there was a rage for negroes without any concern [of] how they were to be paid for." Although a prohibition against the importation of slaves had been passed in 1788, mainly for the purpose of preventing specie from leaving the state, slaves were easily brought in, and in 1803 Governor John Drayton candidly admitted, that "the smuggling . . . has actually taken place in a great degree." Census figures for South Carolina showed that the slave population had increased by nearly 50% in the decade 1791–1800.[37]

Slave population grew remarkably in the period 1775–1790. Curtis Nettels in his recent study of the post Revolutionary economy came to a different conclusion. He claimed that the rate of growth in the slave population declined during the years 1775–1790, rising only 21% as compared to an increase of 34% in the white population. After 1790 Nettels found that the slave population grew at a rate "that was twice that for the fifteen years after 1775." He uses these figures to prove that slavery was declining before the cotton gin. Nettels' case falters through miscalculation. All authorities, including Nettels, agree on a figure

[36] Du Bois, op. cit., 50. Hopkins, Dialogue on Slavery (1785), quoted in Goodell, op. cit., 122. Donnan, "The New England Slave Trade After the Revolution," 255–256.

[37] On the number of slaves imported into South Carolina see Madison to Jefferson, October 3, 1785, Papers of Thomas Jefferson, VIII, 581. For the resumption of slave trade in South Carolina see Rogers, op. cit., 100–103. Rogers is also the source for the reasons for South Carolina's prohibition of the slave trade in 1788. See 131, 161. Drayton, op. cit., 146. In 1790 South Carolina had 107,094 slaves; in 1800, 146, 151.

An interesting figure on the rise of slave population in a state which was unaffected by the growth of cotton in the 1790's is presented by North Carolina. Eli Whitney noted in December, 1802, that "cotton culture had made comparatively little progress in the State of North Carolina." Yet the census showed a great leap in slave population. In 1790 there were 100,783 slaves in North Carolina; in 1800 the slave population numbered 133,296, an increase of 33% in the decade. See "Memoir of the Life of Eli Whitney, Esq. inventor of the Cotton Gin," edited by D. Olmsted, The American Journal of Science and Arts, XXI (July, 1828), 223. Figures on slave population are taken from Negro Population in the United States, 1790–1915 (Washington, 1918), 57.

of 500,000 slaves in 1775. In 1790 the census showed that there were 697,624 slaves. Nettels, however, used the figure of 607,-000, an error of 90,000. In fact, the slave population during the period 1775–1790 grew by nearly 40%, not 21%. It might be noted, in addition, that this growth rate was made despite the fact that Virginia, South Carolina, and Georgia lost over 60,000 slaves to the British during the war years.[38]

The price of slaves should be examined as another good indicator of the position of slavery. A tentative study of the price of slaves in the 1780's and early 90's compared favorably with the price of slaves in the West Indies, the largest market for slaves, and with the colonies before the Revolution. In 1783–84 slaves were selling in Charleston for twice that of the West Indies. After the initial demand levelled off in the late 80's, the price held to 50 pounds sterling, still a notch above West Indian and colonial prices. In 1757 slaves had sold for 31 pounds; in 1771 a "tolerably good price" was 35–37 pounds; in 1773 the price was 40 pounds. In Charleston in 1783–84 the price of slaves "sold on the average of 90 pounds a head." In 1786 Liverpool slavers averaged 41 pounds a slave. In 1787 slaves sold in the West Indies for 40 pounds.[39]

Finally, if slavery were unprofitable one solution would have been to load the slaves aboard ships and sell them in the West

[38] Nettels' error may be found in *The Emergence of a National Economy*, p. 37. There is, in fact, no great break in the pattern of slave growth in the period 1775–1810. Between 1790–1800 the Negro population grew 32% while the white population grew 36%; for 1800–1810 the figures were 37% for Negroes and 36% for whites. See Edward Channing, *A History of the United States*, 6 Volumes, (New York, 1917), IV, 430.

On the Southern loss of slaves see Gray, II, 596. For the most reliable accounts of slave population in America before the first census see Gray, II, 1025, and the Bureau of the Census' *Historical Statistics of the United States, op. cit.*, 756. An important aspect in the growth of slave population before 1800 was that it was achieved *without* northern importations. U. B. Phillips found that "there seems to be no evidence that the traffic across Mason and Dixon's line was ever of large dimensions. . . . The internal trade in the South began to be noticeable about the end of the 18th century." Phillips, *American Negro Slavery* (New York, 1918), 188.

[39] The figures cited in the text are drawn from Elizabeth Donnan, *op. cit.*, IV. Figures on Liverpool traders comes from John B. Spears, *The American Slave Trade* (New York, 1900), 84. Figures on Charleston prices after the Revolution come from Donnan, IV, 483. This has been substantiated by Nettels, *op. cit.*, 50; Gray, *op. cit.*, II, 596. On West Indian prices in the late 1780's see U. B. Phillips, *American Negro Slavery* (New York, 1918), 365.

Indies. The Indies were the largest market and certainly there would have no problem in selling experienced hands. We possess some records of this trade, and it is totally negligible. In 1770 twenty-seven slaves were shipped to the British West Indies from the Southern colonies; in 1771, three, in 1772, one, in 1791, twenty-three.[40]

The figures on American shipment of slaves to Cuba, however, are much more conclusive. In a study of slave shipments from the United States to Cuba during the period 1789–1807, D. C. Corbitt showed that shipments of slaves, although small, did not stop after 1795 but even increased in the following decade. He cites figures taken from the *Papel Periódico de la Havana*. In 1791, seven ships carrying one hundred sixty-one slaves were brought to Havana from American ports. Three ships came from Virginia with a total of fifty slaves; two came from Baltimore with a total of seventy-five slaves, and two came from Charleston with sixty-six slaves. Figures for 1792 and 1793 remains incomplete, but in 1794 of the fifty-three vessels entering Havana from American ports, only one ship, this being from Charleston, brought slaves, and they numbered four. Corbitt did not overlook the importance of these figures. If slave exportation from America stopped at this point, Corbitt commented, "there would then be a perfect 'setup' to prove that Eli Whitney's cotton gin was able in two years to create a demand for slaves that was great enough to stop the small stream that was flowing outward. Unfortunately for this theory, later issues of Havana papers show that shipments did not stop with 1795."[41]

Corbitt found nearly complete records for 1804 and 1805. In the former year, eleven ships entered Havana bringing one hundred and thirteen slaves from America. Ten ships came from Charleston with one hundred seven slaves; the remaining ship came from New York with six slaves. In 1805, twenty-seven

---

[40] Figures on the numbers of slaves sent from Southern states to the West Indies are taken from "Slave Trade by Origin and Destination in 1768 to 1772," in *Historical Statistics of the United States, op. cit.,* 769. Bryan Edwards in *The History of the British Colonies in the West Indies,* 3 Volumes (London, 1801), although listing American products imported into the islands, noticeably fails to enumerate slaves, the figure evidently being so small.

[41] D. C. Corbitt, "Shipments of Slaves from the United States to Cuba, 1789–1807," *Journal of Southern History,* VII, (November, 1941), 545.

American ships brought three hundred nine slaves to Havana. Twenty three came from Charleston with two hundred eighty four slaves; three came from Savanna carrying nineteen slaves, and one came from Baltimore with six slaves.[42]

IV

There is little doubt about the success of cotton and the cotton gin in changing the nature of Southern argriculture. With cotton selling in the 1790's for thirty five to forty cents a pound, planters took acreage out of rice, indigo, tobacco, wheat, and corn and in gold-rush fashion entered the cotton market. Big money was to be made. Wade Hampton earned in 1799 ninety thousand dollars for selling 600 bales of cotton. Cotton was on the way to becoming king before the end of the century. Production of other crops palsied in the wake of cotton, and by 1800 production in rice, indigo, tobacco, and corn fell off drastically. The price of slaves shot up and by 1800 they were selling for twice the price of the previous decade.[43]

[42] *Ibid.*, 545–548.
[43] Wade Hampton's sale of cotton is related in U. B. Phillips, *Life and Labor in the Old South* (Boston, 1929), 98. There are numerous authorities who attest to the fact that the cotton boom took land out of other staples. See, for example, M. B. Hammond, *The Cotton Industry* (New York, 1897), 32. Hammond wrote: [the back country] "which since the war had been meeting with success in the growing of cereals, now abandoned them for cotton, and the recently erected grist mills were left standing idle. Indian corn, which in 1792 had been exported from South Carolina to the extent of nearly one hundred thousand bushels, soon had to be imported for domestic use. Tobacco, hemp, flax, barley and silk had all been articles of export from South Carolina and Georgia, but their cultivation was abandoned." Also *The South in the Building of the Nation*, op. cit., V, 164; Drayton, *op. cit.*, 114.
One of the best contemporary accounts we have of the effect of cotton on the South came from a young merchant in Charleston. Charles Caleb Cotton wrote on October 24, 1799: ". . . the staples of this State which a few years since were tobacco, rice, and indigo, should have ceased to be considered as such. The culture of cotton is now the great staple. . . . Should cotton maintain its present price and demand in England a few years longer. . . . the planters will speadily acquire handsome fortunes. . . . It is supposed that the planters of cotton will make this year 100 pounds sterling to a hand, and as many plantations have 50–80 or 100 working negroes, the profits will be very handsome." Cotton reported eight weeks later that "the price of Negroes is enormous. They average 100 pounds a head by the gang, i.e., men and women included. Prime Negro

The question remains, however, what was the state of slavery before the cotton gin? The cotton gin revolutionized the South. Whether it saved slavery is another matter. The South had too much tied up in slavery to let it quietly go to pieces.[44] The slaveowners, neither in word nor deed, indicated that they were through with their peculiar institution. Evidence would point strongly to the contrary. The agricultural recovery of the region after the Revolution showed the slaveowners to be imaginative and resourceful, possessing a flexible means of labor which could be adopted to new circumstances. The rise of cotton and the invention of the cotton gin should be seen as a product of an economy and system that was viable and creative. *The cotton gin brought slavery from one plateau to one yet higher, not from the desert to the mountain.*

The cotton gin has been used to justify the retention and expansion of slavery. Rather than confronting themselves with the responsibility for the continuation of slavery, Americans in the nineteenth century shifted the burden of guilt onto the cotton gin. It was in keeping with the character of a mechanistic age that they blamed their own failings upon a machine.

Staughton Lynd

American historians in the twentieth century, have downplayed the importance of slavery as an important factor in the formation of the Constitution. However, early and mid-nineteenth century historians saw slavery as the key to an under-

---

fellows are often sold at auction as high as 120 pounds . . ." "The Letters of Charles Caleb Cotton, 1798–1802," edited by Julien Dwight Martin, *The South Carolina Historical and Genealogical Magazine,* 51(1950), 225; 52(1951), 18.

[44] There were, of course, other factors besides the economic one which would have caused the region to hold on to its slaves. The economic argument might, in fact, be of less importance than psychological and numerical factors. What I have tried to do is to focus on the factor which can be most plainly demonstrated. The burden of proof must be shifted on to those historians who claim that slavery after the Revolution was dying and on its last legs. The purpose of this paper has not been to explain everything, but to refocus the question and to shift the burden of proof.

standing of the larger issues which concerned American political life—railroads, national development, land policy, states
rights, power of the central government, the tariff, westward
expansion, civil liberties. But in the latter part of the nineteenth century historians turned their attention away from
slavery. They became interested in the revolutionary changes
that heavy industrialization, large scale capitalism, and agrarian and industrial discontent brought to American society.

This change of emphasis can be seen in the works of the
two most important historians of the early twentieth century,
Frederick Jackson Turner and Charles Beard. Both were very
much influenced by the new industrial order and by the
Populist movement. Turner and Beard turned their attention
from the theme of slavery and abolition and posed one of their
own. They envisioned a conflict going back to the beginnings
of English settlement between democratic and aristocratic
forces, between the conservative older settled areas and the
egalitarian frontier, and later, between the Eastern financiers
and the Western farmers. These themes can be most clearly
seen in Vernon L. Parrington's "Main Currents of American
Thought."

Recently, some historians have returned to an earlier interpretation of American history, and particularly of the Revolutionary period. Professor Staughton Lynd stresses the importance that the question of slavery and slave expansion had
for the Founding Fathers. He discovered that much of the
conflict within the Constitutional Convention owed its origins
to the problem of slavery and a defense of this peculiar interest. As John Rutledge of South Carolina reminded the delegates when the question of the slave trade was raised: "Religion and humanity had nothing to do with the question.
Interest alone is the governing principle with nations. . . ."
It was interest which in the end won out. The South had its
interests secured by the three-fifths provision, the fugitive
slave law, and slave trade compromise.

Professor Lynd not only refocuses the issue, but he takes us
behind the scenes of the Convention to show how the slave
interests were protected. The anti-slavery forces were unable
to put an end to the institution and in the end, they floun-
dered. In "Slavery and the Founding Fathers" Professor Lynd
suggests two basic reasons for their failure. First, "even the

most liberal of the Founding Fathers were unable to imagine a society in which whites and Negroes would live together as fellow-citizens." And secondly, the Founding Fathers were much too committed to the sanctity of private property to envision emancipation.

Professor Lynd is Associate Professor of History at Chicago State College. He is the author of *Antifederalism in Dutchess County*, and editor of *Nonviolence in America*.

SLAVERY AND THE FOUNDING FATHERS

SOURCE: Staughton Lynd, "Slavery and the Founding Fathers." This paper was read at the meeting of the American Historical Association in Washington, D.C., December 30, 1964. Copyright in possession of the author.

From the publication in 1840 of James Madison's journal of the Constitutional Convention until about 1890 interpretation of the Constitution stressed sectional conflict based on slavery. Taking their cue from Madison's repeated statement that "the institution of slavery and its consequences formed the line of discrimination" between the contending groups of states at the Convention, Hildreth, Bancroft, Curtis, Schouler and others established the canon that there had been at the Convention three great compromises. One was the three-fifths compromise regarding representation in the House; the second provided for equal voting in the Senate; the third allowed twenty years of the slave trade in exchange for the provision that laws concerning commerce would require only a simple majority.[1]

Then in the early 1890's Frederick Jackson Turner challenged the concept that the conflict over slavery was the central theme of American history.[2] And in 1903, in a paper on "Compromises of the Constitution," Max Farrand questioned in detail the prevailing abolitionist critique. "It can not be too strongly empha-

[1] Richard Hildreth, *The History of the United States of America*, III (New York, 1849), 520; George Ticknor Curtis, "The Constitution of the United States and its History," *Narrative and Critical History of America*, ed. Justin Winsor, VII (Boston and New York, 1888), 238–239, 243–244; etc.

[2] See my "Turner, Beard and Slavery," *Journal of Negro History*, XLVIII (1963), 237–238.

sized," Farrand wrote, "that in 1787 the slavery question was not the important question, we might say it was not the moral question that it was in 1850." In this and subsequent publications Farrand argued that the three-fifths compromise had been accepted by eleven states before the Convention met, and that the bargain over the slave trade was less significant than compromises about the nature of the Executive and the admission of new states.[3]

A generation of scholars followed Farrand in deemphasizing the importance of slavery at the Convention.[4] Among them was Charles Beard. Beard, laying his stress upon the repugnance for excessive democracy which the Fathers shared rather than upon the sectional conflict which divided them, was uncertain whether slaves were "personalty" or "realty," and left unclarified the role of Southern slaveholders in the ratification drama.[5] For Beard as for Turner, American history was the story of a continuing contest between the capitalist and the farmer. The plantation owner was a kind of farmer. The slave dropped out of sight.

Recent history, of course, has brought him emphatically back into view. Robert E. Brown, for example, has stated that "the really fundamental conflict in American society at the time" of the Constitutional Convention was "the division between slave and free states, between North and South."[6] And John Alden, commenting on the view that a struggle over who should rule at home accompanied the War for Independence, observes: "Had human slavery in the United States disappeared promptly as a result of the social ferment which was stimulated by the Anglo-American conflict, it would indeed be proper to think in terms of an Internal Revolution."[7] In our present mood we are inclined

[3] Max Farrand, "Compromises of the Constitution," *Annual Report of the American Historical Association for the Year 1903*, I (Washington, 1904), 73–84.

[4] Robert Livingston Schuyler, *The Constitution of the United States* (New York, 1923), 100; Andrew C. McLaughlin, *A Constitutional History of the United States* (New York, 1935), 190; etc.

[5] Lynd, "Turner, Beard and Slavery," 246–247.

[6] Robert E. Brown, *Reinterpretation of the Formation of the American Constitution* (Boston, 1963), 48.

[7] John R. Alden, *The South in the Revolution. 1763–1789* (Baton Rouge, 1957), 348.

to agree with Gouverneur Morris' statement at the Convention that "Domestic slavery is the most prominent feature in the aristocratic countenance of the . . . Constitution."[8]

There is a danger that, as in the case of so many other historical controversies, yesterday's view will be discarded only to go back to that which prevailed the day before. The temper of the times tempts one to return to the abolitionist critique, and relax in condemnation of the covenant with death and the agreement with hell. But reality requires a more complex kind of understanding. We must go beyond Beard, not behind him. We must try to understand *why* the Fathers failed to confront this problem with the candor and effectiveness otherwise so habitual to them.

This problem can be made more manageable by breaking it down into two separate questions. First, why did Southerners at the Convention agree to arm the Federal government with greater powers, powers that were ultimately turned against slavery? Second, why did Northerners at the Convention concur in the continuance of a system of labor which, they readily conceded, was flagrantly at odds with the principles of the American Revolution?

Each of these questions has a traditional answer. Southerners, it is said, did not fear to vest new powers in the federal government because sectional conflict was not yet acute in 1787. And Northerners, we are told, did not make an issue of slavery at the Convention because they were confident it would die away gradually of its own accord.

The bulk of the contemporary evidence does not support these familiar explanations.

Sectional conflict *was* already intense in 1787; indeed, Madison referred delegates to the previous votes of Congress for proof of his assertion that the Convention struggle was basically sectional.[9] Diffuse and sporadic before the end of the War for

---

[8] *The Records of the Federal Convention of 1787,* ed. Max Farrand (New Haven, London, Oxford; 1911), II, 222.

[9] On June 29: "The great danger to our general government *is the great southern and northern interests of the continent, being opposed to each other. Look to the votes in congress, and most of them stand divided by the geography of the country, not according to the size of the states* [italics in original]" (*Records of the Convention,* I, 476).

Independence, sectional conflict congealed during the Critical Period into a straight-forward contest for national power.

Consider first the period 1774–1783. When Patrick Henry asserted at the first Continental Congress, "I am not a Virginian, but an American," his point was that Virginia would not insist on counting slaves in apportioning representation.[10] Two South Carolinians at once demurred; and when the discussion was resumed in the summer of 1776, one of them, Lynch of South Carolina, stated: "If it is debated whether their Slaves are their Property, there is an End of the Confederation."[11] Sectional consciousness was evident in Jefferson's 1777 comment that Virginia was apprehensive about a Northern monopoly of commerce; and in the passionate proposal a few months later by William Henry Drayton of South Carolina that some Congressional decisions should require the assent of eleven states.[12] By 1782 James Madison could note in his journal that the Southern states feared the admission of Vermont because of "an habitual jealousy of a predominance of Eastern interest."[13] The mode of repaying the public debt was already so intense a sectional issue that in 1783 Madison wrote to Edmund Randolph that, if the public accounts were not speedily adjusted and discharged, "a dissolution of the Union will be inevitable."[14]

The peace treaty itself with its provision for the repayment of British creditors upset Southerners, who owed five-sixths of these private debts.[15] (Virginians accordingly pushed Jefferson for the French ministry so that at least one Southerner would be on

[10] *Diary and Autobiography of John Adams,* ed. Lyman H. Butterfield (Cambridge, 1961), II, 125.

[11] *Ibid.,* II, 246.

[12] Thomas Jefferson to John Adams, Dec. 17, 1777, *The Papers of Thomas Jefferson,* ed. Julian P. Boyd (Princeton, 1950—), 11, 120; Alden, *South in the Revolution,* 219. Richard Henry Lee voiced fear of a Northern commercial monopoly in 1785: "It seems to me clear, beyond doubt, that the giving Congress a power to Legislate over the Trade of the Union would be dangerous in the extreme to the Southern or Staple States" (R. H. Lee to James Madison, August 11, 1785, *Letters of Congress,* VIII, 181).

[13] "Observations Relating To The Influence Of Vermont, And The Territorial Claims, On The Politics Of Congress," May 1, 1782, *The Papers of James Madison* (Washington, 1840), I, 122–124.

[14] James Madison to Edmund Randolph, Feb. 25, 1783, *ibid.,* I, 511–512.

[15] This necessarily approximate figure is derived from the estimate of the British creditors in 1791. Samuel F. Bemis, *Jay's Treaty: A Study in Commerce and Diplomacy* (New York, 1923), 103n.

the European scene along with Adams, Jay, and Franklin).[16]
Five-sixths of the public debt, on the other hand, was owned in
the North and Southerners continued to resist all plans for
being taxed to pay it.[17] After the Virginia cession of the Northwest Territory, sectional conflict over the admission of new states
took on new intensity. "If a state be first laid off on the [Great]
lakes it will add a vote to the Northern scale," Jefferson wrote
late in 1783 to Benjamin Harrison, "if on the Ohio it will add one
to the Southern."[18] Throughout the 1780's Southerners sought
to hasten the development of the West and to remove all obstacles
to its speedy organization into the largest possible number of new
states.[19]

That group in Congress which contemporaries called "the
Southern Interest" (1786), "the southern party" (1787), or "the
Southern delegation" (1788)[20] was especially aroused when, in
1786, Northern Congressmen moved to surrender America's claim
to use the Mississippi River for its commerce. William Grayson
told the Virginia ratifying convention that the contest over the
Mississippi involved the question, "whether one part of the
continent shall govern the other"; two years earlier he had said
in Congress that if Secretary of State John Jay pursued his plan
of giving up the right to navigate the river, "the Southern States

16 James Monroe to the Governor of Virginia (Benjamin Harrison) and
The Virginia Delegates to same, Mar. 26, 1784 and May 13, 1784, *Letters
of Members of the Continental Congress*, ed. Edmund C. Burnett, VII
(Washington, 1934), 478, 525.
17 E. James Ferguson, *The Power of the Purse* (Chapel Hill, 1961),
181–183. For Southern suspicion of Northern proposals for paying the public
debt, see e.g., Richard Dobbs Spaight to the Gov. of North Carolina
(Alexander Martin), Apr. 30, 1784 (*Letters of Congress*, VII, 509); Jacob
Read to Charles Thomson, Apr. 26, 1785 (*ibid.*, VIII, 105).
18 Thomas Jefferson to the Governor of Virginia (Benjamin Harrison),
Nov. 11, 1783, *Letters of Congress*, VII, 374.
19 See, very much e.g., Hugh Williamson to James Duane, June 8, 1784
and The Virginia Delegates to the Governor of Virginia (Edmund Randolph), Nov. 3, 1787, *ibid.*, VII, 547 and VIII, 672–673. As the Constitution was being ratified, the expiring Congress squabbled bitterly over the
admission of Vermont and Kentucky (*ibid.*, VIII, 708, 714, 724, 733, 741,
757).
20 James Manning to Nathan Miller, May 19, 1786, *ibid.*, VIII, 364; Otto
to Vergennes, Feb. 10, 1787, quoted in George Bancroft, *History of the
Formation of the Constitution of the United States of America* (New York,
1882), II, 410; James Madison to Edmund Randolph, Aug. 11, 1788,
Letters of Congress, VIII, 778.

would never grant those powers which were acknowledged to be essential to the existence of the Union."[21] What most disturbed Southerners about Jay's procedure was that he secured authority from Congress to surrender the Mississippi navigation by a bare majority of seven votes. Two other Virginians were made Antifederalists by the controversy: James Monroe wrote to Patrick Henry that the object of Jay and his associates was "to throw the weight of population eastward and keep it there," and that if it came to disunion every effort should be made to win Pennsylvania and New Jersey for the Southern confederation.[22]

In the autumn of 1786 sectional feeling, inflamed by controversy over opening the Mississippi River to American commerce, was at a height. Timothy Bloodworth of North Carolina wrote to Governor Richard Caswell that the Mississippi controversy had brought all other business to a stop; "it is wel known that the ballance of power is now in the Eastern States," Bloodworth stated, "and they appear determined to keep it in that Direction."[23] Bloodworth, like Monroe, mentioned the possibility of disunion; so did the French minister to America, who reported to Vergennes "that this discussion . . . may be the germ of a future separation of the southern states."[24] In August 1786, Madison wrote Jefferson that he despaired of strengthening Congress through the Annapolis Convention or any other.[25]

A year later, all but four Southern delegates[26] to the Constitutional Convention agreed to a Constitution vastly strengthening the powers of Congress. Why?

Once again, Madison gives us the clue. In nearly-identical letters to Jefferson, Randolph and Washington in the spring of

---

[21] *The Debates in the Several State Conventions, on the Adoption of the Federal Constitution*, ed. Jonathan Elliot (Washington, 1836), III, 343; Charles Thomson, "Minutes of Proceedings, Aug. 18, 1786," *Letters of Congress*, VIII, 438–440.

[22] James Monroe to the Governor of Virginia (Patrick Henry), Aug. 12, 1786, *ibid.*, VIII, 424–425.

[23] Timothy Bloodworth to the Governor of North Carolina (Richard Caswell), Sept. 4, 1786, *ibid.*, VIII, 462.

[24] Otto to Vergennes, Sept. 10, 1786, quoted in *Formation of the Constitution*, II, 391.

[25] James Madison to Thomas Jefferson, Aug. 12, 1786, *The Writings of James Madison*, ed. Gaillard Hunt, II (New York, 1901), 262.

[26] Mason and Randolph of Virginia, Martin and Mercer of Maryland.

1787, Madison stated that if the South were to agree to strengthening Congress, the plan which gave each state one vote would have to be changed in the South's favor. Since the South (Madison assumed) was the more rapidly-growing section, this could be done by proportioning representation to numbers. Such a change would be "recommended to the Eastern States by the actual superiority of their populousness, and to the Southern by their expected superiority."[27] In a word: the South would strengthen the national government if it could be assured of controlling it.

And so it fell out. Over and over again members of the Convention stated, as of something on which all agreed, that "as soon as the Southern & Western population should predominate, which must happen in a few years," the South would be compensated for any advantages wrung from it by the North in the mean time.[28] Northerners insisted on equality of votes in the Senate because they feared what would happen when the South gained its inevitable (as they supposed) majority. "He must be short sighted indeed," declared King on July 12,

who does not foresee that whenever the Southern States shall be more numerous than the Northern, they can & will hold a language that will awe them [the Northern States] into justice. If they threaten to separate now in case injury shall be done them, will their threats be less urgent or effectual, when force shall back their demands?[29]

Gouverneur Morris echoed this gloomy prophecy the next day. "It has been said," Morris stated, "that N.C. [,] S.C. and Georgia only will in a little time have a majority of the people in America. They must in that case include the great interior Country, and every thing was to be apprehended from their getting the power into their hands." Morris said that the prospect would oblige him "to vote for ye. vicious principle of equality in the 2d. branch in order to provide some defense for the N. States agst. it."[30]

[27] James Madison to Thomas Jefferson, Mar. 19 [18], 1787, to Edmund Randolph, Apr. 8, 1787, and to George Washington, Apr. 16, 1787, *Writings of Madison*, II, 327, 340, 345.
[28] These were the words of George Mason on July 11 (*Records of the Convention*, I, 586).
[29] *Ibid.*, I, 595–596.
[30] *Ibid.*, I, 604–605.

The inclusion of slaves in apportioning representation, and the admission of new states represented in Congress on the same basis as the old states, were for the South alternative methods of implementing its expected numerical superiority. Farrand artifically separates these two questions, which were debated together in the crucial week of July 6 to 13. Nor is he correct in asserting that the adoption of the three-fifths formula for representation in the House was a foregone conclusion. The formula had previously been accepted only as a formula for taxation, and it was only as a formula for taxation that it appeared in the New Jersey plan.[31] What was at issue in the Convention was whether the three-fifths formula should be extended to representation as well. The two applications were very different: as William Paterson and Luther Martin remarked, taxing slaves discouraged slavery, while giving them political representation rewarded it.[32] Years later Rufus King stated that the three-fifths clause had been regarded as a great concession; at the Convention, once the crisis was passed, Charles Pinckney affirmed that the rule of representation in the House had been the "condition" of compromise on the rule of representation in the Senate.[33]

The South was victorious in obtaining both the representation of slaves, and the admission of new states on a basis of equality with the old. These agreements were voted by the Convention on July 12 and 13. A circumstance much remarked in the nineteenth century[34] was that on July 13 the Continental Congress in New York City, a body which just then had a decided majority of Southerners, passed the Northwest Ordinance banning slavery north of the Ohio River. Madison told Edward Coles, according to the latter, that the actions of the Convention

[31] For the New Jersey Plan, *ibid.*, I, 243 (Resolution 3).
[32] *Ibid.*, I, 561; III, 197.
[33] Speech in the Senate, Mar. 1819, *Records of the Convention*, III, 428–430; *ibid.*, II, 263.
[34] See *Abridgement of the Debates of Congress, From 1789 To 1856*, VI (Washington, 1858), 359n., 363, 391, 410, 492, and especially 517, for reference to the interconnection of the Ordinance and the Constitution during the Missouri Compromise debates; also Thomas H. Benton, *Historical and Legal Examination Of That Part Of The Decision Of The Supreme Court Of The United States In The Dred Scott Case, Which Declares The Unconstitutionality Of The Missouri Compromise Act* . . . (New York, 1857), 37–39, and sources cited in note 35.

and the Congress were coordinated parts of an overall compromise between the sections. "Many individuals were members of both bodies," Madison said,

and thus were enabled to know what was passing in each—both sitting with closed doors and in secret sessions. The distracting question of slavery was agitating and retarding the labors of both, and led to conferences and inter-communications of the members, which resulted in a compromise by which the northern or anti-slavery portion of the country agreed to incorporate, into the Ordinance and Constitution, the provision to restore fugitive slaves; and this mutual and concurrent action was the cause of the similarity of the provision contained in both, and had its influence, in creating the great unanimity by which the Ordinance passed, and also in making the constitution the more acceptable to the slave holders.[35]

Some evidence regarding these "conferences and inter-communications" survives to support Coles' memory of Madison's words. William Pierce of Georgia returned to New York from the Convention on June 14, just after discussion of the rule of representation had begun, and according to Nathan Dane spoke freely of sectional conflicts.[36] Gouverneur Morris returned to the Convention July 2, after a lengthy New York sojourn; Richard Henry Lee arrived in New York City July 7, after a week in Philadelphia; two North Carolina Congressmen, Blount and Hawkins, visited Philadelphia from June 19 to July 2: On July 10 Hawkins, now back in New York, wrote the Governor of North Carolina that the struggle to safeguard "our right to the free and common use of the navigation of the Mississippi . . . has at length, from a variety of circumstances unnecessary as well perhaps as improper to relate been put in a better situation than heretofore."[37]

[35] Edward Coles, *History Of The Ordinance of 1787* (Philadelphia, 1856), 28–29. The passage begins: "This brings to my recollection what I was told by Mr. Madison, and what I do not remember ever to have seen in print." It is accepted as trustworthy by William Henry Smith, *The Life and Public Services of Arthur St. Clair,* I (Cincinnati, 1882), 134 and by Peter Force, *Life, Journals and Correspondence of Reverend Manasseh Cutler,* II (Cincinnati, 1888), Appendix D, 419.

[36] For the date of Pierce's arrival, William Blount to John Gray Blount, June 15, 1787, *Letters of Congress,* VIII, 610; for his loose tongue regarding "the plans of the Southern, Eastern or Middle States," Nathan Dane to Rufus King, June 19, 1787, *ibid.,* VIII, 225.

[37] Madison noted the date of Morris' return to the Convention (*Records of the Convention,* I, 511); for Lee's itinerary, see *Letters of*

The most suggestive travellers between New York and Philadelphia were Alexander Hamilton and Manasseh Cutler. Hamilton, who left the Convention after his speech of June 29, returned to Philadelphia no earlier than July 10 (when Washington wrote that he wished Hamilton would return) and no later than the evening of July 12, when Manasseh Cutler met with him and other key delegates to the Convention at the Indian Queen tavern.[38] Cutler, we know, left New York City late on July 10 after returning to the Congressional committee working on the Ordinance a draft with "several amendments" including, so he later claimed, that prohibiting slavery. He arrived in Philadelphia late on the 12th and left on the 14th, after a second meeting with a number of Convention delegates.[39] Some of

Congress, VIII, 613n., 627; for that of Blount and Hawkins, ibid., VIII, 610, 613, 618, 623; for Benjamin Hawkins to the Governor of North Carolina (Richard Caswell), July 10, 1787, ibid., VIII, 619. William Blount was one of the largest land speculators in the Southwest and during this summer of 1787 wrote several letters from an imaginary Westerner, urging the opening of the Mississippi to American commerce, which were published in the New York City press; see William Blount to [Thomas Blount], July 30, 1787, The John Gray Blount Papers, ed. Alice Barnwell Keith, I (Raleigh, 1952), 327–328; and William Blount to John Gray Blount, July 19, 1787, Letters of Congress, VIII, 623–624. In December 1787 the Spanish minister to America wrote to his superiors that Lee had come to Congress "at my instance to further our cause [of keeping the Mississippi closed]" (quoted in Samuel F. Bemis, Pinckney's Treaty: America's Advantage from Europe's Distress, 1783–1800 [New Haven, 1960], 95 n.). Lee had invested heavily in lands near the Ohio River; both he and Washington were untypical among Southerners in that they were not enthusiastic for the opening of the Mississippi; see Richard Henry Lee to Francis Lightfoot Lee, July 14, 1787 and to George Washington, July 15, 1787, The Letters of Richard Henry Lee, ed. James Curtis Ballagh, II (New York, 1914), 423–424, 425–427.

[38] Washington's letter (The Papers of Alexander Hamilton, ed. Harold C. Syrett, IV [New York, 1962], 225) shows that Hamilton was not in Philadelphia on the 10th, and a letter from Hamilton to Nathaniel Mitchell, written from New York City on July 20 (ibid., IV, 226) proves that he was back from Philadelphia by that date. Cutler saw "Mr. Hamilton of New York" the evening of July 12, and Strong, Martin, Mason, Williamson, Madison, Rutledge and "Mr. Hamilton, all members of Convention" on the morning of July 14 (Life, Journals and Correspondence, I, 254, 272). Professor Syrett has written to me, July 22, 1964: "You are certainly right about the Cutler citation, and he was obviously referring to Hamilton. I don't have to add that we missed the Cutler citation when we were doing vol. IV."

[39] Life, Journals and Correspondence of Manasseh Cutler, I, 242, 343–344.

the same ambiguity clings about this scientific side-trip as still surrounds a later botanical excursion by Jefferson and Madison. John Sergeant of Pennsylvania, whose father had lunched with Cutler just before the latter left New York for Philadelphia on July 10, told the House of Representatives in 1821 that the Ordinance had "finally adjusted" for the territories the problems of admission of new states and slave representation which were troubling the Convention, "and was therefore eminently calculated to quiet the minds of the advocates of freedom; to remove their objections to the principle of representation, and to secure their assent to the government which contained that principle. . . . It is not to be questioned," Sergeant concluded, "that this ordinance, unanimously adopted, and, as it were, fixing an unchangeable basis, by common consent, had a most powerful influence in bringing about the adoption of the constitution."[40]

Whether such a Compromise of 1787 took place, whether these were among the "several . . . political reasons" which (according to William Grayson)[41] induced the Southern members of Con-

[40] For the luncheon in its relation to the legislative history of the ordinance, see William F. Poole, "The Early Northwest," *Papers of the American Historical Association*, III (New York, 1889), No. 2, 47–49; for the speech, *Abridgement of the Debates of Congress*, VI, 517.

[41] William Grayson to James Monroe, Aug. 8, 1787, *Letters of Congress*, VIII, 632–633. It should be emphasized that the plan adopted by Congress for the Northwest Territory in 1784 dealt with the entire area west of the Appalachians, south as well as north of the Ohio River, and that until July 1787 Congressional discussion of plans for the West regularly referred to the southern as well as the northern area (see *Papers of Jefferson*, VI, 593; *Journals of the Continental Congress, 1774–1789*, ed. Gaillard Hunt [Washington, 1904–1937], XXVI, 118–120, 274–279, XXVIII, 164–165, XXX, 139, 251, 404, 418n., XXXI, 561n., 563, 667n., 669, XXXII, 242, 274, 281–283, 313). John M. Merriam remarks that it is surprising that Dane, who later claimed credit for the anti-slavery clause, was ready to vote for an ordinance without such a clause on May 10, 1787; while B. A. Hinsdale says of the clause: ". . . it had been rejected by Southern men when Mr. Jefferson first brought it forward, and now five of the eight States present are Southern States and eleven of the eighteen men Southern men, and it prevails" ("The Legislative History of the Ordinance of 1787," *Proceedings of the American Antiquarian Society* (Worcester, 1888–1889], New Series, V, 336; *The Old Northwest* [New York, 1899], 266). Hildreth says that the Southern states were doubtless reconciled to the Ordinance "by the idea, afterward acted upon, of securing the continuation of slavery in the territory south of the Ohio, under future terms of cession" (*op. cit.*, III, 528–529).

gress to vote in 1787 for a ban on slavery they had rejected in 1784, remains probable but not proven. What is clear is that Southerners had good reason to consider the votes of the Convention on July 12 and 13 a clear-cut victory which held out hope of ultimate Southern control of the national government.

Thus slavery was written into the United States Constitution. In 1783 members of Congress had "been ashamed," in the phrase of Paterson, to use the word "slave" in framing the three-fifths formula.[42] In wording the Constitution, the "peculiar scruples" of Northerners led them to omit the word "slave" so as to shield the new government from any "stain."[43] These scruples, this shame, this sense of having somehow flawed the new fabric at its moment of inception, were summed up eloquently in Luther Martin's statement that a Revolution

grounded upon the preservation of *those rights* to which God and nature had entitled *us*, not in *particular*, but in *common* with *all the rest of mankind*

had ended by making a Constitution that was an

insult to that God . . . who views with equal eye the poor *African slave* and his *American master*.[44]

Why did they do what they knew to be wrong?

Some Northern delegates at the Convention expressed the belief that Southerners would gradually abandon slavery, but it is difficult to imagine that they placed much confidence in that belief. The delegates of the Deep South were on their feet repeatedly stressing their intention to safeguard the peculiar institution.[45] All knew that South Carolina had resumed slave importation at its pre-war rate.[46] Jefferson, whose own state

---

[42] *Records of the Convention*, I, 561.

[43] *Ibid.*, III, 376–377; *Debates in State Conventions*, IV, 182.

[44] *Records of the Convention*, III, 211.

[45] *Ibid.*, e.g., I, 594 (C. C. Pinckney), 605 (Butler); II, 95 (C. C. Pinckney), 364 (C. Pinckney, 371 (both Pinckneys).

[46] The number of slaves imported by South Carolina between the spring of 1783 and the fall of 1785, two-and-a half years, was variously estimated as 7000 (by John Rutledge, quoted in Ulrich B. Phillips, *American Negro Slavery* [New York and London, 1933], 134) and 12,000 (James Madison to Thomas Jefferson, Oct. 3, 1785, *Writings of Madison*, II, 178 ff.). In the twenty years between 1753 and 1773 the average importation was

could not bring emancipation to a vote in the 1780's, wrote in 1786: "In Maryland and N. Carolina, a very few are disposed to emancipate. In S. Carolina and Georgia not the smallest symptom of it."[47] Madison, who wrote Jefferson before the Convention that South Carolina would no doubt insist on a proviso "against any restraint from importing slaves," wrote him after the Convention that South Carolina and Georgia had been "inflexible on the point of slaves."[48] And at the Convention, George Mason said: "The Western people are already calling out for slaves for their new lands; and will fill that Country with slaves if they can be got thro' S. Carolina and Georgia."[49]

Why did the North acquiesce in this?

Even the most liberal of the Founding Fathers were unable to imagine a society in which whites and Negroes would live together as fellow-citizens. Honor and intellectual consistency drove them to favor abolition; personal distaste, to fear it. Jefferson said just this when he wrote: "Nothing is more certainly written in the book of fate, than that these people are to be free; nor is it less certain that the two races, equally free, cannot live in the same government."[50] These were also the sentiments of Northerners like Otis, Franklin, and John Quincy Adams. Otis condemned slavery in the abstract, but also prided himself that North America was settled "not as the common people of England foolishly imagine, with a compound mongrel mixture of

just over 2000 (Edward McCrady, "Slavery in the Province of South Carolina, 1670–1770," *Annual Report of the American Historical Association for the Year 1895* [Washington, 1896], 669).

[47] Answers to Démeunier's First Queries," Jan. 24, 1786, *Papers of Jefferson*, X, 18.

[48] James Madison to Thomas Jefferson, Oct. 3, 1785 and Oct. 24, 1787, *Writings of Madison*, II, 178 ff. and *Records of the Convention*, III, 131.

[49] *Records of the Convention*, II, 370. Mason's point was that the laws of the Upper South restricting slave importation (so often referred to by historians as evidence of a trend toward emancipation) would be in vain if South Carolina and Georgia could continue to import freely. Mason's opponents charged that he was not interested in emancipation but in raising the price of home-grown Virginian slaves. Evidence for this is that at the Virginia ratifying convention Mason warned that the Constitution might lead to emancipation (*Debates in State Conventions*, III, 262–263).

[50] *The Works of Thomas Jefferson*, ed. Andrew A. Lipscomb, I (Washington, 1904), 72–73.

English, Indian and *Negro,* but with freeborn *British white subjects.*"[51] On the eve of his career as an abolitionist, John Quincy Adams praised Andrew Jackson for destroying the "motley tribe of black, white, and red combatants," the "particolored forces" of the "negro-Indian banditti" in Florida.[52] As for Franklin, the future president of the Pennsylvania Abolition Society wrote in 1751:

. . . the Number of purely white People in the World is proportionably very small. All Africa is black or tawny. Asia chiefly tawny. America (exclusive of the new Comers) wholly so. And in Europe, the Spaniards, Italians, French, Russians and Swedes, are generally of what we call a swarthy Complexion; as are the Germans also, the Saxons only excepted, who with the English, make the principal Body of White People on the Face of the Earth. I could wish their Numbers were increased. And while we are, as I may call it, *Scouring* our Planet, by clearing America of Woods, and so making this Side of our Globe reflect a brighter Light to the Eyes of Inhabitants in Mars or Venus, why should we in the Sight of Superior Beings, darken its People? why increase the Sons of Africa, by Planting them in America, where we have so fair an Opportunity, by excluding all Blacks and Tawneys, of increasing the lovely White and Red?[53]

A second reason why Northern liberals among the Fathers turned aside from an attack on slavery was their commitment to private property. Gouverneur Morris was the Convention's most

---

[51] The quoted phrases are from *The Rights of the British Colonies Asserted and Proved,* 3d. ed. (London, 1766), 36–37, 43, the same pamphlet which also says: "The Colonists are by the law of nature free born, as indeed all men are, white or black. . . . Does it follow that it is right to enslave a man because he is black? Will short curled hair like wool, instead of christian hair, as it is called by those whose hearts are as hard as the nether millstone, help the argument?" etc.

[52] John Quincy Adams to George William Erving, Nov. 28, 1818, *Writings of John Quincy Adams,* ed. Worthington Chauncey Ford, VI (New York, 1916), 477, 488, 496. Adams characterized the struggle of General Jackson's antagonists as "all in the name of South American liberty, of the rights of runaway Negroes, and the wrongs of savage murderers."

[53] "Observations Concerning the Increase of Mankind" (1751), *Papers of Benjamin Franklin,* ed. Leonard W. Labaree (New Haven, 1959—), IV, 234. Contrast Bolivar: "The blood of our citizens is varied: let it be mixed for the sake of unity" (*Selected Writings of Bolivar,* ed. Harold A. Bierck, Jr., I [New York, 1951], 191); and again, to Miranda: "Neither we nor the generation following us will see the glory of the republic which we are founding. There will be a new caste composed of an amalgamation of all races, which will produce a homogeneous people" (Victor Andres Belaunde, *Bolivar and the Political Thought of the Spanish American Revolution* [Baltimore, 1938], 166).

outspoken opponent of slavery, the South Carolina delegates were its frankest defenders; but their identical assumptions about the place of property in society drove them to similar conclusions. Thus, in the Convention debates of July 5 and 6, Morris declared that "life and liberty were generally said to be of more value, than property," but that "an accurate view of the matter would nevertheless prove that property was the main object of Society."[54] This was a view which the South Carolinians could only echo. What it came down to was, as Charles Cotesworth Pinckney put it, that "property in slaves should not be exposed to danger under a Govt. instituted for the protection of property."[55] And so, while Morris stated on July 11 that if compelled to do injustice to human nature or the southern states, he must do it to the latter, that same evening he worked out the formula—proportioning representation to direct taxation —which proved a "bridge" to the three-fifths compromise; and in August it was he who proposed what he termed a "bargain" between North and South over slave importation.[56]

Property, of course, induced the North to compromise in a more substantive way. As late as 1833, Madison could write that the good faith of the North was "sufficiently guarantied by the interest they have, as merchants, as ship owners, and as manufacturers, in preserving a Union with the slave-holding states."[57] But apart from interest, the belief that private property was the indispensable foundation for personal freedom made it more difficult for Northerners to confront the fact of slavery squarely.

Unable to summon the moral imagination required to transcend race prejudice, unwilling to contemplate social experiments which impinged on private property, the Fathers, unhappily, ambivalently, confusedly, passed by on the other side. Their much-praised deistic coolness of temper could not help them here. The compromise of 1787 was a critical, albeit characteristic, failure of the American pragmatic intelligence.

---

[54] *Records of the Convention*, I, 533.

[55] *Ibid.*, I, 534, 542, 593 (latter the Pinckney quotation).

[56] The "bridge" (July 24), *ibid.*, II, 106; the "bargain" (August 22), *ibid.*, II, 374.

[57] James Madison to Henry Clay, June, 1833, *Writings of Madison*, IX, 517.

IV. THE NEGRO RESPONSE

On Tuesday morning the driver Bill came to me and stated that Samuel had become unmanageable, was destroying cotton, that he had ordered Samuel down to be whipped, that Samuel then swore he would not be whipped. Bill then told him he would get the overseer. . . . I then asked Samuel if he had refused to get down for punishment when the driver ordered him, he answered at once, Yes by God, I did and I am not going to be whipped by anybody, either black or white. I told him to stop, as I allowed no negro to talk in that way and that he knew that. I then ordered him to throw down his hoe and get down, he swore God damn him if he would. . . . he turned and ran off. I kept my horse standing and called to the rest of the hands to catch that boy, not one of them paid the least attention to me but kept on at their work. I then started after Samuel myself. . . . he wheeled around, with his raised hoe in both hands and struck at me with his full force . . . his hoe descending I think within one or two feet of my head. [I] pulled my horse up, and drew my pistol. Samuel was then standing with his hoe raised. I fired across my bridle arm when he fell.

CORONOR'S COURT REPORT, *Concordia Parish Louisiana*, 185?.

Benjamin Quarles

From the earliest histories written by Negroes, emphasis has been placed on their participation in American development, and particularly of their loyalty to the country during times of trial (*See* the various studies listed in the bibliography). For the most part white historians have ignored the Negro's part in the nation's struggles. U. B. Phillips in *American Negro Slavery* contemptuously described the Negroes during the American revolution as "a passive element whose fate was affected only so far as the master race determined." Yet Negroes were far from passive. It was a Negro, Crispus Attacks, who was the first man killed by the British in the Boston Massacre. Negroes fought at Lexington, Concord, and Bunker Hill. We have the names of hundreds of Negroes whose exploits are remembered for exceptional bravery and allegiance to the cause of the Revolution.

The Revolutionaries had doubts about the use of Negroes. They feared that recruitment might open the door for mass emancipation. Washington issued an order of July 9, 1775 instructing recruiting officers not to sign up ". . . any stroller, Negro, or vagabond. . . ." The British showed no such reluctance, and in the fall of 1775 they invited Negroes to join their forces. Within two months after the British announcement, Washington modified his policy and agreed to the enlistment of free Negroes. As the war took a turn for the worse and months passed to years, the Revolutionaries let expediency override their prejudices, and Negroes were taken into the army and navy. However, South Carolina and Georgia remained implacably opposed to the recruitment of slaves, even though their own areas remained undefended and open to British devastation. The 5000 Negro soldiers who fought in the Revolution came mainly from the Northern colonies. Three-quarters of the Rhode Island regiment passing in review at Yorktown in 1781 were Negroes. By the war's end, Washington had accepted the Negro soldier, and in the North, Negro participation contributed to the liberalization of the institution of slavery.

However, there is another side of the story that is seldom mentioned by either white or Negro historians. The British promise of freedom to the bondsmen of the rebels caused many thousands of Negroes to find refuge in the British lines, and it is estimated that the Southern colonies alone lost 65,000 slaves. Benjamin Quarles' study of the Negro in the American Revolution is the first major work to show this facet of Negro reaction to slavery. In the context of the Negroes' response it should be interpreted as an act of rebellion for joining the British, as refugees, laborers, or spies, they were American equivalents of the *palmaristas* of Brazil. It illustrates that rebellion was possible when the whites fought among themselves, as happened in Brazil between the Portuguese and Dutch, in Haiti between the Royalists and Revolutionaries, in Jamaica between the Spaniards and British, and in America between the Crown and the colonists.

As the Revolution ended and the British evacuated the major areas they held, they took with them not only American

Loyalists, but Negroes who had come into their lines and who chose to chance it with them rather than return to the lives they had known as slaves. The final evacuation in 1782–83 of Savannah, Charleston, and New York found some 14,000 Negroes sailing off with the British. Previously 5000 had already left with them, some left with the French, others sailed South to British East Florida, some crossed into Canada, and some remained behind as guerrilla bands in the backcountry of South Carolina and Georgia. Throughout the West Indies, Nova Scotia, and England, settlements of Negro refugees sprang up, with the final phase coming in 1791 when 1190 Negroes left Canada for settlement in Africa, in what was to become Sierra Leone. The capitol city was christened Freetown. They had come full circle.

Professor Quarles is Chairman of the History Department of Morgan State College, Baltimore. He is the author of *Frederick Douglass* (1948), *The Negro in the Civil War* (1953), and *Lincoln and the Negro* (1962).

EVACUATION WITH THE BRITISH

SOURCE: Benjamin Quarles, "Evacuation with the British," from *The Negro in the American Revolution* (Chapel Hill: University of North Carolina Press, 1961), pp. 158–59, 163, 167, 172–81.

The chief concern of Americans about Negroes in the thirty months after Yorktown was their disappearance. Whenever the defeated British made their final withdrawals, whether by land or sea, thousands of slaves went with them. Take what precautions they would, the Americans could not prevent mass exodus of their black bondmen, which began immediately after Cornwallis's defeat.

The articles of capitulation at Yorktown stated that any American property held by the British garrison was subject to recovery.[1] The surrender terms were silent, however, about slaves who would try to escape by going aboard the departing warships of the royal navy. Americans did not need to be told that prompt action was necessary to forestall the flight of slaves. On the very day of the Yorktown surrender, General George Weedon placed

---

[1] Tarleton, *History of the Campaigns in the Southern Provinces,* 439.

sentinels "all along the Beach" to prevent them from reaching the vessels of the royal navy. Prompt as was his action, he feared that many runaways had already "secreted" themselves on board the ships. On the next day Weedon sent a letter to Governor Nelson apprising him of the situation.[2]

Virginia's chief executive had not been idle. Within twenty-four hours after the surrender he had written to Cornwallis asking him to prevent Negroes from making their escape by boarding the sloop of war, Bonetta, which was allowed to sail to New York with news of the capitulation. These Negroes, cautioned the Governor, would "endeavor to lie concealed from your Lordship's Notice till the Vessel sails."[3]

General Washington lent his support to the effort to keep Negroes from leaving the state. He was disturbed about the number of slaves who attached themselves to the British or posed as freemen in order to deceive American commanders. To put a stop to such irregularities, Washington on October 25 ordered officers of the allied armies to deliver all Negroes who came into their hands to a guard to be established at Yorktown and Gloucester under the superintendency of David Ross, Virginia's commercial agent. Negroes who could prove they were not escaped slaves would be released. Slaves whose masters lived in the vicinity would be issued a pass enabling them to make their way home unmolested. Slaves whose owners were not Virginians would be advertised in newspapers of their home states. While waiting for their masters to claim them, they would be "sent into the Country to work for their Victuals and Cloathes."[4] . . . .

For some months after the surrender at Yorktown, the British appeared "unable to carry on the war, and too proud to make peace."[5] But by April 1782 His Majesty's ministers had decided to evacuate their troops, using three of the major seaports. The first of these departures took place at Savannah in the summer of 1782.

[2] Weedon to Nelson, Oct. 20, 1781, Cal. of Va. State Papers, II, 561.
[3] Nelson to Cornwallis, Oct. 20, 1781, Off. Letters of Govs. of Va., III, 88.
[4] General Orders, Oct. 25, 1781, Fitzpatrick, ed., Writings of Washington, XXIII, 264–65; Washington to Ross, Oct. 24, 1781, ibid., 262.
[5] Phrase attributed to Benjamin Franklin. Washington to Nathanael Greene, Sept. 23, 1782, Fitzpatrick, ed., Writings of Washington, XXV, 195.

A week before the date set for the evacuation, the Georgia assembly urged Governor John Martin to request of the British commandant of Savannah that no Negroes or other property belonging to Americans be carried off. The legislators also asked Governor Martin to grant permission to citizens having property in British hands to lodge a formal claim. Realizing that Georgia needed all its manpower resources to rebuild the state's economy, the lower house also tried to persuade departing Tories to leave their slaves behind. The commissioners for the sales of forfeited estates were empowered to purchase Negroes from evacuees and sell them to residents, on condition that the purchasers would not carry them out of the state for at least eighteen months.[6]

British military forces formally withdrew from Savannah in July 1782, evacuating loyalists with their slaves as well as troops. On July 6, General Leslie ordered the royal navy to provide shipping accommodations for 50 whites and 1,900 Negroes. An embarkation return of August 10, 1782, lists six ships as having carried 1,568 Negroes to Jamaica. By December 23, 1782, an additional 1,786 Negroes had been taken to St. Augustine; seven months later this figure had reached 1,956, of whom 799 were men, 705 women, and 452 children.[7] . . .

Five months after the British left Savannah, Charleston was evacuated. . . . When, on December 14, 1782, they finally left the city, they took 5,327 Negroes, of whom one-half were destined for Jamaica. Of the remainder, all but 500 went to East Florida, with a few finding their way to St. Lucia, Halifax, England, and New York.[8] . . .

By the time His Majesty's forces officially withdrew from

[6] Candler, ed., *Rev. Rec. of Ga.*, III, 119–20, 122, 127.

[7] Leslie to Captain William Swiney, July 6, 1782, Leslie Letter Book, N.Y. Pub. Lib.; Lists of transports from Savannah to Jamaica, Aug. 10, 1782, C. O. 5/560, 477; Lists of refugees to East Florida, Dec. 23, 1782, authenticated by John Winniett, Inspector of Refugees, C. O. 5/160, 507; Lists of refugees to East Florida, July 18, 1783, C. O. 5/560, 810. For an analytical statement on the number of white and Negro civilian evacuees from Georgia see Kenneth Coleman, *The American Revolution in Georgia, 1763–1789* (Athens, 1958), 145–46.

[8] "Return of People Embarked from South Carolina and Georgia. Charleston, 13 December 1782," Mass. Hist. Soc., *Proc.*, 2nd Ser., 3 (1887), 95. For the specific number coming into Florida as of July 15, 1783, see C. O. 5/560, 811–20.

New York on November 30, 1783, the British commissioners had compiled a detailed list of 3,000 Negroes they had inspected, comprising 1,336 men, 914 women, and 750 children. This massive "Inspection Roll of Negroes" bore eight columns listing the names of the Negroes, their former masters, and the names of the vessels on which they were embarking. One heading was entitled, "Description," and bore such arresting comments as "fine boy," "an idiot," "likely rascal," "snug little wench," and "nearly worn out."

To these 3,000 Negroes who left New York must be added the hundreds of unregistered ones carried away in private vessels. The total number of colored persons who left that city, as well as other ports, can only be guessed. Perhaps it would be safe to say that during the evacuations the numbers of Negroes leaving Savannah was 4,000, Charleston 6,000, and New York 4,000. If anything, these figures are a bit low, and they do not, of course, include those who went off with the French, nor the thousands—perhaps around five thousand—whom the British carried away prior to the surrender of Yorktown.

Many Negroes were carried off without regard for their own wishes. This would be particularly true of slaves belonging to departing loyalists. Likewise, many Negroes who had deserted to the British were not consulted about their being taken off in the evacuations. Perhaps most of these former runaways would have left America voluntarily, since the British had assiduously spread the idea that those who went back to their American masters would be severely whipped and then assigned the hardest kind of labor.

The belief that their former masters would treat them harshly for having fled was no doubt a strong factor in shaping the conduct of Negroes who had a free choice. In peacetime a recovered runaway was not likely to get off lightly; in wartime a slave who not only had taken to his heels but had joined the enemy had reason to feel nervous about the welcome he would receive upon his return to the home plantation. To allay this fear, some masters promised a pardon. Virginia's Theodorick Bland, Jr., sent word to his slaves, Isaac and Kitt, who were in New York, that if they would come back to Framingdell, the

family plantation in Prince George County, he would let bygones be bygones. Neither would listen; Isaac informed Bland's
emissary that he had heard that once a slave had returned to his
master he was "treated with great severity."[9]

Exclusive of the thousand or more youngsters who were born
within the British lines and who therefore might be considered
born free, a small number of adult free Negroes, perhaps a few
hundred, went off in the evacuations. There were 8 free Negroes
among the 2,563 colored refugees who came to East Florida from
South Carolina as of July 15, 1783. Numbered in the 1,956 black
emigrants from Georgia to East Florida as of July 18, 1783, were
3 free Negroes. Accompanying the British from Charleston to
New York late in 1782 was free Negro Bacchus, a smith by
trade. Thirteen free Negroes, 7 men and 6 women, were included in the 232 adults sailing out of New York in November
1783 on the *Peggy, Concord,* and *Diannah.*[10]

One free Negro who was not near an evacuation point be-
sought Carleton's aid in getting out of America. Originally from
England, Towers Bell had been brought to Baltimore and sold
into slavery. His four years in bondage were a time in which he
had "suffered with the Greatest Barbarity in this Rebellious
Country." For the last six years he had been free, but had
neither friends nor money, and needed assistance to get home.[11]

Not all the Negroes within British lines were evacuated.
Aside from a handful successfully reclaimed by Washington's
commissioners, there were some slaves who were deliberately
left behind. They were the sick, the helpless, and the aged,
whom evacuating loyalists simply abandoned.[12] Some departing
masters sold their slaves.

[9] Jacob Morris to Bland, July 17, 1783, Campbell, ed., *Bland Papers,*
II, III.

[10] C. O. 5/560, 810, 811–20; Return of the Civil Branch of Ordnance
and Horse Department, arrived at New York from Charleston in South
Carolina, Jan. 19, 1783, Wray Papers, Clements Lib.; Inspection Roll of
Negroes, taken on board the undernamed vessels, on the 30th day of Nov.
1783 at Anchor near Statten Island, previous to their Sailing for Port-
Mattoon in the province of Nova Scotia, The Papers of the Continental
Congress, LIII, 276–95, National Archives. These lists carry a descriptive
statement on each of the Negroes who embarked on the three transports.

[11] Bell to Carleton, June 7, 1783, Carleton photostats.

[12] Harry B. Yoshpe, *The Disposition of Loyalist Estates in the Southern
District of the State of New York* (New York, 1939), 91–93.

One slave thus disposed of was to have a notable career. James Derham had been the property of a surgeon in the British Sixteenth Regiment. While his master was with the army, Derham was allowed to perform medical duties, since he had already acquired some experience in compounding medicines and acting as a male nurse. At the close of the war, the surgeon sold him to a New Orleans physician, who employed him as a paid assistant. While still in his early twenties, Derham was able to buy his freedom, and by 1789 he had built up a thriving medical practice in Philadelphia, with an income of over $3,000 a year. The celebrated Dr. Benjamin Rush was impressed by his fellow practitioner—by his fluency in French and Spanish, and, more importantly, by his knowledge of the healing arts: "I expected to have suggested some new medicines to him," wrote Rush, "but he suggested many more to me."[13]

While most Negroes whom the British left behind had no choice in the matter, a corps of some three hundred ex-slaves in Georgia remained there by preference. This group had been arms-bearers for the British during the occupation of Savannah, and they proposed neither to return to their masters nor leave in the evacuation. Styling themselves the "King of England's soldiers," they settled along the swamps bordering the Savannah River, plundering by night and disappearing by day. It was not until May 1786 that they were dispersed, following the discovery and burning of their fortified encampment at Bear Creek by militia from Georgia and South Carolina.[14]

The Negroes who left the United States at war's end traveled to widely separated points on the globe. Over a thousand, as will be noted, went to the west coast of Africa. An odder destination was reserved for a Negro drum corps which arrived in central Europe, accompanying General Riedesel to Brunswick, where, on a mid-October day in 1783, it formed part of an infantry battalion received with military honors in a public market place.[15] The overwhelming majority of black evacuees, however,

13 For a sketch of Derham by Rush see *The American Museum*, 5 (Phila., 1789), 61–62.
14 Charles C. Jones, *The Life and Services of the Honorable Major General Samuel Elbert* (Cambridge, 1887), 47; Stevens, *A History of Georgia*, II, 376–78.
15 "The Brunswick Contingent in America, 1776–1783," *Pa. Mag. of Hist. and Biog.*, 15 (1891), 224.

settled in the British Caribbean islands or in Canada, although thousands of these were at first taken into East Florida, where their sojourn proved to be temporary.

Before the British evacuation of Savannah, many Georgia loyalists contemplated a removal to East Florida. Just south of the state border, it offered a climate and conditions to which they were accustomed. Uncertain as to what disposition would be made of the province after the war, they urged British authorities to retain it. Responding to their entreaties, Sir Guy Carleton, successor to Henry Clinton as commander-in-chief, merely informed Governor Leslie that the province would remain as it was. Georgia loyalists construed his remark to mean that the British did not intend to give it up. Accordingly, many of them migrated into the neighboring province, bearing with them a large number of slaves. By the summer of 1783, as we have seen, a total of 1,956 slaves had been taken into East Florida.[16]

Within a few months the newcomers knew that East Florida was destined to go to Spain, and that they would have to move again; Spanish rule had no attraction for Anglo-Americans. The treaty that ceded East Florida to Spain, signed in September 1783, gave the inhabitants of the province eighteen months to get out. The nearly eight thousand Negroes in the province at that time included not more than one thousand who were free and could therefore choose whether to go or stay.[17] The others followed the dictates of their masters.

Of the 6,540 Negroes recorded as leaving the province, over 2,500 were brought back to the United States,[18] many of them to Georgia. As early as October 1782 the Georgia Council voted to permit its citizens to purchase slaves from loyalists who had gone

16 Candler, ed., *Col. Rec. of Ga.*, XV, 664–65; Lists of refugees to East Florida, July 18, 1783, C. O. 5/560, 810; Coleman, *Amer. Rev. in Ga.*, 145–46.

17 Joseph Bryne Lockey, *East Florida, 1783–1785* (Berkeley, 1949), 23, 340.

18 For the specific figures on white and black migrants to the varying destination points see "Return of Persons who emigrated from East Florida to different parts of the British Dominions &c," C. O. 5/561, 817. Dated London, 1786, this return is signed by Colonel William Brown, Commissioner of Embarkation.

to East Florida, and to export produce and lumber to pay for
such purchases. The Council granted individual petitions to those
wishing to go to St. Augustine to recover or to purchase slaves,
such petitions generally specifying the product or commodity to
be used in defraying expenses. In the spring of 1783 the state of
South Carolina sent a commissioner to St. Augustine to seek
recovery of her expatriated blacks.[19] "There is," wrote the
governor of East Florida, "a considerable influx of transient
people from Georgia and South Carolina to recover their
property in Negroes."[20] Apart from such efforts, slaves amounting to "upwards of 1,000" were brought back from St. Augustine
to South Carolina by former loyalists who were legally permitted to return.[21] Some of East Florida's free Negroes returned
to America, but they tended to move northwestward toward the
Mississippi River rather than northeastward toward the Savannah and the Santee.

By no means was all the black emigration out of East Florida
to the United States; over 2,200 Negroes went to the Bahamas,
and lesser numbers went to other points, ranging from the 714
transported to Jamaica to the 35 that crossed the Atlantic to
an English port. In addition to those whose departure was
officially recorded, there were hundreds of refugees, white and
black, who left in small groups, sailing away without authoriza-
tion, leaving not a trace behind. A few hundred Negroes remained in the province; presumably they were of the free class.

As the migration figures illustrate, the Bahamas attracted
slave-owning refugees, not only from East Florida, but from the
United States. Over a twenty-two month span from June 1783
to April 1785 these British islands received from six to seven
thousand refugees, white and colored.[22] A few of the black
newcomers were destined to return to the mainland. Late in
1784 General James Grant sold to three South Carolinians

[19] Candler, ed., *Rev. Rec. of Ga.*, II, 388, 477, 478; James Clitherall to
John Cruden, May 31, 1783, *Amer. MSS in Royal Inst. of G. B.*, IV, 115.
[20] Tonyn to Thomas Townshend, May 15, 1783, C. O. 5/560, 550.
[21] Ralph Izard to Jefferson, with "Reports on the Trade of South Carolina,
June 10, 1785, Boyd, ed., *Papers of Jefferson*, VIII.
[22] Wilbur H. Siebert, "The Legacy of the American Revolution in the
British West Indies, and Bahamas," Ohio State University, *Bulletin*, 17
(1913), 22.

twenty-seven of his slaves—ten men, five women, eleven children and an infant just christened "Providence." But most of the other Negroes remained in the Bahamas, giving its agriculture, particularly its cotton culture, a new impetus.

Thousands of Negroes were taken to other islands in the British West Indies; from 1775 to 1787 the colored population of Jamaica showed an increase of 60,000. Practically all of the black immigrants were slaves. Many had been brought in as slaves, but many others who came expecting to be free were seized by those holding no legal title, and sold for rum, coffee, sugar, and fruits.[23]

Perhaps the most noteworthy of the Negroes taken to Jamaica was George Liele who as a slave and a free man in Georgia had been a dedicated preacher. Brought to Kingston in 1782 as an indentured servant, Liele worked out his time in two years. Once he obtained his certificate of freedom, Liele resumed his work in religion, preaching in private homes and then organizing a church—the only Baptist church on the island. By 1790 more than 450 persons had received baptism at his hands.[24]

Many of the Negroes evacuated from the United States did not go southward; thousands went to Canada. Perhaps their lot may be suggested by focussing on the story of African-born Thomas Peters. Dark-skinned and of large frame, Peters had in 1776 fled from his master and joined the British.[25] During the war he served as a sergeant in a Negro arms-bearing pioneer company, being twice wounded in battle. With the coming of peace, he and his wife settled at Annapolis in Nova Scotia, a province to which many of the Canada-bound Negroes went.

The British had promised Peters and his comrades not only freedom but a farm. His Majesty's officers were slow in making good the promise of a farm, and the civilian authorities were

---

[23] *Ibid.*, 16, 38.

[24] See Carter G. Woodson, *The History of the Negro Church* (Washington, 1921), 43–45; and "Letters showing the Rise and Progress of the early Negro Churches of Georgia and the West Indies," *Journal of Negro History*, I (1916), 69–92, *passim*.

[25] For sketches of Peters see C. H. Fyfe, *Thomas Peters: History and Legend* (a 10-page pamphlet, no date, no place, but republished from *Sierra Leone Studies* [Freetown], Dec. 1953), and F. W. Butt-Thompson, *Sierra Leone in History and Tradition* (London, 1926), 89–96.

likewise dilatory.[26] The black settlers in Nova Scotia felt cheated: either the surveyor was too busy to mark out their lands, or the plots they received were largely thick pine forest and hard to clear. Finding themselves landless, or holders of land that would produce little, many Negroes apprenticed themselves to farmers or congregated in Burchtown, a nearly all-Negro community.

Peters was a patient man, but after six years of waiting he determined to go to England to seek redress from the king's ministers. By virtue of a small sum raised by his fellows, and by working as a "hand" to pay his passage aboard ship, Peters arrived in London early in 1791. Here he received a welcome that must have made up for much of the disappointment of the preceding years. Granville Sharp and his fellow reformers took Peters in tow, and soon the former slave-soldier became a London celebrity. "His eloquence, his passion, his spirit, made him the rage of the newspaper world, the latest fashionable craze, and the newest object of philanthropy."[27]

To assist Peters, his abolitionist friends drew up a memorial in his name and sent it to William W. Granville, secretary of state for foreign affairs. This document described the plight of 102 colored families at Annapolis Royal and 100 families at New Brunswick. These Negroes would remain in those provinces, it was said, if they could obtain the full grant of land and provisions originally promised them; otherwise many would be willing to migrate to any country which would make them a "competent" offer.[28]

This petition, which Peters signed by making his mark, brought quick action. The Secretary of State ordered the governor of Nova Scotia to investigate the matter. If the charges were true, the governor was informed that the province must

[26] There were a number of Negroes at Port Roseway, and some expected at Halifax, "for whom Lands are not yet located, nor other provisions made," wrote Colonel Robert Morse to General H. E. Fox on Aug. 23, 1783, Carleton photostats.

[27] Butt-Thompson, *Sierra Leone*, 93–94.

[28] John Clarkson, Clarkson's Mission to America (478-page handwritten document in diary form, dated from Aug. 6, 1791 to Mar. 18, 1792, is in the N.-Y. Hist. Soc.), 6. Another copy, handwritten but with a different pagination, may be seen at the Moorland Library, Howard University, Washington, D.C. In these footnotes I use the pagination of the former.

fulfill its obligation or send these families to Sierra Leone. A removal to Sierra Leone would entail some expense, but His Majesty's government had an obligation to these Negroes for their wartime services.[29]

The idea of transporting the Canadian Negroes to Africa originated with the directors of the recently incorporated Sierra Leone Company. Founded to enable destitute Negroes in London to make a new start by settling them on the west coast of Africa, the company had acquired a site and begun operations by the time Peters visited London. On its board of directors in 1791 the company counted such well-known abolitionists as Thomas Clarkson, William Wilberforce and Granville Sharp. It was Sharp who introduced Peters to the other board members, and enlisted their interest in the black Nova Scotians. In turn Peters was favorably impressed by the kindness of the board members—by their assurance that he and his associates would be welcome in Sierra Leone, and by their belief that his group would be better off there than in frigid Canada.

With the tacit support of Parliament, and the approval of Peters, the Sierra Leone Company got busy.[30] On August 12, 1791 the company authorized two agents, Lawrence Hartshorn of Halifax and John Clarkson, to screen out the candidates for resettlement and get written testimonials as to their character, sobriety and industry. The agents were authorized to offer twenty acres of land to each prospective migrant, with ten additional acres for his wife and five for each child.

The choice of Clarkson as an agent was a happy one. A former naval lieutenant and the younger brother of Thomas Clarkson, he brought a spirit of dedication to his task. Reaching Halifax in early October 1791, he took the leadership in recruiting prospective emigrants. First he interviewed the applicant, optimistically assuring him that in Sierra Leone he would have every opportunity to become his own master. The

[29] Clarkson's Mission to America, 8, N.-Y. Hist. Soc.

[30] For this Nova Scotian project of the Sierra Leone Company see *Report by Court of Directors of the Sierra Leone Company, 1794* (London, 1794), 3–8; Adams G. Archibald, "Story of the Deportation of Negroes from Nova Scotia to Sierra Leone," Nova Scotia Historical Society, *Collections*, 7 (1889–1891), 129–54.

interview was followed by an investigation, and if the applicant came out well, he received a certificate of character.

The deeply religious and sensitive Clarkson was often moved by the interviews. He noted that the greatest number of applicants were not thinking of their own future but that of their children "whom they wished to see established (as they expressed it) upon a better foundation."[31] Particularly touching to Clarkson was the incident in which a Negro slave, John Coltress, came to enroll his free wife and children. Putting the Atlantic between himself and his family was heart-rending to Coltress, but he was willing to face it because it would bring "a better life for them."[32]

Many of the candidates were personally enlisted by Peters, who returned to the province prior to Clarkson's arrival. Including his family, Peters recruited a total of eighty-four persons from St. John, New Brunswick and Annapolis, and brought them to Halifax. Some applicants made their way alone; many of these arrived at the headquarters city only after hard journeys of up to 340 miles through wooded and little known country.

Once gathered in Halifax and awaiting the date of departure, the migrants kept Clarkson busy with all kinds of requests and petitions. Typical was the request of the thirty-eight residents of the township of Preston (one of whom bore the incongruous name "British Freedom") that in Sierra Leone they be permitted to settle side by side.[33] Another group which sought to keep together and managed to make arrangements to cross the ocean in the same brig, was the congregation of the Baptist minister, David George. George had been a slave until the British seized Savannah and his master fled. He resided in Charleston during the last years of the war, and in 1782 came to Nova Scotia, where for nearly ten years he had preached at Burchtown and Shelburne. When he learned of the Sierra Leone proposal, George enrolled his own family of six, and persuaded fifty-nine of his congregation to sign up.[34]

[31] Clarkson's Mission to America, 86, N.-Y. Hist. Soc.
[32] Ibid., 88.
[33] Ibid., 300.
[34] For a brief sketch of George see Woodson, History of the Negro Church, 41–42.

Thanks to men like George and Peters, there was no problem in recruiting good prospects; indeed, the directors of the Sierra Leone Company were surprised and gratified by the number of applicants. By the end of the year a large enough group had been recruited and the ships chartered. On January 15, 1782, a bit over three months after his arrival at Halifax, agent John Clarkson could joyfully write: "I am now under sail with a fair wind and fine weather, having on board 1190 souls in fifteen ships, properly equipped and I hope destined to be happy."[35]

For the next few weeks the embarking Nova Scotians were not as happy as Clarkson had hoped. The expedition ran into heavy squalls, temporarily separating one ship from another. Some sixty-five of the voyagers died at sea, and another hundred were too ill to be landed when the fleet pulled into Kru Bay in early March. When the remaining thousand stepped ashore they found that little preparation had been made to receive them. They knew they would have to work long hours if they were to succeed in throwing up enough shelters before the rainy season set in. But if at the moment their new dwelling site lacked adequate housing, it bore a sweet sounding name—Freetown.

Kenneth M. Stampp

Looking back at the hundreds of works that American historians have produced since 1865 on the Negro, slavery, and the Civil War, we find that the overwhelming number were written with an anti-Negro bias. It has only been since World War II that the great majority of historians writing on the subject of slavery have tried to shed the *a priori* assumptions that Americans as a whole have held about Negroes. Gone from the new histories was U. B. Phillips view that "American Negroes represented that sort of inert and backward people" (*American Negro Slavery*). "I have assumed," wrote Kenneth M. Stampp in *The Peculiar Institution* "that the slaves were merely ordinary human beings, that innately Negroes *are*, after all, only white men with black skins, nothing more,

[35] Clarkson's Mission to America, 399.

nothing less." Gone also was the insensitivity of historians toward slavery, an insensitivity that allowed Boston-born, Harvard-educated, Samuel Eliot Morison to write in *The Growth
of the American Republic* (4th edition, 1950) that "there is
some reason to believe that he [the slave, whom Morison refers to in the text as "Sambo"] suffered less than any other
class in the South from its 'peculiar institution.'"

The post-World War II period made historians sensitive to
the moral issues involved in the problem of slavery. The war
against Nazism highlighted America's own form of racism.
Negroes at home were demanding an end to discrimination
and segregation. Historians could no longer abdicate responsibility. "How a person thinks about Negro slavery historically," wrote Stanley M. Elkins, "makes a great deal of difference here and now; it tends to locate him morally in relation
to a whole range of very immediate political, social, and philosophical issues which in some way refer back to slavery."

The efforts of Negro historians, who for too long labored
almost alone in the academic wilderness, have been vindicated by contemporary scholarship. No scholar deserves more
credit in helping to bring about this change than Harvard-
educated Dr. Carter G. Woodson, editor of the *Journal of
Negro History* and founder of the Association for the Study
of Negro Life and History. He, almost alone among professional historians, challenged the racially biased history that
dominated American historiography for the large part of the
twentieth century. In 1918, three years after *The Birth of a
Nation*, Ulrich B. Phillips, Georgia-born professor of history
at the University of Michigan, placed a scholarly imprint on
the more popular views held by most Americans regarding
the Negro. In his *American Negro Slavery*, Phillips una-
shamedly paraded his racial prejudices. Slavery, Phillips
wrote in justification of the institution, "was in fact just what
the bulk of the Negroes most needed. They were in an alien
land, in an essentially slow process of transition from barbarism to civilization." Historians were profuse in their praise of
Phillips' book. Woodson answered Phillips in the *Mississippi
Valley Historical Review*. He reduced the issue to fundamental terms. Woodson charged Phillips with falsifying history, with so arranging the facts as to make the reader believe
"that the Negroes were satisfied with it [slavery]." Phillips re-

fused to view the slaves as men and failed to see that it was a "system of exploiting one man for the benefit of another."

However, the great majority of historians refused to accept Woodson's arguments. The most prominent historians writing Southern history, the history of slavery and Reconstruction, were Southerners, and historians accepted the judgement of their colleagues against a few Negro dissenters. Frederick Jackson Turner in *The United States, 1830–1850* justified slavery "as the mode of dealing with the negro," while Charles Beard, according to Professor Staughton Lynd in his article "On Turner, Beard and Slavery," "characterized the attitude of the slaves during the Civil War as a blend of contentment, affection for their owners, inertia, and helplessness."

What was needed, as Professor Lawrence Reddick wrote in "A New Interpretation for Negro History" in 1937, was "a picture of the institution as seen through eyes of the bondsman himself." Kenneth M. Stampp raised the problem again in 1952 while engaged in research on slavery. He argued in "The Historian and Southern Negro Slavery" that a history of slavery had to begin with two basic assumptions. First, that "slavery at its best was still slavery." Secondly, and directing himself to the findings of social psychologists, cultural anthropologists, and sociologists, Stampp charged that "no historian of the institution can be taken seriously unless he begins with the knowledge that there is no valid evidence that the Negro race is innately inferior to the white. . . ."

In 1956 Stampp produced a long awaited *coup de grâce* to Phillips. His *The Peculiar Institution* was received with almost unanimous praise. William M. Brewer, Woodson's successor as editor of the *Journal of Negro History*, wrote with some satisfaction: "*The Peculiar Institution* shows conclusively that slavery violated every fundamental of the dignity of man. . . . At long last slavery is here truthfully described as the most bestial regime that has ever tarnished America."

Kenneth M. Stampp's "The Historian and Southern Negro Slavery," the selection presented here, foreshadowed his own work and that to be done by other contemporary historians. Phillips' racially biased history has been discredited, but its success raises serious questions about American history and historians. That racist historiography could gain such scholarly recognition must remain an indictment of the American historical profession. Moreover, so much time and effort were needed to overturn the Phillips' school that historians were prevented from getting on with the work of studying other phases of Negro history. Possibly, this is fitting for a society which has made a virtue of waste.

Kenneth M. Stampp is Professor of History at the University of California (Berkeley).

THE HISTORIAN AND
SOUTHERN NEGRO SLAVERY

SOURCE: Kenneth M. Stampp, "The Historian and Southern Negro Slavery," *American Historical Review*, LVII (April, 1952), 613–24.

A Survey of the literature dealing with southern Negro slavery reveals one fundamental problem that still remains unresolved. This is the problem of the biased historian. It is, of course, a universal historical problem—one that is not likely to be resolved as long as historians themselves are divided into scientific and so-called "subjectivist-presentist-relativist" schools.[1] These schools seem to agree that historians ought to strive for a maximum of intellectual detachment and ought not to engage in special pleading and pamphleteering. But whether they are entitled to pass moral judgments, whether they can overcome the subjective influences of their own backgrounds and environments, are still debatable questions—at least they are questions which are still being debated. Yet it must be said that so far as Negro slavery is concerned we are still waiting for the first scientific and completely objective study of the institution which is based upon no assumptions whose validity cannot be thoroughly proved. And as long as historians must select their evidence from a great mass of sources, as long as they attempt to organize and interpret their findings, the prospects are not very encouraging.

This does not mean that everyone who has written about slavery has had the *same* bias, or that some have not been more flagrantly biased than others, or more skillful than others in the use of the subtle innuendo. It most certainly does not

[1] Chester McArthur Destler, "Some Observations on Contemporary Historical Thought," *American Historical Review*, LV (April, 1950), 503–29.

imply that further efforts toward a clearer understanding of slavery are futile, or that we are not enormously indebted to the many scholars who have already engaged in research in this field. No student could begin to understand the complexities of the slave system without being thoroughly familiar with the findings and varying points of views of such historians as Ulrich B. Phillips, Herbert Aptheker, Lewis C. Gray, John Hope Franklin, Avery Craven, Carter G. Woodson, Frederic Bancroft, Charles S. Sydnor, John Spencer Bassett, and many others.

Among these scholars, the late Professor Phillips has unquestionably made the largest single contribution to our present understanding of southern slavery. It may be that his most durable monument will be the vast amount of new source material which he uncovered. But Phillips was also an unusually able and prolific writer. Measured only crudely in terms of sheer bulk, his numerous books and articles are impressive.[2] That, taken together with his substantial compilations of fresh factual information, his rare ability to combine scholarship with a fine literary style, and his point of view for which there has been a persistent affinity, explains the deep impression he has made. One needs only to sample the textbooks and monographic literature to appreciate the great influence of Professor Phillips' interpretations and methodology. A historian who recently attempted to evaluate Phillips' investigations of the slave-plantation system arrived at this conclusion: "So thorough was his work that, granted the same purpose, the same materials, and the same methods, his treatment . . . is unlikely to be altered in fundamental respects."[3]

"There is, however," this historian hastened to add, "nothing inevitable about his point of view or his technique." Rather, he contended that "a materially different version" would emerge when scholars with different points of view and different techniques subjected the slave system to a similarly intensive study.[4]

[2] Phillips' findings and conclusions can be studied most conveniently in *American Negro Slavery* (New York, 1918), and in *Life and Labor in the Old South* (Boston, 1929).

[3] Richard Hofstadter, "U. B. Phillips and the Plantation Legend," *Journal of Negro History*, XXIX (April, 1944), 124.

[4] *Ibid.*, pp. 122, 124.

Indeed, he might have noted that a "materially different version" is already emerging. For the most notable additions to the bibliography of slavery during the past three decades have been those which have in some way altered Phillips' classic exposition of the slave regime. This revisionism is the product of new information discovered in both old and new sources, of new research techniques, and, to be sure, of different points of view and different assumptions. In recent years the subject has become less and less an emotional issue between scholarly descendants of the northern abolitionists and of the southern proslavery school. It may only be a sign of the effeteness of the new generation of scholars, but there is a tendency among them to recognize that it is at least conceivable that a colleague on the other side of the Mason and Dixon line could write something significant about slavery. For the new light that is constantly being shed upon the Old South's "peculiar institution" we are indebted to historians of both southern and northern origins—and of both the Negro and white races.

One of these revisionists has raised some searching questions about Phillips' methodology. Professor Richard Hofstadter has discovered a serious flaw in Phillips' sampling technique, which caused him to examine slavery and slaveholders on "types of plantations that were not at all representative of the common slaveholding unit." Phillips made considerable use of the case-study method, and he relied heavily upon the kinds of manuscript records kept primarily by the more substantial planters. Therefore, Hofstadter concludes, "Insofar . . . as Phillips drew his picture of the Old South from plantations of more than 100 slaves [as he usually did], he was sampling about 10% of all the slaves and less than 1% of all the slaveholders."[5] The lesser planters and small slaveholding farmers, who were far more typical, rarely kept diaries and formal records; hence they received considerably less attention from Phillips. The danger is generalizing about the whole regime from an unrepresentative sample is obvious enough.

Getting information about the slaves and masters on the smaller holdings is difficult, but it is nevertheless essential for a

[5] *Ibid.,* pp. 109–19.

comprehensive understanding of the slave system. Professor Frank L. Owsley has already demonstrated the value of county records, court records, and census returns for this purpose.[6] Phillips made only limited use of the evidence gathered by contemporary travelers, especially by Frederick Law Olmsted in whom he had little confidence. The traveler in the South who viewed slavery with an entirely open mind was rare indeed, but it does not necessarily follow that the only accurate reporters among them were those who viewed it sympathetically.

How the picture of slavery will be modified when life on the small plantations and farms has been adequately studied cannot be predicted with as much assurance as some may think. The evidence now available suggests conflicting tendencies. On these units, there was very little absentee ownership, the proverbially harsh overseer was less frequently employed, and contacts between masters and slaves were often more numerous and intimate. Undoubtedly in many cases these conditions tended to make the treatment of the Negroes less harsh and the system less rigid. But it is also necessary to consider other tendencies, as well as the probability that the human factor makes generalization risky. Sometimes the material needs of the slaves were provided for more adequately on the larger plantations than they were on the smaller ones. Sometimes the lower educational and cultural level and the insecure social status of the small slaveholders had an unfavorable effect upon their racial attitudes. There are enough cases in the court records to make it clear that members of this group were, on occasion, capable of extreme cruelty toward their slaves. Nor can the factor of economic competition be overlooked. The lesser planters who were ambitious to rise in the social scale were, to phrase it cautiously, exposed to the temptation not to indulge their slaves while seeking their fortunes in competition with the larger planters. To be sure, as Lewis C. Gray points out, many of these small slaveholders lived in relatively isolated areas where the competitive

---

[6] Frank L. and Harriet C. Owsley, "The Economic Basis of Society in the Late Ante-Bellum South," *Journal of Southern History*, VI (February, 1940), 24–45. Much information about the treatment of slaves on the small plantations and farms can be found in Helen T. Caterall, ed., *Judicial Cases concerning American Slavery and the Negro* (5 vols., New York, 1926–37).

factor was less urgent.[7] But there still is a need for further investigation of these small slaveholders before generalizations about conditions among their slaves will cease to be highly speculative.

A tendency toward loose and glib generalizing is, in fact, one of the chief faults of the classic portrayal of the slave regime— and, incidentally, of some of its critics as well. This is true of descriptions of how the slaves were treated: how long and hard they were worked, how severely they were punished, how well they were fed, housed, and clothed, and how carefully they were attended during illness. It may be that some historians have attached an undue significance to these questions, for there are important philosophical implications in the evaluation of slavery in terms of such mundane matters as what went into the slave's stomach. In any event, the evidence hardly warrants the sweeping pictures of uniform physical comfort or uniform physical misery that are sometimes drawn. The only generalization that can be made with relative confidence is that some masters were harsh and frugal, others were mild and generous, and the rest ran the whole gamut in between. And even this generalization may need qualification, for it is altogether likely that the same master could have been harsh and frugal on some occasions and mild and generous on others. Some men become increasingly mellow and others increasingly irascible with advancing years. Some masters were more generous, or less frugal, in times of economic prosperity than they were in times of economic depression. The treatment of the slaves probably varied with the state of the master's health, with the vicissitudes of his domestic relations, and with the immediate and subsequent impact of alcoholic beverages upon his personality. It would also be logical to suspect—and there is evidence that this was the case—that masters did not treat all their slaves alike, that, being human, they developed personal animosities for some and personal affections for others. The care of slaves under the supervision of overseers might change from year to year as one overseer replaced another in the normally rapid turnover. In

[7] Lewis C. Gray, *History of Agriculture in the Southern United States to 1860* (Washington, 1933), I, 518, 556–57.

short, the human factor introduced a variable that defied generalization.

This same human factor complicates the question of how the Negroes reacted to their bondage. The generalization that the great majority of Negroes were contented as slaves has never been proved, and in the classic picture it was premised on the assumption that certain racial traits caused them to adapt to the system with peculiar ease. If freedom was so far beyond their comprehension, it was a little remarkable that freedom was the very reward considered most suitable for a slave who rendered some extraordinary service to his master or to the state. It is well known that many slaves took advantage of opportunities to purchase their freedom. Resistance by running away and by the damaging of crops and tools occurred frequently enough to cause Dr. Samuel Cartwright of Louisiana to conclude that these acts were the symptoms of exotic diseases peculiar to Negroes.[8] Though there is no way to discover precisely how much of the property damage was deliberate, and how much was merely the by-product of indifference and carelessness, the distinction is perhaps inconsequential. Finally, there were individual acts of violence against masters and overseers, and cases of conspiracy and rebellion. If the significance of these cases has been overstated by Herbert Aptheker,[9] it has been understated by many of his predecessors.

This is not to deny that among the slaves only a minority of undeterminable size fought the system by these various devices. It is simply to give proper emphasis to the fact that such a minority did exist. In all probability it consisted primarily of individuals of exceptional daring, or intelligence, or individuality. Such individuals constitute a minority in all societies.

That the majority of Negroes seemed to submit to their bondage proves neither their special fitness for it nor their contentment with it. It merely proves that men *can* be enslaved

[8] Raymond A. and Alice H. Bauer, "Day to Day Resistance to Slavery," *Jour. Negro Hist.*, XXVII (October, 1942), 388–419. For references to some of Dr. Cartwright's unique views see Felice Swados, "Negro Health on the Ante Bellum Plantations," *Bulletin of the History of Medicine*, X (October, 1941), 462.

[9] Herbert Aptheker, *American Negro Slave Revolts* (New York, 1943). Many acts of violence by individual slaves are recorded in Caterall, *passim*.

when they are kept illiterate, when communication is restricted, and when the instruments of violence are monopolized by the state and the master class.[10] In the light of twentieth-century experience, when white men have also been forced to submit to tyranny and virtual slavery, it would appear to be a little preposterous to generalize about the peculiarities of Negroes in this respect. In both cases the majority has acquiesced. In neither case does it necessarily follow that they have reveled in their bondage.

To be sure, there were plenty of opportunists among the Negroes who played the role assigned to them, acted the clown, and curried the favor of their masters in order to win the maximum rewards within the system, sometimes even at the expense of their fellow slaves. There were others who, in the very human search for personal recognition within their limited social orbit, salvaged what prestige they could from the high sales prices attached to them, or from the high social status of their masters.[11] Nor is it necessary to deny that many slaves sang and danced, enjoyed their holidays, and were adaptable enough to find a measure of happiness in their daily lives. It is enough to note that all of this still proves nothing, except that it is altogether likely that Negroes behaved much as people of other races would have behaved under similar circumstances.

In describing these various types of slave behavior historians must always weigh carefully, or at least recognize, the moral implications and value judgments implicit in the adjectives they use. How, for example, does one distinguish a "good" Negro from a "bad" Negro in the slave regime? Was the "good" Negro the one who was courteous and loyal to his master, and who did his work faithfully and cheerfully? Or was the "good" Negro the defiant one who has sometimes been called "insolent" or "surly" or "unruly"? Was the "brighter" side of slavery to be found in the bonds of love and loyalty that developed between some household servants and some of the more genteel and gentle

[10] The techniques of Negro enslavement are described in Aptheker, pp. 53–78.
[11] Historians who failed to grasp the psychological significance of such slave behavior have sometimes drawn some unjustifiable inferences from it, for example, that Negroes were naturally docile and felt no personal humiliation because of their inferior status.

masters? Or was it to be found among those slaves who would not submit, who fought back, ran away, faked illness, loafed, sabotaged, and never ceased longing for freedom in spite of the heavy odds against them? In short, just what *are* the proper ethical standards for identifying undesirable or even criminal behavior among slaves? There is no answer that is not based upon subjective factors, and the question therefore may not be within the province of "objective" historians. But in that case historians must also avoid the use of morally weighted adjectives when they write about slavery.

The general subject of slave behavior suggests a method of studying the institution which revisionists need to exploit more fully. For proper balance and perspective slavery must be viewed through the eyes of the Negro as well as through the eyes of the white master.[12] This is obviously a difficult task, for slaves rarely wrote letters or kept diaries.[13] But significant clues can be found in scattered sources. The autobiographies and recollections of fugitive slaves and freedmen have value when used with the caution required of all such sources. Slaves were interviewed by a few travelers in the ante-bellum South, and ex-slaves by a few historians in the post-Civil War period;[14] but unfortunately the interviewing was never done systematically until the attempt of the Federal Writers Project in the 1930's.[15] The mind of the slave can also be studied through his external behavior as it is described in plantation manuscripts, court records, and newspaper files. For example, there is undoubtedly some psychological significance in the high frequency of stuttering and of what was loosely called a "downcast look" among the slaves identified in the advertisements for fugitives.[16] Finally,

[12] John Hope Franklin makes a brief attempt to accomplish this in *From Slavery to Freedom* (New York, 1948), pp. 204–12.

[13] *Cf.* Carter G. Woodson, ed., *The Mind of the Negro as Reflected in Letters Written during the Crisis, 1800–1860* (Washington, 1926).

[14] See, for example, Harrison A. Trexler, *Slavery in Missouri, 1804–1865* (Baltimore, 1914), *passim*.

[15] Selections from these interviews are published in Benjamin A. Botkin, ed., *Lay My Burden Down* (Chicago, 1945).

[16] The present writer was impressed by this while searching through thousands of advertisements for fugitive slaves in various southern newspapers.

the historian might find clues to the mental processes of the slaves in the many recent sociological and anthropological studies of the American Negro. The impact of nineteenth-century slavery and of twentieth-century prejudice and discrimination upon the Negro's thought and behavior patterns have some significant similarities.[17]

This kind of perspective is not to be found in the Phillips version of slavery, for he began with a basic assumption which gave a different direction to his writings. That he failed to view the institution through the eyes of the Negro, that he emphasized its mild and humorous side and minimized its grosser aspects, was the result of his belief—implicit always and stated explicitly more than once—in the inherent inferiority of the Negro race. The slaves, he wrote, were "by racial quality" "submissive," "light-hearted," "amiable," "ingratiating," and "imitative." Removing the Negro from Africa to America, he added, "had little more effect upon his temperament than upon his complexion." Hence "the progress of the generality [of slaves] was restricted by the fact of their being negroes."[18] Having isolated and identified their "racial qualities," Phillips' conclusions about slavery followed logically enough.

It is clear in every line Phillips wrote that he felt no animus toward the Negroes. Far from it. He looked upon them with feelings of genuine kindliness and affection. But hearing as he did the still-faintly-ringing laughter of the simple plantation Negroes, the songs sung in their melodious voices, Phillips was unable to take them seriously. Instead he viewed them as lovable, "serio-comic" figures who provided not only a labor supply of sorts but also much of the plantation's social charm. Thus slavery was hardly an institution that could be weighed heavily upon them.

Now, it is probably true that the historian who criticizes slavery per se reveals a subjective bias, or at least certain assumptions he cannot prove. The sociological argument of George Fitzhugh that slavery is a positive good, not only for

[17] Especially suggestive is Robert L. Sutherland, *Color, Class, and Personality* (Washington, 1942).

[18] *American Negro Slavery*, pp. 291–92, 339, 341–42.

the laboring man but for society in general, cannot be conclusively refuted with scientific precision. Those who disagree
with Fitzhugh can only argue from certain unproved premises
and optimistic convictions about the so-called "rights" and
"dignity" of labor and the potentialities of free men in a
democratic society. And the historian may run into all sorts of
difficulties when he deals with such subjective matters.

But to assume that the *Negro* was peculiarly suited for
slavery because of certain inherent racial traits is quite another
matter. This involves not primarily a subjective bias but ignorance of, or disregard for, the overwhelming evidence to the
contrary. Much of this evidence was already available to Phillips,
though it must be noted that he grew up at a time when the
imperialist doctrine of the "white man's burden" and the writings
of such men as John Fiske and John W. Burgess were giving
added strength to the belief in Anglo-Saxon superiority. Nor
should he be blamed for failing to anticipate the findings of
biologists, psychologists, anthropologists, and sociologists subsequent to the publication of his volume *American Negro
Slavery* in 1918. It may be significant that he presented his
own point of view with considerably more restraint in his *Life
and Labor in the Old South* which appeared a decade later.

Nevertheless, it is this point of view which both dates and
outdates the Phillips version of slavery. No historian of the
institution can be taken seriously any longer unless he begins
with the knowledge that there is no valid evidence that the
Negro race is innately inferior to the white, and that there is
growing evidence that both races have approximately the same
potentialities.[19] He must also take into account the equally
important fact that there are tremendous variations in the
capacities and personalities of individuals within each race, and
that it is therefore impossible to make valid generalizations about
races as such.

An awareness of these facts is forcing the revisionists to
discard much of the folklore about Negroes that found a support

[19] For a summary of the evidence and literature on this subject see
Gunnar Myrdal, *An American Dilemma: The Negro Problem and Modern
Democracy* (New York, 1944), esp. chap. VI, including the footnotes to this
chapter, pp. 1212–18.

in the classic portrayal of slavery. Take, for example, the idea that the primitive Negroes brought to America could only adapt to the culture of the civilized white man in the course of many generations of gradual growth. Phillips saw the plantation as "a school constantly training and controlling pupils who were in a backward state of civilization. . . . On the whole the plantations were the best schools yet invented for the mass training of that sort of inert and backward people which the bulk of the American negroes represented."[20]

This idea would seem to imply that the Negroes could only be civilized through a slow evolutionary process, during which they would gradually acquire and transmit to their descendants the white man's patterns of social behavior. In actual fact the first generation of Negroes born in the English colonies in the seventeenth century was as capable of learning these patterns of social behavior—for they were things that were learned, not inherited—and of growing up and living as free men as was the generation alive in 1865. Indeed many of the Negroes of this Civil War generation were *still* unprepared for freedom; and that fact reveals the basic flaw in the whole Phillips concept. It does not show that the plantation school had not had sufficient time to complete its work but rather that it was capable of doing little more than training succeeding generations of slaves. After two centuries of slavery most Negroes had to learn how to live as free men by *starting* to live as free men. The plantation school may have had some limited success as a vocational institution, but in the field of the social sciences it was almost a total failure.

Other discredited aspects of the mythology of slavery can be mentioned only briefly. Revisionists no longer attempt to explain the origin of the institution with a doctrine of "climatic determinism." Since white men did and still do labor long and hard in cotton and tobacco fields there is little point in tracing southern slavery to the generative powers of southern heat.[21] Nor does it appear that the health of Negroes in the fever-infested rice swamps was as flourishing as it has some-

---

[20] *American Negro Slavery*, pp. 342–43.
[21] Oscar and Mary F. Handlin, "Origins of the Southern Labor System," *William and Mary Quarterly*, VII (April, 1950), 199.

times been described.[22] And the fact that unfree labor alone made possible the rise of the plantation system proves neither the "necessity" nor the "inevitability" of slavery. For there was nothing inevitable about the plantation. Without this supply of unfree labor southern agriculture would probably have given less emphasis to the production of staples, and the small-farm unit would have prevailed. But the South would not have remained a wilderness. Moreover, Negroes *might* have been brought to America as servants rather than slaves (as the first ones were). Thus, like the white servants, many of them might have become landowning farmers in the period when land was abundant and cheap.

Slavery, then, was the inevitable product of neither the weather nor some irresistible force in the South's economic evolution. Slaves were used in southern agriculture because men sought greater returns than they could obtain from their own labor alone. It was a man-made institution. It was inevitable only insofar as everything that has happened in history was inevitable, not in terms of immutable or naturalistic laws.

And finally, the revisionists have brought some of the classic conclusions about the economics of slavery under serious scrutiny. Was it really a profitable institution? Although Thomas R. Dew and some other proslavery writers argued that it was and that it would have been abolished had it not been, there has been a persistent tendency, dating back to ante-bellum times, to minimize the question of profits and to emphasize other factors. It was not that slavery was profitable—indeed many contended that it was actually unprofitable for most slaveholders —but rather it was the race question or the masters' feeling of responsibility for the Negroes that explained its preservation. This was also the conclusion of Professor Phillips who believed that, except on the rich and fresh lands of the Southwest, slavery had nearly ceased to be profitable by 1860.[23]

But in recent years there has been much disagreement with

[22] Swados, pp. 460–72; J. H. Easterby, ed., *The South Carolina Rice Plantation as Revealed in the Papers of Robert F. W. Allston* (Chicago, 1945), p. 30; Bennett H. Wall, "Medical Care of Ebenezer Pettigrew's Slaves," *Mississippi Valley Historical Review*, XXXVII (December, 1950), 451–70.

[23] *American Negro Slavery*, pp. 391–92.

this conclusion. Lewis C. Gray, Thomas P. Govan, Robert R. Russel, and Robert Worthington Smith have found evidence that slavery continued to be profitable for the slaveholders as a class down to the very outbreak of the Civil War.[24] Frequently the average money investment in the plantation labor force has been exaggerated; depreciation on this investment has been figured as a cost when the slaves were actually increasing in both numbers and value; and faulty accounting methods have resulted in listing interest on the slave investment as an operational expense. Too often profits have been measured exclusively in terms of staple production, and the value of the natural increase of slaves, of the food they produced for the master and his family, and of the personal services they rendered have been ignored. Many of the debt-burdened planters provided evidence not of the unprofitability of slavery but of their tendency to disregard the middle-class virtue of thrift and to live beyond their means. Nor does slavery appear to be primarily responsible for the crude agricultural methods or for the soil exhaustion that occurred in the South.[25]

Rarely has a group engaged in agriculture earned the returns and achieved the high social status enjoyed by the southern slaveholding class. Certainly no colonial or nineteenth-century farmer could have hoped to reap such fruits from his own labor. The fact that some planters made fortunes while others failed, that the profits were painfully low in times of economic depression, merely demonstrates that the slave-plantation system had many striking similarities to the factory system based on private capitalist production. Is one to generalize about the profits of industrial capitalism from the fortunes accumulated by some, or from the failures suffered by thousands of others? From the high returns in periods of prosperity, or from the low returns

[24] Lewis C. Gray, "Economic Efficiency and Competitive Advantage of Slavery under the Plantation System," *Agricultural History*, IV (April, 1930), 31–47; Thomas P. Govan, "Was Plantation Slavery Profitable?" *Jour. Southern Hist.*, VIII (November, 1942), 513–35; Robert R. Russel, "The General Effects of Slavery upon Southern Economic Progress," *ibid.*, IV (February, 1938), 34–54; Robert Worthington Smith, "Was Slavery Unprofitable in the Ante-Bellum South?" *Agric. Hist.*, XX (January, 1946), 62–64.

[25] Gray, *History of Agriculture*, I, 447–48, 470; Avery O. Craven, *The Repressible Conflict, 1830–1861* (Baton Rouge, 1939), chaps. I, II.

in periods of depression? And what is to be made of the oft-repeated argument that the planters got nowhere because "they bought lands and slaves wherewith to grow cotton, and with the proceeds ever bought more slaves to make more cotton"?[26] If this is the essence of economic futility, then one must also pity the late Andrew Carnegie who built a mill wherewith to make steel, and with the proceeds ever built more mills to make more steel. The economist would not agree that either Carnegie or the planters were in a vicious circle, for they were simply enlarging their capital holdings by reinvesting their surplus profits.

The revisionists still agree that slavery, in the long run, had some unfavorable economic consequences for the South as a whole, especially for the nonslaveholding whites.[27] And some historian may yet point out that slavery was not very profitable for the Negroes. At least he may question the baffling generalization that the southern whites were more enslaved by Negro slavery than were the Negro slaves.[28] For in the final analysis, it was the *Negro* who had the most to gain from emancipation.

Abolitionists have suffered severely at the hands of historians during the past generation. They have been roundly condemned for their distortions and exaggerations. But are historians really being "objective" when they combine warm sympathy for the slaveholders' point of view with cold contempt for those who looked upon the enslavement of four million American Negroes as the most shocking social evil of their day? Perhaps historians need to be told what James Russell Lowell once told the South: "It is time . . . [to] learn . . . that the difficulty of the Slavery question is slavery itself,—nothing more, nothing less."[29] It may be that the most important fact that the historian will

---

[26] Phillips, *American Negro Slavery*, pp. 395–98.

[27] Gray, *History of Agriculture*, II, 940–42.

[28] "In a real sense the whites were more enslaved by the institution than the blacks." James G. Randall, *The Civil War and Reconstruction* (Boston, 1937), p. 73. "As for Sambo . . . there is some reason to believe that he suffered less than any other class in the South from its 'peculiar institution.'" Samuel Eliot Morison and Henry Steele Commager, *The Growth of the American Republic* (4th ed.; New York, 1950), I, 537.

[29] [James Russell Lowell], "The Question of the Hour," *Atlantic Monthly*, VII (1861), 120–21.

ever uncover about the South's "peculiar institution" is that slavery, at its best, was still slavery, and that certain dangers were inherent in a master-slave relationship even among normal men.

E. Franklin Frazier

The abstractions that historians so often invoke to hide the realities of slavery allow us to forget that its essence was the complete exploitation of other human beings. Just what effect slavery had on the Negro is seldom discussed. American history textbooks generally do not get excited about slavery, and when historians finally come around to explaining the system it is in terms of "necessity," "economics," and stereotyped images. U. B. Phillips came to justify slavery on quite sophisticated rounds. He wrote that slavery, for the whites, acted as a "safeguard of civilization and orderly government," and he wrote in *American Negro Slavery,* slavery for the Negroes was "in fact, a school constantly training and controlling pupils who were in a backward state of civilization."

Historians have, therefore, been able to ignore what they cared not to see. Phillips wrote that in his research for *American Negro Slavery,* he was able to find only *one* case of a Negro woman being used as a slave breeder, and that this case occurred in 1636 in Massachusetts. However, Frederic Bancroft was able to uncover in his research for *Slave-Trading in the Old South* twenty one pages of evidence of slave breeding, and it was common to find a Negro woman advertised as a "rattlin good breeder." Stampp's *The Peculiar Institution* supported Bancroft's conclusions. In *American Negro Slavery,* Phillips denied that children "were hardly ever sold separately" from the mother. Bancroft cites evidence to show that "the selling singly of young children privately and publicly was frequent and notorious." Examples of such biased historical investigation can be found in dealing with almost all aspects of Negro history, and this stems in large measure from a refusal to consider Negroes as fellow human beings.

One of the most successful attempts to examine analytically what happened to the Negro under slavery was written by the late E. Franklin Frazier, Professor of Sociology at Howard University, and author of *The Free Negro Family* (1932) and *The Negro Family in the United States* (1939). In *The Negro Family* he set out to show how the Negro family took shape in an environment and under social conditions that were hostile to its development. Frazier, as he was to show again in *Black Bourgeoisie* (1955), had no use for the myths that enveloped the Negro, whether they were presented by Negro or white authors.

In a chapter of *The Negro Family* presented here Frazier examined the problem of how the Negro slave woman managed to cope with a situation in which personal relations with her husband, children, and master were virtually unstable. His results were disturbing. For while Frazier found that many mothers were able through heroic sacrifices to maintain family bonds and feeling, in many cases a woman was shattered by life under slavery, often to the extent of destroying her feelings for her children. Giving birth to unwanted babies in quick succession, many of whom were forced upon her, the mother often withdrew from the children and the family into a schizophrenic world of her own. The myth of the heroic slave mothers leaves out the fact that women, no less than men, broke under the pressure and strain of the system. What is suprising is that so many women managed to survive and make the sacrifices and develop the affection needed to ensure the stability of their children. The whole story of what happened to the human personality under slavery is still to be written. When it is completed it may find its only parallel in the history of our own age.

MOTHERHOOD IN BONDAGE

source: E. Franklin Frazier, "Motherhood in Bondage," from *The Negro Family in the United States,* 2nd revised and abridged edition (Chicago, University of Chicago Press, 1966), pp. 33–45, 45–49.

Strange to say, the idealized picture of the Negro mother has not grown out of the stories of her sacrifices and devotion to her own children but has emerged from the tradition of the Negro mammy—a romantic figure in whom maternal love as a vicarious sentiment has become embodied. There is plenty of

evidence to give a solid background to the familiar picture—
stories of cold, and often inhuman, indifference toward her own
offspring and undying devotion to the children of the master
race. "The devotion of the nurses of these foster-children was
greater than their love for their own" is the comment of one
observer, Susan Smedes, who supports her generalizations with
the following instance which she has recorded in A *Southern
Planter:*

> One of them, with a baby at home very sick, left it to stay with the
> white child. This one she insisted on walking the night through, be-
> cause he was roaring with the colic, though the mistress entirely dis-
> approved and urged her to go home to her own child, whose illness
> was more serious, if less noisy, than the white nursling with its colic.[1]

This seems all the more strange when we recall the universal
testimony of travelers and missionaries that the love of the
African mother for her children is unsurpassed in any part of the
world. "Maternal affection (neither suppressed by the restraints,
nor diverted by the solicitudes of civilized life) is everywhere
conspicuous among them," wrote Mungo Park, "and creates a
correspondent return of tenderness in the child." He reports the
following incident:

> In the course of the day, several women, hearing that I was going
> to Sego, came and begged me to inquire of Mansong, the King, what
> was become of their children. One woman in particular, told me that
> her son's name was Mamadee; that he was no heathen, but prayed to
> God morning and evening, and had been taken from her about three
> years ago, by Mansong's army; since which she had never heard of
> him. She said she often dreamed about him; and begged me, if I
> should see him, either in Bambarra, or in my own country, to tell him
> that his mother and sister were still alive.

Likewise, we learn that in East Africa mothers offered themselves to the slave-raiders in order to save their sons, and
Hottentot women refused food during famines until their children were fed.

How are we to explain this contrast between the native
Negro mother and her descendants in America? Surely transportation to the New World could not have eradicated fundamental impulses and instinctive feelings.

[1] Susan Smedes, A *Southern Planter,* Baltimore, 1887, p. 50.

Elizabeth Donnan, in the *Documents Illustrative of the History of Slave Trade to America,* of which she is editor, gives evidence that the dehumanizing of the Negro began before he left the shores of Africa. An official of the Dutch West India Company on the African coast wrote as follows concerning the Negro's reputed indifference to family ties where the slave trade was carried on: "Not a few in our country fondly imagine that parents here sell their children, men their wives, and one brother the other: but those who think so deceive themselves; for this never happens on any other account but that of necessity, or some great crime. But most of the slaves that are offered to us are prisoners of war, which are sold by the victors as their booty."[2]

To pregnant women who formed a part of the slave caravans motherhood meant only a burden and an accentuation of their miseries. Maternal feeling was choked and dried up in mothers who had to bear children, in addition to loads of corn or rice, on their backs during marches of eight to fourteen hours. Nor did life in the slave pens on the coast, where they were chained and branded and sometimes starved, mitigate the sufferings of motherhood.

In the selection of Negroes for the cargoes of the slave ships, their physical condition and their suitability for the specific requirements of the trade were the only factors of moment to the traders. When William Ellery, the father of one of the signers of the Declaration of Independence, instructed the captain of his slaver: "If you have a good Trade for Negroes may purchase forty or Fifty Negroes. get most of them mere Boys and Girl, some Men, let them be Young, No very small Children," it is unlikely that the faithful captain in obeying his orders cared much about the feelings of the Negro mothers who had to surrender their children. During the Middle Passage that followed the gathering of slaves on the coast, the last spark of maternal feeling was probably smothered in the breasts of many mothers who were packed spoon fashion between decks and often gave birth to children in the scalding perspiration from the human cargo. Then whatever was left of

[2] Elizabeth Donnan (ed), *Documents Illustrative of the History of the Slave Trade to America,* Washington, D.C., 1930, I, 441.

maternal sentiment had to undergo another ordeal in the slave markets of the New World.

Scarcely more regard was shown for the humanity of the slaves in the American markets than in those of Africa. To be sure, humanitarian sentiment was more likely to make itself felt in the American communities than among the adventurers and criminals who frequented the slave markets of Africa. Moreover, in the slave markets of Charleston and Richmond it was to the economic advantage of those who bought and sold slaves to see that infants did not die because of the lack of maternal care. But since, as a South Carolina court held in 1809, "the young of slaves. . . . stand on the same footing as other animals," the relation of mothers to their children was recognized not because of its human or social significance but because of property interests involved in the relationship.

In some cases the affectional ties between mother and children survived the ordeals of the slave markets and the Middle Passage and were perhaps strengthened by common suffering. But the characteristic attitudes and sentiments which the slave mother developed in America grew out of her experiences with pregnancy and childbirth and her relations with her offspring in the new environment. Where slave women were maintained as breeders and enjoyed certain indulgences and privileges because of their position, the experience of pregnancy and childbirth was likely to cause them to look upon their children as the source of these favors.

The following instructions were sent to an agent for the management of a plantation in Virginia in 1759: "The breeding wenches particularly, you must instruct the overseers to be kind and indulgent to, and not to force them when with child upon any service or hardship that will be injurious to them and that they have every necessary when in that condition that is needful for them, and the children to be well looked after and to give them every spring and fall the jerusalem oak seed for a week together and that none of them suffer in time of sickness for want of proper care."[3]

On the other hand, where slave women were forced into

[3] Arthur W. Calhoun, A Social History of the American Family from Colonial Times to the Present, Cleveland, 1917–18, I, 327.

cohabitation and pregnancy, and childbirth brought no release from labor, they might develop a distinct antipathy toward their offspring. A former slave, Moses Grandy, wrote the following concerning the treatment of women by the overseer:

> On the estate I am speaking of, those women who had sucking children suffered much from their breasts becoming full of milk, the infants being left at home; they therefore could not keep up with the other hands: I have seen the overseer beat them with raw hide, so that the blood and milk flew mingled from their breasts. A woman who gives offence in the field, and is large in the family way, is compelled to lie down over a hole made to receive her corpulency, and is flogged with the whip, or beat with a paddle, which had holes in it; at every stroke comes a blister. One of my sisters was so severely punished in this way, that labor was brought on, and the child was born in the field. This very overseer, Mr. Brooks, killed in this manner a girl named Mary: her father and mother were in the field at the time.[4]

Even under the more normal conditions of slavery, childbirth could not have had the same significance for the slave mother as for the African mother. In Africa tribal customs and taboos tended to fix the mother's attitude toward her child before it was born. In America this traditional element in the shaping of maternal feeling was absent. Consequently, the development of maternal feeling was dependent largely upon the physiological and emotional responses of the mother to her child.

Concerning the biologically inherited elements in the so-called "maternal instinct," L. L. Bernard writes:

> It is difficult to separate early acquirements through the imitation process from biological inheritance without considerable intensive investigation. But it is doubtful if more than the response to touch, temperature and odor stimuli from the child by fondling, holding and licking or kissing, a more or less vague unorganized emotional response to its cries, which chiefly manifests itself in movement toward the child, vague answering cries and the discharge of milk upon certain definite stimuli of pressure upon the breast, can be said to be inherited by the human mother.[5]

[4] Moses Grandy, *Narrative of the Life of Moses Grandy; Late a Slave in the United States of America*, Boston, 1844, p. 18.
[5] L. L. Bernard, *Instinct: A Study in Social Psychology*, New York, 1924, p. 326.

Generally, during the period of pregnancy, the slave woman's labor was reduced, and on the birth of a child she received additional clothes and rations. But the following letter of an overseer indicates that the needs of the mothers and their newborn children were not always promptly met:

Charlotte & Venus & Mary & Little Sary have all had children and have not received their baby clothes also Hetty & Sary & Coteler will want baby clothes. I see a Blanket for the old fellow Sampson he is dead. I thought I wrote to you that he was dead. Little Peggy Sarys daughter has not ever drawn any Blanket at all, and when they come I think it would be right to give her the Blanket that was sent to Sampson.[6]

As soon as possible after childbirth, the mother was required to return to the fields, often taking her unweaned child along. A former slave describes the situation as follows:

The bell rings, at four o'clock in the morning, and they have half an hour to get ready. Men and women start together, and the women must work as steadily as the men, and perform the same tasks as the men. If the plantation is far from the house, the sucking children are taken out and kept in the field all day. If the cabins are near, the women are permitted to go in two or three times a day to their infant children. The mother is driven out when the child is three to four weeks old.[7]

In some cases the mothers were permitted to return to the cabin in order to nurse the infant who was left either alone or in the charge of a child. "At this period," writes a former slave, John Brown, "my principal occupation was to nurse my little brother whilst my mother worked in the field. Almost all the slave children have to do the nursing; the big taking care of the small, who often come poorly off in consequence. I know this was my little brother's case. I used to lay him in the shade, under a tree, sometimes, and go to play, or curl myself up under a hedge, and take a sleep."

The following situation described by Frances A. Kemble in her *Journal* was typical of many plantations:

[6] Letter of Elisha Cain, overseer, on Retreat Plantation, Jefferson County, Georgia, to his employer, Miss Mary Telfair, Savannah, November 20, 1836, in Phillips, *Documentary History of American Industrial Society: Plantation and Frontier*, Cleveland, I, 333–34.

[7] Lewis Clarke, *Narrative of the Sufferings of Lewis and Milton Clarke, Sons of a Soldier of the Revolution*, Boston, 1846, p. 127.

It is true that every able-bodied woman is made the most of in being driven afield as long as, under all and any circumstances, she is able to wield a hoe; but, on the other hand, stout, hale, hearty girls and boys, of from eight to twelve and older, are allowed to lounge about, filthy and idle, with no pretense of an occupation but what they call "tend baby," i.e., see to the life and limbs of the little slave infants, to whose mothers, working in distant fields, they carry them during the day to be suckled, and for the rest of the time leave them to crawl and kick in the filthy cabins or on the broiling sand which surrounds them.[8]

Consequently, where such limitations were placed upon the mother's spontaneous emotional responses to the needs of her children and where even her suckling and fondling of them were restricted, it was not unnatural that she often showed little attachment to her offspring.

A slaveholder, who loved "to recall the patriarchal responsibility and tenderness" which her father "felt for his poor, ignorant, dependent slaves," tells the following story to "show that the master's feelings are sometimes even deeper than the

One of my slaves had an infant child two months old who was attacked with an affection of the windpipe. I never saw such extreme suffering; it was one continual spasm and struggle for breath. The physician visited it several times every day, but could give no relief. The poor little sufferer seemed as if it would neither live nor die. These extreme tortures lasted a whole week before it breathed its last; and my own mind was so excited by its sharp and constant convulsive shrieks, that I never left it night or day, and could not sleep, even a moment, sitting by its side; and yet its own mother slept soundly at the foot of the bed, not because she was fatigued, for she was required to do nothing but nurse the dying child.[9]

mother's": While the pathos expressed here is understandable, one would require a knowledge of the mother's experience during pregnancy and childbirth and her subsequent relations with her infant in order to decide whether her behavior was unnatural or extraordinary. However, one might ask: Why were these slave women, in the words of the same informant, "the most enthusiastically fond fostermothers, when they [were] called upon to nurse the infant child of their owners"?

---

[8] Frances A. Kemble, *Journal of a Residence on a Georgian Plantation*, New York, 1863, pp. 121–22.

[9] H. B. Schoolcraft, *By A Southern Lady: Letters on the Condition of the African Race in the United States*, Philadelphia, 1852, pp. 13–14.

Often the relations of the foster-mother or "mammy" to her "white children" offered greater scope for the expression of the emotions and impulses characteristic of maternal love than the contacts which she had with her own offspring. The attachment and devotion which the "mammy" showed for the white children began before the children were born. The "mammy," who was always an important member of the household, attended her mistress during pregnancy and took under her care the infant as soon as it was born. Often she, instead of the mother, suckled the child and if the child was a girl, was never separated from her until she was grown. Miss Bremer has left a picture of one of these foster-mothers sitting "like a horrid specter, black and silent by the altar," during the wedding of her foster-child from whom she "could not bear the thought of parting." If these black foster-mothers showed more maternal affection and devotion for their charges than they or their black sisters showed for their own offspring, it was due to the emotional and biological dependence that developed between them as the result of this intimate association. Moreover, where this intimate association extended over several generations and the "mammy" became assimilated into the master's household, tradition tended to define her role and to inculcate in her sentiments proper to her status.

It should not be inferred from what has been said concerning the Negro woman's devotion to the children of the master race that she never developed a deep and lasting sentiment for her own children. In the slave cabin, where she was generally mistress, she often gathered about her a numerous progeny, in spite of miscarriages and a high infant mortality. Miss Kemble enters in her *Journal*, pp. 190–91, the following information relative to the size of slave families, miscarriages, and infant mortality:

"*Fanny* has had six children; all dead but one. She came to beg to have her work in the field lightened.

"*Nanny* has had three children; two of them dead. She came to implore that the rule of sending them into the field three weeks after their confinement might be altered.

"*Leah*, Caesar's wife, has had six children; three are dead.

"*Sophy*, Lewis's wife, came to beg for some old linen. She is suffering fearfully; has had ten children; five of them are dead. The principal favor she asked was a piece of meat, which I gave her.

"*Sally*, Scipio's wife, has had two miscarriages and three children born, one of whom is dead. She came complaining of incessant pain and weakness in her back. This woman was a mulatto daughter of a slave called Sophy, by a white man of the name of Walker, who visited the plantation.

"*Charlotte*, Renty's wife, had had two miscarriages, and was with child again. She was almost crippled with rheumatism, and showed me a pair of poor swollen knees that made my heart ache. I have promised her a pair of flannel trowsers, which I must forthwith set about making.

"*Sarah*, Stephen's wife—this woman's case and history were alike deplorable. She had had four miscarriages, had brought seven children into the world, five of whom were dead, and was again with child. She complained of dreadful pains in the back, and an internal tumor which swells with the exertion of working in the fields; probably, I think, she is ruptured."

The following entries concerning births and deaths of children were made by an overseer on a plantation in Florida, 1851.

BIRTHS ON THE PLANTATION IN 1851

Florer was confined this morning with a male Child, Jany. 27, 1851.
May 28th, Cate was delivered of a Female Child this morning.
June 4th, Martha was delivered of a male child at 12 o'clock today.
June 13th, Long Mariah was delivered of a male Child today at twelve o'clock.
August 17th, B. Mariah was delivered of a male child this morning.

DEATHS ON THE PLANTATION IN 1851

August 4th, Catherine, a child departed this life today at 2 oclock.
September 18th, one Child Departed this life today at ten oclock; by the name of Amy.
December 31. B. Mariers Child Billy died this morning.

After the day's labor in the field under an unsympathetic overseer, she could find warmth and sympathy and appreciation among her children and kinsmen. There the mother could give full rein to her tender feelings and kindly impulses. "One of my earliest recollections," writes Booker T. Washington, "is that of my mother cooking a chicken late at night, and awakening her children for the purpose of feeding them." The devotion of the mothers to their own children was often demonstrated in their sacrifices to see them when they were separated from them. Douglass' childhood recollections of his mother, who lived twelve miles from him, were of "a few hasty visits made in the night on foot, after the daily tasks were over, and when she was under the necessity of returning in time to respond to the driver's call to the field in the early morning."

It is not surprising, then, to find that slave mothers, instead of viewing with indifference the sale, or loss otherwise, of their children, often put up a stubborn resistance and suffered cruel punishments to prevent separation from them. The fact that slave families were often divided when it was to the economic advantage of the owners is too well established to take seriously the denials of those who have idealized slavery. Washington Irving, who regarded the separation of children from their parents as a peculiar evil of slavery, rationalized thus: "But are not white people so, by schooling, marriage, business, etc."[10]

When Loguen's brothers and sisters were taken from his mother, she was "taken into the room which was used for weaving coarse cloth for the negroes and fastened securely to the loom, where she remained, raving and moaning until morning." Another slave recounts his mother's efforts to prevent her children from being sold:

The master, Billy Grandy, whose slave I was born, was a hard drinking man; he sold away many slaves. I remember four sisters and four brothers; my mother had more children, but they were dead or sold away before I can remember. I was the youngest. I remember well my mother often hid us all in the woods, to prevent master selling us. When we wanted water, she sought for it in any hole or puddle, formed by falling trees or other wise: it was often full of tadpoles and insects: she strained it, and gave it round to each of us in the hollow of her hand. For food, she gathered berries in the woods, got potatoes, raw corn, &c. After a time the master would send word to her to come in, promising he would not sell us. But, at length, persons came, who agreed to give the prices he set on us. His wife, with much to be done, prevailed on him not to sell me; but he sold my brother, who was a little boy. My mother, frantic with grief, resisted their taking her child away; she was beaten and held down: she fainted, and when she came to herself, her boy was gone. She made much outcry, for which the master tied her up to a peach tree in the yard, and flogged her.[11]

[10] *The Journals of Washington Irving*, ed. William P. Trent and George S. Hellman, Boston, 1919, III, 115.
[11] Grandy, *op. cit.*, pp. 5–6.

When Josiah Henson's master died, and it was necessary to sell the slaves in order to divide the estate among the heirs, he says:

We were all put up at auction and sold to the highest bidder, and scattered over various parts of the country. My brothers and sisters were bid off one by one, while my mother, holding my hand, looked on in an agony of grief, the cause of which I but ill understood at first, but which dawned on my mind with dreadful clearness, as the sale proceeded. My mother was then separated from me, and put up in her turn. She was bought by a man named Isaac R., residing in Montgomery county, and then I was offered to the assembled purchasers. My mother, half distracted with the parting forever from all her children, pushed through the crowd, while the bidding for me was going on, to the spot where R. was standing. She fell at his feet, and clung to his knees, entreating him in tones that a mother only could command, to buy her BABY as well as herself, and spare to her one of her little ones at least. Will it, can it be believed that this man, thus appealed to, was capable not merely of turning a deaf ear to her supplication, but of disengaging himself from her with such violent blows and kicks, as to reduce to the necessity of creeping out of his reach.[12]

We need not rely solely on the slave's word concerning the strength of the mother's affection for her children; indirect evidence, as well as contemporary observations, gives the same testimony. Concerning the slave mother's attachment for her children, the remark of an overseer in reply to another who spoke of the danger of losing slaves when they were taken North, is significant:

Oh, stuff and nonsense, I take care when my wife goes North with the children, to send Lucy with her; *her children are down here, and I defy all the Abolitionists in creation to get her to stay North.*

In the following accounts of a sale we learn that the mother's distress at the separation from her child was sufficient to cause it to be purchased with her:

Gambling v. *Read,* Meigs 281, December 1838. 1837, Gambling sold Read, Hannah, a female slave for $1200, ... Hannah had a young child, (a boy, three months old,) and her distress at the separation from it induced Read to propose to purchase it; . . . . agreed that he should have it for 150 dollars.[13]

[12] *The Life of Josiah Henson, Formerly a Slave, Now an Inhabitant of Canada, as Narrated by Himself,* Boston, 1844, pp. 3–4.
[13] Helen Tunnicliff Catterall (ed), *Judicial Cases concerning American Slavery and the Negro,* Washington, D.C., 1929, II, p. 507.

The *Alexandria Gazette*'s comment on the slave trade in the national capital gives a vivid picture of the effect of selling children of the bereft mothers:

Here you may behold fathers and mothers leaving behind them the dearest objects of affection, and moving slowly along in the mute agony of despair; there, the young mother, sobbing over the infant whose innocent smile seems but to increase her misery. From some you will hear the burst of bitter lamentation, while from others the loud hysteric laugh breaks forth, denoting still deeper agony. Such is but a faint picture of the American slave-trade.

Let us return to the cabins at the quarters where the slave mothers lived with their children. A slave described the quarters where he lived as follows:

About a quarter of a mile from the dwelling house, were the huts, or cabins, of the plantation slaves, or field hands, standing in rows; much like the Indian villages which I have seen in the country of the Cherokees. These cabins were thirty-eight in number; generally about fifteen or sixteen feet square; built of hewn logs; covered with shingles, and provided with floors of pine boards. These houses were all dry and comfortable and were provided with chimnies; so that the people when in them, were well sheltered from the inclemencies of the weather. In this practice of keeping their slaves, well sheltered at night, the southern planters are pretty uniform; for they know that upon this circumstance, more than any other in that climate, depends the health of the slave, and consequently his value. In these thirty-eight cabins, were lodged two hundred and fifty people, of all ages, sexes, and sizes. Ten or twelve were generally employed in the garden and about the house[14]

In spite of the numerous separations, the slave mother and her children, especially those under ten, were treated as a group. The following advertisement from the *Charleston* (S.C.) *City Gazette,* February 21, 1825, is typical of a sale of a group of slaves:

VALUABLE NEGROES FOR SALE

A Wench, complete cook, washer and ironer, and her 4 children—a Boy 12, another 9, a Girl 5, that sews; and a Girl about 4 years old.

Another Family—a Wench, complete washer and ironer, and her Daughter, 14 years old, accustomed to the house.

A Wench, a houseservant, and two male Children; one three years old, and the other 4 months.

[14] Charles Ball, *Slavery in the United States,* Lewistown, Pa., 1836, p. 107.

A complete Seamstress and House Servant, with her male Child 7 years old.

Three Young Wenches, 18, 19, 21, all accustomed to house work.

A Mulatto Girl, about 17, a complete Seamstress and Waiting Maid, with her Grandmother.

Two Men, one a complete Coachman, and the other a Waiter. Apply at this Office, or at No. 19 Hasell-street, Feb. 19.

Sometimes more than one family occupied a cabin. "We all lived together with our mother," writes a former slave, "in a long cabin, containing two rooms, one of which we occupied; the other being inhabited by my mother's niece, Annike, and her children." Since the slaves were rationed according to families and under some circumstances were permitted to cultivate gardens for their own use, a sort of family economy gave a material foundation to their sentimental relationships. . . .

Although the families were recognized as more or less distinct units, the fact that life among the slaves was informal and familiar tended to bring them all into intimate relations. The orphans had little difficulty in finding mothers among the women at the quarters. Concerning a former slave, the biographer writes:

Aunt Phyllis showed him tender sympathy and remarked to aunt Betty that it was a pity "ter-tek' dat po' child fum his sick mamma, and brung him on dis place whah he won't meet nobody but a pas'le o' low-down, good-for-nuthin' strangers." This remark attached the boy to aunt Phyllis and he loved her ever afterward. He loved her, too, because she had the same name as his mother. Aunt Phyllis was a big-hearted old soul, and she looked with commiseration on all who suffered affliction or distress.[15]

But, in spite of this seemingly indiscriminate feeling toward children, mothers were likely to show special regard for their own offspring. Douglass, who was among the children placed under care of a cook, says:

She had a strong hold upon old master, for she was a first-rate cook, and very industrious. She was therefore greatly favored by him —as one mark of his favor she was the only mother who was permitted to retain her children around her, and even to these, her own children, she was often fiendishly in her brutality. Cruel, however, as she

[15] Charles Alexander, *Battles and Victories of Allen Allensworth*, Boston, 1914, p. 27.

sometimes was to her own children, she was not destitute of maternal feeling, and in her instinct to satisfy their demands for food, she was often guilty of starving me and the other children.

When the mother was sold away or died, the oldest sister often assumed the role of mother to her brothers and sisters. A former slave wrote recently:

When my mother was sold I had one brother, William, and three sisters, Silva, Agga, and Emma. My father and mother were both pure blooded African Negroes and there is not a drop of white blood in my veins, nor in those of my brother and sisters. When mother was taken away from us, Emma was a baby three years old. Silva, the oldest of the children, was fourteen, and she was a mother to the rest of us children. She took my mother's place in the kitchen as cook for my boss.[16]

We have spoken of the mother as the mistress of the cabin and as the head of the family. There is good reason for this. Not only did she have a more fundamental interest in her children than the father but, as a worker and free agent, except where the master's will was concerned, she developed a spirit of independence and a keen sense of her personal rights. An entry in a plantation journal represents her in one case requesting a divorce because of the burden of having so many children:

Lafayette Renty asked for Leaf to Marry Lear I also gave them Leaf. Rose, Rentys other wife, ses that she dont want to Libe with Renty on the account of his having so Many Children and they weare always quarling so I let them sepperate.

Usually the prospective son-in-law had to get the consent of the girl's mother. A slave complained that the mother of the girl whom he sought to marry opposed him because

she wanted her daughter to marry a slave who belonged to a very rich man living near by, and who was well known to be the son of his master. She thought no doubt that his master or father might chance to set him free before he died, which would enable him to do a better part to her daughter than I could.[17]

16 Robert Anderson, *From Slavery to Affluence; Memories of Robert Anderson, Ex-Slave*, Hemingsford, Neb., 1927, p. 5.

17 Henry Bibb, *The Narrative of the Life and Adventures of Henry Bibb, an American Slave, Written by Himself, with an Introduction by Lucius Matlock*, New York, 1849, pp. 39–40.

The dominating position of the mother is seen in the comment of a former slave on the character of her father and mother. Her father, she said, was "made after the timid kind" and "would never fuss back" at her mother who was constantly warning him: "Bob, I don't want no sorry nigger around me. I can't tolerate you if you ain't got no backbone."

Sometimes it happened that the husband and father played a more aggressive role in the slave family.

In some lists of groups of slaves bought, the father appears:

NEGROES BOUGHT FEBY, 1839

Brave Boy, Carpenter, 40 years old	Pompey, Phillis's son, 16
Phillis, his wife, 35	Jack B. Boy & Phillis's son, 16
Primus B. Boy's son, 21	Chloe child do do
Cato Child, B. Boy's son	Louisa her sister's child who is dead—child, 10
Jenny (Blind) B. Boy's mother	Sarah, Nelly's child, 8
Nelly's husband in town, 30	Jack, Nelly's carpenter boy, 18
Betty, her sister's child who died—child	Ismel, Nelly's, 16
Affey Nelly's child,—child, 11	Lappo Phillis & Brave Boy's, 19

I paid cash for these 16 Negroes, $640. each—$10,240.00

Henson tells the following story of his father's defense of his mother:

The only incident I can remember, which occurred while my mother continued on N.'s farm, was the appearance of my father one day, with his head bloody and his back lacerated. He was in a state of great excitement, and though it was all a mystery to me at the age of three or four years, it was explained at a later period, and I understood that he had been suffering the cruel penalty of the Maryland law for beating a white man. His right ear had been cut off close to his head, and he had received a hundred lashes on his back. He had beaten the overseer for a brutal assault on my mother, and this was his punishment. Furious at such treatment, my father became a different man, and was so morose, disobedient, and intractable, that Mr. N. determined to sell him. He accordingly parted with him, not long after, to his son, who lived in Alabama; and neither mother nor I ever heard of him again.[18]

In some accounts of their families, former slaves included their father. For example, Steward wrote: "Our family consisted of my father and mother—whose names were Robert and Susan

[18] Austin Steward, *Twenty-two Years a Slave, and Forty Years a Freeman*, Rochester, 1857, p. 13.

Steward—a sister, Mary, and myself." But generally the husband made regular visits to his wife and children. According to Bishop Heard, his father, who lived three miles away, "would come in on Wednesday nights after things had closed up at his home, and be back at his home by daylight, Thursday mornings; come again Saturday night, and return by daylight Monday morning."

The strength of the bond that sometimes existed between the father and his family is shown in such advertisements as the following:

$50 REWARD

Ran away from the subscriber his Negro man Pauladore, commonly called Paul. I understand GEN. R. Y. HAYNE* *has purchased his wife and children* from H. L. PINCKNEY, Esq.,** and has them now on his plantation at Goose-creek, where, no doubt, the fellow is frequently lurking. T. DAVIS.

When Ball escaped from slavery in Georgia, he made his way back to his wife and children in Maryland. The apparently insignificant detail in the journal of an overseer: "To Eldesteno, old ben, to see his Grand son Samuel die," is an eloquent testimony to what some men felt in regard to their progeny. On the other hand, many slaves had the same relation with their fathers as Anderson, who says that, after his mother was sold away, "I frequently saw my father after that, but not sufficient to become familiar with him as a father and son should be. A few years later he married another woman from another plantation."

Generally speaking, the mother remained throughout slavery the dominant and important figure in the slave family. Although tradition has represented her as a devoted foster-parent to her master's children and indifferent to her own, it appears that, where this existed, the relations between the slave woman and the white child were similar to the relations which normally exist between mother and child. On the other hand, pregnancy and childbirth often meant only suffering for the slave mother who, because of her limited contacts with her young, never developed that attachment which grows out of physiological and emotional responses to its needs. Nevertheless, there is abundant evidence that slave mothers developed a deep and permanent love for their children, which often caused them to defy their masters and to undergo suffering to prevent separation from their young.

Stanley M. Elkins

Without any doubt, the most controversial piece of work done on slavery in recent times has been Stanley M. Elkins' *Slavery: A Problem in American Institutional and Intellectual Life* (1959). Elkins' book was vigorously attacked by many Negroes and whites. *Freedomways*, an important journal for radical Negro intellectuals, described the work as "vicious" and "chauvinistic," while David Donald, a pupil of James G. Randall, blistered Elkins in the *American Historical Review* for producing a work "in poor taste and worse logic." The *Journal of Negro History* remained noticeably silent. On the other hand, Professor Elkins has not lacked supporters. Sociologist Nathan Glazer of the University of California (Berkeley), in an introduction to Elkins' study, hailed it as raising "the curtain on what must become an important area for research and thinking," and the *British Journal of Sociology* called *Slavery* the "most useful single book on slavery to appear in fifty years." What had Elkins written to provoke such responses?

Elkins presented the most searing indictment of slavery yet made. American slavery took away not only the physical freedom of the Negro, for that had happened elsewhere, but also destroyed his personality, brainwashing him into the "Sambo" of Southern folklore. Leaning heavily on the work of Freyre and Tannenbaum, who showed slavery in Latin America to be a clearly different institution from that of North America, Elkins began to investigate what effect this had on the slaves. Did this explain why North America did not see the appearance of more aggressive slaves, and subsequently great slave rebellions? Elkins' answer was that the Negro under American slavery had been reduced to the "Sambo." Far from being the "freedom fighter," the Negro, who in Africa had been the warrior or farmer, became a dependent, infantile child, "doc-

ile, but irresponsible, loyal but lazy, humble but chronically
given to lying and stealing; his behavior was full of infantile
silliness and his talk inflated with childish exaggeration." The
Negro was psychologically castrated, and could only survive
under American slavery, as a clown, not as a rebel; as a child,
not as an adult. This was in complete contrast to the slave in
Latin America, who, argued Elkins, under a less restrictive
system had been able to retain an adult role, and thereby remained, both a man and a rebel. Latin America saw great
slave rebellions. America, according to Elkins, saw only the
"aimless butchery" of Nat Turner.

Elkins tested his hypothesis against the behavior of victims
of the Nazi concentration camps. While not fully equating
the American slave plantation with the concentration camp,
he did find that the concentration camp produced on Europeans almost the same personality changes that the plantation had on the Negro. The absolute power of a closed system
produced an infantilization, a helpless dependency, an identification with the oppressors, which prevented both the European and the Negro to offer effective resistance against
their captors. The only way to survive was in the form of the
"Sambo."

But before we can accept Elkins' conclusions we need to
raise four points. First, we need to know much more about
the behavior of slaves before accepting the "Sambo" picture
of the Negro. The evidence supplied by Aptheker, Stampp,
Quarles, and James McPherson suggests that the Negro was
far less docile than we have been led to believe. Second, we
need to know more about the dynamics of revolt. An important ingredient would appear to be division, decay, or liberalization in the ranks of the masters. When decay of authority
came during the American Revolution and the Civil War,
slaves found a way to show their discontent. Third, we need
to know more about the specifics of South American and
Caribbean rebellions. Were they the results of a different
type of Negro, or rather environmental factors such as the
proportion of slaves to whites, the accessibility of forests and
mountains, the concentration in one area of freshly imported
Negroes from Africa, or the breakdown of planter control?
Finally, did the emergence of Negroes who were able to escape the debilitating effects of the slave system necessarily
mean that rebellion was soon to follow? Richard C. Wade has
shown in *Slavery in the Cities* that while the slaves in South-

ern cities did have the opportunity to escape from the narrow control of their masters and did develop into "an invaluable pool of potential leadership . . . no actual significant uprising took place in any Southern city."

While we may hold off final judgement on Professor Elkins' thesis, he has already directed historians into examining the comparative nature of slavery, and made us rethink some assumptions concerning the workings of slavery and its effects upon the slaves. Such studies by David B. Davis, Herbert S. Klein, and Marvin Harris owe much to Elkins' preliminary findings.

Stanley M. Elkins is Professor of History at Smith College, Northampton, Massachusetts.

SLAVERY AND PERSONALITY

SOURCE: Stanley M. Elkins, *Slavery: A Problem in American Institutional and Intellectual Life* (Chicago: University of Chicago Press, 1959), 81–85, 86–89, 97–98, 102–4, 111–13, 128–33, 133–39.

Personality Types and Stereotypes

An examination of American slavery, checked at certain critical points against a very different slave system, that of Latin America, reveals that a major key to many of the contrasts between them was an institutional key: The presence or absence of other powerful institutions in society made an immense difference in the character of slavery itself. In Latin America, the very tension and balance among three kinds of organizational concerns—church, crown, and plantation agriculture—prevented slavery from being carried by the planting class to its ultimate logic. For the slave, in terms of the space thus allowed for the development of men and women as moral beings, the result was an "open system": a system of contacts with free society through which ultimate absorption into that society could and did occur with great frequency. The rights of personality implicit in the ancient traditions of slavery and in the church's most venerable assumptions on the nature of the human soul were thus in a vital sense conserved, whereas to a staggering extent the very opposite was true in North American slavery.

The latter system had developed virtually unchecked by institutions having anything like the power of their Latin counterparts; the legal structure which supported it, shaped only by the demands of a staple-raising capitalism, had defined with such nicety the slave's character as chattel that his character as a moral individual was left in the vaguest of legal obscurity. In this sense American slavery operated as a "closed" system—one in which, for the generality of slaves in their nature as men and women, contacts with free society could occur only on the most narrowly circumscribed of terms. The next question is whether living within such a "closed system" might not have produced noticeable effects upon the slave's very personality.

The name "Sambo" has come to be synonymous with "race stereotype." Here is an automatic danger signal, warning that the analytical difficulties of asking questions about slave personality may not be nearly so great as the moral difficulties. The one inhibits the other; the morality of the matter has had a clogging effect on its theoretical development that may not be to the best interests of either. And yet theory on group personality is still in a stage rudimentary enough that this particular body of material—potentially illuminating—ought not to remain morally impounded any longer.

Is it possible to deal with "Sambo" as a type? The characteristics that have been claimed for the type come principally from Southern lore. Sambo, the typical plantation slave, was docile but irresponsible, loyal but lazy, humble but chronically given to lying and stealing; his behavior was full of infantile silliness and his talk inflated with childish exaggeration. His relationship with his master was one of utter dependence and childlike attachment: it was indeed this childlike quality that was the very key to his being. Although the merest hint of Sambo's "manhood" might fill the Southern breast with scorn, the child, "in his place," could be both exasperating and lovable.

Was he real or unreal? What order of existence, what rank of legitimacy, should be accorded him? Is there a "scientific" way to talk about this problem? For most Southerners in 1860 it went without saying not only that Sambo was real—that he was a dominant plantation type—but also that his characteristics were the clear product of racial inheritance. That was one way to deal with Sambo, a way that persisted a good many years after 1860. But in recent times, the discrediting, as unscientific, of racial explanations for any feature of plantation slavery has tended in the case of Sambo to discredit not simply the explanation itself but also the thing it was supposed to explain. Sambo is a mere stereotype—"stereotype" is itself a bad word, insinuating racial inferiority and invidious discrimination. This modern approach to Sambo had a strong counterpart in the way Northern reformers thought about slavery in ante-bellum times: they thought that nothing could actually be said about the Negro's "true" nature because that nature was veiled by the institution of slavery. It could only be revealed by tearing away the veil. In short, no order of reality could be given to assertions about slave character, because those assertions were illegitimately grounded on race, whereas their only basis was a corrupt and "unreal" institution. "To be sure," a recent writer concedes, "there were plenty of opportunists among the Negroes who played the role assigned to them, acted the clown, and curried the favor of their masters in order to win the maximum rewards within the system. . . ."[1] To impeach Sambo's legitimacy in this way is the next thing to talking him out of existence.

There ought, however, to be still a third way of dealing with the Sambo picture, some formula for taking it seriously. The picture has far too many circumstantial details, its hues have been stroked in by too many different brushes, for it to be denounced as counterfeit. Too much folk-knowledge, too much plantation literature, too much of the Negro's own lore, have gone into its making to entitle one in good conscience to condemn it as "conspiracy." One searches in vain through the literature of the Latin-American slave systems for the "Sambo" of our tradition—the perpetual child incapable of maturity. How is this to be explained?[2] If Sambo is not a product of race (that

---

[1] Kenneth Stampp, "The Historian and Southern Negro Slavery," *American Historical Review*, LVII (April, 1952), 617.

[2] There is such a word as "Zambo" in Latin America, but its meaning has no relation to our "Sambo." "A Zambo or Sambo (Spanish, *Zambo*, 'bandy-legged') is a cross between a *Negro* and an Amerindian (sometimes this name is given to the cross between a pure Negro and a mulatto, which the French called 'griffe')." Sir Harry Johnston, *The Negro in the New World* (London: Methuen, 1910), p. 3. I am not implying that racial

"explanation" can be consigned to oblivion) and not simply a product of "slavery" in the abstract (other societies have had slavery), then he must be related to our own peculiar variety of it. And if Sambo is uniquely an American product, then his existence, and the reasons for his character, must be recognized in order to appreciate the very scope of our slave problem and its aftermath. The absoluteness with which such a personality ("real" or "unreal") had been stamped upon the plantation slave does much to make plausible the ante-bellum Southerner's difficulty in imagining that blacks anywhere could be anything but a degraded race—and it goes far to explain his failure to see any sense at all in abolitionism. . . .

If it were taken for granted that a special type existed in significant numbers on American plantations, closer connections might be made with a growing literature on personality and character types, the investigation of which has become a widespread, respectable, and productive enterprise among our psychologists and social scientists. Realizing that, it might then seem not quite so dangerous to add that the type corresponded in its major outlines to "Sambo."

Let the above, then, be a preface to the argument of the present essay. It will be assumed that there were elements in the very structure of the plantation system—its "closed" char-

---

stigma of some kind did not exist in South America (see above, pp. 77–78, n. 113); indeed, anthropological research has shown that the Latin-Americans were, and are, a good deal more conscious of "race" than such writers as Gilberto Freyre have been willing to admit. Even in Brazil, derogatory Negro stereotypes are common, and are apparently of long standing. On this point see Charles Wagley, *Race and Class in Rural Brazil* (Paris: UNESCO, 1952). On the other hand, it would be very difficult to find evidence in the literature of Brazil, or anywhere else in Latin America, of responsible men seriously maintaining that the Negro slave was constitutionally incapable of freedom. The views of a man like James H. Hammond, or for that matter the views of any average Southerner during the ante-bellum period, would have had little meaning in nineteenth-century Latin America. One is even inclined to think that these Latin-American stereotypes would compare more closely with the stereotypes of eastern and southern European immigrants that were held by certain classes in this country early in the twentieth century. See, e.g., Madison Grant's *Passing of the Great Race* (New York: Scribner, 1916). There are stereotypes and stereotypes: it would be quite safe to say that our "Sambo" far exceeds in tenacity and pervasiveness anything comparable in Latin America.

acter—that could sustain infantilism as a normal feature of behavior. These elements, having less to do with "cruelty" per se than simply with the sanctions of authority, were effective and pervasive enough to require that such infantilism be characterized as something much more basic than mere "accommodation." It will be assumed that the sanctions of the system were in themselves sufficient to produce a recognizable personality type.

It should be understood that to identify a social type in this sense is still to generalize on a fairly crude level—and to insist for a limited purpose on the legitimacy of such generalizing is by no means to deny that, on more refined levels, a great profusion of individual types might have been observed in slave society. Nor need it be claimed that the "Sambo" type, even in the relatively crude sense employed here, was a universal type. It was, however, a plantation type, and a plantation existence embraced well over half the slave population.[3] Two kinds of material will be used in the effort to picture the mechanisms whereby this adjustment to absolute power—an adjustment whose end product included infantile features of behavior—may have been effected. One is drawn from the theoretical knowledge presently available in social psychology, and the other, in the form of an analogy, is derived from some of the data that have come out of the German concentration camps. It is recognized in most theory that social behavior is regulated in some general way by adjustment to symbols of authority—however diversely "authority" may be defined either in theory or in culture itself—and that such adjustment is closely related to the very formation of personality. A corollary would be, of course, that the more diverse those symbols of authority may be, the greater is the permissible variety of adjustment to them—and the wider the margin of individuality, consequently, in the development of

---

[3] Although the majority of Southern slaveholders were not planters, the majority of slaves were owned by a planter minority. "Considerably more than half of them lived on plantation units of more than twenty slaves, and one-fourth lived on units of more than fifty. That the majority of slaves belonged to members of the planter class, and not to those who operated small farms with a single slave family, is a fact of crucial importance concerning the nature of bondage in the ante-bellum South." Kenneth M. Stampp, *Peculiar Institution*, (New York, 1956), p. 31.

the self. The question here has to do with the wideness or narrowness of that margin on the ante-bellum plantation.

The other body of material, involving an experience undergone by several million men and women in the concentration camps of our own time, contains certain items of relevance to the problem here being considered. The experience was analogous to that of slavery and was one in which wide-scale instances of infantilization were observed. The material is sufficiently detailed, and sufficiently documented by men who not only took part in the experience itself but who were versed in the use of psychological theory for analyzing it, that the advantages of drawing upon such data for purposes of analogy seem to outweigh the possible risks.

The introduction of this second body of material must to a certain extent govern the theoretical strategy itself. It has been recognized both implicitly and explicitly that the psychic impact and effects of the concentration-camp experience were not anticipated in existing theory and that consequently such theory would require some major supplementation. It might be added, parenthetically, that almost any published discussion of this modern Inferno, no matter how learned, demonstrates how "theory," operating at such a level of shared human experience, tends to shed much of its technical trappings and to take on an almost literary quality. The experience showed, in any event, that infantile personality features could be induced in a relatively short time among large numbers of adult human beings coming from very diverse backgrounds. The particular strain which was thus placed upon prior theory consisted in the need to make room not only for the cultural and environmental sanctions that sustain personality (which in a sense Freudian theory already had) but also for a virtually unanticipated problem: actual change in the personality of masses of adults. It forced a reappraisal and new appreciation of how completely and effectively prior cultural sanctions for behavior and personality could be detached to make way for new and different sanctions, and of how adjustments could be made by individuals to a species of authority vastly different from any previously known. The revelation for theory was the process of detachment.

These cues, accordingly, will guide the argument on Negro slavery. Several million people were detached with a peculiar effectiveness from a great variety of cultural backgrounds in Africa—a detachment operating with infinitely more effectiveness upon those brought to North America than upon those who came to Latin America. It was achieved partly by the shock experience inherent in the very mode of procurement but more specifically by the type of authority-system to which they were introduced and to which they had to adjust for physical and psychic survival. The new adjustment, to absolute power in a closed system, involved infantilization, and the detachment was so complete that little trace of prior (and thus alternative) cultural sanctions for behavior and personality remained for the descendants of the first generation. For them, adjustment to clear and omnipresent authority could be more or less automatic—as much so, or as little, as it is for anyone whose adjustment to a social system begins at birth and to whom that system represents normality. We do not know how generally a full adjustment was made by the first generation of fresh slaves from Africa. But we do know—from a modern experience—that such an adjustment is possible, not only within the same generation but within two or three years. This proved possible for people in a full state of complex civilization, for men and women who were not black and not savages. . . .

But returning to the primary problem: no true picture, cursory or extended, of African culture seems to throw any light at all on the origins of what would emerge, in American plantation society, as the stereotyped "Sambo" personality. The typical West African tribesman was a distinctly warlike individual; he had a profound sense of family and family authority; he took hard work for granted; and he was accustomed to live by a highly formalized set of rules which he himself often helped to administer. If he belonged to the upper classes of tribal society— as did many who later fell victim to the slave trade—he might have had considerable experience as a political or military leader. He was the product, in any case, of cultural traditions essentially heroic in nature.

Something very profound, therefore, would have had to intervene in order to obliterate all this and to produce, on the American plantation, a society of helpless dependents. . . .

The thoroughness with which African Negroes coming to America were detached from prior cultural sanctions should thus be partly explainable by the very shock sequence inherent in the technique of procurement. But it took something more than this to produce "Sambo," and it is possible to overrate—or at least to overgeneralize—this shock sequence in the effort to explain what followed. A comparable experience was also undergone by slaves coming into Latin America, where very little that resembled our "Sambo" tradition would ever develop. We should also remember that, in either case, it was only the first generation that actually experienced these shocks. It could even be argued that the shock sequence is not an absolute necessity for explaining "Sambo" at all.

So whereas the Middle Passage and all that went with it must have been psychologically numbing, and should probably be regarded as a long thrust, at least, toward the end product, it has little meaning considered apart from what came later. It may be assumed that the process of detachment was completed—and, as it were, guaranteed—by the kind of "closed" authority-system into which the slave was introduced and to which he would have to adjust. At any rate, a test of this detachment and its thoroughness is virtually ready-made. Everyone who has looked into the problem of African cultural features surviving among New World Negroes agrees that the contrast between North America and Latin America is immense. In Brazil, survivals from African religion are not only to be encountered everywhere, but such carry-overs are so distinct that they may even be identified with particular tribal groups. "The Negro religions and cults," Arthur Ramos adds, "were not the only form of cultural expression which survived in Brazil. The number of folklore survivals is extremely large, the prolongation of social institutions, habits, practices and events from Africa."[4] Fernando Ortiz,

---

[4] Arthur Ramos, *The Negro in Brazil* (Washington: Associated Publishers, 1939), p. 94. Ramos devotes two full chapters to "The Cultural Heritage of the Brazilian Negro." Donald Pierson, in his *Negroes in Brazil* (Chicago: University of Chicago Press, 1942), likewise devotes two chapters to African influences in the customs of the Negroes of Bahia.

writing of Cuba in 1905, saw the African witchcraft cults flourish-ing on the island as a formidable social problem.[5] One of our own anthropologists, on the other hand, despite much dedicated field work, has been put to great effort to prove that in North American Negro society any African cultural vestiges have survived at all.[6]

Adjustment to Absolute Power in the Concentration Camp

A certain amount of the mellowness in Ulrich Phillips' picture of ante-bellum plantation life has of necessity been discredited by recent efforts not only to refocus attention upon the brutalities of the slave system but also to dispose once and for all of Phillips' assumptions about the slave as a racially inferior being. And yet it is important—particularly in view of the analogy about to be presented—to keep in mind that for all the system's cruelties there were still clear standards of patriarchal benev-olence inherent in its human side, and that such standards were recognized as those of the best Southern families. This aspect, despite the most drastic changes of emphasis, should continue to guarantee for Phillips' view more than just a modicum of legitimacy; the patriarchal quality, whatever measure of benev-olence or lack of it one wants to impute to the regime, still holds a major key to its nature as a social system.

Introducing, therefore, certain elements of the German con-centration-camp experience involves the risky business of trying to balance two necessities—emphasizing both the vast dissimi-larities of the two regimes and the essentially limited purpose for which they are being brought together, and at the same

[5] Fernando Ortiz, Los Negros Brujos (Madrid: Libería de F. Fé, 1906). This entire book is devoted to occult African practices in Cuba, including a chapter called "The Future of Witchcraft."

[6] Herskovits, Myth of the Negro Past (New York, 1941). The real aim of this study seems more often than not to be that of "promoting" African culture in the United States by insisting on its values instead of describing its actual survivals—which the author himself admits are decidedly on the scanty side compared with those to be found in Latin America. Such "Africanisms" do not seem to go much beyond esoteric vestiges of a suspiciously circumstantial nature, in speech rhythms, certain symbols in folk-tales, habits of "temporary mating," etc. Professor Herskovits reveals, perhaps unwittingly, that efforts to convince American Negro audiences that they do, in fact, have an African cultural heritage, have met with hostility and tension.

time justifying the use of the analogy in the first place. The point is perhaps best made by insisting on an order of classification. The American plantation was not even in the metaphorical sense a "concentration camp"; nor was it even "like" a concentration camp, to the extent that any standards comparable to those governing the camps might be imputed to any sector of American society, at any time; but it should at least be permissible to turn the thing around—to speak of the concentration camp as a special and highly perverted instance of human slavery. Doing so, moreover, should actually be of some assistance in the strategy, now universally sanctioned, of demonstrating how little the products and consequences of slavery ever had to do with race. The only mass experience that Western people have had within recorded history comparable in any way with Negro slavery was undergone in the nether world of Nazism. The concentration camp was not only a perverted slave system; it was also—what is less obvious but even more to the point—a perverted patriarchy. . . .

The most immediate aspect of the old inmates' behavior [in concentration camps] which struck observers was its *childlike* quality. "The prisoners developed types of behavior which are characteristic of infancy or early youth. Some of these behaviors developed slowly, others were immediately imposed on the prisoners and developed only in intensity as time went on."[7] Such infantile behavior took innumerable forms. The inmates' sexual impotence brought about a disappearance of sexuality in their talk,[8] instead, excretory functions occupied them endlessly. They lost many of the customary inhibitions as to soiling their beds and their persons.[9] Their humor was shot with silliness

[7] Bettelheim, "Individual and Mass Behavior in Extreme Situations," *Journal of Abnormal Psychology*, XXXVIII (October, 1943), 424.

[8] Says Dr. Cohen, "I am not asserting that sex was never discussed; it was, though not often. Frankl also states 'that in contrast to mass existence in other military communities . . . here (in the concentration camp) there is *no smut talk.*'" *Human Behavior In the Concentration Camp* (New York, 1953), 141.

[9] "With reference to this phenomenon Miss Bluhm has pointed out that it is not at all unusual that people in extraordinary circumstances, for example soldiers in wartime, 'are able to give up their habitual standards of cleanliness without deeper disturbance; yet only up to certain limits.' The rules of anal cleanliness, she adds, are not disregarded. 'Their neglect means return to instinctual behavior of childhood.'" *Ibid.*, p. 175.

and they giggled like children when one of them would expel wind. Their relationships were highly unstable. "Prisoners would, like early adolescents, fight one another tooth and nail . . . only to become close friends within a few minutes."[10] Dishonesty became chronic. "Now they suddenly appeared to be pathological liars, to be unable to restrain themselves, to be unable to make objective evaluation, etc."[11] "In hundreds of ways," writes Colaço Belmonte, "the soldier, and to an even greater extent the prisoner of war, is given to understand that he is a child. . . . Then dishonesty, mendacity, egotistic actions in order to obtain more food or to get out of scrapes reach full development, and theft becomes a veritable affliction of camp life."[12] This was all true, according to Elie Cohen, in the concentration camp as well.[13] Benedikt Kautsky observed such things in his own behavior: "I myself can declare that often I saw myself as I used to be in my school days, when by sly dodges and clever pretexts we avoided being found out, or could 'organize' something."[14] Bruno Bettelheim remarks on the extravagance of the stories told by the prisoners to one another. "They were boastful, telling tales about what they had accomplished in their former lives, or how they succeeded in cheating foremen or guards, and how they sabotaged the work. Like children they felt not at all set back or ashamed when it became known that they had lied about their prowess."[15]

This development of childlike behavior in the old inmates was the counterpart of something even more striking that was happening to them: *"Only very few of the prisoners escaped a more or less intensive identification with the SS."*[16] As Mr. Bettelheim puts it: "A prisoner had reached the final stage of adjustment to the camp situation when he had changed his personality so

[10] Bettelheim, "Individual and Mass Behavior," p. 445.
[11] *Ibid.*, p. 421.
[12] Quoted in Cohen, *Human Behavior*, p. 176.
[13] *Ibid.*
[14] *Ibid.*, p. 174.
[15] Bettelheim, "Individual and Mass Behavior," pp. 445–46. This same phenomenon is noted by Curt Bondy: "They tell great stories about what they have been before and what they have performed." "Problems of Internment Camps," *Journal of Abnormal and Social Psychology*, XXXVIII (October, 1943), 453–75.
[16] Cohen, *Human Behavior*, p. 177. Italics in original.

as to accept as his own the values of the Gestapo."[17] The Bettelheim study furnishes a catalogue of examples. The old prisoners came to share the attitude of the SS toward the "unfit" prisoners; newcomers who behaved badly in the labor groups or who could not withstand the strain became a liability for the others, who were often instrumental in getting rid of them. Many old prisoners actually imitated the SS; they would sew and mend their uniforms in such a way as to make them look more like those of the SS—even though they risked punishment for it. "When asked why they did it, they admitted that they loved to look like . . . the guards." Some took great enjoyment in the fact that during roll call "they really had stood well at attention." There were cases of nonsensical rules, made by the guards, which the older prisoners would continue to observe and try to force on the others long after the SS had forgotten them.[18] Even the most abstract ideals of the SS, such as their intense German nationalism and anti-Semitism, were often absorbed by the old inmates—a phenomenon observed among the politically well-educated and even among the Jews themselves.[19] The final quintessence of all this was seen in the "Kapo"—the prisoner who had been placed in a supervisory position over his fellow inmates. These creatures, many of them professional criminals, not only behaved with slavish servility to the SS, but the way in which they often outdid the SS in sheer brutality became one of the most durable features of the concentration-camp legend.

To all these men, reduced to complete and childish dependence upon their masters, the SS had actually become a

[17] Bettelheim, "Individual and Mass Behavior," p. 447.

[18] *Ibid.*, pp. 448–50. "Once, for instance, a guard on inspecting the prisoners' apparel found that the shoes of some of them were dirty on the inside. He ordered all prisoners to wash their shoes inside and out with water and soap. The heavy shoes treated this way became hard as stone. The order was never repeated, and many prisoners did not execute it when given. Nevertheless there were some old prisoners who not only continued to wash the inside of their shoes every day but cursed all others who did not do so as negligent and dirty. These prisoners firmly believed that the rules set down by the Gestapo were desirable standards of human behavior, at least in the camp situation." *Ibid.*, p. 450.

[19] *Ibid.* See also Cohen, *Human Behavior*, pp. 189–93, for a discussion of anti-Semitism among the Jews.

father-symbol. "The SS man was all-powerful in the camp, he was the lord and master of the prisoner's life. As a cruel father he could, without fear of punishment, even kill the prisoner and as a gentle father he could scatter largesse and afford the prisoner his protection."[20] The result, admits Dr. Cohen, was that "for all of us the SS was a father image. . . ."[21] The closed system, in short, had become a kind of grotesque patriarchy. . . .

It is hoped that the very hideousness of a special example of slavery [the concentration camp] has not disqualified it as a test for certain features of a far milder and more benevolent form of slavery. But it should still be possible to say, with regard to the individuals who lived as slaves within the respective systems, that just as on one level there is every difference between a wretched childhood and a carefree one, there are, for other purposes, limited features which the one may be said to have shared with the other.

Both were closed systems from which all standards based on prior connections had been effectively detached. A working adjustment to either system required a childlike conformity, a limited choice of "significant others." Cruelty per se cannot be considered the primary key to this; of far greater importance was the simple "closedness" of the system, in which all lines of authority descended from the master and in which alternative social bases that might have supported alternative standards were systematically suppressed.[22] The individual, consequently,

[20] Cohen, *Human Behavior,* pp. 176–77.

[21] *Ibid.,* p. 179. On this and other points I must also acknowledge my indebtedness to Mr. Ies Spetter, a former Dutch journalist now living in this country, who was imprisoned for a time at Auschwitz during World War II. Mr. Spetter permitted me to see an unpublished paper, "Some Thoughts on Victims and Criminals in the German Concentration Camps," which he wrote in 1954 at the New School for Social Research; and this, together with a number of conversations I had with him, added much to my understanding of concentration-camp psychology.

[22] The experience of American prisoners taken by the Chinese during the Korean War seems to indicate that profound changes in behavior and values, if not in basic personality itself, can be effected without the use of physical torture or extreme deprivation. The Chinese were able to get large numbers of Americans to act as informers and to co-operate in numerous ways in the effort to indoctrinate all the prisoners with Communist propaganda. The technique contained two key elements. One was that all formal and informal authority structures within the group were systematically destroyed; this was done by isolating officers, non-commissioned officers, and

for his very psychic security, had to picture his master in some way as the "good father," even when, as in the concentration camp, it made no sense at all.[23] But why should it not have made sense for many a simple plantation Negro whose master did exhibit, in all the ways that could be expected, the features of the good father who was really "good"? If the concentration camp could produce in two or three years the results that it did, one wonders how much more pervasive must have been those attitudes, expectations, and values which had, certainly, their benevolent side and which were accepted and transmitted over generations.

For the Negro child, in particular, the plantation offered no really satisfactory father-image other than the master. The "real" father was virtually without authority over his child, since discipline, parental responsibility, and control of rewards and punishments all rested in other hands; the slave father could not even protect the mother of his children except by appealing directly to the master. Indeed, the mother's own role loomed far larger for the slave child than did that of the father. She controlled those few activities—household care, preparation of food, and rearing of children—that were left to the slave family. For that matter, the very etiquette of plantation life removed even

---

any enlisted men who gave indications of leadership capacities. The other element involved the continual emphasizing of the captors' power and influence by judicious manipulation of petty rewards and punishments and by subtle hints of the greater rewards and more severe punishments (repatriation or non-repatriation) that rested with the pleasure of those in authority. See Edgar H. Schein, "Some Observations on Chinese Methods of Handling Prisoners of War," *Public Opinion Quarterly*, XX (Spring, 1956), 321–27.

[23] Bruno Bettelheim tells us of the fantastic efforts of the old prisoners to believe in the benevolence of the officers of the SS. "They insisted that these officers [hid] behind their rough surface a feeling of justice and propriety; he, or they, were supposed to be genuinely interested in the prisoners and even trying, in a small way, to help them. Since nothing of these supposed feelings and efforts ever became apparent, it was explained that he hid them so effectively because otherwise he would not be able to help the prisoners. The eagerness of these prisoners to find reasons for their claims was pitiful. A whole legend was woven around the fact that of two officers inspecting a barrack one had cleaned his shoes from mud before entering. He probably did it automatically, but it was interpreted as a rebuff of the other officer and a clear demonstration of how he felt about the concentration camp." Bettelheim, "Individual and Mass Behavior," p. 451.

the honorific attributes of fatherhood from the Negro male, who was addressed as "boy"—until, when the vigorous years of his prime were past, he was allowed to assume the title of "uncle."

From the master's viewpoint, slaves had been defined in law as property, and the master's power over his property must be absolute. But then this property was still human property. These slaves might never be quite as human as *he* was, but still there were certain standards that could be laid down for their behavior: obedience, fidelity, humility, docility, cheerfulness, and so on. Industry and diligence would of course be demanded, but a final element in the master's situation would undoubtedly qualify that expectation. Absolute power for him meant absolute dependency for the slave—the dependency not of the developing child but of the perpetual child. For the master, the role most aptly fitting such a relationship would naturally be that of the father. As a father he could be either harsh or kind, as he chose, but as a *wise* father he would have, we may suspect, a sense of the limits of his situation. He must be ready to cope with *all* the qualities of the child, exasperating as well as ingratiating. He might conceivably have to expect in this child—besides his loyalty, docility, humility, cheerfulness, and (under supervision) his diligence—such additional qualities as irresponsibility, playfulness, silliness, laziness, and (quite possibly) tendencies to lying and stealing. Should the entire prediction prove accurate, the result would be something resembling "Sambo."

The social and psychological sanctions of role-playing may in the last analysis prove to be the most satisfactory of the several approaches to Sambo, for, without doubt, of all the roles in American life that of Sambo was by far the most pervasive. The outlines of the role might be sketched in by crude necessity, but what of the finer shades? The sanctions against overstepping it were bleak enough,[24] but the rewards—the sweet applause, as it were, for performing it with sincerity and feeling—were something to be appreciated on quite another level. The law, untuned to the deeper harmonies, could command the player to be present for the occasion, and the whip might even warn

[24] Professor Stampp, in a chapter called "To Make Them Stand in Fear," describes the planter's resources for dealing with a recalcitrant slave. *Peculiar Institution*, pp. 141–91.

against his missing the grosser cues, but could those things really insure the performance that melted all hearts? Yet there was many and many a performance, and the audiences (whose standards were high) appear to have been for the most part well pleased. They were actually viewing their own masterpiece. Much labor had been lavished upon this chef d'oeuvre, the most genial resources of Southern society had been available for the work; touch after touch had been applied throughout the years, and the result—embodied not in the unfeeling law but in the richest layers of Southern lore—had been the product of an exquisitely rounded collective creativity. And indeed, in a sense that somehow transcended the merely ironic, it was a labor of love. "I love the simple and unadulterated slave, with his geniality, his mirth, his swagger, and his nonsense," wrote Edward Pollard. "I love to look upon his countenance shining with content and grease; I love to study his affectionate heart; I love to mark that peculiarity in him, which beneath all his buffoonery exhibits him as a creature of the tenderest sensibilities, mingling his joys and his sorrows with those of his master's home.[25] Love, even on those terms, was surely no inconsequential reward.

But what were the terms? The Negro was to be a child forever. "The Negro . . . in his true nature, is always a boy, let him be ever so old. . . ."[26] "He is . . . a dependent upon the white race; dependent for guidance and direction even to the procurement of his most indispensable necessaries. Apart from this protection he has the helplessness of a child—without foresight, without faculty of contrivance, without thrift of any kind."[27] Not only was he a child; he was a happy child. Few Southern writers failed to describe with obvious fondness the bubbling gaiety of a plantation holiday or the perpetual good humor that seemed to mark the Negro character, the good humor of an everlasting childhood.

The role, of course, must have been rather harder for the earliest generations of slaves to learn. "Accommodation," according to John Dollard, "involves the renunciation of protest or

[25] Edward A. Pollard, *Black Diamonds Gathered in the Darkey Homes of the South* (New York: Pudney & Russel, 1859), p. 58.

[26] *Ibid.*, p. viii.

[27] John Pendleton Kennedy, *Swallow Barn* (Philadelphia: Carey & Lea, 1832).

aggression against undesirable conditions of life and the organization of the character so that protest does not appear, but acceptance does. It may come to pass in the end that the unwelcome force is idealized, that one identifies with it and takes it into the personality; it sometimes even happens that what is at first resented and feared is finally loved."[28]

Might the process, on the other hand, be reversed? It is hard to imagine its being reversed overnight. The same role might still be played in the years after slavery—we are told that it was[29] —and yet it was played to more vulgar audiences with cruder standards, who paid much less for what they saw. The lines might be repeated more and more mechanically, with less and less conviction; the incentives to perfection could become hazy and blurred, and the excellent old piece could degenerate over time into low farce. There could come a point, conceivably, with the old zest gone, that it was no longer worth the candle.

[28] John Dollard, *Caste and Class in a Southern Town* (2d ed.; New York: Harper, 1949), p. 255. The lore of "accommodation," taken just in itself, is very rich and is, needless to say, morally very complex. It suggests a delicate psychological balance. On the one hand, as the Dollard citation above implies, accommodation is fraught with dangers for the personalities of those who engage in it. On the other hand, as Bruno Bettelheim has reminded me, this involves a principle that goes well beyond American Negro society and is to be found deeply imbedded in European traditions: the principle of how the powerless can manipulate the powerful through aggressive stupidity, literal-mindedness, servile fawning, and irresponsibility. In this sense the immovably stupid "Good Soldier Schweik" and the fawning Negro in Richard Wright's *Black Boy* who allowed the white man to kick him for a quarter partake of the same tradition. Each has a technique whereby he can in a real sense exploit his powerful superiors, feel contempt for them, and suffer in the process no great damage to his own pride. Jewish lore, as is well known, teems with this sort of thing. There was much of it also in the traditional relationships between peasants and nobles in central Europe.

Still, all this required the existence of some sort of alternative forces for moral and psychological orientation. The problem of the Negro in slavery times involved the virtual absence of such forces. It was with the end of slavery, presumably, that they would first begin to present themselves in generally usable form—a man's neighbors, the Loyal Leagues, white politicians, and so on. It would be in these circumstances that the essentially intermediate technique of accommodation could be used as a protective device beneath which a more independent personality might develop.

[29] Even Negro officeholders during Reconstruction, according to Francis B. Simkins, "were known to observe carefully the etiquette of the Southern caste system." "New Viewpoints of Southern Reconstruction," *Journal of Southern History*, V (February, 1939), 52.

The day might come at last when it dawned on a man's full waking consciousness that he had really grown up, that he was, after all, only playing a part.

Mechanisms of Resistance to Absolute Power

Why should it be, turning once more to Latin America, that there one finds no Sambo, no social tradition, that is, in which slaves were defined by virtually complete consensus as children incapable of being trusted with the full privileges of freedom and adulthood? There, the system surely had its brutalities. The slaves arriving there from Africa had also undergone the capture, the sale, the Middle Passage. They too had been uprooted from a prior culture, from a life very different from the one in which they now found themselves. There, however, the system was not closed.

Here again the concentration camp, paradoxically enough, can be instructive. There were in the camps a very small minority of the survivors who had undergone an experience different in crucial ways from that of the others, an experience which protected them from the full impact of the closed system. These people, mainly by virtue of wretched little jobs in the camp administration which offered them a minute measure of privilege, were able to carry on "underground" activities. In a practical sense the actual operations of such "undergrounds" as were possible may seem to us unheroic and limited: stealing blankets; "organizing" a few bandages, a little medicine, from the camp hospital; black market arrangements with a guard for a bit of extra food and protection for oneself and one's comrades; the circulation of news; and other such apparently trifling activities. But for the psychological balance of those involved, such activities were vital; they made possible a fundamentally different adjustment to the camp. To a prisoner so engaged, there were others who mattered, who gave real point to his existence—the SS was no longer the *only* one. Conversely, the role of the child was not the only one he played. He could take initiative; he could give as well as receive protection; he did things which had meaning in adult terms. He had, in short, alternative roles; this was a fact which made such a prisoner's transition from

his old life to that of the camp less agonizing and destructive;
those very prisoners, moreover, appear to have been the ones
who could, upon liberation, resume normal lives most easily. It
is, in fact, these people—not those of the ranks—who have
described the camps to us.[30]

It was just such a difference—indeed, a much greater one—
that separated the typical slave in Latin America from the typical
slave in the United States. Though he too had experienced the
Middle Passage, he was entering a society where alternatives
were significantly more diverse than those awaiting his kinsman
in North America. Concerned in some sense with his status were
distinct and at certain points competing institutions. This involved multiple and often competing "significant others." His
master was, of course, clearly the chief one—but not the only
one. There could, in fact, be a considerable number: the friar
who boarded his ship to examine his conscience, the confessor;
the priest who made the rounds and who might report irregularities in treatment to the *procurador;* the zealous Jesuit quick to
resent a master's intrusion upon such sacred matters as marriage
and worship (a resentment of no small consequence to the
master); the local magistrate, with his eye on the king's official
protector of slaves, who would find himself in trouble were the
laws too widely evaded; the king's informer who received one-

---

[30] Virtually all the ex-prisoners whose writing I have made use of were
men and women who had certain privileges (as clerks, physicians, and the
like) in the camps. Many of the same persons were also active in the "underground" and could offer some measure of leadership and support for
others. That is to say, both the objectivity necessary for making useful observations and the latitude enabling one to exercise some leadership were
made possible by a certain degree of protection not available to the rank
and file.

I should add, however, that a notable exception was the case of Bruno
Bettelheim, who throughout the period of his detention had no privileged
position of any kind which could afford him what I am calling an "alternative role" to play. And yet I do not think that it would be stretching the
point too far to insist that he did in fact have such a role, one which was
literally self-created: that of the scientific observer. In him, the scientist's
objectivity, his feeling for clinical detail and sense of personal detachment,
amounted virtually to a passion. It would not be fair, however, to expect
such a degree of personal autonomy as this in other cases, except for a very
few. I am told, for instance, that the behavior of many members of this
"underground" toward their fellow prisoners was itself by no means above
moral reproach. The depths to which the system could corrupt a man, it
must be remembered, were profound.

third of the fines. For the slave the result was a certain latitude; the lines did not all converge on one man; the slave's personality, accordingly, did not have to focus on a single role. He was, true enough, primarily a slave. Yet he might in fact perform multiple roles. He could be a husband and a father (for the American slave these roles had virtually no meaning); open to him also were such activities as artisan, peddler, petty merchant, truck gardener (the law reserved to him the necessary time and a share of the proceeds, but such arrangements were against the law for Sambo); he could be a communicant in the church, a member of a religious fraternity[31] (roles guaranteed by the most powerful institution in Latin America—comparable privileges in the American South depended on a master's pleasure). These roles were all legitimized and protected *outside* the plantation; they offered a diversity of channels for the development of personality. Not only did the individual have multiple roles open to him as a slave, but the very nature of these roles made possible a certain range of aspirations should he some day become free. He could have a fantasy-life not limited to catfish and watermelons; it was within his conception to become a priest, an independent farmer, a successful merchant, a military officer.[32] The slave could actually—to an extent quite unthinkable in the United States—conceive of himself *as a rebel*. Bloody slave revolts, actual wars, took place in Latin America; nothing on this order occurred in the United States.[33]

[31] See Frank Tannenbaum, *Slave and Citizen*, (New York, 1946), 64–65.

[32] *Ibid.*, pp. 4ff., 56–57, 90–93; see also Sir Harry Johnston, *Negro in the New World*, (New York, 1910), 90.

[33] Compared with the countless uprisings of the Brazilian Negroes, the slave revolts in our own country appear rather desperate and futile. Only three emerge as worthy of any note, and their seriousness—even when described by a sympathetic historian like Herbert Aptheker—depends largely on the supposed plans of the rebels rather than on the things they actually did. The best organized of such "revolts," those of Vesey and Gabriel, were easily suppressed, while the most dramatic of them—the Nat Turner Rebellion—was characterized by little more than aimless butchery. The Brazilian revolts, on the other hand, were marked by imagination and a sense of direction, and they often involved large-scale military operations. One is impressed both by their scope and their variety. They range from the legendary Palmares Republic of the seventeenth century (a Negro state organized by escaped slaves and successfully defended for over fifty years), to the bloody revolts of the Moslem Negroes of Bahia which, between 1807 and

But even without a rebellion, society here had a network of customary arrangements, rooted in antiquity, which made possible at many points a smooth transition of status from slave to free and which provided much social space for the exfoliation of individual character.

To the typical slave on the ante-bellum plantation in the United States, society of course offered no such alternatives. But that is hardly to say that something of an "underground"—something rather more, indeed, than an underground—could not exist in Southern slave society. And there were those in it who hardly fitted the picture of "Sambo."

The American slave system, compared with that of Latin America, was closed and circumscribed, but, like all social systems, its arrangements were less perfect in practice than they appeared to be in theory. It was possible for significant numbers of slaves, in varying degrees, to escape the full impact of the system and its coercions upon personality. The house servant, the urban mechanic, the slave who arranged his own employment and paid his master a stipulated sum each week, were all figuratively members of the "underground." Even among those working on large plantations, the skilled craftsman or the responsible slave foreman had a measure of independence not shared by his simpler brethren. Even the single slave family owned by a small farmer had a status much closer to that of house servants than to that of a plantation labor gang. For all

---

1835, five times paralyzed a substantial portion of Brazil. Many such wars were launched from the *quilombos* (fortified villages built deep in the jungles by escaped slaves to defend themselves from recapture); there were also the popular rebellions in which the Negroes of an entire area would take part. One is immediately struck by the heroic stature of the Negro leaders: no allowances of any sort need be made for them; they are impressive from any point of view. Arthur Ramos has described a number of them, including Zambi, a fabulous figure of the Palmares Republic; Luiza Mahin, mother of the Negro poet Luiz Gama and "one of the most outstanding leaders of the 1835 insurrection"; and Manoel Francisco dos Anjos Fereira, whose followers in the *Balaiada* (a movement which drew its name from "Baliao," his own nickname) held the *entire province* of Maranhão for three years. Their brilliance, gallantry, and warlike accomplishments give to their histories an almost legendary quality. On the other hand, one could not begin to think of Nat Turner in such a connection. See Ramos, *The Negro in Brazil*, pp. 24–53; Herbert Aptheker, *American Negro Slave Revolts* (New York: Columbia University, 1943), *passim*.

such people there was a margin of space denied to the majority; the system's authority-structure claimed their bodies but not quite their souls.

Out of such groups an individual as complex and as highly developed as William Johnson, the Natchez barber, might emerge. Johnson's diary reveals a personality that one recognizes instantly as a type—but a type whose values came from a sector of society very different from that which formed Sambo. Johnson is the young man on the make, the ambitious free-enterpriser of American legend. He began life as a slave, was manumitted at the age of eleven, and rose from a poor apprentice barber to become one of the wealthiest and most influential Negroes in ante-bellum Mississippi. He was respected by white and black alike, and counted among his friends some of the leading public men of the state.[34]

It is of great interest to note that although the danger of slave revolts (like Communist conspiracies in our own day) was much overrated by touchy Southerners; the revolts that actually did occur were in no instance planned by plantation laborers but rather by Negroes whose qualities of leadership were developed well outside the full coercions of the plantation authority-system. Gabriel, who led the revolt of 1800, was a blacksmith who lived a few miles outside Richmond; Denmark Vesey, leading spirit of the 1822 plot at Charleston, was a freed Negro artisan who had been born in Africa and served several years aboard a slave-trading vessel; and Nat Turner, the Virginia slave who fomented the massacre of 1831, was a literate preacher of recognized intelligence. Of the plots that have been convincingly substantiated (whether they came to anything or not), the majority originated in urban centers.[35]

For a time during Reconstruction, a Negro elite of sorts did emerge in the South. Many of its members were Northern Negroes, but the Southern ex-slaves who also comprised it seem in general to have emerged from the categories just indicated. Vernon Wharton, writing of Mississippi, says:

[34] See William R. Hogan and Edwin A. Davis (eds.), *William Johnson's Natchez: The Ante-Bellum Diary of a Free Negro* (Baton Rouge: Louisiana State University Press, 1951), esp. pp. 1–64.

[35] Herbert Aptheker, *American Negro Slave Revolts* (New York, 1943), pp. 220, 268–69, 295–96, and *passim*.

A large portion of the minor Negro leaders were preachers, lawyers, or teachers from the free states or from Canada. Their education and their independent attitude gained for them immediate favor and leadership. Of the natives who became their rivals, the majority had been urban slaves, blacksmiths, carpenters, clerks, or waiters in hotels and boarding houses; a few of them had been favored body-servants of affluent whites.[36]

The William Johnsons and Denmark Veseys have been accorded, though belatedly, their due honor. They are, indeed, all too easily identified, thanks to the system that enabled them as individuals to be so conspicuous and so exceptional and, as members of a group, so few.

Leon F. Litwack

By 1860 free Negroes in the United States numbered 488,000; slaves numbered nearly 4,000,000. Of the free Negro population a little more than one out of three was a mulatto. Since 1790 much of the increase in the free Negro population was due to white masters freeing their mulatto children. As time went on, however, states passed laws making it much more difficult to manumit slaves, and each decade after 1810 saw a smaller percentage increase in the number of free Negroes. Slaves in the United States, unlike those in Latin America, had less chance of being freed by their masters or of working their way out of slavery. One of the most publicized methods of gaining freedom was by escape. Although we have an extensive literature about the underground railroad, the effect of this means of emancipation has been vastly overestimated. In the most recent study of the subject, Larry Gara found that it had more symbolic than actual value. On the other hand, individuals did manage to escape, the most famous being Frederick Douglass, whose account of life as a slave, *The Life and Times of Frederick Douglass,* is still the most perceptive critique of the system. The free Negro population by 1860 was about evenly divided between North and South, with 25,000 living in

[36] Vernon L. Wharton, *The Negro in Mississippi, 1865–1890* (Chapel Hill: University of North Carolina Press, 1942), p. 164.

Baltimore, 22,000 in Philadelphia, 12,500 in New York, 10,600 in New Orleans, 3200 in Charleston, and 2000 in Boston. Throughout the United States, the free Negro faced numerous restrictions on his freedom, and in few areas did he have the same rights as white Americans. In the North he was allowed the suffrage in only six states (five being in New England), and he was discriminated against in court, public schools, public transportation, and other services. Frequently the free Negro had to contend with mob violence. In the South, the barriers were even greater as many states put restrictions on the physical movement of free Negroes.

What kind of life could Negroes develop under such conditions? In the urban areas the free Negroes had more opportunity to practice a trade, and a large percentage of Negroes worked as tradesmen or semi-skilled laborers. Some were able to establish shops, a few made their way into the ministry, teaching, and law. The most conspicuous characteristic of free Negro communities was the development of their own self-help organizations: churches, benevolent and fraternal societies, educational institutions, abolitionist groups, convention movements, and newspapers. The first Negro newspaper appeared in 1827, the first Negro history textbook in 1841, the first novel written by a Negro in 1853. Where the states did not provide for the education of Negro children, Negro groups set up their own schools, and on the eve of the Civil War, laid the foundation for two colleges (to become Lincoln of Pennsylvania and Wilberforce in Ohio). The record of free Negro activities can be found in Herbert Aptheker's valuable *A Documentary History of the Negro People in the United States.*

One area of free Negro life that has been overlooked until very recently has been his participation in the abolitionist movement. So much attention has been given to Garrison, Wendell Phillips, James G. Birney, Arthur Tappen, and others, that the importance of the Negro abolitionist has been underplayed. Not only did Negroes actively support and help finance white abolitionist enterprises, but they also formed their own abolitionist organizations, newspapers, and pressure groups. Negroes such as Frederick Douglass, James Forten, Jr., Martin Delany, Charles Remond, William C. Neil, William Wells Brown, and Henry H. Garnet took to the rostrum in their own behalf. These abolitionists were more militant than their white allies and they not only rejected schemes for resettlement and colonization, but also disregarded Garrison's faith in moral persuasion, pacificism, and utopian schemes. Possibly the greatest victory of the militant Negro abolitionists came when David Walker and Henry H. Garnet converted the most eloquent and persuasive Negro abolitionist, Frederick Douglass, to their activist position.

William and Jane Pease have recently given us a fresh survey of the abolitionist movement in *The Antislavery Argument* (1965), while Martin Duberman has edited *The Antislavery Vanguard* (1965), which presents a modern defense of the abolitionists and their tactics. The life of free Negroes in the North has been best described in Leon F. Litwack's *North of Slavery*.

Leon F. Litwack, whose essay follows, is Associate Professor of History at the University of California (Berkeley).

THE BLACK ABOLITIONISTS

SOURCE: Leon F. Litwack, "The Black Abolitionists," from *North of Slavery, the Negro in the Free States, 1790–1860* (Chicago: University of Chicago Press, 1961), 230–46.

The widely publicized activities of white antislavery workers and the commanding figures of William Lloyd Garrison, Wendell Phillips, and Theodore Weld have tended to obscure the important and active role of the Negro abolitionist. The antislavery movement was not solely a white man's movement. Through their own newspapers, conventions, tracts, orations, and legislative petitions, Negroes agitated for an end to southern bondage and northern repression. The white abolitionist encountered strong and often violent public opposition, but the Negro abolitionist risked even greater hostility, for his very presence on the antislavery platform challenged those popular notions which had stereotyped his people as passive, meek, and docile. As a common laborer, the Negro might be tolerated, even valued, for his services; as an antislavery agitator, he was frequently mobbed.

Negro abolitionism preceded by several years the appearance of Garrison and *The Liberator*. Encouraged by the post-Revolutionary emancipation movement, Negroes worked with sympathetic whites to remove the last traces of slavery in the North and to call for its abolition in the South. As early as 1797, four illegally manumitted North Carolina Negroes, who had fled to the North to escape re-enslavement, petitioned Congress to consider "our relief as a people." Three years later, a group of Philadelphia free Negroes appealed directly to Congress to revise the federal laws concerning the African trade and fugitive slaves and to adopt "such measures as shall in due course emancipate the whole of their brethren from their present situation."[1] In addition to legislative petitions, meetings commemorating the abolition of the African slave trade or the end of slavery in a particular state afforded opportunities for such prominent Negro leaders as Peter Williams, Nathaniel Paul, William Hamilton, and Joseph Sidney to voice their sentiments on public issues.[2] The organization of independent churches, Free African societies, Masonic lodges, and anticolonization meetings further intensified a growing race consciousness and helped to arouse the Negro community in several areas to a more vigorous defense of its civil rights.

Four years before the publication of the first issue of The Liberator, two Negro leaders, John Russwurm and Samuel E. Cornish, launched the first Negro newspaper—Freedom's Journal —in an effort to disseminate useful ideas and information and to attract public attention to the plight of those still in bondage. In the first issue, the editors announced that Negroes had to plead their own cause: "Too long have other spoken for us. Too long has the publick been deceived by misrepresentations."[3] During its two years of publication, Freedom's Journal featured articles on the evils of slavery and intemperance, the importance of

[1] Herbert Aptheker (ed.), A Documentary History of the Negro people in the United States (New York, 1951), pp. 39–41.

[2] For a convenient guide to the published addresses of these early Negro leaders, see Dorothy P. Porter, "Early American Negro Writings: A Bibliographical Study," Papers of the Bibliographical Society of America, XXXIX (1945), 192–268. Especially valuable for an early Negro's views on national affairs is Joseph Sidney, An Oration, Commemorative of the Abolition of the Slave Trade in the United States; Delivered before the Wilberforce Philanthropic Association, in the City of New York, on the second of January, 1809 (New York, 1809). Copy in Schomburg Collection, New York Public Library.

[3] Freedom's Journal, March 16, 1827.

education and the progress of Negro schools, literary and historical selections, moral lessons, information on the various Afro-American benevolent societies, and a discussion of colonization. Cornish subsequently withdrew from the partnership and established a short-lived newspaper, *The Rights of All*, and Russwurm abandoned his editorial duties to join the colonizationists.[4]

Negro antislavery agitation took on a more aggressive tone in 1829 as David Walker, a Boston clothing dealer and local agent for *Freedom's Journal*, contributed a powerful tract to abolitionist literature—*Walker's Appeal, in Four Articles*. Addressing his sentiments to the "coloured citizens" of the world, but particularly to those of the United States, Walker described American Negroes as "the most degraded, wretched, and abject set of beings that ever lived since the world began." Indeed, he asked, "Can our condition be any worse?—Can it be more mean and abject? If there are any changes, will they not be for the better, though they may appear for the worst at first? Can they get us any lower? Where can they get us? They are afraid to treat us worse, for they know well, the day they do it they are gone."

In Walker's estimation, four major factors accounted for this wretched state of affairs: slavery, ignorance, "the preachers of Jesus Christ," and the African colonization movement. Consequently, Negroes had to strive for economic and educational improvement and resist the encroachments of the colonizationists. ("America is as much our country, as it is yours.") The southern Negro, on the other hand, faced an even greater challenge, for he had to strike directly and perhaps violently for his freedom as a natural right. Once that thrust for liberty had been made, Walker advised, "make sure work—do not trifle, for they will not trifle with you—they want us for their slaves, and think nothing of murdering us in order to subject us to that wretched condition—therefore, if there is an *attempt* made by us, kill or be killed." To prevent the outbreak of racial war, Walker warned the white man, recognize the legal rights of Negroes. There can be no mistaking the alternative. "Remember, Americans, that we must and shall be free and enlightened as you are,

---

[4] For some bitter criticism of Russwurm after his conversion to colonization, see Carter G. Woodson (ed.), *Mind of the Negro*, pp. 160–63. As reflected in letters written during the crisis, 1800–1860 (Washington, D.C., 1926), pp. 160–63.

will you wait until we shall, under God, obtain our liberty by the crushing arm of power? Will it not be dreadful for you? I speak Americans for your good. We must and shall be free I say, in spite of you. . . . And wo, wo, will be to you if we have to obtain our freedom by fighting."[5]

Within a year after its publication, the apparent popularity— or notoriety—of Walker's pamphlet warranted a third edition. The often violent reaction to its contents and the mysterious death of the author in 1830 undoubtedly assisted its circulation.[6] Indeed, it had already caused some consternation in the North, and it understandably created outright alarm in portions of the South. Already beset by a growing fear of slave uprisings, the South could not afford to tolerate the potentially explosive appeal of a Boston clothing dealer. The governor of North Carolina denounced it as "an open appeal to their [the slaves'] natural love of liberty . . . and throughout expressing sentiments totally subversive of all subordination in our slaves"; the mayor of Savannah wrote to the mayor of Boston requesting that Walker be arrested and punished, and Richmond's mayor reported that several copies of *Walker's Appeal* had been found in the possession of local free Negroes; the governors of Georgia and North Carolina submitted the pamphlet to their state legislatures for appropriate action; and the Virginia legislature held secret sessions to consider proper measures to prevent the pamphlet's circulation. Finally, four southern states—Georgia, North Carolina, Mississippi, and Louisiana—seized upon the pamphlet to enact severe restrictions to cope with such "seditious" propaganda.[7]

The South was not alone in its critical reaction. Walker's medicine for the ills of American Negroes was too strong for many white abolitionists. "A more bold, daring, inflammatory publication, perhaps, never issued from the press of any coun-

[5] David Walker, *Walker's Appeal, in Four Articles; together with a Preamble, to the Coloured Citizens of the World, but in particular, and very expressly to those of the United States of America, written in Boston, State of Massachusetts, September 28, 1829* (3d ed.; Boston, 1830).
[6] See Vernon Loggins, *The Negro Author* (New York, 1931), p. 86; Woodson (ed.), *Mind of the Negro,* p. 222.
[7] Clement Eaton, "A Dangerous Pamphlet in the Old South," *Journal of Southern History,* II (1936), 323–34.

try," antislavery publisher Benjamin Lundy declared. "I can do
no less than set the broadest seal of condemnation on it."[8]
Lundy's disciple, William Lloyd Garrison, had just launched his
own career as an aggressive antislavery publicist and was more
equivocal in his reaction. The editor of *The Liberator* found it
difficult to reconcile his belief in nonresistance with his un-
concealed admiration of Walker's courage and forthrightness.
While deploring the circulation of this "most injudicious publication" and "its general spirit," Garrison admitted that it contained "many valuable truths and seasonable warnings."[9]

The appearance of *The Liberator* in 1831 and the formation of
the American Anti-Slavery Society two years later thus found
northern Negroes already engaged in a variety of abolitionist
activities. In addition to publishing a newspaper and several
antislavery tracts, Negroes had taken steps to co-ordinate their
actions through annual national conventions. On September 15,
1830, delegates gathered in Philadelphia's Bethel Church to
launch the first in a series of such conventions. Against a background of increasing repressive legislation in the North, the
delegates adopted an address to the free Negro population,
pointing out that their present "forlorn and deplorable situation"
demanded immediate action. Where Negroes were subjected to
constant harassment and denied even the right of residence, the
most recent and blatant case being Ohio, such action would have
to take the form of emigration to Canada. There, the convention
advised, Negroes could establish themselves "in a land where the
laws and prejudices of society will have no effect in retarding
their advancement to the summit of civil and religious improvement." Meanwhile, those Negroes who chose to remain in the
United States would have to utilize every legal means to improve
their political and economic position. Before adjourning, the
delegates called upon Negroes to establish auxiliary societies and
send delegates to the next annual convention.[10]

Convening annually up to 1835 and periodically thereafter, the
national Negro conventions regularly condemned the American

---

[8] *Genius of Universal Emancipation*, April, 1830; *The Liberator*, January
29, 1831.

[9] *The Liberator*, January 29, 1831.

[10] "The First Colored Convention," *Anglo-African Magazine*, I (October,
1859), 305–10; Aptheker (ed.), *Documentary History*, pp. 102–7.

Colonization Society, deprecated segregation and "oppressive, unjust and unconstitutional" legislation, stressed the importance of organization, education, temperance, and economy, and set aside the Fourth of July as a day of "humiliation, fasting and prayer" when Negroes would ask for divine intervention to break "the shackles of slavery."[11] Meanwhile, the formation of auxiliary state organizations, temperance groups, moral-reform societies, and educational associations created an unprecedented amount of unity and activity among northern Negroes, developed new leadership, and contributed mightily to the strength of the newly formed white antislavery societies.

While engaged in these independent activities, Negro abolitionists also hailed the appearance of a new militancy among their white supporters; they not only welcomed the publication of *The Liberator* but actually outnumbered white subscribers in the early years. "It is a remarkable fact," William Lloyd Garrison wrote in 1834, "that, of the whole number of subscribers to the *Liberator*, only about one-fourth are white. The paper, then, belongs emphatically to the people of color—it is their organ."[12] In addition to contributing articles and letters to the antislavery press, Negroes also attended and addressed abolitionist conventions and, notwithstanding some opposition, served as members of the executive committee and board of managers of both the American Anti-Slavery Society and its later rival, the American and Foreign Anti-Slavery Society.[13]

Negro abolitionists did not confine their activities to the United States. In the 1840's and 1850's, several of them toured the British Isles to promote antislavery sentiment and raise money for abolitionist enterprises. Englishmen crowded into meeting halls to see and hear leading American Negroes tell of the plight of their people and their own experiences as slaves or freemen. Frederick Douglass, for example, described his years of bondage in the South; William G. Allen told of his

[11] Selected proceedings of several of the national Negro conventions may be found in Aptheker (ed.), *Documentary History*, pp. 114–19, 133–37, 141–46, 154–57, 159, 226–33, and 341–57.

[12] Francis and Wendell P. Garrison, *William Lloyd Garrison, 1805–1879* (4 vols., Boston & New York, 1894), I, 432.

[13] Herbert Aptheker, "The Negro in the Abolitionist Movement," *Essays in the History of the American Negro* (New York, 1945), pp. 154–55; Foner (ed.), *Life and Writings of Frederick Douglass*, I, 33, 426.

narrow escape from an enraged northern mob after proposing to marry a white girl; William and Ellen Craft related their flight to freedom and their subsequent exile to avoid prosecution under the Fugitive Slave Act; and Henry Highland Garnet undoubtedly mentioned the mob that ejected him from a Connecticut boys' academy.[14] While arousing their foreign audiences with these tales of slavery and racial violence, Negroes also found much to amaze them. "Here the colored man feels himself among friends, and not among enemies," one Negro "exile" wrote from England, "among a people who, when they treat him well, do it not in the patronizing (and, of course insulting) spirit, even of hundreds of the American abolitionists, but in a spirit rightly appreciative of the doctrine of human equality."[15] For some of these Negro abolitionists, returning home must have been difficult. After extensive travels in England and Europe, for example, William Wells Brown came back to Philadelphia, only to find himself proscribed from the Chestnut Street omnibus on his first day home. "The omnibuses of Paris, Edinburgh, Glasgow, and Liverpool, had stopped to take me up," he recollected, "but what mattered that? My face was not white, my hair was not straight; and, therefore, I must be excluded from a seat in a third-rate American omnibus."[16]

Both Negro and white abolitionists suffered from internal dissension over fundamental questions of policy and ideology. While the white antislavery societies split over the issues of political action, nonresistance, women's rights, disunion, and the nature of the Constitution, Negroes argued the merits of moral suasion and separate conventions. By 1835, the American Moral Reform Society, dominated largely by Philadelphia Negroes, replaced the regular convention movement. Dedicated to "improving the condition of mankind," the new organization urged Negroes to abandon the use of the terms "colored" and "African," to refrain from holding separate colored conventions, to integrate as fully as possible into white society, to support the equality of

[14] Benjamin Quarles, "Ministers Without Portfolio," *Journal of Negro History*, XXXIX (1954), 27–42.
[15] *The Liberator*, July 22, 1853.
[16] William Wells Brown, *The American Fugitive in Europe* (Boston, 1855), pp. 312–14.

women, and to adopt the principles of peace, temperance, brotherly love, and nonresistance "under all circumstances." In adopting such a program, the moral reformers obviously allied themselves with the Garrisonians in the growing factional struggle within the antislavery movement.

The American Moral Reform Society found little support outside the Garrisonian strongholds of Philadelphia and Boston. Meanwhile, New York Negro leaders launched a new weekly newspaper, the *Colored American,* which expressed dismay over the growing split in abolitionist ranks and the activities of the moral reformers. Editor Samuel Cornish noted that the delegates to a recent moral-reform convention had impressed him as "vague, wild, indefinite and confused in their views." Only drastic reorganization and the adoption of a more vigorous program of action could possibly salvage the society. As for their efforts to substitute the term "oppressed Americans" for "colored people," Cornish called this sheer nonsense. "Oppressed Americans! *who are they?*" he asked. "Nonsense brethren!! You are COLORED AMERICANS. The indians are RED AMERICANS, and the white people are WHITE AMERICANS and *you are good as they, and they are no better than you.*"

While scolding the moral reformers, the *Colored American* also engaged in a controversy with the pro-Garrison *National Anti-Slavery Standard* over the advisability of colored conventions. "We oppose all exclusive action on the part of the colored people," the *Standard* announced in June, 1840, "except where the clearest necessity demands it." As long as Negroes contented themselves with separate churches, schools, and conventions, public sentiment would remain unaltered. Instead, Negroes should join with their white friends to demand equal rights as men, not as colored persons, and thus confirm the abolitionists' contention that racial distinctions had no place in American society. The moral reformers enthusiastically indorsed the position of the *Standard.* Other Negro leaders, however, immediately condemned it and upheld the need for independent action. The abolitionists had done much for the Negro, Samuel R. Ward wrote to the editor of the *Standard,* but too many of them "best love the colored man at a distance" and refuse to admit or eradicate their own prejudices. In the meantime, Negroes had to meet and act for themselves.

Although the American Moral Reform Society had a short life, the split in white abolitionist ranks continued to undermine Negro unity. By 1840, Garrisonians shared the field of agitation with the American and Foreign Anti-Slavery Society and the Liberty party. New England and Philadelphia Negroes generally supported the American Anti-Slavery Society and condemned the critics of Garrison as unworthy of confidence or support. New York Negroes, on the other hand, not only dissociated themselves from the moral reformers but generally indorsed direct political action and contributed to the leadership and campaigns of the Liberty party. At one point, the *Colored American* attempted to restore some semblance of sanity and unity to abolitionists by urging them to avoid peripheral issues and petty bickering and get back to opposing slavery. "Why . . . make governments or anti-governments—resistance or non-resistance—women's rights or men's rights—Sabbaths or anti-Sabbaths, a bone of contention?" the Negro newspaper asked. "None of these should have any thing to do with our Anti-Slavery efforts. *They are neither parts nor parcels of that great and holy cause,* nor should they be intruded into its measures." Rather than promote abolitionist harmony, however, such sentiments, coupled with the editors' indorsement of political action and their refusal to censure Garrison's critics, induced some severe attacks and threats to cut off financial support from the paper. Defending their right to differ with Garrison on any issue and to adopt an independent editorial policy, the editors of the *Colored American* warned Negroes that as long as they permitted white abolitionists to act and think for them, "so long they will outwardly treat us as men, while in their hearts they still hold us as slaves."[17]

In a desperate effort to retain their hold on the antislavery movement, Garrison and his associates made every effort to secure Negro support. In Boston and New Bedford, Negro meetings acclaimed Garrison as a "friend and benefactor" and in-

[17] *Colored American,* October 7, 14, 1837, May 11, August 17, October 5, 19, November 2, 1839.

dorsed his antislavery position.[18] Already abandoned by many of his white followers, Garrison expressed gratification over such reactions. The opposition knew, he wrote, "that, so long as I retain the confidence of my colored friends, all of their machinations against me will prove abortive."[19] Had Garrison known that his most important Negro ally, Frederick Douglass, was about to desert him, he would have had much less cause for optimism.

As late as September 4, 1849, Douglass had insisted that he was a loyal Garrisonian abolitionist, and there was little reason to doubt him. According to the tenets of that faith, he had excoriated the Constitution as "a most foul and bloody conspiracy" against the rights of three million slaves, had supported disunion as the most effective means to remove federal protection from the "peculiar institution," had belittled political action as futile and necessarily compromising, and had advocated moral persuasion rather than violence in attacking slavery.[20] Nevertheless, signs of revolt became increasingly apparent. After founding the *North Star* in 1847 against the advice of his Boston friends and moving from New England to Rochester, Douglass carefully re-evaluated his position and listened to the arguments of various New York abolitionists who had already broken with Garrison. Before long, the Negro leader reached the conclusion that disunion would only place the slaves at the complete mercy of the South, that political action constituted "a legitimate and powerful means for abolishing slavery," that southern bondage would probably have to expire in violence, and that the Constitution made no guarantees to slavery but in fact implied its eventual extinction.[21] In May, 1851, Douglass utilized the annual convention of the American Anti-Slavery Society to proclaim his heresy publicly. "There is roguery somewhere," Garrison re-

[18] *The Liberator*, June 7, 21, 1839. See also *Eighth Annual Report of the Board of Managers of the Massachusetts Anti-Slavery Society* (Boston, 1840), pp. 36–37; *The Liberator*, October 6, 1837, April 3, 1840; Dwight L. Dumond (ed.), *Letters of James Gillepsie Birney, 1831–1857* (2 vols.; New York, 1938), I, 575–79.

[19] William Lloyd Garrison to Elizabeth Pease, September 1, 1840, Garrison Papers.

[20] Foner (ed.), *Life and Writings of Frederick Douglass*, II, 49–52.

[21] Douglass, *Life and Times*, pp. 322–24; Foner (ed.), *Life and Writings of Frederick Douglass*, II, 52–53, 149–50, 152–53, 155–57.

putedly declared as he moved to strike the *North Star* from the list of approved abolitionist publications.[22] Douglass had gone over to the enemy.

Although he voiced his new position on the lecture platform and in the *North Star*, Douglass hoped to avert a complete break with Garrison. "I stand in relation to him something like that of a child to a parent," he wrote to Charles Sumner.[23] Nevertheless, Garrisonian anxiety and alarm soon changed to vigorous denunciation and even personal defamation. *The Liberator* now placed Douglass' editorials in the section usually reserved for proslavery sentiments, and it charged that the Negro leader had betrayed his former friends for the sake of financial gain, that he possessed ambitions to become the spokesman of the colored race, and that he had lost much of his moral fervor and influence.[24] When Douglass reduced the size of his newspaper, one Garrisonian gleefully wrote to an English friend that the Negro editor "has the confidence of very few, the respect . . . of none. Do what he may, we shall take no notice of him, and I think his career—on professedly anti-slavery grounds —will soon come to an end." Although Garrison generally allowed his followers to deal editorially with the Negro upstart, he confided to friends that he regarded Douglass as a malignant enemy, "thoroughly base and selfish," "destitute of every principle of honor, ungrateful to the last degree, and malevolent in spirit," and unworthy of "respect, confidence, or countenance." Such was the thoroughness of the Garrison indictment.[25]

Replying to his critics with equal bitterness, Douglass called them "vigilant enemies" and labeled their Negro followers as "practical enemies of the colored people" and contemptible tools. The Garrisonians had first attempted to silence his newspaper, he charged, and now they sought to expel him from the anti-slavery fold as a dangerous heretic. "They talk down there [Boston] just as if the Anti-Slavery Cause belonged to them—

---

[22] Foner (ed.), *Life and Writings of Frederick Douglass*, II, 53–54, 155–56.

[23] *Ibid.*, II, 210–11.

[24] *The Liberator*, September 16, 23, 30, December 16, 30, 1853.

[25] Samuel May, Jr., to Richard Davis Webb, February 8, 1857, May Papers; William Lloyd Garrison to Samuel J. May, September 5, 1857, September 28, 1860, Garrison Papers.

and as if all Anti-Slavery ideas originated with them and that no man has a right to 'peep or mutter' on the subject, who does not hold letters patent from them."[26] Douglass also sought to clarify his differences with Garrison, but these appeared to be lost in the bitter editorial war. Before long, Negroes in various parts of the country were meeting to discuss the conflict and to choose sides. Chicago Negroes condemned Garrison's "vile crusade" against "the voice of the colored people"; a Rhode Island convention hailed Douglass as "our acknowledged leader"; and an Ohio gathering decisively defeated a proposal calling on Negroes to abstain from voting in those areas where they enjoyed the franchise. Meanwhile, Garrisonian Negro leaders reiterated the charges of *The Liberator* and claimed to speak for "all the true colored men in the country."[27]

Efforts to reconcile the two antislavery leaders met with no success—only time could heal the deep wounds left by this useless and wasteful struggle. To many Negro and white abolitionists, the entire affair presented a rather sordid and dreary spectacle. "Where is this work of excommunication to end?" Harriet Beecher Stowe wrote Garrison. "Is there but one true anti-slavery church and all others infidels?—Who shall declare which it is."[28] While the dispute helped to reduce the effectiveness of the antislavery movement, it also clearly demonstrated some of the weaknesses in Garrison's ideological and tactical position. Nonresistance, the rejection of political action, disunion, and a proslavery interpretation of the Constitution did not strike many abolitionists in the 1840's and 1850's as being either suitable or realistic weapons with which to abolish southern bondage or northern proscription. Indeed, the final triumph of Garrisonian objectives resulted almost entirely from the employment of strictly non-Garrisonian methods—political agitation and armed force.

Internal dissension hampered but did not stifle the independent activities of Negro abolitionists. Despite the Garrisonian

[26] *Frederick Douglass' Paper*, December 9, 1853; Foner (ed.), *Life and Writings of Frederick Douglass*, II, 270.
[27] Foner (ed.), *Life and Writings of Frederick Douglass*, II, 61–62; *Minutes of the State Convention of the Colored Citizens of Ohio* (Columbus, 1851), pp. 11–12.
[28] Foner (ed.), *Life and Writings of Frederick Douglass*, II, 64.

antipathy to "complexional conventions," local and state organizations continued to meet in the 1840's, and several national conventions revived interstate co-operation. On August 15, 1843, Negroes from various states met in Buffalo to consider "their moral and political condition as American citizens." After several heated debates—which partly reflected the growing split in abolitionist ranks—the convention adopted a series of resolutions which denounced the American Colonization Society and the proslavery churches, indorsed the Liberty party, stressed the value of temperance, education, the mechanical arts, and agriculture, and attributed the plight of free Negroes—North and South—to the evils of slavery.[29]

Henry Highland Garnet, a New York Negro leader, hoped to secure from the Buffalo delegates a more aggressive stand against slavery. Indicting the cruelties of southern bondage and praising as martyrs those Negroes who had led revolts for freedom, Garnet delivered a powerful plea to the slave population in tones reminiscent of David Walker's *Appeal.* "Brethren arise, arise!" he declared. "Strike for your lives and liberties. Now is the day and the hour. Let every slave throughout the land do this, and the days of slavery are numbered. You cannot be more oppressed than you have been—you cannot suffer greater cruelties than you have already. *Rather die freemen than live to be slaves.* Remember that you are FOUR MILLIONS! . . . Let your motto be resistance! resistance! RESISTANCE!" Although the Garrisonians had suffered a defeat on the issue of political action, they managed to steer the convention away from such a commitment to physical violence in overthrowing slavery. By a vote of nineteen to eighteen, the delegates refused to indorse Garnet's address. Instead, the convention affirmed its faith in the ultimate righteousness of human government and the abolition of slavery through its instrumentality.[30] Relieved at this outcome, one Garrisonian intimated that Garnet, who had also been one of the first Negroes to

[29] *National Colored Convention, Buffalo, 1843,* pp. 11, 14–16, 19–22, 25, 27, 31–36.

[30] Carter G. Woodson (ed.), *Negro Orators and Their Orations,* (Washington, D.C., 1925), pp. 150–57; William M. Brewer, "Henry Highland Garnet," *Journal of Negro History,* XIII (1928), p. 46; *National Colored Convention, Buffalo, 1843,* p. 16.

indorse the Liberty party, had fallen under the influence of bad advisers. "If it has come to this," Garnet replied, "that I must think as you do, because you are an abolitionist, or be exterminated by your thunder, then I do not hesitate to say that your abolitionism is abject slavery."[31]

Although the Buffalo delegates refused to indorse Garnet's address, its contents and the closeness of the convention vote indicated the emergence of a new militancy among Negro abolitionists. Six years later, Garnet's address and Walker's appeal appeared together in a published pamphlet—reportedly at the expense of an obscure New York farmer, John Brown.[32] An Ohio Negro convention immediately ordered five hundred copies to be "gratuitously" circulated.[33] That same year, a New York Negro editor reminded the governor and legislature of Louisiana that their recent expressions of sympathy for Hungarian rebels might be equally applicable to their own bondsmen. "Strike for your freedom now, at the suggestion of your enslavers," the editor wrote. "Make up your minds to die, rather than bequeath a state of slavery to your posterity."[34]

By the end of the 1840's, the appeals of Garnet and Walker— once deemed too radical—received growing support in Negro conventions, newspapers, and antislavery tracts. Even Frederick Douglass, who had bitterly opposed Garnet's address, abandoned his previous conviction that moral persuasion and nonresistance alone could abolish slavery. While still a loyal Garrisonian, he created a "marked sensation" in 1849 when he told a Faneuil Hall audience that he would "welcome the intelligence tomorrow, should it come, that the slaves had risen in the South, and that the sable arms which had been engaged in beautifying and adorning the South were engaged in spreading death and devastation there." Three years later, Douglass told the national Free Soil party convention that the slaveholders had forfeited their right to live. The potential horrors of a slave insurrection should no longer be allowed to obstruct the path to freedom.

[31] *The Liberator*, December 3, 1843.
[32] Loggins, *The Negro Author*, p. 192; Woodson (ed.), *Negro Orators and Their Orations*, p. 150.
[33] *Ohio Colored Convention of 1849*, p. 18.
[34] Aptheker (ed.), *Documentary History*, pp. 290–91.

"The slaveholder has been tried and sentenced," he declared in 1857. "He is training his own executioners." The following year, John Brown visited the Douglass home and remained there for several weeks, devoting most of his time to writing financial appeals for a yet unrevealed plan.[35]

[35] *North Star*, June 15, 1849; *Frederick Douglass' Paper*, August 20, 1852; Chambers, *American Slavery and Colour*, p. 174 n.; Foner (ed.), *Life and Writings of Frederick Douglass*, II, 88.

V. THE STRUGGLE FOR FREEDOM

Anoder ting is, suppose you had kept your freedom without enlisting in dis army; your chillen might have grown up free and been well cultuvated so as to be equal to any business, but it would have been flung in dere faces—"Your fader never fought for he own freedom."

PRIVATE THOMAS LONG, 1st South Carolina
Regiment of Volunteers

I never believed in niggers before, but by Jasus, they are hell for fighting.

UNION OFFICER, 3rd Wisconsin Cavalry

Arthur M. Schlesinger, Jr.

The leading figures in twentieth century Civil War historiography, Charles Beard, James G. Randall, Avery Craven, Allan Nevins, have dominated historical thinking with two theses which in their own separate ways, managed to eliminate the Negro and the issue of slavery from its central place as the cause of the war.

Beard, for his part, stated that "the institution of slavery as a question of ethics was not the fundamental issue in the years preceding the bombardment of Fort Sumter." The Civil War was an irrepressible conflict "in which the capitalists, laborers, and farmers of the North and West drove from power in the national government the planting aristocracy of the South."

Randall, Craven, and Nevins (up to a point), on the other hand, argued that the war could have been avoided if the fanatics on both sides, particularly the abolitionists, had not inflamed public opinion over the issue of slavery and its defense, and if political leadership on both sides had been less blundering. Randall denied that "fundamental motives produce war," while Professor Craven, being more explicit, wrote that slavery "played a rather minor part in the life of the South and of the Negro." The war in their view was, to use the title of one of Craven's books, *The Repressible Conflict*.

Both groups of historians were very much influenced in their interpretation of the causes of the Civil War by their own post-Civil War experiences. Beard was influenced by the Populist movement of his youth and the quasi-Marxist conflict between Midwestern agrarianism and Eastern capitalism. Randall and Craven were part of a post-World War I generation disillusioned by the effectiveness of war as a means of solving basic problems. As for the question of slavery and the Negro, Beard argued that slavery was incidental to the economic conflict between Northern bourgeoisie and free farmers and the Southern planters; Randall and Craven said that slavery would have passed away in time without war.

But in the aftermath of the New Deal and World War II a younger generation of historians learned that there are times when a stand should be taken against injustice. They were less ready to reconcile the unpleasantness found in American history with the harmonious picture demanded by American ideals. Their concern with those groups that had been left out of the American pantheon led them to write about the working classes, Negroes, immigrants, midwestern farmers, poor whites. These motifs can be seen in the work of Arthur M. Schlesinger, Jr., Richard Hofstadter, John Hope Franklin, C. Vann Woodward, Oscar Handlin, and Kenneth M. Stampp. For many historians of the postwar generation, history was not filled with glory but with irony and tragedy.

Arthur M. Schlesinger, Jr., writing in the *Partisan Review* in 1949, spoke for this generation when he attacked the "revisionist" ideas of Professors Randall and Craven. Historians could no longer hide from the unpleasant realities of life, hoping that they would disappear. One of these unpleasant realities was slavery, and Schlesinger saw this as the crux of the conflict between North and South. "It was the moral issue of slavery, for example, that gave the struggles over slavery in the territories or over the enforcement of the fugitive slave laws their significance." To argue, as did Randall, Craven, and their followers, that the issue of slavery was artificial, that the abolitionists were to be faulted for their concern over slavery, and that politicians should have been able to skirt great moral problems, like the "revisionist" hero, Senator Stephen A. Douglas, was totally unreal. "There are certain essential issues," Schlesinger argued, "on which it is necessary for the historian to have a position if he is to understand the great conflicts of history." We could not pretend that these moral issues did not exist. For the "revisionists," who decried the Civil War, the central problem, which they did not answer, was how slavery could have been abolished without war. Schlesinger's argument was to be prophetic, for although written in 1949, it sounded much like the credo of the civil rights advocates a decade hence. (For American historiography Schlesinger helped restore perspective to the question of slavery, and the place of the Negro in American history.)

Arthur M. Schlesinger, Jr., is Professor of History at the City University of New York. Among his many books are *The Age of Jackson;* the series, *The Age of Roosevelt;* and *A Thousand Days,* a study of the Kennedy administration.

THE CAUSES OF THE CIVIL WAR: A NOTE ON HISTORICAL SENTIMENTALISM

SOURCE: Arthur M. Schlesinger, Jr., "The Causes of the Civil War: A Note on Historical Sentimentalism," *Partisan Review,* XVI (October, 1949), pp. 969–81.

The Civil War was our great national trauma. A savage fraternal conflict, it released deep sentiments of guilt and remorse—sentiments which have reverberated through our history and our literature ever since. Literature in the end came to terms with these sentiments by yielding to the South in fantasy the victory it had been denied in fact; this tendency culminated on the popular level in *Gone with the Wind* and on the highbrow level in the Nashville cult of agrarianism. But history, a less malleable medium, was constricted by the intractable fact that the war had taken place, and by the related assumption that it was, in William H. Seward's phrase, an "irrepressible conflict," and hence a justified one.

As short a time ago as 1937, for example, even Professor James G. Randall could describe himself as "unprepared to go to the point of denying that the great American tragedy could have been avoided." Yet in a few years the writing of history would succumb to the psychological imperatives which had produced *I'll Take My Stand* and *Gone with the Wind;* and Professor Randall would emerge as the leader of a triumphant new school of self-styled "revisionists." The publication of two vigorous books by Professor Avery Craven—*The Repressible Conflict* (1939) and *The Coming of the Civil War* (1942)—and the appearance of Professor Randall's own notable volumes on Lincoln—*Lincoln the President: Springfield to Gettysburg* (1945), *Lincoln and the South* (1946), and *Lincoln the Liberal Statesman* (1947)—brought about a profound reversal of the professional historian's attitude toward the Civil War. Scholars now denied the traditional assumption of the inevitability of the war and boldly advanced the thesis that a "blundering generation" had transformed a "repressible conflict" into a "needless war."

The swift triumph of revisionism came about with very little resistance or even expressed reservations on the part of the profession. Indeed, the only adequate evaluation of the revisionist thesis that I know was made, not by an academic historian at all, but by that illustrious semi-pro, Mr. Bernard DeVoto; and Mr. DeVoto's two brilliant articles in *Harper's* in 1945 unfortunately had little influence within the guild. By 1947 Professor Allan Nevins, summing up the most recent scholarship in *Ordeal of the Union,* his able general history of the 1850's, could define the basic problem of the period in terms which indicated a measured but entire acceptance of revisionism. "The primary task of statesmanship in this era," Nevins wrote, "was to furnish a workable adjustment between the two sections, while offering strong inducements to the southern people to regard their labor system not as static but evolutionary, and equal persuasions to the northern people to assume a helpful rather than scolding attitude."

This new interpretation surely deserves at least as meticulous an examination as Professor Randall is prepared to give, for example, to such a question as whether or not Lincoln was playing fives when he received the news of his nomination in

1860. The following notes are presented in the interests of stimulating such an examination.

The revisionist case, as expounded by Professors Randall and Craven, has three main premises.

First: that the Civil War was caused by the irresponsible emotionalization of politics far out of proportion to the real problems involved. The war, as Randall put it, was certainly not caused by cultural variations nor by economic rivalries nor by sectional differences; these all existed, but it was "stupid," as he declared, to think that they required war as a solution. "One of the most colossal of misconceptions" was the "theory" that "fundamental motives produce war. The glaring and obvious fact is the artificiality of war-making agitation." After all, Randall pointed out, agrarian and industrial interests had been in conflict under Coolidge and Hoover; yet no war resulted. "In Illinois," he added, "major controversies (not mere transient differences) between downstate and metropolis have stopped short of war."

Nor was slavery the cause. The issues arising over slavery were in Randall's judgment "highly artificial, almost fabricated. . . . They produced quarrels out of things that would have settled themselves were it not for political agitation." Slavery, Craven observed, was in any case a much overrated problem. It is "perfectly clear," he wrote, "that slavery played a rather minor part in the life of the South and of the Negro."

What then was the cause of war? "If one word or phrase were selected to account for the war," wrote Randall, ". . . it would have to be such a word as fanaticism (on both sides), misunderstanding, misrepresentation, or perhaps politics." Phrases like "whipped-up crisis" and "psychopathic case" adorned Randall's explanation. Craven similarly described the growing sense of sectional differences as "an artificial creation of inflamed minds." The "molders of public opinion steadily created the fiction of two distinct peoples." As a result, "distortion led a people into bloody war."

If uncontrolled emotionalism and fanaticism caused the war, how did they get out of hand? Who whipped up the "whipped-up crisis"?

Thus the second revisionist thesis: that sectional friction was permitted to develop into needless war by the inexcusable failure of political leadership in the '50's. "It is difficult to achieve a full realization of how Lincoln's generation stumbled into a ghastly war," wrote Randall. ". . . If one questions the term 'blundering generation,' let him inquire how many measures of the time he would wish copied or repeated if the period were to be approached with a clean slate and to be lived again."

It was the politicians, charged Craven, who systematically sacrificed peace to their pursuit of power. Calhoun and Adams, "seeking political advantage," mixed up slavery and expansion; Wilmot introduced his "trouble-making Proviso as part of the political game"; the repeal clause in the Kansas-Nebraska Act was "the afterthought of a mere handful of politicians"; Chase's "Appeal to the Independent Democrats" was "false in its assertions and unfair in its purposes, but it was politically effective"; the "damaging" section in the Dred Scott decision was forced "by the political ambitions of dissenting judges." "These uncalled-for moves and this irresponsible leadership," concluded Craven, blew up a "crackpot" crusade into a national conflict.

It is hard to tell which was under attack here—the performance of a particular generation or democratic politics in general. But, if the indictment "blundering generation" meant no more than a general complaint that democratic politics placed a premium on emotionalism, then the Civil War would have been no more nor less "needless" than any event in our blundering history. The phrase "blundering generation" must consequently imply that the generation in power in the '50's was *below* the human or historical or democratic average in its blundering.

Hence the third revisionist thesis: that the slavery problem could have been solved without war. For, even if slavery were as unimportant as the revisionists have insisted, they would presumably admit that it constituted the real sticking-point in the relation between the sections. They must show therefore that there were policies with which a nonblundering generation could have resolved the slavery crisis and averted war; and that these policies were so obvious that the failure to adopt them indicated blundering and stupidity of a peculiarly irresponsible nature. If no such policies could be produced even by hindsight, then it would seem excessive to condemn the politicians of the '50's for failing to discover them at the time.

The revisionists have shown only a most vague and sporadic awareness of this problem. "Any kind of sane policy in Washington in 1860 might have saved the day for nationalism," remarked Craven; but he did not vouchsafe the details of these sane policies; we would be satisfied to know about one.[1] Similarly Randall declared that there were few policies of the '50's he would wish repeated if the period were to be lived over again; but he was not communicative about the policies he would wish pursued. Nevins likewise blamed the war on the "collapse of American statesmanship," but restrained himself from suggesting how a noncollapsible statesmanship would have solved the hard problems of the '50's.

In view of this reticence on a point so crucial to the revisionist argument, it is necessary to reconstruct the possibilities that might lie in the back of revisionism. Clearly there could be only two "solutions" to the slavery problem: the preservation of slavery or its abolition.

Presumably the revisionists would not regard the preservation of slavery as a possible solution. Craven, it is true, has argued that "most of the incentives to honest and sustained effort, to a contented, well-rounded life, might be found under slavery. . . . What owning and being owned added to the normal relationship of employer and employee is very hard to say." In describing incidents in which slaves beat up masters, he has even noted that "happenings and reactions like these were the rule [sic], not the exception." But Craven would doubtless admit that, however jolly this system might have been, its perpetuation would have been, to say the least, impracticable.

If, then, revisionism has rested on the assumption that the non-violent abolition of slavery was possible, such abolition could conceivably have come about through internal reform in the South; through economic exhaustion of the slavery system in the South; or through some government project for gradual and compensated emancipation. Let us examine these possibilities.

1. *The internal reform argument.* The South, the revisionists have suggested, might have ended the slavery system if left to its

[1] It is fair to say that Professor Craven seems in recent years to have modified his earlier extreme position; see his article "The Civil War and the Democratic Process," *Abraham Lincoln Quarterly*, June 1947.

own devices; only the abolitionists spoiled everything by letting loose a hysteria which caused the southern ranks to close in self-defense.

This revisionist argument would have been more convincing if the decades of alleged antislavery feeling in the South had produced any concrete results. As one judicious southern historian, Professor Charles S. Sydnor, recently put it, "Although the abolition movement was followed by a decline of antislavery sentiment in the South, it must be remembered that in all the long years before that movement began no part of the South had made substantial progress toward ending slavery. . . . Southern liberalism had not ended slavery in any state."

In any case, it is difficult for historians seriously to suppose that northerners could have denied themselves feelings of disapproval over slavery. To say that there "should" have been no abolitionists in America before the Civil War is about as sensible as to say that there "should" have been no anti-Nazis in the 1930's or that there "should" be no anti-Communists today. People who indulge in criticism of remote evils may not be so pure of heart as they imagine; but that fact does not affect their inevitability as part of the historic situation.

Any theory, in short, which expects people to repress such spontaneous aversions is profoundly unhistorical. If revisionism has based itself on the conviction that things would have been different if only there had been no abolitionists, it has forgotten that abolitionism was as definite and irrevocable a factor in the historic situation as was slavery itself. And, just as abolitionism was inevitable, so too was the southern reaction against it—a reaction which, as Professor Clement Eaton has ably shown, steadily drove the free discussion of slavery out of the South. The extinction of free discussion meant, of course, the absolute extinction of any hope of abolition through internal reform.

2. *The economic exhaustion argument.* Slavery, it has been pointed out, was on the skids economically. It was overcapitalized and inefficient; it immobilized both capital and labor; its one-crop system was draining the soil of fertility; it stood in the way of industrialization. As the South came to realize these facts, a revisionist might argue, it would have moved to abolish

slavery for its own economic good. As Craven put it, slavery "may have been almost ready to break down of its own weight."[2] This argument assumed, of course, that southerners would have recognized the causes of their economic predicament and taken the appropriate measures. Yet such an assumption would be plainly contrary to history and to experience. From the beginning the South has always blamed its economic shortcomings, not on its own economic ruling class and its own inefficient use of resources, but on northern exploitation. Hard times in the 1850's produced in the South, not a reconsideration of the slavery system, but blasts against the North for the high prices of manufactured goods. The overcapitalization of slavery led not to criticisms of the system but to increasingly insistent demands for the reopening of the slave trade. Advanced southern writers like George Fitzhugh and James D. B. DeBow were even arguing that slavery was adapted to industrialism. When Hinton R. Helper did advance before the Civil War an early version of Craven's argument, asserting that emancipation was necessary to save the southern economy, the South burned his book. Nothing in the historical record suggests that the southern ruling class was preparing to deviate from its traditional pattern of self-exculpation long enough to take such a drastic step as the abolition of slavery.

3. *Compensated emancipation.* Abraham Lincoln made repeated proposals of compensated emancipation. In his annual message to Congress of December 1, 1862, he set forth a detailed plan by which states, on an agreement to abolish slavery by 1900, would receive government bonds in proportion to the number of slaves emancipated. Yet, even though Lincoln's proposals represented a solution of the problem conceivably gratifying to the slave-holder's purse as well as to his pride, they got nowhere. Two-thirds of the border representatives rejected the scheme, even when personally presented to them by Lincoln himself. And, of course, only the pressure of war brought compensated emancipation its limited hearing of 1862.

Still, granted these difficulties, does it not remain true that

[2] This, at least, was the belief in 1949. Subsequent investigations by Alfred Conrad and John Meyer challenge the assumption that slavery was becoming uneconomic. [footnote added by author, 1962]

other countries abolished slavery without internal convulsion? If emotionalism had not aggravated the situation beyond hope, Craven has written, then slavery "might have been faced as a national question and dealt with as successfully as the South American countries dealt with the same problem." If Brazil could free its slaves and Russia its serfs in the middle of the 19th century without civil war, why could not the United States have done as well?

The analogies are appealing but not, I think, really persuasive. There are essential differences between the slavery question in the United States and the problems in Brazil or in Russia. In the first place, Brazil and Russia were able to face servitude "as a national question" because it was, in fact, a national question. Neither country had the American problem of the identification of compact sectional interests with the survival of the slavery system. In the second place, there was no race problem at all in Russia, and, though there was a race problem in Brazil, the more civilized folkways of that country relieved racial differences of the extreme tension which they breed in the South of the United States. In the third place, neither in Russia nor in Brazil did the abolition of servitude involve constitutional issues; and the existence of these issues played a great part in determining the form of the American struggle.

It is hard to draw much comfort, therefore, from the fact that other nations abolished servitude peaceably. The problem in America was peculiarly recalcitrant. The schemes for gradual emancipation got nowhere. Neither internal reform nor economic exhaustion contained much promise for a peaceful solution. The hard fact, indeed, is that the revisionists have not tried seriously to describe the policies by which the slavery problem could have been peacefully resolved. They have resorted instead to broad affirmations of faith: if only the conflict could have been staved off long enough, then somehow, somewhere, we could have worked something out. It is legitimate, I think, to ask how? where? what?—at least, if these affirmations of faith are to be used as the premise for castigating the unhappy men who had the practical responsibility for finding solutions and failed.

Where have the revisionists gone astray? In part, the popu-

larity of revisionism obviously parallels that of *Gone with the
Wind*—the victors paying for victory by pretending literary
defeat. But the essential problem is why history should be so
vulnerable to this literary fashion; and this problem, I believe,
raises basic questions about the whole modern view of history.
It is perhaps stating the issue in too portentous terms. Yet
I cannot escape the feeling that the vogue of revisionism is
connected with the modern tendency to seek in optimistic
sentimentalism an escape from the severe demands of moral
decision; that it is the offspring of our modern sentimentality
which at once evades the essential moral problems in the name
of a superficial objectivity and asserts their unimportance in
the name of an invincible progress.

The revisionists first glided over the implications of the fact
that the slavery system was producing a closed society in the
South. Yet that society increasingly had justified itself by a
political and philosophical repudiation of free society; southern
thinkers swiftly developed the anti-libertarian potentialities in a
social system whose cornerstone, in Alexander H. Stephens' proud
phrase, was human bondage. In theory and in practice, the
South organized itself with mounting rigor against ideas of
human dignity and freedom, because such ideas inevitably
threatened the basis of their own system. Professor Frank L.
Owsley, the southern agrarian, has described inadvertently but
accurately the direction in which the slave South was moving.
"The abolitionists and their political allies were threatening the
existence of the South as seriously as the Nazis threaten the
existence of England," wrote Owsley in 1940; ". . . Under such
circumstances the surprising thing is that so little was done by
the South to defend its existence."

There can be no question that many southerners in the '50's
had similar sentiments; that they regarded their system of control
as ridiculously inadequate; and that, with the book-burning, the
censorship of the mails, the gradual illegalization of dissent, the
South was in process of creating a real machinery of repression
in order more effectively "to defend its existence." No society, I
suppose, encourages criticism of its basic institutions. Yet, when a
democratic society acts in self-defense, it does so at least in the
name of human dignity and freedom. When a society based on

bond slavery acts to eliminate criticism of its peculiar institution, it outlaws what a believer in democracy can only regard as the abiding values of man. When the basic institutions are evil, in other words, the effect of attempts to defend their existence can only be the moral and intellectual stultification of the society.

A society closed in the defense of evil institutions thus creates moral differences far too profound to be solved by compromise. Such a society forces upon everyone, both those living at the time and those writing about it later, the necessity for a moral judgment; and the moral judgment in such cases becomes an indispensable factor in the historical understanding.

The revisionists were commendably anxious to avoid the vulgar errors of the post-Civil War historians who pronounced smug individual judgments on the persons involuntarily involved in the tragedy of the slave system. Consequently they tried hard to pronounce no moral judgments at all on slavery. Slavery became important, in Craven's phrase, "only as a very ancient labor system, probably at this time rather near the end of its existence"; the attempt to charge this labor system with moral meanings was "a creation of inflamed imaginations." Randall, talking of the Kansas-Nebraska Act, could describe it as "a law intended to subordinate the slavery question and hold it in *proper* proportion" (my italics). I have quoted Randall's even more astonishing argument that, because major controversies between downstate and metropolis in Illinois stopped short of war, there was reason to believe that the Civil War could have been avoided. Are we to take it that the revisionists seriously believe that the downstate-metropolis fight in Illinois—or the agrarian-industrial fight in the Coolidge and Hoover administrations—were in any useful sense comparable to the difference between the North and South in 1861?

Because the revisionists felt no moral urgency themselves, they deplored as fanatics those who did feel it, or brushed aside their feelings as the artificial product of emotion and propaganda. The revisionist hero was Stephen A. Douglas, who always thought that the great moral problems could be solved by sleight-of-hand. The phrase "northern man of southern sentiments," Randall remarked was "said opprobriously . . . as if it were a base thing for a northern man to work with his southern fellows."

By denying themselves insight into the moral dimension of the slavery crisis, in other words, the revisionists denied themselves a historical understanding of the intensities that caused the crisis. It was the moral issue of slavery, for example, that gave the struggles over slavery in the territories or over the enforcement of the fugitive slave laws their significance. These issues, as the revisionists have shown with cogency, were not in themselves basic. But they were the available issues; they were almost the only points within the existing constitutional framework where the moral conflict could be faced; as a consequence, they became charged with the moral and political dynamism of the central issue. To say that the Civil War was fought over the "unreal" issue of slavery in the territories is like saying that the Second World War was fought over the "unreal" issue of the invasion of Poland. The democracies could not challenge fascism inside Germany any more than opponents of slavery could challenge slavery inside the South; but the extension of slavery, like the extension of fascism, was an act of aggression which made a moral choice inescapable.

Let us be clear what the relationship of moral judgment to history is. Every historian, as we all know in an argument that surely does not have to be repeated in 1949, imports his own set of moral judgments into the writing of history by the very process of interpretation; and the phrase "every historian" includes the category "revisionist." Mr. DeVoto in his paraphrases of the revisionist position has put admirably the contradictions on this point: as for "moral questions, God forbid. History will not put itself in the position of saying that any thesis may have been wrong, any cause evil. . . . History will not deal with moral values, though of course the Republican radicals were, well, culpable." The whole revisionist attitude toward abolitionists and radicals, repeatedly characterized by Randall as "unctuous" and "intolerant," overflows with the moral feeling which is so virtuously excluded from discussions of slavery.

An acceptance of the fact of moral responsibility does not license the historian to roam through the past ladling out individual praise and blame: such an attitude would ignore the fact that all individuals, including historians, are trapped in a web of circumstance which curtails their moral possibilities. But it does mean that there are certain essential issues on which it is necessary for the historian to have a position if he is to understand the great conflicts of history. These great conflicts are relatively few because there are few enough historical phenomena which we can confidently identify as evil. The essential issues appear, moreover, not in pure and absolute form, but incomplete and imperfect, compromised by the deep complexity of history. Their proponents may often be neurotics and fanatics, like the abolitionists. They may attain a social importance only when a configuration of nonmoral factors—economic, political, social, military—permit them to do so.

Yet neither the nature of the context nor the pretensions of the proponents alter the character of the issue. And human slavery is certainly one of the few issues of whose evil we can be sure. It is not just "a very ancient labor system"; it is also a betrayal of the basic values of our Christian and democratic tradition. No historian can understand the circumstances which led to its abolition until he writes about it in its fundamental moral context. "History is supposed to understand the difference between a decaying economy and an expanding one," as Mr. DeVoto well said, "between solvency and bankruptcy, between a dying social idea and one coming to world acceptance. . . . It is even supposed to understand implications of the difference between a man who is legally a slave and one who is legally free."

"Revisionism in general has no position," DeVoto continues, "but only a vague sentiment." Professor Randall well suggested the uncritical optimism of that sentiment when he remarked, "To suppose that the Union could not have been continued or slavery outmoded without the war and without the corrupt concomitants of war is hardly an enlightened assumption." We have here a touching afterglow of the admirable 19th-century faith in the full rationality and perfectibility of man; the faith that the errors of the world would all in time be "outmoded" (Professor Randall's use of this word is suggestive) by progress. Yet the experience of the 20th century has made it clear that we gravely overrated man's capacity to solve the problems of existence within the terms of history.

This conclusion about man may disturb our complacencies

about human nature. Yet it is certainly more in accord with history than Professor Randall's "enlightened" assumption that man can solve peaceably all the problems which overwhelm him. The unhappy fact is that man occasionally works himself into a log-jam; and that the log-jam must be burst by violence. We know that well enough from the experience of the last decade. Are we to suppose that some future historian will echo Professor Nevins' version of the "failure" of the 1850's and write: "The primary task of statesmanship in the 1930's was to furnish a workable adjustment between the United States and Germany, while offering strong inducements to the German people to abandon the police state and equal persuasions to the Americans to help the Nazis rather than scold them"? Will some future historian adapt Professor Randall's formula and write that the word "appeaser" was used "opprobriously" as if it were a "base" thing for an American to work with his Nazi fellow? Obviously this revisionism of the future (already foreshadowed in the work of Charles A. Beard) would represent, as we now see it, a fantastic evasion of the hard and unpleasant problems of the '30's. I doubt whether our present revisionism would make much more sense to the men of the 1850's.

The problem of the inevitability of the Civil War, of course, is in its essence a problem devoid of meaning. The revisionist attempt to argue that the war could have been avoided by "any kind of sane policy" is of interest less in its own right than as an expression of a characteristically sentimental conception of man and of history. And the great vogue of revisionism in the historical profession suggests, in my judgment, ominous weaknesses in the contemporary attitude toward history.

We delude ourselves when we think that history teaches us that evil will be "outmoded" by progress and that politics consequently does not impose on us the necessity for decision and for struggle. If historians are to understand the fullness of the social dilemma they seek to reconstruct, they must understand that sometimes there is no escape from the implacabilities of moral decision. When social conflicts embody great moral issues, these conflicts cannot be assigned for solution to the invincible march of progress; nor can they be by-passed with "objective" neutrality. Not many problems perhaps force this decision upon the historian. But, if any problem does in our history, it is the Civil War.

To reject the moral actuality of the Civil War is to foreclose the possibility of an adequate account of its causes. More than that, it is to misconceive and grotesquely to sentimentalize the nature of history. For history is not a redeemer, promising to solve all human problems in time; nor is man capable of transcending the limitations of his being. Man generally is entangled in insoluble problems; history is consequently a tragedy in which we are all involved, whose keynote is anxiety and frustration, not progress and fulfillment. Nothing exists in history to assure us that the great moral dilemmas can be resolved without pain; we cannot therefore be relieved from the duty of moral judgment on issues so appalling and inescapable as those involved in human slavery; nor can we be consoled by sentimental theories about the needlessness of the Civil War into regarding our own struggles against evil as equally needless.

One must emphasize, however, that this duty of judgment applies to issues. Because we are all implicated in the same tragedy, we must judge the men of the past with the same forbearance and charity which we hope the future will apply toward us.

James M. McPherson

History has dealt very harshly with the abolitionists. To many historians, they were the villains, the fanatics who drove the South into secession and thereby threatened the existence of the nation. Historians have characterized them as psychologically maladjusted (Avery Craven), men without responsibility (Stanley M. Elkins), a displaced elite (David Donald), paranoic (C. Vann Woodward),.and fanatics (Frank L. Owsley). Even those more sympathetic to the abolitionists, such as Leon F. Litwack, have admitted that the antislavery movement suffered from "factionalism, extreme partisanship, narrow class attitudes, prejudice, and even hypocrisy." The Negro abolitionist and editor, Martin Delany, charged that the white abolitionists always "presumed to *think* for, dictate to, and *know* better what suited colored people, than they know for themselves" (Litwack).

However, this picture has been recently challenged by a number of historians. One of the most fruitful studies in defense of the abolitionists has come from James M. McPherson who examined the activities of the abolitionists during and after the Civil War. In *The Struggle For Equality*, he found that the abolitionists were sincere in their efforts for Negro rights, and that their agitation and propaganda laid the basis for many of the Negroes' gains. "Early in the war, abolitionists outlined a broad program of emancipation, employment of Negro soldiers in the Union Army, creation of a Freedmen's Bureau, government assistance for the education of the freedman, civil and political equality for all black men, and grants of confiscated land to the freed slaves. Under the military pressures of war and the political pressures of Reconstruction, the Republican party adopted all of these policies except the wholesale confiscation of southern plantations."

But one of the most formidable undertakings of the abolitionists was a full-scale defense of Negro equality. The underpinnings of prejudice in the United States was the belief in Negro inferiority. "In truth," Frederick Douglass wrote, "this question is at the bottom of the whole [slavery] controversy." As Professors William R. Stanton and Thomas F. Gossett have shown, the nineteenth-century view of inequality became recognized as a scientific theory, justified by academic and scholarly opinion. The Negroes were a race apart, and as Louis Agassiz of Harvard contended, it was an error to ascribe "to all living beings upon earth one common centre of origin" (Thomas F. Gossett, *Race: The History of An Idea in America*).

It was in these circumstances that the abolitionists, Negro and white, defended the equality of the Negro. Through books, newspapers, and on the lecture platform, they set out to convince the American public that the Negro was not only entitled to freedom, but that he could contribute to American life and democracy. They pointed to Negro contributions of the past; they popularized scientific evidence supporting equality, documented the culture of Africa and Africans, and supported the idea of environmental rather than racial determinates. They tackled the problem of intermarriage, and at-

tacked commonly held racial stereotypes. Although the abolitionists were a tiny minority, through their persistence they
helped forge the attitudes that ended slavery, enfranchised
the Negro, and gave him citizenship. The abolitionists proved
themselves to be more than "sunshine patriots." McPherson
has shown that they deserve better at the hands of historians.
James M. McPherson is Associate Professor of History at
Princeton University. In addition to writing *The Struggle for
Equality*, he is the editor of *The Negro's Civil War* (1965).

THE NEGRO: INNATELY INFERIOR
OR EQUAL?

SOURCE: James M. McPherson, "The Negro: Innately Inferior or Equal,"
from *The Struggle for Equality: Abolitionists and the Negro in the Civil
War and Reconstruction* (Princeton: Princeton University Press), 134–53.

One of the most formidable obstacles to the abolition of slavery
and the extension of equal rights to free Negroes was the
widespread popular and scientific belief, North as well as South,
in the innate inferiority of the Negro race. Most white Americans
took it for granted that Negroes were by nature shiftless,
slovenly, childlike, savage, and incapable of assimilation as
equals into white society. Since the beginning of the antislavery
movement abolitionists had been confronted by arguments that
Negroes belonged to a separate and inferior species of mankind;
that they would work only under compulsion; that they could
not take care of themselves in freedom and would revert to
barbarism; and that emancipation would bring economic and
social ruin to the South and the nation.[1]

For thirty years abolitionists had worked tirelessly but without

[1] The following studies treat this subject in considerable detail: William S.
Jenkins, *Pro-Slavery Thought in the Old South* (Chapel Hill, 1935),
242–84; Guion G. Johnson, "A History of Racial Ideologies in the United
States with Reference to the Negro," MS in the Schomburg Collection,
NYPL; William R. Stanton, *The Leopard's Spots: Scientific Attitudes Toward
Race in America, 1815–59* (Chicago, 1960). For a good example of the
many pamphlets and books arguing that innate inferiority of the Negro, see
J. H. Van Evrie, *Negroes and Negro "Slavery"; The First an Inferior Race—
the Latter its Normal Condition* (New York, 1853).

much success to combat these arguments. When war came in 1861 and emancipation became an imminent possibility, the debate about the Negro's racial character reached new heights of intensity and bitterness. Conservatives urged their thesis of Negro inferiority and unfitness for freedom with desperate energy; abolitionists argued from the pulpit, platform, and press that a hostile environment, not innate inferiority, had created the servile, comic creature that was the American concept of the Negro in 1860. The abolitionists affirmed that if this environment were transformed by the abolition of slavery and of racial discrimination, the Negro would prove himself a constructive, capable, and creative member of society.

Abolitionists were well aware that the common belief in the Negro's racial inferiority constituted one of the main justifications for slavery. In the final analysis, wrote Sydney Howard Gay in 1860, slavery was based "upon the assumed fact that the negroes are an inferior race, over whom the whites possess not merely an artificial superiority dependent upon the existing circumstances of their mutual position, but a natural superiority, which exists and ever must exist." Frederick Douglass said, "In truth, this question is at the bottom of the whole [slavery] controversy." Until the doctrine of the diversity and inequality of races was discredited, abolitionists reasoned, the theory and practice of slavery would remain strongly entrenched in America. "We cannot expect," said Gilbert Haven, the militant, red-headed Methodist clergyman, "the complete removal of this curse from our land until we stand boldly and heartily upon the divine foundation—the perfect unity of the human race."[2]

With the coming of war in 1861 and the impending prospect of emancipation, proslavery advocates roused themselves to even greater efforts to show that bondage was the normal and only possible condition of the Negro. When the emancipationist drive was gathering momentum at the end of 1861, the *New York Journal of Commerce* published a concise summary of the conservative argument against abolition. "A year ago, no thoroughly sane man in America would have consented to a decree of absolute emancipation," declared the *Journal,* and the war was no reason why the nation should suddenly go insane. "Let no man say this is a base and sordid view of a question of personal freedom." It was a matter of racial common sense. The Negro simply could not take care of himself in freedom. "Unless the reformer can, with his emancipation scheme, introduce new and superhuman industry, economy, thrift and perseverance into the negro, it will result that he will not earn a support for himself alone, much less for his family." The attempt "to make use of the war for the purposes of emancipation," concluded the *Journal,* "is virtually a proposition to plunge the South into the depths of poverty."[3] The northern proslavery press echoed these sentiments throughout the war.

The abolitionist attack on the concept of racial inequality centered on two fronts: one, an attempt to demonstrate, from the Bible, from science, from history, and from observed facts, the essential unity and equality of races; and two, an attempt to show that the unfavorable environmental conditions of slavery and segregation, rather than natural inferiority, had caused the vices and disabilities of the American Negro.

The antebellum generation was fond of quoting the Bible as a weapon in the slavery controversy, and abolitionists could point to several passages of scripture which "proved" the unity of the human race. The book of Genesis told the story of the creation of *man* (not men) in God's own image. In his famous sermon on Mars Hill, St. Paul told the people of Athens that God "hath made of one blood all nations of men for to dwell on the face of the earth." Gilbert Haven contended that the Bible sanctioned the complete equality and fraternity of the races. Solomon treated the Queen of Sheba, an Ethiopian, "with the utmost respect and cordiality." Moses married an Ethiopian; a Negro was called by God to be one of the prophets and teachers of the Church at Antioch. "More than this," declared Haven, "the Bible constantly proclaims the absolute oneness of the race of man, in Adam, Noah, and Christ."[4]

By 1860, however, the Bible argument was pretty well played

---

[3] *New York Journal of Commerce,* quoted in *Liberator,* Jan. 3, 1862.
[4] Haven, *National Sermons,* 137.

out. Thirty years of controversy had only shown that the Bible could be quoted effectively on both sides of the slavery issue. Science, especially ethnology and anthropology, commanded a large and growing influence in the mid-nineteenth century. Ethnology in the hands of Josiah Nott, Louis Agassiz, Samuel G. Morton, and George Gliddon (a group that came to be known as the "American School" of anthropology), who taught that the various races of mankind constituted separate species with the Negro at the bottom of the scale, had become a major weapon in the defense of slavery. Abolitionists realized that to combat these teachings they must themselves use the weapons of ethnology. Few abolitionists had any formal anthropological training, but as a group they were well educated and highly literate; and given the rather crude state of nineteenth-century ethnological knowledge, the industrious layman could become almost as well informed as the professional scientist.

Several abolitionists made intensive studies of the question of race. To refute the "American School" of anthropology, abolitionists quoted prominent European naturalists who argued for the unity and equality of races. In 1861, for example, the *Anti-Slavery Standard* published a review of *L'Unité de l'Espèce Humaine*, by M. de Quatrefarges, professor of natural history and ethnology at the Museum of Natural History in Paris. Using the classifications of Linnaeus and Lamarck, M. de Quatrefarges defined mankind as a single species; racial differences were the result of varieties within the species developed by conditions of environment and transmitted by heredity. M. de Quatrefarges used his vast knowledge to deny the existence of any fundamental and immutable differences in the mental capacities of various races.[5]

Abolitionists cited several other outstanding European scientists who maintained the unity and equality of races: Dr. R. G. Latham, the British ethnologist; Dumont d'Urville, the French geographer and navigator; George Louis Leclerc Buffon, the brilliant naturalist; and finally, most important of all, the renowned Alexander von Humboldt, who wrote: "Whilst we maintain the unity of the human species, we at the same time repel the depressing assumption of superior and inferior races of men."

[5] *N.A.S. Standard*, Nov. 9, 1861.

Through Humboldt, said Charles Sumner, "Science is enlisted for the Equal Rights of All."[6]

Sumner may have overstated his case, since American science, at least, spoke overwhelmingly for inequality. But the ethnologists of the world spoke with a discordant and divided voice on the subject of race in 1860. Abolitionists argued forcefully and accurately that science had failed to *prove* the racial inferiority of the Negro. "You may read Prichard, and Pinkerton, and Morton, and Pickering, and Latham, and all the rest—the whole library of Ethnology," said Theodore Tilton in 1863, "and in the confusion of knowledge you will find one thing clear—and that is, science has not yet proved, in advance, that the negro race is not to be a high-cultured, dominant race—rulers of their own continent, and perhaps dictators to the world."[7]

The endless refinements of the scientific racial arguments probably passed over the heads of the general public. The average man was more interested in concrete examples; and the advocates of Negro inferiority thought they had one incontrovertible example to show him: the supposed barbarous and uncivilized condition of Africa. What contribution to civilization and progress had Africa ever made, asked proslavery writers derisively?

This was a potentially damaging argument, and abolitionists advanced boldly to meet it. Negro abolitionists were in the forefront of the struggle to vindicate Africa. The central theme of their argument was that the inhabitants of ancient Egypt, fountainhead of western civilization, were a Negroid or partially Negroid race. "The ancient Egyptians were not white people," declared Frederick Douglass, "but were, undoubtedly, just about as dark in complexion as many in this country who are considered Negroes." Their hair "was far from being of that graceful lankness which adorns the fair Anglo-Saxon head." William Wells Brown, a prominent Negro abolitionist, lecturer, and author, said in 1862, "I claim that the blacks are the legitimate descend-

---

[6] Charles Sumner, *Works of Charles Sumner* (15 vols., Boston, 1870–73), XIII, 155–57. Curiously enough, none of the disputants in the racial controversy referred to Darwin before 1866, although *The Origin of Species* was known in America soon after its publication in 1859.

[7] Theodore Tilton, *The Negro* (New York, 1863), 5. This was a speech delivered by Tilton at the annual meeting of the American Anti-Slavery Society in 1863. Several thousand copies were published and distributed by the Society.

ants of the Egyptians." While the ancestors of the proud Anglo-Saxons were roaming the forests of northern Europe as savages, declared Brown, Africa had created the foundations of western civilization and passed on this precious heritage to the Jews, Greeks, Romans, and ultimately to western Europe.[8] Martin Delany, another Negro abolitionist, cited the historians Herodotus and Diodorus Siculus in support of his contention that the world was indebted to ancient Egypt and Ethiopia "for the propagation of that glorious light of progressive civilization—religion, philosophy, arts, science and literature in general, which now illuminate the world." In reply to a derisive reference to Negroes by Senator William L. Yancey of Alabama, William Wells Brown told a group of Boston abolitionists in 1860: "When Mr. Yancey's ancestors were bending their backs to the yoke of William the Conqueror, the ancestors of his slaves were revelling in the halls of science and learning. If the Hon. Senator from Alabama wants antecedents, he shall have them; and upon such, I claim a superiority for the negro. (Loud applause)"[9]

These arguments were most vigorously advanced by Brown in a book entitled *The Black Man, His Antecedents, His Genius, and His Achievements,* published in 1863. Brown wrote the book for the express purpose of dispelling popular notions about the Negro in order to help mobilize popular support for Lincoln's newly adopted emancipation policy. The book was an immediate success; the first edition was sold out soon after publication, and in the next three years ten printings came off the presses. "Such a rapid sale of a book devoted entirely to an exhibition of the genius, the talent and the heroism of the hated Negro," said the *Anti-Slavery Standard,* "shows that a great change has come over the minds of the American people, and that justice to a long injured race is not far off." Lewis Tappan exclaimed, "This is just the book for the hour. It will do more for the colored man's elevation than any work yet published."[10]

[8] Foner, *Douglass,* II, 296; *Liberator,* June 6, 1862, quoting speech by William Wells Brown.

[9] Martin Delany, *Principia of Ethnology: The Origin of Races and Color* (Philadelphia, 1879), 42–48; Brown was quoted in *Liberator,* Oct. 26, 1860.

[10] *N.A.S. Standard,* Aug. 1, 1863; Tappan was quoted in William Wells Brown, *The Rising Son* (Boston, 1874), introduction by Alonzo D. Moore, 24. See also *Commonwealth,* Oct. 30, 1863; and Samuel May, Jr., to Richard Webb, Sept. 19, 1865, Samuel May, Jr., Papers, BPL.

But the glories of ancient Ethiopia were not sufficient to convince many skeptics of the inherent equality of Negroes. Modern Africa stood in the way. Most nineteenth century Americans considered Africa a backward, barbaric continent, devoid of any trace of civilization or culture. Most world travelers who visited the dark continent concurred with Bayard Taylor's opinion that the Negro was "the lowest type of humanity on the face of the earth." Not being world travelers themselves, abolitionists perforce obtained much of their information on Africa from such unflattering sources. Consequently they admitted that contemporary Africa stood low in the scale of civilization, but they advanced a kind of cyclical theory of history, by which nations rose and fell, and would rise again. At one time Africa was the center of learning and culture, said Gerrit Smith, but in the course of events she declined in importance. Africa's "inherent, inborn faculties," however, "are neither multiplied nor diminished because developed in one age, and undeveloped in another. . . . Changes of circumstances, along with other causes, alternately lift up and depress a people." Theodore Tilton asked in 1863:

"Do you call the negro race inferior? No man can yet pronounce that judgment safely. How will you compare races, to give each its due rank? . . . You must compare them in their fulfillments, not in their beginnings. . . . How will you estimate the rank of the Roman people? By its beginnings? By its decline? By neither. You rank it at the height of its civilization. . . . The Germans, today, give philosophy to Europe—but you can count the years backward when the Germans, now philosophers, were barbarians. . . . No man can now predict the destiny of the negro race. That race is yet so undeveloped—that destiny is yet so unfulfilled—that no man can say, and no wise man pretends to say, what the negro race shall finally become."[11]

Some abolitionists, moreover, did not entirely accept the dark portrait of modern Africa drawn by most travelers. Several months after the outbreak of the Civil War a remarkable little book, written anonymously and entitled *Record of an Obscure Man*, was published in Boston. It purported to be the memoir of a man who had visited a friend in the South in 1842 and had talked with him about the capabilities of the Negro race. In reality it was a fictional essay by Mrs. Mary Putnam, elder sister

[11] Gerrit Smith to Montgomery Blair, Apr. 2, 1862, in *Liberator*, Apr. 18; Tilton, *The Negro*, 4–5.

of James Russell Lowell and an abolitionist sympathizer. Mary Putnam asserted that most travelers who visited Africa penetrated no farther than the coastal areas, whose inhabitants had been subjected to debasing contact with rapacious slave traders, "to which their degradation is to be attributed, rather than to inherent depravity or stupidity." Travelers who had ventured into the interior of Africa found people of finer appearance, gentler manners, greater industry and honesty. "When Central Africa has been fully laid open to the world," she argued, "we shall be called upon to revise many of our opinions."[12]

Displaying great learning, Mrs. Putnam quoted from world-famous travelers and explorers who had ventured into Central Africa: Hugh Clapperton, Mungo Park, and Dixon Denham. "Read what Denham says of the inhabitants of the interior," she urged; "of their industry, their skill in weaving and dyeing, of their love of music and poetry." Denham described the natives as "hospitable, kind-hearted, honest, and liberal." Anticipating the findings of modern scholars, Mrs. Putnam decried the notion that Negroes had been civilized and uplifted by slavery and Christianity. Slavery, she said, had only suppressed their native virtues and intelligence.[13]

In one of the best expressions of "cultural relativism" to come out of the nineteenth century, Mary Putnam warned against accepting at face value the somber descriptions of Africa by certain westerners. "All men are prone to judge the manners of other countries by the standard of their own," she wrote, "and the civilized world views from its own stand-point that which it calls savage. We find the Africans barbarians, wherever customs differ from ours; but they are on the road to civilization, when their nonsense suits our nonsense."[14]

Abolitionists praised Mary Putnam's little book. "Such a studied tribute to the negro, in this way, we have never had the fortune to see," said Garrison in his review of *Record of an Obscure Man*. "The African is contemplated as a man apart from his accidents, and heavy must be the load of prejudice against color that is not lightened by the spirit and the truthfulness with which his claims

---

[12] [Mary Putnam], *Record of an Obscure Man* (Boston, 1861), 91–92.
[13] *Ibid.*, 92–96.
[14] *Ibid.*, 123.

are urged."[15] Abolitionists adopted many of Mrs. Putnam's arguments in their crusade for emancipation and equal rights.

The advocates of racial equality did not have to confine their researches to Africa to find persuasive examples of the manhood, ability, and achievements of the Negro race. There were plenty of authentic black heroes in the western hemisphere. By all odds, the greatest of these was Toussaint L'Ouverture, the Haitian liberator who led his people out of slavery and defeated the armies of Napoleon when the French tried to reenslave the Caribbean island. One of Wendell Phillips' most powerful and compelling lectures was a biography of Haiti's warrior statesman. In 1862–63 Phillips gave this lecture to dozens of audiences throughout the Northeast as a means of dramatizing the Negro's fitness for freedom. "The negro race, instead of being that object of pity and contempt which we usually consider it, is entitled, judged by the facts of history, to a place close by the side of the Saxon," said Phillips. Did anyone doubt the Negro's courage? "Go to 50,000 graves of the best soldiers France ever had, and ask them what they think of the negro's sword." Could the Negro take care of himself in freedom? "Hayti, from the ruins of her colonial dependence, is become a civilized state, the seventh nation in the catalogue of commerce with this country, inferior in morals and education to none of the West Indian isles. Toussaint made her what she is. Courage, purpose, endurance—they are the tests." The *Semi-Weekly New York Tribune* printed a special edition containing Phillips' speech on March 13, 1863, for circulation among the troops in the Union army.[16]

The Negro had proved his physical courage in Haiti, in the

---

[15] *Liberator*, Nov. 29, 1861. The *Anglo-African*, a weekly newspaper published by Negroes in New York City, pronounced *Record of an Obscure Man* "the fullest and most satisfactory record it has been our fortune to meet with, after reading all we could find in print on the subject. . . . She recognizes in the negro an original, inherent germ force of his own, solemn, grand, endowed with energy and vitality enough to develop civil, social, and intellectual greatness out of his own resources." *Anglo-African*, Feb. 15, 1862.

[16] *New York Tribune* (Daily), Mar. 12, 14, 1863; *Semi-Weekly Tribune*, Mar. 13, 1863. In 1863 James Redpath edited and published an old biography of Toussaint by John R. Beard as a part of the effort to win public respect for the courage and resourcefulness of the Negro race. James Redpath, ed., *Toussaint L'Ouverture: a Biography and Autobiography* (Boston, 1863).

American Revolution and War of 1812, and would soon prove it again in the Civil War; but what about mental ability and intellectual achievement? It was while asking himself this question that Moncure Conway stumbled across the remarkable story of Benjamin Banneker. Conway did some research on Banneker's life and published an article on him in the *Atlantic Monthly* at the end of 1862. A free-born, self-taught Maryland Negro, Banneker had devoted all his spare time to scientific research. He corrected some of the errors of the greatest astronomers of his age; in 1790 he compiled an accurate almanac based on his studies, and continued to publish annual almanacs until shortly before his death in 1804. His work was praised by Jefferson and internationally acclaimed by scientists. "History must record," concluded Conway, "that the most original scientific intellect which the South has yet produced was that of the pure African, Benjamin Banneker."[17]

Abolitionists industriously gathered statistics on the intellectual, professional, and business achievements of free Negroes. The American Anti-Slavery Society's *Annual Report* for 1859 pointed to the Negro actor Ira Aldridge, who was delighting European audiences with his portrayal of Othello; to three young Haitian students who had won highest honors at the concourse of all French colleges in Paris; to the New York Negro, Ditz, who had submitted a plan for a Broadway railroad; and the Philadelphia Negro, Aaron Roberts, who had developed a new and improved fire-extinguishing apparatus. These and many other accomplishments by Negroes demonstrated "the black man's capacity for mental culture and improvement . . . wherever a fair chance to test it has been given." In the business world Negroes boasted George T. Downing of Rhode Island and Stephen Smith of Philadelphia, both of them wealthy men by any standards. Some Negro lawyers of mark were John Mercer Langston of Ohio, and Robert Morris and John Rock of Boston. Frederick Douglass was one of the foremost orators in America, and in the pulpit the Reverend Henry Highland Garnet of New York and the Reverend J. Sella Martin of Boston ranked high. In sum, wrote William Wells Brown, the Negroes of the North,

---

[17] Moncure D. Conway, "Benjamin Banneker, the Negro Astronomer," *Atlantic Monthly*, xi (Jan. 1863), 79–84.

though "shut out, by a cruel prejudice, from nearly all the mechanical branches, and all the professions," had "learned trades, become artists, gone into the professions. . . . If this is not an exhibition of capacity, I don't understand the meaning of the term."[18]

Many abolitionists, while arguing vigorously for the inherent equality of the Negro race, nevertheless believed in racial *differences*. "It is a mistake to speak of the African as an inferior race to the Caucasian," said James Freeman Clarke. "It is doubtless *different* from this, just as this is also different from the Malay, the Indian, the Mongolian. There are many varieties in the human family." This was an accurate statement by today's ethnological standards, but Clarke parlayed it into a more questionable thesis: that the Negro was innately inferior to the Caucasian in some respects and superior in others. He stated:

"The colored man has not so much invention as the white, but more imitation. He has not so much of the reflective, but more of the perceptive powers. The black child will learn to read and write as fast or faster than the white child, having equal advantages. The blacks have not the indomitable perseverance and will, which make the Caucasian, at least the Saxon portion of it, *masters* wherever they go—but they have a native courtesy, a civility like that from which the word "gentleman" has its etymological meaning, and a capacity for the highest refinement of character. More than all, they have almost universally, a strong religious tendency, and that strength of attachment which is capable of any kind of self-denial, and self-sacrifice. Is this an inferior race—so inferior as to be only fit for chains?"[19]

Several other abolitionists subscribed to the notion of the Negro's superiority in the realm of manners, religion, and the arts, and inferiority in certain aspects of the hard-headed, practical business world. In an effort to convince readers of the Negro's ability to make positive contributions to American culture, Moncure Conway penned an article for the *Boston Commonwealth* in 1862, signing himself "A Native of the South." Negroes were a graceful people, he said, full of exuberance and picturesque

---

[18] *Annual Report of the American Anti-Slavery Society for the Year Ending May 1, 1859* (New York, 1860), 77–78; Brown, *Black Man*, 49. This book contains short biographies of 57 eminent Negroes.

[19] James Freeman Clarke, *Slavery in the United States: A Sermon Delivered on Thanksgiving Day, 1842* (Boston, 1843), 24.

charm. It was the Negro who gave to the South its warmth and radiance. The colored people had fertile, poetic imaginations. They had contributed much to southern culture, and would contribute more in freedom. "In our practical, anxious, unimaginative country, we need an infusion of this fervid African element, so child-like, exuberant, and hopeful," wrote Conway. "We ought to prize it, as we do rare woods and glowing gems imported from the gorgeous tropics." One year later, writing for an English audience, Conway stated that Negroes "seem to me to be weaker in the direction of the understanding, strictly speaking, but to have strength and elegance of imagination and expression. Negro sermons, fables, and descriptions are in the highest degree pictorial, abounding in mystic interpretations which would delight a German transcendentalist. My belief is, that there is a vast deal of high art yet to come out of that people in America. Their songs and hymns are the only original melodies we have."[20]

In his widely publicized speech on "The Negro," Theodore Tilton proclaimed the Negro "the most religious man among men. Is not the religious nature the highest part of human nature? Strike out the negro then, and you destroy the highest development of the highest part of human nature." It was a mistake, thought Tilton,

"to rank men only by a superiority of intellectual faculties. God has given to man a higher dignity than the reason. It is the moral nature. . . . In all those intellectual activities which take their strange quickening from the moral faculties—processes which we call instincts, or intuitions—the negro is superior to the white man—equal to the white woman. The negro race is the feminine race of the world. . . .

"We have need of the negro for his . . . aesthetic faculties. . . . We have need of the negro for his music. . . . But let us stop questioning whether the negro is a man. In many respects he is a superior man. In a few respects, he is the greatest of men. I think he is certainly greater than those men who clamor against giving him a chance in the world, as if they feared something from the competition."[21]

Among American natural scientists of the mid-nineteenth century, Louis Agassiz was foremost in prestige and authority. His

[20] *Commonwealth*, Oct. 18, 1862; Conway, *Testimonies Concerning Slavery*, 71. Conway had gone to England in 1863 as a sort of ambassador of good will from the American abolitionists. He liked London so well that he settled down and lived there for the next 20 years.
[21] Tilton, *The Negro*, 11–13.

adherence to the "American School" of anthropology gave it an influence it could not otherwise have commanded. As a Harvard Professor, Agassiz had many acquaintances in Boston's intellectual circles; several of these acquaintances were abolitionists, and Agassiz's racial ideas could not help but have some effect on their thinking. Samuel Gridley Howe was one such friend. In 1863–1864 Howe served as a member of the American Freedmen's Inquiry Commission. In connection with his research for the Commission, Howe asked Agassiz for his view on the effect of race on the problems of emancipation and reconstruction. Agassiz replied that he welcomed the prospect of emancipation, but warned against granting equal political and social rights to freedmen. He reviewed the history of the Negro in Africa and the western hemisphere, and concluded that Negroes were "indolent, playful, sensual, imitative, subservient, good-natured, versatile, unsteady in their purpose, devoted and affectionate." The Negro had never shown himself qualified for self-government. "I cannot," concluded Agassiz, "think it just or safe to grant at once to the negro all the privileges which we ourselves have acquired by long struggles. . . . Let us beware of granting too much to the negro race in the beginning, lest it become necessary hereafter to deprive them of some of the privileges which they may use to their own and our detriment."[22]

Howe was torn between his respect for Agassiz's learning and his own equalitarian principles. "I would not only advocate entire freedom, equal rights and privileges," he told Agassiz, but "open competition for social distinction." Howe was nevertheless influenced by some of Agassiz's notions regarding the mental inferiority of Negroes. In a book on Canadian Negroes published in 1864, Howe lamented that the younger generation, who had never known slavery and who enjoyed equal civil and political rights in Canada, had failed to produce as many outstanding individuals, in proportion to their numbers, as the white community. Howe took into account the prejudice, discrimination, and lack of opportunity that might account for this failure, but concluded

[22] Howe to Agassiz, Aug. 3, 1863; Agassiz to Howe, Aug. 9, 10, 1863, in Elizabeth C. Agassiz, *Louis Agassiz: His Life and Correspondence* (2 vols., Boston, 1885), II, 591–608.

that even with these disabilities the Negro community should have produced more superior men. Teachers to whom he talked testified that Negroes learned just as fast as whites in the lower grades, but fell behind at the higher levels "when they come to studies which tax the higher mental powers, or the reasoning and combining faculties." Colored people, thought Howe, were "quick of perception; very imitative; and they rapidly become intelligent. But they are rather knowing, than thinking people. They occupy useful stations in life; but such as require quick perceptions, rather than strong sense."[23]

To the modern reader familiar with the view of contemporary anthropology that there is no proof of significant differences in the mental capacities of various races, the opinions of Howe and other abolitionists who thought like him appear to border on racism. Even the belief of Tilton, Conway, and others in the inherent superiority of the Negro in the "feminine" virtues—religion and the arts—imply an assumption of Negro *inferiority* in the "masculine" virtues of reason and enterprise. Thus a case of modified racism could be made out against certain of the abolitionists, but only by ignoring the fact that in the contemporary spectrum of opinion on race, the abolitionists were far in the liberal vanguard. The remarkable fact about the abolitionists was not that as champions of the Negro *some* of them believed in racial differences, but that in a nation where popular belief *and* scientific learning overwhelmingly proclaimed the Negro's absolute inferiority, there were men and women who dared to affirm their faith in the innate equality of all men, regardless of race.

Then as now, one of the most explosive aspects of the race question was the issue of intermarriage. "Would you like your daughter to marry a nigger?" was the derisive question hurled at abolitionists hundreds of times through the years. It is not recorded whether any daughter of a white abolitionist did marry a Negro, but it is known that the abolitionists did not shrink from discussing the issue. In the face of popular odium and violence, abolitionists struggled to remove laws barring intermarriage from

[23] Howe to Agassiz, Aug. 18, 1863, *ibid.*, 614; Samuel G. Howe, *The Refugees from Slavery in Canada West* (Boston, 1864), 81–82.

the statute books of Massachusetts and other states. Marriage "is a personal and private matter, with which neither Congress nor any other law-makers have aught to do," said Gerrit Smith. "When a man and woman want to be married it is *their* business, not mine, nor anybody's else," declared Theodore Tilton. "But to read what some newspapers say of the 'monstrous doctrine of amalgamation,' one would think it consisted in stationing a prov-ost-marshal at street corners, to seize first a white man and then a black woman, and to marry them on the spot, against their will, for a testimony to human equality." Tilton pointed out the obvious fact, usually ignored by proslavery partisans, that amalgamation occurred under slavery, not freedom, at the bid-ding of the white man, not the Negro. Tilton declared that "a slave-woman's master, who makes himself the father of her chil-dren, is in honor bound to make himself her husband. So far from denouncing the marriage of blacks and whites, I would be glad if the banns of a hundred thousand such marriages could be published next Sunday."[24]

Abolitionists Louisa May Alcott, Lydia Maria Child, and Anna Dickinson defended intermarriage in short stories and novels. Gilbert Haven frequently vindicated amalgamation from his pul-pit.[25] Moncure Conway proclaimed boldly that "I, for one, am firmly persuaded that the mixture of the blacks and whites is good; that the person so produced is, under ordinarily favour-able circumstances, healthy, handsome, and intelligent. Under the best circumstances, I believe that such a combination would evolve a more complete character than the unmitigated Anglo-Saxon," because it would combine the best traits of both races. "Amalgamation!" exclaimed Wendell Phillips dramatically. "Re-member this, the youngest of you; that, on the 4th of July, 1863, you heard a man say, that in the light of all history, in virtue of every page he ever read, he was an amalgamationist to the ut-most extent. (Applause)" Phillips had no hope for the future "but in that sublime mingling of races which is God's own

[24] Gerrit Smith to the Hon. John Gurley, Dec. 16, 1861, in *Liberator*, Jan. 3, 1862; Tilton, *The Negro*, 10.
[25] Louisa May Alcott, "M. L.," a short story published serially in the *Commonwealth*, Jan. 24, 31, Feb. 7, 14, 21, 1863; Lydia M. Child, *A Romance of the Republic* (Boston, 1867); Anna Dickinson, *What Answer?* (Boston, 1868); Haven, *National Sermons*, 146.

method of civilizing and elevating the world. (Loud applause) Not the amalgamation of licentiousness, born of slavery, . . . but that gradual and harmonizing union, in honorable marriage, which has mingled all other races, and from which springs the present phase of European and Northern civilization."[26]

Most modern sociologists and psychologists agree that discrimination, segregation, and "cultural deprivation" rather than innate inferiority are responsible for the inferior status which the Negro occupies in American society. Abolitionists advanced this argument more than a century ago. Like modern sociologists, they maintained that environment, not racial deficiency, was the cause of the Negro's inferiority.

"I well remember what amazement was excited when Mr. Garrison and his partner first took a black boy as an apprentice in the office of 'The Liberator,'" wrote Oliver Johnson in his memoirs. "It was declared on every side that no 'nigger' could learn the art of printing, and it was held to be evidence of arrant folly to try the experiment. If the negroes, under such circumstances, sometimes seemed dull and even stupid, who can wonder? What race or class of men is strong enough to keep its feet under such a load of prejudice and contumely?" Theodore Tilton agreed that discrimination was responsible for the Negro's disabilities. "We put a stigma upon the black man's color, and then plead that prejudice against the commonest fair dealing," he stated. "We shut him out of schools, and then bitterly inveigh against the ignorance of his kind. We shut up all learned professions from his reach, and withhold the motives for ordinary enterprise, and then declare that he is an inferior being, fitted only for menial services."[27]

Prejudice and discrimination against the free Negro were debilitating enough, but the effects of slavery were worse still. "Take any race you please, French, English, Irish, or Scotch," said Frederick Douglass; "subject them to slavery for ages—regard and treat them every where, every way, as property. . . .

[26] Conway, *Testimonies Concerning Slavery*, 76; Phillips' speech quoted in *Commonwealth*, July 17, 1863.
[27] Oliver Johnson, *William Lloyd Garrison and His Times* (2nd ed., Boston, 1885), 101–02; *Independent*, May 29, 1862.

Let them be loaded with chains, scarred with the whip, branded with hot irons, sold in the market, kept in ignorance . . . and I venture to say that the same doubt would spring up concerning either of them, which now confronts the negro." It was little wonder that "the colored people in America appear stupid, helpless and degraded. The wonder is that they evince so much spirit and manhood as they do." Theodore Tilton conceded that "slavery has reduced the blacks to the lowest point of ignorance and humiliation of which humanity . . . is capable." The "peculiar institution" had produced some singular effects on the Negro, making him childlike and dependent, lacking in initiative and self-respect. "Man is, to a certain extent, the creature of circumstances," argued Tilton, "and two centuries of slavery must needs have molded the character of the slave. . . . The faults of the slave . . . come of training, rather than of natural endowment."[28]

In the *New York Tribune* of February 5, 1863, Sydney Gay presented a cogent and eloquent summary of the environmentalist argument. "We have never supposed that the liberation of so many human beings, heretofore irresponsible, would be without some embarrassments," he wrote in reply to proslavery arguments that slaves were not fit for freedom. "It is Freedom that fits men for Freedom. . . . The crime of Slavery has been that it has found the incapacity of its victims an argument for the continuation of its emasculating influences, and has continually pointed to the ruin it has wrought as an apology for postponing reparation." Nobody in his right senses, continued Gay,

"has expected to find the Freedman . . . a miracle of virtue, a wonder of wit, a paragon of prudence, and a marvel of industry. In him who was yesterday a Slave, we should expect to find the vices of the Slave—the traces of that falsehood which heretofore had been his sole protection against cruelty—of that thievishness which may have saved him from the pangs of hunger, or guarded him from the inclemency of the elements—of that insubordination of the animal passions which his superiors in society have encouraged for their own profit and by their own example. . . . Emancipation will not remove the scars which Slavery has inflicted. There is many a brow from which the

[28] Speech by Douglass in Cooper Union, Feb. 12, 1862, published in *New York Tribune*, Feb. 13; article by Tilton in *Independent*, Aug. 20, 1863.

brand can never be erased. . . . So much the sooner should we, with all the courage of a genuine repentance, dock this entail of human misery, and at least turn the faces of future generations toward kindlier opportunities and less discouraging vicissitudes!"[29]

The effects of slavery and racial discrimination on the Negro's character, according to abolitionists, were felt primarily in three areas: intelligence, industry, and morals. The Negro's defects of intelligence, remarked Douglass, could be found among the peasants, laborers, and lower classes of all races. "A man is worked upon by what *he* works on. He may carve out his circumstances, but his circumstances will carve him out as well." Douglass recalled his trip to Ireland in the 1840's, where he found the population of the poorer districts much like plantation slaves in every respect save color. "The open, uneducated mouth —the long, gaunt arm—the badly formed foot and ankle—the shuffling gait—the retreating forehead and vacant expression— and, their petty quarrels and fights—all reminded me of the plantation, and my own cruelly abused people."[30]

Moncure Conway, born and raised on a Virginia plantation, recounted the story of a companion of his youth, a slave boy who was popular with the white boys of the neighborhood and excelled in telling stories, playing games, and so on. The boy had a great native intelligence. He accompanied young Moncure to school every day, but of course was not allowed in the schoolroom. He wanted to know what happened in there, and when he found out he too wanted to learn to read. He could not understand why he was denied this privilege, and soon grew bewildered, then saddened, and finally rebellious, forcing Moncure's father to sell him South. Conway never forgot the boy. "I have dwelt upon this case," he wrote in his *Testimonies Concerning Slavery*, "because it is that which represents, in my own experience, one of the most tragical forms in which Slavery outrages human nature." On the basis of his experience, Conway also denied the theory that because of some natural disability, Negroes learned quickly until the age of ten or twelve, and then fell behind. "It has been my lot to have much to do with the poor whites of the South, and I have observed precisely the

[29] *New York Tribune*, Feb. 5, 1863. See also J. M. McKim to Gay, Jan. 28, 1863, Gay Papers, cu.
[30] Foner, *Douglass*, II, 304-05.

same arrest of development, both physical and mental, in those poor whites. . . . They learn well at first, even with a kind of voracity; but, at about the same age with the Negro child, they become dull." This was the result, not of inherent inferiority, but of the child's sudden realization of the cramped circumstances, limited opportunities, and unhappy future that faced the poor whites, as well as Negroes, of the South.[31]

The lazy, shiftless Negro who would work only under compulsion was a byword among those who defended slavery and ridiculed the idea of emancipation. Of course slaves were lazy, wrote Lydia Maria Child in her study of emancipation in the West Indies. Slavery "takes away the motive power from the laborers, who naturally desire to shirk as much as possible of the work, which brings them no pay. . . . It makes them indifferent to the destruction of property on estates, in whose prosperity they have no interest. . . . It kills their ingenuity and enterprise." She cited the testimony of planters and missionaries in the West Indies, who said that emancipation had "almost wholly put an end to sulking, or pretending to be sick. . . . Planters treat their laborers more like fellow-men, and that leads them to be respectful, in their turn. They have now a growing regard for character; a feeling unknown to them in the days of slavery."[32]

The alleged immorality, dishonesty and untruthfulness of the Negro were cited by proslavery propagandists as additional proofs of his inferiority. Of course the slave was immoral, replied abolitionists. Under slavery promiscuity was encouraged, marriage had no legal validity, and the father had no personal responsibility for his children, who belonged, not to their parents, but to their master. "Being regarded as animals, and treated like live-stock, [slaves] unavoidably lived like animals," wrote Mrs. Child. "Modesty and self-respect were impossible to their brutalized condition." In the West Indies, she contended, there was much less immorality a generation after emancipation than there had been under slavery.[33]

"To tell us that Slavery fosters in the enslaved habits of de-

[31] Conway, *Testimonies Concerning Slavery*, 4–7, 65–66.
[32] Lydia Maria Child, *The Right Way the Safe Way* (2d ed., New York, 1862), 5–6, 15–16.
[33] Charles K. Whipple, *The Family Relation, as Affected by Slavery* (Cincinnati, 1858), passim; Child, *Right Way Safe Way*, 6.

ception, is not to communicate to us any startling novelty," wrote Sydney Gay in 1862. Gay and Conway admitted that Negroes were prone to petty thievery, "but it should be remembered that the rights of property involve some very refined problems," said Conway. "If the Negro is inclined to sympathize with the views of Rousseau on such questions more than the English schools would approve, it must be admitted that the systematic disregard of his own right to his earnings is scarcely the best method of giving him better views. I have never heard yet of a slave who had managed to filch back so much as had been filched from him." Samuel Gridley Howe declared that "the offences against property, with which by public voice the [Negroes] are charged, . . . grow directly out of slavery. . . . The owner, in his daily practice, violates the most sacred right of property, by taking the slave's labor without pay; and the slave imitates him by violating the less sacred right of property, in stealing what he can lay his hands on." Upon the basis of his observations of free Negroes in Canada, Howe concluded that "with freedom and the ownership of property, the instinct of family will be developed, marriages will increase, and promiscuous intercourse decrease. . . . [Canadian Negroes] are, upon the whole, sober, industrious, and thrifty, and have proved themselves to be capable of self-guidance and self-support."[34]

"The difference between the Black and White," thought Sydney Gay, "is no other than the difference between the White and the White—differences occasioned by the accidents of location, and susceptible of removal by the opportunities of culture." Abolitionists realized, however, that these differences would not be wiped out in a year or two. "Men going from slavery to freedom cannot change their habits as they change their garments," wrote Howe. "The effects of Slavery will last more than one generation or even two," predicted Wendell Phillips. "It were a very slight evil if they could be done away sooner." The Negro was potentially the equal of the white man, but he had a long, hard road to travel before he reached that potentiality.[35]

[34] *New York Tribune*, Jan. 13, 1862; Conway, *Testimonies Concerning Slavery*, 70; Howe, *Refugees in Canada West*, 86–87, 101, 103.
[35] *New York Tribune*, Sept. 17, 1863; Howe, *Refugees in Canada West*, 86; speech by Wendell Phillips in Boston Music Hall, Dec. 16, 1860, in *New York Tribune*, Dec. 18.

In the final analysis, argued abolitionists, the question was not one of race, but of human rights. "I think races are of secondary importance," said Wendell Phillips in 1863. "I despise an empire resting its claims on the blood of a single race. My pride in the future is in the banner that welcomes every race and every blood, and under whose shelter all races stand up equal. (Applause)" Theodore Tilton proclaimed, "Looked at through the centuries, the question of races sinks into insignificance. The only generalization that will stand is, not that there are five races of men, or seven, or twelve, but only one—the universal human race in which all men are brothers, and God is father over all!"[36]

Dudley T. Cornish

Nearly 200,000 Negro soldiers fought in the Union army. This is rarely mentioned in history books. Where historians have recognized the Negro contribution, it has often been referred to in a derisive manner. For example, W. E. Woodward, whose popular histories had considerable acceptance in the 1920s and 30s, could find only seven lines for Negro soldiers in his 517-page biography of General Grant, and in those seven lines he made *six* errors of fact. Woodward wrote:

The employment of negroes as soldiers began in 1863 [1], and colored troops were first used, in an experimental way at the siege of Vicksburg [2]. Before the end of the war there were about one hundred thousand [3] negroes in the Union Army. Most of the officers of high rank were not favorably impressed by the Negro troops [4]. Sherman considered them a joke [5], and Grant usually kept them in the rear, guarding his wagon trains [6].

In fact, Negro soldiers were first employed in 1862 along the coasts of South Carolina, Georgia, and Florida, and before the end of the war some 178,000 Negro soldiers served in the army. Initial prejudice against the Negro soldier diminished in proportion to the use of Negroes, and as early as 1863 President Lincoln could state that "some of the commanders of our armies in the field who have given us our most im-

---

[36] *Liberator*, May 29, 1863; Tilton, *The Negro*, 8.

portant successes, believe the emancipation policy, and the use of colored troops, constitute the heaviest blow yet dealt to the rebellion." Negro troops made up an important segment of Sherman's army that marched on Atlanta, and he received commendable reports from his commanders about the fighting quality of the Negro regiments under his command. In Grant's great battles in Virginia, the all-Negro XXV Army Corps impressed Grant with their performance. Negro troops were among the first to enter Richmond and Charleston, and played a very significant part in the great Battle of the Crater in 1864.

The prejudice against the Negro soldier in the beginning of the war made their lot a good deal harder than the average soldier's. "We don't want to fight side and side with a nigger," wrote a Union corporal from New York. "We think we are too superior [a] race for that." Negro soldiers received less pay than whites, were ineligible until the very end of the war from becoming officers, and if captured, could not be expected to be treated as prisoners of war.

Yet the abolitionists and others realized the importance of having Negroes in the Union army. Not only would Negro troops help shorten the war, and bring about the freedom of the slaves, but their participation would be their passport to citizenship. Douglass wrote in 1863: "Once let the black man get upon his person the brass letters, U.S.; let him get an eagle on his button, and a musket on his shoulder and bullets in his pocket, and there is not power on earth which can deny that he had earned the rights to citizenship in the United States" (*The Life and Times of Frederick Douglass*). General Lorenzo Thomas noted that white prejudice against Negro soldiers diminished "since the blacks have fully shown their fighting qualities and manliness."

An important aspect of Negro involvement is the fact that most of the Negro soldiers came from the South and were former slaves. Over forty percent of the Negro soldiers were recruited in the lower Mississippi area alone. John Hope Franklin estimated that 93,000 Negro troops were recruited from the seceded states, 40,000 came from the border slave states which remained in the Union, and 52,000 came from the free states. These figures should modify the view held by many historians about the loyalty of slaves during the war.

Dudley T. Cornish, Professor of History at Kansas State

College (Pittsburg, Kansas), presents us with a full-scale account of the Negro soldier as combatant. Concerned less with policy behind the lines than performance in the field, Professor Cornish has tried to see the war as it might have been viewed by the Negro soldier. He skillfully made use of the 128 volume *Official Records,* the War Records Division of the National Archives, and a number of collections of important papers including those of Lorenzo Thomas, Adjutant General, United States Army, who was instrumental in recruiting large numbers of Negro troops in the lower Mississippi Valley. The results are found in Professor Cornish's *The Sable Arm: Negro Troops in the Union Army, 1861–1865.* Historians can no longer ignore the contribution of the Negro soldier to the winning of the war and to gaining his own freedom.

". . . EVEN THE SLAVE BECOMES A MAN . . ."

SOURCE: Dudley T. Cornish, ". . . even the slave becomes a man . . ." from *The Sable Arm: Negro Troops in the Union Army, 1861–1865* (New York: Longmans, Green and Company, 1956), pp. 261–66, 285–87, 287–91.

> *We called upon them in the day of our trial, when volunteering had ceased, when the draft was a partial failure, and the bounty system a senseless extravagance. They were ineligible for promotion, they were not to be treated as prisoners of war. Nothing was definite except that they could be shot and hanged as soldiers. Fortunate indeed it is for us, as well as for them, that they were equal to the crisis; that the grand historic moment which comes to a race only once in many centuries came to them, and that they recognized it . . .*
>
> NORWOOD PENROSE HALLOWELL, 1892
> Colonel, 55th Massachusetts Infantry

"Gentlemen, the question is settled; negroes will fight."

This is the verdict pronounced by Major General George H. Thomas as he rode over the battlefield of Nashville in December, 1864, and observed "the bodies of colored men side by side with the foremost on the very works of the enemy." Thomas was neither the first nor the last Union commander to reach that verdict.

Rufus Saxton had expressed the same opinion back in 1862. The behavior of Negro troops at Port Hudson, Milliken's Bend, Honey Springs, and Fort Wagner in mid-1863 had proved its validity. But throughout the war, whenever Negro soldiers fought, they had to prove it all over again. As late as April 13, 1865, four days after Lee had surrendered to Grant at Appomattox, Colonel Charles A. Gilchrist, commanding the 50th U.S. Colored Infantry, thought it necessary to conclude his report of the conduct of his troops in the siege and assault on Fort Blakely, guarding Mobile, with this statement: "The conduct of none could be criticized to their discredit, and the behavior of the men when constructing trenches under fire, than which there could scarcely be a more trying position, was a convincing proof that the former slaves of the South cannot be excelled as soldiers." Colonel A. Watson Webber, commanding the 51st U.S. Colored in the same operations, concluded his report in almost the same language: "There can be no doubt now, in the minds of their officers at least, but that our colored soldiers are brave and will fight."

It is hard to realize, ninety years after the Civil War, how revolutionary the experiment of permitting Negroes to bear arms was considered, how fraught with imagined dangers to the Union cause, how galling to white pride, how difficult of popular acceptance. And yet today, ninety years after Appomattox, the same questions are still asked when Negro soldiers are mentioned: how did they behave? did they fight or did they run? did they dare to face their former masters? did they require white soldiers with them to sustain their courage—and perhaps to keep them from running? Now, as then, the Negro soldier is a stereotype in the public mind, and the actual performance of actual Negro soldiers, which shows the stereotype for what it really is, is still slow to be accepted. Only through steady repetition of steady soldierly conduct could the Negro soldier break the stereotype. Even with integration officially a fact in the armed forces of the United States, the stereotype lingers, and now as then Negro soldiers, airmen, seamen, and marines, officers and men alike, have always to prove themselves over and over again.

Daniel Ullmann was no social scientist, and yet some of his

observations on Negro troops and popular conceptions regarding
them are worth noting. The common error in judging them,
Ullmann thought, was "to look at them as a unit, as a whole, as
being all alike—the inferior specimens are selected as examples
of all—" and he asked a searching question: "How would the
white races stand such a test?"

Of the quality of colored troops Ullmann had this to say:
"Now, I have commanded colored regiments, as good troops as
need be, and I have commanded some indifferent, and some
very inferior. In their abnormal state, they require good officers
more than other soldiers. I have seen colored regiments—weak,
disorganized, inefficient—which stripped of their miserable officers, and placed in the hands of men who both knew their duty
and discharged it, were raised speedily to a high degree of discipline and effectiveness." Few readers with any military experience will disagree that Ullmann could have been speaking of
white troops as well. "The privates of the Colored Troops," he
continued, "were pretty uniformly reported to me to be sober,
docile, subordinate, obedient, attentive, and, as soldiers, enthusiastic. As sentinels, and on general picket duty, they have no
superiors. On a march, it was generally necessary to check them.
Their powers of endurance none will question. As to their fighting qualities, it is surprising that doubts were so extensively
entertained . . ." Extensively, stubbornly, exasperatingly, and,
it almost seems, eternally.

Despite their painfully accumulated battle record, there was
widespread lack of agreement on the ability of the Negro soldiers throughout and after the Civil War. Although the problem
had ceased to exist as far as the promulgation of national policy
was concerned, the complex details of the problem continued to
plague president, War Department, and Negro soldiers themselves. The insistent and persisting questions of proper employment of Negro troops—as garrison soldiers, labor battalions, prison guards, infantry and cavalry in the field; of their
pay; of their recruitment in the sensitive Border states; of their
impressment into service, of their treatment when captured, of
their ability to re-form and return to the fight after having once
been driven back; of their self-control in the heat of battle—
these and others of less importance continued to be asked even

after the answers were obvious. The Nashville *Daily Union* came close to the heart of the matter when it asserted on August 1, 1863, that "Copperhead officers would have called [the 54th Massachusetts] cowardly if they had stormed and carried the gates of hell . . ." There were persons in the United States who simply refused to believe that Negroes could and would make good soldiers, for whom the evidence was never sufficient, the testimony of commanding generals never convincing. Their descendants have stubbornly survived to this day.

From the beginning of 1864 on through the rest of the war Negro soldiers were permitted to do soldiers' work. They had given definite indications during 1863 of what could be expected of them. If doubt still remained in some minds—as it did—their combat performance during 1864 and 1865 should have removed a great deal of it.

The increasing contribution of colored troops to actual fighting is clearly shown in the number of engagements in which they participated in the different years of the war. The *Official Army Register* in 1867 listed the total of "battles" in which colored troops took part as 250: 1 in 1862, 28 in 1863, 170 in 1864, and 51 in 1865. This is patently an incomplete list: for example, it shows only one engagement for 1862, the minor engagement of Island Mound, Missouri, in which the 1st Kansas Colored made its debut as a fighting organization. The *Official Records*, however, contain reports of a number of other engagements in the fall of 1862 in which Negroes fought: two expeditions by portions of the 1st South Carolina Colored and several operations in which Butler's Louisiana regiments took part. There are omissions in the listings for the other years also. The expeditions against Fort Fisher near Wilmington, North Carolina, in December, 1864, and January, 1865, are the most obvious of these omissions.

The *Army Register* list of "battles" deserves further criticism because it makes no differentiation as between minor skirmishes, brushes with Confederate pickets, affairs, and major battles, sieges, and campaigns. The operations around Petersburg, lasting from May, 1864, through April of the next year, are disposed of in this list as one "battle" and, aside from the number of colored regiments involved, there is no indication that this "battle" was of any greater significance than the skirmish at Magnolia, Tennessee, on January 7, 1865, in which the 15th U.S. Colored suffered no casualties at all. One explanation of these errors is that when the *Register* was published in 1867 reports and records were still being collected and many were probably not available to the War Department compilers.

Frederick Dyer's well-known *Compendium,* published in 1908, drew on the relatively complete records published between 1880 and 1901 in the *Official Records.* Dyer listed 449 engagements in which colored troops fought, 200 more than the *Register.* Of these, Dyer rated 39 as major engagements. He also took the trouble to differentiate between battles, campaigns, brushes, and affairs, so that his list is more meaningful and of greater value to any analysis of the combat contribution of the Negro.

For all its obvious faults, the *Army Register* list still has value. It shows clearly, if inaccurately, how the military employment of colored troops increased steadily from an extremely small number of engagements in the first year of their organization to a substantial number in 1863, and to wide use as combat troops in 1864. In 1862 the organization of Negro regiments was merely beginning. The idea was new, tentative, extremely unpopular. Accordingly, Negro soldiers were given few opportunities to show their fighting ability. In 1863 they were still on an experimental basis; they were still expected to make their contribution to the war by providing a labor force for the armies, by garrisoning forts, by relieving white troops for combat. Circumstances forced the issue: colored regiments in a few scattered actions demonstrated that as combat troops Negroes could perform with courage and skill and determination. After serving their apprenticeship in 1863, it was logical and natural that Negro soldiers should have found themselves more and more in action in 1864.

They continued to serve as garrison troops, of course, with and without the company of white soldiers. With the freeing of the Mississippi in 1863, the main theater of war shifted toward the east and the battle of behemoths in Virginia, but Union garrisons from Columbus, Kentucky, to Forts Jackson and St.

Philip downstream from New Orleans, continued to be necessary, and Negro troops made up the bulk of them. General E. R. S. Canby's statement of "troops left in garrison on the Mississippi" in March, 1865, showed a total effective strength of 27,876 Union soldiers. Of this total, 18,299—65 per cent— were colored soldiers of 27 different regiments. But this was by no means the end of their participation in the closing rounds of the war.

Instead, Negro soldiers won an enviable reputation by their stubborn fighting with the Army of the Frontier under Blunt and Schofield and Steele. They fought repeatedly against Forrest in Tennessee and Mississippi. They aided materially in the defeat and demolition of Hood's army at Nashville. Nine Negro regiments were in on the difficult assignment of reducing Fort Blakely in the final assualt on Mobile, and victory rode their bayonets. Other Negro regiments fought in Florida, South Carolina, Georgia, and North Carolina, but by far the greatest number in any single theater of war were involved in the slow, bloody work of wearing down the Army of Northern Virginia from May, 1864, though April, 1865.

Mere numbers of colored troops engaged in Virginia in the last twelve months of war are impressive. Thirteen Negro regiments fought at Chaffin's Farm at the end of September, and of a total of thirty-seven Congressional Medals of Honor awarded to participants in that two-day struggle, fourteen went to members of colored organizations. Four of those same regiments fought again at Darbytown Road on October 13, six at Fair Oaks, five at Hatcher's Run, and five at Deep Bottom toward the end of the month. Twenty-two regiments were at one time or another engaged in the terrible and costly fighting before Petersburg in 1864 and 1865. Fifteen regiments served in the XVIII Corps of Butler's Army of the James; eight served in the IX Corps of the Army of the Potomac, fifteen in the X Corps. Finally, in December of 1864, the XXV Corps was organized under General Godfrey Weitzel. Unique in American military history, it was an entire army corps made up of Negro regiments, thirty-two in all. When the Confederacy had been defeated and the war was over, more than thirty Negro regiments (substantially the whole XXV Corps) were transferred to the

Department of Texas for duty along the Rio Grande, to give force to State Department protests against French interference and the puppet empire of Maximilian in Mexico. In the closing years of the war, and particularly during the last twelve months of conflict, the American Negro soldier proved himself worthy of the uniform he wore and the flag he defended.

To measure the contribution of the Negro soldier to final Union victory in the Civil War involves more than counting casualties and listing engagements. Actual combat takes a relatively small part of a soldier's time and energy. While some organizations seem to have been kept pretty constantly in forward positions, others, although actively engaged in prosecuting the war, found themselves in less harrowing situations, fighting the boredom that is a constant in the soldier's equation, guarding prisoners, preparing fortifications, escorting wagon trains, standing retreat parade for visiting dignitaries, drilling, working, and "wishing for the war to cease." It was like that with all who fought in the Civil War, white or colored, Union or Confederate. By and large, colored soldiers shared every kind of soldiers' duty with their white comrades.

Had Negro soldiers been used uniformly throughout the armies of the Union only as garrison troops, or labor battalions, or assault infantry, the task of assessing their contribution would be less difficult. As it was, their uneven employment in all the variety of duties incident to the conduct of total war—civil war at that—makes the task the more involved. In the trans-Mississippi West, colored troops were used as an integral part of the Army of the Frontier, working, foraging, fighting, and dying, side by side with white troops in Kansas, Missouri, Oklahoma, and Arkansas, from 1862 on through the war. In the Mississippi Valley, Negro regiments were used as commanding generals saw fit and as the changing tactical situation demanded. They fought against small bands of guerrillas or Forrest's roving columns; they garrisoned forts from Cairo to the Gulf; they dug in the parallels approaching the Confederate fortifications surrounding Mobile, and they came out of those parallels with a shout in the last assault wave of the war. They protected contrabands chopping cotton on captured plantations. They worked

in the swirling waters of the Red River to build Colonel Joseph
Bailey's dams and save Porter's fleet in the ill-starred Banks
expedition of the spring of 1864. At the end of the war, Bailey,
then a general commanding a brigade of engineers at Mobile,
was careful to mention them by name in his final report. "No
troops during this war have labored more severely or ardu-
ously," he wrote of his engineers, "but those to whom most
credit is due are the Ninety-sixth and Ninety-seventh U.S. Colored Engineer Regiments. Night and day without complaint
those regiments worked, and it is difficult to comprehend how
they endured through it. The regiments manifest very great
care and ability in their organization and discipline. The officers of both, with two exceptions, now out of service, labored
assiduously. Of none of them can I do other than speak in the
highest terms."

Captain J. M. Addeman of the 14th Rhode Island Heavy
Artillery (colored) served from the organization of his regiment through to the end of the war. It was the fate of the 14th
to have various garrison, picket, and outpost duty in the river
parishes of Louisiana, at Plaquemine and Donaldsonville. They
never knew the mingled panic and enthusiasm, the pain and
the glory of full combat with bugles and colors and three rous-
ing cheers from the white regiment on their left. They lasted
out the war near Plaquemine, the officers caught in the routine
of reports, courts-martial, inspections, staff work, and the like,
the enlisted men painfully learning to read and write in the
regimental schools, building forts, standing guard, or doing
picket duty. Their greatest enemies were not Confederates but
"yellow jack," "breakbone fever," and boredom. But Nathaniel
Banks complimented them in orders, and Thomas W. Sherman
called them "a noble regiment." They wanted to fight, Addeman
maintained: "The call was hopefully expected but disappoint-
ingly unheard. Yet," he asked, "may they not fairly claim to
share in the glory of the result, and to them may not the words
of the poet justly apply,—'They also serve who only stand and
wait.'"

Along the Atlantic coast Negro soldiers saw more mixed duty
as occasion demanded. They sweated in the Union trenches
around Charleston. They died in such ill-planned and badly

executed battles as Olustee and Honey Hill. In Northern Virginia they fought, dug, entrenched, reconnoitered the enemy's lines, and fought again, as the need arose. They guarded Confederate prisoners at Rock Island, Illinois, at Point Lookout, Maryland, and on the Dry Tortugas. Negro soldiers, in whatever theater of war they found themselves, seem to have done everything that soldiers might conceivably be expected to do. . . .

In numbers alone Negro troops made a measurable contribution to the strength of Union arms. Under the draft call of December, 1864, some ten thousand colored soldiers were added to the force already enrolled. On July 15, 1865, a total of 123,156 Negro soldiers were in the Union Army, organized into 120 infantry regiments, 12 regiments of heavy artillery, 10 batteries of light artillery, and 7 regiments of cavalry. They made up, at war's end, a good 12 per cent of the estimated one million men then in the armies of the Union. The whole number of colored troops recruited and organized during the war is usually given as 186,017, but since that figure includes 7,122 officers, a more nearly correct total is 178,895. The exact total will never be known, since records in some regiments were incorrectly kept or lost and since some organizations may have had their own rather irregular methods of securing replacements without either entering the casualties on the muster roll or changing the names on the roll. Joseph T. Wilson insisted that sometimes "if a company on picket or scouting lost ten men, the officers would immediately put ten new men in their places and have them answer to the dead men's names." Wilson asserted that this practice was followed in Missouri, Tennessee, and Virginia. As a consequence, Wilson suggested, the total number of colored troops who served in the Union Army may run as high as 200,000. But accepting the figure of 180,000 as probable, Negro troops made up between 9 and 10 per cent of the total number of Union soldiers. Losses among Negro troops were high: 68,178 from all causes were reported, or over one-third of the total enrolled. Of these, 2,751 were killed in action; the balance died of wounds or disease or were missing. Disease took far more lives than bullets; this was true of the entire Union Army, and of the Negro troops serving in it, too. To cite an extreme case: the 56th U.S. Colored saw over two years of service, chiefly post and garrison duty at Helena, Arkansas, and participated in three minor engagements, with a battle loss of 4 officers and 21 enlisted men killed or mortally wounded. But this regiment lost 6 officers and 647 men from disease.

Whatever duties they performed, Negro soldiers responded to the Union call when war weariness and anti-Negro feeling were at high tide in the North. Despite impressment, discrimination in pay and duty, and the constant threat of death or return to slavery if captured, Negro soldiers did not desert in abnormally large numbers. Some 14,887 went "over the hill" permanently, or roughly 7 per cent of the total desertions from the Union Army of over 200,000. Negro soldiers worked hard and they fought hard; they improved themselves by study when more pressing demands of a military nature permitted; they were generally a challenge to their officers. It is not in the province of the historian to speculate on what might have been, but it is tempting to wonder how many Negro regiments might have been raised if the pay scale for colored troops had been the same as that for the rest of the Union Army from August, 1862—or even from January, 1863—through the war. It is tempting, too, to wonder how a hundred colored regiments, adequately armed and trained in the use of those arms, might have performed as an independent army corps under sympathetic and intelligent officers who appreciated their worth and their potential.

Hindsight and speculation on the basis of hindsight seldom win battles or campaigns. Soldiers are seldom adequately trained until a war is over. Conditions are never ideal. It is enough that they served as soldiers, that they were admitted finally into the ranks of armies organized to preserve the Union and to win freedom for the Negro. In summing up the part his colored troops had played in the battle of Nashville, Colonel Thomas Morgan used words appropriate to their role in the war: "Colored soldiers had fought side by side with white troops. They had mingled together in the charge. They had supported each other.

They had assisted each other from the field when wounded, and they lay side by side in death. The survivors rejoiced together over a hard-fought field, won by common valor. All who witnessed their conduct gave them equal praise. The day we longed to see had come and gone, and the sun went down upon a record of coolness, bravery, manliness, never to be unmade. A new chapter in the history of liberty had been written. It had been shown that marching under the flag of freedom, animated by a love of liberty, even the slave becomes a man and a hero."

The new chapter had been written. Negro soldiers had helped write it. And, as Frederick Douglass had foreseen in the opening weeks of war, they had helped themselves enormously by their soldierly participation. As occasion provided, they had learned their first lessons in reading and writing at company and regimental schools. Of more significance, Negro soldiers learned their first lessons in self-reliance and in the exercise of authority, choice, and discretion. They bore arms like white men, and as officers and noncommissioned officers they gave orders, kept records, and shouldered new responsibilities. They learned important lessons in loyalty to the Union, and after the war they found respectful treatment and honor when, as veterans of the Union Army, they joined the Grand Army of the Republic. In the G.A.R., Negro veterans rose to positions of trust and distinction: George Washington Williams in 1888 signed himself "Colonel and Late Judge Advocate in the Grand Army of the Republic." Joseph Wilson became aide-de-camp to the commander in chief of the G.A.R.

In the period between the close of the Civil War and the end of the century, the Negro veteran enjoyed wide respect and some equality of treatment and consideration throughout the North. In the rather florid language of Ben Butler, the Negro soldier had "with the bayonet . . . unlocked the iron-barred gates of prejudice, and opened new fields of freedom, liberty, and equality of right." Opportunity was his after the war: he served in state and local elective offices; he went to constitutional conventions in Southern states; he went to the Congress of the United States. He was permitted to become an integral part of the regular army. As a part of that army he helped to garrison the conquered South and to guard the westward marches. As infantryman and especially as cavalryman on the western plains, he added new laurels to those won at Petersburg, New Market Heights, and Nashville.

If there had been a better integrated and more widely accepted Negro soldier policy in the Lincoln administration and in the Union Army earlier, very probably Negro soldiers might have been allowed a larger share of what William Birney called the "glory" of the closing campaigns. But the Negro soldier had won glory enough. He had fought his way into the Union Army by his courage and tenacity and sacrifice. Once he had been officially recognized as a soldier, he had fought to maintain his position as a soldier and to broaden the scope of his military usefulness. As a soldier, he had gradually subdued much of the Negro's worst enemy, white prejudice. As a soldier in the Union Army, the American Negro proved his manhood and established a strong claim to equality of treatment and opportunity. In the 14th and 15th amendments to the Constitution of the United States, his manhood and his claim were recognized by the nation.

Had the Negro played a merely passive role as spectator during the Civil War, had he served only in his traditional menial capacity as cook and teamster and laborer, that national recognition of him as man and as citizen must have been postponed indefinitely. The Southern position that slaves could not bear arms was essentially correct: a slave was not a man. The war ended slavery. The Negro soldier proved that the slave could become a man.

William Edward Burghardt Du Bois

Why should Du Bois' essay in defense of Reconstruction, originally published in 1910, be reprinted in a collection of essays whose purpose it is to present recent interpretations of Negro history? The answer lies in the history of American historiography.

Du Bois' defense of Reconstruction first appeared in an article, "The Freedmen's Bureau" in the *Atlantic Monthly* of March 1901, and it was reprinted in *The Souls of Black Folk* two years later. However, the tide of Reconstruction scholarship then being produced in American universities was decidedly opposed to Du Bois' position. The leading historians of Reconstruction, John W. Burgess and William Dunning of Columbia University, and their graduate students, produced a number of scholarly monographs that were very critical of Reconstruction. By the time Du Bois presented a full-scale defense of Reconstruction in December 1909, he was nearly alone in his views.

Speaking calmly and without rancor to the members of the American Historical Association, Du Bois pointed to the accomplishments of Reconstruction governments. He called attention to the new democratic constitutions, to the beginnings of a public school system, to the reconstruction of war-ravaged public facilities, and to various social reforms. He reminded his colleagues of all that Negroes had done to help themselves—their churches, schools and colleges, and self-help projects. He defended the Freedmen's Bureau and justified Negro suffrage. He placed the corruption and malfeasance of Reconstruction in the larger light of American history, arguing that it was not restricted to carpetbaggers and Negroes. He supported the character and quality of many of the important Negro officeholders. Finally, Du Bois remained unrepentant about Reconstruction. He concluded with bitter irony: "Practically the whole new growth of the South has been accomplished under laws which black men helped to frame thirty years ago. I know of no greater compliment to Negro suffrage." The irony, of course, was in the fact that Negroes had over the previous decade been eliminated from the polls.

Du Bois' paper was printed in the *American Historical Review* in 1910, but his thesis was ignored by contemporary historiography. What Du Bois had to say did not fit into the spirit of the times. Five years later D. W. Griffiths' movie version of Reconstruction, *The Birth of a Nation*, swept the country, as did a revival of the Ku Klux Klan. Du Bois' essay, while not completely forgotten, was consigned, along with the works of the Negro historian, A. A. Taylor, to the category of "special pleading."

However, the findings of Du Bois, Taylor, and Horace Mann Bond were gradually supported by a number of studies, written by a new generation of historians. One of the most significant facts about these new studies was that for the most part they were written by young white Southern historians, among whom were Francis Simkins, Robert H. Woody, Roger W. Shugg, C. Vann Woodward, David Donald, Vernon L. Wharton, George B. Tindall, and Joel Williamson.

The picture of Reconstruction that emerges from contemporary scholarship is very similar to that which Du Bois drew in 1910. His study still retains its freshness after more than five decades and is reprinted here in its entirety.

RECONSTRUCTION AND ITS BENEFITS[1]

SOURCE: W. E. B. Du Bois, "Reconstruction and Its Benefits," *American Historical Review*, XV (July, 1910), pp. 781–99.

There is danger to-day that between the intense feeling of the South and the conciliatory spirit of the North grave injustice will be done the negro American in the history of Reconstruction. Those who see in negro suffrage the cause of the main evils of Reconstruction must remember that if there had not been a single freedman left in the South after the war the problems of Reconstruction would still have been grave. Property in slaves to the extent of perhaps two thousand million dollars had suddenly disappeared. One thousand five hundred more millions, representing the Confederate war debt, had largely disappeared. Large amounts of real estate and other property had been destroyed, industry had been disorganized, 250,000 men had been killed and many more maimed. With this went the moral effect of an unsuccessful war with all its letting down of social standards and quickening of hatred and discouragement —a situation which would make it difficult under any circumstances to reconstruct a new government and a new civilization. Add to all this the presence of four million freedmen and the

[1] Paper read at the annual meeting of the American Historical Association in New York, December, 1909.

situation is further complicated. But this complication is very largely a matter of well-known historical causes. Any human being "doomed in his own person, and his posterity, to live without knowledge, and without the capacity to make anything his own, and to toil that another may reap the fruits,"[2] is bound, on sudden emancipation, to loom like a great dread on the horizon.

How to train and treat these ex-slaves easily became a central problem of Reconstruction, although by no means the only problem. Three agencies undertook the solution of this problem at first and their influence is apt to be forgotten. Without them the problems of Reconstruction would have been far graver than they were. These agencies were: (a) the negro church, (b) the negro school, and (c) the Freedmen's Bureau. After the war the white churches of the South got rid of their negro members and the negro church organizations of the North invaded the South. The 20,000 members of the African Methodist Episcopal Church in 1856 leaped to 75,000 in 1866 and 200,000 in 1876, while their property increased sevenfold. The negro Baptists with 150,000 members in 1850 has fully a half million in 1870. There were, before the end of Reconstruction, perhaps 10,000 local bodies touching the majority of the freed population, centring almost the whole of their social life, and teaching them organization and autonomy. They were primitive, ill-governed, at times fantastic groups of human beings, and yet it is difficult to exaggerate the influence of this new responsibility—the first social institution fully controlled by black men in America, with traditions that rooted back to Africa and with possibilities which made the 35,000 negro American churches to-day, with their three and one-half million members, the most powerful negro institutions in the world.

With the negro church, but separate from it, arose the school as the first expression of the missionary activity of Northern religious bodies. Seldom in the history of the world has an almost totally illiterate population been given the means of self-education in so short a time. The movement started with the negroes themselves and they continued to form the dynamic

[2] State *v.* Mann, *North Carolina Reports*, 2 Devereux 263.

force behind it. "This great multitude rose up simultaneously and asked for intelligence."[3] The education of this mass had to begin at the top with the training of teachers, and within a few years a dozen colleges and normal schools started; by 1877, 571,506 negro children were in school. There can be no doubt that these schools were a great conservative steadying force to which the South owes much. It must not be forgotten that among the agents of the Freedmen's Bureau were not only soldiers and politicians but school-teachers and educational leaders like Ware and Cravath.

Granted that the situation was in any case bad and that negro churches and schools stood as conservative educative forces, how far did negro suffrage hinder progress, and was it expedient? The difficulties that stared Reconstruction politicians in the face were these: (a) They must act quickly. (b) Emancipation had increased the political power of the South by one-sixth: could this increased political power be put in the hands of those who, in defense of slavery, had disrupted the Union? (c) How was the abolition of slavery to be made effective? (d) What was to be the political position of the freedmen?

Andrew Johnson said in 1864, in regard to calling a convention to restore the state of Tennessee,

who shall restore and re-establish it? Shall the man who gave his influence and his means to destroy the Government? Is he to participate in the great work of re-organization? Shall he who brought this misery upon the State be permitted to control its destinies? If this be so, then all this precious blood of our brave soldiers and officers so freely poured out will have been wantonly spilled.[4]

To settle these and other difficulties, three ways were suggested: (1) the Freedmen's Bureau, (2) partial negro suffrage, and (3) full manhood suffrage for negroes.

The Freedmen's Bureau was an attempt to establish a government guardianship over the negroes and insure their economic and civil rights. Its establishment was a herculean task both physically and socially, and it not only met the solid opposition of the white South, but even the North looked at the

[3] First General Report of the Inspector of Schools, Freedmen's Bureau.
[4] Edward McPherson, *The Political History of the United States during the Period of Reconstruction* (1871), p. 46.

new thing as socialistic and over-paternal. It accomplished a
great task but it was repudiated. Carl Schurz in 1865 felt warranted in saying

that not half of the labor that has been done in the south this year, or
will be done there next year, would have been or would be done but
for the exertions of the Freedmen's Bureau. . . . No other agency, except one placed there by the national government, could have wielded
that moral power whose interposition was so necessary to prevent the
southern society from falling at once into the chaos of a general col-
lision between its different elements.[5]

Notwithstanding this the Bureau was temporary, was regarded
as a makeshift and soon abandoned.

Meantime, partial negro suffrage seemed not only just but
almost inevitable. Lincoln in 1864 "cautiously suggested" to
Louisiana's private consideration, "whether some of the colored
people may not be let in, as, for instance, the very intelligent,
and especially those who have fought gallantly in our ranks.
They would probably help, in some trying time to come, to keep
the jewel of liberty in the family of freedom."[6] Indeed, the
"family of freedom" in Louisiana being somewhat small just
then, who else was to be intrusted with the "jewel"? Later and
for different reasons, Johnson in 1865 wrote to Mississippi:

If you could extend the elective franchise to all persons of color
who can read the Constitution of the United States in English and
write their names, and to all persons of color who own real estate
valued at not less than two hundred and fifty dollars, and pay taxes
thereon, you would completely disarm the adversary and set an example the other States will follow. This you can do with perfect safety,
and you thus place the southern States, in reference to free persons of
color, upon the same basis with the free States. I hope and trust your
convention will do this.[7]

Meantime the negroes themselves began to ask for the suffrage—
the Georgia Convention in Augusta, 1866, advocating "a proposition to give those who could write and read well, and possessed
a certain property qualification, the right of suffrage." The reply

[5] Schurz. Report to the President, 1865. *Senate Ex. Doc. No. 2*, 39
Cong., 1 sess., p. 40.
[6] Letter to Hahn, March 13. McPherson, p. 20.
[7] Johnson to Sharkey, August 15. *Ibid.*, p. 19.

of the South to these suggestions was decisive. In Tennessee alone was any action attempted that even suggested possible negro suffrage in the future, and that failed. In all other states the "Black Codes" adopted were certainly not reassuring to friends of freedom. To be sure it was not a time to look for calm, cool, thoughtful action on the part of the white South. Their economic condition was pitiable, their fear of negro freedom genuine; yet it was reasonable to expect from them something less than repression and utter reaction toward slavery. To some extent this expectation was fulfilled: the abolition of slavery was recognized and the civil rights of owning property and appearing as a witness in cases in which he was a party were generally granted the negro; yet with these went in many cases harsh and unbearable regulations which largely neutralized the concessions and certainly gave ground for the assumption that once free the South would virtually re-enslave the negro. The colored people themselves naturally feared this and protested as in Mississippi "against the reactionary policy prevailing, and expressing the fear that the Legislature will pass such proscriptive laws as will drive the freedmen from the State, or practically re-enslave them."[8]

The Codes spoke for themselves. They have often been re-printed and quoted. No open-minded student can read them without being convinced that they meant nothing more nor less than slavery in daily toil. Not only this but as Professor Burgess (whom no one accuses of being negrophile) says:

Almost every act, word or gesture of the Negro, not consonant with good taste and good manners as well as good morals, was made a crime or misdemeanor, for which he could first be fined by the magistrates and then be consigned to a condition of almost slavery for an indefinite time, if he could not pay the bill.

These laws might have been interpreted and applied liberally, but the picture painted by Carl Schurz does not lead one to anticipate this:

Some planters held back their former slaves on their plantations by brute force. Armed bands of white men patrolled the country roads to drive back the negroes wandering about. Dead bodies of murdered

[8] October 7, 1865.

negroes were found on and near the highways and by-paths. Gruesome reports came from the hospitals—reports of colored men and women whose ears had been cut off, whose skulls had been broken by blows, whose bodies had been slashed by knives or lacerated with scourges. A number of such cases I had occasion to examine myself. A veritable reign of terror prevailed in many parts of the South. The negro found scant justice in the local courts against the white man. He could look for protection only to the military forces of the United States still garrisoning the "States lately in rebellion" and to the Freedmen's Bureau.

All things considered, it seems probable that if the South had been permitted to have its way in 1865 the harshness of negro slavery would have been mitigated so as to make slave-trading difficult, and to make it possible for a negro to hold property and appear in some cases in court; but that in most other respects the blacks would have remained in slavery.

What could prevent this? A Freedmen's Bureau, established for ten, twenty or forty years with a careful distribution of land and capital and a system of education for the children, might have prevented such an extension of slavery. But the country would not listen to such a comprehensive plan. A restricted grant of the suffrage voluntarily made by the states would have been a reassuring proof of a desire to treat the freedmen fairly, and would have balanced, in part at least, the increased political power of the South. There was no such disposition evident. On the other hand, there was ground for the conclusion in the Reconstruction report of June 18, 1866, that so far as slavery was concerned "the language of all the provisions and ordinances of these States on the subject amounts to nothing more than an unwilling admission of an unwelcome truth." This was of course natural, but was it unnatural that the North should feel that better guarantees were needed to abolish slavery? Carl Schurz wrote:

I deem it proper, however, to offer a few remarks on the assertion frequently put forth, that the franchise is likely to be extended to the colored man by the voluntary action of the Southern whites themselves. My observation leads me to a contrary opinion. Aside from a very few enlightened men, I found but one class of people in favor of the enfranchisement of the blacks: it was the class of Unionists who found themselves politically ostracised and looked upon the enfranchisement of the loyal negroes as the salvation of the whole loyal element. . . . The masses are strongly opposed to colored suffrage; anybody that dares to advocate it is stigmatized as a dangerous fanatic. The only manner in which, in my opinion, the southern people can be induced to grant to the freedman some measure of self-protecting power in the form of suffrage, is to make it a condition precedent to "readmission."[9]

Even in Louisiana, under the proposed reconstruction

not one negro was allowed to vote, though at that very time the wealthy intelligent free colored people of the state paid taxes on property assessed at $15,000,000 and many of them were well known for their patriotic zeal and love for the Union. Thousands of colored men whose homes were in Louisiana, served bravely in the national army and navy, and many of the so-called negroes in New Orleans could not be distinguished by the most intelligent strangers from the best class of white gentlemen, either by color or manner, dress or language, still, as it was known by tradition and common fame that they were not of pure Caucasian descent, they could not vote.[10]

The United States government might now have taken any one of three courses:

1. Allowed the whites to reorganize the states and take no measures to enfranchise the freedmen.

2. Allowed the whites to reorganize the states but provided that after the lapse of a reasonable length of time there should be no discrimination in the right of suffrage on account of "race, color or previous condition of servitude."

3. Admitted all men, black and white, to take part in reorganizing the states and then provided that future restrictions on the suffrage should be made on any basis except "race, color and previous condition of servitude."

The first course was clearly inadmissible since it meant virtually giving up the great principle of which the war was largely fought and won, i.e., human freedom; a giving of freedom which contented itself with an edict, and then turned the "freed" slaves over to the tender mercies of their impoverished and angry ex-masters was no gift at all. The second course was theoretically attractive but practically impossible. It meant at least a prolongation of slavery and instead of attempts to raise the freedmen, it gave the white community strong incentives

[9] Report to the President, 1865. *Senate Ex. Doc. No. 2*, 39 Cong., 1 sess., p. 44.
[10] Brewster, *Sketches of Southern Mystery, Treason, and Murder*, p. 116.

for keeping the blacks down so that as few as possible would ever qualify for the suffrage. Negro schools would have been discouraged and economic fetters would have held the black man as a serf for an indefinite time. On the other hand, the arguments for universal negro suffrage from the start were strong and are still strong, and no one would question their strength were it not for the assumption that the experiment failed. Frederick Douglass said to President Johnson: "Your noble and humane predecessor placed in our hands the sword to assist in saving the nation, and we do hope that you, his able successor, will favorably regard the placing in our hands the ballot with which to save ourselves."[11] And when Johnson demurred on account of the hostility between blacks and poor whites, a committee of prominent colored men replied:

Even if it were true, as you allege, that the hostility of the blacks toward the poor whites must necessarily project itself into a state of freedom, and that this enmity between the two races is even more intense in a state of freedom than in a state of slavery, in the name of Heaven, we reverently ask, how can you, in view of your professed desire to promote the welfare of the black man, deprive him of all means of defence, and clothe him whom you regard as his enemy in the panoply of political power?[12]

Carl Schurz expressed this argument most emphatically:

The emancipation of the slaves is submitted to only in so far as chattel slavery in the old form could not be kept up. But although the freedman is no longer considered the property of the individual master, he is considered the slave of society, and all independent State legislation will share the tendency to make him such.

The solution of the problem would be very much facilitated by enabling all the loyal and free-labor elements in the south to exercise a healthy influence upon legislation. It will hardly be possible to secure the freedmen against oppressive class legislation and private persecution, unless he be endowed with a certain measure of political power.[13]

To the argument of ignorance Schurz replied:

The effect of the extension of the franchise to the colored people upon the development of free labor and upon the security of human rights in the south being the principal object in view, the objections

[11] Frederick Douglass to Johnson, February 7, 1866. McPherson, p. 52.
[12] McPherson, p. 56.
[13] Report to the President, 1865. *Senate Ex. Doc. No. 2*, 39 Cong., 1 sess., p. 45.

raised on the ground of the ignorance of the freedmen become unimportant. Practical liberty is a good school. . . . It is idle to say that it will be time to speak of negro suffrage when the whole colored race will be educated, for the ballot may be necessary to him to secure his education.[14]

The granting of full negro suffrage meant one of two alternatives to the South: (a) the uplift of the negro for sheer self-preservation; this is what Schurz and the saner North expected; as one Southern superintendent said: "the elevation of this class is a matter of prime importance since a ballot in the hands of a black citizen is quite as potent as in the hands of a white one." Or (b) a determined concentration of Southern effort by actual force to deprive the negro of the ballot or nullify its use. This is what happened, but even in this case so much energy was taken in keeping the negro from voting that the plan for keeping him in virtual slavery and denying him education failed. It took ten years to nullify negro suffrage in part and twenty years to escape the fear of federal intervention. In these twenty years a vast number of negroes had risen so far as to escape slavery forever. Debt peonage could be fastened on part of the rural South, and was, but even here the new negro landholder appeared. Thus despite everything the Fifteenth Amendment and that alone struck the death knell of slavery.

The steps that ended in the Fifteenth Amendment were not, however, taken suddenly. The negroes were given the right by universal suffrage to join in reconstructing the state governments and the reasons for it were cogently set forth in the report of the Joint Committee on Reconstruction in 1866, which began as follows:

A large proportion of the population had become, instead of mere chattels, free men and citizens. Through all the past struggle these had remained true and loyal, and had, in large numbers, fought on the side of the Union. It was impossible to abandon them without securing them their rights as free men and citizens. The whole civilized world would have cried out against such base ingratitude, and the bare idea is offensive to all right-thinking men. Hence it became important to inquire what could be done to secure their rights, civil and political.[15]

[14] *Ibid.*, p. 43.
[15] *House Reports No. 30*, 39 Cong., 1 sess., p. xiii.

The report then proceeded to emphasize the increased political power of the South and recommended the Fourteenth Amendment, since

It appeared to your committee that the rights of these persons by whom the basis of representation had been thus increased should be recognized by the General Government. While slaves, they were not considered as having any rights, civil or political. It did not seem just or proper that all the political advantages derived from their becoming free should be confined to their former masters, who had fought against the Union, and withheld from themselves, who had always been loyal.[16]

It was soon seen that this expedient of the Fourteenth Amendment was going to prove abortive and that determined and organized effort would be used to deprive the freedmen of the ballot. Thereupon the United States said the final word of simple justice, namely: the states may still regulate the suffrage as they please but they may not deprive a man of the right to vote simply because he is a negro.

For such reasons the negro was enfranchised. What was the result? No language has been spared to describe these results as the worst imaginable. Nor is it necessary to dispute for a moment that there were bad results, and bad results arising from negro suffrage; but it may be questioned if the results were as bad as painted or if negro suffrage was the prime cause.

Let us not forget that the white South believed it to be of vital interest to its welfare that the experiment of negro suffrage should fail ignominiously, and that almost to a man the whites were willing to insure this failure either by active force or passive acquiescence; that beside this there were, as might be expected, men, black and white, Northern and Southern, only too eager to take advantage of such a situation for feathering their own nests. The results in such case had to be evil but to charge the evil to negro suffrage is unfair. It may be charged to anger, poverty, venality, and ignorance; but the anger and poverty were the almost inevitable aftermath of war; the venality was much greater among whites than negroes, and while ignorance was the curse of the negroes, the fault was not theirs, and they took the initiative to correct it.

The chief charges against the negro governments are extrava-

16 *Ibid.*

gance, theft, and incompetency of officials. There is no serious
charge that these governments threatened civilization or the
foundations of social order. The charge is that they threatened
property, and that they were inefficient. These charges are in
part undoubtedly true, but they are often exaggerated. When a
man has, in his opinion, been robbed and maltreated he is
sensitive about money matters. The South had been terribly impoverished and saddled with new social burdens. In other words,
a state with smaller resources was asked not only to do a work of
restoration but a larger social work. The property-holders were
aghast. They not only demurred, but, predicting ruin and revolution, they appealed to secret societies, to intimidation, force,
and murder. They refused to believe that these novices in government and their friends were aught but scamps and fools.
Under the circumstances occurring directly after the war, the
wisest statesman would have been compelled to resort to increased taxation and would in turn have been execrated as extravagant and even dishonest. When now, in addition to this, the
new legislators, white and black, were undoubtedly in a large
number of cases extravagant, dishonest, and incompetent, it is
easy to see what flaming and incredible stories of Reconstruction
governments could gain wide currency and belief. In fact, the
extravagance, although great, was not universal, and much of it
was due to the extravagant spirit pervading the whole country
in a day of inflated currency and speculation. The ignorance
was deplorable but a deliberate legacy from the past, and some
of the extravagance and much of the effort was to remedy this
ignorance. The incompetency was in part real and in part emphasized by the attitude of the whites of the better class.

When incompetency gains political power in an extravagant
age the result is widespread dishonesty. The dishonesty in the
reconstruction of the South was helped on by three circumstances:

1. The former dishonesty in the political South.

2. The presence of many dishonest Northern politicians.

3. The temptation to Southern politicians at once to profit by
dishonesty and to discredit negro government.

4. The poverty of the negro.

(1) Dishonesty in public life has no monopoly of time or

place in America. To take one state: In 1839 it was reported in Mississippi that ninety per cent of the fines collected by sheriffs and clerks were unaccounted for. In 1841 the state treasurer acknowledges himself "at a loss to determine the precise liabilities of the state and her means of paying the same." And in 1839 the auditor's books had not been posted for eighteen months, no entries made for a year, and no vouchers examined for three years. Congress gave Jefferson College, Natchez, more than 46,000 acres of land; before the war this whole property had "disappeared" and the college was closed. Congress gave to Mississippi among other states the "16th section" of the public lands for schools. In thirty years the proceeds of this land in Mississippi were embezzled to the amount of at least one and a half millions of dollars. In Columbus, Mississippi, a receiver of public moneys stole $100,000 and resigned. His successor stole $55,000, and a treasury agent wrote: "Another receiver would probably follow in the footsteps of the two. You will not be surprised if I recommend his being retained in preference to another appointment." From 1830 to 1860 Southern men in federal offices alone embezzled more than a million dollars—a far larger sum then than now. There might have been less stealing in the South during Reconstruction without negro suffrage but it is certainly highly instructive to remember that the mark of the thief which dragged its slime across nearly every great Northern state and almost up to the presidential chair could not certainly in those cases be charged against the vote of black men. This was the day when a national secretary of war was caught stealing, a vice-president presumably took bribes, a private secretary of the president, a chief clerk of the Treasury, and eighty-six government officials stole millions in the whiskey frauds, while the Credit Mobilier filched fifty millions and bribed the government to an extent never fully revealed; not to mention less distinguished thieves like Tweed.

Is it surprising that in such an atmosphere a new race learning the a-b-c of government should have become the tools of thieves? And when they did was the stealing their fault or was it justly chargeable to their enfranchisement?

Undoubtedly there were many ridiculous things connected with Reconstruction governments: the placing of ignorant field-hands who could neither read nor write in the legislature, the gold spittoons of South Carolina, the enormous public printing bill of Mississippi—all these were extravagant and funny, and yet somehow, to one who sees beneath all that is bizarre, the real human tragedy of the upward striving of down-trodden men, the groping for light among people born in darkness, there is less tendency to laugh and gibe than among shallower minds and easier consciences. All that is funny is not bad.

Then too a careful examination of the alleged stealing in the South reveals much. First, there is repeated exaggeration. For instance it is said that the taxation in Mississippi was fourteen times as great in 1874 as in 1869. This sounds staggering until we learn that the state taxation in 1869 was only ten cents on one hundred dollars, and that the expenses of government in 1874 were only twice as great as in 1860, and that too with a depreciated currency. It could certainly be argued that the state government in Mississippi was doing enough additional work in 1874 to warrant greatly increased cost. A Southern white historian acknowledges that

the work of restoration which the government was obliged to undertake, made increased expenses necessary. During the period of the war, and for several years thereafter, public buildings and state institutions were permitted to fall into decay. The state house and grounds, the executive mansion, the penitentiary, the insane asylum, and the buildings for the blind, deaf, and dumb were in a dilapidated condition, and had to be extended and repaired. A new building for the blind was purchased and fitted up. The reconstructionists established a public school system and spent money to maintain and support it, perhaps too freely, in view of the impoverishment of the people. When they took hold, warrants were worth but sixty or seventy cents on the dollar, a fact which made the price of building materials used in the work of construction correspondingly higher. So far as the conduct of state officials who were intrusted with the custody of public funds is concerned, it may be said that there were no great embezzlements or other cases of misappropriation during the period of Republican rule.[17]

The state debt of Mississippi was said to have been increased from a half million to twenty million when in fact it had not been increased at all.

[17] James W. Garner, *Reconstruction in Mississippi,* (1901), p. 322.

The character of the real thieving shows that white men must have been the chief beneficiaries and that as a former South Carolina slaveholder said:

> The legislature, ignorant as it is, could not have been bribed without money, that must have been furnished from some source that it is our duty to discover. A legislature composed chiefly of our former slaves has been bribed. One prominent feature of this transaction is the part which native Carolinians have played in it, some of our own household men whom the state, in the past, has delighted to honor, appealing to their cupidity and avarice make them the instruments to effect the robbery of their impoverished white brethren. Our former slaves have been bribed by these men to give them the privilege by law of plundering the property-holders of the state.[18]

The character of much of the stealing shows who were the thieves. The frauds through the manipulation of state and railway bonds and of bank-notes must have inured chiefly to the benefit of experienced white men, and this must have been largely the case in the furnishing and printing frauds. It was chiefly in the extravagance for "sundries and incidentals" and direct money payments for votes that the negroes received their share.

That the negroes led by astute thieves became tools and received a small share of the spoils is true. But two considerations must be added: much of the legislation which resulted in fraud was represented to the negroes as good legislation, and thus their votes were secured by deliberate misrepresentation. Take for instance the land frauds of South Carolina. A wise negro leader of that state, advocating the state purchase of lands, said:

> One of the greatest of slavery bulwarks was the infernal plantation system, one man owning his thousand, another his twenty, another fifty thousand acres of land. This is the only way by which we will break up that system, and I maintain that our freedom will be of no effect if we allow it to continue. What is the main cause of the prosperity of the North? It is because every man has his own farm and is free and independent. Let the lands of the South be similarly divided.

From such arguments the negroes were induced to aid a scheme to buy land and distribute it; yet a large part of $800,000 appropriated was wasted and went to the white land-holder's pockets. The railroad schemes were in most cases feasible

18 Hon. F. F. Warley in Brewster's *Sketches*, p. 150.

and eventually carried out; it was not the object but the method that was wrong.

Granted then that the negroes were to some extent venal but to a much larger extent ignorant and deceived, the question is: did they show any signs of a disposition to learn better things? The theory of democratic government is not that the will of the people is always right, but rather that normal human beings of average intelligence will, if given a chance, learn the right and best course by bitter experience. This is precisely what the negro voters showed indubitable signs of doing. First, they strove for schools to abolish ignorance, and, second, a large and growing number of them revolted against the carnival of extravagance and stealing that marred the beginning of Reconstruction, and joined with the best elements to institute reform; and the greatest stigma on the white South is not that it opposed negro suffrage and resented theft and incompetence, but that when it saw the reform movement growing and even in some cases triumphing, and a larger and larger number of black voters learning to vote for honesty and ability, it still preferred a Reign of Terror to a campaign of education, and disfranchised negroes instead of punishing rascals. . . .

In the midst of all these difficulties the negro governments in the South accomplished much of positive good. We may recognize three things which negro rule gave to the South:

1. Democratic government.
2. Free public schools.
3. New social legislation.

Two states will illustrate conditions of government in the South before and after negro rule. In South Carolina there was before the war a property qualification for office-holders, and, in part, for voters. The Constitution of 1868, on the other hand, was a modern democratic document starting (in marked contrast to the old constitutions) with a declaration that "We, the People", framed it, and preceded by a broad Declaration of Rights which did away with property qualifications and based representation directly on population instead of property. It especially took up new subjects of social legislation, declaring navigable rivers free public highways, instituting homestead exemptions, establishing boards of county commissioners, providing for a new penal code of laws, establishing universal manhood suffrage "without distinction of race or color", devoting six sections to charitable and penal institutions and six to corporations, providing separate property for married women, etc. Above all, eleven sections of the Tenth Article were devoted to the establishment of a complete public-school system.

So satisfactory was the constitution thus adopted by negro suffrage and by a convention composed of a majority of blacks that the state lived twenty-seven years under it without essential change and when the constitution was revised in 1895, the revision was practically nothing more than an amplification of the Constitution of 1868. No essential advance step of the former document was changed except the suffrage article.

In Mississippi the Constitution of 1868 was, as compared with that before the war, more democratic. It not only forbade distinctions on account of color but abolished all property qualifications for jury service, and property and educational qualifications for suffrage; it required less rigorous qualifications for office; it prohibited the lending of the credit of the state for private corporations—an abuse dating back as far as 1830. It increased the powers of the governor, raised the low state salaries, and increased the number of state officials. New ideas like the public-school system and the immigration bureau were introduced and in general the activity of the state greatly and necessarily enlarged. Finally, that was the only constitution ever submitted to popular approval at the polls. This constitution remained in force twenty-two years. . . .

A thorough study of the legislation accompanying these constitutions and its changes since would of course be necessary before a full picture of the situation could be given. This has not been done, but so far as my studies have gone I have been surprised at the comparatively small amount of change in law and government which the overthrow of negro rule brought about. There were sharp and often hurtful economies introduced marking the return of property to power, there was a sweeping change of officials, but the main body of Reconstruction legislation stood.

This democracy brought forward new leaders and men and definitely overthrew the old Southern aristocracy. Among these new men were negroes of worth and ability. John R. Lynch when speaker of the Mississippi house of representatives was given a public testimonial by Republicans and Democrats and the leading Democratic paper said:

His bearing in office had been so proper, and his rulings in such marked contrast to the partisan conduct of the ignoble whites of his party who have aspired to be leaders of the blacks, that the conservatives cheerfully joined in the testimonial.[19]

Of the colored treasurer of South Carolina, Governor Chamberlain said:

I have never heard one word or seen one act of Mr. Cardozo's which did not confirm my confidence in his personal integrity and his political honor and zeal for the honest administration of the State Government. On every occasion, and under all circumstances, he has been against fraud and jobbery, and in favor of good measures and good men.[20]

Jonathan C. Gibbs, a colored man and the first state superintendent of instruction in Florida, was a graduate of Dartmouth. He established the system and brought it to success, dying in harness in 1874. Such men—and there were others—ought not to be forgotten or confounded with other types of colored and white Reconstruction leaders.

There is no doubt but that the thirst of the black man for knowledge—a thirst which has been too persistent and durable to be mere curiosity of whim—gave birth to the public free-school system of the South. It was the question upon which black voters and legislators insisted more than anything else and while it is possible to find some vestiges of free schools in some of the Southern States before the war yet a universal, well-established system dates from the day that the black man got political power. Common-school instruction in the South, in the modern sense of the term, was begun for negroes by the Freedmen's Bureau and missionary societies, and the state public-school systems for all children were formed mainly by negro Reconstruction governments. The earlier state constitutions of Mississippi "from 1817 to 1865 contained a declaration that 'Religion, morality and knowledge being necessary to good gov-

[19] Jackson (Mississippi) *Clarion*, April 24, 1873.
[20] Allen, *Governor Chamberlain's Administration in South Carolina*, p. 82.

ernment, the preservation of liberty and the happiness of mankind, schools and the means of education shall forever be encouraged.' It was not, however, until 1868 that encouragement
was given to any general system of public schools meant to
embrace the whole youthful population." The Constitution of
1868 makes it the duty of the legislature to establish "a uniform
system of free public schools, by taxation or otherwise, for all
children between the ages of five and twenty-one years." In
Alabama the Reconstruction Constitution of 1868 provided that
"It shall be the duty of the Board of Education to establish
throughout the State, in each township or other school district
which it may have created, one or more schools at which all
the children of the State between the ages of five and twenty-
one years may attend free of charge." Arkansas in 1868, Florida
in 1869, Louisiana in 1868, North Carolina in 1869, South
Carolina in 1868, and Virginia in 1870, established school systems. The Constitution of 1868 in Louisiana required the general
assembly to establish "at least one free public school in every
parish", and that these schools should make no "distinction
of race, color or previous condition." Georgia's system was not
fully established until 1873.

We are apt to forget that in all human probability the granting
of negro manhood suffrage and the passage of the Fifteenth
Amendment were decisive in rendering permanent the foundation of the negro common school. Even after the overthrow of
the negro governments, if the negroes had been left a servile
caste, personally free, but politically powerless, it is not reasonable to think that a system of common schools would have
been provided for them by the Southern States. Serfdom and
education have ever proven contradictory terms. But when Congress, backed by the nation, determined to make the negroes
full-fledged voting citizens, the South had a hard dilemma before
her: either to keep the negroes under as an ignorant proletariat and stand the chance of being ruled eventually from
the slums and jails, or to join in helping to raise these wards
of the nation to a position of intelligence and thrift by means
of a public-school system. The "carpet-bag" governments hastened the decision of the South, and although there was a
period of hesitation and retrogression after the overthrow of

negro rule in the early seventies, yet the South saw that to
abolish negro schools in addition to nullifying the negro vote
would invite Northern interference; and thus eventually every
Southern state confirmed the work of the negro legislators and
maintained the negro public schools along with the white.

Finally, in legislation covering property, the wider functions
of the state, the punishment of crime and the like, it is sufficient to say that the laws on these points established by
Reconstruction legislatures were not only different from and
even revolutionary to the laws in the older South, but they
were so wise and so well suited to the needs of the new South
that in spite of a retrogressive movement following the overthrow of the negro governments the mass of this legislation,
with elaboration and development, still stands on the statute
books of the South.

Reconstruction constitutions, practically unaltered, were kept
in

Florida, 1868–1885	17 years.
Virginia, 1870–1902	32 years.
South Carolina, 1868–1895	27 years.
Mississippi, 1868–1890	22 years.

Even in the case of states like Alabama, Georgia, North
Carolina, and Louisiana, which adopted new constitutions to
signify the overthrow of negro rule, the new constitutions are
nearer the model of the Reconstruction document than they are
to the previous constitutions. They differ from the negro constitutions in minor details but very little in general conception.

Besides this there stands on the statute books of the South
to-day law after law passed between 1868 and 1876, and which
has been found wise, effective, and worthy of preservation.

Paint the "carpet-bag" governments and negro rule as black
as may be, the fact remains that the essence of the revolution
which the overturning of the negro governments made was to
put these black men and their friends out of power. Outside
the curtailing of expenses and stopping of extravagance, not
only did their successors make few changes in the work which
these legislatures and conventions had done, but they largely
carried out their plans, followed their suggestions, and strength-

ened their institutions. Practically the whole new growth of the South has been accomplished under laws which black men helped to frame thirty years ago. I know of no greater compliment to negro suffrage.

C. Vann Woodward

Among historians and laymen, interest in the Reconstruction period has replaced the interest that Civil War historiography formerly held. In large measure, this change reflects the Negro's struggle to end segregation, discrimination, and disenfranchisement.

Looking back at Reconstruction and considering American attitudes toward Negroes it must appear strange, not that it failed, but that it was tried at all. Reconstruction was the boldest social experiment ever attempted in the United States up till the New Deal. Yet for such an undertaking, the North, which held the key to the successful conclusion of Reconstruction, had serious reservations. In the light of recent developments in the United States regarding the civil rights struggle, it might be instructive to examine the causes for the failure of Reconstruction.

During the Civil War the North went further than anyone would have predicted in 1860. It freed the slaves, armed the freedmen, enfranchised the ex-slaves, and protected their newly given civil rights. Still, in 1865 most Northern states denied the franchise to Negroes. But when Negro enfranchisement came to be seen as the means of ensuring Republican and Northern capitalistic ascendancy, expediency overrode popular prejudice. As C. Vann Woodward in *Reunion and Reaction* has shown, Negro suffrage would be jettisoned once the Northern political and economic leaders decided they no longer needed the Negro vote to ensure their own interests. By the mid-eighteen seventies, Northern businessmen realized that their economic program would be protected by the old time Whigs who now controlled the Democratic party in the South. "They spoke," Professor Woodward has written in the following essay of the Southern leaders, "much the same type of economic interests as the Republicans—railroads, industries, business enterprise of one kind or another."

The North was tired of the Negro problem and retreated from its commitments. Even former friends of the Negroes lost hope as American society turned from reformism and sunk into the materialism that Vernon L. Parrington called "the Great Barbecue." Pro-Negro sentiment in the Republican party was considerably lessened after 1872 as Charles Sumner, Charles Francis Adams, and Carl Schurz left the party. By 1878 Thomas Wentworth Higginson who commanded the Negro 1st South Carolina Volunteers during the Civil War advised the Negro to either emigrate or trust in the benevolence of the Southern gentlemen of the Wade Hampton variety. The sections slowly began to heal the wounds left by the war, and the price for this reunion was to allow the South to deal exclusively with the Negro.

The Negro was left in the end to fend for himself. Without a Marshall Plan to rebuild the Southern economy or a permanent and large Freedman's Bureau to aid the Negro, the South had to settle for what it could get from the Northern business interests. Both the Negro and the South were disappointed. The Southern states did not get the large-scale Northern industrial governmental investment it needed. The Negroes' political gains were eroded and eventually taken away.

In the day of the Northern backlash and the growing white estrangement from the civil rights movement, the 1970s may prove to repeat the history of the 1870s. The history of the first Reconstruction should give no one overconfidence about the future of the Negro in the South or in the United States.

No historian has given us greater understanding of the complex problem of Reconstruction than C. Vann Woodward, Professor of History at Yale University. His studies, *Tom Watson, Reunion and Reaction, Origins of the New South,* and *The Strange Career of Jim Crow,* have done more to recast the whole history of Reconstruction than any other recent works. The following essay, which originally appeared in *The Journal of Negro Education,* XXVI (1957), was reprinted in *The Burden of Southern History.*

THE POLITICAL LEGACY OF RECONSTRUCTION

SOURCE: C. Vann Woodward, "The Political Legacy of Reconstruction," *The Journal of Negro Education*, XXVI (1957), pp. 231–40.

Of all the revolutionary proposals that eventually received the sanction of law in the upheaval of Reconstruction, the proposal to give the freedmen the unrestricted right to vote was one of the most difficult for contemporaries to accept, in the North as well as in the South. Emancipation itself had been repeatedly disavowed as a war aim until the war was well under way. Civil rights for freedmen was another cautiously advanced afterthought. Enfranchisement came in belatedly, surreptitiously, almost disingenuously advanced by its proponents, grudgingly accepted by a North that moved under duress and the argument of necessity and greeted with gloomy forebodings of failure, if not disaster. These attitudes were widespread, and they were not confined to copperheads, doughfaces, and mossback conservatives.

Representative of the skeptical and negative attitude of the time is the following pronouncement: "When was it ever known that liberation from bondage was accompanied by a recognition of political equality? Chattels personal may be instantly translated from the auction-block into freemen; but when were they ever taken at the same time to the ballot-box, and invested with all political rights and immunities? According to the laws of development and progress, it is not practicable. . . . Nor, if the freed blacks were admitted to the polls by Presidential fiat, do I see any permanent advantage likely to be secured by it; for, submitted to as a necessity at the outset, as soon as the state was organized and left to manage its own affairs, the white population, with their superior intelligence, wealth, and power, would unquestionably alter the franchise in accordance with their prejudices, and exclude those thus summarily brought to the polls. Coercion would gain nothing."

The author of these sentiments, written in 1864, was none other than William Lloyd Garrison of the *Liberator*, the man who swore to be "harsh as truth and uncompromising as justice." Nor was he alone among the abolitionists in these sentiments, for the radicals themselves were divided on the matter of Negro suffrage. Even Senator Charles Sumner, one of the earlier and most powerful advocates of placing the ballot in the freedman's hands, was prepared in a Senate speech on February 5, 1866, to admit that educational qualifications for the suffrage would be advisable. At that time, of course, educational restrictions, even a literacy test fairly administered, would have limited the franchise to a small minority of the freedmen. Horace Greeley of the New York *Tribune,* an old friend of the slave, would "limit the voting privilege to the competent and deserving" and suggested such qualifications as ability to read and write, payment of taxes, or establishment in a trade. General O. O. Howard, head of the Freedmen's Bureau, hoped that the franchise would be limited "at least by an educational qualification." This far, of course, President Lincoln and President Johnson were prepared to go, and both in fact did unsuccessfully recommend to Southern states such franchise laws.

To go further than that in 1866 or even later was to incur grave political risks, that even the most radical of Republicans were reluctant to assume. Only five states in the North, all with a negligible percentage of colored population, provided for Negro franchise. In 1865 Wisconsin, Minnesota, and Connecticut defeated proposals to allow the Negroes to vote, and the Nebraska constitution of 1866 confined suffrage to whites. New Jersey and Ohio in 1867 and Michigan and Pennsylvania in 1868 turned down proposals for Negro suffrage. Dr. W. E. B. Du Bois, who contends that in 1861 "probably not one white American in a hundred believed that Negroes could become an integral part of American democracy," concludes that even by 1868 "the country was not ready for Negro suffrage."

Yet Negro suffrage did come. It came very quickly. In fact, by 1868 it had already come in the South. How it came and why are important determinants in the political legacy left the South and the American Negro by Reconstruction.

Thaddeus Stevens, foremost champion of the freedmen, master of the Republican House majority, and leader of Radical Reconstruction, was advocating some extremely radical measures.

He was quite ready to disfranchise Southern whites in great numbers and to confiscate great quantities of their land. "It is intended to revolutionize their feelings and principles," he declared. "This may startle feeble minds and shake weak nerves. So do all great improvements." To those who objected to humiliating the defeated foe, he replied: "Why not? Do not they deserve humiliation? If they do not, who does? What criminal, what felon deserves it more?"

But for all his radicalism, Stevens was not yet prepared to enfranchise the Negro freedmen. For one thing, of course, he knew that public opinion would not support it and that the majority of his own party was against it. But apart from political reasons he had other doubts about the wisdom of the measure, some of them similar to those expressed by Garrison, Greeley, Howard, and, for that matter, President Andrew Johnson.

On this vital matter Stevens, contrary to his reputation, can be classified as a moderate or conservative. For one thing he doubted that the freedmen were prepared for intelligent voting. The conditions and laws of slavery, he said on December 18, 1865, "have prevented them from acquiring an education, understanding the commonest laws of contract, or of managing the ordinary business of life." The following month, on January 31, 1866, while urging a constitutional amendment basing representation in the House on the number of qualified voters in a state, Stevens actually expressed hope that the Southern states would not immediately grant the freedmen suffrage and thereby increase Southern voting power in Congress. He assumed that the Negroes would fall under the political influence of their former masters. "I do not therefore want to grant them this privilege for some years . . . four or five years hence, when the freedmen shall have been made free indeed, when they shall have become intelligent enough, and there are sufficient loyal men there to control the representation from those States," Negro voting would be safe enough. In fact, at this time, Stevens adopted a states' rights position: "I hold that the States have the right, and always have had it, to fix the elective franchise within their own States."

Stevens' solution to the freedmen's suffrage problem was to force upon the Southern states the dilemma posed by the proposed Fourteenth Amendment. According to these terms the states would have to choose between excluding the freedmen from the ballot box, thus reducing their number of representatives to about forty-six, or on the other hand, enfranchising them, thereby increasing their representatives to about eighty-three but running the grave risk of losing control to the Republic party. To ensure the adoption of the amendment Stevens proposed that it be submitted only to the non-Southern states and declared adopted when approved by three-fourths of these states, exclusive of the South. This solution was rejected by his party, and the Southern states voted the amendment down when it was submitted to them along with the other states.

Still hesitant, still reluctant to accept immediate freedman's suffrage and impose it by force, Stevens temporized with still another proposal. This was contained in a bill he introduced on December 13, 1866, for the reconstruction of North Carolina. In this he proposed to restrict the ballot to those of both races who could read and write or who owned real estate assessed at a value of a hundred dollars or more. Loyal men who had voted before (whites) were not to be disfranchised, but certain classes of Confederates were. There was at times, as Ralph Korngold has suggested, something of Lincoln's hesitant approach to emancipation about Stevens' approach to enfranchisement. Hesitation ceased, however, early in 1867, almost two years after the war. He now went the whole way of military rule, disfranchisement of large numbers of Southern whites and immediate and universal Negro suffrage—full scale Radical Reconstruction.

Reasons for the conversion of Thaddeus Stevens will always be debated. A few facts stand out, however, with inescapable clarity. President Johnson's plan of reconstruction would have increased the Southern delegation in the House of Representatives by some thirteen members, since all the freedmen instead of three-fifths would have been counted in apportionment. Without Negro ballots it was probable that all the additional seats, plus all the rest of the seats of the eleven states, would be filled by Democrats and not Republicans. These same estates would not only swell the opposition votes in Congress but the electoral votes in presidential contests. About thirty-seven of the Southern seats in the House would be accounted for by Negro population, who had no votes, and likely filled by sworn opponents of the party that took credit for Negro freedom. To ask an over-whelmingly Republican Congress—radical or conservative—to ap-prove such a plan was to ask water to run uphill. Conservative Republicans were no more ready to commit political hara-kiri than Radical Republicans.

"Another good reason is," said Stevens in support of his plan, "it would insure the ascendancy of the Union [Republican] party. Do you avow the party purpose? exclaims some horror stricken demagogue. I do. For I believe, on my conscience, that on the continued ascendancy of that party depends the safety of this great nation. If impartial [Negro] suffrage is excluded in the rebel States then every one of them is sure to send a solid rebel [Democratic] representation to Congress, and cast a solid rebel electoral vote. They, with their kindred Copperheads [Democrats] of the North, would always elect the President and control Congress."

Stevens' follower, Roscoe Conkling of New York, was quite as blunt and more specific. "Shall one hundred and twenty-seven thousand white people in New York cast but one vote in this House and have but one voice here, while the same number of white people in Mississippi have three votes in three voices? Shall the death of slavery add two fifths to the entire power which slavery had when slavery was living? Shall one white man have as much share in the Government as three other white men merely because he lives where blacks out-number whites two to one? . . . No sir; not if I can help it."

In addition to "the party purpose" so frankly avowed by Stevens, there was another purpose which was not frankly declared. It was more often disavowed, concealed, deprecated. This was the purpose of the business community. Although there were significant divisions within the community, a power-ful group saw in the return of a disaffected and Democratic South a menace to the economic order that had been estab-lished during the absence of the seceding states from the Union. On nearly every delicate and disturbing economic issue of the day—taxation, the National Bank, the national debt, government bonds and their funding, railroads and their financ-

ing, regulation of corporations, government grants and sub-
sidies to business, protective tariff legislation—on one and all
the business community recognized in the unreconstructed South
an antagonist of long standing. In combination with traditional
allies in the West and North, the South could upset the new
order. Under these circumstances, the Northern business community, except for the banking and mercantile interests allied
with the Democrats, put aside conservative habits and politics
and threw its support to Radical Reconstruction.

Neither the party purpose, the business purpose, nor the two
combined constituted a reputable justification with which to
persuade the public to support a radical and unpopular program. But there was a purpose that *was* both reputable and
persuasive—the philanthropic purpose, the argument that the
freedmen needed the ballot to defend and protect their dearly
bought freedom, their newly won civil rights, their welfare and
livelihood. Of their philanthropic argument the Radicals could
make a persuasive and cogent case. And it is undoubtedly true
that some of the Radicals were motivated almost entirely by
their idealism and their genuine concern for the rights and
welfare of the freedmen. What is doubtful is that these were the
effective or primary motives, or that they took priority over
the pragmatic and materialistic motives of party advantage and
sectional economic interests. It is clear at any rate that, until
the latter were aroused and marshalled, the former made little
progress. On the whole the skepticism of Secretary Gideon Welles
would seem to be justified. "It is evident," he wrote in his
diary, "that intense partisanship instead of philanthropy is the
root of the movement."

This ulterior motivation, then, is the incubus with which the
Negro was burdened before he was ever awakened into political
life. The operative and effective motives of his political genesis
were extraneous to his own interests and calculated to serve other
ends. If there ever came a time when those ends—party advantage and sectional business interests—were better served in
some other way, even in a way destructive of the basic political
rights of the race, then the political prospects of the Negro
would darken. Another incubus was the strongly partisan identi-
fications of his political origins. The major national party of

opposition took no part in those origins, regarded them as wholly inimical to its interests, and consequently felt no real commitment to the movement nor to the preservation of its fruits. If there came a time when that party was in the ascendancy, even locally, the political future of the Negro again would darken. To these evil portents should be added the strong resistance to Negro suffrage in the Northern states, the obvious reluctance and hesitance of radical leaders to commit the party to that course, and the grudging acquiescence of the North in the coercive use of it in the South.

After enfranchisement was in full effect in the Southern states, the Republican party felt obliged to give specific promise to the people of the North that they would be left free to keep the Negro disfranchised in their own states. In the Republican platform of 1868 appeared the following: "The guaranty by Congress of equal suffrage to all loyal men at the South was demanded by every consideration of public safety, of gratitude, and of justice, and must be maintained; while the question of suffrage in all loyal [non-Southern] States properly belongs to the people of those States." Only after the presidential election was over and General Grant had won did the party dare bring forward the Fifteenth Amendment denying the right of any state to disfranchise the Negro, and not until 1870 was its ratification completed.

In the meantime a political revolution was under way in the Southern states, a revolution that is the first chapter in the history of the Negro voter in America. The initial step under military government, after the destruction of the old civil governments, was the creation of the new electorate in 1867 and 1868. In all, more than 703,000 Negroes and some 627,000 whites were registered as qualified voters in the reconstructed states. The processes of disfranchisement and enfranchisement were going on simultaneously. The number of whites disfranchised is unknown and unknowable, but it is evident from a comparison of population and registration figures that the number was rather large in some states. While only two states had a colored majority of population, five states were given a colored majority of registered voters. The male population of voting age in Louisiana in 1860 was 94,711 whites and 92,502 Negroes, but only 45,218 whites were registered as against 84,436 Negroes. Alabama's voting age population in 1860 was 113,871 whites and 92,404 Negroes, but only 61,295 whites were registered against 104,518 Negroes. While some states with white majorities in population were given colored majorities in their electorate, others had their white majorities drastically reduced, and the two states with a preponderance of Negroes in population, South Carolina and Mississippi, had overwhelming majorities of colored voters.

This new-born electorate of freedmen was plunged immediately into action by the election of delegates to constitutional conventions. They followed by electing legislative bodies, state and local officials, and by full-scale and continuous participation in all phases and aspects of political life in a period that was abnormally active in a political way. To characterize the quality of the performance of this many people over a decade of time and in a multiplicity of activities with sweeping adjectives, "good" or "bad" or "indifferent," would be to indulge in empty generalities. That the mass of these people had less education, less experience in public affairs, and less property of all sorts than the white voters is obvious. As for the more intangible endowments of status and inner security that the psychologists stress, their relative impoverishment was appalling, unprecedented among American or any other known electorates. Their very appearance at the polls in mass, wearing the rags of slave days and bearing the ancient stigmata of oppression, conjured up every gloomy prognostication of the fate of democracies from Aristotle to the Federalists. Not Athens, nor Rome, nor Paris at greatest turbulence had confronted their like. Here was the Federalist beast who would turn every garden into a pigsty. Here was old John Adams' shiftless and improvident Demos, pawn of demagogues and plutocrats and menace to all order. Here in the flesh was Hamilton's "turbulent and changing" mass who "seldom judge or determine right" and who made it necessary to give to "the rich and well born" that "distinct, permanent share in the government," which alone would insure stability. Here was the ultimate test of the democratic dogma in the most extreme form ever attempted.

The records left by that revolutionary experiment have been

widely used to discredit both the experiment itself and democratic faith in general. Yet those records need not put democracy
out of countenance, nor are they wholly devoid of comfort for
those of that faith. No red glow of anarchy lit up the southern
horizon as a consequence of the revolution, and the enfranchised
freedmen did not prove the unleashed beast of Federalist
imagination. Moral pigsties undoubtedly developed, but they
were oftener than not the creation of the other race, and more
of them were to be found outside the South than within.

The new electorate of freedmen proved on the whole remarkably modest in their demands, unaggressive in their conduct, and deferential in their attitude. In no state did they
hold place and power in anything approaching their actual
numbers and voting strength. The possible exception was South
Carolina, and there they held a majority of seats only in the
lower house of the legislature. In the first legislature under the
new constitution of Mississippi, the other state with a large
Negro majority of population, Negro representatives constituted
only two-sevenths of the membership of the House and an
even smaller proportion of the Senate. Freedmen of that state
almost never took advantage of their numbers to seize control
in local government, for a Negro majority in a municipal government seems to have been unknown. There was only one
Negro mayor of a city in the state and a record of only
twelve sheriffs. Only three Negroes were elected in the whole
country to the Forty-first Congress, the first to which they were
eligible, and there were never more than eight at one time
out of a total of more than one hundred members from the
Southern states. In view of the subordinate role and the few
offices that the freedmen took, no state in the South could
properly be said to have been under Negro rule or "domination"
at any time.

Yet in varying numbers and different states Negroes occupied
all the varieties of public office in existence, up to but not
including the governorship. They served as policemen and supreme court justices, recorders of deeds and lieutenant-governors,
sheriffs and prosecuting attorneys, justices of the peace and
state superintendents of education, mayors and United States
senators. Without doubt some of them made awkward efforts

and a few of them cut some grotesque capers, but upon the crude stage of frontier democracy comic figures had appeared before this time, and none of them could have been taken for colored minstrels before 1868. In an age of low public morals the country over, some of the neophyte politicians were as guilty of corruption as the old hands, but the neophytes rarely seem to have received their fair share of graft.

In retrospect, one is more impressed with the success that a people of such meager resources and limited experience enjoyed in producing the number of sober, honest, and capable leaders and public servants they did. The appearance of some of this sort in every state is the main comfort the record provides to the democratic faith. They give the impression of people struggling conscientiously under desperate odds to live up to a test such as no other people had ever been subjected to in all the long testing of the democratic theory. Their success varied from state to state. With regard to Mississippi the conclusions of Vernon Wharton are that "altogether, as governments go, that supplied by the Negro and white Republicans in Mississippi between 1870 and 1876 was not a bad government. Never, in states, counties, or towns, did the Negroes hold office in proportion to their numbers. . . . The Negroes who held county offices were often ignorant, but under the control of white Democrats or Republicans they supplied a form of government which differed little from that in counties where they held no offices. The three who represented the state in Congress were above reproach. Those in the legislature sought no special advantages for their race, and in one of their very first acts they petitioned Congress to remove all political disabilities from the whites. With their white Republican colleagues, they gave to the state a government of greatly expanded functions at a cost that was low in comparison with that of almost any other state."

By the operation of a sort of historical color bar, the history of the Negro's political experience in Reconstruction has been studied too much in isolation and pictured as unique. There were unique features in that history, of course, but it does not constitute the only, nor the last, instance of the sudden enfranchisement of large numbers of politically inexperienced people. Nor does it support the stereotype of the Negro as the political tyro and neophyte of the western world, the laggard in the race for political maturity. After the Reconstruction episode was over, millions of people entered this country. Of the more than twelve million white immigrants who poured into the stream of American citizenship in the fifty years after 1880 from southern and eastern European countries, it is doubtful that more than a very small percentage had ever enjoyed any significant experience of direct political participation in the democratic sense. Their first taste of such experience came in the 1880's, the 1890's, or 1900's, or later when they took out citizenship papers. Here were the real political neophytes of the American electorate. They greatly outnumber the Negro population. They too were dominated by bosses and influenced by handouts and small favors. The record of the inexperience, naïveté, and ineptitude of these erstwhile peasants in the big city slums is written in the history of corrupt city bosses, rings, and machines, a history that can match some of the darker chapters of Reconstruction government. The Mugwump reformers turned against them, as they turned against the Radical Republicans, because of the corruption associated with their regimes. Eventually the immigrants learned the ropes, gained experience and assurance, helped clean up some of the messes their inexperience had created, and gained acceptance as respected members of the body politic.

The immigrants had their own handicaps of language and prejudice to deal with, but they never had anything approaching the handicaps against which the Negro had to struggle to gain acceptance. The prejudices that the immigrants confronted were nothing like the race prejudice with which the Negro had to cope. Nor was the white immigrant's enfranchisement accompanied by the disfranchisement of the ruling and propertied classes of the community in which he settled. Neither did the exercise of his franchise have to be protected by the bayonets of federal troops, nor did the gaining of his political rights appear to old settlers as a penalty and punishment inflicted upon them, a deliberate humiliation of them by their conquerors. Political leaders of the immigrants were not ordinarily regarded by the old settlers as "carpetbaggers," intruders, and puppets of a hostile government sent to rule over them; immigrants did not regard the old settlers as their former owners, any more than the old settlers looked upon the immigrants as their former slaves. The situation of the latest political neophytes was, after all, in many ways quite different from that of the neophytes of the seventies.

The time eventually came when the incubus of their political genesis returned to haunt the freedmen and destroy their future. That was the time when the two dominant operative motives of Radical Reconstruction, party advantage and sectional business interests, became inactive—the time when it became apparent that those mighty ends could better be served by abandoning the experiment and leaving the freedmen to shift for themselves. The philanthropic motive was still a factor, and in many minds still strong, but it was not enough without the support of the two powerful props of party advantage and sectional interests. The moment of collapse came at different times in different states, but the climax and consolidation of the decision came with the disputed presidential election of 1876 and the settlement that resolved it in the Compromise of 1877.

It would be neither fair nor accurate to place all the blame upon the North and its selfish interests. There had been plenty of willing co-operation on the part of Southern whites. They had used craft and guile, force and violence, economic pressure and physical terror, and all the subtle psychological devices of race prejudice and propaganda at their command. But the Southern whites were after all a minority, and not a strong minority at that. The North had not only numbers and power on its side, but the law and the Constitution as well. When the moment of crisis arrived, however, the old doubts and skepticism of the North returned, the doubts that had kept the Negro disfranchised in the North after freedman's suffrage had been imposed upon the South. After the Fifteenth Amendment was passed, the North rapidly lost interest in the Negro voters. They were pushed out of the limelight by other interests, beset by prejudices, and neglected by politicians. The Northern Negro did not enjoy a fraction of the political success the Southern Negro enjoyed, as modest as that was. Reformers and

Mugwumps of the North identified corruption with the Radical wing of the Republican party, lost interest in the Negro allies of the Radicals, and looked upon them as a means of perpetuating corrupt government all over the nation as well as in the South. In this mood they came to the conclusion that the Negro voter had been given a fair chance to prove his worth as a responsible citizen and that the experiment had proved a failure. This conclusion appeared in many places, most strangely perhaps in the columns of that old champion of the race, the New York *Tribune* (April 7, 1877), which declared that the Negroes had been given "ample opportunity to develop their own latent capacities," and had only succeeded in proving that "as a race they are idle, ignorant, and vicious."

The North's loss of faith in its own cause is reflected in many surprising places. One example must suffice. It is of special interest because it comes from the supreme official charged with enforcing the Fifteenth Amendment and guaranteeing to the freedmen their political rights, the President whose administration coincided with Radical Reconstruction and the whole great experiment—General U. S. Grant. According to the diary of Secretary Hamilton Fish, entry of January 17, 1877: "He [Grant] says he opposed the Fifteenth Amendment and thinks it was a mistake, that it had done the Negro no good, and had been a hindrance to the South, and by no means a political advantage to the North."

During the present struggle for Negro rights, which might be called the Second Reconstruction—though one of quite a different sort—I have noticed among Negro intellectuals at times a tendency to look back upon the First Reconstruction as if it were in some ways a sort of Golden Age. In this nostalgic view that period takes the shape of the race's finest hour, a time of heroic leaders and deeds, of high faith and firm resolution, a time of forthright and passionate action, with no bowing to compromises of "deliberate speed." I think I understand their feeling. Reconstruction will always have a special and powerful meaning for the Negro. It is undoubtedly a period full of rich and tragic and meaningful history, a period that should be studiously searched for its meanings, a period that has many meanings yet to yield. But I seriously doubt that it will ever serve satisfactorily as a Golden Age—for anybody. There is too much irony mixed with the tragedy.

John Hope Franklin

One of the most persistent myths of American history has to do with the leaders of radical Reconstruction. They are known to all as carpetbaggers and scalawags. *Webster's* defines a carpetbagger as "A Northerner who went to the South after the Civil War, esp. to make money by taking advantage of unsettled conditions or political corruption." The myth of the grasping Yankees who went South, goading on the ignorant ex-slaves against their white friends, and lining their own pockets through corruption, has been applied to all Northerners who settled in the South after the Civil War and participated in the reconstruction governments. The story of the carpetbaggers and their Southern white allies, the scalawags, has been, in fact, too useful to give up. It has been one of those political myths that justified the disenfranchisement of the Negro and the rejection of the Republican party. The picture of the vicious carpetbaggers in alliance with ignorant Negroes has become part of American historical folklore, beginning with James S. Pike's *The Prostrate State* (1873), and culminating with Margaret Mitchell's *Gone With the Wind*.

But as historians have recently discovered in taking a fresh look at Reconstruction, the problem is much more complicated than dividing the leading figures into heroes and villains. The starting point in speaking of radical Reconstruction is to realize that Negroes, who have been blamed for the excesses of Reconstruction, did not dominate the state governments, the constitutional conventions, or the judicial systems. They did, however, vote, hold public office, serve in the militia, and sit in Congress and state legislatures. Secondly, Negroes in office, far from being radicals, showed themselves to be moderate in their demands. As a Negro delegate Tom Lee told the Alabama Constitutional Convention of 1867, "I have no desire to take away any rights of the white man. All I want is equal rights in the court house and equal rights when I go to vote." The picture of Reconstruction presented in such propagandistic works as *The Birth of a Nation* is wholly fabrication, such as the famous scene near the end of the movie showing Negroes joyously greeting the news that the law prohibiting intermarriage had been repealed by the Negro-dominated legislature.

Historians have also shed new light on the carpetbaggers and scalawags. Most of the carpetbaggers were young veterans of the Union army who came South after the war seeking land and opportunity. As Kenneth M. Stampp has shown in *The Era of Reconstruction* (1965) the scalawags represented a variety of interests. Some such as General Beauregard and other prominent Confederates were opportunists who threw in their lot with the winners. Others, such as Republican Governor James L. Alcorn of Mississippi were former Whigs, who either joined the Republicans because they agreed with the party's economic program or opposed secession in 1860. Many scalawags were poor white farmers who resented the earlier control of their states by planter interests, and now hoped that the radical governments might provide them with some tangible economic benefits. Altogether, historians have found that the radical coalition of Negroes, carpetbaggers, and scalawags was more complex and looser than we had been led to believe. Above all, they were far from being the villains and rascals that older historians such as E. M. Coulter have made them out to be.

On the other hand, it is a serious mistake to see the so-called scalawags and carpetbaggers—as some liberals and Negroes would like—as selfless and philanthropic. Even the white allies of the Negroes in Reconstruction governments were often contaminated by large doses of Negrophobia.

John Hope Franklin has in *Reconstruction After the Civil War* written a new history of the period based on contemporary research. His analysis of the leadership of Reconstruction governments, presented in the following essay, should lay to rest one of the myths of American history. Professor Franklin is the author of *From Slavery to Freedom, The Militant South,* and *The Emancipation Proclamation.* He is Professor of American History and Chairman of the History Department at the University of Chicago.

THE SOUTH'S NEW LEADERS

SOURCE: John Hope Franklin, "The South's New Leaders," from *Reconstruction After the Civil War* (Chicago: University of Chicago Press, 1961), pp. 85–103.

The Act of March 2, 1867, was specific about the qualifications of those who were to have a voice in the new program of reconstruction. Constitutions were to be written by delegates "to be elected by the male citizens of the state, twenty-one years old and upward, of whatever race, color, or previous condition, who have been resident in said state for one year . . . except such as may be disfranchised for participation in the rebellion or for felony at common law." It was no easy task to administer satisfactorily these provisions of the Act. The commanding generals in the Southern military districts were hard pressed to find competent and qualified registrars to enroll the electorate. They used Union Army officers and Freedmen's Bureau agents; and a few of them used some Negroes. Travel into remote areas was difficult, and in some instances weeks elapsed before registrations were received, compiled, and made ready for elections.

Some of the commanding generals felt a deep responsibility to provide a little political education for those voters who had never had the experience or the opportunity to participate in politics. Several of them gave explicit instructions to registration officials to provide the freedmen with adequate information regarding their political rights. Freedmen's Bureau officers and agents engaged by the generals to work in the registration program helped the new voters understand their rights and duties. When Bureau officials had no political literature of their own to distribute, they disseminated materials prepared by the Union League, which was, as we shall see, easily the most active organization in the political education of the Negro.

When the criteria for becoming electors were applied to the people of the South, three groups qualified. One group was the vast majority of Negroes whose loyalty to the Union was unquestioned and who merely had to prove that they were not felons and had lived in the state one year. Another was the Northerners who had taken up residence in the South. If they met the residence requirements, they were enrolled. Finally, there were the native Southerners who qualified to take the "ironclad oath," and who were scrutinized with the greatest care. The rank and file among these groups was to be the center of the controversy that raged over the ensuing decade. Out of these groups were to come the leaders who bore the major responsibility for both the good and the evils flowing from the difficult tasks of rebuilding the South.

The entrance of Negroes into the political arena was the most revolutionary aspect of the reconstruction program. Out of a population of approximately four million, some 700,000 qualified as voters, but the most of them were without the qualifications to participate effectively in a democracy. In this they were not unlike the large number of Americans who were enfranchised during the age of Jackson or the large number of immigrants who were being voted in herds by political bosses in New York, Boston, and other American cities at this time. They were the first to admit their deficiencies. Beverly Nash, an unlettered former slave sitting in the South Carolina convention, expressed the views of many when he said: "I believe, my friends and fellow-citizens, we are not prepared for this suffrage. But we can learn. Give a man tools and let him commence to use them, and in time he will learn a trade. So it is with voting. We may not understand it at the start, but in time we shall learn to do our duty."

Like Nash most of the Negroes were illiterate. A slave existence could hardly be expected to prepare one for the responsibilities of citizenship, especially when there were laws, as there were in all slave states, banning the teaching of slaves. Even if Negroes were free, as were more than 200,000 in the slave states before the war, laws forbade their being taught to read and write. Indeed, when they came out of slavery many Negroes did not know their own names; many did not even have family names. It goes without saying that a considerable number had not the vaguest notion of what registering and voting meant.

None of this is surprising. It had been only two years since emancipation from a system that for more than two centuries had denied slaves most rights as human beings. And it must be remembered that in these two years the former Confederates, in power all over the South, did nothing to promote the social and political education of the former slaves. What is surprising is that there were some—and no paltry number—who in 1867 were able to assume the responsibilities of citizens and leaders.

Among South Carolina's Negro leaders was state treasurer Francis L. Cardozo, educated at Glasgow and London, who had been a minister in New Haven and, after the war, was principal of a Negro school in Charleston. Robert B. Elliott, born in Massachusetts, trained at Eton College in England, and elected to Congress in 1870, was urbane and articulate. J. J. Wright, a state supreme court justice, had studied at the University of Pennsylvania and had been a respected member of the Pennsylvania bar before moving to South Carolina after the war. Congressman James Rapier's white father sent him to school in Canada, and when he returned to his native Alabama after the war he had not only an ample formal education but a world of experience gained from travel and work in the North. Florida's secretary of state, Jonathan C. Gibbs, graduated from Dartmouth College and had been a Presbyterian minister for several years when reconstruction began. Among the Negro leaders of North Carolina James W. Hood, assistant superintendent of public instruction, and James H. Harris, an important figure in the 1868 constitutional convention, were educated, respectively, in Pennsylvania and Ohio. Many others, among them Henry M. Turner of the Georgia legislature, Hiram Revels, United States senator from Mississippi, and Richard H. Gleaves, member of Congress from South Carolina, had much more than the rudiments of a formal education when they entered upon their official duties.

Significant among Negro leaders were those who were almost wholly self-educated. Robert Smalls of South Carolina pursued his studies diligently until he had mastered the rudiments. Later he went to the United States House of Representatives. In Mississippi, John Roy Lynch regularly took time off from his duties in a photographer's studio to gaze across the alley into a white schoolroom, where he kept up with the class until he had mastered the courses taught there. When he became speaker of the Mississippi house and later a member of Congress, he relied on this earlier training. Before Jefferson Long went into Congress from Georgia, he had educated himself and had become a merchant tailor in Macon. There were numerous other self-educated Negro leaders, including John Carraway and Peyton Finley of Alabama, James O'Hara and A. H. Galloway of North Carolina, and James W. Bland and Lewis Lindsay of Virginia. From this educated element came the articulate, responsible Negroes who contributed substantially to the writing of the new constitutions and the establishment of the new governments in the former slave states.

Most of the Negro leaders were ministers. A fair number taught school. Some were employees of the Freedmen's Bureau or another federal agency. Here and there one found a Negro who had been trained in the law. There were, of course, farmers; and there were some artisans engaged in a variety of occupations. The economic interests and aspirations of the Negro leaders varied widely. It would be wrong to assume that they had no economic interests or that they had no views regarding the economic future of the South.

One of the really remarkable features of the Negro leadership was the small amount of vindictiveness in their words and their actions. There was no bully, no swagger, as they took their places in the state and federal governments traditionally occupied by the white planters of the South. The spirit of conciliation pervaded most of the public utterances the Negroes made. In his first speech in the South Carolina convention Beverly Nash asserted that the Southern white man was the "true friend of the black man." Pointing to the banner containing the words "United we stand, divided we fall," Nash said, "If you could see the scroll of the society that banner represents, you would see the white man and the black man standing with their arms locked together, as the type of friendship and union which we desire."

Negroes generally wished to see political disabilities removed from the whites. In South Carolina several Negroes presented a resolution asking Congress to remove all such disabilities, and it was passed. In Louisiana the Negroes requested that former

Confederates be permitted to vote but, for the time being, not to hold office. In Alabama James T. Rapier, a Negro delegate to the constitutional convention, successfully sponsored a resolution asking Congress to remove the political disabilities of those who might aid in reconstruction. In Mississippi a Democratic paper, the Jackson *Clarion,* admitted that in their general conduct Negroes "have shown consideration for the feelings of the whites. . . . In other words, the colored people had manifested no disposition to rule or dominate the whites, and the only Color Line which had existed, grew out of the unwise policy which had previously been pursued by the Democratic Party in its efforts to prevent the enjoyment by the newly-emancipated race of the rights and privileges to which they were entitled, under the Constitution and laws of the country." In South Carolina Beverly Nash declared that in public affairs "we must unite with our white fellow-citizens. They tell us that they have been disfranchised, yet we tell the North that we shall never let the halls of Congress be silent until we remove that disability."

Negroes attempted no revolution in the social relations of the races in the South. Francis B. Simkins in his "New Viewpoints of Southern Reconstruction" has accurately observed that "the defiance of the traditional caste division occasionally expressed in an official reception or in an act of the legislature was not reflected generally in common social relations." Negroes, as a rule conceded to the insistence of whites that they were a race apart; and they made little or no attempt to invade social privacies. They did not even attempt to destroy white supremacy except where such supremacy rejected Negroes altogether as human beings, and there was almost nowhere any serious consideration given to providing legal approbation of interracial marriages. While Negroes sought equality as human beings, they manifested no desire to involve themselves in the purely social relations of whites as individuals or as groups. "It is false, it is a wholesale falsehood to say that we wish to force ourselves upon white people," declared the near-white P. B. S. Pinchback of Louisiana.

Nor did any considerable number of Negroes seek to effect an economic revolution in the South. Henry McNeal Turner, the fearless Negro leader who was almost universally disliked by white Georgians, did what he could to assist the whites in recovering their economic strength. In the Georgia convention he secured the passage of two resolutions that indicated a remarkable willingness to stabilize the economic life of the white community. One sought to prevent the sale of property whose owners were unable to pay their taxes; the other provided for the relief of banks. In South Carolina Negro leaders such as Robert DeLarge and Francis Cardozo supported relief measures with the full knowledge that whites would benefit as much as Negroes.

The movement of Northerners into the South after the Civil War is a part of the exciting drama of the migrations that had seen the continent populated from ocean to ocean and had taken Americans, new and old, wherever opportunity beckoned. The movement into the South was greatly stimulated by the favorable observations of scores of thousands of Union soldiers who had seen action on Southern battlefields. Some were mustered out of the army while still in the South and, despite some Southern feelings of hostility against them, decided to adopt the South as their home. Others, back in their Northern homes, waited only for the first opportunity to return to the South. By the fall of 1866, for example, more than five thousand Union soldiers had settled in Louisiana alone. The movement was also stimulated by the large number of industrialists and investors who saw in the underdeveloped South an important new economic frontier. Those committed to the view that the South's recovery from the war would be accompanied by an era of unparalleled expansion began to move into the region, bringing with them their own resources, and often the resources of others, with which to build railroads and factories and to purchase farm land and other properties.

Many federal agents—some from the Department of the Treasury, others from the Freedmen's Bureau—settled in the South and called it home. Northern teachers, men and women, braved numerous indignities at the hands of hostile whites in order to teach Negroes, and they cast their lot with the South. There were those from the North, moreover, who saw new political opportunities in the South. They hoped to use the newly enfranchised element and the problems arising out of reconstruction to achieve political power and economic gain. For them the South was a "happy hunting ground" that they could not resist. As to any frontier, there went to the South the adventurers, those who wanted to "get rich quick," and ne'er-do-wells who were fully prepared to embrace *any* cause, including Radical Reconstruction, that would benefit them.

These were the people who have been called "carpetbaggers" for the last ninety years. This opprobrious term, used as early as 1846 to describe any suspicious stranger, was applied indiscriminately to all Northerners in the South during reconstruction. It has generally implied that as a group they had nothing in the way of worldly possessions and were thoroughly unprincipled in their determination to fleece and exploit the South until their carpetbags fairly bulged with the possessions of Southerners and they were forced to acquire new coffers in which to place their ill-gotten gains. They have been described as a group at work on a grand master plan to Africanize the country. One historian described them as "gangs of itinerant adventurers, vagrant interlopers" who were "too depraved, dissolute, dishonest and degraded to get the lowest of places in the states they had just left." These descriptions fall far short of the mark. They impugn the integrity and good intentions of thousands whose motives were otherwise. Even more important, perhaps, is the fact that such descriptions show no understanding of the variety and complexity of the motives underlying the migrations and no appreciation for the economic and political relationships that grew out of such motives.

There is no evidence that even the considerable number of Negro migrants from the North were interested in "Africanizing" the country. Indeed the term was an extravagance, a flourish—like "Negro rule"—used to express disgust. The other common descriptions are equally inaccurate. As Thomas Conway pointed out a few months after the war, many Northerners, including the teacher, preacher, merchant, husbandman, mechanic, laborer, and discharged Union soldier, were ready to move South. He had persuaded Northern men to take $3,000,000 into the South to purchase land, make loans, and advances on crops. Their only fears were whether there was sufficient law and order to maintain security for their investments. But they went South, and they continued to go all during the reconstruction period. In November, 1865, Sidney Andrews observed that already several Massachusetts men were in business in Charleston; and he estimated that at least half the stores on the principal streets of the city were run by Northern men.

The careers of Captain H. S. Chamberlain and General John T. Wilder, both of Ohio, illustrate the kind of activities in which numerous so-called carpetbaggers were engaged. When Chamberlain was mustered out of the Union army in Knoxville, Tennessee, in 1865, he at once entered the iron and coal business in Knoxville and is regarded by some as the real founder of the modern iron industry south of the Ohio. In 1867 Chamberlain joined with General Wilder, late of Wilder's Lightning Brigade of Ohio, to organize the Roane Iron Company, which bought large tracts of coal and iron land and engaged extensively in the operation of coke works, iron mines, and furnaces. Together they became involved in many industrial and financial ventures, including the Dixie Portland Cement Company, the Brookside Cotton Mills of Knoxville, and the First National Bank of Chattanooga.

That all so-called carpetbaggers were not simply Radicals with no consideration for the welfare and development of the South can be seen also in the life of Willard Warner, planter, politician, and iron manufacturer. Born in Granville, Ohio, and educated at Marietta College, Warner served in the Union army and went to the Ohio senate in 1865. Two years later he moved to Alabama, and with his ample resources engaged in cotton planting for several years. He became active in Republican politics and served in the United States Senate from 1868 to 1871. Then he organized the Tecumseh Iron Company and served as president and manager until 1873. For this venture more than $100,000 was supplied by his Northern associates. Later he moved to Tennessee, where he had extensive investments and blast furnaces. The overthrow of reconstruction seems not to have affected this "carpetbagger," for as late as 1900 the Conservatives (the Democrats) in his adopted state elected him to the Tennessee legislature.

If recent historians have reviled Northerners who settled in the South after the Civil War, their Southern contemporaries were inclined to be grateful to them for their contributions to Southern development. Clinton A. Cilley, born in New Hampshire and a Harvard graduate, settled in North Carolina in 1866. After a career in the law, including several years as a judge of the Lenoir Superior Court, he was called in 1900 "one of North Carolina's ablest lawyers and finest citizens." General Wilder, the iron manufacturer, was very popular among Southerners, including former Confederates. During the Spanish-American War the governor of Tennessee named the training camp near Knoxville "Camp Wilder," in honor of the carpetbagger from Ohio. Lieutenant B. H. True of the 136th New York Volunteers, who settled in Georgia in 1865, was consistently popular with his new neighbors; they not only supported his newspaper, the *Appeal and Advertiser*, but elected him, as the "celebrated farmer from Morgan County," to the State Agricultural Society.

The interest of such men and groups of men in the political future of the South was real. With so much at stake in the way of investments and with full appreciation of the economic potential of the South they could not be indifferent to the uncertain political winds that were blowing across their adopted home. Their interest transformed itself into a strong desire to attain certain specific political goals for the South. One was the achievement and maintenance of law and order. They had seen enough hostility and lawlessness in many Southern communities to cause considerable uneasiness about the safety of their investments. They wanted governments that would insure this safety; and if they could facilitate the establishment of such governments, they would certainly do so. Another was the maintenance of a close alliance between government and the business community. They had seen the importance of such an alliance in numerous developments in Washington during the war and in the effective service that several state governments in the North had rendered the business community. Favorable banking and insurance laws, tax exemptions or rebates, land grants and other assistance to railroads were among the favors the government could and would, under certain desirable circumstances, grant to business and industry. If at all possible, Northerners would see that this was done in the South.

Finally, most Northerners in the South were convinced that their goals could best be attained through a vigorous, well-organized Republican party throughout the South. This was, after all, the party responsible for the intimate relationship between government and business on the national level and in several Northern state governments. They knew that there was little chance of luring the former Confederates into the Republican party and that the Democratic party would oppose at every turn whatever Republicans attempted to do. Southern Democrats tended to equate Republicans with abolitionists and thus to regard them as the destroyers of the South's cherished economic and social system. Northern Republicans had to look to others in the South for political support.

A Republican in the South did not have to belong to the Thaddeus Stevens-Charles Sumner wing of the party to reach the conclusion that Negro suffrage was not only desirable but imperative. For the conclusion was inescapable that the party's strength would come from Negroes and from whatever support they could secure from loyal native Southerners. They did all they could to promote the enfranchisement of the Negro and draw him into the Republican party. This did not mean, however, that the so-called carpetbaggers were interested in "Africanizing" the South. Even when they undertook to "Northernize" the South, there was no revolution in the general social relations between Negroes and whites. B. H. True, a New Yorker living in Georgia, said that he was as friendly toward the Negro as anyone, "but there is an antagonism which we all have against the race; that I cannot get rid of; I do not believe any man can." Had these Radicals been radical on social questions, they would have opposed the laws against intermarriage that were enacted during the Radical regime. They would also have stood for one system of public schools open to all races, but their infrequent expressions in favor of such a system were feeble indeed. These matters—unlike Negro suffrage—were not among their primary interests, and they gave them scant attention.

It was only natural that Northerners in the South could wield political influence and exercise power far out of proportion to their numbers. They were the best prepared to step into the vacuum created by the disfranchisement of the former Confederates. They had training and experience in political and economic matters that neither Negroes nor loyal native Southerners had. They clearly knew what their interests were and how best they could be secured. Finally they had the support of the powerful, victorious party that was in control of affairs in Washington. While their influence in the South was not always decisive or even critical, it was invariably a factor in the determination of affairs, present and future, in the Southern states.

No group of postwar Southern leaders has been reviled or castigated—or misunderstood—more than loyal native Southerners, commonly known as "scalawags." The term came in all likelihood from Scalloway, a district in the Shetland Islands where small, runty cattle and horses were bred. It was used in western New York before the Civil War in referring to a "mean fellow, a scape grace." In the South the term was used by the opponents of reconstruction to describe those they regarded as the lowest, meanest element in society. These were the Southerners who could swear that they had never voluntarily given aid, countenance, counsel, or encouragement to persons in rebellion and had exercised or attempted to exercise the functions of no office under the Confederacy. They were largely men who had opposed secession. The votes against secession in some state legislatures, together with the known sentiment against such drastic action, indicate that a considerable number of Southerners dragged their feet or refused to have any part in the Confederate cause. Many had for years smarted under a system that gave every advantage to the planter class, to which very few of them belonged. They bitterly resented the course of action, pursued by the planter class, which had led to a war that, from their point of view, became more and more a "poor man's fight."

It is impossible to determine how many so-called scalawags were qualified to participate in reconstruction under the terms of the several acts of Congress. Likewise it is impossible to determine the extent to which those who took the "ironclad oath" were eligible to do so. After June, 1867, those who took the oath were, as President Johnson had indicated to the commanding generals, judges of their own honesty. Since the machinery as well as the personnel of registration was of questionable efficiency, it is entirely possible that many who were clearly not eligible registered anyway. There were some eligibles who refused to register, and many who were not eligible advised the loyal Southerners to have no part in the Radical regime. Others advised the eligibles to register and then defeat the Radical effort by voting against it. "If we are to wear manacles," said Governor Perry of South Carolina, "let them be put on by our tyrants, not ourselves."

But there were those in the South who counseled loyal Southerners to participate in the new reconstruction program and then to restrain any excessive or revolutionary tendencies that might militate against the best interests of the South. The fact that Negroes were to participate did not degrade white Southerners or diminish their influence unless they purposely abandoned the field to Negroes. The New Orleans *Picayune* told its readers that promptness in registering and voting would convince the North "that we mean to take care of our own affairs." The Savannah *News* gave similar advice when it declared that Georgia expected every man to do his duty and register without delay to show his reverence for his "noble commonwealth." The Charleston *Daily Courier* echoed the same view: "That you should register is an imperative duty which each man owes to himself, to his community and to his state."

A curious assortment of native Southerners thus became eligible to participate in Radical Reconstruction. And the number increased as the President granted individual pardons or issued new proclamations of amnesty. It became increasingly difficult to make a distinction between the views of the loyal Southerners and the views of those whose citizenship was being restored. On political and social questions they ranged from the radicalism of James W. Hunnicut of Virginia, who stood for the full legal and social equality of Negroes and whites, to the conservatism of Milton Candler, a Georgia senator who claimed that Negroes were not citizens and therefore were not eligible to hold office. Certainly the majority of these loyal Southerners could not be described as Radicals in the sense of embracing the policies and programs for Negroes set forth by the Radicals in Congress. Often they advocated segregation of Negroes and whites in educational and other institutions. Often they spoke as vigorously for the rights of the South as did any former Confederate. Their primary interest was in supporting a party that would build the South on a broader base than the plantation aristocracy of ante-bellum days. They found it expedient to do business with Negroes and so-called carpetbaggers; but often they returned to the Democratic party as it gained sufficient strength to be a factor in Southern politics.

These were the people who were called scalawags by their adversaries. They hardly deserved the name, nor did they deserve the numerous other opprobrious labels pinned on them by hostile critics. Wade Hampton called them "the mean, lousy and filthy kind that are not fit for butchers or dogs." Another called them "scaly, scabby runts in a herd of cattle." Even the historians have joined in the verbal assault on these loyal native Southerners. One describes scalawags as "vile, blatant, vindictive, unprincipled." Perhaps during the period of their ascendancy the scalawags committed many offenses against the social order; for the graft and corruption they must take at least a part of the blame. But their most serious offense was to have been loyal to the Union during the Civil War or to have declared that they had been loyal and thereby to have enjoyed full citizenship during the period of Radical Reconstruction.

It is extremely difficult to determine the strength of the three groups that dominated the South during Radical Reconstruction. There was constant fluctuation in the show of strength, particularly among the native Southerners and the Northerners living in the South. And there was constant defection, with Negroes dropping out of the picture under Ku Klux Klan or other pressures, with Northerners leaving or going over to the Conservatives, as the opponents of Radical Reconstruction were called, and with "loyal" Southerners deviating from or deserting the Radical cause altogether. The best that one can do is look at the comparative numerical strength of the three groups and draw some inferences from the observation. A likely time for such a comparison is 1867–68, when the several state conventions wrote the new constitutions required by the Reconstruction Acts (see table).

The figures in the table illustrate several significant points. In the first place, except for South Carolina, Negroes enjoyed no numerical domination in the conventions. The only other state in which they were nearly a majority was Louisiana, where by agreement they were to constitute 50 per cent of the delegates.

MEMBERSHIP OF STATE CONVENTIONS, 1867–68

STATE	NEGRO	WHITE			Total	PERCENTAGE		
						Negro	White	
		Native	North-ern	TOTAL			Native	North-ern
Alabama	18	59	31	90	108	17	55	28
Arkansas	8	35	23	58	66	13	52	35
Florida	18	12	15	27	45	40	27	33
Georgia	33	128	9	137	170	19	74	7
Louisiana	49	*	*	49	98	50	*	*
Mississippi	17	29	54	83	100	17	29	54
North Carolina	15	100	18	118	133	11	75	14
South Carolina	76	27	21	48	124	61	22	17
Virginia	25	33	47	80	105	24	31	45
Texas	9	*	*	81	90	10	*	*

* Further breakdown unavailable.

Thus "Negro rule," as reconstruction has been erroneously described, had an inauspicious beginning and, indeed, was never to materialize. Second, the so-called carpetbaggers were in the minority in every state except Mississippi. Many were so preoccupied with personal undertakings, or with setting up schools and churches, that they had no time for public service. Their position, however, was adequately represented by those new settlers who did find time to serve. Finally, the native whites had a larger numerical representation in the conventions than is usually recognized. Dominating several conventions, such as those in Alabama, Georgia, and North Carolina, and having substantial numbers in others, they were prepared to play a significant part in the deliberations and in the administration of affairs in their states.

Although leadership in the South came from these three groups, at least in the early days of congressional reconstruction, it does not follow that the leaders invariably worked together in promoting a Radical program. Their motives, values, and goals were not the same and their effort to work together was often strained because of these differences. Far from entering into any conspiracy to degrade and destroy the Southern way of life, they frequently worked at cross purposes. At times the position of the Negro leaders approached that of the crusading abolitionists. Meanwhile, the so-called carpetbaggers frequently preoccupied themselves with building up the alliance between the business community and the Republican-controlled state government. All too often, moreover, the loyal Southerners talked and acted like the conservative former Confederates whom they presumably opposed. Co-operation was at best loose and irregular, forced at times only by the threat of their common destruction. It was under these circumstances that the three groups of leaders forged a program for the reconstruction of the Southern states. How such a program actually emerged is one of the fascinating chapters in American history.

VI. PATTERNS OF NEGRO LIFE
AND THOUGHT, 1880–1930

*Make your own little heaven right here and now. Do it by
putting business methods into your farming, by growing
things in your garden the year around, by building and keeping attractive and comfortable homes for your children so that
they will stay at home and not go to the cities, . . . by staying in one place, by getting a good teacher and a good
preacher, . . . by keeping out of debt, and by cultivating
friendly relations with your neighbors both black and white.*
BOOKER T. WASHINGTON

The cost of liberty is less than the price of repression.
W. E. B. DU BOIS

A race without authority and power is a race without respect.
MARCUS GARVEY

C. Vann Woodward

Nineteen fifty-four was to be in more ways than one the *an-
nus mirabilis* for the civil rights movement. The Supreme
Court decision came in May, and Martin Luther King, Jr.,
settled in Montgomery, Alabama, in the fall. On the campus
of Jefferson's University of Virginia an event quietly took
place that was to have great significance for later political and
social developments. Southern born and educated C. Vann
Woodward, Professor of History at Johns Hopkins University,
delivered the James W. Richard lectures entitled *The Strange
Career of Jim Crow*. Published as a book the following year,
it soon became not only standard reading in undergraduate
American history courses, but also received the general pub-

lic's attention. Woodward's thesis made a deep impression on the minds of civil rights proponents.

His basic proposition was that segregation and the total elimination of the Negro from Southern political and social life has come about, not in the full flourish of the overthrow of Reconstruction, but only gradually. There was an important period between the end of Reconstruction and the establishment of white supremacy when the Negro still retained his civil rights and, in modified form, freedom from total segregation. It was a period when some options remained open for a reconciliation of the races. This began to change in the 1890s as the forces that restrained racism weakened. Supreme Court decisions, American racism abroad, Northern disinterest, an economic depression, political disillusionment, all came together to open the floodgates of extreme racism. The forces in the South that wanted to disenfranchise and segregate the Negro now had a free hand.

The position that the South had established for the Negro between 1890–1910 soon took on the appearance of a time honored method of dealing with racial matters, a folkway of Southern life. Professor Woodward showed that what seemed to be a time-honored tradition had been a relatively recent man-made development. Contrary to the belief that "legislation cannot make mores," the historical fact was that Southern segregation laws engendered folkways and customs. The implication of Woodward's thesis in *The Strange Career of Jim Crow* was that what had once been made by legislation could now be undone by a repeal of segregationist statutes. Race relations in the South had not always been so fixed. In earlier days the Negro "could do many things in the South that in the latter part of the period, under different conditions, he was prevented from doing."

A second point was made in *The Strange Career of Jim Crow*, the implications of which were equally as far-reaching. There was a period in the 1880s and early 1890s, Professor Woodward found, when Southern Negroes and whites were able to make, however tentative, a political coalition in the Populist movement based on common economic needs rather than on race. A permanent alliance of poor whites and Negroes would have had revolutionary implications for Southern politics. Populists realized that Negroes "are in the ditch just like we are," and a combination of both groups would have overturned the conservative forces that controlled Southern politics.

During the Montgomery March of 1965, Martin Luther King, Jr., speaking to some 25,000 marchers in front of the Alabama State Capitol, and millions more who saw and heard his speech on nationwide television, invoked the name of Professor Woodward and his book for the purpose of illustrating that out of the strife of the civil rights struggle a new movement of Negroes and whites similar to that envisioned by the Populists years earlier might emerge.

But it is also important to remember that Tom Watson, the Georgia Populist leader, who thought of this interracial alliance for the common good, was the same man who out of frustration turned to the more successful occupation of championing racism. Continued rebuffs to Negroes in seeking relief from poverty and social deprivation may yet see in our own time the emergence of Negro Tom Watsons.

CAPITULATION TO RACISM

SOURCE: C. Vann Woodward, "Capitulation to Racism," from *The Strange Career of Jim Crow*, second revised edition, (New York: Oxford University Press, 1966), pp. 67–69, 97–109.

Up to the year 1898 South Carolina had resisted the Jim Crow car movement which had swept the western states of the South completely by that time. In that year, however, after several attempts, the proponents of the Jim Crow law were on the eve of victory. The Charleston *News and Courier*, the oldest newspaper in the South and a consistent spokesman of conservatism, fired a final broadside against extremists in behalf of the conservative creed of race policy.

'As we have got on fairly well for a third of a century, including a long period of reconstruction, without such a measure,' wrote the editor, 'we can probably get on as well hereafter without it, and certainly so extreme a measure should not be adopted and enforced without added and urgent cause.' He then called attention to what he considered the absurd consequences to which such a law might lead once the principle of the thing were conceded. 'If there must be Jim Crow cars on the railroads, there should be Jim Crow cars on the street railways. Also on all passenger boats. . . . If there are to be Jim Crow cars, moreover, there should be Jim Crow waiting saloons at all stations, and Jim Crow eating houses. . . . There should be Jim Crow sections of the jury box, and a separate Jim Crow dock and witness stand in every court—and a Jim Crow Bible for colored witnesses to kiss. It would be advisable also to have a Jim Crow section in county auditors' and treasurers' officers for the accommodation of colored taxpayers. The two races are dreadfully mixed in these offices for weeks every year, especially about Christmas. . . . There should be a Jim Crow department for making returns and paying for the privileges and blessings of citizenship. Perhaps, the best plan would be, after all, to take the short cut to the general end . . . by establishing two or three Jim Crow counties at once, and turning them over to our colored citizens for their special and exclusive accommodation.'

In resorting to the tactics of *reductio ad absurdum* the editor doubtless believed that he had dealt the Jim Crow principle a telling blow with his heavy irony. But there is now apparent to us an irony in his argument of which the author was unconscious. For what he intended as a *reductio ad absurdum* and obviously regarded as an absurdity became in a very short time a reality, and not only that but a reality that was regarded as the only sensible solution to a vexing problem, a solution having the sanction of tradition and long usage. Apart from the Jim Crow counties and Jim Crow witness stand, all the improbable applications of the principle suggested by the editor in derision had been put into practice—down to and including the Jim Crow Bible.

The South's adoption of extreme racism was due not so much to a conversion as it was to a relaxation of the opposition. All the elements of fear, jealousy, proscription, hatred, and fanaticism had long been present, as they are present in various degrees of intensity in any society. What enabled them to rise to dominance was not so much cleverness or ingenuity as it was a general weakening and discrediting of the numerous forces that had hitherto kept them in check. The restraining forces included not only Northern liberal opinion in the press, the courts, and the government, but also internal checks imposed by the prestige and influence of the Southern conservatives, as well as by the idealism and zeal of the Southern radicals. What happened toward the end of the century was an almost simultaneous—and sometimes not unrelated—decline in the effectiveness of restraint that had been exercised by all three forces: Northern liberalism, Southern conservatism, and Southern radicalism. . . .

Within this context of growing pessimism, mounting tension, and unleashed phobias the structure of segregation and discrimination was extended by the adoption of a great number of the Jim Crow type of laws. Up to 1900 the only law of this type adopted by the majority of Southern states was that applying to passengers aboard trains. And South Carolina did not adopt that until 1898,[1] North Carolina in 1899, and Virginia, the last, in 1900. Only three states had required or authorized the Jim Crow waiting room in railway stations before 1899, but in the next decade nearly all of the other Southern states fell in line. The adoption of laws applying to new subjects tended to take place in waves of popularity. Street cars had been common in Southern cities since the 'eighties, but only Georgia had a segregation law applying to them before the end of the century. Then in quick succession North Carolina and Virginia adopted such a law in 1901, Louisiana in 1902, Arkansas, South Carolina, and Tennessee in 1903, Mississippi and Maryland in 1904, Florida in 1905, and Oklahoma in 1907. These laws referred to separation within cars, but a Montgomery city ordinance of 1906 was the first to require a completely separate Jim Crow street car. During these years the older seaboard states of the South also extended the segregation laws to steamboats.

The mushroom growth of discriminatory and segregation laws during the first two decades of this century piled up a huge bulk of legislation. Much of the code was contributed by city ordinances or by local regulations and rules enforced without the formality of laws. Only a sampling is possible here. For up and down the avenues and byways of Southern life appeared with increasing profusion the little signs: 'Whites Only'

[1] For first-class coaches only, and not until 1900 was the law amended to apply to second class as well.

or 'Colored.' Sometimes the law prescribed their dimensions in inches, and in one case the kind and color of paint. Many appeared without requirement by law—over entrances and exits, at theaters and boarding houses, toilets and water fountains, waiting rooms and ticket windows.

A large body of law grew up concerned with the segregation of employees and their working conditions. The South Carolina code of 1915, with subsequent elaborations, prohibited textile factories from permitting laborers of different races from working together in the same room, or using the same entrances, pay windows, exits, doorways, stairways, 'or windows [sic]' at the same time, or the same 'lavatories, toilets, drinking water buckets, pails, cups, dippers or glasses' at any time. Exceptions were made of firemen, floor scrubbers, and repair men, who were permitted association with the white proletarian elite on an emergency basis. In most instances segregation in employment was established without the aid of statute. And in many crafts and trades the written or unwritten policies of Jim Crow unionism made segregation superfluous by excluding Negroes from employment.

State institutions for the care of the dependent or incapacitated were naturally the subject of more legislation than private institutions of the same sort, but ordinarily the latter followed pretty closely the segregation practices of the public institutions. Both types had usually made it a practice all along. The fact that only Mississippi and South Carolina specifically provided by law for general segregation in hospitals does not indicate that non-segregation was the rule in the hospitals of other states. The two states named also required Negro nurses for Negro patients, and Alabama prohibited white female nurses from attending Negro male patients. Thirteen Southern and border states required the separation of patients by races in mental hospitals, and ten states specified segregation of inmates in penal institutions. Some of the latter went into detail regarding the chaining, transportation, feeding, and working of the prisoners on a segregated basis. Segregation of the races in homes for the aged, the indigent, the orphans, the blind, the deaf, and the dumb was the subject of numerous state laws.

Much ingenuity and effort went into the separation of the

races in their amusements, diversions, recreations, and sports. The Separate Park Law of Georgia, adopted in 1905, appears to have been the first venture of a state legislature into this field, though city ordinances and local custom were quite active in pushing the Negro out of the public parks. Circuses and tent shows, including side shows, fell under a law adopted by Louisiana in 1914, which required separate entrances, exits, ticket windows, and ticket sellers that would be kept at least twenty-five feet apart. The city of Birmingham applied the principle to 'any room, hall, theatre, picture house, auditorium, yard, court, ball park, or other indoor or outdoor place' and specified that the races be 'distinctly separated . . . by well defined physical barriers.' North Carolina and Virginia interdicted all fraternal orders or societies that permitted members of both races to address each other as brother.

Residential segregation in cities, still rare in the older seaboard towns, developed along five different patterns in the second decade of the century. The type originating in Baltimore in 1910 designated all-white and all-Negro blocks in areas occupied by both races. This experiment was imitated in Atlanta and Greenville. Virginia sought to legalize segregation by a state law that authorized city councils to divide territories into segregated districts and to prohibit either race from living in the other's district, a method adopted by Roanoke and Portsmouth, Virginia. The third method, invented by Richmond, designated blocks throughout the city black or white according to the majority of the residents and forbade any person to live in any block 'where the majority of residents on such streets are occupied by those with whom said person is forbidden to intermarry.' This one was later copied by Ashland, Virginia, and Winston-Salem, North Carolina. A still more complicated law originated in Norfolk, which applied to both mixed and unmixed blocks and fixed the color status by ownership as well as occupancy. And finally New Orleans developed a law requiring a person of either race to secure consent of the majority of persons living in an area before establishing a residence therein. After these devices were frustrated by a Supreme Court decision in 1917, attempts continued to be made to circumvent the decision. Probably the most effective of these was the restrictive covenant, a private contract limiting the sale of property in an area to purchasers of the favored race.

The most prevalent and widespread segregation of living areas was accomplished without need for legal sanction. The black ghettos of the 'Darktown' slums in every Southern city were the consequence mainly of the Negro's economic status, his relegation to the lowest rung of the ladder. Smaller towns sometimes excluded Negro residents completely simply by letting it be known in forceful ways that their presence would not be tolerated. In 1914 there were six such towns in Texas, five in Oklahoma, and two in Alabama. On the other hand there were by that time some thirty towns in the South, besides a number of unincorporated settlements, inhabited exclusively by Negroes. In August 1913, Clarence Poe, editor of the *Progressive Farmer*, secured the unanimous endorsement of a convention of the North Carolina Farmer's Union for a movement to segregate the races in rural districts.

The extremes to which caste penalties and separation were carried in parts of the South could hardly find a counterpart short of the latitudes of India and South Africa. In 1909 Mobile passed a curfew law applying exclusively to Negroes and requiring them to be off the streets by 10 p.m. The Oklahoma legislature in 1915 authorized its Corporation Commission to require telephone companies 'to maintain separate booths for white and colored patrons.' North Carolina and Florida required that textbooks used by the public-school children of one race be kept separate from those used by the other, and the Florida law specified separation even while the books were in storage. South Carolina for a time segregated a third caste by establishing separate schools for mulatto as well as for white and Negro children. A New Orleans ordinance segregated white and Negro prostitutes in separate districts. Ray Stannard Baker found Jim Crow Bibles for Negro witnesses in Atlanta courts and Jim Crow elevators for Negro passengers in Atlanta buildings.

A search of the statute books fails to disclose any state law or city ordinance specifying separate Bibles and separate elevators. Right here it is well to admit, and even to emphasize, that *laws are not an adequate index of the extent and prev-*

alence of segregation and discriminatory practices in the South.
The practices often anticipated and sometimes exceeded the
laws. It may be confidently assumed—and it could be verified
by present observation—that there is more Jim Crowism practiced in the South than there are Jim Crow laws on the books.

To say that, however, is not to concede the position so often
taken by Southern as well as Northern writers that the laws
were of little consequence anyway. This view consciously or
unconsciously voices a laissez-faire bias and often leans for support upon the authority of William Graham Sumner. It was
the contention of Sumner's classic *Folkways,* published in 1907,
that 'legislation cannot make mores' and that 'stateways cannot
change folkways.' Sumner described these 'folkways' as 'uniform,
universal in the group, imperative, and invariable.' Perhaps it
was not his intention, but Sumner's teachings lent credence to
the existence of a primeval rock of human nature upon which
the waves of legislation beat in vain. This concept as it was
applied to Southern race practices and caste penalties was
further buttressed by an American apostle of Herbert Spencer,
the sociologist Franklin Henry Giddings. His emphasis upon
'consciousness of kind' in works appearing in 1896 and the decade
following gave aid and comfort to the followers of Sumner. So
did the racist interpretations of the psychologist William Mc-
Dougall, whose *Introduction to Social Psychology* appeared in
1908.

Since the works mentioned represented the dominant American social theory of the early twentieth century, and since they
appeared in the years when the wave of Southern and American
racism was reaching its crest, it was natural that they should
have influenced thinking upon the South's major social preoccupation. Their influence was to encourage the notion that there
was something inevitable and rigidly inflexible about the existing patterns of segregation and race relations in the South;
that these patterns had not been and could not be altered by
conscious effort; and that it was, indeed, folly to attempt to
meddle with them by means of legislation. These early twentieth-
century theories have been characterized by a present-day psychologist, Kenneth B. Clark, as 'the modern attempt at acceptable restatement of the medieval doctrine of *innate ideas.*'

Conceived of as biological or social imperatives, these modern 'innate ideas' were presented as 'folkways' or 'mores' which explained and, by inference, justified the existing structure of society, the privileges and policies of the dominant race, and the subordination of the minority race.

This body of social theory, though outmoded by later discovery and disproved by recent experience, continued to be pressed into use for various purposes down to quite recent times. Thus David L. Cohn of Mississippi wrote in the *Atlantic Monthly* of January 1944, 'It is William Graham Sumner's dictum that you cannot change the mores of a people by law, and since the social segregation of the races is the most deepseated and pervasive of the Southern mores, it is evident that he who attempts to change it by law runs risks of incalculable gravity.' Among such risks he cited 'civil war' as one.

There was a curious contradiction or inconsistency implicit in the theory of this school in so far as it was applied to the history of race relations in the South. When William Graham Sumner wrote that 'The whites [in the South] have never been converted from the old mores' and that 'Vain attempts have been made to control the new order by legislation,' he was thinking of the legislative efforts of radical Reconstruction. Those were the laws he had in mind when he said that 'The only result is the proof that legislation cannot make mores.' It was the same experiment that the historian William H. Dunning, Giddings's colleague at Columbia, referred to in saying, 'The enfranchisement of the freedman was as reckless a species of statecraft, as that which marked "the blind hysterics of the Celt" in 1789–95.' And yet Southerners cited these authorities upon the utter futility of legislation in the alteration of relations between races to justify and support an elaborate program of legislation to change the relations between races in a different direction. The inference would seem to be that while sound scientific theory proved that folkways and mores could not be changed for some purposes, it proved at the same time that they could be changed for other purposes.

At any rate, the findings of the present investigation tend to bear out the testimony of Negroes from various parts of the South, as reported by the Swedish writer Gunnar Myrdal, to the effect that 'the Jim Crow statutes were effective means of tightening and freezing—in many cases instigating—segregation and discrimination.' The evidence has indicated that under conditions prevailing in the earlier part of the period reviewed the Negro could and did do many things in the South that in the latter part of the period, under different conditions, he was prevented from doing.

We have seen that in the 'seventies, 'eighties, and 'nineties the Negroes voted in large numbers. White leaders of opposing parties encouraged them to vote and earnestly solicited their votes. Qualified and acknowledged leaders of Southern white opinion were on record as saying that it was proper, inevitable, and desirable that they should vote. Yet after the disfranchisement measures were passed around 1900 the Negroes ceased to vote. And at that time qualified and acknowledged leaders of white opinion said that it was unthinkable that they should ever be permitted to vote. In the earlier decades Negroes still took an active, if modest, part in public life. They held offices, served on the jury, sat on the bench, and were represented in local councils, state legislatures, and the national Congress. Later on these things were simply not so, and the last of the Negroes disappeared from these forums.

It has also been seen that their presence on trains upon equal terms with white men was once regarded in some states as normal, acceptable, and unobjectionable. Whether railways qualify as folkways or stateways, black man and white man once rode them together and without a partition between them. Later on the stateways apparently changed the folkways—or at any rate the railways—for the partitions and Jim Crow cars became universal. And the new seating arrangement came to seem as normal, unchangeable, and inevitable as the old ways. And so it was with the soda fountains, bars, waiting rooms, street cars, and circuses. And so it probably was with the parks in Atlanta, and with cemeteries in Mississippi. There must even have been a time in Oklahoma when a colored man could walk into any old telephone booth he took a notion to and pick up the receiver.

What was once said in extenuation of the harshness of the black codes of slavery times—that they were more honored in the breach than in the observance—cannot be said of the Jim Crow codes. Any Southerner of middle age, of course, could think of exceptions: the old 'auntie' who came to talk with one's grandmother on Saturday afternoons when the weather was nice; the privileged 'uncle' who preferred and was permitted to attend the white church; the defiant 'mammy' on the white day coach; and the old retainer who lorded it over the family larder and put the grocer's white delivery boy in his place. But we recognize them all as belated survivors of the old times— relics now gone with the second wind of history.

Barring those disappearing exceptions, the Jim Crow laws applied to *all* Negroes—not merely to the rowdy, or drunken, or surly, or ignorant ones. The new laws did not countenance the old conservative tendency to distinguish between classes of the race, to encourage the 'better' element, and to draw it into a white alliance. Those laws backed up the Alabamian who told the disfranchising convention of his state that no Negro in the world was the equal of 'the least, poorest, lowest-down white man I ever knew'; but not ex-Governor Oates, who replied: 'I would not trust him as quickly as I would a negro of intelligence and good character.' The Jim Crow laws put the authority of the state or city in the voice of the street-car conductor, the railway brakeman, the bus driver, the theater usher, and also into the voice of the hoodlum of the public parks and playgrounds. They gave free rein and the majesty of the law to mass aggressions that might otherwise have been curbed, blunted, or deflected.

The Jim Crow laws, unlike feudal laws, did not assign the subordinate group a fixed status in society. They were constantly pushing the Negro farther down. In seeking to distinguish between the Southern white attitudes toward the Negro during Reconstruction and the era following and the attitudes later developed, Edgar Gardner Murphy in 1911 called the one 'defensive' and 'conservative' and the other 'increasingly aggressive' and 'destructive.' 'The new mood,' he wrote, 'makes few professions of conservatism. It does not claim to be necessary to the state's existence . . . These new antipathies are not defensive, but assertive and combative . . . frankly and ruthlessly destructive.' The movement had proceeded in mounting stages of aggression. 'Its spirit is that of an all-absorbing autocracy of race, an animus of aggrandizement which makes, in the imagination of the white man, an absolute identification of the stronger race with the very being of the state.'

We have come a long way since that time and since that mood prevailed in the South. But most of the distance we have traveled has been covered in very recent years. The most common observation upon recent developments in race relations by intelligent white people of the South is almost invariably prefaced by the phrase: 'Ten (or twenty) years ago I would never have believed that . . .' And, indeed, there was then little reason to believe, or to expect, that things would change in the South at any more than a glacial pace. For as recently as that the doctrine according to Sumner prevailed almost unchallenged in the mind of the laity—as well as in the minds of a good part of the 'experts' on social problems. And that doctrine had it that however crying the need for change, those immovable 'folkways' and irresistible 'mores' made the whole idea impracticable, or slowed down change to the pace of evolution.

When a scientific theory ceases to account for the observed facts of common experience, however, it would seem to be time to discard the theory. In lieu of another to offer in its place, we can at least try to understand what has happened.

August Meier

After the end of Reconstruction, Negro leaders sought desperately to find some program and solution to their problems. They responded to their worsening conditions by protesting against and boycotting segregated facilities, appealing to the Republican party, forming alliances with the Populists, supporting Democratic or Independent candidates, proposing schemes for emigrating to Africa, migrating to the West and North, and trying to revive among white Northerners interest in Negro rights.

Yet nothing seemed to stem the tide of lynchings, disenfranchisements, segregation, and poverty. With the exceptions of a few patronage jobs to the faithful, and pious statements before election time, Negroes could show few gains for their efforts on behalf of the Republican party. The Republican party, caught between loyalty to the Negroes or building a lily-white party in the South, chose the latter. Even supposed friends of the Negroes, such as President Theodore Roosevelt, held them privately in contempt. "Now as to the Negroes!" Roosevelt wrote to a friend in 1906, "I entirely agree with you that as a race and in the mass they are altogether inferior to the whites."

In this atmosphere the stage was set for the appearance of Booker T. Washington, Principal of Tuskegee Normal and Industrial Institute. Professor Rayford Logan found that Washington's Atlanta Exposition address of 1895 ("In all things that are purely social we can be as separate as the fingers, yet one as the hand in all things essential to mutual progress") was hailed by white political leaders and the press throughout the nation. Negroes were less enthusiastic, and the Negro Washington *Bee* noted that "Prof. Washington's speech suited the white prejudiced element in the country." Nevertheless, Washington soon became the foremost spokesman of the Negro community. A year after the Atlanta speech, Harvard awarded Washington an honorary Master of Arts. Within a short time Booker T. Washington had become the arbiter of Negro affairs as white philanthropists and organizations channeled political patronage, educational funds, and newspaper advertisements through him. From 1895 almost until his death in 1915, Washington served as the paramount intermediary between the Negro and white communities.

In his public life, Washington said what white Americans thought Negroes should say: Work hard, be thrifty, do not push too hard for political or social equality, be satisfied in building your own separate community, and avoid the appeals of agitators, radicals, Socialists, and labor unions. But as August Meier has discovered by a close examination of the Washington papers, Washington presented quite a different image in private. Secretly he provided funds for lawyers to challenge segregationist laws and defend Negroes, and quietly worked against many of the things and people which he appeared to condone in public.

This seemed to be the price Washington was willing to pay for leadership. Certainly he cracked down hard on those Negroes who challenged his leadership and programs. Today even Washington's most sincere defenders are hard-pressed to justify his course of action. It is often said in his behalf that under the circumstances of American life at the time what could he or anyone else have done differently. For an answer to that question, we may read Francis L. Broderick's essay on the career of W. E. B. Du Bois. (*See* pages 358– 372.)

August Meier is among the most productive young scholars now working in the field of contemporary Negro history. He has taught at Tougaloo, Fisk, Morgan State, and Roosevelt University, and is now Professor of History at Kent State University. He is the author of *From Plantation to Ghetto* (with Elliott M. Rudwick), and editor of *Negro Protest Thought in the Twentieth Century* (with Francis L. Broderick). Meier began his reassessment of Washington in the 1950s, and a fully developed reinterpretation appeared in *Negro Thought in America, 1880–1915* (1963) from which the following essay is taken.

BOOKER T. WASHINGTON:
AN INTERPRETATION

SOURCE: August Meier, "Booker T. Washington: An Interpretation," from *Negro Thought in America, 1880–1915* (Ann Arbor, Michigan: University of Michigan Press, 1963), pp. 100–3, 103–5, 105–6, 107–10, 110–11, 113– 15, 116, 118.

Booker T. Washington had assiduously cultivated a good press and from time to time had received the attention accorded leaders who were, as the phrase went, "succeeding." Yet it was with relative suddenness that he emerged at the Atlanta Exposition in September 1895 as a figure of national reputation and the acknowledged leader of Negroes in America.

To Washington the solution of the race problem lay essentially in an application of the gospel of wealth, and he opened and closed his address that memorable afternoon with references to material prosperity. He urged Negroes to stay in the South, since when it came to business, pure and simple, it was in the South that the Negro was given a man's chance. Whites were urged to lend a helping hand in the uplifting of the

Negroes in order to further the prosperity and well-being of their region. Coupled with this appeal to the self-interest of the white South was a conciliatory phraseology and a criticism of Negroes. Washington deprecated politics and the Reconstruction experience. He criticized Negroes for forgetting that the masses of the race were to live by the production of their hands and for permitting their grievances to overshadow their opportunities. He grew lyrical in reciting the loyalty and fidelity of Negroes—"the most patient, faithful, law-abiding and unresentful people that the world had seen." He denied any interest in social equality when he said: "In all things that are purely social we can be as separate as the five fingers, yet one as the hand in all things essential to mutual progress." In conclusion he asked for justice and an elimination of sectional differences and racial animosities, which, combined with material prosperity would usher in a new era for "our beloved South."[1]

Washington's emphasis upon economic prosperity was the hallmark of the age. The pledges of loyalty to the South and the identification of Negro uplift with the cause of the New South satisfied the "better class" of Southern whites and Northern investors; the generalities about justice to the Negro, of interracial co-operation in things essential to mutual progress, coupled with a denial of interest in social equality, encompassed a wide range of views that could be satisfied by ambiguous phraseology. Washington's generalized references to justice and progress and uplift soothed the pallid consciences of the dominant groups in the nation and at the same time allowed the white South to assume that justice could be achieved without granting Negroes political and civil rights. Yet a careful reading of the address indicates that it could also be interpreted as including ultimate goals more advanced than white Southerners could possibly support. Negroes must begin at the bottom, but surely Washington believed that eventually they would arrive at the top. Most Negroes interpreted social equality as meaning simply intimate social relationships which they did not desire, though most whites interpreted it as meaning the abolition of segregation. Even though Washington said that "it is important and

[1] Address . . . Delivered at the Opening of the Cotton States and International Exposition, 1895 (no imprint, n.d.), 6–11.

right that all privileges of the law be ours; but it is vastly more important that we be prepared for the exercise of these privileges," and that "the opportunity to earn a dollar in a factory just now is worth infinitely more than the opportunity to spend a dollar in an opera house," his Negro supporters emphasized the future implications of his remarks, and his statement that "no race that has anything to contribute to the markets of the world is long in any degree ostracized." Unlike Negroes, the dominant whites were impressed by his conciliatory phraseology, confused his means for his ends, and were satisfied with the immediate program that he enunciated.

Washington captured his audience and assured his ascendancy primarily because his ideas accorded with the climate of opinion at the time. His association with industrial education, his emphasis upon the economic, and his conciliatory approach were undoubtedly important reasons why he was selected to speak on this prominent occasion. As Charles S. Johnson has suggested, Washington was effectively manipulating the symbols and myths dear to the majority of Americans.[2] It cannot be overemphasized that Washington's philosophy represents in large measure the basic tendencies of Negro thought in the period under consideration. Armstrong at Hampton had expressed the identical program as a ground of compromise between the white North, the white South, and the Negro. Indeed, it is clear that the chief source of Washington's philosophy was his experience at Hampton Institute, for he unmistakably bore the stamp of its founder.

How much the youthful Washington was shaped by his Hampton experience it is hard to say. He later recounted his strenuous efforts to obtain an education while working in the salt and coal mines at Malden, West Virginia, his lessons of cleanliness, thoroughness, and honesty as the servant of the wife of Yankee General Lewis Ruffner, and his bold trip, largely on foot, of five hundred miles from his home to Hampton. These were all evidences of the self-reliant personality that was his. Consequently, Yankee, Puritan, industrious Hampton and this ambitious and industrious youth of sixteen, who presented himself

[2] Charles S. Johnson, "The Social Philosophy of Booker T. Washington," 1940, MS lent to the author by the late Dr. Johnson.

at its doors in the fall of 1872, clicked from the first. "At Hampton," he wrote later, "I found the opportunities . . . to learn thrift, economy and push. I was surrounded by an atmosphere of business, Christian influences, and the spirit of self-help, that seemed to have awakened every faculty in me."[3]

Armstrong was undoubtedly the most influential person in Washington's life, and his viewpoint contained the major ingredients of Washington's philosophy. Yet Washington was not fully committed to the Hampton idea when he left the school in 1875. He taught for two years in his home town in West Virginia, attended briefly the liberal arts Wayman Seminary in Washington, toyed with the idea of a political career, and started the study of law. Like the majority of his future students he at no time seriously considered practicing a trade for a livelihood. All questions were settled, however, when he was asked to return to Hampton to teach in 1879. Then, in 1881 Washington set forth to establish his own school at Tuskegee, Alabama, on the meager appropriations that resulted—paradoxically enough—from a political deal on the part of an ex-Confederate colonel who solicited Negro votes by promising to introduce a bill for a Negro industrial school in the legislature.[4] From then until 1895 Washington was engaged in building the school—a story of trial and success in the best Hampton tradition.

In discussing Washington's ideology it will be necessary to examine both his overtly expressed philosophy of accommodation and his covertly conducted attack on racial discrimination. His conciliatory approach was an important factor in his achieving eminence, and his continued ascendancy in Negro affairs, due as it was to the support of dominant white elements, depended upon his playing this tactful role to the fullest extent. Yet his very prominence brought him into situations that led to secret activities that directly contradicted the ideology he officially espoused. . . .

The central theme in Washington's philosophy was that through thrift, industry, and Christian character Negroes would

<hr />

[3] *Future of the American Negro* (Boston, 1899), 107. Biographical details are supplied in *Up From Slavery* (New York, 1901), and in the more revealing *Story of My Life and Work* (Naperville, 1900).

[4] Emmett J. Scott and Lyman B. Stowe, *Booker T. Washington: Builder of a Civilization* (New York, 1916), 3–4.

eventually attain their constitutional rights. To Washington it seemed but proper that Negroes would have to measure up to American standards of morality and material prosperity if they were to succeed in the Social Darwinist race of life. Just as the individual who succeeds can do something that the world wants done well, so with a race. Things would be on a different footing if it became common to associate the possession of wealth with a black skin. "It is not within the province of human nature that the man who is intelligent and virtuous, and owns and cultivates the best farm in his county, shall very long be denied the proper respect and consideration."[5]

Consequently Negroes, he felt, must learn trades in order to compete with whites. He blamed Negroes for neglecting skills acquired under slavery, for the loss of what had been practically a monopoly of the skilled labor in the South at the close of the Civil War. He feared that unless industrial schools filled the breach, the next twenty years would witness the economic demise of the Negro. He was often critical of higher education. He never tired of retelling the anecdotes about the rosewood piano in the tumble-down cabin, or about the young man he found sitting in an unkempt cabin, studying from a French grammar. He denied that he intended to minimize the value of higher education, and his own children in fact enjoyed its advantages, but practical education, he believed, should come first in the rise of a people toward civilization. Occasionally, he praised higher education, but he often cited cases of college graduates who were accomplishing nothing, and once at least he referred to "the college bacillus."[6]

Fundamentally, Washington did not think in terms of a subordinate place in the American economy for Negroes. Though his language was ambiguous, he thought in terms of developing a substantial propertied class of landowners and businessmen. There was, as he often put it, a great need for "captains of industry." He felt a deep sympathy with the wealthy, and he preferred to talk most of all to audiences of businessmen who, he found, were quick to grasp what he was saying. In all this he

[5] *Future of the American Negro,* 176.
[6] "A University Education for Negroes," *Independent,* LXVIII (March 24, 1910), 613–18; "What I am Trying to Do," *World's Work,* XXVII (Nov., 1913), 103.

was thoroughly in accord with the New South philosophy. He praised Robert C. Ogden of Wanamaker's (a trustee of Tuskegee and Hampton and chairman of the General Education Board) and H. H. Rogers, the Standard Oil and railroad magnate, as men whose interest in uplifting the Negro was partly motivated by their desire to develop one of the neglected resources of the South.[7]

Part of Washington's outlook toward capital and the New South was his antagonistic attitude toward labor unions. He recollected that before the days of strikes in the West Virginia coal mines where he had worked, he had known miners with considerable sums in the bank, "but as soon as the professional labor agitators got control, the savings of even the more thrifty ones began disappearing." To some extent, he felt, the loss of the Negro's hold on the skilled trades was due to the unions. He boasted that Negro labor was, if fairly treated, "the best free labor in the world," not given to striking. Later, writing in the *Atlantic Monthly* in 1913, Washington, though still basically hostile, appeared somewhat more favorable toward unions. He admitted that there were cases in which labor unions had used their influence on behalf of Negroes even in the South, and he knew of instances in which Negroes had taken a leading part in the work of their unions. Nevertheless, he felt that unions would cease to discriminate only to the extent that they feared Negro strikebreakers.[8]

Exceedingly important in Washington's outlook was an emphasis on agriculture and rural landownership that has ordinarily been overlooked. He constantly deprecated migration to cities where, he said, the Negro was at his worst and insisted that Negroes should stay on the farmlands of the South. Since all peoples who had gained wealth and recognition had come up from the soil, agriculture should be the chief occupation of Negroes, who should be encouraged to own and cultivate the soil. While he called Negroes the best labor for Southern farms,

---

[7] *My Larger Education*, 72–73, 76–77.
[8] *Up From Slavery*, 68–69; "The Best Free Labor in the World," *Southern State Farm Magazine* (Jan., 1898), 496–98 (clipping in BTW Papers); "The Negro and the Labor Unions," *Atlantic Monthly*, CXI (June, 1913), 756–67.

he optimistically looked forward to an independent yeomanry, respected in their communities. . . .

While whites had some responsibility, the most important part in the Negro's progress was to be played by the Negro himself; the race's future recognition lay within its own hands. On the negative side this emphasis on self-help involved a tendency to blame Negroes for their condition. Washington constantly criticized them for seeking higher rather than practical education, for their loss of places in the skilled trades, for their lack of morality and economic virtues, and for their tendency toward agitation and complaint. But in its positive aspects this emphasis involved race pride and solidarity. Negroes should be proud of their history and their great men. For a race to grow strong and powerful it must honor its heroes. Negroes should not expect any great success until they learned to imitate the Jews, who through unity and faith in themselves were becoming more and more influential. He showed considerable pride in the all-Negro communities. At times he espoused a high degree of racial solidarity and economic nationalism. On one occasion he declared: "We are a nation within a nation." While Negroes should be the last to draw the color line, at the same time they should see to it that "in every wise and legitimate way our people are taught to patronise racial enterprises."[9]

If emphasis upon racial pride and self-help through economic and moral development formed one side of Washington's thinking, another was his insistence that interracial harmony and white good will were prerequisite to the Negro's advancement. In appealing to whites Washington spoke in both moral and practical terms. Southern whites should aid Negroes out of economic self-interest and should act justly since to do less would corrupt their moral fiber. Washington constantly reiterated his love for the South, his faith in the Southern white man's sense of justice, his belief that the South afforded Negroes more economic opportunity than the North. In 1912, answering the question "Is the Negro Having a Fair Chance?" he did go so far as to admit the existence of the standard grievances, but declared that nowhere were there ten million black people who had greater opportunities or were making greater progress

[9] Detroit *Leader*, Sept. 8, 1911 (in BTW Clipping Books).

than the Negroes of the South; nowhere had any race "had the assistance, the direction, and the sympathy of another race in all its efforts to rise to such an extent as the Negro in the United States." Washington devoted one whole book, *The Man Farthest Down* (1912), to the thesis that American Negroes were better off than the depressed classes in Europe. In general, Washington appealed to the highest sentiments and motives of the whites and brushed lightly over their prejudices and injustices in an attempt to create the favorable sentiment without which Negro progress was doomed. He frequently referred to the friendship Southern whites exhibited toward Negroes and constantly cited examples of harmonious relations between the races. At a time when Mississippi was notorious for "whitecapping" (the attacking of business establishments owned by prosperous Negroes who were then run out of town), he opined that "there, more than anywhere else, the colored people seem to have discovered that, in gaining habits of thrift and industry, in getting property, and in making themselves useful, there is a door of hope open for them which the South has no disposition to close." He was incurably optimistic in his utterances—as he said, "We owe it not only to ourselves, but to our children, to look always upon the bright side of life." . . .[10]

While Washington never changed his basic ideology, before 1895 he tended to be more frank, though always tactful, regarding the Negro's goals. In 1894, for example, he admitted that conventions and organizations whose aims were to redress certain grievances were "right and proper," though they should not be the chief reliance of the race, and went on to declare that if his approach did not in time bring every political and civil right then everything, even the teaching of Christ, was false. As conditions grew worse Washington became more rather than less conciliatory. The outstanding exception to his general policy was his address at the Jubilee celebration held in Chicago after the Spanish-American War, where with President McKinley in the audience, he made one of his famous *faux pas*. Reviewing the valorous deeds of Negroes in the military history

---

[10] "Is the Negro Having a Fair Chance?" *Century*, LXXXV (Nov., 1912), 46, 50–55; *My Larger Education*, 189, 197–98; "Fundamental Needs for the Progress of the Race" (1904, MS at Tuskegee Institute Department of Records and Research).

of the United States, especially in the recent war, he contended that a race that was thus willing to die for its country should be given the highest opportunity to live for its country. Americans had won every conflict in which they had been engaged, "except the effort to conquer ourselves in the blotting out of racial prejudice. . . . Until we thus conquer ourselves I make no empty statement when I say that we shall have a cancer gnawing at the heart of this republic that shall some day prove to be as dangerous as an attack from an army without or within." This statement aroused considerable ire in the Southern press, and Washington characteristically qualified his remarks. He explained that he seldom referred to prejudice because it was something to be lived down rather than talked down, but since that meeting symbolized the end of sectional feelings he had thought it an appropriate time to ask for "the blotting out of racial prejudice as far as possible in 'business and civil relations.' "[11]

On the three major issues of segregation, lynching, and the franchise, the Tuskegeean expressed himself with characteristic circumspection. Prior to the Atlanta address he had made it clear that he opposed segregation in transportation. Speaking in 1884 he had said that "the Governor of Alabama would probably count it no disgrace to ride in the same railroad coach with a colored man." As late as 1894 he urged Negroes to follow the example of Atlanta citizens who had boycotted the newly segregated streetcars and predicted that such economic pressures would make it respectable for both races to ride in the same railway coach as well. But after 1895 he held that separate but equal facilities would be satisfactory. As he once put it: "All . . . parts of the world have their own peculiar customs and prejudices. For that reason it is a part of commonsense to respect them."[12] And he did respect the customs of other parts of the world. He accepted President Roosevelt's dinner invitation in 1901 after careful consideration. He was on

---

[11] "Taking Advantage of Our Disadvantages," A.M.E. *Review*, XX (April, 1894), 480; *Story of My Life and Work*, 265–66, 274–76.

[12] *Selected Speeches* . . . , 2–3; "Taking Advantage of Our Disadvantages," 480; *My Larger Education*, 178.

intimate terms with distinguished philanthropists and was entertained in circles in the North and abroad that few white Southerners could have entered. Yet he declared that the objection to the Jim Crow car was "not the separation, but the inadequacy of the accommodations." Again, speaking in 1914 on the matter of municipal segregation ordinances, Washington stirred up a hornet's nest of criticism by remarking: "Let us, in the future, spend less time talking about the part of the city that we cannot live in, and more time in making the part of the city that we can live in beautiful and attractive." Yet in a posthumously published account of "My View of Segregation Laws" Washington—or his ghostwriter—tactfully gave his reasons for condemning them, and in a most unusual concluding statement openly declared that segregation was "ill-advised" because it was unjust and all thoughtful Negroes resented injustice. There was no case of segregation, he said, that had not widened the breach between the two races. That Negroes did not constantly express their embitterment, he added, was not proof that they did not feel it.[13]

Even on lynching Washington expressed himself rarely, but when he did his statements received considerable attention. He generally emphasized the harm lynching did to the whites—to their moral fiber, to economic conditions, and to the reputation of the South—and at the same time counseled Negroes to cultivate industry and cease the idleness that led to crime. Yet he could be forthright in his condemnation of mob violence. "Within the last fortnight," he said in a statement issued to the press in 1904,

three members of my race have been burned at the stake; one of them was a woman. No one . . . was charged with any crime even remotely connected with the abuse of a white woman. . . . Two of them occurred on Sunday afternoon in sight of a Christian church. . . . The custom of burning human beings has become so common as scarcely to excite interest. . . . There is no shadow of excuse for departure from legal methods in the cases of individuals accused of murder.[14]

[13] "Is the Negro Having a Fair Chance?" 51; *Report of the Fifteenth Annual Convention of the National Negro Business League . . . 1914* (no imprint [1914]), 82; "My View of Segregation Laws," *New Republic*, V (Dec. 4, 1915), 113–14.
[14] *Recorder*, March 17, 1904.

Ordinarily, Washington did not discuss politics, but there were occasions when he did admit that "I do not favor the Negro's giving up anything which is fundamental and which has been guaranteed to him by the Constitution. . . . It is not best for him to relinquish his rights; nor would his doing so be best for the Southern white man." He was critical of Reconstruction, when Negroes had started at the top instead of the bottom, in the senate instead of at the plow, and had been the unwitting instruments of corrupt carpet-bagger politicians. "In a word, too much stress had been placed upon the mere matter of voting and holding political office rather than upon the preparation for the highest citizenship." Washington's solution to the question of political rights was suffrage restriction applied to both races— a notion that had been growing in popularity since about 1890. "The permanent cure for our present evils will come through a property and educational test for voting that shall apply honestly and fairly to both races." In a letter to the Louisiana Constitutional Convention of 1898 he outlined his views. He was, he said, no politician, but had always advised Negroes to acquire property, intelligence, and character as the basis of good citizenship, rather than to engage in political agitation. He agreed that franchise restrictions were necessary to rid the South of ignorant and corrupt government, but suggested that no state could pass a law that would permit an ignorant white man to vote and disfranchise ignorant Negroes "without dwarfing for all time the morals of the white man in the South." In 1899, in referring to the disfranchisement bill before the Georgia legislature, he had forcefully declared that its object was to disfranchise the Negroes. Yet three years later he became notorious for his defense of the disfranchisement constitutions: "Every revised constitution throughout the Southern States has put a premium upon intelligence, ownership of property, thrift and character," he wrote in a general letter to the press.[15] But his hope that these qualifications would be equitably applied remained unfulfilled, and after 1905 Washington no longer rationalized about the disfranchisement constitutions, as he had done, but simply held

[15] *Future of the American Negro*, 141, 13, 153; *An Open Letter to the Louisiana Constitutional Convention*, Feb. 19, 1898 (no imprint [1900?]), 1–2; interview reprinted from Atlanta *Constitution*, ———, 1899 in *ibid.*, 6; *Gazette*, Dec. 20, 1902.

that the acquisition of character, wealth, and education would break down racial discrimination.

All in all, in viewing Washington's philosophy, one is most impressed by his accommodating approach. By carefully selected ambiguities in language, by mentioning political and civil rights but seldom and then only in tactful and vague terms, he effectively masked the ultimate implications of his philosophy. For this reason his philosophy must be viewed as an accommodating one in the context of Southern race relations. In the context of the Negro thinking of the period, perhaps the most significant thing in his philosophy was his emphasis upon self-help and racial solidarity. . . .

Although overtly Washington minimized the importance of the franchise and civil rights, covertly he was deeply involved in political affairs and in efforts to prevent disfranchisement and other forms of discrimination.

For example, he lobbied against the Hardwick disfranchisement bill in Georgia in 1899. While his public ambiguities permitted Southern whites to think that he accepted disfranchisement if they chose to, through the same ambiguities and by private communications Washington tried to keep Negroes thinking otherwise. In 1903 when the Atlanta editor Clark Howell implied that Washington opposed Negro officeholding, he did not openly contradict him, but asked T. Thomas Fortune to editorialize in the *Age* that Howell had no grounds for placing Washington in such a position, for it was "well understood that he, while from the first deprecating the Negro's making political agitation and office-holding the most prominent and fundamental part of his career, has not gone any farther."[16] Again, while Washington opposed proposals to enforce the representation provisions of the fourteenth amendment (because he felt that the South would accept reduction in representation and thus stamp disfranchisement with the seal of constitutionality), he was secretly engaged in attacking the disfranchisement constitutions by court action. As early as 1900 he was asking certain philanthropists for money to fight the electoral provisions of the Louisiana constititution. Subsequently, he worked secretly

[16] BTW to Garrison, Nov. 28, 1899 in Garrison Papers; BTW to T. Thomas Fortune, Nov. 10, 1899, June 23, 1903.

through the financial secretary of the Afro-American Council's legal bureau, personally spending a great deal of money and energy fighting the Louisiana test case.[17] At the time of the Alabama Constitutional Convention in 1901 he used his influence with important whites in an attempt to prevent discriminatory provisions that would apply to Negroes only.[18] He was later deeply involved in testing the Alabama disfranchisement laws in the federal courts in 1903 and 1904. So circumspect was he in this instance that his secretary, Emmett J. Scott, and the New York lawyer Wilford Smith corresponded about the cases under pseudonyms and represented the sums involved in code. Washington was also interested in efforts to prevent or undermine disfranchisement in other states. For example, in Maryland, where disfranchisement later failed, he had a Catholic lawyer, F. L. McGhee of St. Paul, approach the Catholic hierarchy in an attempt to secure its opposition to disfranchisement and urged the Episcopal divine George Freeman Bragg of Baltimore to use his influence among important whites.[19] Washington contributed money generously to the test cases and other efforts, though, except in the border states, they were unsuccessful. In 1903 and 1904 he personally "spent at least four thousand dollars in cash, out of my own pocket . . . in advancing the rights of the black man." . . .[20]

In areas other than politics Washington also played an active behind-the-scenes role. On the Seth Carter (Texas) and Dan Rogers (Alabama) cases involving discrimination in the matter of representation on juries, Washington worked closely with the lawyer Wilford Smith and contributed liberally to their financ-

[17] BTW to Garrison, Feb. 27, and March 11, 1900, Garrison Papers; Jesse Lawson to BTW, March 29, June 26, July 30, Oct. 2, Dec. 30, 1901; April 30, June 24, 1902; BTW to Lawson, Dec. 11, 1903. On BTW's opposition to reduced representation for Southern states, see BTW to R. C. Ogden, May 15, 1903; BTW to W. H. Baldwin, March 4, 1904.

[18] E.g., Correspondence with A. D. Wimbs, 1901.

[19] Correspondence of Wilford Smith (alias J. C. May) and Emmett J. Scott (alias R. C. Black) 1903 and 1904; F. L. McGhee to BTW, Jan. 12, 1904; BTW to George F. Bragg, March 10, 1904. For fuller documentation of this and other points made in this section see August Meier, "Toward a Reinterpretation of Booker T. Washington," JSH, XXIII (May, 1957), 220–27.

[20] BTW to J. W. E. Bowen, Dec. 27, 1904.

ing.[21] He was interested in preventing Negro tenants who had accidentally or in ignorance violated their contracts from being sentenced to the chain gang.[22] He was concerned in the Alonzo Bailey Peonage Case, and when the Supreme Court declared peonage illegal, confided to friends that he and his associates had been working at the case for over two years, securing the free services of some of the best lawyers in Montgomery and the assistance of other leading white people. Yet Washington characteristically interceded to reduce the sentence of the convicted man, who was soon released.[23]

Of special interest are Washington's efforts against railroad segregation. At Washington's suggestion Giles B. Jackson of Richmond undertook the legal fight against the Jim Crow Law in Virginia in 1901.[24] When Tennessee in 1903 in effect prohibited Pullman accommodations for Negroes by requiring that such facilities be entirely separate, he stepped into the breach. He worked closely with Napier in Nashville and enlisted the aid of Atlanta leaders like W. E. B. Du Bois. This group, however, did not succeed in discussing the matter with Pullman Company president Robert Todd Lincoln, in spite of the intercession of another railroad leader, William H. Baldwin, president of the Long Island Rail Road, an important figure in the Pennsylvania and Southern systems, and Washington's closest white friend. And, though Washington wanted to start a suit, the Nashville people failed to act.[25] Again, in 1906, employing the Howard University Professor Kelly Miller and the Boston lawyer Archibald W. Grimké as intermediaries, Washington discreetly supplied funds to pay ex-Senator Henry W. Blair of New Hampshire to lobby against the Warner-Foraker Amendment to the Hepburn Railway Act.[26] This amendment, by requiring

[21] E.g., J. C. May to R. C. Black, July 15, 1903; BTW to Smith, Feb. 2, March 3, 1904; Smith to BTW, Feb. 4, 1904.

[22] BTW to Villard, Sept. 7, 1908; Villard to BTW, Sept. 8, 1908.

[23] BTW to Anderson, Jan. 6, 1911; BTW to R. W. Thompson, Jan. 7, 1911; BTW to Hilles, ——,1911; *Crisis*, II(Aug., 1911), 139.

[24] Jackson to BTW, Jan. 24, 1901.

[25] Napier to BTW, Oct. 28, Dec. 11, 1903; BTW to Napier, Nov. 2, 1903; BTW to Lawson, Nov. 5, 1903; BTW to Du Bois, Dec. 14, 1903, Feb. 27, June 4, 1904; Baldwin to BTW, Jan. 7, 1904.

[26] Miller to BTW, May 22, 1906; Grimké to BTW, May 25, June 10, 1906; BTW to Grimké, June 2, 4, 10, 1906; Scott to Thompson, June 5, 1906.

equality of accommodations in interstate travel, would have impliedly condoned segregation throughout the country, under the separate-but-equal doctrine. The amendment was defeated, but whether due to Blair's lobbying or to the protests of Negro organizations is hard to say.

Thus, in spite of his accommodating tone and his verbal emphasis upon economy as the solution to the race problem, Washington was surreptitiously engaged in undermining the American race system by a direct attack upon disfranchisement and segregation, and in spite of his strictures against political activity he was a powerful politician in his own right.

Comparable to Washington's influence in politics was his position with the philanthropists. He wielded an enormous influence in appropriations made by Carnegie, Rosenwald, the General Education Board, and the Phelps-Stokes and Jeanes Funds. Negro schools that received Carnegie libraries received them at Washington's suggestion, and even applied for them upon his advice.[27] Contributors sought his advice on the worthiness of schools; college administrators asked his advice on personnel. His weight was especially appreciated by the liberal arts colleges. Washington accepted a place on the boards of trustees of Howard University in 1907 and of Fisk University in 1909. In the case of Fisk he proved exceedingly helpful in attracting philanthropic contributions.[28] So complete was Washington's control over educational philanthropy that John Hope, president of Atlanta Baptist College, and a member of the anti-Bookerite Niagara Movement, found the doors of the foundations entirely closed to him. Only through the intercession of his friend Robert Russua Moton, a member of the Hampton circle and Washington's successor at Tuskegee, was Hope able to obtain Washington's necessary endorsement of his school to philanthropists such as Carnegie.[29]

Washington's popularity with leading whites and his power in philanthropic and political circles enhanced his prestige and

[27] See correspondence with various college presidents 1904 and 1905.
[28] BTW to President J. G. Merrill of Fisk, April 26, 1905; James C. Bertram (Carnegie's secretary) to BTW, Jan. 15, 1908; BTW to Carnegie, Oct. 18, 1910; BTW to Bertram, April 28, 1913, etc.
[29] Ridgely Torrence, *The Story of John Hope* (New York, 1948), 159–63; correspondence between Hope and BTW, 1909.

power within the Negro community. His influence was felt in multifarious ways beyond his control over philanthropy and political appointments. His power over the Negro press was considerable and in large measure stifled criticism of his policies. His influence extended into the Negro churches, and his friendship and assistance were eagerly sought by those seeking positions in the church. Between 1902 and 1904 and perhaps longer, Washington controlled the avowedly protest Afro-American Council, the leading Negro rights organization prior to 1905. Whether or not Washington was a "benevolent despot" as one recent biographer has asserted,[30] is an open question, but that he wielded enormous power over the Negro community is undeniable.

It was this quasi-dictatorial power as much as anything else that alienated W. E. B. Du Bois from Washington and his program. Once Washington had achieved eminence he grew extremely sensitive to adverse criticism from Negroes. From the first some had opposed his viewpoint, and while many rushed to his support after he became the puissant adviser to Theodore Roosevelt, somehow "the opposition" (as Washington often referred to his critics) grew apace. Objections were raised to the arbitrary power of the "Tuskegee machine," as Du Bois called it, and to Washington's soft-pedaling of political and civil rights. From 1903 on Washington found himself increasingly under attack. He used every means at his disposal to combat his critics— his influence with the press, placing spies in the opposition movements, depriving their members of church and political positions. The high point of the attack on Washington, the formation of the National Association for the Advancement of Colored People in 1909–10, came at the very time when his political power was slipping, and after 1913 he had no political influence at all, while the N.A.A.C.P. was becoming stronger. By the time he died Washington had lost much of his power. . . .

Thus, although Washington held to full citizenship rights and integration as his objective, he masked this goal beneath an approach that satisfied influential elements that were either indifferent or hostile to its fulfillment. He was not the first to combine a constructive, even militant emphasis upon self-help,

[30] Spencer, *Booker T. Washington*, chap. x.

racial co-operation and economic development with a conciliatory, ingratiating, and accommodating approach to the white
South. But his name is the one most indissolubly linked with
this combination. He was, as one of his followers put it, attempting to bring the wooden horse within the walls of Troy.

Washington apparently really believed that in the face of an
economic and moral development that assimilated Negroes to
American middle-class standards, prejudice would diminish and
the barriers of discrimination would crumble. He emphasized
duties rather than rights; the Negro's faults rather than his
grievances; his opportunities rather than his difficulties. He
stressed means rather than ends. He was optimistic rather than
pessimistic. He stressed economics above politics, industrial above
liberal education, self-help above dependence on the national
government. He taught that rural life was superior to urban life.
He professed a deep love for the South and a profound faith
in the goodness of the Southern whites—at least of the "better
class." He appealed more to the self-interest of the whites—their
economic and moral good—than to their sense of justice. . . .

His program also appealed to a substantial group of Negroes—
to those Negroes who were coming to count for most—in large
part to a rising middle class. In fact, stress upon economics as
an indirect route to the solution of the race problem, interest
in industrial education, the appeal to race pride and solidarity,
and denial of any interest in social equality were all ideas that
had become dominant in the Negro community. The older upper-
class Negroes in certain Northern centers, who had their economic and sometimes their social roots in the white communities,
were less sympathetic to Washington. But to self-made middle-
class Negroes, and to lower middle-class Negroes on the make,
to the leaders and supporters of Negro fraternal enterprises, to
businessmen who depended on the Negro community for their
livelihood, Washington's message seemed common sense. Interestingly enough, this group, especially in the North, did not
always express Washington's conciliatory tone, but assumed that
Washington was using it to placate the white South.

To what extent Washington directly influenced Negro thought
is difficult to evaluate. Washington was acceptable to Negroes
partly because of the prestige and power he held among whites,

and partly because his views—except for his conciliatory phrase-ology—were dominant in the Negro community throughout the country, and his accommodating approach was general throughout the South. Then, too, his Negro supporters read a great deal into his generalizations about eventual justice and constitutional rights. The fact that Negroes tended to see in his words what they already believed would appear to minimize his direct influence. Yet his prestige, the teachers sent out by Tuskegee and her daughter schools, and the widespread publicity generated by the National Negro Business League of which Washington was the founder and president, undoubtedly had a significant impact on Negro thought, reinforcing tendencies already in the foreground.

Francis L. Broderick

Du Bois remains, and will continue to remain one of the most difficult figures of twentieth-century American history to neatly categorize. Almost all of what he did and wrote during his ninety-five years (1868–1963) depended on how regional, national, or international developments affected the Negro people. Therefore, depending on how Negroes fared, he could be found advocating moderation or retaliatory violence, integration or separatism, Pan-Africanism or anti-Garveyism, reform or radicalism, anti-Communism or Communism, elitism or proletarian involvement.

But two themes which remained constant are the seemingly conflicting ideas of *integration* and *racial solidarity*. Du Bois was conscious of "this double-consciousness." "One ever feels this two-ness," he wrote in *The Souls of Black Folk,* "an American, a Negro; two souls, two thoughts, two unreconciled strivings; two warring ideals in one dark body, whose dogged strength alone keeps it from being torn asunder."

Du Bois knew at first hand the blessings and agonies of being both. Born of free mulatto parents in a small western Massachusetts town where Negroes numbered a mere fifty out of a population of five thousand, Du Bois encountered, as he wrote later, "almost no experience of segregation or color dis-

crimination." He did so well in mastering the college prepara-
tory program that he envisioned himself going onto Harvard
or Amherst. Instead he received a scholarship to Fisk University in Nashville, and here he made his first contact with
Southern Negroes. Far from maintaining a sense of aloofness
or superiority, he completely identified with his classmates.
"I am a Negro; and I glory in the name!" he told his fellow
students during an address. "I am proud of the black blood
that flows in my veins. From all the recollections dear to my
boyhood have I come here, not to pose as a critic but to join
hands with this, my people." After three years at Fisk, he
transferred to Harvard where he spent the next two years
and received his B.A. in 1890. At Harvard he studied with
some of the great minds of American scholarship—Josiah
Royce, William James, George Santayana, and Albert Bush-
nell Hart. Yet he always felt himself as an outsider, and never
developed the affection for Harvard that he felt for Fisk. In
1892–94, he traveled throughout Europe and studied for a
time at Berlin. He came back to Harvard to complete his
doctoral thesis in history, which was chosen in 1896 to inau-
gurate the Harvard Historical Studies series.

Although Du Bois had an academic training that few American students could match, he was still denied access to a
teaching position at a leading white university. In 1897, after
finishing research at the University of Pennsylvania on the
Negroes of Philadelphia, he accepted a position in Sociology
at Atlanta University. For the next thirteen years he produced
a great body of important work. Besides teaching, he directed
and edited the Atlanta University *Publications* on the study
of Negro life, began his investigation into Reconstruction,
published numerous essays on the condition of the Negro in
leading "white" magazines, organized the Niagara Movement, edited its magazine, *Horizon*, and wrote an uncompromising biography of John Brown. However, Du Bois'
activities also brought him into conflict with Booker T. Washington and the "Tuskegee Machine." With his school being
passed over for educational grants, his own research budget
reduced, and the Niagara Movement falling apart, Du Bois
had in 1910 reached the low ebb of his career.

When the recently formed National Association for the Advancement of Colored People offered Du Bois the job as di-

rector of publicity and research and editor of the *Crisis,* he saw this as a way out of a dismal situation. For the first time in his career Du Bois could be assured of adequate financial backing and a platform from which to disseminate his views. But his program was always to be more radical than that of the liberal whites who governed the NAACP, and in 1914 a break almost came between them.

In his writings for the *Crisis,* he reflected the dual nature of the Negroes' American experience. Du Bois fought against segregation and discrimination, but he also urged Negroes to form Negro businesses, cooperatives, and political organizations, not for the purpose of duplicating Washington's program, but as a means of confronting—of challenging—the white world on an even basis. Organized power was something that white Americans could understand. As individuals, Negroes could do little; as large and effective blocs, they could do a great deal. Only at this point, wrote Du Bois, would true integration become a possibility.

He constantly encouraged Negroes—as Negroes and in groups—to fight back. "If we are to die," he angrily wrote after a Pennsylvania mob lynched a Negro in 1911, "in God's name let us perish like men and not like bales of hay." Five years later he advised Florida Negroes to answer the mob "by effective guns in the hands of people determined to sell their soul dearly." A few weeks later he wrote that no human group ever achieved its freedom "without being compelled to murder" thousands of oppressors. Though he hoped that this would not be true for Negroes, "it may be necessary" (Broderick).

Du Bois was a complex personality, and it takes a careful reading of his works to follow the development of his ideas. But already by 1900, one can see in Du Bois' thought the great tug between integrationists' goals and racial solidarity. These motifs continued throughout his later work, and through the Negro community in the coming years.

Francis L. Broderick, Dean at Lawrence University, Appleton, Wisconsin, is the author of *W. E. B. Du Bois: Negro Leader in a Time of Crisis* (1959). The following selection is taken from Broderick's biography of Du Bois, and deals with his early career with the NAACP, when for the first time Du Bois was in an influential position.

W. E. B. DU BOIS:
ENTENTE WITH WHITE LIBERALS, 1910–1920

SOURCE: Francis L. Broderick, "W. E. B. Du Bois: Entente with White Liberals," from *W. E. B. Du Bois: Negro Leaders in a Time of Crisis* (Stanford: Stanford University Press, 1959), 90, 92, 92–94, 101–106, 112–113, 113–14, 115–20.

The National Association for the Advancement of Colored People gave Du Bois an entente with white liberals who had enough money to sustain an organ of protest and enough allegiance to American democracy to tolerate the "radical" Negro point of view. With the relatively secure financial backing that the *Horizon* lacked, the *Crisis*, the Association's monthly magazine, gave Du Bois a secure editorial chair and an independent forum. . . .

The alliance of liberals who made up the new Association gave breath to Du Bois's stifled hopes at Atlanta. With support for his scholarship dwindling, with the *Horizon* losing money on each issue, and with the Niagara Movement collapsing, the offer from the Association, then only several months old, opened up white support previously denied to him. On the other side, the Association turned to him because his record of agitation together with his academic experience made him the ideal candidate for editor of the *Crisis* and director of research. . . .

Working with Progressives

In his inaugural address in 1913, a classic statement of progressivism, Woodrow Wilson spoke of returning America to its first principles. The method was the spread of knowledge—"science" he called it—and the spirit was to be the "hearthfire of every man's conscience and vision of the right." Wilson was speaking of the New Freedom; he could as easily have been talking about the program of the Association.

Though the initial statements of the Association were a bit vague, they clearly aligned the new group with the Progressive movement. Progressives were intent on removing hindrances to the free development of the individual; the Association focussed on the great impediment to Negro individuals—discrimination, especially segregation. To fight this discrimination, the Association proposed education, legal action, and organization: education of the American people in their abuses of Negro rights; appeals to courts and legislatures to remove obstacles blocking Negro progress; and organization into a single articulate group of those Americans, white and black, whose democratic faith abhorred the color line. The new organization started simply as a national office that released public statements on Negro matters. The board of directors met monthly for policy decisions, and in the intervals Du Bois, Miss Ovington, Villard, and Joel E. Spingarn, a professor at Columbia University, gave part of their time to routine matters. As the membership grew, NAACP branches, first in the Northeast and then all over the country, bridged the gap between the national office and the members. The branches supplied the national office with information and in turn served as rallying points and distributing centers for material prepared in New York. A natural division of labor developed, the New York office handling national questions and the branches dealing with local matters. All concentrated on the spread of information. The Association, like the progressives, assumed that when Americans knew of injustice, their intelligence and moral principles would demand reform from legislatures and courts.

To this program Du Bois gave ready assent. He wanted no special treatment for the Negro, merely an equal chance. He was glad to link the Negro's progress to progressivism, to free the Negro from concentration on his own progress and unite him with every cause of world uplift, with the "people who are revolutionizing the world."[1] Even before the first issue of the *Crisis* appeared, he called upon a Negro audience to escape its provincialism and to give moral and financial support to the new group. The following year he mailed out a characteristic appeal to a thousand of the most prominent Negroes in the United States, urging them to join the Association and to secure three additional subscribers to the *Crisis* in order to link colored people themselves with the drive for their own freedom. The Association—

[1] Du Bois, "The Forward Movement," ms. of speech, October 1910, Du Bois papers.

and the *Crisis*—would speed the arrival of democratic justice: "Evolution is evolving the millennium, but one of the unescapable factors in evolution are [*sic*] the men who hate wickedness and oppression with perfect hatred, who will not equivocate, will not excuse, and will be heard."[2] The lead editorial in the first issue of the *Crisis* presented his apocalyptic vision: "Catholicity and tolerance, reason and forebearance can to-day make the world-old dream of human brotherhood approach realization; while bigotry and prejudice, emphasized race prejudice and force can repeat the awful history of the contact of nations and groups in the past. We strive for this higher and broader vision of Peace and Good Will."[3]

Though jealous of the *Crisis'* independence, Du Bois recorded and supported the work of the Association. He joined in the Association's campaign against lynching and suggested methods other than publicity for fighting it: better administration of present laws, court action in all possible instances, new legislation, and federal intervention when the states were incompetent to deal with outrages. In 1910, when Chicago, Philadelphia, Columbus, and Atlantic City were considering the establishment of segregated public schools, he condemned the move as "an argument against democracy and an attempt to shift public responsibility from the shoulders of the public to the shoulders of some class who are unable to defend themselves." In 1913 he joined Storey and Villard in a written protest to Wilson against the growing practice of segregation in governmental agencies in Washington. They condemned the humiliating stigma of segregation, especially when inflicted by the federal government itself, and reminded Wilson pointedly that the Negro also expected to share in the New Freedom. . . .

Du Bois's own program, the main lines of which were drawn together in 1915 in an article, "The Immediate Program of the American Negro,"[4] attested to the division between him and the Association. One part paralleled the Association's program, though Du Bois was more explicit in condemning the barriers created by the "oppression of shrewd capitalists," the "jealousy

2 *Crisis*, VIII (May 1914), 26.
3 *Ibid.*, I (November 1910), i, 10.
4 Du Bois, "The Immediate Program of the American Negro," *ibid.*, IX (April 1915), 310–12.

of trade unions," and the "shackles on social intercourse from the President and the so-called church of Christ down to bootblacks." Yet this merely negative program of fighting obstructions was not enough. Negroes needed to work out their own projects for moving ahead, not assuming that "God or his vice-[regent] the White Man" would do it for them. "Conscious self-realization and self-direction," Du Bois said, "is the watchword of modern man, and the first article in the program of any group that will survive must be the great aim, equality and power among men." Negroes had to plan their own building and loan associations, cooperatives for production and distribution, and blueprints for systematic charity. They should embark on a planned migration from "mob rule and robbery" in the South. In art and literature, Du Bois said, the black man must set loose the tremendous emotional wealth and "dramatic strength" of his problems; in politics, he must organize—the next year Du Bois would speak of a Negro party.

For all this, Du Bois said, organization was essential. He thanked God that most of the Association's support came from black hands, but he called for a still larger proportion, and added: "We must not only support but control this and similar organizations and hold them unswervingly to our objects, our aims, and our ideals." Negro objects, Negro aims, Negro ideals—not the shared goals of a biracial group fighting for democratic equality. The distinction was important, and would grow in importance.

Over the years Du Bois had become aware of the dilemma of Negro separatism. Striving for integration (a long-range goal) and striving for security (a short-range goal) frequently drove Du Bois in opposite directions, and he tells in *The Souls of Black Folk* how the conflict split his personality: "One feels ever his two-ness—an American, a Negro; two souls, two thoughts, two unreconciled strivings; two warring ideals in one dark body, whose dogged strength alone keeps it from being torn asunder." He made there what was perhaps his first reference to "that curious double movement where real progress may be negative and actual advance be relative retrogression." Three years later he pointed out that Negroes were forcing their way into white labor markets, but they were doing it at the price of increased anti-Negro prejudice. He wondered if perhaps the Negro's "only path of escape" was to organize a closed Negro business community—this would "provincialize" the Negro and perhaps also increase prejudice against him, but it would produce income.[5] When the same sentiment appeared in *The Negro in the South*— a book of four lectures, two by Du Bois and two by Washington —E. H. Clement of the editorial staff of the Boston *Evening Transcript* assumed that Du Bois had come to accept segregation. Du Bois denied this interpretation: he was opposed to physical segregation, but he was "perfectly willing" to accept "spiritual segregation and an economic segregation on the spiritual side"— that is, Negroes were to live alongside their white fellow men, but were to trade at their own stores and serve themselves. He was quite sure that this arrangement was "going to be the rule for some time."[6]

From 1910 until after the first World War, Du Bois continued to pick his way through this thorny problem. Each decision reflected an *ad hoc*, pragmatic test rather than a sustained point of view. He accepted segregated YMCA branches, for example, because the Negro's urgent need for social and recreational opportunities overbalanced the endorsement of segregation implied by the use of segregated facilities. In general, his alliance with white progressives seems to have drawn him back briefly to the policy of slow integration. In 1911 he said that the absence of intense racial separateness in the North gave more hope for a "slower but larger integration" than the intense Negro self-consciousness and cooperation in the South.[7] The same year he warned that the acceptance of separation indicated a willingness to "sacrifice the foundations of democracy for peace."[8] On the other hand, he could speak of "Blessed Discrimination" which provided concrete economic advantage—the *Crisis*, for example, was "capitalized race prejudice." Significantly, this last comment came latest: Du Bois moved irregularly toward the acceptance of segregation

[5] Du Bois, "The Economic Future of the Negro," *Publications of the American Economic Association*, 3d series, VII (February 1906), 230, 239.

[6] E. H. Clement to Du Bois, December 18, 1907; Du Bois to Clement, December 30, 1907, Du Bois papers.

[7] Du Bois, "The Social Evolution of the Black South," *American Negro Monograph*, I (March 1911), iv, especially 7–10.

[8] *Crisis*, I (February 1911), iv, 20.

which gave some economic compensation. In 1917 he told his readers: "We see more and more clearly that economic survival for the Negro in America means . . . that he must employ labor, that he must organize industry, that he must enter American industrial development as a group, capable of offensive and defensive action, and not simply as an individual, liable to be made the victim of the white employer and of such of the white labor unions as dare." American Negroes, he said, were singularly well endowed to work out efficient industrial cooperation; they were all in approximately the same economic group, and they shared a mounting group loyalty and an imperative need for a change in their industrial life.[9] Two years later his editorial, "Jim Crow," suggested his indecision: he insisted that Negroes work with their own people in art, industry, and social life to build a "new and great Negro ethos," yet he condemned segregation as impossible and impolitic. In these years Du Bois avoided saying right out that chance advantages justified approval of segregation. For the present he preferred to speculate on both policies, recognizing always a dilemma calling for "thought and forebearance."[10]

To achieve his complex ends, an appeal to truth and to the conscience of America were Du Bois's familiar weapons, and he continued to use them in this decade. In 1910, when Washington gave Europe an unusually sanguine picture of Negro conditions in the South, Du Bois joined with thirty-one other Negro Americans in protesting Washington's report as a violation of truth: "It is one thing to be optimistic, self-forgetful and forgiving, but it is quite a different thing, consciously or unconsciously, to misrepresent the truth."[11] And the hard core of truth had to include disfranchisement, 2,500 lynchings in the previous twenty-five years, and unprotected women.

But the road to truth was far from smooth, and America's conscience seemed remarkably abdurate. Du Bois was a sensitive Negro in white America, where the experience of discrimination touched the Negro at almost every facet of his life. Caught in the vise of his emotion, he could not respond directly to what

[9] *Ibid.*, XIV (August 1917), 166.
[10] *Ibid.*, XVII (January 1919), 112–13.
[11] Du Bois *et al.*, "Race Relations in the United States," press release, October 26, 1910, Du Bois papers.

went on around him. He recorded the poignancy of being a Negro in America: the "real tragedy" was "the inner degradation, the hurt hound feeling" which caused joy "at the sheerest and most negative decency." A prejudiced white man confirmed the Negro's expectation of American discrimination, but a non-prejudiced white did not necessarily undo the damage, for far from showing a brighter picture, he might by contrast merely point up the gloom. Spingarn's ability to reach behind Du Bois's wall of reserve made him a "knight," but the occasion of Spingarn's illness in 1918 led Du Bois to lament how few were the men who could work *with* Negroes as well as work *for* them. The tone of Du Bois's columns in the *Crisis* vacillated between hopefulness and despair, for he saw at the same time how far the Negro had come and how far he still had to go in achieving an equal place in American society. An editorial appointment, a philanthropic gift, a biracial sociological meeting in the South would raise hopes that in a month could be crushed by a lynching or by the spread of prejudice into a new area. The resolutions of the Southern Sociological Congress in 1913, which, according to Du Bois, was the first occasion in American history when Southern blacks and whites had met under Southern auspices to discuss the race problem, contained "scarcely a word" which the *Crisis* could not endorse. But even this small step forward was balanced by the conduct of the Atlanta *Georgian* which, he said, tried to foment a lynching. In an early issue of the new magazine Du Bois had hailed recent court decisions as the "glimmerings of a new dawn," but seven months later when the Newburyport, Massachusetts, *Herald*, reprinted an editorial, "The Negro Vote as an Annoying Factor," from the Nashville *Tennessean and American*, the *Crisis* mourned that the soul of New England, as well as the Middle West, was being poisoned by Negro haters in the South. Du Bois was convinced—and the conviction weighed heavily on him—that race prejudice in the United States was a "deliberately cultivated and encouraged state of mind."[12]

Sometimes after recurrent exasperation, or under severe provocation, Du Bois abandoned reason and cajolery and turned frankly to a threat of force. After a bloody lynching at Coates-

[12] *Ibid.*, I (February 1911), iv, 20; II (September 1911), 196–97; II (May 1911), 19.

ville, Pennsylvania, in 1911, he warned that Negroes had had enough: they had crawled and pleaded for justice, he said, and they had been "cheerfully spit upon and murdered and burned." "If we are to die," he went on, "in God's name let us perish like men and not like bales of hay." When Negroes in Gainesville, Florida, failed to resist an attacking white mob in 1916, an editorial, "Cowardice," insisted that they should have fought in self-defense to the last ditch if they killed every white man in the country and were themselves killed in turn. A striking generalization followed: lynching, he said, would stop in the South "when the cowardly mob is faced by effective guns in the hands of people determined to sell their souls dearly." Later the same year, in reply to a young woman who wanted more refinement and fewer overtones of violence in the *Crisis,* Du Bois reminded her that no human group had "ever" achieved its freedom "without being compelled to murder" thousands of oppressors. Though he hoped that this would not be true for American Negroes, "*it may be necessary.*"[13]

Du Bois's threats of violence were only the most extreme manifestations of his divergences from his white associates. While the Association cautiously assailed legal barriers, Du Bois's shots ranged freely over the church, industrialists, labor unions, philanthropic foundations, and even hit his white liberal colleagues. When he went one step further and suggested the possibility of separate, independent Negro development, perhaps through an Association more tightly geared to "our objects, our aims, and our ideals," he left white liberalism far behind. In Du Bois's view, the path upward was blocked by hurdles uncleared by progressivism.

But though programs diverged and tempers wore thin, the entente with the Association held. The Association could ill afford to lose Du Bois's superb editorial talents on a successful magazine. His columns of editorials sparkled; his news columns contained the fullest available record of information about colored men here and abroad. As the years went on, the *Crisis,* largely because of Du Bois's prestige, attracted young Negro

[13] *Ibid.,* II (September 1911), 195.
 Ibid., XII (October 1916), 270–71.
 Ibid., XIII (December 1916), 63.

writers whose articles, short stories, and poems complemented his own contributions. The Association could not afford to sacrifice the prestige of his mounting reputation. When he appeared as a principal speaker at the International Congress of Races in London in 1911, for example, his success there reflected credit back on his organization. Conversely, the *Crisis* gave Du Bois a secure berth which, without hampering his writing and his nation-wide lecturing, gave him both an opportunity and a continuing obligation to plan the emancipation of the Negro.

The Loudest Voice in the Race

During the decade from 1910 to 1920 the balance of power among Negro leaders shifted from the "conservative" to the "radical" wing, and as the most articulate "radical," Du Bois stood at the head of a conquering legion. The terrain had changed: 1915 was not 1895; Du Bois had acquired some heavy artillery in the *Crisis* and the Association; and the death of Washington gave the "conservatives" a chance to capitulate gracefully. . . .

By 1915 Washington's world had changed and was about to change even more rapidly. The Negro was leaving the farm and going to the city; more important, he was moving North in substantial numbers. He was impelled to these migrations both by the "push" of Southern agriculture and the "pull" of Northern industry: the failure of Southern farms, because of crop losses, floods, and the boll weevil, forced tenant farmers to seek new means of support; industrial opportunities in the North, especially during the war when the abrupt end to immigration cut off the foreign supply of unskilled labor, invited Southern Negroes to a new life. From 1910 to 1920, when the increase of Negro population in the South was negligible, the northeastern states gained by 40 per cent and the north central states by 46 per cent. The number of Negroes in Detroit multiplied seven times in the period, and in Chicago, which in 1910 already had a substantial Negro group of 44,000, went up to 109,000. Philadelphia, one of the great Northern Negro centers, had to find room for almost 60 per cent more. For this sizable group, Washington's ideas no longer had meaning: these Negroes had turned their backs on farming and on handicraft industry, and instead of prudently casting down their buckets where they were, as Washington had suggested, they had snatched their pails and run to a new life. Gathered in urban ghettoes, especially Northern ghettoes, they had strength of numbers and the right to vote— powerful weapons for their own defense. Significantly enough, the protest against Washington's philosophy had come from educated Northern urban Negroes—Du Bois, Trotter, Morgan, Forbes, Chesnutt, Mrs. Wells-Barnett. . . .

The changing conditions of Negro life which diminished Washington's power enhanced Du Bois's position. As Negroes left the rural South, residence in Northern cities made them receptive to more advanced views. While maintaining their own independence, the Cleveland *Gazette* and the Chicago *Defender* did locally, or in several cities, what the *Crisis* was doing for a national audience, and their soaring constituencies were prepared to absorb uncompromising statements of the Negro position. Du Bois caught the significance of these new areas in supporting "radical" thought. After a trip to the West Coast in 1913, he speculated on the notion that the state of Washington might become a major Negro area, for already the four thousand Negroes in Tacoma and Seattle meant "much more to themselves and the world" than a hundred thousand in Alabama and Georgia because they had education and ambition. (The admiration was reciprocated: the Seattle *Searchlight* and, further south, the Los Angeles *Liberator* and *New Age* gave Du Bois unusually favorable press notices.)

The *Crisis* and the Association gave Du Bois a springboard to power. In the Negro world Du Bois was the symbol of the Association and of its work. White officers came and went. Before 1920, when James Weldon Johnson joined the staff, the Association never had an executive secretary who made his will felt as an independent force. As a result, local branches all over the nation identified the work of the Association with the personality of the vigorous editor whose views they received every month. Unaware of frictions in New York, they saw behind the *Crisis* and the Association a single figure—the austere, uncompromising, scholarly Dr. Du Bois, unapproachable and unafraid. Even in 1910, the Cleveland *Gazette* said that "all loyal and intelligent Afro-Americans" recognize Du Bois as the real leader of the race.

His connection with the NAACP gave him the local contacts useful for national speaking tours. In the seven months ending April, 1911, he reached 21,000 people in fifty-eight lectures. His 1913 trip carried him seven thousand miles in thirty states, and he returned in a glow. Having found the urban Negro (significantly, the *urban* Negro) "pulsing and alive with a new ambition and determinedness," he "thanked God for this the kindliest race on his green earth, for whom I had the privilege of working and to whom I had the pride of belonging."[14]

The mounting circulation of the *Crisis* was a tribute to his influence, and with each gain he set his goals higher. In April 1911, his 10,000 subscribers made him anxious for 25,000; a year later he had reached 22,000, and another three years later 35,000. In 1919, when the Association had seventy thousand members from thirty-four states, the *Crisis* reached its pinnacle of 104,000 subscribers.

Du Bois moved confidently into his position of leadership. Indeed he could hardly resist a Messianic interpretation of his own role. Occasionally he voiced it quite explicitly: his attack on Indianapolis schools should not produce resentment against him, he said, for he was not attacking, but merely making "straight the way of the Lord."[15] In a Thanksgiving proclamation, mimicking the form of executive declarations, he announced: "We, THE CRISIS, By the grace of God, Guardian of the Liberties of ten dark millions in this land and of countless millions over seas," established a day of rest and thanksgiving.[16] Aloof from the throng, Du Bois equated his monthly judgments with truth, not vulnerable to attack from others whom he presumed to be less informed. With urbane superiority, he urged three unnamed Negro monthlies in 1913 to stop throwing mud, for the Negro had enough to fight about without engaging in unseemly squabbling. The following year Du Bois engaged in some squabbling of his own: an almost blanket attack on the whole Negro press as deficient in facts, wretched in English, and soft in the defense of freedom. Yet when this produced a torrent of rage from insulted editors, he calmly denied any partisan role: "Here as in so many other cases THE CRISIS has but frankly voiced current criticism

[14] *Crisis*, VI (July 1913), 130–31.
[15] *Ibid.*, IV (June 1912), 75.
[16] *Ibid.*, III (November 1911), 21.

and the personality of the editor has little to do with it."[17] And, incredibly enough, he probably believed it.

The early issues of the *Crisis* gave startling confirmation to the charge from "conservatives" that Du Bois's concern for Negro rights touched the upper classes more intimately than the lower, that he was more interested in the few than in the many. Three striking examples appeared in the first fifteen months of publication. In the opening issue he noted that when discrimination comes, "it comes with crushing weight upon those other Negroes to whom the reasons for discrimination do not apply in the slightest respect, and thus they are made to bear a double burden."[18] Sometimes the unstated implications went far beyond what Du Bois meant to say: "To treat all Negroes alike is treating evil as good and good as evil."[19] In 1912 he published a two-page photograph of the colored midwinter assembly in Baltimore in which he appeared prominently in a large gathering of Negroes in evening clothes. Even as Du Bois later recognized the rise to social respectability of more and more of his people, he undermined his praise by patronizing tolerance: "Many a colored man in our day called to conference with his own and rather dreading the contact with uncultivated people even though they were of his own blood has been astonished and deeply gratified at the kind of people he has met—at the evidence of good manners and thoughtfulness among his own."[20]

The role of a "brown Brahmin" came as no new departure for Du Bois. The more surprising fact is that from this supercilious podium he succeeded in making himself the loudest voice in the Negro race. The Great Barrington observer and the Boston outsider now had a national forum from which to lash and encourage his people. Month by month the *Crisis* bestowed praise or let loose its wrath. A Negro audience was chided for laughing as Othello strangled Desdemona. Young college graduates were urged to take on the mantle of leadership slowly lest they lose it in an overwrap of self-importance—Du Bois had changed his views since his own college days. He gave counsel, unsolicited, to businesses and colleges. The Negro church was a

[17] *Ibid.*, VIII (May 1914), 17.
[18] *Ibid.*, I (November 1910) i, 10.
[19] *Ibid.*, (December 1910), ii, 16.
[20] *Ibid.*, XVII (January 1919), 112.

favorite whipping boy: its undue premium on "finesse and personal influence," he said, made the way of "upright and businesslike" candidates for higher positions difficult. Still choked with pretentious, ill-trained men, many dishonest and otherwise immoral, it needed an overwhelming reform, he said, in order to create a place "where colored men and women of education and energy can work for the best things regardless of their belief or disbelief in unimportant dogmas and ancient and outworn creeds."[21] Du Bois's estimate of the bankruptcy of white Christianity made this program seem especially urgent.

The spectrum of moods from month to month gave variety not only in the subject matter of the *Crisis*, but even to its point of view. Yet Du Bois's thought remained consistent on one point: his insistence on full Negro rights left him continuously opposed to the Tuskegee philosophy of compromise and retreat. While Washington lived, it would have been difficult to argue that Du Bois had eclipsed him. After Du Bois left Atlanta, the contest went on for five years until Washington's death in 1915, and finally the balance tipped in Du Bois's favor, for Washington's successor lacked the personal appeal on which the Tuskegee founder had capitalized.

Du Bois's restraint over the five-year period had been, for him, remarkable. On several occasions he prodded Washington a bit, but this was nothing like the monthly peppering that he and his partners on the *Horizon* had delivered. But when Washington finally died in 1915, the *Crisis* obituary gave Du Bois the last word in the long battle. He called his dead opponent the greatest leader since Douglass and the most distinguished man to come out of the South since the Civil War. He listed his achievements: alerting the American Negro to the necessity of economic development, emphasizing technical education, paving the way for black-white understanding. But at the same time Du Bois punctured each item of praise: Washington never recognized the links between industry and politics, he did not understand the "deeper foundations of human training," and his program for Negro-white relations rested on caste. Negroes acknowledged a debt, Du Bois said, but "in stern justice, we must lay on the soul of this man a heavy responsibility for the consummation of Negro dis-

[21] *Crisis*, IV (May 1915), 25.

franchisement, the decline of the Negro college and public school, and the firmer establishment of color caste in this land."

With the death of the chief protagonist, the famous battle lost much of its point. The time had come for reconciliation, especially since so much of the conflict had centered on personality rather than on policy. Washington's position had demanded that he dominate any Negro group in which he took an overt part, and the 1904 meeting had shown that he could keep the initiative from passing even to a well-organized opposition. At his death the "conservatives" were left without a comparable leader; Moton, the new principal of Tuskegee, had to grow into rather than step into the shoes of the master, and, in any case, Moton was moderate in his views.[22] Sensing the moment for tact, Du Bois urged the Association's officers to call off a meeting scheduled for Lincoln's birthday, 1916, to avoid the appearance of staging a counterattraction the day after a memorial service that had been arranged in Washington's memory. The same year, with Moton still uncommitted, the Association called a conference of Negro leaders—of all views, from Trotter to Scott —for a frank discussion of the principal Negro goals. Though conducted under the auspices of the Association, the Amenia conference (1916) was carefully dissociated from the NAACP's official policy. With a minimum of oratory it arrived at generally acceptable resolutions: that all forms of education were desirable for the Negro and should be encouraged, that political freedom was necessary to achieve highest development, that Negro advancement needed an organization and the practical working understanding of Negro leaders, and that old controversies were best forgotten. Finally, the conference "realizes the peculiar difficulties . . . in the South. . . . It has learned to understand and respect the good faith, methods and ideals of those who are

[22] Though Moton had assured Washington that he was "absolutely" on Washington's side (Moton to Washington, April 8, 1914, Washington papers), he had refused to join in the abusive attacks on Du Bois. H. B. Frisell, the principal of Hampton Institute, told Ray Stannard Baker that Moton thought it was a good thing to have men like Du Bois stand up for Negro rights. (Frisell to Baker, May 1, 1908, Ray Stannard Baker Papers, Library of Congress.) August Meier records Moton's attempt to make peace between the two wings of the race, and he regards Moton's selection as Washington's successor at Tuskegee as a victory for moderation. "Booker T. Washington and the Rise of the NAACP," *Crisis*, LXI (February 1954), 118–22.

working for the solution of the problem in various sections of the country."[23] The unanimity of the conference stood as a real victory for Du Bois's wing of the race, a victory achieved by respecting necessary methodological differences in the South. Ironically, the resolutions contained little which would have evoked Washington's criticism in the last years of his life.

The achievement of this unity through the initiative of Du Bois's organization left him as the new major voice of the race. After America's entry into the war, the extent of his victory became apparent when both the Washington conference of leaders in 1917 and the statement of the thirty-one Negro editors the following year repeated the principal items on Du Bois's program and even used his words to express the will of the whole Negro people. Du Bois wrote the second manifesto, and may have written the first as well. The program of the "radicals" had now been accepted as the dominant philosophy of the articulate race leaders.

Gilbert Osofsky

In the long run, the most important event in post-Civil War Negro history went by relatively quietly. It had no philosophy, no messianic beliefs, no revolutionary ardor, no great leaders or literature. The event was the migration, first in trickles, then in hundreds, soon in thousands, of Negroes out of the rural South, first into Southern cities and then more forcefully, into the great industrial complexes of the North and the Midwest. The black masses—the agricultural proletariat—denigrated, short-changed, terrorized, voted with their feet, and like their contemporaries among the Southern Italians, Slavic peoples, Eastern European Jews, and Greeks, Southern Negroes were attracted to the newly expanding industrial cities of America by the promise of a better life and greater opportunities for themselves and their children.

Despite the efforts of Booker T. Washington and the traditional Negro leadership to discourage Negroes from moving

[23] Du Bois, "The Amenia Conference: An Historic Negro Gathering" (*Troutbeck Leaflets*, VIII) (Amenia, N.Y., 1925), 14–15.

North, telling them that their best friends were in the South and their future was in agriculture, many Negroes saw things differently. "I should have been here twenty years ago," a recent arrival from the South wrote home. "I just begin to feel like a man. . . . My children are going to the same school with the whites and I don't have to humble to no one. I have registered. Will vote in the next election and there isn't any yes Sir or no Sir. It's all yes and no, Sam and Bill" (Woodson; *A Century of Negro Migration*).

"The flight from feudal America," as Franklin Frazier termed this migration, in *The Negro Family in the United States*, began before World War I. By 1910 a little over a million Negroes lived in the North; by 1920 the figure was nearly a million and a half; by 1930 it was nearly two and a half million. Overnight Northern cities found themselves with considerable Negro populations. New York had 91,000 Negroes in 1910, 152,000 in 1920, 327,000 in 1930. Chicago had 44,000 Negroes in 1910, 109,000 in 1920, 233,000 in 1930. Detroit's Negro population increased from 40,000 in 1920 to 120,000 in 1930. The migration continued throughout the next three decades, and the 1960 census showed that for the first time a majority of Negroes lived outside the South.

But the North was not all milk and honey. Not only did Negroes face fierce competition for jobs from European immigrants, but they also suffered a great sense of alienation in the impersonal urban world, cut off from traditional community, church, and culture. This rootlessness and alienation is most profoundly described by Richard Wright in *Native Son* (1940) and James Baldwin in *Go Tell It on the Mountain* (1953). During the period of the first great migration (1915–20) a series of race riots occurred in the North, most notably in East St. Louis in 1917 and Chicago in 1919. In the face of hostility from the police, mobs, and Ku Klux Klan, Negroes fought back fiercely. The East St. Louis riot found nine whites dead along with thirty-nine Negroes; in Chicago the figures were fifteen whites and twenty-three Negroes dead. A new militancy and pride was evident in the Negro community, making it clear that Negroes were not going to stand idly by while whites vented their frustrations upon them. Claude McKay sensed this new spirit when he wrote in 1917:

If we must die, let it not be like hogs
Hunted and penned in an inglorious spot. . . .
If we must die, O let us nobly die,
So that our precious blood may not be shed
In vain; . . .
Like men we'll face the murderous, cowardly pack,
Pressed to the wall, dying but fighting back!

The Northern Negro was, in addition, less inclined to listen to the voices of the older leadership with the result that no one man or organization could claim, as did Douglass or Washington, to speak for him. The second and third decades of the century saw the rise of the NAACP and Du Bois, Negro Socialists and A. Philip Randolph, Negro Communists and Claude McKay, the Universal Negro Improvement Association and Marcus Garvey, the National Urban League and Eugene K. Jones. Concurrently there was a great decline in the prestige of the Negro clergyman. Negroes began in increasing numbers to vote the Democratic ticket, and by 1936 the majority of Negroes who voted in the North preferred Roosevelt over his Republican rival. These new loyalties indicated the profound changes that had taken place in the Negro community over twenty-five years.

Gilbert Osofsky gives us the historical background of the Negro migration and examines its effect on New York in the period 1900–14. Dr. Osofsky is the author of Harlem: The Making of a Ghetto, and is Assistant Professor of History at the University of Illinois (Chicago Circle).

"COME OUT FROM AMONG THEM":
NEGRO MIGRATION AND SETTLEMENT,
1890–1914

SOURCE: Gilbert Osofsky, " 'Come out from Among Them': Negro Migration and Settlement, 1890–1914," Harlem: The Making of a Ghetto, (New York: Harper and Row, 1966), pp. 17–24, 33–34.

The most important factor underlying the establishment of Harlem as a Negro community was the substantial increase of Negro population in New York City in the years 1890–1914. That Harlem became the specific center of Negro settlement was the result of circumstance; that *some* section of the city was destined to become a Negro ghetto was the inevitable consequence of the Negro's migration from the South. This pre-World War I population movement, the advance guard of the Great Migration (as the movement of Negroes during the First Wold War is generally called), laid the foundations for present-day Negro communities in Chicago and Philadelphia as well. These were the formative years for the development of Negro communities throughout the North.

In spite of the high Negro death rate, the colored population increased by "leaps and bounds" in New York City in the early twentieth century. By 1910 there were 91,709 Negroes in the metropolis, the majority southern-born: "A Census of the Negroes in any city of the North," said a speaker at the first organizational meeting of the NAACP in 1909, "would show that the majority of . . . them . . . were more or less recent arrivals from the South." Mary White Ovington, in her excellent study *Half A Man: The Status of the Negro in New York,* found that most of the Negro neighborhoods were populated by southerners. Only 14,309 of the 60,534 Negroes in Manhattan in 1910 were born in New York State. The majority of the others (61 per cent) came from other states, practically all in the South. Virginia, North Carolina, South Carolina, Georgia and Florida, in perfect geographical order, were the major southern sources of New York's migrant population.

Contemporaries in both the North and South, Negro and white, were aware of this movement. Unable to foresee that the First World War would bring even larger numbers of Negroes northward, they were staggered by the myriad problems this migration created for them: "There are more Southern Negroes in the North and West than original Northern ones, and they are coming all . . . the time," wrote a Negro journalist in 1913. "What to do with the needy and those who fall by the wayside is becoming a problem of the greatest magnitude. . . ."[1] Historians, impressed by the enormity of changes that occurred at the time of the "Great War," have tended to overlook or underestimate the significance of the pre-World War I migration of Negroes to northern cities.

[1] *The New York Age,* June 5, 1913.

II

Since the end of the Civil War there was a steady but small movement of Negroes northward. It averaged 41,378 persons for each decade between 1870 and 1890. In the following ten years, however, the migration more than doubled as at least 107,796 southern Negroes moved north and west. The Negro populations of the states of New Jersey, Pennsylvania and Illinois increased some two and a half times between 1890 and 1910 and that of New York almost tripled.[2] In 1910, New York City was the second largest Negro urban center in America (just behind Washington, D.C.); Philadelphia was fifth; and Chicago eighth. By 1920, they were ranked first, second and fourth respectively. A total of some 200,000 Negroes migrated from the South and to the North and West, primarily to cities, between 1890 and 1910. In the decade 1900–1910, for the first time since their establishments as states in the early nineteenth century, Mississippi and Louisiana lost Negro population through emigration. Practically every southern state showed the first significant deficit in its Negro birth-residence index (the index that measures population increase and decrease through migration) for the decade 1890–1900. "Prior to 1890," observes one student of population movement, "the migration of Negroes was not great and seems to have been local, from state to state, and only to a slight extent out of the South. But after 1890, the northward direction of the movement has been steadfastly maintained and has increased in amount decade after decade."[3] The number of Negroes migrating to the principal southern cities declined significantly in the years 1890–1900. The Negro population in these cities increased 38.7 per cent between 1880 and 1890, but the growth amounted to only 20.6 per cent in the next ten years. Northern cities were draining off the residents of, and prospective migrants to, the larger southern cities at the turn of the century.

A few discerning analysts were aware of this new shift in Negro migration in the 1890's. Working with census data, Frederick

[2] United States Census, *Negro Population, 1790–1915*, (Washington, 1918), p. 68.
[3] C. Warren Thornthwaite, *Internal Migration in the United States* (Philadelphia, 1934), p. 12 and map opposite p. 12.

J. Brown pointed to the new northward migration from the Border States in 1897.[4] In 1898, W. E. B. DuBois noted the decline of Negro population in Farmville, Virginia, and explained it as "a fact due doubtless to the large emigration to Northern cities."[5] In his pioneering study of Philadelphia Negroes (1899), DuBois showed a significant increase in southern immigration since 1887, and later depicted the "typical colored man" of Philadelphia as a young person "from the South, from twenty to forty years of age. . . ."[6] Similar conclusions were made by a student of New York City's Negro community in 1898,[7] and the United States Department of Labor undertook a detailed analysis of the movement of Negroes to urban areas in these same years.

By the first decade of the twentieth century the migration was well recognized: "It needs no long argument to prove the existence of a large movement of Negroes northward," a social scientist recorded in 1905.[8] An entire issue of the social service magazine *Charities* was devoted to a survey of the migration and the problems that arose from it in the first decade of the twentieth century. New York's leading Negro journal, *The New York Age*, carried innumerable articles in the early 1900's on the "marvelous increase of Afro-American population," "the enormous and steady growth in the Negro population," "the young people in New York City from our Southern States who are constantly coming," and so on. In 1901 a Negro minister delivered a public lecture on what seemed to him to be "The Wholesale Exodus of the Negro from the South."[9]

This pre-World War I exodus has sometimes been characterized as the "Migration of the Talented Tenth." Politicians, busi-

---

[4] Frederick J. Brown, *The Northward Movement of the Colored Population: A Statistical Study* (Baltimore, 1897).

[5] W. E. B. DuBois, "The Negro in Farmville, Virginia: A Social Study," United States Department of Labor, *Bulletin No. 14* (Washington, D.C., 1895), p. 5.

[6] W. E. B. DuBois, "The Black Vote of Philadelphia," *Charities: A Review of Local and General Philanthropy*, XV (October 7, 1905), 31.

[7] John P. Clyde, "The Negro in New York City" (M.A. thesis, Columbia University, 1899), p. 3.

[8] Carl Kelsey, "Some Causes of Negro Emigration: The Men," *Charities*, XV (October 7, 1905), 16.

[9] *The New York Times*, March 18, 1901.

nessmen, the educated, and especially skilled workmen, are supposed to have constituted the majority of people who left the South in these years. Southern Negroes, it has been said, were robbed of their leadership as the talented fled north.[10]

It is undoubtedly true that many educated and gifted Negroes did come north then. William Lewis Bulkley, for example, a South Carolinian born a slave, became a principal in the New York school system and a leader of the Negro community during these years. P. B. S. Pinchback, for a time Reconstruction governor of Louisiana and thereafter an active Republican politician, worked in the New York City Custom House a short while. He used the influence of Booker T. Washington and the Negro Republican leader of New York City, Charles W. Anderson, to get the position. Pinchback's friend, J. Ross Stewart, a former member of the Louisiana legislature, worked there too. North Carolinian George Henry White, member of Congress 1897–1901, practiced law and became a banker in Philadelphia when Negroes were disfranchised in his state. White later established an all-Negro community in New Jersey. T. Thomas Fortune, editor of *The New York Age,* was a Floridian by birth. There were, in fact, *very few* prominent Negroes in New York City in the early twentieth century—lawyers, physicians, businessmen, clergymen, politicians—who were not born in the South.

These people were not typical urban Negro migrants, however. The majority, like all migrant populations, were young people, generally unskilled and unmarried, the earliest Negro generations born in freedom. W. E. B. DuBois described them as "the Southern freedman's sons and daughters," "untrained and poorly educated countrymen, rushing from the hovels of the country or the cottages of the country towns. . . ." Most contemporaries spoke of them as such.[11]

In one group of 240 Negroes interviewed in New York City in 1907, for example, only eighteen were born in New York, and just three of the 222 others were over forty when they migrated. The vast majority were between the ages of fifteen and thirty,

[10] Carter G. Woodson, *A Century of Negro Migration* (Washington, D.C., 1918), pp. 159–166.

[11] Lillian Brandt, "The Make-Up of Negro City Groups," *Charities,* XV (October 7, 1905), 7–11.

and 96 per cent had arrived in New York City after 1887. Another survey of 365 workers found that 68 per cent were born in the South, the largest number single young men and women.

III

There were as many individual and varied reasons for migration as there were people who moved. The less respectable as well as the educated came north. Negroes themselves characterized some as a "hoodlum element," "rovers," "wanderers," "vagrants," "criminals in search of a sporting life."[12] "Many of the worthless people of the race are making their way northward," said *The New York Age* in an editorial. Some wayward husbands—the "wandering men" of Negro folk songs—abandoned their families and responsibilities and sought the anonymity of a city: "I was raised in the country, I been there all my life/Lord I had to run off and leave my children and my wife."

Others came north on excursion trains to get a look at the big city and never returned. One man "heard so much of this town," he said, "that he decided to look it over." Another stated that he "didn't want to remain in one little place all my days. I wanted to get out and see something of the world." Migratory laborers found work on New Jersey, Pennsylvania and New York farms every spring and summer. Some traveled back and forth each year; others simply went to the nearest city when winter came. "Tired of the South," "Wanted to make a change," "Ran away from home," were some of the reasons advanced by Negroes for coming north. All received nominally higher wages in the North, and this was certainly a great attraction. One woman who came to New York City from Virginia, for example, said she was "willing to live anywhere, if the wages were good."[13]

There were also those who fled social proscription and violence in the South. C. Vann Woodward has described the "Capitulation to Racism" that characterized the southern attitude toward the Negro from the late 1880's through the early twentieth

[12] W. E. B. DuBois, "The Northern Negro Problem," *The New York Age*, October 3, 1907; R. R. Wright, Jr., "The Migration of Negroes to the North," *The Annals*, XLIX (September 1913), 570.

[13] Seymour Paul, "A Group of Virginia Negroes in New York City" (M.A. thesis, Columbia University, 1912), p. 41.

century. Vast numbers of Jim Crow laws were passed in these years as the forces which held virulent southern racism in check suddenly crumbled. The conservative, *noblesse oblige* attitude of former Whig leaders ("it is a mark of breeding to treat Negroes with courtesy") was replaced by a violently racist white supremacy movement; the paternalism of a Wade Hampton was followed by the viciousness of a Ben Tillman (whose racist tirades even embarrassed his southern colleagues). Free rein was given to mass aggressions as all forces joined together in an active program of "keeping the Negro down." The great heresy that proclaimed the Negro capable of attaining equality with the white had to be rooted out at all costs, it was argued. There were more Negroes lynched, burned, tortured and disfranchised in the late eighties, nineties and first decade of the twentieth century than at any other time in our history. The militant Negro Ida B. Wells graphically and sadly described this *Red Record* in 1895. It was not surprising to find that the American Colonization Society, organized in 1817, experienced a long-hoped-for revival in the 1890's, and various other plans to colonize Negroes in Africa were rekindled in these years. "I used to love what I thought was the grand old flag, and sing with ecstasy about the stars and stripes," wrote Negro Bishop Henry McNeal Turner of Georgia, "but to the Negro in this country today the American flag is a dirty contemptible rag. . . . Hell is an improvement upon the United States when the Negro is involved." "No man hates this Nation more than I do," Turner said on another occasion. He looked longingly to Africa as the only possible place of Negro freedom.[14]

Negro leaders and the Negro press continually stressed their belief that migration was primarily a movement away from racism: "The large cities of the North and West have had a

[14] There actually were some Negroes who did go to Africa in these years. An Abraham Lincoln African Aid and Colonization Society was established in Oklahoma in 1909. "Chief Sam" (Alfred Charles Sam), a bogus African chief, outfitted a steamer which left Galveston in 1914. T. McCants Stewart, Negro clergyman and lawyer of New York, finally settled in Liberia in 1906. *The New York Age*, April 27, 1905, November 30, 1905, February 26, 1906, September 20, 1906, January 3, 1907, July 11, 1907, September 16, 1909, January 22, 1914, January 29, 1914, April 2, 1914, July 9, 1914. William E. Bittle and Gilbert Geis, *The Longest Way Home: Chief Alfred C. Sam's Back to Africa Movement* (Detroit, 1964).

marvelous increase of Afro-American population in the last ten years, and the increase is growing . . . because of the conditions in the Southern States which make for unrest"; "the terrors of mob wrath."[15] When T. Thomas Fortune, William Lewis Bulkley, and North Carolina educator and politician Edward A. Johnson came north, each emphasized he could no longer live under Jim Crow and racial violence. George Henry White said he left North Carolina because he "couldn't live there and be a man and be treated like a man." He believed that thousands of others would follow him. Booker T. Washington told the Board of Trustees of Tuskegee, in 1903, that "for every lynching that takes place . . . a score of colored people leave . . . for the city."

In general, however, the migration could best be considered not so much a flight from racial violence, as it was a desire for expanded opportunity. This is best summarized in a phrase commonly used by the migrants themselves—the attempt "to better my condition." People moved away from the South in search of a better and more fulfilling life. A Negro shoemaker came north, for example, because he felt "choked" by the "narrow and petty life" he was forced to lead in a small Virginia town. To him, the great attraction of New York City was the "wider scope allowed the Negro." One woman who "never could work . . . in a menial way" was proud that she could earn a living as an independent seamstress in New York. Moving north, wrote DuBois in 1907, offered "the possibility of escaping caste at least in its most aggravating personal features. . . . A certain sort of soul, a certain kind of spirit, finds the narrow repression and provincialism of the South simple unbearable."[16]

The *possibilities* for such movement resulted from two basic changes in American life. One was the overwhelming industrial expansion of the late nineteenth century. The Industrial Revolution created economic opportunities for rural people, Negro and white, and both migrated to industrial and urban centers in the North. For the Negro, hedged about by union restrictions and racial antagonism, employment was usually found in the fringe

[15] *The New York Age,* January 10, 1907, July 4, 1912.
[16] *The New York Age,* October 3, 1907; W. E. B. DuBois, "The Black North," *The New York Times,* December 15, 1901.

jobs that an industrial and commercial society creates—as jani-
tors, elevator operators, general laborers of all kinds, longshore-
men, servants. Negro women almost always worked as domestics.
During periods of labor disputes, Negroes were commonly
found among the strikebreakers.[17]

There was, however, an added factor that influenced Negro
migration and distinguished it from the general rural migration
to cities. Why, it might be asked, had Negroes not moved in
similar numbers in response to industrialization in the 1870's
—the period of great social upheaval and dislocation that followed
the destruction of slavery? The answer undoubtedly lies in an
understanding of the differences between the slave and post-
slave generations. The Negroes who came north now were the
first descendants of former slaves. They had listened to tales of
slavery, gentle and harsh, but had not experienced and lived its
blight—the denial of full manhood. To them, *"War, Hell, and
Slavery were but childhood tales. . . ."*[18] Their parents and
grandparents, psychologically and economically unprepared to
enter what contemporaries called the "competition for life,"
tended to remain as tenants, sharecroppers or laborers on their
former plantations or on places similar to them. They continued
in freedom to live the only life they had knowledge of. "There
were great upheavals in political and labor conditions at the
time of emancipation, but there was little shifting in the populations. For the most part, the freedmen stayed on in the states
and counties where they had formerly existed as slaves," writes
one historian of Negro life.[19] In 1900, practically all southern
Negroes continued to work on the land and some 75 per cent

---

[17] R. R. Wright, Jr., "The Negro in Times of Industrial Unrest,"
Charities, XV (October 7, 1905), 69, 73; James Samuel Stemons, "The
Industrial Color-Line in the North," *The Century Magazine,* LX (July
1900), 477–478; Mary White Ovington, "The Negro in the Trades Unions
of New York," *The Annals,* XXVII (May 1906), 555–556.

[18] W. E. B. DuBois, *The Souls of Black Folk* (New York, 1953), p. 68.

[19] Edwin R. Embree, *Brown America* (New York, 1931), p. 37. "The
Government by whom we were emancipated left us completely in the
power of our former owners." Frederick Douglass, *Three Addresses on the
Relations Subsisting between the White and Colored People of the United
States* (Washington, D.C., 1886), p. 16. Also see Alrutheus Ambush Taylor,
The Negro in South Carolina During Reconstruction (Washington, D.C.,
1924), pp. 25, 55; Alrutheus Ambush Taylor, *The Negro in the Reconstruc-
tion of Virginia* (Washington, D.C., 1926), pp. 90–97.

remained sharecroppers, tenants and laborers. On one Georgia plantation in 1901, as on others, lived many Negroes who had been slaves there: "I have men," the white owner testified, "who were slaves on the place. . . . They have always lived there and will probably die there, right on the plantation where they were born." "It was predicted [during the Civil War] that the Negroes would leave the . . . fields and fill the towns in case of emancipation," said a southern planter at the turn of the century. "That prediction has not been realized suddenly as we anticipated it would be, but it seems to be approaching."

Those who migrated to the North in the 1890's were a new generation. Many Negroes no longer felt any strong attachment to the soil. They could at least *conceive* of life in a new and different way. For some, the discontented and restless, there was now both the ability and willingness to move. They left a South in which their futures were sealed: "There is absolutely nothing before them on the farm. . . . Working year in and year out with . . . no prospect . . . but to continue until they die." In many rural communities of the South, it was reported in 1907, a "number of youths have expressed their conviction that since their fathers and mothers have accumulated nothing after years on the land, they did not intend to stay on the plantation to repeat the process." A leading Republican politician and defender of Negro civil rights, James S. Clarkson, took a trip to the South in the 1890's and "saw many a grey head . . . talking to the young people . . . encouraging the young people to become content," he wrote a Negro confidant.[20] The migrants who came north were aptly described by George Edmund Haynes as "groping seekers for something better. . . ."[21]

Migration to the city [New York] created possibilities for economic mobility that were largely absent from southern life. Many of the businesses which provided services for Negroes were owned by migrants themselves. Some recent arrivals began as small entrepreneurs but made modest fortunes in a relatively short time.

[20] J. S. Clarkson to J. E. Bruce, March 21, 1891. Bruce Manuscripts, Schomburg Collection.
[21] George Edmund Haynes, "Conditions Among Negroes in the Cities," *The Annals,* XLIX (September 1913), 105–119.

Perhaps the most interesting and among the most successful was Lillian Harris, born in a shanty on the Mississippi Delta in 1870. She came north as a teenager and, in 1901, after having knocked around many northern cities for a decade, hitched her way from Boston to New York City on hay, milk and vegetable wagons. Miss Harris had $5.00, and with this capital went into business. She spent $3.00 for an old baby carriage and boiler and $2.00 for pigs' feet. This was the beginning of her career as New York's most widely known Negro peddler. Her converted buggy became a "traveling restaurant."

Hawking her wares in Negro sections, specializing in southern cooking (hog-maws, chitterlings), Lillian Harris was popularly called "Pig Foot Mary." She lived in a tiny room and scrimped and saved for years: "Saving for a respectable old age," she always said. When Negroes began moving to Harlem this astute street-corner saleswoman grasped at opportunity and invested her savings in Harlem property. By the First World War "Pig Foot Mary" (now Mrs. Lillian H. Dean) was a wealthy land-lord—"one of the wealthiest women in Harlem"; "one of the most successful colored business women in New York." "Send it and send it damn quick," she wrote tenants who fell behind in their rent. "Pig Foot Mary" spent her "respectable old age" in retirement in California, where she died in 1929.[22]

William Mack Felton was another southern Negro who made good in New York. He arrived in the city in 1898 with a dollar tucked away in his shoe: "Heeding the call to the Big City," he said. Felton grew up on a small farm in Georgia with little opportunity for formal education. He was naturally bright, however, and gifted with mechanical ability. When he came to New York he worked as a longshoreman long enough to save some money to open a repair shop. The first big job that came his way called for the repair of dozens of clocks left in a Manhattan pawnshop. Most of them had simply stopped running because they had picked up dust and dirt lying around the shelves. Felton realized this, bought a large washtub, filled it with gallons of kerosene and oil and cleaned all the stripped-

[22] Odette Harper, "Sketch of Pig Foot Mary" (WPA research paper, Schomburg Collection); *The New York Age*, November 12, 1927, July 20, 27, 1929.

down clocks in one day. He used this same ingenuity to fix watches, pistols, bicycles—anything that needed repairing. In 1901, when wealthy New Yorkers began to buy new automobiles, Felton opened an auto school and garage. He later invented a device that washed cars automatically. By 1913 his Auto Transportation and Sales Company employed fifteen people and was housed in a seven-story building which he owned. Felton rode back to Georgia in his new car to visit his family and old friends and tell them of life in the "Big City."[23]

Success came to other southern migrants who arrived in New York City in these years. Madame C. J. Walker, born in Louisiana in 1867, was a laundress before she discovered a hair-straightening process (the "Walker System") which brought her great fortune. In 1913 she built a mansion for herself on West One Hundred and Thirty-sixth Street and four years later built a magnificent country estate, Villa Lewaro, in exclusive Irvington-on-the-Hudson.[24] H. C. Haynes, formerly a southern barber, founded a company which manufactured razor strops; Edward E. Lee, a Virginian, was Negro Democratic leader of New York County for fifteen years; J. Franklin Smallwood became chief collector of the State Bank of New York; J. S. Montague ran a mortgage and loan company on Wall Street; Ferdinand Q. Morton, of Macon, Mississippi, was prominent in Democratic politics and ruled "Black Tammany" from the First World War through the Great Depression.[25]

Practically all of these migrants were born in the direst southern poverty and achieved their positions, as the Reverend Dr. Adam Clayton Powell, Sr., later wrote, "Against the Tide." Very few southern Negroes had such fortune, however. The majority of those who came to New York City ended in the ranks of the poor and swelled the slum populations of the Tenderloin, San Juan Hill or Harlem. To many northern Negroes, who had

---

[23] *The New York Age*, February 13, 1913.

[24] Mary McFadden, "Madame Walker" and Odette Harper, "Biographical Sketch of Madame C. J. Walker" (WPA research papers, Schomburg Collection); *Baltimore Afro-American*, March 5, 1932. For pictures of the cabin in which Madame Walker was born and her villa in New York see *The Messenger*, VI (August, 1924), 255.

[25] Biographical sketches of these and many other successful Negro migrants are scattered throughout the issues of *The New York Age*.

never known or had since forgotten the restrictive conditions in the South, the life of the typical migrant seemed no great improvement on his former condition.

The average Negro migrant to New York City obviously found life harsh and difficult. For those who came, however, conditions in the North did offer a measure of self-respect and the possibility for future advancement that was generally denied the Negro in the South. "To many of them oppressed within the limitations set up by the South," wrote Ray Stannard Baker, "it is indeed the promised land."[26]

E. David Cronon

The upheaval which shook Negro life in the wake of the great migration necessitated the formation of a new identity and philosophy to express Negro aspirations and mirror their discontents. One of the strangest episodes was the meteoric rise (and fall) of a Jamaican immigrant, Marcus Garvey, and his Universal Negro Improvement Association. The UNIA caught the imagination of the Negro masses with its program of black nationalism, "back to Africa," and Negro economic independence. Garvey claimed that the UNIA had six million members, although the true figure never reached more than a hundred thousand. Nevertheless, Garvey's sympathizers did number into the hundreds of thousands, which caused John Hope Franklin in *From Slavery to Freedom* to see the UNIA as "the first and only mass movement among Negroes in the history of the United States."

Why had Garvey managed to reach the Negro masses when Washington and Du Bois failed? Garvey came to New York in 1916, aged twenty-eight. He had been trained as a printer in Jamaica and later spent two years in London, where his reading of *Up From Slavery* kindled in him the desire of "being a race leader" by "uniting all the Negro peoples of the world into one great body to establish a country and Government absolutely their own" (Cronon). He was stirred by the idea of Negro independence and wrote to Washington telling him

[26] Ray Stannard Baker, *Following the Color Line* (New York, 1908), *passim; The New York Age,* January 27, 1910.

that he wanted to establish a version of Tuskegee in Jamaica. By the time Garvey arrived in the United States, Washington had been dead for a year, but Garvey sensed that an audience existed for his form of Negro nationalism. And so after touring thirty-eight states and meeting what he termed the "so-called Negro leaders" who, he believed, had no program and lived off the philanthropy of white millionaires, he set up headquarters in Harlem, intent on developing his program which would activate the masses. His fiery speeches and superior editing of the UNIA newspaper, *Negro World*, initially attracted fellow West Indian immigrants, but by 1920 his fame had spread to such an extent that twenty-five thousand flocked to Madison Square Garden to hear him speak. His vision of a Negro-owned merchant marine sailing to Africa, of Negro financed and run factories, co-operatives, groceries, and industrial enterprises caused Negroes to invest hundreds of thousands of dollars into UNIA common stock. Garvey proclaimed himself Provisional President of the African Republic, and he and his followers paraded through Northern cities, resplendent in uniforms garnished with medals that would have done justice to a Shriners' parade. Garvey's African Legionnaires, Black Cross Nurses, or Knights of the Nile seem less exotic when we remember the American penchant for genealogy, parades, and uniforms.

Garvey had caught the imagination of the Negro population at the right time, and his message of race solidarity and pride reached an audience eager to hear these ideas preached. But the ground for Garvey had been laid by a number of developments within the Negro community itself. Garvey's emphasis on Negro history, African ancestry, and race pride had already been foreshadowed by the formation in 1911 of the Negro Society for Historical Research, by Carter Woodson's Association for the Study of Negro Life and History and the *Journal of Negro History*, and by Du Bois' Pan-Africanism, which went back to the turn of the century. Radical newspapers such as A. Philip Randolph's *Messenger* were urging Negroes to resist white racists. President Wilson's call for democracy and self-determination overseas encouraged Negroes to speak out for the same at home, especially since 400,000 Negroes had been taken into the armed forces, and Negro civilians had bought a quarter of a billion dollars worth of war bonds.

But Garvey's initial success was not to last. His financial schemes ended in utter disaster, notably the much publicized Black Star Line, and soon Garvey was brought up on Federal charges of using the mails to defraud. In 1923 he was found guilty, and in 1925 he began a prison term in the Atlanta Federal Penitentiary. Garvey's attacks upon the Negro leadership, both of the left and right, alienated almost the entire Negro press and leadership. Du Bois, Garvey's most vociferous critic, reacted violently when in 1922 Garvey met with the Imperial Giant of the Ku Klux Klan to gain its support for his "back to Africa" program, and to exchange pronunciamentos on each other's segregationist and race-purification plans. "Marcus Garvey," wrote Du Bois in the *Crisis*, "is without doubt, the most dangerous enemy of the Negro race in America and the world. . . . He is either a lunatic or a traitor." Garvey lost support also because his ideas on Negro resettlement in Africa was something that few Negroes wanted, no matter how much interest they showed in their past. James Weldon Johnson in *Black Manhattan* thought that "the main reason for Garvey's failure with thoughtful American Negroes was his African scheme. It was recognized at once by them to be impractical and fantastic." In 1927, Garvey, his movement shattered, was released from prison and deported to England where he died in obscurity in 1940.

Yet times and opinions change. Du Bois, who had been called by Garvey "an enemy of the black people of the world," later praised Garvey as "a master of propaganda" whose ideas spread throughout the world, especially to Africa. One of the Africans who read Garvey, Kwame Nkrumah, wrote in his *Autobiography* in 1957 that "of all the literature that I studied, the book that did more than any other to fire my enthusiasm was [the] *Philosophy and Opinions of Marcus Garvey*. . . ." And, Malcolm Little, better known as Malcolm X, was brought up by his father, a devout follower of Garvey, to believe in the ideas of the black nationalist from Jamaica. "He believed," wrote Malcolm X of his father, "as did Marcus Garvey, that freedom, independence, and self-respect could never be achieved by the Negro in America. . . ."

Garveyism was a symptom of a much greater malaise that affected the Negro community, and interest in Garvey will continue to be shown as long as Negroes remain frustrated in their pursuit of the American promise.

E. David Cronon, Professor of History at the University of Wisconsin, has written a brilliant analysis of Garvey and the UNIA in *Black Moses*.

MARCUS GARVEY:
"ONE AIM! ONE GOD! ONE DESTINY!"

SOURCE: E. David Cronon, "Marcus Garvey: 'One Aim! One God! One Destiny!'" *Black Moses: The Story of Marcus Garvey and the Universal Negro Improvement Association* (Madison, Wisconsin: University of Wisconsin Press, 1955), pp. 170–73, 173–74, 175–76, 176–77, 183–85, 186–99, 200–1.

Although Marcus Garvey never set foot on African soil, the basis for his race philosophy was Africa, the Negro homeland. For out of the moist green depths of the African jungle had come the endless files of hapless Negro slaves, a seemingly inexhaustible labor force to be devoured by the hungry plantations of the Americas. And in spite of the substantial but largely unrecognized contribution of these black slaves to the building of a New World civilization, their life of servitude under white masters had tended to destroy their African culture and to tear down their national and personal self-respect. To Garvey it seemed axiomatic that a redemption of the Negroes of the world must come only through a rebuilding of their shattered racial pride and a restoration of a truly Negro culture. Race pride and African nationalism were inextricably woven together in the Garvey philosophy, therefore, and the program of the Universal Negro Improvement Association centered around these two complementary objectives.

To understand Marcus Garvey and his extraordinary movement, it is necessary to consider in detail this strong emphasis on racism and African nationalism. Such a study helps not only to illumine the ideas of the man but also to show the basis for his wide appeal. Garvey's unparalleled success in capturing the imagination of masses of Negroes throughout the world can be explained only by recognizing that he put into words—and what magnificent inspiring words they were—what large numbers of his people were thinking. Garveyism as a social movement, reflecting as it did the hopes and aspirations of a substantial section of the Negro world, may best be studied by considering the ideas of its founder and leader, since these contain the key to Garvey's remarkable success.

In trying to establish a philosophy of Garveyism, however, it is important to place the movement in the context of general Negro thought in the period immediately following World War I. This was the era of the New Negro reaction to the race riots and frustrated hopes of the war years, and it was an age distinguished by the great artistic and literary activity that has been justly called the Negro Renaissance. Garveyism was for the most part decisively repudiated by the Negro intellectuals and it is thus difficult to give Garvey any credit for the flowering of the Negro Renaissance. Certainly his unceasing efforts to restore a strong sense of pride in things Negro was a march down the same path as that trod by the New Negroes, however, and the same forces that stimulated the Negro Renaissance helped to create an audience for Garveyism. Garvey's bombastic efforts to whip up an intense black nationalism were a logical counterpart to the more subtle but equally militant contemporary verse of such Negro poets as Claude McKay, Langston Hughes, and Countee Cullen.

The significance of Garveyism lies in its appeal to the dreams of millions of Negroes throughout the world. The amazingly loyal support given Marcus Garvey by the Negro masses, particularly in the United States and the West Indies, was forthcoming because he told his followers what they most wanted to hear, or, as E. Franklin Frazier has said, he made them "feel like somebody among white people who have said they were nobody." Two decades after Garvey's inglorious departure for Atlanta penitentiary a new Harlem generation still remembered him as the man who "brought to the Negro people for the first time a sense of pride in being black."[1] This is the core of Marcus Garvey's philosophy; around this ideal he centered his life.

[1] Adam Clayton Powell, *Marching Blacks* (New York, 1945), p. 50.

Coming at a time when Negroes generally had so little of which to be proud, Garvey's appeal to race pride quite naturally stirred a powerful response in the hearts of his eager black listeners. "I am the equal of any white man," Garvey told his followers. "I want you to feel the same way."[2] "We have come now to the turning point of the Negro," he declared with calm assurance, "where we have changed from the old cringing weakling, and transformed into full-grown men, demanding our portion as MEN."[3] One of the delegates to the first U.N.I.A. convention in Harlem in 1920 served notice that "it takes 1,000 white men to lick one Negro" and gave an illuminating preview of the type of Negro leadership needed in the future. "The Uncle Tom nigger has got to go, and his place must be taken by the new leader of the Negro race," he asserted. "That man will not be a white man with a black heart, nor a black man with a white heart, but a black man with a black heart."[4]

Garvey felt strongly that only through concerted action could Negroes achieve any betterment of their lowly status. "The world ought to know that it could not keep 400,000,000 Negroes down forever," he once remarked, and he constantly spoke optimistically of the Negroes of the world "standing together as one man." The black man could hope to better himself, Garvey believed, only by joining his own actions with those of others of his race. "It has been said that the Negro has never yet found cause to engage himself in anything in common with his brother," the U.N.I.A. founder admitted, "but the dawn of a new day is upon us and we see things differently. We see now, not as individuals, but as a collective whole, having one common interest."[5]. . . .

"It is obvious, according to the commonest principles of human action," Garvey told his followers, "that no man will do as much for you as you will do for yourself." Accordingly, he counseled Negroes to work for a strong and united black nation

---

[2] Quoted in R. L. Hartt, "The Negro Moses and His Campaign to Lead the Black Millions into Their Promised Land," *Independent*, CV (February 26, 1921), p. 206.

[3] Amy Jacques Garvey, editor, *Philosophy and Opinions of Marcus Garvey*, 2 Vols. (New York, 1923–1926), I, p. 9.

[4] New York *World*, August 7, 1920.

[5] Garvey, *Philosophy and Opinions*, I, p. 9; II, p. 15.

able to demand justice instead of sympathy from the ruling powers of the world. "If we must have justice, we must be strong," he explained; "if we must be strong, we must come together; if we must come together, we can only do so through the system of organization." "Let us not waste time in breathless appeals to the strong while we are weak," he advised, "but lend our time, energy, and effort to the accumulation of strength among ourselves by which we will voluntarily attract the attention of others."[6] Create a strong Negro nation, Garvey said in essence, and never more will you fear oppression at the hands of other races.

This spirit of race confidence and solidarity pervaded all of the many activities of the Garvey movement. The Black Star Line and its successor, the Black Cross Navigation and Trading Company, the Negro Factories Corporation, and indeed the African Legion, the Black Cross Nurses, and the other components of the U.N.I.A. itself were all a part of the general plan to weld the Negro people into a racially conscious, united group for effective mass action. Outsiders might laugh or scoff at some of the antics of the various Garvey organizations, their serious members ludicrous with high-toned titles and elaborate uniforms, but the importance of this aspect of the movement in restoring the all but shattered Negro self-confidence should not be overlooked. . . .

It is perhaps significant that from this period of intensified race consciousness dates the first large-scale production of Negro dolls. Whether or not Negro children had any instinctive preference for dolls of their own color, their parents now came to believe in increasing numbers that their children should play with colored dolls. In 1919 the Harlem firm of Berry and Ross started the profitable production of dolls of a dusky hue designed to satisfy the most discriminating young mistress—or parent. The Universal Negro Improvement Association encouraged this revolutionary toy development, and Garvey's *Negro World* plugged the sale of black dolls. "Little Thelma Miller, eight years old, is very fond of her little colored doll," ran the caption under a U.N.I.A. photograph of a happy young mother proudly holding her very black toy baby. "She has never had the

[6] *Ibid.*, II, p. 12.

opportunity and pleasure of playing with no other doll except a colored doll. She is a real Garveyite." The fact that most of these Negro dolls were advertised as "light-brown," "high-brown," or "mulatto," however, seems to indicate that Negroes continued to look upon lightness of color as a desirable characteristic.

One of the methods used by Garvey to build up a sense of pride in the Negro heritage was his constant reference to the exploits of Negro heroes and to the land from which the race had come. He angrily accused white scholars of distorting Negro history to make in unfavorable to colored people. "Every student of history, of impartial mind," Garvey taught, "knows that the Negro once ruled the world, when white men were savages and barbarians living in caves; that thousands of Negro professors . . . taught in the universities in Alexandria."[7] The intent Negro audiences in Liberty Hall delighted in Garvey's vivid recollections of a creative black civilization at a time when white men were nothing:

When Europe was inhabited by a race of cannibals, a race of savages, naked men, heathens and pagans, Africa was peopled with a race of cultured black men, who were masters in art, science and literature; men who were cultured and refined; men, who, it was said, were like the gods. Even the great poets of old sang in beautiful sonnets of the delight it afforded the gods to be in companionship with the Ethiopians. Why, then, should we lose hope? Black men, you were once great; you shall be great again. Lose not courage, lose not faith, go forward. The thing to do is to get organized. . . .[8]

Not only were white men of a low breed, far below their darker brothers, but the time had come to tell the world about the great heroes of Negro history. "Negroes, teach your children they are direct descendants of the greatest and proudest race who ever peopled the earth," Garvey preached with earnest intensity. Wherever Negroes had lived they had produced eminent men and accomplished notable achievements. "Sojurner Truth is worthy of the place of sainthood alongside of Joan of Arc; Crispus Attucks and George William Gordon are entitled to the halo of martyrdom with no less glory than that of the martyrs of any other race," Garvey cried. "Toussaint L'Ouver-

---

[7] *Ibid.*, II, p. 19.
[8] *Ibid.*, I, p. 77.

ture's brilliancy as a soldier and statesman outshone that of a
Cromwell, Napoleon, and Washington; hence he is entitled to
the highest place as a hero among men."[9] . . . The Garvey
historical examination might not be as critical as more objective
scholars would desire, but it did act as a massive dose of adren-
alin to the nationalism now beginning to throb in Negro breasts.

Much more important in the stimulation of black nationalism
was the U.N.I.A. program to lead Negroes back to their African
homeland. With customary flamboyance Garvey assured his followers that a few years would see Africa as completely dominated
by Negroes as Europe was by whites. "No one knows when
the hour of Africa's Redemption cometh," he warned mysteri-
ously. "It is in the wind. It is coming. One day, like a storm, it will
be here." To his Liberty Hall supporters Garvey exclaimed, "Let
Africa be our guiding star—our star of destiny," while to the
dark motherland he called, "Wake up Ethiopia! Wake up Africa!
Let us work towards the one glorious end of a free, redeemed
and mighty nation. Let Africa be a bright star among the
constellation of nations."[10]
A great independent African nation was the essential ingredient in the Garvey recipe for race redemption and he was
earnestly convinced that Negroes needed the dark continent to
achieve their destiny as a great people. Like another ardent
disciple of racial nationalism, Garvey demanded *Lebensraum*
for his people. It fell to the U.N.I.A. to lead the struggle to
regain Africa and in the fight Garvey foresaw divine intervention.
"At this moment methinks I see Ethiopia stretching forth her
hands unto God," he declared fervently, "and methinks I see the
angel of God taking up the standard of the Red, and Black,
and the Green, and saying, 'Men of the Negro race, Men of
Ethiopia, follow me!' It falls to our lot to tear off the shackles
that bind Mother Africa." "Climb ye the heights of liberty,"
Garvey exhorted the U.N.I.A. legions, "and cease not in well-
doing until you have planted the banner of the Red, the Black,
and the Green upon the hilltops of Africa."
But what of the powerful European nations that had carved

[9] *Ibid.*, II, p. 82, p. 415.
[10] *Ibid.*, I, p. 6, 10.

up the African continent and now controlled the homeland? Garvey frequently disclaimed any animus against the white race, but at the same time he pointedly told his followers: "We shall not ask England or France or Italy or Belgium, 'Why are you here?' We shall only command them, 'Get out of here.'" The barrier to a free Africa was the white man, and Garvey warned ominously: "We say to the white man who now dominates Africa that it is to his interest to clear out of Africa now, because we are coming . . . 400,000,000 strong." Garvey loved to speculate on the tremendous power that would belong to the Negro people once they discovered what their numerical strength could do for them."[11] We are going home after a long vacation," he told the U.N.I.A., "and are giving notice to the tenant to get out. If he doesn't there is such a thing as forcible ejection." "You will find ten years from now, or 100 years from now," he warned a white audience, "Garvey was not an idle buffoon but was representing the new vision of the Negro who was looking forward to great accomplishments in the future."[12]

It was never Garvey's intention that all Negroes in the New World would return to Africa and in this sense it is misleading to call his scheme a Back to Africa movement. Rather he believed like many Zionists that once a strong African nation was established Negroes everywhere would automatically gain needed prestige and strength and could look to it for protection if necessary.[13] "At no time did he visualize all American Negroes returning to Africa," says his widow. "We do not want all the Negroes in Africa," Garvey informed a U.N.I.A. audience in Madison Square Garden in 1924. "Some are no good here, and naturally will be no good there."[14] Those particularly needed for the work in Africa would be engineers, artisans, and willing workers of all sorts—in short, the pioneering elements upon which all civilizations are built. . . .

It is interesting to note that the idea of setting up an independent African state remained a part of Garvey's program

[11] *Ibid.*, I, p. 39.
[12] Marcus Garvey, *Minutes of a Speech at the Century Theatre, London, Sunday, September 2, 1928* (London, 1928), p. 29.
[13] Hartt in *Independent*, CV, p. 206.
[14] Amy Jacques Garvey, Kingston, Jamaica, to the author, February 19, 1949, and February 14, 1951.

to the end of his life. One of the last issues of his monthly magazine, the *Black Man*, contained an earnest plea for support of U. S. Senator Theodore G. Bilbo's bill for the repatriation of American Negroes to Africa. Garvey admitted that the motives of this bigoted southern racist might "not be as idealistic as Negroes may want," but he gave the Bilbo bill his endorsement because "independent nationality is the greatest guarantee of the ability of any people to stand up in our present civilization." He therefore asked all divisions of the Universal Negro Improvement Association in the United States "to give their undivided and whole-hearted support to Senator Bilbo's Bill."[15]

Garvey's passionate interest in Africa was a logical development of his firm conviction that Negroes could expect no permanent progress in a land dominated by white men.[16] No doubt he would have agreed completely with Mr. Dooley's shrewd analysis of the American race problem: "Th' throuble is that th' naygurs iv th' North have lived too long among th' white people, an' th' white people iv th' South have lived too long among th' naygurs." Garvey said essentially the same thing when he told Negroes to develop "a government, a nation of our own, strong enough to lend protection to the members of our race scattered all over the world, and to compel the respect of the nations and the races of the earth." When Garvey spoke of discrimination, he touched a subject painfully familiar to every Negro: "If you cannot live alongside the white man in peace, if you cannot get the same chance and opportunity alongside the white man, even though you are his fellow citizen; if he claims that you are not entitled to this chance or opportunity because the country is his by force of numbers, then find a country of your own and rise to the highest position within that country."[17] The Garvey solution for Negro ills was to make the race "so strong as to strike fear" into the hearts of the oppressor white race.[18] Only when Negroes could compel respect and justice

[15] *Black Man*, III (November, 1938), p. 19. See also Chicago *Defender*, June 15, 1940.
[16] Garvey, *Philosophy and Opinions*, II, pp. 3, 40, 46, 49, and 97.
[17] Quoted in Hartt in *Independent*, CV, p. 206.
[18] *Ibid.*, p. 218.

through their connection with a strong Negro government would the position of the race be secure.

Garvey had no illusions about the white man's Christian love and believed that it would be used only when conveniently suitable. The U.N.I.A. therefore conceded the right of whites to do as they pleased in their own lands provided that Negroes were allowed to develop a nation of their own in Africa.[19] "Political, social and industrial America," Garvey cautioned, "will never become so converted as to be willing to share up equitably between black and white." Though Negroes might live as useful citizens in the United States for thousands of years, Garvey believed that as long as the white population was numerically superior to them the blacks could never hope for political justice or social equality.

Garvey's plain abdication of Negro rights in America quickly brought him the open support of such white supremacy groups as the Ku Klux Klan and the Anglo-Saxon Clubs, both flourishing mightily in the postwar years. Garvey's major book, the second volume of his *Philosophy and Opinions,* carried an advertisement for Major Earnest Sevier Cox's *White America,* a polemical work strongly preaching the separation of the races. Major Cox sometimes spoke to U.N.I.A. audiences at Liberty Hall in New York, and he even dedicated a pamphlet on racial purity to Garvey, whom he called "a martyr for the independence and integrity of the Negro race."[20] Another white supporter was John Powell, the fanatical organizer of the Anglo-Saxon Clubs of America. Garvey expressed great admiration for men like Cox and Powell because of "their honesty and lack of hypocrisy" in openly working to maintain the power of the white race.[21] Speaking at Liberty Hall late in 1925, Powell congratulated the U.N.I.A. on its racial improvement program and reaffirmed the mutual desire of blacks and whites to preserve the purity of their respective races. Garvey also received support from some southern whites who looked upon his movement with favor because it was likely to attract Negroes who might otherwise be

[19] Garvey, *Philosophy and Opinions,* II, p. 46.

[20] E. S. Cox, *Let My People Go* (Richmond, 1925), p. 4. See also Cox, *The South's Part in Mongrelizing the Nation* (Richmond, 1926), pp. 8–9, 93–94, 103, 108.

[21] Garvey, *Philosophy and Opinions,* II, p. 338.

resentful of their subordinate caste position in the United States.[22] After he was deported, some of Garvey's white friends were active in a campaign to permit the return of the exiled U.N.I.A. leader.

"Lynchings and race riots," said Garvey with reference to the grim postwar period of racial strife and violence, "all work to our advantage by teaching the Negro that he must build a civilization of his own or forever remain the white man's victim." Bishop McGuire, the religious leader of the U.N.I.A. and spiritual head of the African Orthodox Church, declared frankly that the Ku Klux Klan's campaign of intimidation and violence would benefit the movement by driving harassed Negroes into the Garvey organization.[23] In 1922 Garvey indicated his tacit support of the dread Klan, an alliance his opponents had suspected for some time. "The Ku Klux Klan is going to make this a white man's country," Garvey asserted in stating his belief that the K.K.K. was the invisible government of America. "They are perfectly honest and frank about it. Fighting them is not going to get you anywhere."[24]

Early in 1922 Garvey went to Atlanta, Georgia, for a conference with Edward Young Clarke, Imperial Giant of the Klan.[25] The purpose of the meeting was apparently to see how strong the Klan was and whether or not Garvey could hope for its support for the Back to Africa program of the U.N.I.A. Garvey's widow explains that far from approving of the Klan's violent actions against Negroes, her husband merely believed "that the prejudice exhibited by the Klan in hysteria, hate, cruelty, and mob violence was the prejudice common to most white Americans, which deep in their hearts they felt, but culture and refinement prevented many from showing any trace of it."[26] The meeting was one of expediency, then, rather than of

[22] Kelsey Blanton, *Color-Blind and Skin-Deep Democracy* (Tampa, Florida, 1924), pp. 61–62.

[23] Chicago *Defender*, August 16, 1924.

[24] *New York Times*, July 10, 1922.

[25] Chicago *Defender*, July 8, 1922; *New York Times*, February 8, 1923; W. E. B. Du Bois, "Back to Africa," *Century*, CV, (February, 1923), p. 547. Burgit Aron, "The Garvey Movement." Unpublished Master of Arts thesis, Columbia University, 1947.

[26] Amy Jacques Garvey, Kingston, Jamaica, to the author, February 19, 1949.

mutual admiration, but it was nonetheless a serious tactical blunder.

Although details of the Atlanta conference were withheld, the mere thought that a responsible Negro leader would collaborate with the leading avowed enemy of his race brought down a storm of criticism upon Garvey's head. Alderman George Harris, editor of the New York *News*, denounced Garvey as "misrepresenting the attitude of 100 per cent of our native-born Americans and 75 per cent of the foreign-born group" when he surrendered to Clarke. "When Garvey agrees with the Klan's theory that this is a white man's country," Harris complained angrily, "he sadly misrepresents our people." William Pickens, who had at one time very nearly accepted a high U.N.I.A. post, now spurned with contempt a Garvey title of nobility because of this rumored alliance with the Ku Klux Klan. W. E. B. Du Bois let go a powerful blast against the U.N.I.A. president in *Crisis*, the organ of the National Association for the Advancement of Colored People. "Marcus Garvey is, without doubt, the most dangerous enemy of the Negro race in America and the world," sputtered the indignant editor of *Crisis*. "He is either a lunatic or a traitor."[27] Unperturbed by this barrage of Negro criticism, Garvey countered with a candid appraisal of white America. "I regard the Klan, the Anglo-Saxon Clubs and White American Societies," he maintained, "as better friends of the race than all other groups of hypocritical whites put together. I like honesty and fair play. You may call me a Klansman if you will, but, potentially every white man is a Klansman, as far as the Negro in competition with whites socially, economically and politically is concerned, and there is no use lying about it."[28]

The main reason that Garvey and his organization were acceptable to the Ku Klux Klan and other white supremacy groups was that the U.N.I.A. leader preached race purity to his followers. He thundered that racial amalgamation must cease forthwith and warned that any member of the Universal Negro Improvement Association who married a white would be summarily expelled. Not only did Garvey advocate race purity, but as a

[27] "A Lunatic or a Traitor," *Crisis*, XXVIII, pp. 8-9.
[28] Garvey, *Philosophy and Opinions*, II, p. 71. Roi Ottley, *"New World A-Coming": Inside Black America* (Boston, 1943), p. 74.

Jamaican black he attempted to transfer the West Indian three-way color caste system to the United States by attacking mulatto leaders. He laughed at the light-skinned mulattoes, who, he said, were always seeking "excuses to get out of the Negro Race," and he scornfully accused his mulatto opponents of being "time-serving, boot-licking agencies of subserviency to the whites." The average Negro leader, Garvey said, sought to establish himself as "the pet of some philanthropist of another race," thereby selling out the interests of his own people.[29]

The U.N.I.A. catered to the darker Negroes; in fact, Garvey's definition of Negro seemed to require a purity of racial origin. At first the anti-mulatto propaganda helped to inflate the egos of darker Negroes, but it was doomed to failure in the United States where neither whites nor Negroes make any appreciable distinction between Negroes of different shades of color. American blacks lacked the fierce resentment toward the favored position of mulattoes that had been a part of Garvey's Jamaican conditioning. The U.N.I.A. continued to preach racial purity, however, and its founder maintained his attack on his light-skinned critics by asserting that they favored racial amalgamation. "I believe in racial purity, and in maintaining the standard of racial purity," he asserted. "I am proud I am a Negro. It is only the so-called 'colored' man who talks of social equality." "We are not seeking social equality," Garvey told whites. "We do not seek intermarriage, nor do we hanker after the impossible. We want the right to have a country of our own, and there foster and re-establish a culture and civilization exclusively ours." Garvey's advocacy of racial purity was noticed even in Germany, where the so-called German Emergency League against the Black Horror sought to enlist his aid in securing the removal of French Negro occupation troops from the Rhineland.[30]

In Garvey's vocabulary, as in that of most southern whites, social equality meant "the social intermingling of both races, intermarriages, and general social co-relationship." Believing that such intermingling would inevitably lead to "an American race, that will neither be white nor black," Garvey directed a constant stream of criticism against Dr. W. E. B. Du Bois of the N.A.A.C.P.

[29] Garvey, *Philosophy and Opinions*, I, pp. 29–30.
[30] Cited in *Nation*, CXIII (December 28, 1921), p. 769.

for his efforts on behalf of Negro social and political equality.[31] At least part of this animosity was doubtless due to Du Bois' own dignified attacks on the U.N.I.A. and to the fact that the cultured editor of *Crisis* possessed an excellent formal education of the sort Garvey had always desired but had never been able to obtain. E. Franklin Frazier suggests that "Garvey constantly directed the animosity of his followers against the intellectuals because of his own lack of formal education."[32] Though the *Negro World* in 1922 listed Du Bois as one of the "twelve greatest living Negroes" (Garvey was of course also on the list), the 1924 convention of the U.N.I.A. resolved to ostracize Du Bois "from the Negro race, so far as the U.N.I.A. is concerned," declaring him "an enemy of the black people of the world."[33]

Garvey denounced other Negro leaders as being bent on cultural assimilation, cravenly seeking white support, and miserably compromising between accommodation and protest. The National Association for the Advancement of Colored People was the worst offender in Garvey's mind, because, he said, it "wants us all to become white by amalgamation, but they are not honest enough to come out with the truth." "To be a Negro is no disgrace, but an honor," Garvey indignantly affirmed, "and we of the U.N.I.A. do not want to become white."[34] He warned both whites and blacks that the purity of the two races was endangered by the false prophets of amalgamation. "It is the duty of the virtuous and morally pure of both the white and black races," he announced, "to thoughtfully and actively protect the future of the two peoples, by vigorously opposing the destructive propaganda and vile efforts of the miscegenationists of the white race, and their associates, the hybrids of the Negro race." "I believe in a pure black race," Garvey proclaimed loudly, "just as how all self-respecting whites believe in a pure white race, as far as that can be." The U.N.I.A. chief felt constrained to warn the white world of the dangers inherent in social equality.

---

[31] Garvey, *Philosophy and Opinions*, II, pp. 39, 57, 86, and 324–325; Garvey, "A Barefaced Coloured Leader," *Black Man*, I (July, 1935), pp. 5–8; New York *World*, August 4, 1920.

[32] E. Franklin Frazier, "The Garvey Movement," *Opportunity*, IV (November, 1926), p. 346.

[33] Chicago *Defender*, September 6, 1924.

[34] Garvey, *Philosophy and Opinions*, II, pp. 325–326. John Hope Franklin, *From Slavery to Freedom* (New York, 1948), p. 482.

"Some Negroes believe in social equality," he cautioned. "They want to intermarry with the white women of this country, and it is going to cause trouble later on. Some Negroes want the same jobs you have. They want to be Presidents of the nation."

On the other hand, white Americans need have no fears of the aims of the Universal Negro Improvement Association, which Garvey declared was stoutly opposed to "miscegenation and race suicide" and believed strongly "in the purity of the Negro race and the purity of the white race."[35] So intent was Garvey on the goal of complete racial compartmentalization that he even went so far as to warn individual whites of the danger of allowing Negroes to become elected officials, artisans, or skilled laborers while white workers were unemployed. Such ill-considered opportunities for blacks, he believed, would only lead to "bloody . . . wholesale mob violence."[36] This abandonment of Negro economic rights was too much for former sympathizer William Pickens, who exploded wrathfully, "This squat, energetic, gorilla-jawed black man is one of the worst enemies of his own Race." Garvey intended, of course, that Negroes should create their own economic opportunities through such race enterprises as the Black Star Line and the Negro Factories Corporation. In this connection it is of interest to note, however, that at least five of the important operational posts in the Black Star Line were at one time or another filled by white men, including three ship captains, a first assistant engineer, and a marine superintendent. Apparently, suitably skilled Negroes were not easy to find, even for service with a Negro steamship company.

In October, 1921, President Warren G. Harding made a controversial speech on race relations while visiting Birmingham, Alabama. Quoting from Lothrop Stoddard's alarmist book, *The Rising Tide of Color against White World Supremacy*, Harding asserted his belief in the old Booker T. Washington ideal of the social separation of the two races. "There shall be recognition of the absolute divergence in things social and racial," the President declared. "Men of both races may well stand uncompromisingly against every suggestion of social equality. . . . Racial

---

[35] Garvey, *Philosophy and Opinions*, II, p. 81.
[36] Chicago *Defender*, March 29, 1924.

amalgamation there cannot be."[37] Though southern Negroes may have agreed with the Washington *Bee's* appraisal of the Harding speech as "a brave, courageous, fearless, heroic deed," the more militant Negro leadership in the North indicated its stunned dismay at the President's apparently unfriendly attitude. Garvey, however, immediately telegraphed his congratulations to President Harding and expressed "the heartfelt thanks of four hundred million Negroes of the world for the splendid interpretation you have given the race problem." "All true Negroes are against social equality," the U.N.I.A. president asserted, "believing that all races should develop on their own social lines."[38] Harding's Birmingham address, Garvey later wrote, "was one that revealed his depth of thought for the Negro." Those Negroes with an eye for the *double-entendre* could find a wry bit of humor in the assertion. Others might criticize both Harding and his predecessor, Woodrow Wilson, for their lack of sympathetic activity on behalf of colored citizens, but to Garvey they "came nearest to playing the Christ in the leadership of the American people."

How well Garvey's aggressive philosophy of racial purity and social separation permeated the lowest echelons of the Universal Negro Improvement Association may be shown by a letter to the mayor of New Orleans from the women's auxiliary of the local division of the organization:

We like your "Jim Crow" laws, in that they defend the purity of races and any person married to any but a Negro cannot become a member of our organization. We are not members . . . of that class who are spending their time imitating the rich whites . . . studying Spanish so as to be able to pass for anything but a Negro, thereby getting a chance to associate with you. We are not ashamed of the Race to which we belong and we feel sure that God made black skin and kinky hair because he desired to express Himself in that type.[39]

It is not hard to see from the foregoing why Garvey was opposed so vigorously by the militant Negro rights organizations like the N.A.A.C.P., and conversely, why he received open encouragement from such white supremacy groups as the Ku Klux Klan.

[37] *New York Times,* October 27, 1921.
[38] *Ibid.*
[39] Chicago *Defender,* March 31, 1923.

Garvey had a strong distaste for any alliance with white labor organizations, a skepticism that probably stemmed in part from his early failure as a strike leader in Jamaica. This distrust of the labor movement also reflected a feeling that the white worker was the Negro's greatest competitor and most dangerous rival. Rather than seek an alliance with white workers, Garvey told Negroes that the white employer was their best friend until such time as the race had achieved economic independence.[40] The Negro Factories Corporation and the Black Star Line were direct moves to set up Negro-owned business enterprises so that Negroes would not have to beg for employment from whites. It seemed self-evident to Garvey that "the only convenient friend" of the American Negro worker was "the white capitalist," who "being selfish—seeking only the largest profit out of labor— is willing and glad to use Negro labor wherever possible on a scale 'reasonably' below the standard white union wage." The white employer would "tolerate the Negro" only if he accepted "a lower standard of wage than the white union man." Garvey's solution for the black worker, therefore, was to "keep his scale of wage a little lower than the whites" and thereby "keep the goodwill of the white employer," all the time husbanding Negro resources so that the race could ultimately become economically free.[41] Needless to say, this cheerful rejection of trade unionism did little to endear Garvey to Negro labor leaders, and it early won for him the bitter hostility of men like Chandler Owen and A. Philip Randolph, who were currently engaged in a successful campaign to establish a union of Negro sleeping car porters.

Similarly, Garvey refused to have anything to do with socialism and communism, despite the alarmist attempts of the Lusk Committee and the Department of Justice to portray him as a dangerous radical agitator. He felt that these movements of the left, although they made a pretense of helping the Negro, were inherently prejudiced against the black race, since they were dominated by whites. "Fundamentally what racial difference is

[40] Ralph J. Bunche, "The Programs, Ideologies, Tactics, and Achievements of Negro Betterment and Interracial Organizations." Unpublished monograph prepared for the Carnegie-Myrdal study, 1940. Schomburg Collection, N. Y. Public Library.

[41] Garvey, *Philosophy and Opinions*, II, pp. 69–70.

there between a white Communist, Republican or Democrat?" Garvey demanded to know. "On the appeal of race interest the Communist is as ready as either to show his racial . . . superiority over the Negro." The U.N.I.A. leader suspected that for all his fine talk the Communist would just as quickly join a lynch mob as would the less radical white citizen, and consequently he believed that communism must first prove itself as a really new reform movement before the Negro could safely accept it. The Communists were not initially opposed to Garvey's Universal Negro Improvement Association, though they deplored his emphasis on African Zionism. Party members inside the U.N.I.A. were ordered to push the fight for Negro equality within the United States, but they were so few in number that they were never able either to "capture" the association or to challenge successfully Garvey's leadership.[42] The Communist Party was greatly impressed with the amazing lower-class appeal of the U.N.I.A., however, and after the organization had begun to disintegrate in 1926 Robert Minor wrote disconsolately: "A breaking up of this Negro association would be a calamity to the Negro people and to the working class as a whole. . . . It is composed very largely, if not almost entirely, of Negro workers and impoverished farmers, although there is a sprinkling of small business men."[43]

In spite of Garvey's announced opposition to communism as a reform movement, he publicly mourned the death of Nikolai Lenin, the founder of the Soviet Union, in 1924. In a *Negro World* editorial he called Lenin "probably the world's greatest man between 1917 and . . . 1924," and announced that the U.N.I.A. had dispatched a cablegram to Moscow "expressing the sorrow and condolence of the 400,000,000 Negroes of the world."[44] This action need not to be seen as a startling reversal of Garvey's earlier views, but merely as an example of his unexcelled flair for the dramatic and his egotistical desire to be associated with the important men of the day.

[42] Wilson Record, *The Negro and the Communist Party*, (Chapel Hill, 1951), pp. 40–41.
[43] Robert Minor, "Death or a Program," *Workers Monthly*, V (April, 1926), p. 270, quoted in Record, p. 41. Cf. I. Amter, *The World Liberative Movement of the Negroes* (Moscow: Soviet State Publishing House, 1925).
[44] *Negro World*, February 2, 1924.

Although Garvey had once defined "radical" as "a label that is always applied to people who are endeavoring to get freedom," he never hesitated to use the confusing term to discredit his opponents. In January, 1923, for example, after the "Committee of Eight" had written the Department of Justice protesting the delay in the trial of the four Black Star officials, Garvey wired the United States Attorney General to assure him of the patriotic loyalty of the U.N.I.A. In his telegram Garvey sought to smear his Negro critics. The National Association for the Advancement of Colored People was dominated by Socialists, Garvey declared, and he called the Friends of Negro Freedom "a red Socialistic organization." He accused the African Blood Brotherhood, another hostile group, of being composed of "representatives of the Bolsheviki of Russia."[45] This was a shady dodge as old as the game of politics itself: discredit your opponents by fair means or foul and perhaps they will stop asking embarrassing questions. There was just enough truth in Garvey's allegations, however, to warrant making the charges in this period of general reaction against leftist movements.

The Universal Negro Improvement Association, far from being oriented to the left, may be classified as a movement of the extreme right. Its intense nationalism and narrow racial outlook had little in common with liberal groups that were seeking to tear down these barriers between men and nations. In 1937, after Italy's legions had overrun Ethiopia, Garvey boasted that he had been the first prophet of fascism. "We were the first Fascists," he told a friend. "We had disciplined men, women, and children in training for the liberation of Africa. The black masses saw that in this extreme nationalism lay their only hope and readily supported it. Mussolini copied Fascism from me but the Negro reactionaries sabotaged it."[46]

One may question whether Garvey was aware of all the connotations of either fascism or communism, but certainly his U.N.I.A., with its fierce chauvinistic nationalism and strongly centralized leadership, had fascist characteristics. Garvey talked of a democratic African republic but it is a little hard to imagine

[45] New York Times, January 21, 1923.
[46] Quoted in Joel Rogers, World's Great Men of Color, Vol. II (New York, 1946), II, p. 602.

him in such a government. Much more likely would have been a black empire with Garvey upon its throne. "Liberty and true Democracy means," he once said, "that if one man can be the President, King, Premier or Chancellor of a country then the other fellow can be the same also." There never was much doubt in the mind of this supremely confident black man as to just what his personal role in the "democratic" shift of power would be. . . .

Marcus Garvey's philosophy of race relations was inextricably bound up in his staunch belief that it was useless for the Negro to attempt to better his condition in a country dominated by another, inherently hostile race. Firmly convinced that the United States would always be a white man's country, and concerned lest the Negro should forget his racial and cultural background, Garvey willingly relinquished Negro rights in America for the dubious right to establish a black nation in Africa. His zeal in securing this Negro state led him to co-operate with the most reactionary and anti-Negro groups in the United States. It is both a mistake and an injustice to assume, however, as some careless writers have done, that Garvey was merely an opportunistic demagogue anxious to build up a powerful following for personal gain. Demagogue he most certainly was, but his motives, mistaken as they often seemed to many Negro Americans eager to win full status as citizens of the only country they had ever known, were much more complex than that. Garvey was determined to help his suffering people and his devotion often led him to act in a way that was incomprehensible to American-born Negroes.

In 1919, the year Garvey first began to be noticed in the United States, Walter Lippmann concluded that Americans would have to work out a civilization where "no Negro need dream of a white heaven and of bleached angels." "Pride of race will come to the Negro when a dark skin is no longer associated with poverty, ignorance, misery, terror and insult," Lippmann declared. "When this pride arises every white man in America will be the happier for it. He will be able then, as he is not now, to enjoy the finest quality of civilized living—the fellowship of different men."[47] The creation of a powerful feeling of race pride is perhaps Garvey's greatest and most lasting contribution to the American race scene. Marcus Garvey is gone and with him many of the more spectacular yet ephemeral aspects of his colorful movement, but the awakened spirit of Negro pride that he so ardently championed remains an important legacy to the Negro people.

Robert A. Bone

The Harlem Renaissance should be seen as the literary version of the new mood that came over Negro life in the years following World War I. The primary figures of the Renaissance—Claude McKay, Langston Hughes, Jean Toomer, Countee Cullen—consciously identified with the Negro masses. These writers gloried in lower-class Negro life, in their African past, in their blackness, and in the folkways of the great mass of Negroes. They tried to capture the feeling of Negro life—the beat, rhythm, style—and portrayed their characters with a warmth which earlier Negro writers shunned, as if afraid to show themselves to the white world for the fear of bringing disgrace upon themselves. The writers of the Harlem Renaissance were no longer defensive, but like Negro musicians, dancers, and actors of the time they felt secure enough to present part of their real selves to the world.

This had not always been the case. Early Negro writers were mainly didactic. In the antebellum period writers from Frederick Douglass to William Wells Brown attempted to inform white audiences of the horrors of slavery. In the postwar period, Negro writers, far from being radical, strove to prove to white audiences that they could be responsible and respectable. Such writers as Pauline Hopkins, Charles Chesnutt, Paul Laurence Dunbar, Sutton Griggs, did not engage in race pleading or write specifically Negro novels. When they did write about Negroes it was from the point of view of the talented tenth, the educated middle class. Dunbar in 1902 warned the Negro about the dangers of the city, of

[47] Walter Lippmann's Introduction in Carl Sandburg, *The Chicago Race Riots* (New York, 1919), p. iv.

going North to "false ideals and unreal ambitions." Charles Chesnutt and Pauline Hopkins, like many Negro intellectuals at the turn of the century, objected to segregation on the grounds that it discriminated against the better class of Negroes. Chesnutt's hero, Dr. Miller in *The Marrow of Tradition* (1901), dislikes being made to share a segregated car with Negro laborers. "These people," Miller thinks, "were just as offensive to him as to the whites in the other end of the train." And Pauline Hopkins in *Lillian Simmons* (1915) has her Negro heroine believing that Jim Crow railroad cars were necessary "but she could not feel that it was fair to treat all colored people alike, because all were not alike." Few novelists had their characters identify with the masses, and when lower-class characters were depicted, it was in the same condescending manner as used by Joel Chandler Harris or Thomas Nelson Page. Negro intellectuals still were under the Booker Washington influence, which believed that the answer to the race problem could be found in an alliance between the better class of colored people and the quality white folks. Gentility was preferred to social realism or even race pride.

By the early 1920s Negro writers felt less of a need to show the white reader how "civilized" the Negro had become. The shackles of respectability were thrown off and in their poetry and novels Negro writers felt free to tell what it was really like to be black in white America. At the same time the white avant-garde, in their revolt against the narrow morality of the older generation, discovered in Negro life the spontaneity, freedom, and life-giving forces that white America suppressed. For the first time in American life, Negro artists found themselves with allies, who far from desiring to change or reform them, tried to learn from and emulate them. In Eugene O'Neill, George Gershwin, Paul Whiteman, Sherwood Anderson, Dubose Hayward, Waldo Frank, Carl Van Vechten, in countless musicians and artists, we have creative artists discovering in Negro life values and ideas that contained universal meanings. America slowly learned the meaning of Du Bois' query in his *The Souls of Black Folk*, "Would America have been America without her Negro people?"

Robert A. Bone is Professor of English at Teachers College, Columbia University. His study *The Negro Novel in America* is the basic work on the subject.

THE BACKGROUND OF
THE NEGRO RENAISSANCE

SOURCE: Robert A. Bone, "The Background of the Negro Renaissance," *The Negro Novel in America*, revised edition, (New Haven: Yale University Press, 1965), pp. 53–64.

The Great Migration

Alain Locke has described the Negro Renaissance as "the mass movement of the urban immigration of Negroes, projected on the plane of an increasingly articulate elite."[1] The Great Migration to which Locke refers was the most important event in the history of the American Negro since his emancipation from slavery. In the course of this migration, centuries of historical development were traversed in a few decades. It was not merely a movement of the colored population from South to North, or from country to city; it was the sudden transplanting of a debased feudal folk from medieval to modern America.

From 1890 to 1920, while the business and professional class was fighting for the right to rise, the base of the Negro social pyramid was shifting from a peasantry to an urban proletariat. In these decades more than 2,000,000 Negroes left the farm for the factory.[2] As growing numbers of Negro sharecroppers were pushed off the land by erosion and drought, by an exhausted soil, and by the mechanical cotton-picker, they were drawn to the cities by the demands of American industry for cheap labor. Competition from the European immigrant was conveniently eliminated by World War I and by the immigration laws of 1924. At the same time, the war encouraged a vast expansion of American industry, creating a labor market for thousands of black workers. Under these circumstances, the urbanization of the American Negro took place at an unprecedented rate.

The Great Migration brought the Negro masses into contact with the quickened pulse of the modern city. There they were

[1] "The Negro's Contribution to American Culture," *Journal of Negro Education*, 8 (1939), 521–29.
[2] Myrdal, *An American Dilemma*, pp. 191–96.

faced with a mass of strange experiences which forced them to revise their traditional ways of thinking. The crowded ghetto, unlike the isolated farm, provided a basis for a vigorous group life. A rising standard of living and better educational opportunities fostered new attitudes of self-respect and independence. In a word, the Negro's urban environment lifted him to a new plane of consciousness. Such a profound transformation could hardly occur among the masses without reverberations in the world of letters. The new group experience called for a new literary movement to interpret it.

It was a foregone conclusion that Harlem should become the center of the new movement. The largest Negro community in the world, Harlem was itself a product of the Great Migration. Doubling its population from 1900 to 1920, it was wrested from the whites by sheer weight of numbers. As it grew to metropolitan proportions, it gradually acquired the character of a race capital. Negroes from Africa and the West Indies, from North and South, and from all classes and backgrounds poured into the crucible of dark Manhattan. Harlem thus provided the Negro artist with an infinite variety of human subjects, as well as an opportunity to observe urban life at its maximum intensity.

Moreover, this black metropolis evolved within the womb of a city which was the literary, musical, and theatrical capital of America. Harlem meant proximity to Broadway, to the little magazines and the big publishing houses, to Greenwich Village and its white intellectuals, to avant-garde literary groups and successful, established writers. It offered a unique, cosmopolitan milieu, where artists and intellectuals of all kinds could find mutual stimulation. Under the circumstances, it is hardly surprising that Harlem became the cultural center of Negro America.

Rise of an Intelligentsia

Before any group can prosper artistically, as Arthur Koestler notes, it must produce an intelligentsia.[3] This social layer arises in bourgeois society, according to Koestler, when enough gifted individuals have broken with their middle-class background

[3] *The Yogi and the Commissar* (New York, 1945), pp. 61–76.

to form a community of emancipated intellectuals. Shortly after World War I just such an intellectual community began to form in Harlem. Young men and women of introspective leanings came to Harlem from every corner of the nation, drawn by the changing kaleidoscope of metropolitan life.

These young intellectuals were a different breed from the Negro writers of the prewar period. Like their contemporaries of the Lost Generation, they reached maturity in a world of crumbling values. "I had no reason to think," wrote Claude McKay, "that the world I lived in was permanent, solid, and unshakable."[4] Lacking the comforting assurance of an integrated moral universe, they were forced to cope at best they could with what Henry Adams called 20th-century multiplicity. Unsure of their positive goals, they began by sweeping aside the moral debris of the previous era. At one stroke they cut through the taboos of the Victorian Age, demolished its shallow optimism, repudiated its value system, and entered the mainstream of contemporary intellectual life.

The significance of the Negro intelligentsia, which emerged for the first time in the 1920's, lay precisely in this realm of values. The middle-class writer, as Koestler suggests, is inclined not toward new hierarchies of values but toward climbing to the top of the existing hierarchy. The intelligentsia, more independent in outlook, debunks existing values and attempts to replace them with values of its own. Koestler's theoretical point may thus serve to sharpen the contrast between the early Negro novelist and his Renaissance successor. The early novelists were loyal members of the middle class who desired only equal rights within the status quo. The younger writers of the 1920's were the second generation of educated Negroes; they were the wayward sons of the rising middle class.[5] In psychological terms, they were rebelling against their fathers and their fathers' way of life.

This pattern of rebellion appears in the lives of many Renaissance authors. Langston Hughes, for example, observes in his autobiography, "My father was what the Mexicans call *muy americano,* a typical American. . . . He was interested only in

---

[4] *A Long Way from Home* (New York, Lee Furman, 1937), p. 69.
[5] The *parents* of the Renaissance novelists were 55 per cent professionals and 45 per cent white collar (compare 13 per cent and 20 per cent in the early period).

making money."[6] Hughès' most vivid memory of his father was
his constant injunction to hurry up. His father tried to hurry
him through a course in bookkeeping and then through Columbia
University, but Hughes left college to ship out, taking his Grand
Tour on a tramp steamer. Claude McKay's rebellion carried him
from Greenwich Village to the Left Bank, and from militant
Negro nationalism to the early Communist party. Jean Toomer
abandoned a law career for literature and the Gurdjieff Institute.
Countee Cullen, whose father was a minister, has recorded his
rebellion against religious formalism in his novel *One Way to
Heaven.*

The rebellious mood of the emerging Negro intelligentsia is
revealed by the little magazines they founded. *The Messenger,*
for example, displayed as its credo:

> I am an Iconoclast
> I break the limbs of idols
> And smash the traditions of men.

Fire, according to one of its founders, was intended "to burn up
a lot of the old, dead, conventional Negro ideas of the past." In
their rebelliousness and defiance the Negro writers of the 1920's
were no different from their white contemporaries, who were engaged in a similar labor of destruction in such little magazines as
Broom, transition, and *Secession.* The younger Negro intellectuals, whose consciousness was formed during the war years, were
members of an uprooted generation. Critical, skeptical, icono-
clastic, they raised the banner of the New Negro against the
stubborn guardians of the Victorian tradition.

The New Negro Movement

The term "New Negro" presents certain difficulties, for it has
been used to describe both a racial attitude and a literary movement. The extension of the term from its original meaning was
the work of Alain Locke, who in 1925 published an anthology of
younger writers entitled *The New Negro.* The title struck a re-
sponsive chord, and it soon became the accepted designation of
the new literary movement. From the standpoint of literary his-

[6] *The Big Sea* (New York and London, Knopf, 1940), p. 39.

tory this was unfortunate. "New Negro" is not a descriptive term in any literary sense; basically it indicates a rejection of racial conservatism on the part of those who employ it. It is nonetheless of considerable subjective importance that Renaissance writers should think of themselves as "New Negroes." To establish the primary meaning of the term may therefore cast additional light on the period.

The New Negro, with his uncompromising demand for equal rights, was the end product of a long historical process which began when the Negro middle class emerged from slavery and entered upon a new kind of social relations. As the patriarchal relations of slavery were replaced by the contractual relations of bourgeois society, a corresponding psychological transformation took place. Feudal attitudes of servility and dependence were abandoned in favor of the sturdy bourgeois virtues of initiative and self-reliance. This psychological transformation crystallized politically when Du Bois challenged the "accommodating" leadership of Booker T. Washington in the name of universal manhood suffrage. Manhood suffrage, the basic aim of Du Bois' Niagara Movement, became a symbol of the new spirit which animated the Negro middle class. This sense of manhood, greatly enhanced by the Negro's participation in World War I, was passed on to the Renaissance generation as part of its spiritual heritage.

There is a direct line from the Niagara Movement of the early 1900's to the New Negro Movement of the 1920's. The descent may be traced through Negro defense organizations such as the NAACP and the National Urban League, and more precisely through their house organs, Crisis and Opportunity. These two periodicals and their editors, Jesse Fauset and Charles S. Johnson, did yeoman's work for the Negro Renaissance. They encouraged new talent, opened their pages to young writers, and offered cash prizes for outstanding literary achievement. In this manner, as well as through overt patronage, the Negro middle class made a substantial contribution to the birth of the New Negro Movement. Whether they were prepared to acknowledge the lusty and sometimes ungrateful infant which they sired is another matter.

As the Negro Renaissance gained momentum and its break with the tradition of Chesnutt and Dunbar became apparent, the term "New Negro" began to take on an additional connotation of modernism. As a result, it became intellectually fashionable to declare oneself a member of the New Negro coterie. Yet if the New Negro slogan created something of a vogue, it also provided the literary movement of the 1920's with a unifying idea. "New Negro" literary societies sprang up in several large cities[7]; New Negro magazines were founded by avant-garde writers; and one novelist playfully christened his first-born "the New Negro"! This self-consciousness, this sense of belonging to a movement, made for a high group morale, and for an atmosphere which encouraged literary effort. Moreover, in its own way the New Negro Movement expressed that determination to ring out the old and ring in the new which was the central theme of the decade.

Cultural Collaboration in the Jazz Age

The years following World War I were marked by a sudden upsurge of interest in Negro life and culture among the white intelligentsia. Manifestations of this interest were numerous and varied. Throughout the 1920's books on the Negro by white authors appeared in ever-increasing numbers. *Survey Graphic* came out with an issue devoted entirely to Harlem, while Albert and Charles Boni offered a prize of $1,000 for the best novel written by an American Negro. Musical reviews which featured Negro performers broke downtown box-office records, and nightly throngs of white "tourists" invaded Harlem, drawn to night club and cabaret by colored celebrities of musical and theatrical fame. By the mid-1920's the Negro had become a national pastime.

What had happened to change the intellectual climate from hostility and indifference to sympathetic, if often misguided, interest? For one thing the Jazz Age, which derived its very character from the Negro's music, was in full swing. With "flaming youth" leading the way, a popular uprising was in progress against the stuffiness and artificial restraint of the Victorian era. These were the years of postwar catharsis—of

[7] The Writers' Guild, New York; Black Opals, Philadelphia; The Saturday Evening Quill Club, Boston; The Ink-Slingers, Los Angeles; Book and Bench, Topeka, Kansas, etc.

Freud and the sexual revolution, of heavy drinking in defiance of authority, of a wild dance called the Charleston, and of a wilder music which made its way from the bordellos of New Orleans to the night clubs of Chicago and New York. Somewhat to his surprise and not entirely to his liking, the Negro suddenly found himself called upon to uphold a new stereotype: he became a symbol of that freedom from restraint for which the white intellectual longed so ardently.

In the sophisticated art centers of Europe and America, interest in the Negro focused around the cult of the primitive. Insofar as it idealizes simpler cultures, primitivism is a romantic retreat from the complexities of modern life. Reflecting the writings of Sigmund Freud, it exalts instinct over intellect, Id over Super-Ego, and is thus a revolt against the Puritan spirit. For such an artistic movement the Negro had obvious uses: he represented the unspoiled child of nature, the noble savage—carefree, spontaneous, and sexually uninhibited. The discovery of primitive African sculpture and the ascendancy of jazz reinforced the development of this new stereotype.

Like all previous stereotypes, that of the primitive Negro exercised a coercive effect on the Negro novelist. As in the past, the degree of accommodation was astonishing; with a few exceptions the Negro intelligentsia accepted this exotic image of themselves. Perhaps they found in primitivism a useful support for the cultural dualism which they espoused during the Renaissance period. In any event, the younger Negro writers were quite carried away. Langston Hughes wrote ecstatically of jazz as "the tom-tom of revolt," while Countee Cullen discovered "elemental" religion in a Harlem revival meeting. Claude McKay glorified the instinctive Negro in all of his novels, and proudly proclaimed the "primitive sexuality" of the Negro race. Jean Toomer, perhaps the most authentic exponent of Renaissance primitivism, wrote in a sophisticated vein of "the zoo-restrictions and keeper-taboos" of modern civilization.

Whatever its excesses, primitivism provided the common ground for a fruitful period of cultural collaboration. Works like Eugene O'Neill's *The Emperor Jones* (1920) and *All God's Chillun Got Wings* (1924), Waldo Frank's *Holiday* (1923), Sherwood Anderson's *Dark Laughter* (1925), Dubose Heyward's

Porgy (1925) and *Mamba's Daughters* (1927), and Carl Van Vechten's *Nigger Heaven* (1926), acted as a spur to Negro writers and created a sympathetic audience for the serious treatment of Negro subjects. Personal association with white authors meant an end of cultural isolation and provincialism, and an immense gain in technical maturity for the Negro writer. In economic terms alone, considerable patronage and sponsorship occurred, while publishing forts and editorial desks capitulated in the face of a growing market for novels of Negro life. In the forefront of these developments, consciously promoting this cultural exchange, was a white *littérateur* named Carl Van Vechten.

Van Vechten's role in furthering the Negro Renaissance was unique. His literary salons provided a warm atmosphere in which artists and intellectuals of both races could break down their taboos against personal association. His one-man "know the Negro" campaign was eminently successful in overcoming prejudice and awkwardness among his white contemporaries. His efforts on behalf of individual Negro writers and artists were indefatigable, and were amply rewarded in later years when many of his former protégés entrusted their literary effects to his care.[8]

A more questionable contribution, at least in the eyes of some Negro critics, was Van Vechten's *Nigger Heaven,* a novel which appeared in 1926 and quickly ran through several editions. Emphasizing the bawdy and exotic aspects of Harlem life, and heavily influenced by primitivistic conceptions, *Nigger Heaven* shattered the complacency of the Negro intelligentsia by threatening to steal their literary thunder. For most of the Negro middle class the title of the novel was enough. Bitterly attacked in some quarters as a slander against the race, *Nigger Heaven* has been ably defended by James Weldon Johnson,[9] and requires no apologia here. It is sufficient to acknowledge its role in creating an audience for the exotic novel of Harlem life, and its influence on certain members of the so-called Harlem School.

The influence of white intellectuals on the Negro Renaissance

[8] Most of this material is presently housed in the James Weldon Johnson Collection of Negro Arts and Letters at Yale University.

[9] See *Along This Way,* pp. 381–82.

ought not to be overestimated. Some Negro critics have charged the New Negro Movement with white domination, but a sober appraisal leaves no doubt of its indigenous character. The New Negro Movement was not a "vogue" initiated by white "literary faddists,"[10] but a serious attempt by the Negro artist to interpret his own group life. There were excesses, to be sure, for which the whites must bear their share of responsibility. Insofar as the Negro novelist adopted a pose in response to the "primitive" effusions of the white intellectual, it produced a certain shallowness in his work, and a legitimate suspicion that his novels, like his cabarets, were designed to entertain the white folks. In the long run, however, the Negro novelist outgrew his primitive phase; meanwhile it helped him to discover unsuspected values in his own folk culture.

The Essence of the Negro Renaissance

There is a phase in the growth of a derivative literature which corresponds to the adolescent rebellion in an individual—a time when it must cut loose from the parent literature and establish an independent existence. This phase occurred in American literature during the flowering of New England; it was highlighted by Emerson's famous Phi Beta Kappa address, in which he protests, "We have listened too long to the courtly Muses of Europe." The Negro Renaissance represents a similar impulse toward cultural autonomy on the part of the American Negro.

The Negro Renaissance was essentially a period of self-discovery, marked by a sudden growth of interest in things Negro. The Renaissance thus reversed the assimilationist trend of the prewar period, with its conscious imitation of white norms and its deliberate suppression of "racial" elements. The motivation for this sudden reversal was not primarily literary but sociological. The Negro Renaissance, as E. Franklin Frazier has observed, reflects a pattern of adjustment common to all ethnic minorities in America: "At first the group attempts to lose itself in the majority group, disdaining its own characteristics. When this is not possible, there is a new valuation placed upon these very same

10 See Hugh Gloster, "The Van Vechten Vogue," *Negro Voices in American Fiction*, pp. 157–73.

characteristics, and they are glorified in the eyes of the group."[11]

The discovery of autonomous "racial" values by the Renaissance generation was prompted by a wave of Negro nationalism which swept over the colored community in the wake of World War I. As a direct result of his war experience the American Negro became bitterly disillusioned with the promises of the white majority. Discrimination in the armed forces, brutal attacks on returning veterans, and the bloody riots of the summer of 1919 convinced the Negro that his sacrifices for the nation would be acknowledged only by renewed oppression. With every avenue of assimilation apparently closed, a strongly nationalistic reflex occurred on all levels of Negro society.

Among the Negro masses this reflex took the form of recruitment to Marcus Garvey's "Back to Africa" movement. Garvey's program, in spite of its utterly Utopian content, deserves the closest scrutiny, for it stirred the imagination of the Negro masses as never before or since.[12] Garvey held that the Negro must renounce all hope of assistance or understanding from American whites, leave the country, and build a new civilization in Africa. His secessionist movement preyed upon a dissatisfaction so deep that it amounted to despair of ever achieving a full life in America. His immense popularity stands as a sober warning to all who would underestimate the nationalism of the Negro masses.

Meanwhile the logic of events forced the Negro middle class to adopt what might be called a tactical nationalism. As the fluid patterns of the post-Reconstruction period hardened into a rigid and unyielding color line, it became increasingly clear to the Talented Tenth that they could never hope to breach this caste barrier as a special class of "white" Negroes. The war years in particular convinced them that they could not succeed short of an all-out assault on Jim Crow. Abandoning their former strategy, they turned to the Negro masses for support in the coming struggle.

This *rapprochement* with the black masses could not be consummated without great psychological effort. The habit of em-

---

[11] "Racial Self-Expression," *Ebony and Topaz* (1927), pp. 119–21 (special supplement to *Opportunity*).

[12] The numerical strength of the Garvey movement has been estimated at one to four million.

phatically differentiating themselves from the "lower classes" was not easily relinquished by the Talented Tenth. Race leaders perceived at once that they would have to cultivate a mild nationalism in order to achieve a decent show of racial solidarity. One of their number, Jesse Fauset, has preserved this insight for posterity in her novel *Plum Bun:*

Those of us who have forged forward are not able as yet to go our separate ways apart from the unwashed, untutored herd. We must still look back and render service to our less fortunate, weaker brethren. And the first step toward making this a workable attitude is the acquisition not so much of a racial love as a racial pride. A pride that enables us to find our own beautiful and praiseworthy, an intense chauvinism that is content with its own types, that finds completeness within its own group, that loves its own as the French love their country.[13]

The nationalist reflex of the Negro intelligentsia consisted of a withdrawal of allegiance from the values of the dominant culture, and a search for alternative values within their own tradition. Unlike the nationalism of the masses or of the middle class, that of the intelligentsia was not based on racial considerations alone. It was motivated by factors larger than, but including, race—factors related to the universal revolt of the modern artist from bourgeois civilization. The Negro intellectual of the 1920's shared fully in the spiritual alienation of the Lost Generation. Like the white expatriate, he rejected the chromium plate of American culture. His alienation as an artist caused him in turn to alter his goals as a Negro. Instead of advocating blind assimilation into a hopelessly materialistic culture, he began to think in terms of preserving his racial individuality.

The search for a distinctive tradition led in many directions. The alienated Negro intellectual fell back predominantly on the folk culture, with its antecedents in slavery, its roots in the rural South, and its final flowering on the city pavements. Where the folk culture seemed inadequate to his needs, he turned to the cult of African origins, and to primitivism. At the same time, a new concept of the Negro's manifest destiny arose, to replace the old faith in race progress. Along with a sophisticated critique of (white) European civilization, the thesis was advanced that cer-

[13] *Plum Bun* (1928), p. 218.

tain enduring qualities in the racial temperament would redeem the decadent and enervated West. The sum and substance of these explorations was an unequivocal cultural dualism—a conscious attempt to endow Negro literature with a life of its own, apart from the dominant literary tradition.

The frank espousal of cultural dualism by the Negro intelligentsia was viewed with great alarm by the Negro middle class, whose long-range strategy called for eradicating cultural differences. Even at the peak of Renaissance nationalism the middle-class writer could never muster more than token enthusiasm for a distinctive Negro culture. The issues posed by cultural dualism therefore divided the novelists of the period into two schools. The Harlem School, pursuing the nationalist impulse to its logical conclusion, turned to the black masses for literary material. The Old Guard, still intent upon portraying "respectable" Negroes, remained prisoners of the Genteel Tradition.

VII. TOWARD A SECOND
RECONSTRUCTION, 1933–

"We want our freedom now: we want it all; we want it here!"
MARTIN LUTHER KING
*"I want very much to talk with you. About Africa. You see,
Mr. Asagai, I am looking for my* identity!"
LORRAINE HANSBERRY
A Raisin in the Sun

Anthony Lewis

The Supreme Court decision of May 17, 1954, *Brown v.
Board of Education*, appeared to many Americans to be an
unprecedented action by the Supreme Court of the United
States. The Court not only overturned the "separate but
equal" provision of the *Plessy v. Ferguson* decision, but also
accepted evidence of social scientists and psychologists which
showed that segregation, even if facilities were equal, had a
detrimental effect on Negro youngsters. The Court said in
part: "To separate them from others of similar age and qualifications solely because of their race generates a feeling of
inferiority as to their status in the community that may effect
their hearts and minds in a way unlikely ever to be done."

The decision, as Anthony Lewis shows, appears less startling when seen in historical perspective. Behind the decision
lay almost two decades of intensive effort by the NAACP and
its Legal Defense Committee to end segregation. The unsung
hero was Charles Hamilton Houston, Dean of the Law School
of Howard University, and later special counsel to the
NAACP. Under the guidance of Mordecai Johnson, the first
Negro president of Howard, Houston built the Law School
into a leading center for civil rights law, attracting to it a
number of outstanding teachers and students including Wil-

liam Hastie, James Narbit, and Thurgood Marshall, now Associate Justice of the U. S. Supreme Court. In 1938 Houston turned over his position as special counsel to one of his former students, Thurgood Marshall. Marshall and his staff, part of which included Robert L. Carter, Constance Baker, and Jack Greenberg, were to argue in the next decade hundreds of cases across the country in their attempt to end segregation and civil rights violations. In 1950, the NAACP won important victories in the *Sweatt* and *McLaurin* cases on the grounds that Negro educational facilities were inferior to those offered whites, and, therefore, violated the "separate but equal" yardstick. Southern states sensed the changing judicial temper, and in the early fifties they began a massive effort to physically upgrade the Negro school systems. It was their hope that if Negro schools were substantially improved, school integration would be thwarted.

It was at this point that the NAACP made a crucial decision. They would gamble on a new approach, arguing "that racial segregation, without regard to equality of facilities, damaged Negro children." [Kenneth B. Clark, *Prejudice and Your Child* (1963), Appendix 4.] In February, 1951, Robert L. Carter approached Kenneth B. Clark, Professor of Psychology at the City College of New York, and asked him to "inquire whether psychologists had any findings which were relevant to the effects of racial segregation on the personality development of Negro children." [The words are those of Dr. Clark, paraphrasing Mr. Carter; see Clark, *Prejudice and Your Child*, Appendix 4.] In the cases argued by the NAACP in 1951–52, they relied heavily on the studies done by Professor Clark and his wife, Mamie P. Clark, particularly the now famous "Effect of Prejudice and Discrimination on Personality Developments," which the Clarks wrote for the 1950 White House Conference on Children and Youth.

The lawyers for the NAACP also asked Dr. Clark and his colleagues, Stuart Cook and Isidor Chein, to summarize the latest social psychological data on the effects of discrimination on Negro children which the NAACP would then present to the Supreme Court as a special social science brief. Their summary, "The Effects of Segregation and the Consequences of Desegregation: A Social Science Statement" was reviewed and endorsed by thirty-two other social scientists in America, including such figures as Gordon W. Allport of Harvard, Robert K. Merton of Columbia, and Gardner Murphy of the Menninger Clinic in Kansas.

In its decision the Supreme Court took cognizance of the social-science evidence, and voiced the opinion that "segregation of white and colored children in public schools has a detrimental effect upon the colored children." It is still debated whether the social-science evidence provided the determining factor in the Court's decision, but it seems clear that it substantially aided the NAACP lawyers, and that their calculated risk had proven successful.

Anthony Lewis won his first Pulitzer Prize for his coverage of the Supreme Court for the New York *Times*. He was awarded his second Pulitzer Prize for *Gideon's Trumpet*. Mr. Lewis is presently London bureau chief of the *Times*.

THE SCHOOL SEGREGATION CASES

SOURCE: Anthony Lewis, "The School Segregation Cases," *Portrait of a Decade, The Second American Revolution* (New York, 1964), pp. 12–19, 21–28.

We boast of the freedom enjoyed by our people above all other peoples. But it is difficult to reconcile that boast with a state of the law which, practically, puts the brand of servitude and degradation upon a large class of our fellow citizens.
                               JUSTICE HARLAN, dissenting in
                               Plessy v. Ferguson, 1896.

The official southern myth sees the School Segregation decision of 1954 as a sudden and unjustified break with history, a misuse of the judicial power, a departure from the Constitution itself. The myth rests on several assumptions: that our constitutional history placed hallowed sanction on the custom of providing separate-but-equal facilities for Negroes; that the South, in faithful observance of that rule, created substantial equality for the Negro in schools and other public facilities; and that the Supreme Court relied on sociology, not law, in overruling the segregation doctrine.

But the assumptions are false, and the myth is no more than a myth. The separate-but-equal doctrine does not go back to some distant constitutional fount; it was read into the Constitution by judges at a fairly recent date, in what historians would call a political act. Through most of its history the doctrine drew only lip service from the South; there was separation but no equality whatsoever. The Supreme Court's abandonment of the rule was anything but sudden, the step being taken with the greatest care and only after many previous decisions had pointed in that direction. Nor was it unusual for the Court to overrule what it regarded as its own mistake, in the light of experience, and return to the true spirit of the Constitution.

History has to be explored at least briefly in any meaningful discussion of the 1954 decision. For it was no isolated event but the climax of a lengthy historical process—the rise and fall of racial segregation imposed by law. It is a rich history, combining strands of war and politics and economics and the special role of judges in this country.

Many of the forces that still move race relations in the United States were loosed in the Civil War. Not that the racial issue was the dominant cause of the war; most historians have concluded otherwise. But by the end of the war the Union was altogether committed to the abolition of slavery and the up-lifting of the Negro from his degraded status. The Thirteenth Amendment, prohibiting slavery, was adopted in 1865, immediately after the war. The southern states responded by enacting the Black Codes, which restricted the rights of the newly freed Negroes and effectively made them serfs. Some of these laws, for example, forbade Negroes to own land outside towns or do any work but farming without a special license. Congress, dominated by the so-called Radical Republicans, set about to overcome the southern schemes for keeping the Negro submerged. Some of the Radicals doubtless had motives of revenge or plunder, but others were moved by sincere egalitarianism. Whatever the motive, the post-Civil War Congresses assuredly did march under the banner of Negro rights.

In 1866 Congress passed the first Civil Rights Act. Specifically designed to wipe out the disabilities imposed by the Black Codes, it provided that Negroes should have the same right as white men "to make and enforce contracts, to sue, be parties and give evidence, to inherit, purchase, lease, sell, hold and convey real and personal property, . . . and shall be subject to like punishment, pains and penalties, and to none other, any law, statute, ordinance, regulation or custom to the contrary notwithstanding."

President Andrew Johnson vetoed the bill, saying that it attempted to legislate in areas where Congress had no power— matters of "internal policy and economy" that the Constitution reserved for the state governments. Congress passed the act over the President's veto, but doubts remained about its constitutionality. To provide a broad constitutional basis for federal action insuring individual rights in any aspect of life, Congress proposed the Fourteenth Amendment later in 1866. It was ratified in 1868.

The Fourteenth Amendment began by declaring that all persons born or naturalized in the United States were citizens. This overruled the Supreme Court's decision in 1857 in the Dred Scott case, holding that Negroes could not be citizens. Then came the spacious language that has been the subject of so many lawsuits and so many political debates:

"No State shall make or enforce any law which shall abridge the privileges or immunities of citizens of the United States; nor shall any State deprive any person of life, liberty, or property, without due process of law; nor deny to any person within its jurisdiction the equal protection of the laws."

The one thing tolerably clear, as a matter of history, is that the primary, original purpose of the amendment was to protect the newly freed slaves. A contemporaneous Supreme Court so held. In 1873 a butchers' monopoly granted by the Louisiana legislature was attacked as a violation of the Fourteenth Amendment. In the Slaughterhouse cases, decided in 1873, a five-to-four majority of the Supreme Court held that the amendment did not extend to such an economic restriction unrelated to race. Justice Samuel F. Miller, for the majority, said the amendment's "pervading purpose" had been to secure the rights of the Negro and protect him "from the oppressions of those who had formerly exercised unlimited dominion over him." The dissenters did not disagree about this purpose of the amendment but thought "the mischief to be remedied was not merely slavery and its incidents and consequences."

The classic exposition of the Fourteenth Amendment by

judges who had lived through its birth came in 1880. West Virginia law excluded Negroes from serving on juries. The Supreme Court, with only two dissents, held the law unconstitutional. Justice William Strong, for the majority, said the Fourteenth Amendment had been "designed to assure to the colored race the enjoyment of all the civil rights that under the law are enjoyed by white persons." Quoting the language of the amendment, he went on:

"What is this but declaring that the law in the States shall be the same for the black as for the white; that all persons, whether colored or white, shall stand equal before the laws of the States, and, in regard to the colored race, for whose protection the amendment was primarily designed, that no discrimination shall be made against them by law because of their color? . . . The very fact that colored people are singled out and expressly denied by a statute all right to participate in the administration of the law, as jurors, because of their color, though they are citizens, and may be in other respects fully qualified, is practically a brand upon them, affixed by law, an assertion of their inferiority, and a stimulant to that race prejudice which is an impediment to securing to individuals of the race that equal justice which the law aims to secure to all others."

But that was the end of an era. By that time northern politicians had lost interest in the cause of justice for the Negro. The Republican party was dedicated not to human egalitarianism but to laissez-faire economics and the growth of industrial empires that dominated the last part of the nineteenth century. The disputed Hayes-Tilden election of 1876 marked the political watershed. The award of the Presidency to Hayes was a bargain that historians have summarized as giving the Republicans control of the national government and economy while letting the whites of the South do as they would with the Negro.

The South began taking advantage of the bargain in the late 1880's. Jim Crow statutes segregating Negroes in railroads and streetcars were enacted by the southern legislatures. A poll tax was levied and restrictive qualifications adopted to keep Negroes from voting; the white primary completed the process of disenfranchisement. Ironically, poor whites and Populism hastened the subjugation of the Negro. Recent research has uncovered a body of upper-class southern opinion at the end of the century that wanted to absorb the Negro into society.

As the political situation changed, so did the Supreme Court's interpretation of the Fourteenth Amendment. The justices, like the country's business and political leaders, became more interested in economics than in race relations. The protection of economic rights that the Court had refused to see in the amendment in the Slaughterhouse cases was now found. The Court redefined the "persons" protected by the language of the amendment to include corporations and found various state regulations of business invalid.

As for the meaning of the Fourteenth Amendment to Negroes, that was redefined in *Plessy v. Ferguson* in 1896. Louisiana had enacted a Jim Crow transportation law in 1890. When Homer Adolph Plessy, who was one-eighth Negro, entered a railroad car reserved for whites, he was arrested. He challenged the constitutionality of the statute. The Supreme Court, by a vote of seven to one, found it valid.

"The underlying fallacy" of Plessy's argument, wrote Justice Henry B. Brown for the majority, was its "assumption that the enforced separation of the two races stamps the colored race with a badge of inferiority. If this be so, it is not by reason of anything found in the act but solely because the colored race chooses to put that construction upon it."

Justice Brown did not cite any legal authorities for that proposition. Nor could he, for it was nothing but a psychological or sociological thesis, doubtless widely accepted in his day but not universally even then. There is nothing wrong with the Supreme Court's interpreting language as broad as "equal protection of the laws" in light of the best contemporary understanding of human behavior. Indeed, there is nothing else the Court can do. But it is somewhat ironic to realize the purely sociological basis of *Plessy v. Ferguson,* a decision so admired by the same southerners who used "sociology" as a term of derision against the Court when it overruled Plessy in 1954.

The dissenter in *Plessy,* Justice John Marshall Harlan, did not accept the majority's premise. "The destinies of the two races in this country are indissolubly linked together," he wrote, "and the interests of both require that the common government of all shall not permit the seeds of race hate to be planted under the sanction of law. What can more certainly arouse race hate, what more certainly create and perpetuate a feeling of distrust between these races, than state enactments which in fact proceed on the ground that colored citizens are so inferior and degraded that they cannot be allowed to sit in public coaches occupied by white citizens? That, as all will admit, is the real meaning of such legislation as was enacted in Louisiana. . . . The thin disguise of 'equal' accommodations for passengers in railroad coaches will not mislead anyone, or atone for the wrong this day done."

Certainly the spirit of Justice Harlan's dissent was much closer to what the Court had said sixteen years earlier, in *Strauder v. West Virginia*, about laws affixing upon Negroes "a brand . . . , an assertion of their inferiority, and a stimulant to that race prejudice. . . ." The Supreme Court in 1896 had simply turned its back on the aspirations of that earlier day. It had introduced the new thesis that the Constitution's demand for equal protection of the laws could be met by legislation treating whites and Negroes as separate classes of people.

Plessy v. Ferguson was necessarily prophecy in good part. Justice Brown said: "A statute which implies merely a legal distinction between the white and colored races . . . has no tendency to destroy the legal equality of the two races." Justice Harlan, in contrast, predicted that the *Plessy* doctrine of separate but equal would "stimulate aggressions, more or less brutal and irritating, upon the admitted rights of colored citizens."

As a prophet Justice Harlan prevailed. *Plessy v. Ferguson* did help to stimulate the proliferation of segregation laws in every corner of life, from cradle to grave—literally, for Negroes were barred from both white hospitals and white cemeteries. Nor was there any real pretense at equality in the decades following the *Plessy* decision. In 1915 South Carolina spent $23.76 on the average white child in public school, $2.91 on the average Negro child. As late as 1931 six southeastern states (Alabama, Arkansas, Florida, Georgia, North and South Carolina) spent less than a third as much per Negro public-school pupil as per white child. Ten years later spending for the Negro had risen only to forty-four per cent of the white figure. At the time of the 1954 decision the South as a whole was spending $165 a year for the average white pupil, $115 for the Negro.

Other public facilities, such as hospitals, were just as inferior for the Negro as schools. Nor was this physical inequality the only result of the climate fostered by segregation. Negroes were purged wholesale from the voting rolls. They were rigorously excluded from almost all except menial jobs. Their very lives were at the hazard of terror and mass injustice; and by the turn of the century more than one hundred Negroes were being lynched every year.

Through the early decades of this century it became clearer and clearer to any detached observer that segregation was part of a deliberate pattern to degrade Negroes and deprive them of the rights they had been given after the Civil War. The Supreme Court was not blind to this change in the informed understanding of society. Slowly but with growing inevitability it eroded the foundations of *Plessy v. Ferguson.*

In 1917 the Court held unconstitutional a Louisville ordinance forbidding Negroes and whites to move into houses on city blocks occupied mostly by the other race. The opinion said: "It is urged that this proposed segregation will promote the public peace by preventing race conflicts. Desirable as this is, and important as is the preservation of the public peace, this aim cannot be accomplished by laws or ordinances which deny rights created or protected by the Federal Constitution."

In 1927 the Court held that state laws barring Negroes from voting in primary elections violated the Fourteenth Amendment. Justice Oliver Wendell Holmes said: "States may do a good deal of classifying that it is difficult to believe rational, but there are limits, and it is too clear for extended argument that color cannot be made the basis of a statutory classification affecting the right [to vote]."

Then, beginning in 1938, there came a series of cases in the field of higher education. The first held that Missouri could not meet the test of separate but equal by offering to pay the tuition of a Negro applicant for the Missouri Law School at an out-of-state school. Chief Justice Charles Evans Hughes said the state had to provide equal facilities itself. The decision drew a dissent —the last in any major Supreme Court decision on racial segregation. Justice James C. McReynolds wrote:

"For a long time Missouri has acted upon the view that the best interest of her people demands separation of whites and Negroes in schools. Under the opinion just announced, I presume she may abandon her law school and thereby disadvantage her white citizens without impairing petitioner's opportunities for legal instruction; or she may break down the settled practice concerning separate schools and thereby, as indicated by experience, damnify both races."

Professor Paul A. Freund of the Harvard Law School has made a perceptive comment on the McReynolds dissent. "It is of course dangerous," he said, "to accept a dissenting opinion as an objective guide to the meaning of a decision. But in this instance Mr. Justice McReynolds saw which way the winds of doctrine were blowing, and he did not like what he saw. What he saw was a steady, unmistakable progression on the part of the Court in applying the guarantee of equal protection of the laws to a series of issues: the right to serve on juries, the right to vote in primaries, the right to choose a place of residence without a legal color bar, the right to be considered for admission to a state professional school without discrimination because of race. The Court was recognizing the developing consciousness of the country that equal protection of the laws was to be given a full and not a qualified meaning."

In 1950 the Court held that a new law school set up by the State of Texas for Negroes did not provide equal protection of the laws because, as Chief Justice Fred M. Vinson put it,

"the University of Texas Law School [for whites] possesses to a far greater degree those qualities which are incapable of objective measurement but which make for greatness in a law school. Such qualities, to name but a few, include reputation of the faculty, experience of the administration, position and influence of the alumni, standing in the community, traditions and prestige. It is difficult to believe that one who had a free choice between these law schools would consider the question close."

When such intangible factors were placed in the scale, how could any separate school ever be termed "equal"? In the *New York Times* the day after the Texas Law School decision Arthur Krock said the separate-but-equal doctrine was now "a mass of tatters."

It was in that context that the Supreme Court came to the great issue of public-school segregation—the context of a legal history showing a developing momentum against the separate-but-equal rule. But it was not an easy next step. For here, unlike voting or juries or graduate education, there was involved the compulsory association of children day after day and year after year, and it was just such association that southern whites most feared.

Moreover, the Court was dealing with a practice that covered a large part of the country. Seventeen southern and border states and the District of Columbia, with forty per cent of the country's public-school enrollment, required segregation in the schools. (The states were Alabama, Arkansas, Delaware, Florida, Georgia, Kentucky, Louisiana, Maryland, Mississippi, Missouri, North Carolina, Oklahoma, South Carolina, Tennessee, Texas, Virginia and West Virginia.) There were some segregated schools also in three other states whose statutes permitted the practice: Arizona, Kansas and New Mexico.

The Supreme Court, fully aware of the delicacy of the issue, handled it with exceptional care and deliberation. It should also be pointed out, as Professor Freund reminds us, that the Court did not go out looking for the school-segregation issue. It was brought there by Negro individuals and civil-rights groups desperate to improve Negro educational opportunities. Originally in fact, in the 1930's, the N.A.A.C.P. had proposed lawsuits to attack only the inequality of Negro school facilities and teachers' salaries; but the victories in the graduate-school cases inevitably led to a direct assault on the institution of segregation.

The first school case came to the Supreme Court in 1951, from Clarendon County, South Carolina. A three-judge federal district court had upheld the constitutionality of segregated schools by a vote of two-to-one, but ordered prompt action to correct the admitted inequality of the Negro schools. (The dissenter, Judge J. Waties Waring of South Carolina, was virtually driven out of the state by ostracism for his courage.) On January 28, 1952, the Supreme Court acted to avoid an early constitutional decision in the case. It sent the matter back to the lower court to get its views on a report filed by the school board concerning the program to equalize facilities. Justices Hugo L. Black and William O. Douglas dissented, saying the report was "irrelevant to the constitutional questions" and urging that those questions be argued at once.

In the fall of 1952 the South Carolina case was back, along now with others from Kansas, Delaware, Virginia and the District of Columbia. Because the Kansas case was listed first, it gave its name to the historic litigation: *Oliver Brown et al. v. Board of Education of Topeka, Kansas.*

The cause of the Negro plaintiffs now received a most significant boost. The Federal Government, in the last days of the Truman Administration, filed a brief as a friend of the Court attacking the constitutionality of segregation. It was prepared by Philip Elman, a career Justice Department lawyer of unusual scholarship and imagination, who had been a law clerk to Justice Felix Frankfurter of the Supreme Court.

The brief argued that the separate-but-equal doctrine was, when laid down in 1896, "an unwarranted departure, based upon dubious assumptions of fact combined with a disregard of the basic purposes of the Fourteenth Amendment, from the fundamental principle that all Americans, whatever their race or color, stand equal and alike before the law." Nor did the age of the precedent "give it immunity from re-examination and rejection," the brief went on. The Court had overruled its own decisions dozens of times. In 1944 it had said: "When convinced of former error, this Court has never felt constrained to follow precedent. In constitutional questions, where correction depends upon amendment and not upon legislative action, this Court throughout its history has freely exercised its power to re-examine the basis of its constitutional decisions."

The conclusion was that the Court should, if it reached the ultimate question, overrule the separate-but-equal doctrine. "Compulsory racial segregation is itself an unconstitutional discrimination." But this was not the only significance of the brief. Perhaps even more vital was a suggestion advanced as to the procedure for carrying out any decision against school segregation. The government said the Court would not have to order all segregation ended everywhere at once. Instead, the Court should send the cases back to the district courts so that those local tribunals could work with local authorities to devise plans for desegregation. The brief said the Court might even want to issue no final decrees with its decision but order a further argument on the question of implementation. In short, the government put forward a moderate approach that recognized, as it said, "the practical difficulties" in ending a custom with such deep roots.

What made that suggestion so significant was that the practical difficulties were just what concerned some of the members of the Supreme Court. The deliberations of the justices have not been disclosed. But it is known that some deeply feared the reaction that might be aroused by an order for immediate, total desegregation. If that had been the only course open, they might well not have voted to declare segregation unconstitutional. They might, as one alternative, have said that the magnitude of the issue made it appropriate for resolution not by the Court but by Congress, which is empowered by Section Five of the Fourteenth Amendment to enforce its terms. In this regard the position of Justice Frankfurter is believed to have been critical. For while he was personally a dedicated opponent of racial discrimination, he had often expressed concern about the effect on the Court as an institution if it tried to go too far too fast in constitutional decisions.

The Court heard the cases and then, at the end of the term in June, 1953, put them over the reargument in the term beginning the following October. The Court posed a series of broad questions now, asking counsel to deal with them in their briefs and argument. First there was a historical inquiry: Had the men who framed and ratified the Fourteenth Amendment understood that it would prohibit segregation in public schools? Then, interestingly, the Court asked about the relative powers of Congress and the judiciary in interpreting the amendment: Had its framers contemplated that future Congresses might abolish segregation? Was it "within the judicial power, in light of [changed] conditions, to construe the amendment as abolishing such segregation of its own force?" The Court also took up the suggestion in the Justice Department's brief and asked whether, if it held segregation unconstitutional, it could properly allow "gradual adjustment" and whether the proper way to carry that out was to remand the cases to the district courts.

The Government answered those questions in a lengthy new brief the following November. There was political as well as legal import in the brief, for a new Administration had taken office since the first Government presentation. President Eisenhower himself took a hand in determining the position. In charge at the Justice Department were Attorney General Herbert Brownell, Jr., and Assistant Attorney General J. Lee Rankin. Mr. Elman again did the major part of the drafting.

The brief examined in great detail the legislative history of the Fourteenth Amendment as proposed by Congress and ratified in the state legislatures. While there were some references to school segregation, the Government said, they were "too few and scattered to justify any definite conclusion as to the existence of a general understanding . . . as to the effect which the amendment would have on school segregation." But "the primary and pervasive purpose of the Fourteenth Amendment" was "to secure for Negroes full and complete equality before the law and to abolish all legal distinctions based on race or color."

And the fact was that the amendment had been framed in the broadest, most general language. It did not mention schools, a point often raised by southerners as if it had some relevance. But neither did it mention voting or housing or juries or corporations, all areas in which the Supreme Court had repeatedly—and with general assent—held that the amendment barred discriminatory state action. And of course the amendment did not contain the words "separate but equal." The framers might have written a detailed code of what was and was not permissible in race relations. But they wisely had not; they had followed the example of those who wrote the original Constitution in using expansive phrases that would be given contemporary meaning by each generation. As Justice Holmes said of another constitutional provision: "When we are dealing with words that also are a constituent act, like the Constitution of the United States, we must realize that they have called into life a being the development of which could not have been forseen completely by the most gifted of its begetters. . . . The case before us must be considered in the light of our whole experience and not merely in that of what was said a hundred years ago."

The demand of the Fourteenth Amendment was for "equal protection of the laws." There was no talisman in the history of the amendment that defined those words for all times. The separate-but-equal doctrine had itself been a fresh interpretation, a departure in 1896 from the spirit of earlier decisions. It was in the great tradition of the Constitution, the Government said, to read the words now in light of conditions now. A provision such as the equal-protection clause expresses "broad principles of government, the essence of which is their vitality and adaptability to the progressive changes and needs of the nation."

Nor did the Government's brief see anything in the suggestion that Congress rather than the Court should deal with the issue. The Supreme Court had applied the Fourteenth Amendment in hundreds of cases without reference to Congress—in the racial field most recently in the graduate-school cases. What was posed now was "a question not of legislative policy but of constitutional power—and it is a question which under our system of government must ultimately be determined by this Court."

When the brief was filed, it puzzled some observers in one respect. It did not directly urge the Court, as the previous Administration's brief had, to hold racial segregation in the public schools unconstitutional. Instead the 188-page document was confined to what was termed "an objective nonadversary discussion" of the questions posed by the Court the previous June. The brief concluded, for instance, with a conditional statement: "If the Court holds that laws providing for separate schools are unconstitutional, it should remand the instant cases to the lower courts with directions to carry out the Court's decision as the particular circumstances permit."

Just how the brief emerged in this form is disputed. Some who participated in the drafting say that it contained a direct call for a finding of unconstitutionality when the draft was submitted to Attorney General Brownell, and that it was softened by either Brownell or President Eisenhower. But Brownell states that the draft "did not include any such conclusion . . . when it reached my desk and, so far as I know, never did include it. Mr. Rankin . . . and I agreed at all times that since the brief was filed in direct response to questions asked of the department by the Court, it should answer those questions solely." The truth is probably that Rankin and Brownell would personally have liked to include a direct statement on the unconstitutionality of segregation but did not believe President Eisenhower would approve it. The Attorney General did advise the President that Rankin, if asked by a member of the Supreme Court during the oral argument what the Justice Department's position was, would say that segregation should be struck down. The President evidently made no objection, and the question was asked and answered as planned. In any event the thrust of the new brief, for all its lack of a firm conclusion, was plainly against segregation. It told the justices that they had the power and the duty to give the Fourteenth Amendment a contemporary interpretation. And it said that the import of decisions up through the graduate-school cases was to make it "unreasonable and unconstitutional . . . for a state to establish or enforce legal distinctions based on race or color."

When the cases were reargued, in December, 1953, fate had made a most important change in the Supreme Court. Chief Justice Vinson had died during the summer, and President Eisenhower had appointed in his place the Governor of California, Earl Warren. Only when some future historians have access to the judicial papers of that period will it be possible to state accurately the impact of the new Chief Justice on the School cases. But enough has been said or hinted to make it clear that the change of membership on the Court made a real difference in the way *Brown v. Board of Education* looks to history. Chief Justice Vinson's inclination was to carry on the approach of the Texas Law School case, further tightening up the standard of equality within the separate-but-equal doctrine. In short, he thought it was not the time to challenge segregation per se; the most he was likely to have done was to say that the Negro pupils here did not have real equality. The indications were that he might have carried one or more of his colleagues with him, and there is also reason to believe that at least two members of the Court were inclined to put the whole issue to Congress. There was certainly no unanimity of desire on the Court to face up to the ultimate question—whether segregation itself denied the equal protection of the laws. In all likelihood, as things stood during the Vinson period, the Brown case would have produced a collection of differing opinions.

Unanimity was the most striking aspect of the actual decision when it came down on May 17, 1954. Chief Justice Warren delivered the opinion; there was no dissent, not even a separate concurrence.

The opinion found the history of the Fourteenth Amendment "inconclusive" in relation to school segregation, as the Justice Department had argued. In any case, history could not give an adequate answer because public education was just beginning in the 1860's. "We cannot turn the clock back to 1868 when the amendment was adopted, or even to 1896 when *Plessy v. Ferguson* was written. We must consider public education in the light of its full development and its present place in American life. . . . Today, education is perhaps the most important function of state and local governments. . . . In these days, it is doubtful that any child may reasonably be expected to succeed in life if he is denied the opportunity of an education. Such an opportunity, where the state has undertaken to provide it, is a right which must be made available to all on equal terms. We come then to the question presented: Does segregation of children in public schools solely on the basis of race, even though the physical facilities and other 'tangible' factors may be equal, deprive the children of the minority group of equal educational opportunities? We believe that it does."

The Chief Justice noted the Texas Law School case and its emphasis on intangible differences in schools. "Such considerations," he said, "apply with added force to children in grade and high schools. To separate them from others of similar age and qualifications solely because of their race generates a feeling of inferiority as to their status in the community that may affect their hearts and minds in a way unlikely ever to be undone. . . . Whatever may have been the extent of psychological knowledge at the time of *Plessy v. Ferguson*, this finding is amply supported by modern authority." Here the opinion, in a footnote that has been much criticized, cited the writings of various social scientists, including Myrdal.

"We conclude," the Chief Justice said, "that in the field of public education the doctrine of 'separate but equal' has no place. Separate educational facilities are inherently unequal."

The Court ordered still further argument the next term on problems of implementing its decision. Simon E. Sobeloff, who had now become Solicitor General, submitted a brief for the Federal Government suggesting—as the Justice Department had earlier indicated—that the cases be remanded to the trial courts to work out local problems. President Eisenhower personally inserted a passage in the brief. Where it said that the Court had outlawed "a social institution which has existed for a long time in many areas throughout the country," he added "—an institution, it may be noted, which during its existence not only has had the sanction of decisions of this Court but has been fervently supported by great numbers of people as justifiable on legal and moral grounds. The Court's holding in the present cases that segregation is a denial of constitutional rights involved an express recognition of the importance of psychological and emotional factors; the impact of segregation upon children, the Court found, can so affect their entire lives as to preclude their full enjoyment of constitutional rights. In similar fashion, psychological and emotional factors are involved—and must be met with understanding and good will—in the alterations that must now take place in order to bring about compliance with the Court's decision."

On May 31, 1955, after what was surely one of the most exhaustive considerations it had ever given to any issue, the Supreme Court finally disposed of *Brown v. Board of Education*. Chief Justice Warren's opinion on implementation generally followed the line suggested by the Justice Department but was even more gradualist in one respect: The Court did not, as proposed by the department, direct the lower courts to make local school authorities present desegregation plans within a specified time. It said only that the lower courts must require "a prompt and reasonable start toward full compliance." The process of desegregation, the opinion concluded, must proceed "with all deliberate speed"—a phrase first used in the Supreme Court in 1911, by Justice Holmes, and often invoked in recent years by Holmes's great admirer, Justice Frankfurter.

One item especially in Chief Justice Warren's 1954 opinion was seized upon by southerners as proof that the decision did not rest upon "law." This was the footnote citing social scientists as "modern authority" for the statement that segregation generated feelings of inferiority. But the footnote was at worst pretentious superfluity. It took no reference to social scientists to know that state-enforced separation of human beings on account of their race was a calculated device to exalt one group and debase another. Justice Brown had simply been proved wrong in his sociological hypothesis, in *Plessy v. Ferguson*, that there was nothing invidious about segregation unless the Negro chose "to put that construction upon it." After Adolf Hitler the world knew, and the Supreme Court would have been blind not to see, that it was invidious to separate out one group in society, whether Negroes or Jews or some other. Justice Harlan had been right when he said that segregation "puts the brand of servitude and degradation" on the Negro. The Court had moved toward his dissenting view in *Plessy v. Ferguson:* "Our Constitution is color-blind, and neither knows nor tolerates classes among citizens." Segregation was not the equal protection of the laws.

August Meier

Martin Luther King, Jr., came to national attention in 1955 when the twenty-six year old clergyman emerged as leader of the Montgomery bus boycott, the first massive and sustained Negro protest in the South following the Supreme Court's decision of May 1954, overturning the *Plessy v. Ferguson* ruling. The eventual success of King's protest movement obscured the fact that the Negro American had been actively engaged in protesting segregation and job discrimination for some time. Many of the tactics which were used by King, CORE, and SNCC in the South were derived from the experiences of the Negroes in the North at a much earlier date.

The labor unions of the thirties, in particular the CIO locals, perfected the sit-ins. Adam Clayton Powell, who rose to prominence in the middle to late thirties, led a successful campaign in New York to open up jobs and end discrimination, using the boycott and the power of the Negro community to win concessions from the public utilities, the City of New York, and private businessmen. The use of the churches by King and Ralph Abernathy in Montgomery had been already developed by Powell. He showed how the pulpit and the church could cement the community using as his base the loyalty that Negroes placed in their churches. A. Philip Randolph, who won his long fight in the late thirties to organize the sleeping-car porters and break the company union, won an even greater victory in 1941 by threatening a March on Washington by Negro and liberal forces. At that time he forced President Roosevelt to issue his now famous executive order outlawing job discrimination in defense industries.

While taking his theological degree at Crozier Theological Seminary, King received first-hand accounts of Gandhi's campaign of civil disobedience and philosophy of passive resistance from President Morecai Johnson of Howard University who had just come back from a trip to India. From the theologian and philosopher Howard Thurman, King was encouraged to commit himself to the idea of the Christian Witness.

In addition, King and his allies could look behind them to the court decisions restoring civil rights to the Negroes, to the armed forces integrating the services, and across the seas, to the growing nationalistic movements by the colored peoples of Asia and Africa. So when the Montgomery movement began in 1955, the Negroes had both the moral support and practical tools to wage their struggle against Jim Crow. In the end, however, it was to prove the grit of the Montgomery Negroes which saw them through to victory.

King and his associates went on to form the Southern Christian Leadership Conference in 1957. They aided in the organization of the Student Non-Violent Coordinating Committee in 1960, and lead the Birmingham protests of 1963 which more than any other event (with the possible exception of the murder of President Kennedy, and the subsequent wave of national guilt for having opposed Kennedy's civil rights program) led to the major civil rights legislation of 1964 and 1965.

King's non-violent philosophy won for him the Nobel Peace Prize in 1965, yet he still faced difficulties. He expanded his interests to the Northern ghettos with less immediate success. The acceleration of American involvement in the Vietnam war had turned King's attentions to the problems of international war and peace, with King advocating an American disengagement. King argued that not only had the American action unloosened new and greater violence, but the war was draining federal funds and interest from the Negro community, while Negroes were being called on to serve in large numbers in the war.

With all of Dr. King's success, he found himself losing ground in the Negro community. He was hard pressed to hold to his non-violent philosophy when Negroes had discovered that whites would listen much quicker to Negro grievances after a violent, rather than non-violent confrontation. Evidently, many Negroes are concluding, riots and engagements with the police are the only things that will make the white people listen. Whether Dr. King could have kept to his Christian non-violence principles and still have maintained his position of leadership with the advent of the new phase of the civil rights movement is left unresolved by his assassination.

On the other hand, as Professor Meier reminds us in his incisive critique of Dr. King's program and methods, "It is . . . no easier . . . than it has been in past years to predict the course of the Negro protest movement. . . ."

There is no better introduction to Dr. King's ideas and struggles than three volumes of his own work: *Stride Toward Freedom, Why We Can't Wait,* and *Strength to Love.* Lawrence D. Reddick has written a sympathetic biography based on King's career to 1958, *Crusader Without Violence: Martin Luther King, Jr.* Although Dr. Meier's article which follows was written in 1965, it stands up remarkably well, although it should be regarded, as all contemporary judgments, as tentative.

August Meier is Professor of History at Kent State University and is the author of *Negro Thought in America, 1880–1915,* co-editor of *Negro Protest Thought in the Twentieth Century,* and co-author of *From Plantation to Ghetto: History of the American Negro.*

ON THE ROLE OF MARTIN LUTHER KING

SOURCE: August Meier, "On the Role of Martin Luther King," *New Politics,* IV (Winter, 1965), pp. 52–59.

The phenomenon that is Martin Luther King consists of a number of striking paradoxes. The Nobel Prize winner is accepted by the outside world as *the* leader of the nonviolent direct action movement, but he is criticized by many activists within the movement. He is criticized for what appears, at times, as indecisiveness, and more often denounced for a tendency to accept compromise. Yet, in the eyes of most Americans, both black and white, he remains the symbol of militant direct action. So potent is this symbol of King as direct actionist, that a new myth is arising about his historic role. The real credit for developing and projecting the techniques and philosophy of nonviolent direct action in the civil rights arena must be given to the Congress of Racial Equality which was founded in 1942, more than a dozen years before the Montgomery bus boycott projected King into international fame. And the idea of mass action by Negroes themselves to secure redress of their grievances must, in large part, be ascribed to the vision of A. Philip Randolph, architect of the March on Washington Movement during World War II. Yet, as we were told in Montgomery on March 25, 1965, King and his followers now assert, apparently without serious contradiction, that a new type of civil rights strategy was born at Montgomery in 1955 under King's auspices.

In a movement in which respect is accorded in direct proportion to the number of times one has been arrested, King appears to keep the number of times he goes to jail to a minimum. In a movement in which successful leaders are those who share in the hardships of their followers, in the risks they take, in the beatings they receive, in the length of time they spend in jail, King tends to leave prison for other important engagements, rather than remaining there and suffering with his followers. In a movement in which leadership ordinarily devolves upon persons who mix democratically with their followers, King remains isolated and aloof. In a movement which prides itself on militancy and "no compromise" with racial discrimination or with the white "power structure," King maintains close relationships with, and appears to be influenced by, Democratic presidents and their emissaries, seems amenable to compromises considered by some half a load or less, and often appears willing to postpone or avoid a direct confrontation in the streets.

King's career has been characterized by failures that, in the larger sense, must be accounted triumphs. The buses in Montgomery were desegregated only after lengthy judicial proceedings conducted by the NAACP Legal Defense Fund secured a favorable decision from the U. S. Supreme Court. Nevertheless, the events in Montgomery were a triumph for direct action, and gave this tactic a popularity unknown when identified solely with CORE. King's subsequent major campaigns—in Albany, Georgia; in Danville, Virginia; in Birmingham, Alabama; and in St. Augustine, Florida—ended as failures or with only token accomplishments in those cities. But each of them, chiefly because of his presence, dramatically focused national and international attention on the plight of the Southern Negro, thereby facilitating overall progress. In Birmingham, in particular, demonstrations which fell short of their local goals were directly responsible for a major Federal Civil Rights Act. Essentially, this pattern of local failure and national victory was recently enacted at Selma, Alabama.

King is ideologically committed to disobeying unjust laws and court orders, in the Gandhian tradition, but generally he follows a policy of not disobeying Federal Court orders. In his recent Montgomery speech, he expressed a crude, neo-Marxist interpretation of history romanticizing the Populist movement as a genuine union of black and white common people, ascribing race prejudice to capitalists playing white workers against black. Yet, in practice, he is amenable to compromise with the white bourgeois political and economic Establishment. More important, King enunciates a superficial and eclectic philosophy and by virtue of it he has profoundly awakened the moral conscience of America.

In short, King can be described as a "Conservative Militant."

In this combination of militancy with conservatism and caution, of righteousness with respectability, lies the secret of King's enormous success.

Certain important civil rights leaders have dismissed King's position as the product of publicity generated by the mass communications media. But this can be said of the successes of the civil rights nonviolent action movement generally. Without publicity it is hard to conceive that much progress would have been made. In fact, contrary to the official nonviolent direct action philosophy, demonstrations have secured their results not by changing the hearts of the oppressors through a display of nonviolent love, but through the national and international pressures generated by the publicity arising from mass arrests and incidents of violence. And no one has employed this strategy of securing publicity through mass arrests and precipitating violence from white hoodlums and law enforcement officers more than King himself. King abhors violence; as at Selma, for example, he constantly retreats from situations that might result in the deaths of his followers. But he is precisely most successful when, contrary to his deepest wishes, his demonstrations precipitate violence from Southern whites against Negro and white demonstrators. We need only cite Birmingham and Selma to illustrate this point.

Publicity alone does not explain the durability of King's image, or why he remains for the rank and file of whites and blacks alike, the symbol of the direct action movement, the nearest thing to a charismatic leader that the civil rights movement has ever had. At the heart of King's continuing influence and popularity are two facts. First, better than anyone else, he articulates the aspirations of Negroes who respond to the cadence of his addresses, his religious phraseology and manner of speaking, and the vision of his dream for them and for America. King has intuitively adopted the style of the old fashioned Negro Baptist preacher and transformed it into a new art form; he has, indeed, restored oratory to its place among the arts. Second, he communicates Negro aspirations to white America more effectively than anyone else. His religious terminology and manipulation of the Christian symbols of love and nonresistance are partly responsible for his appeal among whites. To talk in terms of Christianity, love, nonviolence is reassuring to the mentality of white America. At the same time, the very superficialities of his philosophy—that rich and eclectic amalgam of Jesus, Hegel, Gandhi and others as outlined in his *Stride Toward Freedom*—makes him appear intellectually profound to the superficially educated middle class white American. Actually, if he were a truly profound religious thinker, like Tillich or Niebuhr, his influence would of necessity be limited to a select audience. But by uttering moral clichés, the Christian pieties, in a magnificent display of oratory, King becomes enormously effective.

If his success with Negroes is largely due to the style of his utterance, his success with whites is a much more complicated matter. For one thing, he unerringly knows how to exploit to maximum effectiveness their growing feeling of guilt. King, of course, is not unique in attaining fame and popularity among whites through playing upon their guilt feelings. James Baldwin is the most conspicuous example of a man who has achieved success with this formula. The incredible fascination which the Black Muslims have for white people, and the posthumous near-sanctification of Malcolm X by many naive whites (in addition to many Negroes whose motivations are, of course, very different), must in large part be attributed to the same source. But King goes beyond this. With intuitive, but extraordinary skill, he not only castigates whites for their sins but, in contrast to angry young writers like Baldwin, he explicitly states his belief in their salvation. Not only will direct action bring fulfillment of the "American Dream" to Negroes but the Negroes' use of direct action will help whites to live up to their Christian and democratic values; it will purify, cleanse and heal the sickness in white society. Whites will benefit as well as Negroes. He has faith that the white man will redeem himself. Negroes must not hate whites, but love them. In this manner, King first arouses the guilt feelings of whites, and then relieves them—though always leaving the lingering feeling in his white listeners that they should support his nonviolent crusade. Like a Greek tragedy, King's performance provides an extraordinary catharsis for the white listener.

King thus gives white men the feeling that he is their good friend, that he poses no threat to them. It is interesting to note that this was the same feeling white men received from Booker T. Washington, the noted early 20th Century accommodator. Both men stressed their faith in the white man; both expressed the belief that the white man could be brought to accord Negroes their rights. Both stressed the importance of whites recognizing the rights of Negroes for the moral health and well-being of white society. Like King, Washington had an extraordinary following among whites. Like King, Washington symbolized for most whites the whole program of Negro advancement. While there are important similarities in the functioning of both men vis-à-vis the community, needless to say, in most respects, their philosophies are in disagreement.

It is not surprising, therefore, to find that King is the recipient of contributions from organizations and individuals who fail to eradicate evidence of prejudice in their own backyards. For example, certain liberal trade union leaders who are philosophically committed to full racial equality, who feel the need to identify their organizations with the cause of militant civil rights, although they are unable to defeat racist elements in their unions, contribute hundreds of thousands of dollars to King's Southern Christian Leadership Conference (SCLC). One might attribute this phenomenon to the fact that SCLC works in the South rather than the North, but this is true also for SNCC which does not benefit similarly from union treasuries. And the fact is that ever since the college students started their sit-ins in 1960, it is SNCC which has been the real spearhead of direct action in most of the South, and has performed the lion's share of work in local communities, while SCLC has received most of the publicity and most of the money. However, while King provides a verbal catharsis for whites, leaving them feeling purified and comfortable, SNCC's uncompromising militancy makes whites feel less comfortable and less beneficent.

(The above is not to suggest that SNCC and SCLC are responsible for all, or nearly all, the direct action in the South. The NAACP has actively engaged in direct action, especially in Savannah under the leadership of W. W. Law, in South Carolina under I. DeQuincy Newman, and in Clarksdale, Mississippi, under Aaron Henry. The work of CORE—including most of the direct action in Louisiana, much of the nonviolent work in Florida and Mississippi, the famous Freedom Ride of 1961—has been most important. In addition, one should note the work of SCLC affiliates, such as those in Lynchburg, Virginia, led by Reverend Virgil Wood; in Birmingham led by Reverend Fred Shuttlesworth, and in Savannah, by Hosea Williams.

(There are other reasons for SNCC's lesser popularity with whites than King's. These are connected with the great changes that have occurred in SNCC since it was founded in 1960, changes reflected in the half-jocular epigram circulating in SNCC circles that the student Nonviolent Coordinating Com-

mittee has now become the "Non-Student Violent Non-Coordi-
nating Committee." The point is, however, that even when
SNCC thrilled the nation in 1960–1961 with the student sit-ins
that swept the South, it did not enjoy the popularity and
financial support accorded to King.)

King's very tendencies toward compromise and caution, his
willingness to negotiate and bargain with White House emissaries, his hesitancy to risk the precipitation of mass violence upon
demonstrators, further endear him to whites. He appears to
them a "responsible" and "moderate" man. To militant activists,
King's failure to march past the State Police on that famous
Tuesday morning outside Selma indicated either a lack of
courage, or a desire to advance himself by currying Presidential
favor. But King's shrinking from a possible bloodbath, his acces-
sion to the entreaties of the political Establishment, his acceptance of face-saving compromise in this, as in other instances,
are fundamental to the particular role he is playing, and
essential for achieving and sustaining his image as a leader of
heroic moral stature in the eyes of white men. His caution and
compromise keep open the channels of communication between
the activists and the majority of the white community. In brief:
King makes the nonviolent direct action movement respectable.

Of course, many, if not most, activists reject the notion that
the movement should be made respectable. Yet, American history
shows that for any reform movement to succeed, it must attain
respectability. It must attract moderates, even conservatives, to
its ranks. The March on Washington made direct action respectable; Selma made it fashionable. More than any other force, it
is Martin Luther King who impressed the civil rights revolution
on the American conscience and is attracting that great middle
body of American public opinion to its support. It is this
revolution of conscience that will undoubtedly lead fairly soon
to the elimination of all violations of Negroes' constitutional
rights, thereby creating the conditions for the economic and
social changes that are necessary if we are to achieve full racial
equality. This is not to deny the dangers to the civil rights
movement in becoming respectable. Respectability, for example,
encourages the attempts of political machines to capture civil
rights organizations. Respectability can also become an end in

itself, thereby dulling the cutting edge of its protest activities. Indeed, the history of the labor movement reveals how attaining respectability can produce loss of original purpose and character. These perils, however, do not contradict the importance of achieving respectability—even a degree of modishness—if racial equality is ever to be realized.

There is another side to the picture: King would be neither respected nor respectable if there were not more militant activists on his left, engaged in more radical forms of direct action. Without CORE and, especially, SNCC, King would appear "radical" and "irresponsible" rather than "moderate" and "respectable."

King occupies a position of strategic importance as the "vital center" within the civil rights movement. Though he has lieutenants who are far more militant and "radical" than he is, SCLC acts, in effect, as the most cautious, deliberate and "conservative" of the direct action groups because of King's leadership. This permits King and the SCLC to function—almost certainly unintentionally—not only as an organ of communication with the Establishment and majority white public opinion, but as something of a bridge between the activist and more traditionalist or "conservative" civil rights groups, as well. For example, it appears unlikely that the Urban League and NAACP, which supplied most of the funds, would have participated in the 1963 March on Washington if King had not done so. Because King agreed to go along with SNCC and CORE, the NAACP found it mandatory to join if it was to maintain its image as a protest organization. King's identification with the March was also essential for securing the support of large numbers of white clergymen and their moderate followers. The March was the brainchild of the civil rights movement's ablest strategist and tactician, Bayard Rustin, and the call was issued by A. Philip Randolph. But it would have been a minor episode in the history of the civil rights movement without King's support.

Yet curiously enough, despite his charisma and international reputation, King thus far has been more a symbol than a power in the civil rights movement. Indeed his strength in the movement has derived less from an organizational base than from his symbolic role. Seven or eight years ago, one might have expected King to achieve an organizationally dominant position in the civil rights movement, at least in its direct action wing. The fact is that in the period after the Montgomery bus boycott, King developed no program and, it is generally agreed, revealed himself as an ineffective administrator who failed to capitalize upon his popularity among Negroes. In 1957, he founded SCLC to coordinate the work of direct action groups that had sprung up in Southern cities. Composed of autonomous units, usually led by Baptist ministers, SCLC does not appear to have developed an overall sense of direction or a program of real breadth and scope. Although the leaders of SCLC affiliates became the race leaders in their communities—displacing the established local conservative leadership of teachers, old-line ministers, businessmen—it is hard for an observer (who admittedly has not been close to SCLC) to perceive exactly what SCLC did before the 1960's except to advance the image and personality of King. King appeared not to direct but to float with the tide of militant direct action. For example, King did not supply the initiative for the bus boycott in Montgomery, but was pushed into the leadership by others, as he himself records in *Stride Toward Freedom*. Similarly, in the late Fifties and early Sixties, he appeared to let events shape his course. In the last two years, this has changed, but until the Birmingham demonstrations of 1963, King epitomized conservative militancy.

SCLC under King's leadership called the Raleigh Conference of April 1960 which gave birth to SNCC. Incredibly, within a year, the SNCC youth had lost their faith in the man they now satirically call "De Lawd," and had struck out on their own independent path. By that time, the Spring of 1961, King's power in the Southern direct action movement had been further curtailed by CORE's stunning Freedom Ride to Alabama and Mississippi.

The limited extent of King's actual power in the civil rights movement was illustrated by the efforts made to invest King with the qualities of a Messiah during the recent ceremonies at the state capital in Montgomery. Reverend Abernathy's constant iteration of the theme that King is "our Leader," the Moses of the race, chosen by God, and King's claim that he originated the nonviolent direct action movement at Montgomery a decade ago, are all assertions that would have been superfluous if King's power in the movement was very substantial.

It is, of course, no easier today than it has been in the past few years to predict the course of the Negro protest movement, and it is always possible that the current state of affairs may change quite abruptly. It is conceivable that the ambitious program that SCLC is now projecting—both in Southern voter registration and in Northern urban direct action programs—may give it a position of commanding importance in civil rights. As a result of the recent demonstrations in Selma and Montgomery, King's prestige is now higher than ever. At the same time, the nature of CORE and NAACP direct action activities at the moment has created a programmatic vacuum which SCLC may be able to exploit. Given this convergence of circumstances, SCLC leaders may be able to establish an organizational base upon which to build a power commensurate with the symbolic position of their president.

It is indeed fortunate that King has not obtained a predominance of power in the movement commensurate with his prestige. For today, as in the past, a diversity of approaches is necessary. Needed in the movement are those who view the struggle chiefly as a conflict situation, in which the power of demonstrations, the power of Negroes, will force recognition of the race's humanity and citizenship rights, and the achievement of equality. Equally needed are those who see the movement's strategy to be chiefly one of capitalizing on the basic consensus of values in American society by awakening the conscience of the white man to the contradiction between his professions and the facts of discrimination. And just as necessary to the movement as both of these are those who operate skillfully, recognizing and yet exploiting the deeply held American belief that compromise among competing interest groups is the best *modus operandi* in public life.

King is unique in that he maintains a delicate balance among all three of these basic strategy assumptions. The traditional approaches of the Urban League (conciliation of the white businessmen) and of the NAACP (most pre-eminently appeals to the courts and appeals to the sense of fair play in the American public), basically attempted to exploit the consensus in American values. It would of course be a gross oversimplification to say that the Urban League and NAACP strategies are based simply on attempting to capitalize on the consensus of values, while SNCC and CORE act simply as if the situation were purely a conflict situation. Implicit in the actions of all civil rights organizations are both sets of assumptions—even where people are not conscious of the theoretical assumptions under which, in effect, they operate. The NAACP especially encompasses a broad spectrum of strategies and types of activities, ranging from time-tested court procedures to militant direct action. Sophisticated CORE activists know very well when a judicious compromise is necessary or valuable. But I hold that King is in the middle, acting in effect as if he were basing his strategy upon all three assumptions described above. He maintains a delicate balance between a purely moral appeal and a militant display of power. He talks of the power of the bodies of Negro demonstrators in the streets, but unlike CORE and SNCC activists, he accepts compromises at times that consist of token improvements, and calls them impressive victories. More than any of the other groups, King and SCLC can, up to this point at least, be described as exploiting all three tactical assumptions to an approximately equal degree. King's continued success, I suspect, will depend to a considerable degree upon the difficult feat of maintaining his position at the "vital center" of the civil rights movement.

Viewed from another angle King's failure to achieve a position of power on a level with his prestige is fortunate because rivalries between personalities and organizations remain an essential ingredient of the dynamics of the movement and a precondition for its success as each current tries to outdo the others in effectiveness and in maintaining a good public image. Without this competitive stimulus, the civil rights revolution would slow down.

I have already noted that one of King's functions is to serve as a bridge between the militant and conservative wings of the movement. In addition, by gathering support for SCLC, he generates wider support for CORE and SNCC, as well. The most striking example is the recent series of demonstrations in Selma where SNCC had been operating for nearly two years with

only moderate amounts of publicity before King chose that city
as his own target. As usual, it was King's presence that focused
world attention on Selma. In the course of subsequent events,
the rift between King and SNCC assumed the proportions of a
serious conflict. Yet people who otherwise would have been
hesitant to support SNCC's efforts, even people who had become
disillusioned with certain aspects of SNCC's policies during the
Mississippi Summer Project of 1964, were drawn to demonstrate
in Selma and Montgomery. Moreover, although King received
the major share of credit for the demonstrations, it seems likely
that in the controversy between King and SNCC, the latter
emerged with more power and influence in the civil rights movement than ever before. It is now possible that the Administration will, in the future, regard SNCC as more of a force to be
reckoned with than it has heretofore.

Major dailies like the *New York Times* and the *Washington
Post*, basically sympathetic to civil rights and racial equality,
though more gradualist than the activist organizations, have
congratulated the nation upon its good fortune in having a
"responsible and moderate" leader like King at the head of the
nonviolent action movement (though they overestimate his
power and underestimate the symbolic nature of his role). It
would be more appropriate to congratulate the civil rights movement for *its* good fortune in having as its symbolic leader a man
like King. The fact that he has more prestige than power; the
fact that he not only criticizes whites but explicitly believes in
their redemption; his ability to arouse creative tension combined
with his inclination to shrink from carrying demonstrations to
the point where major bloodshed might result; the intellectual
simplicity of his philosophy; his tendency to compromise and
exert caution, even his seeming indecisiveness on some occasions;
the sparing use he makes of going to or staying in jail himself;
his friendship with the man in the White House—all are essential
to the role he plays, and invaluable for the success of the movement. It is well, of course, that not all civil rights leaders are
cut of the same cloth—that King is unique among them. Like
Randolph, who functions very differently, King is really an
institution. His most important function, I believe, is that of

effectively communicating Negro aspirations to white people, of making nonviolent direct action respectable in the eyes of the white majority. In addition, he functions within the movement by occupying a vital center position between its "conservative" and "radical" wings, by symbolizing direct action and attracting people to participate in it without dominating either the civil rights movement or its activist wing. Viewed in this context, traits that many activists criticize in King actually function not as sources of weakness, but as the foundations of his strength.

C. Eric Lincoln

For white Americans the Black Muslims appear to be very much of an enigma, some strange blend of religious fanaticism and black nationalism. And although the adherence to the strict codes of the Muslim religion finds few sympathizers among Negroes, there is an immediate response to the Muslim indictment of white society. In a Muslim morality play entitled *Orgena* (*a Negro* spelled backward) a prosecutor presents the following charge against the white man: "I charge the white man with being the greatest robber on earth. I charge the white man with being the greatest deceiver on earth. I charge the white man with being the greatest troublemaker on earth. So, therefore, ladies and gentlemen of the jury, I ask you, bring back a verdict of guilty as charged!" The all-Muslim stage jury finds the white man guilty, and he is sentenced to death as the audience cheers. It is a verdict with which many non-Muslim Negroes would agree.

The Muslims were not the first Negroes who espoused colonization or immigration from an America they felt offered them no future. Escaped slaves chose British rule and passage to Sierra Leone rather than return to a newly independent United States. Twelve thousand others sailed for Africa under the patronage of the American Colonization Society. A number of prominent Negro leaders who had at first opposed African colonization or repatriation eventually came out for emigration. These included Paul Cuffee, a hero of the revolution, John B. Russworm, co-editor of the first Negro-

American newspaper, Martin Delany, Harvard-educated physician and colleague of Frederick Douglass, Bishop Alexander Crummel, Cambridge University-educated and a leading Episcopalian clergyman, and Bishop Henry McNeal Turner, militant leader of black Reconstruction in Georgia. The Garveyites resurrected this idea, and when the Muslims first made their appearance in 1930, the belief in emigration or colonization in a separate land was still held by some. The Muslims, while vague on resettlement in Africa, have insisted that their ultimate aim is a complete separatism from white America, possibly somewhere in the southwestern United States. A similar proposal was adopted by the Communists in 1928 and only officially abandoned in the late fifties.

In place of the American dream, which Negroes have seldom realized, the Muslims counter with a number of ideas of their own: black supremacy as an answer to Negro inferiority, an Afro-Asian past as against American slavery, a brotherhood with other "colored" peoples as opposed to Europeans, and a religion of Islam in contrast to the white man's Christianity. On the other hand, the Muslims foster a respect for those techniques which have enabled the white man to succeed. "Observe the operations of the white man," they tell their members. "He is successful" (C. Eric Lincoln, *The Black Muslims in America*). Muslims believe that one day they will beat the white man at his own game. To this end they have adopted a code of behavior that follows the Puritan ethic of capitalism: discipline, thrift, hard work, upright behavior, businesslike methods, respect for authority. Seen in a larger context, Muslims practice all the virtues which Negroes are reputed to lack.

But while the Muslims would like their members to imitate the businesslike methods of the whites, they aim to have the Negro reject everything having to do with his American experience: his church and religion, his music and "soul," his nationality and outlook. The Muslims also show an ambiguity about their African past. Elijah Muhammad has sought an Asian ancestry and a Near Eastern religion to represent the true spirituality and identity of the Africans. However, Islam in Africa proved to be no respecter of indigenous African culture or institutions. Islam displayed the same arrogance as

Christianity in treating African society, and the Moslem Arabs vied with the Europeans for the reputation of being the most brutal slavetraders. Even the Garveyites, for all their fanciful titles and "make believe" history, did not want to return to an Islamized Africa. In their attempt to escape the stigma that whites have attached to Africa, the Muslims have created new myths that will only complicate the task of the Negro in coming to terms with his own identity.

The ideology of the Black Muslims have been examined by E. U. Essien-Udom in *Black Nationalism* (1962), Morroe Berger in "The Black Muslims," *Horizon* (January, 1964), and C. Eric Lincoln in *The Black Muslims in America* (1961). Dr. Lincoln first became acquainted with the Muslims in 1956 when teaching at Clark College, Atlanta, and subsequently became close friends with many of the Muslim leaders, particularly Malcolm X.

Dr. Lincoln now holds a chair in social philosophy at the Union Theological Seminary, New York. He is the author of *My Face Is Black*, and a contributor to the *American Negro Reference Book*.

THE BLACK MUSLIMS AS
A PROTEST MOVEMENT

SOURCE: C. Eric Lincoln, "The Black Muslims as a Protest Movement," Arnold M. Rose, editor, *Assuring Freedom to the Free* (Detroit: Wayne State University Press, 1964), pp. 226–40.

. . . The Black Muslim movement had its beginning in the black ghetto of Detroit. The time was 1930. It was the first year of the Great Depression—a time of hunger, confusion, disillusionment, despair, and discontent. It was a period of widespread fear and anxiety. Between 1900 and 1930 two-and-a-quarter-million Negroes left the farms and plantations of the South. Most of them emigrated to selected urban areas of the North—New York, Philadelphia, Chicago, and Detroit being among the most popular destinations. The Negro population of Detroit, for example, increased 611 per cent during the ten years of 1910 to 1920. During the same period, the total Negro population in the North increased from a mere 75,000 to 300,000, an increase of 400 per cent.

Floods, crop failures, boll weevils, and the revival of the Ku Klux Klan all served to hasten the Negro's departure from the South. One hundred Negroes were lynched during the first year of the twentieth century. By the outbreak of the First World War in 1914, the number stood at 1,100. When the war was over, the practice was resumed—28 Negroes being burned alive between 1918 and 1921. Scores of others were hanged, dragged behind automobiles, shot, drowned, or hacked to death.

The Negroes who left the South were temporarily welcomed in the North, although the congenialities of the North have always been of a most impersonal sort. Many industries sent agents into the South to lure the Negroes north with promises of good jobs. But the Negro was soon to find that it was his labor, not his presence, that was wanted. It was a common practice for the agents to purchase tickets for whole families and to move them *en masse* for resettlement in the great industrial cities. The war had drained away the white manpower needed to build the ships, work the steel, pack the meat, and man the machines; and it had also cut off the normal supply of immigrant labor from Europe.

After the war was over, the Negro's welcome wore thin. It became increasingly hard for Negroes to get jobs except as strike-breakers. Soon there were not enough jobs to go around, and thousands of Negroes were fired and replaced with white men. There was not enough housing, and most Negroes were crowded into the black ghettos in the most deteriorated part of the inner city. Landlords and law-enforcement agencies alike were unsympathetic. But still the Negroes came out of the South. Few had skills; many were illiterate. All were filled with hope for something better than what they had left. Soon there was hunger and crime and delinquency—and trouble with the police. The bright promise of the North had failed. Hope turned to desperation. In desperation is the onset of anxiety.

It is an interesting historical phenomenon that when a people reach the precipice of despair, there is so often waiting in the wings a savior—a messiah to snatch them back from the edge of

the abyss. So it was that in Detroit there appeared in the black
ghetto a mysterious Mullah who called himself W. D. Farad
Muhammad. He had come, he told the handful of Negroes who
gathered to hear him, from the holy city of Mecca. His mission,
as he described it, was "to wake the 'Dead Nation in the West'[1];
to teach [them] the truth about the white man, and to prepare
[them] for the Armageddon." The Armageddon? What did this
apocalyptic concept have to do with the problems of the Negro
in America? Farad was explicit on the point: In the Book of
Revelation it is promised that there will be a final battle between good and evil, and that this decisive battle will take place
at Har-Magedon, "the Mountain of Megiddo," in the Great Plain
of Esdraelon in Asia Minor.[2] But the Bible has a cryptic message
for the initiated of Black Islam (even as it has for more familiar
sects). The forces of "good and evil" are the forces of "black
and white." "The Valley of Esdraelon" symbolizes "the Wilderness of North America." The Battle of Armageddon is to be the
Black Man's final confrontation of the race which has so long
oppressed him.

At first Farad (who was at the time thought to be a prophet,
but who was after his departure recognized as Allah himself)
met from house to house with small groups of Negroes. He went
about his mission as unobtrusively as possible, listening to the
problems of the destitute Negroes, sharing whatever they had to
offer him. A contemporary convert recalls his *modus operandi*:

He came first to our house selling raincoats, and afterwards silks. In
this way he could get into the people's houses. . . . If we asked him
to eat with us, he would eat whatever we had on the table, but after
the meal he began to talk. . . .[3]

What he had to say must have been electrifying. Another
Muslim describes his first encounter with the Prophet as follows:

Up to that time I always went to the Baptist church. After I heard
that sermon from the Prophet, I was turned around completely.
When I went home and heard that dinner was ready, I said: "I don't

---

[1] I.e., American Negroes.

[2] "Armageddon" is Greek transliteration from the Hebrew "Har-Magedon."

[3] Eradmann Beynon, "The Voodoo Cult Among Negro Migrants in
Detroit," *The American Journal of Sociology*, XLIII (July 1937–May 1938),
895.

want any dinner, I just want to go back to the meetings." I wouldn't eat my meals but I [went] back that night and I [went] to every meeting after that. . . . That changed everything for me.[4]

The fame of the Prophet spread and he soon established in Detroit the first of the Temples of Islam. As his following increased he grew more bold in his attacks upon the habits and the culture symbols the Negroes had always taken for granted. In the first place, he taught his followers that they were not "Negroes," but "Black Men." The word "Negro" was alleged to be an invention of the white man designed to identify his victims better and to separate them from their Asian and African brothers. Further, the so-called Negro was not an American, but an "Asiatic," for his forefathers had been stolen from the Afro-Asian continent by the white slavemasters who came in the name of Jesus. Christianity, the Prophet taught, was a white man's religion, a contrivance designed for the enslavement of nonwhite peoples. Wherever Christianity has gone, he declared, men have lost their liberty and their freedom. Islam was declared to be "the natural religion of the Black Man." Only in Islam could the so-called Negroes find freedom, justice, and equality.

Little by little the Prophet began to enlighten these disillusioned migrants from the South about their true history and their place in the future. Black Man was the "Original Man," he taught. On the continent of Afro-Asia black civilizations flourished "long before the white man stood up on his hind legs and crept out of the caves of Europe." Further, the white man was pictured as "a devil by nature." He is, the Prophet taught, the physical embodiment of the principle of evil, and he is incapable of doing good. Further, said Farad, "the white man is the eternal adversary of the one true God whose right and proper name is Allah."

By "tricknology" the blue-eyed devils had enslaved the Black Man, the chosen people of Allah. The devils had taken away the slaves' native language (which was Arabic), and forced them to speak a foreign tongue. The white devils had taken away their names (i.e. their identity), and given them European names (which are to be hated as badges of slavery). Above all, the

[4] *Ibid*, p. 896.

cruel slavemasters took away their natural religion (which is Islam) and made them worship a blue-eyed Jesus with blond hair, telling them that this was their God.

The so-called Negroes, although unknown to themselves, comprised "The Nation of Islam in the West." They had been brainwashed and given a false image of themselves by their white teachers, especially the Christian preachers who lulled them into submission by promising them a home "over Jordan" when they would no longer hew the wood and draw the water for the white man's comfort.

"The wheel must turn," the Prophet insisted. The Nation of Islam had a manifest destiny. The Armageddon must come. It would come as soon as the Black Man in America learned who he himself was, and accepted the truth about the white man, which the Prophet had been sent to declare.

Not all of Farad's energies were spent in attacking the white man. He taught his followers cleanliness and thrift. He persuaded them to give up liquor and such "unclean" foods as pork, cornbread, peas, possums, and catfish, bidding them to separate themselves from the habits they acquired in slavery. He established a school where homemaking, Negro history, Arabic, and other subjects of interest to the Muslims were taught. He demanded that his followers be clean at all times, bathing at least once each day. He taught them to give an honest day's work for an honest day's pay. He taught them to be respectful of others, and above all, to respect themselves. They must obey "all constituted authority," but they must require an eye for an eye and a tooth for a tooth. The *lex talionis* was the law of survival.

The Prophet's first appearance in Detroit is dated as July 4, 1930, and no one remembers seeing him after June 30, 1934. There are many legends, but no authentic information on where he came from, or where he went. But four years of preaching left a legacy of good and evil for eight thousand Negroes who had come to call themselves Muslims.

In the troubled times of the early 1930's, men and women everywhere were looking for some panacea to save them from the desperate circumstances of the Depression. Large numbers of people found that they could not cope rationally with the excruciating anxiety—the uncertainties with which they were confronted from day to day. Some escapists leaped from the roof-tops of the very buildings which were symbols of more stable times. Some clairvoyants, who thought they could discern the wave of the future in Marxist philosophy, found their panacea in the Communist party. The Negro's ecapism tended to be of a more practical nature. Instead of taking the long route to heaven, he built himself "heavens" here on earth in the cults of Father Divine and Daddy Grace.

The followers of Farad were both escapists and clairvoyants. Farad himself was the messiah who had come to lead the so-called Negroes into the millennium which was to follow the Battle of Armageddon. He was the Prophet who had foreseen and foretold the Golden Age that would be theirs when the Black Nation in the West had thrown off the yoke of the white slavemasters. But Farad had disappeared.

The Prophet had not left himself without a witness. Very early in his brief ministry in Detroit he had attracted the admiration and the loyalty of a young Negro from the town of Sandersville, Georgia. Elijah Poole, son of a Baptist minister, was already embittered by the harshness of race relations in the South when he left Georgia and migrated to Detroit with his family in the early 1920's. In Detroit, his disillusionment with the "promised land" was almost immediate, for he soon discovered that the limitations which prescribed his place in the North differed only in degree from the familiar pattern of circumscription in the South. For a time, better jobs were available in the North, but Poole was soon to discover that job security operated on a racial basis. Housing was more strictly segregated than in the South, and living conditions in the black ghetto were often worse than they had been in the sharecropper's cabin. The lynchings in the South had their counterparts in the race riots of the North. There seemed to exist a universal conspiracy to make life in America as untenable as possible for Negroes.

The belittling paternalism of the South had been replaced by the cold indifference of the North, and Elijah Poole found himself and his family with no better chance of assimilation in the great "melting pot" of the North than he had left in the South.

As a matter of fact, his daily contact with foreign-born elements speaking in strange "unAmerican" accents and wearing "foreign" clothes increased his feelings of isolation and resentment. He saw the jobs of Negroes taken from them and given to white men who had not fought for this country, and who in some cases had fought against it. Inevitably, the Georgia-born Poole arrived at the conclusion that even in the North the color of a man's skin, not the fact of his citizenship nor the quality of his intrinsic worth, was the determining factor in all his social relationships.

Elijah was now ready for the racist doctrines of Wali Farad. From their first meeting he became the Prophet's most dedicated apostle and his chief amanuensis. Farad had identified the Black Man's oppressor in terms never before heard in the Negro community. He had exposed the white man as a devil—a *literal* devil, created on the Isle of Patmos by a mad scientist whose name was Yakub. This was the secret of the white man's power, his cruelty, *and* his vulnerability. Allah had given the devil a certain time to rule, and the time of the devil was up. *The Black Man must prepare himself for the Armageddon!* Poole was impressed. Farad had the explanation of the white man's cruelty as well as the key to his power. Eventually, Farad entrusted his mantle and his mission to Elijah. He made Poole First Minister of Islam and put the Muslim school, the training of ministers, and the highly secret FOI (the Fruit of Islam, the leadership training corps "for the coming Armageddon") under his direction. Later, Poole was sent to Chicago to found Temple No. 2, the present headquarters of the movement.

In recognition of Poole's dedicated leadership, Farad relieved him of his "slave-name" (i.e. "Poole") and honored him with the Muslim name "Muhammad." Thereafter, Farad's public appearances were progressively less frequent until the day of his final disappearance.

Under Elijah Muhammad, the new "Messenger of Islam," the movement spread from the initial temple in Detroit to almost every major city in the country where there is a sizable Negro population. In most of these cities there is a temple; in others, where the movement is less strong, there are missions. Where there are no missions there are likely to be representatives of the movement who are in contact with the Muslim leadership in nearby cities.

The black ghetto is the principal source of Muslim recruitment. There, in the dirty streets and crowded tenements where life is cheap and hope is minimal, where isolation from the common values of society and from the common privileges of citizenship is most acute, the voice of the Messenger does not fall upon deaf ears. So often, his is the only message directed to the pimps, the prostitutes, the con-men, the prisoners, the ex-cons, the alcoholics, the addicts, the unemployed, whom the responsible society has forgotten. It is a voice challenging them to recover their self-respect, urging them to repudiate the white man's religion and the white man's culture, daring them to believe in black supremacy, offering them a Black God and a Black Nation, promising them that the day will come when "we will be masters . . . and we are going to treat the white man the way he should be treated,"[5] demanding of them that "if anyone comes to take advantage of you, *lay down your life!* and the Black Man will be respected all over the Planet Earth."[6]

"Never be the aggressor," the voice proclaims, "never look for trouble. But if any man molests you, may Allah bless you."[7]

"We must take things into our own hands," the Messenger insists. "We must return to the Mosaic law of an eye for an eye and a tooth for a tooth. What does it matter if 10 million of us die? There will be 7 million of us left and they will enjoy justice and freedom."[8]

Such is the challenge of Elijah Muhammad who is hailed by his ministers as "the most fearless black man in America." His followers are, with few exceptions, from America's most underprivileged class. They are denizens of the black ghetto. To them, the voice of Elijah Muhammad is a voice raised against injustice —real or imagined. Muhammad is a paladin who has taken up the cudgel against the "devil" responsible for all of their miseries and their failures. The resentments and the hostilities that

[5] *Chicago's American*, February 22, 1960.
[6] See "Tensions Outside the Movement," C. Eric Lincoln, *The Black Muslims in America* (Boston: Beacon Press, 1961), pp. 135–78.
[7] *Op. cit.*, p. 5.
[8] *Chicago's American*, February 23, 1960.

breed in the ghetto are finally brought to focus upon a single object—*the white man*. Outside the black ghetto there are Muslim units in many of the state and federal prisons across the country. Here the movement finds its prison audiences to be ready made and highly receptive, for the racial character of the law-enforcement agencies, the courts and the custodial personnel, is a key factor in sharpening the Negro prisoner's resentments and his sense of persecution.

I have tried to present a developmental background for the Black Muslim movement against which we may now more profitably examine their demands as a protest group. Generally speaking, the movement has been a protest directed at the whole value-construct of the white Christian society of which the Black Muslims feel themselves (as Negroes) to be an isolated and unappreciated appendage. Hence, the burden of their protest is against their "retention" in a society where they are not wanted. This is the soft side of the "Armageddon complex" which looks to the removal of the source of their discomfiture rather than to going anywhere themselves. Mr. Muhammad teaches that "the white man's home is in Europe," and that "there will be no peace until every man is in his own country."

In a recent issue of the official Muslim newspaper, *Mr. Muhammad Speaks*, the Muslims stated their protest in the form of the following ten propositions:

1. We want freedom. We want a full and complete freedom.
2. We want justice. Equal justice under the law. We want justice applied equally to all, regardless of creed or class or color.
3. We want equality of opportunity. We want equal membership in society with the best in civilized society.
4. We want our people in America whose parents or grandparents were descendants from slaves, to be allowed to establish a separate state or territory of their own. . . .
5. We want freedom for all Believers of Islam now held in federal prisons. We want freedom for all black men and women now under death sentence in innumerable prisons in the North as well as the South.
   We want every black man and woman to have the freedom to accept or reject being separated from the slave master's children and establish a land of their own. . . .

6. We want an immediate end to the police brutality and mob attacks against the so-called Negro throughout the United States.
7. As long as we are not allowed to establish a state or territory of our own, we demand not only equal justice under the laws of the United States, but equal employment opportunities—NOW! . . . .
8. We want the government of the United States to exempt our people from ALL taxation as long as we are deprived of equal justice under the laws of the land.
9. We want equal education—but separate schools up to 16 for boys and 18 for girls on the condition that the girls be sent to women's colleges and universities. We want all black children educated, taught without hindrance or suppression.
10. We believe that intermarriage or race mixing should be prohibited. We want the religion of Islam taught without hindrance or suppression.

These are some of the things that we, the Muslims, want for our people in North America.[9]

Some of the proposals of the Muslims are obviously unrealistic, and we need not discuss them here. Other tests and demands of the Black Muslims are stated in the foregoing propositions do not seem unreasonable. I do not know any Americans who do not "want freedom," for example. Justice under the law, equality of opportunity, and freedom of worship are all "approved values" in our society, and they find their sanctions in the American creed. Further, they are objectives which are implicit in the programs of all other movements within the Negro spectrum of protest. What, then, are the factors which qualify the Muslim protest movement and make it unacceptable to the general American public?

The fundamental differences between the attitudes, the behavior, and the goals of the Black Muslims as compared to other Negro protest organizations may be explained in terms of their differing degrees of dissociation deriving from the unusual anxiety and frustration incident to their status in the American social arrangement. Negroes, as a caste, are *all* outside the assimilative process, and they exhibit from time to time the frustrations which are the corollaries of their marginality. However, the dissociation of the Muslim membership from the larger society, and even from the general Negro subgroup (which ordinarily seeks to identify itself with the American mainstream), may be

[9] July 31, 1962.

considered extreme. In reacting to the unique pressures of their day-to-day experiences as low-caste Negroes in a white-oriented society, the Muslims have abandoned the fundamental principles of the American creed and have substituted in its place a new system of values perceived as more consistent with the realities of their circumstances.

It is meaningless to label the Muslims as "unAmerican," for the American creed is not a legal or constitutional document against which the political loyalty of a group may be measured.[10] The American creed is a common set of beliefs and values in which all Americans have normally found consensus. It is a body of ideals, a social philosophy which affirms the basic dignity of every individual and the existence of certain inalienable rights without reference to race, creed, or color. The roots of the American creed are deep in the equalitarian doctrines of the eighteenth-century Enlightenment, Protestant Christianity and English law. For most of us, it has been the cultural matrix within which all discordant socio-political attitudes converge, and from which derives the great diversity of social and political interpretations which makes democracy possible in a society of widely variant populations.

The Black Muslims, by the nature of certain of their goals and institutions, have excepted themselves from the aegis of the American creed. The Black Muslims repudiate American citizenship in favor of a somewhat dubious membership in a mystical "Asiatic" confraternity, and they are violently opposed to Christianity, the principles of which are fundamental to our understanding of the democratic ideal. Not only do they resist assimilation and avoid interracial participation in the life of the community, but the Muslim creed assigns all nonblacks to the subhuman status of "devils" (and promises to treat them as such); the sustaining philosophy is one of black supremacy nurtured by a careful inculcation of hatred for the white man and his characteristic institutions. By their own choice the Black Muslims exclude themselves from the body of principles and the system of values within the framework of which Americans have customarily sought to negotiate their grievances.

[10] For an excellent interpretation of the American creed see Arnold Rose, *The Negro in America* (Boston: Beacon Press, 1957), pp. 1 ff.

Other groups advocate white supremacy, resist the assimilation of Negroes and others, and practice hatred rather than love, yet they retain an idealistic loyalty to the principles of the American creed. The point is that although the creed is violated constantly in practice, it remains an *ideal* to which all give their asseveration—in which all believe, and from which we continue to derive our laws and our moral values in spite of our failures to honor them completely.

The Black Muslim movement does not conceive itself to be in violation of the principles and values of the American creed. Rather, the movement views itself as having substituted new principles, new values, and a new creed based on a radically different interpretation of history from that expressed in the American creed. Muhammad promises a new order based on the primacy of a nation of Black Men with a manifest destiny under a Black God. His is a nation radically different from those now shaping the existing American society. In spite of the fact that the Black Muslim movement shares at some points the immediate goals of the lesser Negro protest movements, its oppugnance to traditional values limits its general acceptability as a protest organization. The action impact of the movement on the general Negro community has been negligible considering the fact that most of America's twenty million black citizens live under conditions considerably more iniquitous than those which at other times and places have been productive of the gravest social consequences. This is not to suggest that Negroes are not aware of the movement. They are. And there are important pockets of sympathy among Negroes for the Muslims as a class more oppressed than other Negro classes, and a certain covert admiration for their militant, nonaccommodative stance against the traditional aggressions of the white man.

Nevertheless, the depth of the Negro's commitment *as a class* to the democratic procedures implicit in the American creed has operated successfully to contain the Muslim movement—eliminating it as a serious threat to racial peace or national security. But the Black Muslims remain a somber symbol of the social callousness that is possible even in an equalitarian democracy. Such movements do not "just happen." The Muslims are the most insistent symptoms of the failure of this society to meet effectively the minimum needs of one-tenth of its population to find a meaningful level of participation in the significant social values most Americans take for granted.

The Muslims represent that segment of the Negro sub-group who, being most deprived of traditional incentives, have finally turned to search for alternatives outside the commonly accepted value structure. They are the products of social anxiety —people who are repeatedly frustrated in their attempts to make satisfactory adjustments in a society unaware of their existence except as the faceless subjects of statistical data. As Negroes, their future was unpromising. As Muslims, theirs is a creed of futility. As Americans, the responsibility for what they are, or what they will become, is our own.

I. F. Stone

One of the most remarkable autobiographical accounts in the whole of American letters was published in 1965 with the appearance of *The Autobiography of Malcolm X* (written with the assistance of Alex Haley). For sheer frankness about himself and the life led by Negroes in the ghettos of the North, the work has had few equals. Malcolm X's story is not, like Richard Wright's *Black Boy* (1944), about the known horrors of growing up in the South. It is rather about the North and the Midwest, areas that were supposedly free from the intense race problem of the South. For an autobiography, it is different from the classic success story, although in its own way, Malcolm's life was a success. He became the voice of the disinherited, the lumpenproletariat, the rootless ones who hopelessly inhabit the Negro ghettos of America.

The most interesting part of his career is Malcolm's growth and development from a Black Muslim to a militant civil rights oriented black nationalist, and in a broader sense, from a follower of a sectarian cult to a significant figure on the larger world scene. In 1963 Malcolm was suspended from his post as Minister of the New York Muslim temple, ostensibly for his statement made after the murder of President Kennedy about "chickens coming home to roost." As Malcolm X explained it in his autobiography: "I said that the hate in white men had not stopped with the killing of defenseless black people, but that hate, allowed to spread unchecked, finally had struck down this country's Chief of State. I said it was the same thing that had happened with Medgar Evers, with Patrice Lumumba, with Madame Nhu's husband." But there were more fundamental reasons for Malcolm X's suspension and eventual murder. As C. Eric Lincoln found in 1961, Malcolm X had already become an outstanding Muslim figure in his own right, and there were fears that he would challenge for the leadership of the movement. Jealousy developed among the leaders, and some said that Malcolm was becoming too important. Malcolm X gave as the cause of his disenchantment with Mr. Muhammad the news that the head of the Muslims had been involved in personal scandal. But with his suspension, Malcolm X's intellectual development and outlook changed quickly.

He traveled for eighteen weeks in 1964 to the Near East and Africa where he made a pilgrimage to Mecca, met with the heads of states, and had time to get some perspective on his own ideas. He realized for the first time that the Islam of the Black Muslims was not the same as the Islam practiced by most of the world's 400 million Muslims. He became less racist. "My trip to Mecca has opened my eyes," said Malcolm X. "I no longer subscribe to racism. I have adjusted my thinking to the point where I believe that whites are human beings —as long as this is borne out by their humane attitude toward Negroes." Equally important, Malcolm X began to "think internationally." Like Garvey and Du Bois before him, he realized the power that an independent Africa could have to influence American policy toward Negroes at home. He told students in Nigeria that he "was convinced that it was time for all Afro-Americans to join the world's Pan-Africanists." Returning to the United States, Malcolm X began to organize a broadly based movement called the Organization of Afro-American Unity. While dropping the Muslim religious ideology, Malcolm X still held to their concept of black nationalism and their rejection of non-violence. He wanted a program that would be more immediate than that of the Muslims. As he wrote in his autobiography, "twenty-two million of our people . . . still here in America need better food, clothing, housing, education and jobs right now."

But before the OAAU could get firmly started, Malcolm X was brutally murdered on February 21, 1965, in the Audubon Ballroom in upper Harlem by three men, two of whom were later shown to be members of the Black Muslims. In his *autobiography*, which he finished only a short time before his death, he told Alex Haley his co-author, that he expected the Muslims to make an attempt on his life. He knew well the penalty for apostasy. Malcolm X recalled that he had taught the Muslims to protect themselves, and how to use force when necessary. "He had no right to reject me," Elijah Muhammad declared a few days after Malcolm's murder. "He was a star, who went astray!" (Alex Haley, "Epilogue," *The Autobiography of Malcolm X*).

I. F. Stone, has been for many years one of America's most perceptive and incisive political commentators and reporters. Mr. Stone wrote the following piece for the *New York Review of Books*. He is the editor/author of *I. F. Stone's Weekly* (Washington, D.C.).

THE PILGRIMAGE OF MALCOLM X

SOURCE: I. F. Stone, "The Pilgrimage of Malcolm X," *New York Review of Books*, V (November 11, 1965), pp. 3–5.

Malcolm X was born into Black Nationalism. His father was a follower of Marcus Garvey, the West Indian who launched a "Back to Africa" movement in the Twenties. Malcolm's first clash with white men took place when his mother was pregnant with him; a mob of Klansmen in Omaha, Nebraska, waving shotguns and rifles, warned her one night to move out of town because her husband was spreading trouble among the "good" Negroes with Garvey's teachings. One of his earliest memories was of seeing their home burned down in Lansing, Michigan, in 1929, because the Black Legion, a white Fascist organization, considered his father an "uppity" Negro. The body of his father, a tall, powerful black man from Georgia, soon afterward was found literally cut to pieces in one of those mysterious accidents that often veil a racial killing.

His mother was a West Indian who looked like a white woman. Her unknown father was white. She slowly went to pieces mentally under the burden of raising eight children. When the family was broken up, Malcolm was sent to a detention home, from which he attended a white school. He must have been a bright and attractive lad, for he was at the top of his class and was elected class president in the seventh grade. Many years later, in a speech on the Black Revolution which is included in the collection, *Malcom X Speaks*, he was able to boast bitterly, "I grew up with white people. I was integrated before they even invented the word." The reason for the bitterness was an incident that changed his life. His English teacher told him he ought to begin thinking about his career. Malcolm said he would like to be a lawyer. His teacher suggested carpentry instead. "We all here like you, you know that," the teacher said, "but you've got to be realistic about being a nigger."

Malcolm X left Lansing deeply alienated and in the slums of Boston and New York he became a "hustler," selling numbers, women, and dope. "All of us," he says in his *Autobiography* of his friends in the human jungle, "who might have probed space or cured cancer or built industries, were instead black victims of the white man's American social system." Insofar as he was concerned, this was no exaggeration. He was an extraordinary man. Had he been wholly white, instead of irretrievably "Negro" by American standards, he might easily have become a leader of the bar. In the underworld he went from marijuana to cocaine. To meet the cost he took up burglary. He was arrested with a white mistress who had become his look-out woman. In February, 1940, not quite twenty-one, he was sentenced to ten years in prison in Massachusetts. The heavy sentence reflected the revulsion created in the judge by the discovery that Malcolm had made a white woman his "love slave." In prison, he went on nutmeg, reefers, Nembutal, and benzedrine in a desperate effort to replace the drugs. He was a vicious prisoner, often in solitary. The other prisoners nicknamed him "Satan." But the prison had an unusually well stocked library to which he was introduced by a fellow prisoner, an old-time burglar named Bimbi. Through him, Malcolm first encountered Thoreau. Prison became his university; there also he was converted to the Nation of Islam, the sect the press calls Black Muslims.

The important word here is conversion. To understand Malcolm's experience, one must go to the literature of conversion. "Were we writing the history of the mind from the purely natural history point of view," William James concludes in his *Varieties of Religious Experience,* "we would still have to write down man's liability to sudden and complete conversion as one of his most curious peculiarities." The convert's sense of being born anew, the sudden change from despair to elation, bears an obvious resemblance to the manic-depressive cycle, except that the change in the personality is often permanent. But those who experience it must first—to borrow Gospel language—be brought low. James quotes the theological maxim, "Man's extremity is God's opportunity." It is only out of the depths that men on occasion experience this phenomenon of renewal. The success of the Black Muslims in converting and rehabilitating criminals and dope addicts like Malcolm X recalls the mighty phrases James quotes from Luther. "God," he preached, "is the God . . . of those that are brought even to nothing . . . and his nature is . . . to save the very desperate and damned." Malcolm had been brought to nothing, he was one of those very desperate and damned when he was "saved" by Elijah Muhammad, the self-proclaimed Messenger of Allah to the lost Black Nation of that imaginary Islam he preaches.

The tendency is to dismiss Elijah Muhammad's weird doctrine as another example of the superstitions, old and new, that thrive in the Negro ghetto. It is not really any more absurd than the Virgin Birth or the Sacrifice of Isaac. The rational absurdity does not detract from the psychic therapy. Indeed the therapy may lie in the absurdity. Converts to any creed talk of the joy in complete surrender; a rape of the mind occurs. "*Credo quia absurdum,*" Tertullian, the first really cultivated apologist for Christianity, is said to have exulted, "I believe because it *is* absurd." Tertullian was himself a convert. Black Nationalists may even claim him as an African, for his home was Carthage.

There is a special reason for the efficacy of the Black Muslims in reaching the Negro damned. The sickness of the Negro in America is that he has been made to feel a nigger; the genocide is psychic. The Negro must rid himself of this feeling if he is to stand erect again. He can do so in two ways. He can change the outer world of white supremacy, or he

can change his inner world by "conversion." The teachings of
the Black Muslims may be fantastic but they are superbly suited
to the task of shaking off the feeling of nigger-ness. Elijah
Muhammad teaches that the original man was black, that
Caucasians are "white devils" created almost 6,000 years ago by
a black genius named Yakub. He bleached a number of blacks
by a process of mutation into pale-faced blue-eyed devils in
order to test the mettle of the Black Nation. This inferior breed
has ruled by deviltry but their time will soon be up, at the end
of the sixth millenium, which may be by 1970 or thereabouts.
To explain the white man as a devil is, as Malcolm X says in
the *Autobiography,* to strike "a nerve center in the American
black man" for "when he thinks about his own life, he is going
to see where, to him personally, the white man sure has acted
like a devil." To see the white man this way is, in Gospel
imagery, to cast out the devil. With him go his values, as he
has impressed them on the Black Man, above all the inner feeling of being a nigger. To lose that feeling is to be fully
emancipated. For the poor Negro no drug could be a stronger
opiate than this black religion.

With rejection of the white man's values goes rejection of the
white man's God. "We're worshipping a Jesus," Malcolm protested in one of his sermons after he became a Black Muslim
Minister, "who doesn't even *look* like us." The white man, he
declared, "has brainwashed us black people to fasten our gaze
upon a blond-haired, blue-eyed Jesus." This Black Muslim doctrine may seem a blasphemous joke until one makes the effort
to imagine how whites would feel if taught to worship a black
God with thick African lips. Men prefer to create a God in
their own image. "The Ethiopians," one of the pre-Socratic
Greek philosophers observed a half millenium before Christ,
"assert that their gods are snub-nosed and black" while the
"Nordic" Thracians said theirs were "blue-eyed and red-haired."
When Marcus Garvey, the first apostle of Pan-Africanism, toured
Africa, urging expulsion of the white man, he called for a Negro
religion with a Negro Christ. Just as Malcolm Little, in accordance with Black Muslim practice, rejected his "slave name"
and became Malcolm X, so Malcolm X, son of a Baptist preacher,
rejected Christianity as a slave religion. His teacher, Elijah

Muhammad, did not have to read Nietszche to discover that Christianity was admirably suited to make Rome's slaves submissive. In our ante-bellum South the value of Christian teaching in making slaves tractable was widely recognized even by slaveholders themselves agnostic.[1] The Negro converted to Christianity was cut off from the disturbing memory of his own gods and of his lost freedom, and reconciled to his lot in the white man's chains. Here again the primitivistic fantasies of the Black Muslims unerringly focus on a crucial point. It is in the Christian mission that what Malcolm X called the "brainwashing" of the blacks began.

Racism and nationalism are poisons. Sometimes a poison may be prescribed as a medicine, and Negroes have found in racism a way to restore their self-respect. But black racism is still racism, with all its primitive irrationality and danger. There are passages in the *Autobiography* in which Malcolm, recounting some of his Black Muslim sermons, sounds like a Southern white supremacist in reverse, vibrating with anger and sexual obsession over the horrors of race pollution. There is the same preoccupation with rape, the same revulsion about mixed breeds. "Why," he cried out, "the white man's raping of the black race's woman began right on those slave ships!" A psychoanalyst might see in his fury the feeling of rejection by the race of his white grandfather. A biologist might see in the achievements of this tall sandy-complexioned Negro—his friends called him "Red" —an example of the possibilities of successful racial mixture. But Malcolm's feelings on the subject were as outraged as those of a Daughter of the Confederacy. He returned revulsion for revulsion and hate for hate. He named his first child, a daughter, Attilah, and explained that he named her for the Hun who sacked Rome.

But hidden under the surface of the Black Nationalist creed to which he was won there lay a peculiar anti-Negroism. The true nationalist loves his people and their peculiarities; he wants to preserve them; he is filled with filial piety. But there is in Elijah Muhammad's Black Muslim creed none of the love for the Negro one finds in W. E. B. Du Bois, or of that yearning

[1] See Stampp's *The Peculiar Institution*, pps. 158–60.

for the ancestral Africa which obsessed Garvey. Elijah Muhammad—who himself looks more Chinese than Negro—teaches his people that they are Asians, not Africans; that their original tongue is Arabic. He turns his people into middle-class Americans. Their clothes are conservative, almost Ivy League. Their religious services eschew that rich antiphony between preacher and congregation which one finds in Negro churches. The Nigerian, E. U. Essien-Udom, whose *Black Nationalism* is the best book on the Black Muslims, was struck by their middle-class attitudes and coldness to Africa and African ways. In Black Muslim homes, when jazz was played, he writes that he was "often tempted to tap his feet to the tune of jazz" but was inhibited because his Black Muslim hosts "listened to it without ostensible response to the rhythm." In their own way the Black Muslims are as much in flight from Negritude as was Booker T. Washington. Indeed Elijah Muhammad's stress on Negro private business and his hostility to trade unionism in his own dealings with Negroes are very much in the Booker T. Washington pattern. The virtues of bourgeois America are what Elijah Muhammad seeks to recreate in his separate Black Nation. This is the banal reality which lies behind all his hocus-pocus about the Koran, and here lie the roots of his split with Malcolm X.

For Elijah Muhammad practices separation not only from American life but from the American Negro community, and from its concrete struggles for racial justice. Malcolm X was drawn more and more to engagement in that struggle. In the midst of describing in the *Autobiography* his happy and successful years as a Black Muslim organizer, Malcolm X says:

If I harbored any personal disappointment, whatsoever, it was that privately I was convinced that our Nation of Islam could be an even greater force in the American black man's overall struggle—if we engaged in more *action*. By that I mean I thought privately that we should have amended or relaxed, our general non-engagement policy. I felt that, wherever black people committed themselves, in the Little Rocks and Birminghams and other places, militantly disciplined Muslims should also be there—for all the world to see, and respect and discuss. It could be heard increasingly in the Negro communities: "Those Muslims *talk* tough, but they never *do* anything, unless somebody bothers Muslims." [Italics in original.]

This alone was bound to divide the prophet and disciple. But there were also personal factors. Elijah Muhammad won Malcolm's devotion by his kindness in corresponding with the young convict when Malcolm was still in prison. But Malcolm's intellectual horizons were already far wider than those of the rather narrow, ill-educated, and suspicious Messenger of Allah. In the prison library Malcolm X was finding substantiation for the Black Muslim creed in *Paradise Lost* and in Herodotus; this passionate curiosity and voracious reading were bound to make him outgrow Elijah's dream-book theology. On the one side envy and on the other disillusion were to drive the two men apart. The crowds drawn by Malcolm and his very organizing success made Elijah Muhammad and his family jealous. On the other hand, Malcolm, who had kept the sect's vows of chastity, was shocked when former secretaries of Elijah Muhammad filed paternity suits against the prophet. Malcolm had nothing but a small salary and the house the sect had provided for him. Elijah Muhammad's cars (two Cadillacs and a Lincoln Continental), his $200 pin-striped banker-style suits, his elegantly furnished 18-room house in one of the better sections of Chicago's Hyde Park, began to make a sour impression on Malcolm. The hierarchy lives well in practically all religions, and their worldly affluence fosters schism. Malcolm was too big, too smart, too able, to fit into the confines of this little sect and remain submissive to its family oligarchy. He began to open up a larger world, and this endangered Elijah Muhammad's hold on the little band of unsophisticated faithful he had recruited.

Muhammad Speaks, the weekly organ of the Black Muslims, had begun to play down Malcolm's activities. The break came over Malcolm's comment on Kennedy's assassination. Within hours after the President's killing, Elijah Muhammad sent out a directive ordering the cult's ministers to make no comment on the murder. Malcolm, speaking at Manhattan Center a few days afterward, was asked in the question period what he thought of the assassination. He answered it was a case of "the chickens coming home to roost." Malcolm explains in the *Autobiography,* "I said that the hate in white men had not stopped with the killing of defenseless black people but . . . finally had struck down the President." He complains that "some of the world's

most important personages were saying in various ways, and in
far stronger ways than I did, that America's climate of hate had
been responsible for the President's death. But when Malcolm
X said the same thing it was ominous." Elijah Muhammad
called him in. "That was a very bad statement," he said. "The
country loved this man." He ordered Malcolm silenced for ninety
days so that the Black Muslims could be "disassociated from
the blunder." Malcolm agreed and submitted. But three days
later he heard that a Mosque official was suggesting his own
assassination. Soon after, another Black Muslim told him of a
plan to wire his car so that it would explode when he turned
the ignition key. Malcolm decided to build a Muslim Mosque
of his own, and open its doors to black men of all faiths for
common action. To prepare himself he decided to make the
pilgrimage to Mecca.

This visit to Mecca was a turning-point for Malcolm. His
warm reception in the Arabic world, the sight of white men in
equal fraternity with black and brown, marked a second conversion in his life. "For the past week," Malcolm wrote home, "I
have been utterly speechless and spellbound by the graciousness
I see displayed all around me by people *of all colors.*" The
italics were his. The man who made the seven circuits around
the Ka'ba and drank the waters of Zem-Zem emerged from his
pilgrimage no longer a racist or a Black Muslim. He took the
title of El Hajj earned by his visit to Mecca and called himself
henceforth El-Hajj Malik El-Shabazz. He turned Muslim in the
true sense of the word. How indelibly he also remained an
American go-getter is deliciously reflected in a passage of the
Autobiography where he says that while in Mecca:

I saw that Islam's conversions around the world could double and
triple if the colorfulness and the true spiritualness of the Hajj pilgrimage were properly advertised and communicated to the outside world.
I saw that the Arabs are poor at understanding the psychology of non-
Arabs and the importance of public relations. The Arabs said "Inshah
Allah" ("God willing")—then they waited for converts, but I knew
that with improved public relations methods the new converts turning
to Allah could be turned into millions.

He had become a Hajj but remained in some ways a Babbitt,
the salesman, archtype of our American society. A creed was

something to *sell*. Allah, the Merciful, needed better merchandising.

Malcolm returned from abroad May 21, 1964. Several attempts were made on his life. On February 21, 1965, he was killed by gunmen when he got up to speak at a meeting in New York's Audubon Ballroom. He was not quite forty when he died. The most revealing tribute paid him was the complaint by Elijah Muhammad after Malcolm was killed. "He came back preaching that we should not hate the enemy . . . He was a star who went astray." What nobler way to go astray? In Africa and in America there was almost unanimous recognition that the Negro race had lost a gifted son; only the then head of the U. S. Information Agency, Carl Rowan, immortalized himself with a monumental Uncle Tomism. "All this about an ex-convict, ex-dope peddler who became a racial fanatic," was Rowan's obtuse and ugly comment; it ranks with his discovery, as USIA Director, of what he called the public's "right *not* to know."

From tape-recorded conversations, a Negro writer, Alex Haley, put together the *Autobiography;* he did his job with sensitivity and with devotion. Here one may read, in the agony of this brilliant Negro's self-creation, the agony of an entire people in their search for identity. But more fully to understand this remarkable man, one must turn to *Malcolm X Speaks*, which supplements the *Autobiography*. All but one of the speeches were made in those last eight tumultuous months of his life after his break with the Black Muslims when he was seeking a new path. In their pages one can begin to understand his power as a speaker and to see, more clearly than in the *Autobiography*, the political legacy he left his people in its struggle for full emancipation.

Over and over again in simple imagery, savagely uncompromising, he drove home the real truth about the Negro's position in America. It may not be pleasant but it must be faced. "Those Hunkies that just got off the boat," he said in one of his favorite comparisons, "they're already Americans. Polacks are already Americans; the Italian refugees are already Americans. Everything that comes out of Europe, every blue-eyed thing, is already an American. And as long as you and I have been over here, we aren't Americans yet. They don't have to pass civil rights legislation to make a Polack an American." In a favorite metaphor, he said "I'm not going to sit at your table and watch you eat, with nothing on my plate, and call myself a diner. Sitting at the table doesn't make you a diner, unless you eat some of what's on the plate. Being here in America doesn't make you an American. Being born here in America doesn't make you an American." He often said, "Don't be shocked when I say that I was in prison. You're still in prison. That's what America means—prison." Who can deny that this is true for the black man? No matter how high he rises, he never loses consciousness of the invisible bars which hem him in. "We didn't land on Plymouth Rock," Malcolm was fond of saying. "It landed on us."

He counselled violence but he defended this as an answer to white violence. "If they make the Klan non-violent," he said over and over again, "I'll be non-violent." In another speech he said, "If violence is wrong in America, violence is wrong abroad. If it is wrong to be violent defending black women and black children and black babies and black men, then it is wrong for America to draft us and make us violent abroad in defense of her." He taunted his people in the same speech that "As long as the white man sent you to Korea, you bled . . . You bleed for white people, but when it comes to seeing your own churches being bombed and little black girls murdered, you haven't any blood." In a speech he made about the brutal beating of Fannie Lou Hamer of Mississippi, he said of the white man, "if he only understands the language of a rifle, get a rifle. If he only understands the language of a rope, get a rope. But don't waste time talking the wrong language to a man if you really want to communicate with him." In preaching Pan-Africanism, he reached down into the aching roots of Negro self-hatred as few men have ever done. "You can't hate Africa and not hate yourself," he said in one speech. "This is what the white man knows. So they make you and me hate our African identity . . . We hated our heads, we hated the shape of our nose, we wanted one of those long dove-like noses, you know; we hated the color of our skin, hated the blood of Africa that was in our veins. And in hating our features and our skin and our blood, we had to end up hating ourselves." No man has better expressed his people's trapped anguish.

Malcolm's most important message to his people is muted in the *Autobiography*, perhaps because Alex Haley, its writer, is politically conventional, but it comes out sharply in *Malcolm X Speaks* which was edited and published by a group of Trotskyists. This was the idea that while the Negro is a minority in this country, he is part of a majority if he thinks of common action with the rest of the world's colored peoples. "The first thing the American power structure doesn't want any Negroes to start," he says in the *Autobiography*, "is thinking internationally." In a speech at Ibadan University in Nigeria, he relates in the *Autobiography*, he urged the Africans to bring the American Negro's plight before the United Nations: "I said that just as the American Jew is in political, cultural, and economic harmony with world Jewry, I was convinced that it was time for all Afro-Americans to join the world's Pan-Africanists." Malcolm persuaded the Organization of African Unity at its Cairo conference to pass a resolution saying that discrimination against Negroes in the United States was "a matter of deep concern" to the Africans, and *The New York Times* in August 1964 reported that the State and Justice Departments had begun "to take an interest in Malcolm's campaign because it might create 'a touchy problem' for the U.S. if raised at the UN." In the UN debate over U.S. intervention to save white lives in the Congo, African delegates at the UN for the first time accused the U.S. of being indifferent to similar atrocities against blacks in Mississippi. This is what Malcolm wanted when he spoke of putting the Negro struggle in a world context.

An Italian writer, Vittorio Lanternari, published a remarkable book five years ago, which appeared here in 1963 as *The Religions of the Oppressed: A Study of Modern Messianic Cults*. It suggests that wherever white men have driven out or subdued colored men, whether in the case of the American Indians, or in Africa, or with the Maoris in New Zealand, as with the Tai-Pings in China and the Cao Dai in Vietnam or among the uprooted blacks and harried Indians in the Caribbean and Latin America, Messianic cults have arisen, rejecting white men's values and seeking the restoration of shattered cultural identities as the first step toward political freedom. He did not include in his survey the cults which thrive in our Negro ghettoes though they are of the same character. One striking common bond among all these sects of the oppressed has been their effort to free their people from drinking the white man's "firewater" or (in China) smoking his opium. To see the Black Muslims and Malcolm's life in this perspective is to begin to understand the psychic havoc wrought around the world by white imperialism in the centuries since America was discovered and Afro-Asia opened up to white penetration. There are few places on earth where whites have not grown rich robbing the colored races. It was Malcolm's great contribution to help make us all aware of this.

His assassination was a loss to the country as well as to his race. These two books will have a permanent place in the literature of the Afro-American struggle. It is tantalizing to speculate on what he might have become had he lived. What makes his life so moving a story was his capacity to learn and grow. New disillusions, and a richer view of the human condition, lay ahead for the man who could say, as he did in one of his last speeches, when discussing the first Bandung conference, "Once they excluded the white man, they found they could get together." Since then India and Pakistan, Singapore and Malaysia, the rebellion against the Arabs in Zanzibar and the splits in Black Africa itself have demonstrated that fratricide does not end with the eviction of the white devil. Various Left sects, Maoist and Trotzkyist and Communist, sought to recruit him, but he was trying to build a movement of his own. He was shopping around for new political ideas. He was also becoming active in the South instead of merely talking about a Dixie Mau-Mau from the relative safety of Harlem. I believe there was in him a readiness painfully to find and face new truths which might have made him one of the great Negroes, and Americans, of our time.

Harold R. Isaacs

W. E. B. Du Bois remains the most important symbolic figure for contemporary Negro history. Du Bois seems larger than life, with a productive career that spanned nearly a century. Throughout his life he remained a fighter and non-compromiser, a romantic and a revolutionary in a world given to appeasement and inaction. None could ever accuse him of selling out to the white man.

He was fundamentally a *race man*. Everything Du Bois wrote centered around the question, and he judged all events and actions on this basis. Du Bois reacted to the actions of nations and peoples by how well they treated Negro or non-white peoples. Du Bois was clearly conscious of this racial preoccupation in his own work. He wrote in the autobiographical *Dusk of Dawn* (1940): "In my life the chief fact has been race. . . . Into the spiritual provincialism of this belief I have been born and this fact has guided, embittered, illuminated and enshrouded my life."

This racial view of history helps to explain his early pro-Japanese sympathies, his rationalization of the Moslem slave trade, and his suspicion of the white working class. It is also the key to his pro-Soviet sympathies, for despite all the attacks leveled against it, Russia has in fact been less an exploiter and enemy of colored peoples than the Western nations. For Du Bois, it was France, Britain, Holland, Belgium, Italy, and Portugal who had subjugated Africa and Asia. America practiced dollar imperialism overseas and at home did nothing to stop the merciless exploitation of its Negro citizens. And while Du Bois' interpretation of history was narrow, it did allow him to predict with great accuracy much of the course of twentieth century developments. He had prophesied in 1900 that "the problem of the twentieth century is the problem of the color-line, the relation of the darker to the lighter races of men in Asia and Africa, in America and the islands of the sea." (Du Bois, *The Souls of Black Folk*) He anticipated Lenin by seeing in imperialism the roots of the World War ("The African Roots of the War," *Atlantic Monthly*, May,

1915), and in 1920, after finding that the great powers had no interest in freeing the colonial peoples, Du Bois wrote: "The World War was primarily the jealous and avaricious struggle for the largest share in exploiting darker races. As such it is and must be but the prelude to the armed and indignant protests of these despised and raped peoples." Far from being the war that ended all wars, it is but the beginning!

But this interpretation of events also had its weaknesses, as Du Bois' later career clearly showed. Du Bois had so long fought against Western imperialism that he failed to take note of a Soviet variety. After he left Atlanta University in 1944, he rejoined the NAACP for a few years, only to break with the organization over the question of foreign policy. The NAACP wanted to concentrate on civil rights matters at home while Du Bois became more and more involved with foreign affairs. After he left the NAACP only the Communists presented him with a forum to vent his hatred of imperialism. From the late forties to his death in 1963, Du Bois remained virtually outside the American civil rights movement. Much that he had fought so hard to achieve in the lean years before World War II, was realized without his actual help. Du Bois receded more and more into the shadows of the Cold War. By the late fifties, a prominent professor at a large Negro university found that his students knew little of Du Bois other than that he was a "'a great man.' Some didn't know his name at all" (Harold R. Isaacs, *The New World of Negro Americans*).

In 1961 Du Bois applied for membership in the American Communist party. He was then ninety-three. Soon afterward, he and his wife gave up their fashionable home in Brooklyn Heights, and accepted President Nkrumah's invitation to settle in Ghana. He died there two years later, having lived to see many of his dreams in America and Africa fulfilled.

Du Bois' career is of such proportions and his achievements so considerable that it is not necessary to mythologize his life. It can stand the test of critical appraisal. Harold R. Isaac's candid portrait originally appeared as part of his chapter "Du Bois and Africa," in *The New World of Negro Americans* (1963). Professor Isaacs is a research associate at the Center for International Studies at the Massachusetts Institute of Technology.

DU BOIS: A CONTEMPORARY ASSESSMENT

SOURCE: Harold R. Isaacs, "Du Bois: A Contemporary Assessment," from a chapter "Du Bois and Africa," *The New World of Negro Americans* (New York, 1964), pp. 197–200, 225–30.

The lifetime of William E. Burghardt Du Bois, the most prolific of all American Negro writers and intellectuals, spans nearly the whole century back to Emancipation. He was born in 1868, had his first book published in 1896, and has been writing continuously ever since. His works include sociological studies, essays and sketches, biography and autobiography, history, novels, and poetry. As editor of several different series of scholarly papers and pamphlets and of several periodicals, he fathered still more words, especially in the volumes of *Crisis*, which he founded in 1910 and edited until 1933, the period of' his greatest personal impact on the affairs of Negroes in the United States. Never a successful leader or organizer or even a popular public figure, Du Bois with his words alone scratched deep, life-changing marks on the minds of a whole emergent generation of aspiring Negroes as it came to its youth and maturity in the first three decades of this century.

Du Bois' impact began in 1903 with the publication of *The Souls of Black Folk*, still his most famous and best-remembered book. In it he openly took issue with Booker T. Washington, until then the undisputed and unchallenged leader of American Negroes. Du Bois called upon Negroes to abandon the posture of submissiveness and modest aspiration that Washington counseled them to hold, and instead urged them to stand up to and fight for their rights as men and citizens in the American society. Instead of the limited system of education-for-work that Washington promoted at Tuskegee, Du Bois called upon Negroes to reach for the heights of all learning and to produce that famous "Talented Tenth" to lead Negroes to the full enjoyment of freedom. In 1905 he and a group of cothinkers launched the Niagara movement to promote these aims, and in 1910 he joined with a group of white liberals to found the National Association for the Advancement of Colored People, becoming its research director and the editor of its organ, *Crisis*.

In the columns of *Crisis* for the next 23 years Du Bois made himself the most eloquent tribune of the fight for civil rights and equality of opportunity for Negroes, lashing, arguing, cajoling, pontificating, fighting white injustices with slashing journalism, savage wit, and fierce polemics, and fighting black weaknesses with every weapon he could grasp. He fostered pride in Negro history, Negro achievements, and Negro good looks. He coaxed out artistic talent, ran issues devoted to college graduates, budding writers and artists, and beautiful babies. And ever and always he set forth in his own articles and editorials his own strong views of issues big and small in the Negro's fight for equality. In addition, almost as an extracurricular activity to which even his Negro readers paid scant attention, Du Bois organized between 1919 and 1927 four Pan-African Conferences in an unsuccessful attempt to give world scope to the black man's struggle for freedom from the oppression of the white. But his editorial performance was spectacular enough, pushing *Crisis* from an initial subscription of 10,000 to a top of 104,000, a figure small in looks but large in meaning because it included all Negroes who had set their faces upward and were pushing at the barriers for better education, political freedom, and better economic opportunity. It was a stormy editorship, because Du Bois, a prickly and vain man, was no easy associate. His object was to influence people, not to make friends, and he succeeded to a remarkable degree. Du Bois has written, sometimes sadly but more often complacently, of his special aloofness, and especially his aloofness from any personal contact with whites. From his earliest days he preferred to accept being glassed in—a figure of speech he has himself used. It was a withdrawal he liked to see as proud and austere, but it was really much more like the shrinking of a porcupine inside his armor of rising spines. A biographer will one day pursue this thread of self-separation through all the reams of Du Bois' writing about himself and about the world. It will help explain why, when he reached a time of despair after 30 years' struggle for integration and equality, he reverted to a program of self-imposed isolation for Negroes, a plan for growth-within-the-ghetto that took him all the way back into the shadow of Booker T. Washington.

In the same way, a biographer who seeks to put this man's parts together again will have to see the links and the spaces between his persistent elitism, his delight in elegance and aristocracy, his half-digested Marxism, his belief in power and authority and in a "Talented Tenth" to lead the slower-moving mass, and his slow gravitation toward the international Communist movement, ending in the last decades of his long life in a close embrace—indeed, a marriage—with totalitarian Communist world power. Over most of his active years Du Bois' attitudes toward the Soviet Union and the Communist Party were conditioned, like everything else in his life, by considerations of race. He held the Communist Party in rather scornful disdain most of the time for its gross ineptitude in the "Negro question," but he warmed to the Soviet Union early for its anticolonialism and for what he believed to be its abdication of the color line. In the 30 years since he left the editorship of *Crisis*, Du Bois moved first for a confused interval toward self-segregation and then more and more steadily into the camp of the Communists. In doing so he drifted into greater and greater isolation from Negroes in general, from most of those who still admired him for the great days of his past, and indeed from any significant contact with American or Western society. It is hardly accidental that Du Bois finally turned for his compensations and realizations to the emergent world of Communist power only when he could begin to see in it the verification of some of his prophecies of doom for the Western white world, the instrument for the defeat on the largest possible scale of the Anglo-Saxon dominators who were always his prime foes. In return, the Communist empire has given Du Bois the eminence and recognition of which he felt deprived in his homeland and even among his fellow Negroes in these last decades of his long life. In 1958–59, Du Bois made a long journey across the Soviet half world from Prague to Peking, and he was showered with honors by Communist universities and leaders in country after country. Responding to encomiums offered on his ninety-first birthday on February 23, 1959, in a speech broadcast over the Peking radio,

Du Bois gave his thanks and he said: "In my own country for nearly a century, I have been nothing but a nigger."[1]

When I was finally granted an hour's audience with Dr. Du Bois on a winter day not long before his ninety-second birthday, I knew it would be impossible to re-explore much of all this past, that most of my questions would have to go unasked, that I would be lucky enough to catch a glimpse of how he now saw the future, of how the long story was ending. One wanted this glimpse, even knowing that for a quarter of a century what Du Bois thought had ceased to echo in the thinking of others, that he had passed from behind his famous veil to a new place behind an even more famous curtain.

In his half of a comfortable house in well-to-do Brooklyn Heights, I was shown into Du Bois' study, heavy with his life's accumulation of books, including his own on a long shelf. In spaces on the walls were the parchments of some of his recently acquired honors from Communist institutions in Eastern Europe. Over the mantel hung a portrait of what I took to be one of his prized ancestors, a handsome, fair-skinned patrician-looking man. Du Bois walked in slowly, short but of good carriage, fingering the gold chain across his gray waistcoated middle with a polished Phi Beta Kappa key gleaming upon it. With his small goatee, his high bald crown, his sharp and clear light eyes, his acquiline face, his tone and air of authority, he was the breakfast-table autocrat, only semiretired, calmly scornful of a world too unintelligent to accept the verities of which he was now the venerable guardian. But he was graciously willing to measure them out in quiet and genteel and clean sentences. His politeness, nearly punctilious, gave an odd contrapuntal effect to his words, especially when he was offering up, like verses out of scripture, bits of crude Communist hagiography.

He began by asking me what went on at the Center for International Studies, and when I spoke of its interest in world problems, he tapped his fingertips knowingly together and said: "I suppose this all has to do with investments." It became clear that what he pictured was a roomful of men with top hats, beaked noses, big bellies, and clawed hands grasping great big moneybags, drooling over the outlook for new profits in Asia

[1] *The New York Times*, March 5, 1959.

and Africa. I murmured a small denial and changed the subject, but at first this did not help at all. When we began to discuss the impact of world affairs on Negroes, he said: "There is really no way for the young Negro to get to know about world affairs. All the news here is suppressed and distorted. He has no way of learning what is going on in the Soviet Union or in China." Any young Negro traveling abroad, he went on, is "coached as to what to say. It means that a young man when he goes abroad has to be more or less a traitor to his people. He either keeps his mouth shut abroad or else he lies." When I opened the matter of his early recollections about Africa, he tapped a fat manuscript on the desk before him. "I have dealt with this in a new autobiography I have just finished," he said. "I will offer it for publication here, but I doubt that it will get published. Of course it *will* be published, in Russia, Czechoslovakia, and East Germany." I looked over his head at the shelf of his own works, all issued here over the many years, and I thought that I might ask him if in all the Soviet Union or China he could find such a shelf of books, or even a single volume, written by anyone who was even in small part the critic, opponent, and rebel against the society that Du Bois had been all his life in America. But I pressed on to other things, and although Du Bois has never been a man lightly turned away from his obsessions, we did cover some small patches of new and higher ground, enough to show me that even in this latest and perhaps last of his outlooks an impressive intelligence survives.

It quickly became clear that Du Bois, who had despaired 25 years before of winning through to Negro integration in American life, was now concerned with the effects of integration, seeing its success as already assured. He had leapfrogged ahead to new problems: "The Negro child gets into a school which is integrated, and the chances are nine out of ten that he will have an unsympathetic teacher who won't know or care anything about the history of Negroes. How will he ever get to know anything about it?" He was worried much more by the fear that with growing economic opportunity and well being, Negroes were getting to be just like whites: "Why, most of the Negroes who went to Ghana for the independence celebration or have gone there since have been interested in business and investments, in what money they could make . . . In Ghana there was a flood of Americans, Negro and white, who just wanted to make money. It was the same when Nkrumah was here." And the principal difference from the past was that "the Negro now assumes he has the same chance" as the white man to profit. "This is the sickness of the whole American civilization, money! The insidious thing is that Negroes are taking white Americans as their pattern, to make a life out of buying and selling and become rich, spending for show."

What were the alternatives for the Negro? I asked. Alienation? Migration? Integration?

Du Bois ruled out alienation, and he credited this to the Communist world. "The thing that will stop any new alienation of Negroes from whites will be the attitudes of the Soviet Union and China. The Negro gets more consideration in the Soviet Union and China than he ever got in England or France or elsewhere. You can't have another movement like Garvey's [i.e., against whites] because you would have to include as whites the two hundred million Russians, Czechs, and so on. And now countries that can't get capital on satisfactory terms from the West can turn to the Soviet Union, and eventually to China, and get it at two percent."

Migration? He thought not. "Of course it is true that for a long time many Negroes had come to think that there was no hope of winning equality in the United States and that it was best to get out. But they were disappointed in Liberia and disappointed in Garvey and had to be content with the emphasis, sometimes the overemphasis, on Africa and race pride in books like Carter Woodson's. . . . But there will be no reproduction of any urge to migrate. Negroes now have the chance to go into business, opportunities are opening up. You now have Negro millionaires!"

Integration, then?

"The real question is: after there is no more discrimination based on race and color, what do you do? Where do you go? I have somewhere drawn the analogy of being on a train, and having a fight with my fellow passengers over my treatment on that train while I should be thinking: Where is this train going? We have fought down discrimination. There has been tremendous improvement. Negroes are becoming Americans. But then what are Americans to become?"

Well, what is the prospect, then, and what about Africa?

"I don't know," replied Du Bois. "The Negro is not working it out. He doesn't really see the problem yet. In the next ten to twenty years there will be a change of thought regarding the relationship of the American Negro to Africa and to the world. We used to think that because they were educated, and had some chance, American Negroes would lead Africans to progress. But the chances are now that Africa will lead American Negroes. But into what kind of world? And what kind of world will there be to be led into? I do not know where the American people will decide to move, but I am sure that the organization of Africa will have a decisive effect on what American Negroes will do and think about the future. I don't think they will leave the United States. Negroes will be more and more integrated. There will be more and more intermarriage . . . But this will be a longtime development of a hundred years or more. The question even then is: What culture of Africa and what culture of the American Negro will succeed in surviving? What in general of the culture of the world? The question really is what will all human society be like? We prefer varieties. What will the varieties be? I don't think it is really important for the future of mankind what color skin men will have or what their racial characteristics will be. I don't think the issue of race is central, that the color of skin is the important thing. The Negro has been trying to unmake the situation in which this was important and he should not be drawn back toward it. I don't really care what the racial identity of people will be in the twenty-third century. I don't think the future of 'Negritude' is important. What will be important is what people will be thinking and doing by then."

This was Du Bois, at ninety-two, straining his eyes harder than ever from his lonely hilltop, and now, as at the beginning, glimpsing dreams and ideas far, far away, across a foreground pitted and barred by the grotesque shapes and distortions of the nearby reality. For him these were the enshrouding distortions of racism, and to fight debasement he made himself into a racist, genteel, intelligent and literate, but still a racist. When he came, in his late age, to abandon the racist view—if that indeed is what he has really done—it has been to embrace as more humane the greater inhumanities of Communist totalitarianism. All his life Du Bois scornfully rejected the preachers of pie in the sky, believing that in heaven a man was nothing and had to win his freedom on earth, only in his last years to surrender to those for whom a man's freedom is nothing, neither in heaven nor, most of all, on earth.

Du Bois did not settle the Negro score. It is being settled by the great glacial pressures that do finally move human society. But he did make himself part of those pressures and the "settlement," as it comes, resembles much of what he wanted for black men in America and in Africa, and from this he must gather what satisfaction he can. But Du Bois did not settle his own score either. He wanted recognition, acceptance, eminence, a life among peers. When he was denied, he cut himself off. Today he still stands apart from all except the Communists, who cynically do him honor for his use as a symbol now, especially abroad, and some older Negroes who remember with respect what he did for them in a distant past. It is impossible for me to know whether all of Du Bois' unsatisfied urges and dreams for himself are gratified and realized in the recognition extended to him by the Communist world. He may insist that he sees Communist world power as man's last best hope; it is hard not to imagine that he also sees in it history's means for finally settling the white world's accounts with him and with his fellow nonwhites. Either way, he helps explain the nature of his failure and leaves one only to guess what a great man he might have become had he been able to set himself resolutely all his life against *all* forms of tyranny over the minds of men.

George Shepperson

It has generally been assumed that Negro Americans became interested in Africa only in recent years. On analysis, however, this assumption proved to be incorrect.

Since the late eighteenth century Negroes have not only shown an interest in Africa, but a considerable number decided to emigrate to Sierra Leone and Liberia. For the great majority that remained, Africa was never far from their consciousness, as shown when free Negroes affixed the name "African" to their organizations, e.g., New York African Free School (1787), African Methodist Episcopal Church (1799), *The Anglo-African Magazine* (1859).

After the Civil War, Negroes increased their activities in Africa. Leading the way were Negro missionaries and churchmen. As early as 1862 Bishop Alexander Crummell foresaw the positive role in educational and missionary work that Negroes from America might play in Africa's future. A. M. E. Bishop Henry McNeal Turner toured Africa in the 1890s and advocated the return to Africa of American Negroes. Bishop Alexander Walters of the A.M.E.Z. Church took an active part in the first Pan-African Conference held in 1900. Negro churchmen gathered together in Atlanta in 1895 to discuss developments in Africa, and their report, *Africa and the American Negro,* constituted, according to Professor George Shepperson, the largest body of accurate information then available anywhere on Africa.

Interest in Africa was not just confined to the higher clergy, but was passed down to members of almost every Negro congregation. Professor Rayford Logan remembers that as a boy he "heard the great Negro missionary [William Henry] Sheppard, who told us about the mutilation in the Congo. It made an indelible impression on me. In the humblest Negro church there was a willingness to give in order to send missionaries, an interest in people's need of the Gospel and a special interest in Africa because we knew we were descendants of Africans" (Isaac's *The New World of Negro Americans*).

These missionaries brought more than the Gospel. Negro American missionaries were viewed with great suspicion as teaching subversive ideas, and many of the African students who came home from training in America reinforced this view by becoming agitators and revolutionaries. For example, Daniel Chilembwe of Nyasaland (Malawi), trained at the Negro Virginia Theological Seminary and, supported in his works by Negro American Baptists, led a rebellion in 1915. Three American-educated Africans were active in the formation and growth of the African Native National Congress in South Africa.

Other Negroes took an active part in fostering an interest

in Africa. Du Bois' work is well known, but mention should
be made of Dr. Carter G. Woodson who, through the *Journal
of Negro History*, encouraged research in African history.
Booker T. Washington was very much interested in African
affairs, and in 1912 he sponsored a major conference on
Africa at Tuskegee Institute.

African students continued to come to America. Nkrumah of
Ghana, Hastings Banda of Malawi, and Nnamdi Azikiwe of
Nigeria were among the most famous. The African students
learned from the Negro American experience. Dr. Nkrumah
told the Sixth Pan-African Congress in 1958 that "before
many of us were conscious of our own degradation, it was
the New World Negroes who raised the banner of African
liberation." Other Africans were influenced by reading the
writings of Negro American poets. Leopold Senghor, President of Senegal, poet, philosopher, and exponent of negritude,
discovered Negro-American writers through the works of
Haitian intellectuals. Alain Locke of Howard University influenced Senghor's concept of negritude, and when visiting
the United States in 1962, Senghor paid tribute to the poets
of the Harlem Renaissance for providing him and other African intellectuals with the inspiration to pursue their ideas of
African cultural nationalism.

George Shepperson is Professor of Commonwealth and
American History at the University of Edinburgh, where he
specializes in African and American history. With Thomas
Price he wrote *Independent African, John Chilembwe and
. . . the Nyasaland Native Uprising of 1915* (1958).

NOTES ON NEGRO AMERICAN INFLUENCES
ON THE EMERGENCE OF
AFRICAN NATIONALISM

SOURCE: George Shepperson, *Journal of African History*, 1, 2 (1960), pp.
299–312.

The first British Empire owed much to the triangular trade
between Africa, the West Indies and North America. The last
British Empire has not been uninfluenced by another triangular
trade, a trade not of pocatille, slaves and molasses, but a com-

merce of ideas and politics between the descendants of the slaves in the West Indies and North America and their ancestral continent. Until the imposition of immigrant quotas by the United States in the 1920s, West Indian Negroes[1] contributed a distinct element to the coloured American's interest in and influence on Africa.

Edward Blyden, who was born in St. Thomas in 1832, went to New York in 1847 but was refused admission to an American university because of his colour and, therefore, emigrated to Liberia in 1850 to become a leading politician and pioneer theorist of the 'African personality', is the outstanding example of this three-way process. At the peak of his powers, 1872 to 1888, Blyden visited America eleven times. He knew many Negro Americans and the sentiments he offered them are exemplified in his address at the Hampton Institute, Virginia, in 1883. Warning his Negro audience against European travellers' accounts of Africa, he declared that 'No people can interpret Africans but Africans'.[2] It was ideas of this kind which made the Gold Coast nationalist Casely Hayford dub the writings on racial questions by some Negro Americans as 'exclusive and provincial' and led him to praise Blyden's conceptions as 'universal among the entire race and the entire race problem'.[3]

The two other outstanding West Indians in this ideological triangle are obvious: Marcus Garvey, the Jamaican Negro whose eleven years in the States, through his militant Universal Negro Improvement Association (U.N.I.A.), 'awakened a race consciousness that made Harlem felt around the world'[4]; and George Padmore of Trinidad whose last and best book, *Pan-Africanism or*

---

[1] With the exception of Ira De A. Reid's *The Negro Immigrant* (New York, 1939), there has been almost no serious study of West Indian Negro influence on Negro Americans.

[2] *Southern Workman* (Hampton, Va.), 1883, 9. See also Edward Blyden, *The African Problem and other Discourses delivered in America in 1890* (London, 1890).

[3] Casely Hayford, *Ethiopia Unbound* (London, 1911), 163: cf. Hayford's introduction to *Africa and the Africans. Proceedings . . . of a Banquet . . . to Edward W. Blyden, Ll.D., by West Africans in London* (London, 1903), especially p. 18. See also James S. Coleman, *Nigeria* (Berkeley, 1958), 175-6, 183-4, 452-3; L. J. Coppin, *Unwritten History* (Philadelphia, 1919), 316-17.

[4] Clayton Powell, Snr., *Against the Tide* (1938), 70-1. See also Edmund D. Cronon, *Black Moses* (Madison, 1955).

Communism? (London, 1956) is one of the few studies which has recognized the existence of this triangle and tried to estimate its significance for Africa.

There are many lesser names which indicate that this is not inconsiderable: for example, the Barbadian Dr Albert Thorne,[5] a precursor of Garvey, who tried from 1897 to the 1920s to launch in America a movement for the Negro colonization of Central Africa; the Antiguan George Alexander McGuire, first American Bishop in 1921 of the African Orthodox Church of the Garvey movement[6] which made its mark on independent African churches in South and East Africa; and the Jamaican Claude McKay whose militant verse of the 'Harlem Renaissance' period has influenced emerging Negro literature everywhere. Thorne's belief that 'Africa is the only quarter of the world where we will be permanently respected as a race'[7] illustrates one of the main factors linking the *avante-garde* of American and West Indian Negroes in a common interest in Africa.

Both groups shared a common challenge: the challenge implicit in such statements as that by a white sympathizer of the Negro in America in 1909 that 'at the background of every Negro, however wise, or well educated, or brave, or good, is contemporary Africa which has no collective achievement . . . like other nationalities'.[8] Two responses, at least, were possible: to recognize that this view was correct and to seek every means to lay a basis for African nationality and collective achievement; or to claim that it was wrong and to demonstrate this by searching into the African past for achievements which the biased eye of the white man had overlooked. In the intermin-

[5] *Illustrated Missionary News* (London, 1897), 70–2, 105, 113; *New York Age*, 12 August 1922, 'African Colonization Schemes'.
[6] A. C. Terry Thomas, *The History of the African Orthodox Church* (New York, 1956). See also Cronon, op. cit. 69, 103, 160, 178–80, 189; *The African Yearly Register*, ed. T. D. Mweli Skota (Johannesburg, 1932), 128, 172, etc. G. A. McGuire (misspelt as 'Maguire') is now immortalized as an 'American Negro' in *Historical Survey of the Origins and Growth of Mau Mau* (Cmnd. 1030, London, 1960), 173: cf. also pp. 45, 174–5, 178.
[7] *An Appeal addressed to the Friends of the African Race* (c. 1896), 30, in Church of Scotland Papers, Miscellaneous Bundle, Pamphlets No. 1, National Library of Scotland.
[8] Edgar Gardner Murphy, *The Basis of Ascendency* (New York, 1909), 42.

gling of these two responses may be seen most of the elements in the Negro American's influence on Africa.

This influence would not be expected to make itself felt to any degree until after the American Civil War and the emancipation of the slaves. Nevertheless, some Negroes in America showed an interest in Africa before the 1860s—usually in the face of the criticism of black abolitionists such as Frederick Douglass who considered the African dream a dangerous diversification of energies which were needed in the fight for emancipation and civil rights at home[9]—which provided a basis on which coloured Americans' aspirations could build after the Civil War.

Liberia, of course, supplied them with a focus. Its American-style Constitution and Declaration of Independence in 1847 seemed to demonstrate 'beyond all reasonable doubt that the Black Man is capable of self-government'[10]—though there have been cynics, Negro as well as white, who have felt that the existence of Liberia has done as much to delay as to advance African self-government.[11]

But, for one of the major pre-Civil War Negro American exponents of the 'Back-to-Africa' dream, Martin R. Delany, Harvard-trained physician and first Negro to be commissioned with field rank by president Lincoln, the Liberians were a 'noble band of brothers'.[12] He visited Liberia in July 1859 and saw in the proposed Liberian College 'a grand stride in the march of African Regeneration and Negro Nationality'.[13] Half a century later, however, Sir Harry Johnston castigated the 'obstinate adhesion' of the Liberians and their College 'to the ideals of New England' and warned that they 'must turn their

---

[9] E.g. *Life and Writings of Frederick Douglass,* ed. Philip S. Foner (New York, 1950), II, 251–4, 387–8, 441–6.

[10] John Says, U.S. agent for liberated Africans in Liberia: Rhodes House Library, Mic. Afr. 349, Roll 10.

[11] George S. Schuyler, *Slaves To-day* (New York, 1931); Charles S. Johnson (Negro American member of 1930 League of Nations Commission on Forced Labour in Liberia), *Bitter Canaan,* unpublished typescript in C. S. Johnson papers, Fisk University. But cf. N. Azikiwe, *Liberia in World Politics* (London, 1934), 233 et seq.

[12] Martin R. Delany, *Official Report of the Niger Valley Exploring Party* (New York, 1861), 24.

[13] Ibid. 23.

backs on America and their faces towards Africa, or they will dwindle to nothing'.[14] That Delany was also seriously concerned with this problem of loss of identity was seen in September 1859 when he visited Abeokuta and concluded an agreement with the Egba chiefs. He criticized the Christian missionaries' habit of changing the names of their African converts on the grounds that this would lead to 'a loss of identity'.[15] For Delany, the only answer was 'Africa for the African': with Blyden, he appears to have been one of the first to use this magnetic slogan.[16]

Delany's emphasis was political. Other Negro Americans looked for the joint regeneration of the coloured man in America and Africa through Negro-led Christian missions. As early as the 1790s, Negroes from America were interested in the independent churches of Sierra Leone. By the Civil War, the outstanding theoretician of the Negro missionary movement to Africa was Alexander Crummell,[17] Bachelor of Arts of Queen's College, Cambridge, and a coloured Anglican divine. It was to be the connexion between the Negro churches of America and Africa which, after the Civil War, was to provide a channel for increasing numbers of Africans to gain an education in coloured American schools and colleges.

After the Civil War and the so-called Reconstruction of the Southern States, when the civil rights which the Negro had expected from a Northern victory were denied to him in many parts of the Union, numerous Negro Americans, despairing of a redress of their grievances in the United States, sought consolation in the 'Back-to-Africa' dream. At the same time, the partition of Africa by the European Powers and the many overt injustices which this created, gave the Negro American, already highly

[14] *Liberia* (London, 1906), 368–70.

[15] Delany, op. cit. 52.

[16] Ibid. 61. See also George Shepperson and Thomas Price, *Independent African* (Edinburgh, 1958), 504.

[17] Crummell's life is one of the great missed opportunities of American biographers, although most of his papers are conveniently collected in the Schomburg Collection of the New York Public Library. There is a brief sketch in William H. Ferris, *Alexander Crummell* (Washington, D.C., 1920). See also the moving tribute in ch. XII of W. E. B. Dubois's *The Souls of Black Folk* (New York, 1955 reprint). An example of Crummell's interest in Africa is his *The Future of Africa* (New York, 1862).

conscious of injustice, the added incentive of rendering service in Africa to his 'own people'.

After the Civil War, as before, the 'Back-to-Africa' movement was strenuously opposed by leading Negro politicians.[18] But it never lost its attractions. Up to the first World War, its major exponent was the African Methodist Episcopal Church Bishop, Henry M. Turner,[19] who urged Negro Americans passionately that it was their only way to salvation. For all its idealism, the movement did not lack its racketeers.[20] Nor was there any shortage of colourful characters, such as the Negro stockbroker, William Henry Ellis,[21] who led an expedition to Ethiopia in 1903, supported by Turner, which had the unusual effect of eliciting a letter in Amharic from Menelik II to thank Andrew Carnegie for his gifts to the education of 'African Americans' in the United States.[22] All such schemes, fair or foul, kept the idea of Negro colonization and a roseate image of Africa alive amongst Negro Americans until the time was ripe for an outburst of Negro grievances which could make use of them.

This occurred immediately after the first World War when, as at the end of the Civil War, the raising of Negro hopes had proved abortive and fresh disillusionment ensued. Into this setting, in 1914, stepped Marcus Garvey, with a ready-made programme, the manifesto of his Universal Negro Improvement Association and African Committees League which had been founded on 1 August 1914, in Jamaica. The U.N.I.A. stressed race pride and power and declared that it aimed 'to strengthen

[18] A good example of modern criticisms is Charles I. Glicksberg's 'Negro Americans and the African Dream', *Phylon* (Atlanta, Ga.), VIII, 4, 323–30.

[19] The best indication of Turner's interest in African colonization is his newspaper, *The Voice of the People*, 1901–7 (copy on loan in the library of Morris Brown College, Atlanta, Ga.) See also, for example, W. K. Roberts, *An African Canaan for American Negroes* (Birmingham, Ala., 1896), 18–19.

[20] E.g. Deluding the Negroes: 'The United States and Congo National Emigration Steamship Company'. A ticket to Africa and a Farm for One Dollar. From *'The (Washington) Post'*, 19 January 1891 (Library of Congress).

[21] *Voice of the People*, op. cit. 33, 1 Oct. 1903, 3, 34, ? Nov. 1903, 1; *African Methodist Episcopal Church Review* (Philadelphia, 1903), xx, 302, 'Menelik the Negus'.

[22] The original letter and a small file about it are in the Carnegie Birthplace Museum, Dunfermline.

the imperialism of independent African states'.[23] At its 1920
New York convention a 'Declaration of Rights of the Negro
Peoples of the World' was drawn up which set out these aims
in greater detail and demanded 'Africa for the Africans at home
and abroad'.[24] If Garvey's 'Back-to-Africa' scheme, his Black
Star Line, collapsed when he was deported from America in
1927, his massive propaganda for pride, not shame, in a black
skin left an ineradicable mark on African nationalism everywhere, all the criticisms which were made of him by men of his
own colour notwithstanding.[25] Kwame Nkrumah has stated
unequivocally that the *Philosophy and Opinions of Marcus
Garvey* influenced him more than anything else during his
period in America.[26] And Garvey's pride of colour, through his
organ, *The Negro World,* reached out into West Africa, its
independent church and nationalist movements[27]; into South
and Central Africa, where it had some effect on the followers of
Clements Kadalie of the Industrial and Commercial Workers
Union of Africa and the remains of the Nyasaland Chilembwe-
ite movement[28]; and into the messianic nationalism of the
Kimbangu movement in the Congo.[29]

The 1920s, the main years of the Garvey movement, was the
period when European governments in Africa were most wary of
Negro American influences in their territories. Garvey's U.N.I.A.,
certainly, had brought this suspicion to a head: but it had much
earlier roots. The phenomenon of 'Ethiopianism'[30] in South
Africa went back to 1896–8 when separatist South African

[23] Booker T. Washington Papers, Library of Congress (hereafter cited as
B.T.W.), Container 939, Miscellaneous Correspondence, 1915, E–H: Garvey to Washington, 12 April, 1915.

[24] Raymond Leslie Buell, *The Native Problem in Africa* (New York,
1928), II, 967.

[25] E.g. M. Mokete Manoedi (Basuto), *Garvey and Africa* (n.d.), in
Schomburg Collection, N.Y.

[26] *The Autobiography of Kwame Nkrumah* (Edinburgh, 1957), 45.

[27] Coleman, op. cit. 189–91. See also correspondence between Akinambi
Agbebi (Lagos Black Star line agent), E. M. E. Agbebi and John Edward Bruce in the John Edward Bruce Papers (hereafter cited as J.E.B.)
in the Schomburg Collection, N.Y.

[28] Shepperson and Price, op. cit. 433–5, 504; *Nyasaland Times,* 24
September 1926, 3.

[29] Efraim Andersson, *Messianic Popular Movements in the Lower Congo*
(Uppsala, 1958), 250–6.

[30] Shepperson and Price, op. cit. passim.

churches had sought affiliation with the pioneer Negro American independent church, the African Methodist Episcopal Church,[31] and its fiery Bishop, H. M. Turner, had made his trip to Africa.[32] Through such connexions, numbers of Africans from South Africa were to visit the United States, often in search of an education which seemed to them easier to obtain in Negro American colleges than at home. Three names stand out in this process: John L. Dube,[33] Solomon Plaatje[34] and D. D. T. Jabavu,[35] all of whom played important roles in the growth of the South African Native National Congress. The list could be extended considerably[36] until a pattern emerges which makes intelligible

[31] L. J. Coppin, *Observations of Persons and Things in South Africa* (Philadelphia, n.d.), 8–18. See also references to James Dwane in the A.M.E. Church *Episcopal Handbook*, 1900, ed. B. W. Arnett, especially pp. 8–17.

[32] His first trip was in 1892: see *African Methodist Episcopal Church Review* (Philadelphia), 1892, 446–98.

[33] Edward Roux, *Times Longer Than Rope* (London, 1949), 108, 117–18, 258, 260, 296, 306, 357; Shepperson and Price, op. cit. 91–2, 102, 145, 162, 203, 461; *Southern Workman* (1897), 141–2; John L. Dube, *A Zulu's Message to Afro-Americans* in J.E.B. Papers and *A Talk about my Native Land* (Rochester, N.Y., 1892).

[34] Roux, op. cit. 118–19; Shepperson and Price, op. cit. 202; Sol. T. Plaatje, *The Mote and the Beam* (New York, 1921) in Howard University Library; Sol. T. Plaatje, *Native Life in South Africa* (London, 5th edn., n.d.), 16, 286, 368, indicate the influence of W. E. B. Du Bois; Plaatje's pamphlet on the 1913 South African Natives' Land Act was sent to B. T. Washington's secretary, E. J. Scott, by Plaatje, 27 Aug. 1914 (B.T.W. Papers, Container 13, O–R); J. E. Bruce to Carter G. Woodson, 17 Jan. 1923, in Carter G. Woodson Papers, Library of Congress (hereafter cited as C.G.W.).

[35] Roux, op. cit. 65, 85, 182, 295–96, 299, 301, 306; D. D. T. Jabavu, *The Black Problem* (Lovedale, C. P., 1920), i, 25–96, 103.

[36] A representative list of some of the many South African Africans who visited America or corresponded with Negro Americans might include: The Lincoln University group—22 between 1896 and 1924 and none, apparently, thereafter (figures from an unpublished history of Lincoln University kindly supplied by Dr. Horace Mann Bond)—of which one of the most interesting was Livingstone N. Mzimba, son of P. J. Mzimba, separatist church leader (see *Lincoln University Herald*, Oxford, Pa., xiii, May, 1909, 1–2, and L. N. Mzimba, 'The African Church', 86–95, *Christianity and the Natives of South Africa*, ed. J. Dexter Taylor, Lovedale, 1927). A. K. Soga, editor of *Izwi LaBantu* (to Bruce, 23 Feb. 1907, J.E.B. Papers). Representatives of the 'Ethiopian Church of South Africa' at 1912 Tuskegee Africa Conference, Reverends Henry Reed and Isaiah Goda Shishuba (C.G.W. Papers, Box 13, galley proof). P. K. Isaka Seme, initiator of the South African Native National Congress (see the reprint of his 1906 Colum-

the South African Government's fear that Negro Americans were inflaming Bantu racial consciousness. This fear reached unreasonable heights at the time of the 1906 Natal Zulu Rebellion[37] and flamed up again in the 1920s, not only because of Garveyism but also because of the 1921 'Bulhoek Massacre' episode, for Enoch Mgijima, the leading figure in the affair, was known to have been in communion once with the primitive communistic Negro American Church of God and Saints of Christ.[38] If John Buchan's 1910 *Prester John* is the classical literary expression of this fear, Senator George Heaton Nicholl's hysterical novel *Bayete!* of 1923 shows it in its most frenzied form. It was a fear which manifested itself in British Central Africa from 1902, when two Negro American missionaries *en route* for Nyasaland were detained at Chinde for nine days,[39] until at least a decade after the 1915 Chilembwe Rising.[40]

If it was in South Africa and Nyasaland that the fear of Negroes from America disturbed most European Governments,

bia University address, 'The Regeneration of Africa', 436–9, William H. Ferris, *The African Abroad,* I, New Haven, 1913). Columbus Kamba Simango, 'The African and Civilization', *Southern Workman* (Hampton, Va., 1917), 552–5. Jeannie Somtuuzi, 'African Contributions to Civilization', address at 34th annual meeting of the Negro National Baptist Convention, Sept. 1914 (in B.T.W. Papers, Container 12, L–N). Simbini Mamba Nkomo, *The Tribal Life of the People of South Africa* (Oration delivered at College Commencement, Greenville, Ill., June, 1917) in Howard University Library. Abraham Le Fleux, 'who came to London to get justice for land out of which his people had been cheated' (letters sent by Alice Werner to Carter G. Woodson, C.G.W. Papers, Boxes 4 and 5); etc. It will be noticed that this very brief selection includes one African (P. K. I. Seme) who went to a non-Negro university. In general, such students often had deficiencies in their education made up at Negro American schools and colleges before proceeding to white institutions. A present-day example is Dr. Hastings K. Banda, who attended the Negro Wilberforce Academy at Wilberforce, Ohio, in 1928, before he went to Indiana and Chicago Universities.

37 Cf. C. S. Smith (A.M.E. Church Bishop in South Africa, 1904–6), *The Relations of the British Government to the Natives of South Africa* (Washington, D.C., 1906), 12–13; *Southern Workman,* 1906, 664–5.

38 *Reports . . . relative to 'Israelites' at Bulhoek and Occurrences in May, 1921* (Cape Town, 1921), I; Elmer T. Clark, *The Small Sects in America* (Nashville, 1949), 151–3.

39 *Review and Herald* (Seventh-day Adventist, Washington, D.C.), 18 Nov. 1902, 17: cf. George Shepperson, "The Literature of British Central Africa', *Rhodes-Livingstone Journal* (Manchester, 1958), XXIII, 42.

40 Shepperson and Price, op. cit. 390–1.

other parts of Africa were affected by it. In the Congo, the Belgians, as early as 1878,[41] had shown interest in Negro Americans because of their long experience with the white man's methods of work. But by the 1890s,[42] although they were still interested, a critical attitude was developing amongst the Negro American intelligentsia towards the Leopold régime which was not calculated to ensure a warm welcome for the coloured American in the future by the Congo authorities. George Washington Williams, whose *History of the Negro Race* was one of the first historical studies by a Negro American writer to quicken the imagination of African nationalists,[43] played a small part in gaining American support for the Congo Free State; but in 1890, after a journalistic visit to the Congo, he became increasingly critical of conditions there.[44] Similarly, by the 1890s, the Negro American Presbyterian missionary, William Henry Sheppard, had begun his outspoken criticisms of the Belgian Congo régime which were to bring upon him a libel charge and eight months' imprisonment in 1908.[45] Beginning with Williams and Sheppard, an image of the Belgian Congo as the quintessence of European exploitation of Africa was created amongst Negro Americans which played no small part in shaping their attitude to Africa.[46] On the West Coast, the 'Back-to-Africa' movement of 'Chief Alfred Sam' and the Akim Trading Company seems to have had the effect, by 1914, of getting the

[41] H. S. Sanford Papers in process at Tennessee State Archives, Nashville: H. M. Stanley to Sanford, Rotterdam, 20 Dec. 1878. See also Leo T. Molloy, *Henry Shelton Sanford* (Derby, Conn., private print), 27.

[42] Sanford Papers: Senator J. T. Morgan to Sanford, 19 ? 1890.

[43] Frederick Alexander Durham, *The Lone Star of Liberia* (London, 1892), XII.

[44] Paul McStallworth, *The United States and the Congo Question, 1884–1914* (Ph.D., Ohio State University, 1954), 196 et seq.; John Hope Franklin, 'George Washington Williams, Historian', *Journal of Negro History* (Washington, D.C., 1946), XXXI, 1, 89–90.

[45] Ruth M. Slade, *English-Speaking Missions in the Congo Independent State, 1878–1908* (Brussels, 1959), 104–6, 254–6, 368–70; *Southern Workman* (1910), 8–12; *Africa in the World Democracy . . . N.A.A.C.P. . . . 6 January 1919* (New York, 1919), 25–6.

[46] Samuel Barrett, *A Plea for Unity among American Negroes and the Negroes of the World* (Waterloo, Iowa, 1926), 65, copy in Howard University Library; Horace R. Cayton and St. Clair Drake, *Black Metropolis* (London, 1946), 720.

Gold Coast to tighten up its immigration regulations in order to keep 'undesirable' Negro Americans out of its area.[47] Altogether, by the mid-1920s, the problem of Negroes from the United States in Africa had become so serious that the 1926 International Conference on the Christian Mission in Africa addressed itself specially to the question.[48]

By the 1920s, the ideological influence on emerging African nationalism of the writings and political activities of such militant Negro Americans as W. E. B. Du Bois and Carter G. Woodson was making itself felt. Du Bois's role as a pioneer of Pan-Africanism through the Pan-African Conferences which he initiated or encouraged in 1919 (Paris), 1921 (London), 1923 (London and Lisbon), 1927 (New York) and 1945 (Manchester), to which Kwame Nkrumah paid tribute in his speech at the opening session of the 1958 All-African People's Conference at Accra, is relatively well known.[49] What is not so well known, however, is that the first so-called Pan-African Conference was held in London in 1900.[50] Although Du Bois was present at this Conference and became chairman of its 'Committee on Address to the Nations of the World', it was started by H. Sylvester Williams, a West Indian barrister, and a moving spirit was Bishop Alexander Walters of the African Methodist Episcopal Zion Church, a neglected figure of Negro American

---

[47] Arna Bontemps and Jack Conroy, *They Seek a City* (New York, 1945), 171; Sydney H. French, 'Chief Sam and His "Back-to-Africa" Movement', W.P.A. paper, Schomburg Collection, N.Y.; *Sierra Leone Weekly News*, 23 Jan. 1915, 6–7, 9, 12; Rhodes House Library, Press Cuttings, 1914–15, 'Back to Africa', Anti-Slavery Society Papers; *African Times and Orient Review*, 7 July, 1914, 380, 'Accra Native' letter.

[48] Milton Stauffer, *Thinking With Africa* (New York, 1927), 154–6. See also 'The Contribution of the American Negro to Africa', *Christian Action in Africa, Report of the Church Conference on African Affairs held at Otterbein College, Westerville, Ohio, June 19–25, 1942* (New York, 1942), 140–1.

[49] See, for example, Padmore, op. cit. 89–170; Thomas Hodgkin, *Nationalism in Colonial Africa* (London, 1956), 21, 23–4, 161, 175, 181–2, 184, 188; Ch. du Bus de Warnaffe, 'Le mouvement pan-nègre aux Etats-Unis et ailleurs', *Congo* (Brussels), May 1922.

[50] W. E. B. Du Bois, *The World and Africa* (New York, 1947), 7; George Padmore, *Pan-Africanism or Communism?* (London, 1956), 117–18. The fullest account is Alexander Walters, *My Life and Work* (New York, 1917), ch. xx. I am indebted to Mr Harold Isaacs of the Centre for International Studies, Boston, for drawing my attention to Bishop Walters. See also *The Times* (London, 1900), 24 July, 7, 25 July, 15, 26 July, 11.

history and a believer in the inevitability of a 'Negro Cecil Rhodes'.[51] The Conference sent a memorial to Queen Victoria protesting against the treatment of Africans in South Africa and Rhodesia and succeeded in eliciting from Joseph Chamberlain a pledge that 'Her Majesty's Government will not overlook the interests and welfare of the native races'.[52]

It was at the 1900 Pan-African Conference, in a memorial which he drafted to be sent 'to the sovereigns in whose realms are subjects of African descent', that Du Bois first made the statement that 'The problem of the Twentieth Century is the color line'—those famous words which, three years later, headed his influential book, *The Souls of Black Folk*.[53] It is important to remember that this often-quoted slogan started not in the opening paragraph to his first notable book but at the time of Du Bois's introduction to Pan-Africanism.

Until 1914, Pan-Africanism, if not forgotten,[54] was dormant amongst Negro Americans, probably because the increase of colour problems in the United States temporarily narrowed their horizons. The outbreak of the first World War, however, flung these horizons wide open again. In 1915, Du Bois published his important article 'The African Roots of the War' in *The Atlantic Monthly*. Although he had not yet become converted to Marxism, Du Bois demonstrated in this article how close he was to its tenets. 'The African Roots of the War' anticipates Lenin's thesis on the colonial origins of the War in his *Imperialism* and even uses the term 'aristocracy of labor'[55] which is often considered to be Lenin's invention. Such writings stimulated a new interest in Africa amongst the members of the National Association for the Advancement of Colored People. As the editorials of James Weldon Johnson in the Harlem *New York Age* indicated,[56] the

[51] B.T.W. Papers: Box 917, 1912 Conference, prospectus of Conference for Walters' paper.

[52] Walters, *Life*, op. cit. 257.

[53] In first paragraph of 'Forethought' in 1903 ed.: vii in New York, 1953, reprint.

[54] J.E.B. Papers: ALS. Ms. 235, 1492, letter of 25 March 1907, 'the Pan-African League Department of the Niagara Movement'. Cf. Casely Hayford, op. cit. 179.

[55] *Atlantic Monthly* May, 1915, 711.

[56] James Weldon Johnson Collection, Yale University, Scrapbook X, see especially clippings for 7 Dec. 1918, and 11 Jan. and 8 Feb. 1919.

Negro in the United States felt that the 1914–18 War was crucial in his own struggle for greater civil rights. Africa and America joined hands. When James Weldon Johnson in a 1919 N.A.A.C.P. pamphlet, *Africa in the World Democracy*, contributed an essay on 'Africa at the Peace Table' and declared that 'Self-determination will be secured only by those who are in a position to force it',[57] he was speaking not only to the African in Africa but also—and perhaps primarily—to the Negro in America.

The association of these two motives was seen after the War when the N.A.A.C.P. sent Du Bois to Europe to collect material for a history of the Negro's part in the War and to call, if possible, a Pan-African Congress.[58] Out of this visit came Du Bois's ambitious plan, which the N.A.A.C.P. backed, for the internationalization of a great belt of Central African territory which would, in some measure, it was hoped, make up for the mistakes of the Scramble for Africa.[59]

Du Bois and James Weldon Johnson were not alone in their eloquence on the significance of the first World War for Africans. The Negro scholar, Benjamin Brawley, in his 1918 *Africa and the War* claimed that: 'The great war of our day is to determine the future of the Negro in the World. Alsace-Lorraine, Belgium, the Balkans, and even Russia all become second in importance.'[60] L. G. Jordan, Foreign Mission Secretary of the Negro American National Baptist Convention and mentor of John Chilembwe, leader of the Nyasaland Native Rising of 1915, rose to even more bitter heights of eloquence:

With 600,000 Africans fighting in the trenches with the allies and an equal number in arms in various parts of Africa under governments who have taken over the continent, it can never be hoped to again make the African a docile creature, to be dumb driven like a brute, which his oppressors have been 100 years or more in the making.[61]

[57] Op. cit., 15.
[58] Francis L. Broderick, *W. E. B. Du Bois* (Stanford, 1959), 129.
[59] Cf. Kelly Miller, 'The German Colonies', *Southern Workman* (1919), 52–3.
[60] (New York, 1918), preface, p. i.
[61] Lewis Garnett Jordan, *Pebbles from an African Beach* (Philadelphia, 1918), 2.

How much such sentiments exercised a direct influence on
Africans is a matter for speculation, though it should be remembered that coloured American soldiers, through their contacts with French troops in Europe, may have helped to disseminate them.[62] Similarly, in the present state of research, one
can only speculate on the influence of the 1919 and 1921
Pan-African Congresses at which Du Bois and his Negro American colleagues associated with Blaise Diagne, the French
Senegalese deputy, on the emergence of the Mandates System.
Du Bois himself has claimed that:

> The Congress specifically asked that the German colonies be turned
> over to an international organization instead of being handled by the
> various colonial powers. Out of this idea came the Mandates Commis-
> sion.[63]

No speculation, however, is necessary about the influence on
emerging African nationalism of the cultural, as distinct from
the organizational side of Pan-Africanism: pan-Africanism with
a small rather than a large 'p'. Blyden, of course, was the pioneer
of the Negro history movement: the search for roots, often
romanticized, but a search which, without doubt, has brought
to the surface important elements in the Negro and African
past which the white investigator may easily overlook. Du Bois,
like Blyden, realized that such a movement was necessary to
bolster both Negro American and emergent African nationalist
self-esteem. To this end, he produced in 1915 his little Home
University volume, *The Negro*, the first of many books of its kind.
Yet, as Rayford W. Logan, Du Bois's associate in the early
post-1919 Pan-African movement has pointed out,[64] the popu-
larization of the study of the African past probably owes more to
one of the moving spirits of the Association for the Study of

---

[62] The problem of Negro American relations with French Africans is
almost completely unstudied.

[63] Du Bois, *World and Africa*, op. cit. 11. Cf. also Padmore, op. cit.
122–4; Rayford W. Logan, *The African Mandates in World Politics* (Washington, D.C., 1948), iv, 42; *League of Nations. Mandates. Second Pan-
African Congress. August–September, 1921*; George Louis Beer, *African
Questions at the Paris Peace Conference* (New York, 1923), 285–6.

[64] Rayford W. Logan, 'The American Negro's View of Africa', *Africa
Seen by American Negroes*, ed. John A. Davis (American Society of
African Culture, New York, 1958), 220.

Negro History and the founder of the *Journal of Negro History*, Carter G. Woodson, than to W. E. B. Du Bois. Woodson's papers in the Library of Congress reveal an intense interest amongst early African nationalists in his work.[65] Aggrey of Achimota, for example, spoke enthusiastically of the importance of Woodson's efforts.[66]

But, if Woodson's contributions to that essential part of any nationalist movement, the myth—in the widest sense—of its past, are as great or greater than Du Bois's own immense efforts, one other name, hitherto grossly neglected by almost all writers on Negro history, must be mentioned: John Edward Bruce (1856–1924),[67] a New York Negro journalist who formed with Arthur Schomburg in 1911 the Negro Society for Historical Research, which included amongst its original honorary presidents, vice-presidents and members, Lewanika of Barotseland, Blyden, Casely Hayford, and Duse Mohammed Effendi,[68] who became later one of the leading ideologists of the Garvey movement, to which Bruce himself subsequently gave his allegiance. Blyden, Hayford, Dube[69] and numerous other Africans who visited America or who wrote to Bruce, bear witness to his influence on their thought about the African past and their desire to gain from it a pride in their blackness. Bruce's own pride in his colour was shown when he acted as American agent for Casely Hayford's *Ethiopia Unbound*.[70] To Aggrey, Bruce was 'Daddy'.[71] Furthermore, he maintained close relations with

[65] E.g. C.G.W. Papers: Box 5—from Amanzimtoti Institute, Natal, 13 March, 1917; Box 6—from Kodwo Nsaaku, Gold Coast, 29 April and 21 July, 1923, from Casely Hayford, 15 June 1916, and 11 Nov. 1917, from D. E. Carney, Sierra Leone, 19 Jan. 1921, from W. Esuman-Awira Sekyi, Gold Coast, 14 Oct. 1920, from Dada Adeshigbin, Lagos, 10 Jan. 1917, from Majola Agbebi, Lagos, 5 July, 1916; Box 16—from Casely Hayford, 7 July 1923, and 4 Jan. 1924, from Dada Adeshigbin, 25 Sept. 1918; etc.

[66] C.G.W. Papers: Box 6—from Aggrey, 13 July, 1927.

[67] There is a biographical sketch in J.E.B. Papers; see also Ferris, op. cit. II, 862–3.

[68] Ferris, op. cit. II, 865. Cf. also C.G.W. Papers: Box 16—Bruce on Duse Mohammed, 25 Jan. 1922.

[69] Blyden, Hayford, Dube items are well indexed in J.E.B. Papers, Schomburg Collection, N.Y.: one interesting item in the Papers is a letter from James Cluny, Sierra Leone, to Blyden, 21 June, 1909, defending clithorodechtomy on 'nationalist' lines.

[70] Casely Hayford, *William Waddy Harris* (London, 1915), xi–xii.

[71] J.E.B. Papers: Aggrey to Bruce, 28 June 1922.

Majola Agbebi,[72] Baptist Yoruba founder of what has been called 'the first independent Native African church in West Africa',[73] who was introduced to Bruce by Blyden during a visit to America in 1903.[74] The importance in the development of West African nationalism of Agbebi's inaugural sermon to the 'African Church' in Lagos on 21 December 1902, has yet to be appreciated. Blyden believed that it showed that 'Africa is struggling for a separate personality'.[75] Bruce responded enthusiastically, too, and asked Agbebi's permission to publish it in a Negro American newspaper in a letter which shows that the African's address had drawn out of him the full sentiment of *négritude*: 'I am a negro and all negro. I am black all over, and proud of my beautiful black skin. . . .'[76] So enthusiastic was Bruce, that in 1907 he led a group of coloured Americans in New York, who sought to get 11 October observed each year by Negro Americans as 'Majola Agbebi Day',[77] 'to immortalize in him an African personality'. The very use of the last two words of this phrase suggests that the Ghanaian concept of 'African personality' and its corresponding idea of *négritude* have complicated origins in the commerce of ideas over many years amongst peoples of African descent on both sides of the Atlantic. An honourable place in this commerce must be found for George

[72] There is a brief reference to Agbebi's paper, 'The West African Problem' at the London 1911 First Universal Races Congress (in ed. G. Spiller, *Papers on Inter-Racial Problems*, London, 1911, 341–8) in Coleman, op. cit. 187. Agbebi remains, however, a neglected pioneer of Nigerian nationalism. In addition to the references below, see Ferris, op. cit. II, 822, 848; *Southern Workman*, 1896, 15; *An Account of Dr Majola Agbebi's Work in West Africa* (n.d.), copy in Howard University Library; *African Times and Orient Review* (London), Sept. 1912, 92, March 1914, 64; Majola Agbebi, *The Christian Handbook. New Calabar, West Africa* (n.d.), copy in Schomburg Collection, N.Y.; letters by and about M. Agbebi and his family in J.E.B. Papers, Schomburg Collection, N.Y. There is a photograph of Agbebi in Lewis G. Jordan, *Negro Baptist History, U.S.A.* (Nashville, Tenn., 1930).

[73] *African Times* (*London*), 5 July 1899, quoted in *Account of Dr Agbebi's Work*, op. cit.

[74] *Christian* (London), 27 Aug. 1903, quoted in *Account of Dr Agbebi's Work*, op. cit.

[75] Majola Agbebi, *Inaugural Sermon. Delivered at the Celebration of the First Anniversary of the 'African Church'*, Lagos, West Africa, December 21, 1902 (copy in Schomburg Collection, N.Y.), 17.

[76] Ibid. 27.

[77] J.E.B. Papers: A.L.S. Ms. 167 (1493); see also A.8. (1504), 27 Aug. 1907, Agbebi to Bruce.

W. Ellis, Negro American Secretary from 1901 to 1910 of the
United States Legation in Liberia, who took as the aim of his
pioneer study, *Negro Culture in West Africa* (New York, 1914),
in the words of Edward Blyden: 'To show the world—Africans
helping in the work—that the African has a culture of his own—
to explain that culture and to assist him to develop it.'[78]

A less militant figure than those which have been examined
must now be included in a brief examination of this commerce
of ideas: Booker T. Washington whose self-help, educational
ideal for coloured people had profound effects on African nationalism, particularly through its influence on Aggrey of
Achimota[79] and John L. Dube of the Ohlange Institute, Natal.[80]
(Not all the Negro American educationalists of the self-help
school, however, exercised a 'reformist', Booker-T.-Washington
kind of influence on their African charges, as the effects of the
militantly independent Principal of the Virginia Theological
Seminary and College at Lynchburg, Gregory Willis Hayes, on
John Chilembwe of Nyasaland indicate.) Sir Harry Johnston,
who visited the Hampton Institute and Booker T. Washington's
Tuskegee Institute when gathering material for his *The Negro in
the New World* (London, 1910), saw the influence of this
educational idea and claimed correctly that it would 'spread
"American" influence amongst the coloured peoples of the
world'.[81]

Booker T. Washington's interest in Africa has been disguised
by the juxtaposition of his ideas with those of W. E. B. Du Bois
in so many works on Negro American history.[82] The great
conference on Africa which he called at Tuskegee in 1912,[83]

[78] Title page.
[79] Edwin W. Smith, *Aggrey of Achimota* (London, 1929), 121.
[80] B.T.W. Papers: Box 1060, 1912 Scrapbook, cutting from *South Africa*,
16 March, 1912, and *The Trailer* (West Point, Pa.), 25 April 1912.
[81] 408. See also A. Victory Murray, *The School in the Rush* (London,
1929), 291–310.
[82] Blyden knew better: see his article, 'The Negro in the United States',
African Methodist Episcopal Church Review (Philadelphia, 1900), XVI,
330.
[83] C.G.W. Papers: Box 13, galley proof. B.T.W. Papers: Box 917, Miscellaneous Correspondence (1912), CL, Conference CZ; Box 1060, 1912
Scrapbook. *Southern Workman* (1912), 347–86. *African Times and Orient
Review* (London, 1912), I, 1, 9–12. Alfred Tildsley, *The Remarkable Work
of Dr. Mark Hayford* (London, 1926), 33.

although it followed in the line of descent of the 1895 Africa Conference at the Negro Gammon Theological Seminary, Atlanta, Georgia,[84] shows that Washington was no Negro American isolationist.[85] This is also clear from his interest in coloured American business ventures in Africa, a good example of which is the Africa Union Company,[86] a carefully organized scheme for promoting trade between Negro America and the Gold Coast that was destroyed by the 1914 War's interruption of Atlantic commerce. Casely Hayford, whose 1911 *Ethiopia Unbound* had been sceptical of Negro American interest in Africa, by 1914 was welcoming this coloured American enterprise.[87]

The failure of the Garvey movement in the 1920s[88] and the coming of the Depression forced the attention of most Negroes in the United States closely upon their own country. Yet, if there was a decline in interest in Africa, coloured American influence on emerging African nationalism did not cease. Negro American missionary activity, orthodox and unorthodox, continued to influence the African political scene.[89] Negro American schools and colleges still attracted increasing numbers of African students. As in the period before the first World War, this was one of the main ways in which Negro American ideas and methods of political organization entered Africa. This is obvious from the careers of Kwame Nkrumah, Nnamdi Azikiwe and Hastings

[84] *Africa and the American Negro*, ed. J. W. E. Bowen (Atlanta, Ga., 1896), passim.

[85] Cf. Washington's opposition to proposed 1915 U. S. Immigration Bill on the grounds that it was likely to keep out African students: B.T.W. Papers, Container 77, 1915.

[86] B.T.W. Papers: Personal Correspondence (Container 9), 1914–15, file on Africa Union Company; cf. 'Afro-Americans and the Gold Coast', *African Times and Orient Review* (London, 1914), 21 April, 99–100.

[87] Hayford, '. . . marks the beginning of a new era here in the Gold Coast': B.T.W. Papers, Personal Correspondence (Container 9), 1914–15, extract in letter of Charles W. Chapelle to J. L. Jones, 15 July 1914. Hayford's attitude seems to have changed at the time of the 1912 Tuskegee Africa Conference: see his letter to the Conference in C.G.W. Papers, Box 13, press release of 17 April 1912.

[88] See Cronon, op. cit. 138–69.

[89] See Wilbur C. Harr, *The Negro as an American Protestant Missionary in Africa* (Ph.D., University of Chicago, 1945); Shepperson and Price, op. cit. passim; C. P. Groves, *The Planting of Christianity in Africa* (London, 1958), IV, 62–3, 79–80, 113–14, 128–9, 187. See also ref. 6 above.

Kamazu Banda. Furthermore, in South and Central Africa a glorified image of the Negro American as the liberator of Africa from European imperialism developed between the 1920s when Aggrey visited Africa with the Phelps-Stokes Commission and was seen as the spearhead of a coloured American invasion of South Africa[90] to the 1947 Madagascar Rising, when the rumor spread that Negro American troops had arrived to bring arms to the insurgents. But, amongst the emerging African middle-class, a more compelling image of Negro America has probably been that of the *Ebony* magazine variety, with its emphasis on respectable achievement.[91] What influence this may have had on African nationalism is an open question: for Du Bois, certainly, it seemed at one time to show 'symptoms of following in the footsteps of western acquisitive society'.[92]

No nationalism draws its strength from outside sources primarily, though a period of exile—if only in Harlem, Chicago or a Negro American college—has been a recognized mechanism for the political education of nationalist leaders at least since the 1848 revolutions in Europe. These notes make no claim that Negro Americans have themselves played a primary organizational role in African politics. But from the beginnings of Du Bois's interest in Africa and the 1900 Pan-African Conference, through the George Padmore period of African nationalism, to the 1959 London Kenya conference at which Thurgood Marshall, N.A.A.C.P. lawyer, acted as an adviser to the African delegation, they often appear to have acted at least secondary or tertiary parts. A more reliable measurement must await further research into all the avenues—unofficial as well as official, minor as well as major—of both Negro American and African history.[93]

Even in the present state of pioneering investigation into these fields, one thing is clear: Negro Americans, in a complicated Atlantic triangle of influences, have played a considerable part

[90] E. W. Smith, op. cit. 181. See forthcoming paper, George Shepperson, 'Nyasaland and the Millennium', *Comparative Studies in Society and History;* R. L. Buell, op. cit. II, 603.

[91] Roi Ottley, *No Green Pastures* (London, 1952), 12.

[92] W. E. B. Du Bois, *In Battle for Peace* (New York, 1952), 154.

[93] Two useful guides to present-day Negro American interest in Africa are *Africa Seen by American Negroes*, op. cit. and Harold R. Isaacs, 'The American Negro and Africa: Some Notes', *Phylon* (Atlanta, Ga., 1959), XX, 3, 219–33.

ideologically in the emergence of African nationalism: in con-
ceptualization, evocation of attitudes and through the provision
of the raw material of history. If, today, the new African nations
may be said to be of more value to Negro America than Negro
America to them, this should not be allowed to conceal the
historical role of the coloured American in their emergence.

Victor H. Bernstein

Although a number of great victories have been won by
Negroes since the 1940s, the Negro community remains discontented and unsatisfied. The civil rights movement of "black
and white together" and "non-violent resistance" has just
about disintegrated. Black nationalism is the current fashion although it remains without a program or organization.
The Negro leaders who rose to prominence in the 1950s,
Martin Luther King, Jr., Bayard Rustin, James Farmer, Thurgood Marshall, Roy Wilkens, must now share the spotlight
with younger and more militant Negro spokesmen such as
Stokely Carmichael, LeRoi Jones, Cassius Clay, Floyd McKis-
sick, and the memory of Malcolm X. The malaise, especially
among youths in the ghettos, originates from the fact that
they have yet to benefit from the vaunted talk of civil rights
accomplishments. They are unable to overcome the slum-
lords, the Jim Crow unions, the exploitative shopkeepers, the
insensitive police forces, and the defeatist school officials. Employment has been the most frustrating problem Negroes face.
Here the civil rights movement has been weakest, and on this
point all talk of progress breaks down.

Looking back over the fifties and early sixties we see that
what the civil rights movement accomplished was the destruction of discriminatory barriers (housing excluded). Integration
was the key word. In Southern cities Negroes could now eat
and sleep in the facilities of their choice. Some universities
were opened to Negro students. Professional societies and
clubs were desegregated. These developments, however, were
of benefit mainly to the Negro middle class. For the working
class Negro the immediate question was putting food on the
table, keeping the white police off his back, improving the

quality of the local school, and keeping healthy. Little was done to solve these problems. Ralph Bunche foresaw in 1940 that the civil rights movement would divide over the issue of economics. The NAACP and the middle class have been strong on integration, weak on economic solutions. Bunche wrote: "The escape that the Negro mass seeks is one from economic deprivation, from destitution and imminent starvation. To these people, appealing for livelihood, the NAACP answers: give them educational facilities, let them sit next to whites in streetcars, restaurants, and theaters. They cry for bread and are offered political cake" (Wilson Record, *Race and Radicalism*).

The Negro in the ghetto sees that the present American political system is incapable of producing the jobs necessary to put bread on the table and to keep families together. Experts such as Herbert Hill, National Labor Secretary of the NAACP, have shown in countless studies the pattern of union discrimination against Negro job applicants. Daniel Moynihan and C. Eric Lincoln, building on the work of E. Franklin Frazier, have documented the extent of the disintegration of Negro families when employment cannot be found for the male of the family. Kenneth Clark in *Dark Ghetto* (1965) and Claude Brown in *Manchild in the Promised Land* (1966) have through sociology and autobiography given us a picture of what poverty does to people in the ghetto. Everyone speaks in terms of long-range solutions when millions must live from day to day. Before the riots of 1966 awakened America to the problem of the ghetto, James Baldwin had predicted what would occur. Yet nothing dramatic happened to curb economic deprivation except the Vietnam war, which skims off the cream of Negro unemployed into the armed forces. Meanwhile the country waits for its now annual summer of riots, and busily reinforces its frightened and nervous police forces. American leaders blame the disturbances on the heat, or on outside agitators, yet the riots continue to grow in intensity and volume. Young Negro intellectuals, who have already discarded Martin Luther King's *Stride Toward Freedom*, put down their copy of Malcolm X's Autobiography, and go out to seek the latest work of Frantz Fanon, whose *The Wretched of the Earth* may well be the revolutionary textbook of the 1970s.

Meanwhile, white Americans, frustrated by the protracted

Vietnam war, listen more and more to those politicians who declare that the answer to the Negro problem is stronger police measures. Both sides arm themselves, and it would be an optimist indeed who would be hopeful about the peaceful resolution of the racial conflict in the United States.

Victor H. Bernstein is the former Managing Editor of *The Nation*. His article, "Why Negroes Are Still Angry," which appeared in *Redbook Magazine*, skillfully summarizes the work of recent students on the racial problem today and accurately catches the angry mood of the Negro masses.

WHY NEGROES ARE STILL ANGRY

SOURCE: Victor H. Bernstein, "Why Negroes Are Still Angry," *Redbook Magazine* (July 1966), 54, 114-15, 121-23, 126-27.

Many people are saying that the civil rights movement is in a state of crisis. Some even say that success has spoiled it. I suggest that those who think this way exaggerate the success and misplace the crisis. Many of the movement's successes are more apparent than real. And the crisis exists not so much *in* the movement as outside it—among millions of white Americans who have always sympathized with the Negro, who still profess sympathy for him, but who today regard his continued militancy with increasing bafflement and resentment.

Even as this summer's White House Conference on Civil Rights makes news, some national polls reflect a spreading conviction among whites that Negroes are pushing too far too fast. More is involved in this change of attitude than the "white backlash" from the occasional outburst of racial violence. The civil rights movement has reached the point where it has taken up the slack of white tolerance and is beginning to tug hard at basic American institutions—schools, neighborhood patterns, the competitive job market. It doesn't cost anything to move up a few feet along a hamburger counter to make room for a Negro. But the cost—economic, social, psychological—of abolishing forever a Negro ghetto of half a million souls is only now becoming apparent.

White resentment of continued Negro pressure is intensified

by the evidence, plain to see, of the enormous strides made by many Negroes in recent years. As I write this a Negro has been appointed to the President's Cabinet, another to a state board of regents, a third (this one, unprecedently, a woman) to a federal judgeship—all within a single fortnight. On television, a Negro regularly broadcasts the late-evening news from New York and another Negro shares top billing on a weekly spy thriller. In a TV commercial a brewer shows a roomful of handsome colored people drinking his product; at least Negroes will agree that he is doing *something* right. In the world of books, opera and the theater, black Americans are getting to be as prominent as they long have been in sports and jazz.

Politics? In the office of the National Committee Against Discrimination in Housing, I chatted with Margaret Fisher, a Southern white woman who for more than a quarter of a century has devoted herself to civil rights causes. We talked of that distant day in Atlanta, Georgia, in the early 1940s when she guided me to various polling places around town so that I could report to my newspaper how Negro college teachers, some of them Ph.D.s, were banned from the ballot on the grounds of "illiteracy." Today, Miss Fisher reminded me, Georgia has more Negro state legislators than any state in the Union except Michigan. And in the Alabama and Texas primaries in May, Negroes succeeded in nominating 12 of their number to various offices. In Texas, three were nominated for the state legislature. In Alabama, nine ran highest in primary balloting.

There are many statistics to support a picture of Negro overall progress. In the years 1940 to 1960 the percentage of male Negro workers who follow professional, technical and kindred occupations has more than doubled; the percentage of clerks, salespeople and skilled workers has risen two and a half times. Today there are nearly 20 times as many Negro engineers in the United States as there were in 1940, six times as many chemists, more than three times as many accountants and auditors, twice as many lawyers and judges. In the years 1939 to 1964 the median wage of the Negro male worker rose more than sevenfold, that of the white only fivefold.

In the legal field the country has done more for its Negro citizens in the last decade than it did in the previous half century. The flood of legislation and court decisions, the proliferation of human-relations commissions at federal, state and local levels, make it appear that we have embarked on nothing less than a Second Reconstruction—a repetition of the years following the Civil War during which the North tried to smash forever the South's overpowering white power structure.

Judged by accepted American standards, who can deny that all this represents real and dramatic progress? Admittedly, there are areas in the Deep South where the Negro's situation is still intolerable, where the last to uphold the law are those who are sworn to do so. Everyone agrees that something must be done about this. But today most Negroes live in the North, where public accommodations have generally been open; where the Negro is not only free to vote but is constantly urged (and, like many whites, has sometimes secretly been paid) to vote; and where tens of thousands of Negro children go to school with white children.

What, then, many whites are asking, does the Negro want now—and especially the Northern Negro? That there be no Negro poor? But, they say, there are millions more white poor than Negro poor. That every Negro have a white neighbor? There must be something very wrong, say these whites, with people who don't want to live among their own. That every Negro child have white schoolmates? What an admission of racial inferiority! It is saying that a school in Nigeria, for instance, where there are no white children, can't ever attain acceptable standards of education.

And why all these laws on behalf of the Negro? Other minorities—the Irish, the Jews, the Italians—made it on their own; why can't the black man?

Questions like these are on the minds of millions of Americans. And they were on my mind as I discussed with Miss Fisher the clear evidence of Negro progress since the school desegregation decision of 1954.

"So far," Miss Fisher warned, "you've been looking at the top of the iceberg. It's about time you began to look underneath."

In my search for the undersides of the "iceberg" I talked to civil rights leaders, black and white, and read many of their books; I plowed through news clippings, magazine articles and official documents; and I renewed an old acquaintanceship with Harlem, or at least that part of it where I lived as a boy. It was not Harlem then; mine had been a quiet, lower-middle-class neighborhood, mostly Jewish but with an admixture of Irish. The nearest Negroes lived at least ten blocks away; today one would have to walk at least 20 blocks to find the home of the nearest whites. My family lived on the third floor of an old slightly shabby but still serviceable and clean apartment house. Five of us lived in seven rooms: three bedrooms, bathroom, kitchen, a "parlor" and a dining room. Today the apartment house has been made over into a rooming house. Seventeen people, including eight children, now occupy the space we five lived in more than 40 years ago.

I wanted very much to take a complete census of the old building, including the rats. There wasn't time; and there was no need, really. The building is one of tens of thousands just like it in ghettos spread over America, and what they add up to is becoming increasingly clear as sociologists, in behalf of the war on poverty, busily add up sums in human misery. Since Negroes are only one tenth of our population, it is not surprising that there are more poor whites than poor blacks. But the burden of this poverty is unequally shared to a shocking degree. Negro unemployment runs twice that of white; for males between the ages of 18 and 24 the ratio is five to one. And when the Negro male does have a job, his median income is barely more than half that of his white fellow worker. The rare Negro who completes four years of college can expect to earn only as much in his lifetime as a white man who has not gone beyond the eighth grade in grammar school. In Chicago, says Edwin Berry, of the National Urban League in that city, the white high-school dropout earns ten per cent more than the Negro college graduate.

Sargent Shriver, director of President Johnson's war on poverty, once defined as poverty-stricken any family whose food budget provided for no more than 22 cents per capita per meal. *In Negro families with children under 18 years of age, 62 per cent of all the children in these families are being raised in poverty under this definition.* If Mr. Shriver's allotment is raised by four cents to 26 cents, *81 per cent of these children are being raised in poverty.*

In the stultifying atmosphere of the ghetto, Negro family life is crumbling. Nearly a quarter of all urban Negro marriages are dissolved; nearly a quarter of all Negro families are headed by females—a mother, grandmother, aunt or older sister. *Nearly one Negro child in four is illegitimate;* in some areas in Harlem, the rate is closer to 50 per cent. (There are well-meaning partisans of the Negro cause who say that these illegitimacy rates are misleading in comparison with the relatively low white rates. "The rate of white sexual promiscuity," say these critics, "is hidden by the use of contraceptives, abortion, and births in private hospitals where illegitimacy can be effectively hidden." True, but what of it? The statistics show not that the Negro woman is more promiscuous than the white, but merely that through poverty and ignorance she more often has to pay the price.)

Against this background the Negro child plays out his tragic role. More than a third of all Negro children lack either a father or a mother living at home; the comparable figure for white children is one tenth. At the third grade in elementary school the median IQ for children from central Harlem is eight points below the city average; by the sixth grade the gap has widened to 13.5 (Reviewing these figures with me, Dr. Kenneth B. Clark, distinguished Negro social psychologist and director of the Social Dynamics Research Institute at New York's City College, asked pointedly: "Why should these children show a relative drop in IQ from the third to the sixth grades? Are our Harlem schools educating them or *dis*educating them?") Juvenile delinquency among Negroes runs two to three times higher than among whites in most of our great cities. At draft age, reports Daniel P. Moynihan, former Assistant Secretary of Labor and principal author of a controversial Labor Department document entitled *The Negro Family,* 56 per cent of Negro youths fail to pass the elementary Armed Forces Qualification Test; the comparable rate for white boys is 15 per cent.

In school desegregation, where the Negro has won an almost

unbroken series of legal and legislative victories, he has met with an equally unbroken series of practical setbacks. In the South, where by now nine of every ten school districts are "officially" desegregated, 84 per cent of Negro children still attend segregated schools. And in the North there are more segregated schools today than there were ten years ago. "Seventy-eight New York schools below high school became segregated between 1958 and 1963," Dr. Clark told me. The public-school systems of our great cities are becoming progressively Negrofied as black ghettos grow and more and more whites retreat to the suburbs. In Detroit, Cleveland and Philadelphia, from 40 to 60 per cent of all public-school children are Negro; in Chicago, the proportion is 48 per cent; in New York's borough of Manhattan, where Harlem is located, the proportion is 73 per cent. In ten years the proportion of Negro students in the public schools of the nation's capital rose from one third to more than three quarters.

Housing? Again the Negro victories have been in law, not in fact. John A. Morsell, associate director of the National Association for the Advancement of Colored People (N.A.A.C.P.), told me: "Despite all our laws, there's no place in the United States where you can say there is really an open housing market." Was this, perhaps, because the "open housing" laws are comparatively new and, like all "revolutionary" laws, must be given a reasonable time to take effect? Miss Fisher smiled when I put the question to her. Picking up a pamphlet from her desk, she riffled through it until she found what she wanted. "Let me read you something," she said. "*'All citizens of the United States shall have the same right, in every State and Territory, as is enjoyed by white citizens thereof to inherit, purchase, lease, sell, hold and convey real and personal property.'*" She put the booklet down. "That," she said, "is from the text of the Federal Civil Rights Act of 1866—and it has never been repealed."

Law is only a promise; fulfillment lies in enforcement. The Negro masses have learned that a vast gap often exists between the two. The entire federal housing and urban renewal program is designed, on paper, to encourage integrated housing. Yet in Danbury, Connecticut, the small city near which I live, the following has taken place: (a) Negro families rendered homeless by federally financed slum clearance were never properly relocated; (b) the only land so far allotted to badly needed low-income public housing lies next to the municipal sewage plant—and even this has been held up for nearly three years now by a court suit brought by whites who don't want Negroes in their neighborhood; (c) with other sites available for low-income public housing, the city administration has decided instead to use federal funds for housing for the elderly (in which, no doubt, one or two Negro couples will be installed to satisfy federal nondiscrimination requirements).

The situation in this Connecticut town is duplicated many times over throughout the country. It is no wonder that so many Negro intellectuals like James Baldwin savagely denounce the white power structure as incapable of giving the black minority the justice it is demanding. Baldwin, in his anger, speaks for millions of Negroes who have never read his books, who may never even have heard of him. And the restiveness of the Negro masses has had its effect on many hitherto moderate civil rights spokesmen who have always believed, and would like to continue to believe, that justice for the Negro must and will come through the cooperation of the whites. Today they are forced to echo Gandhi: "There go my people; I must catch them, for I am their leader."

"The most difficult fact for white Americans to understand," notes Mr. Moynihan in the U. S. Labor Department document *The Negro Family,* "is that . . . the circumstances of the Negro American community in recent years have probably been getting *worse,* not *better.*" Does this mean that the so-called Negro revolution that began in 1954 with the Supreme Court decision on public schools has been in vain? Were the Freedom Rides, the sit-ins, the marches, the bombed churches and murdered children—were they for nothing? Were the score of persons, most of them Negroes, who died last year in racial strife martyrs to a doomed cause?

I posed the question to several persons, among them Henry Schwarzschild, executive secretary of the Lawyers Constitutional Defense Committee, which provides legal defense for civil rights workers and is a cooperative effort of the N.A.A.C.P., the Congress of Racial Equality (CORE), the Student Non-Violent

Coordinating Committee (SNICK) and other interested organizations.

"The civil rights movement has accomplished two things since 1954," said Mr. Schwarzschild. "First, through court decisions and legislation it has succeeded in destroying the legal institutions, upholding segregation; the courts will no longer uphold a race law. Second, it has awakened the Negro masses to a sense of their power potential. Indeed, one can argue that the Negro revolution dates back not to the 1954 Supreme Court decision that separate schools mean unequal schools, but to the decision of a Negro housewife not to yield her bus seat to a white man in Montgomery, Alabama, in 1955. Mrs. Rosa Parks's act of defiance, followed by the bus boycott that the Reverend Martin Luther King organized, taught Negro Americans that they were not forever doomed to be the *objects* of law. Given the opportunity, they could *make* law."

What the Negro needs now, Mr. Schwarzschild continued, is an economic and political power base from which he can operate effectively. "This presents a much more complex problem," he said, "than opening a park, a beach or a lunchroom to a Negro. What some of us call 'hamburger integration' was never, in itself, an important objective; the civil rights movement fought so hard for it because of its importance as a symbol of the dignity of the black man and of the rights of all men. Now the thrust of the movement must be in the direction of education, jobs, housing—curing the whole pathology of the ghetto. And because the solution to these complex problems may involve readjustment of the American socioeconomic structure, the whites are beginning to feel fearful—and resentful."

Charles E. Silberman, author of *Crisis in Black and White,* developed the thesis in another direction. "Ten years ago," he told me, "the Negro was seeking equality of opportunity. Today he is seeking equality of *results.* And this is where he is finding himself in trouble. For most Negroes lack the education and skills necessary to exploit the opportunities given them. This is not their fault; it is the inevitable outcome of three centuries of oppression and denial.

"The truth is that today there is not one Negro problem, but two—the white man's Negro problem and the Negro's Negro problem. The old-line civil rights leaders have been overrating what the whites can do for the Negro and underrating what the Negro can and must do for himself. Negro backwardness, Negro apathy—these are the Negro's problem. And I blame the old-line Negro leadership, which still looks to a white minority for its chief support instead of to the majority of blacks. Most of the time, Negro leaders are talking with their backs to their own people."

"You sound like a Black Muslim," I said.

"Don't underestimate the Black Muslims," Mr. Silberman retorted. "They get their people *involved*. Have you ever seen the young men who used to gather around Malcolm X in the Muslim restaurant in Harlem? Slim, well-dressed, shoes shined, courteous—ironically, the very embodiment of the white, middle-class ideal they profess to hate so much. They were imbued with a pride, a self-respect, not shared by many of their Harlem brethren.

"Of course, their goal, a Negro nation on sequestered American soil, is sheer madness; they have made a farrago of something they call the Moslem religion; implicit in their program is the ultimate threat of violence; far from fighting racism, they have simply turned it against whites. But when Malcolm X told his Muslim brothers that 'we can't change the white man's image of the black man until we change our image of ourselves,' he was speaking a profound psychological truth.

"This does not mean that the white man is not responsible for the Negro's image of himself and for his social and economic plight. Considering what our society has inflicted on Negroes, merely that they endured is marvel enough. And certainly," Mr. Silberman continued, "the Negro cannot right these wrongs by himself: it is still very much a white man's Negro problem. Some sociologists say the Negro is simply a new 'immigrant' to our cities and given time, will adapt himself just as the Irish, Italian, and Jewish immigrants adapted themselves to our culture. I disagree. For one thing, the great European migrations to this country came when there were tremendous shortages of unskilled labor, so that the newcomers could find jobs; today the demand is increasingly for skilled labor, which the Negro is in no position yet to supply. But beyond this is the central fact of skin color. The white man's ethnic and religious background is lost in a crowd; the Negro can never lay down what our society has proclaimed to be his cross."

Because the whites have burdened the Negro with the cross, the civil rights movement argues, they must go out of their way to lift it from him. So the movement has come to a relatively new concept: Not equal, but preferential, treatment is now appropriate. When jobs open or promotion is possible or scholarships are available, the Negro applicant should get preference—even at the cost of stretching the "merit" principle. This is doubly essential, it is argued, because the menial tasks to which the Negroes have been restricted for so long are now disappearing with the advance of automation. How can a man keep up with the pack in a 100-yard dash if he has to start ten yards behind the others?

This marks an odd turn in the evolution of civil rights concepts. Where once proponents of the Negro cause argued for a *color-blind* society, where all men would be treated alike regardless of color, they are now arguing for a more *color-conscious* society—at least temporarily. "Remember," they seem to be saying to the employer, the educator, the government official, "this man is black. He has for so long been the *victim* of special treatment that he now deserves to be its *beneficiary*." Thus the birth of the phrase "benign quota," representing the civil rights movement's demand on employers and institutions that they go out of their way to employ, or to involve, a reasonable number of Negroes.

It is difficult to deny the justice of this argument, yet it is a prickly one for whites to accept—and especially well-meaning whites who have never knowingly discriminated against the Negro. "Why should I have to pay for other people's prejudices?" they ask. "Why should a Negro be favored over me for a job, a promotion, an apartment, because of what the slave owners or the Ku Klux Klan or white supremacists did, or are doing, to the black people? If the Negro has to climb over someone to take his rightful place in society, let him do it over those who have injured him—not over me."

But it is one of the tenets of democracy that each individual must share in a collective responsibility for the kind of society in which he lives. The Negro might say to the fair-minded white: "You have never done anything *against* me; but have you ever done anything *for* me?" And he might recall Edmund Burke's words of a long time ago: "The only thing necessary for the triumph of evil is that good men do nothing."

Integration has always been the key word in the lexicon of the civil rights movement. "In the context of race," Dr. Clark says, "the integrated society is one in which color is no longer a factor in determining a person's job, education, place of residence or social milieu. Though certain Negro intellectuals, such as James Baldwin and LeRoi Jones, have no wish to integrate with a white society they feel is itself disintegrating, most spokesmen for civil rights agree that integration is still the ultimate goal. But integration in which direction first? And at what speed? The public schools in big-city ghettos? There is growing opposition by thoughtful leaders to the idea that immediate and total integration in public schools is feasible, whether by busing white children to ghetto schools or by other methods.

"This type of wholesale, forced integration," Dr. Clark impressed upon me, "will only drive more whites out into the suburbs. In the minds of the white middle class, inferior schools and Negroes go together—and unhappily, in schools such as we find in Harlem they *do* go together. Ghetto schools are inferior because the children in them are treated as if they are uneducable, and children treated that way inevitably become uneducable.

"Busing is needful in certain situations, but even more needful is quality education in the ghetto schools—better teachers, better methods and, most important, a conviction of the teachability of the Negro child. Pilot programs have shown repeatedly that when properly taught, 'culturally deprived' children—whether black or white—can learn as rapidly as more advantaged children. The trouble is that pilot programs are begun, completed and then forgotten. No school system ever seems willing to apply the lessons of its own successful experiments.

"Once white parents are convinced that schools in which Negroes predominate are not inferior, but actually superior, they will stop running away, and the necessary conditions for genuine integration will exist."

One way to abolish the ghetto school, of course, is to abolish the ghetto. I spoke with Mrs. Constance Baker Motley in her office as Borough President of Manhattan (it is becoming traditional in New York that this office be held by a Negro). Harlem is in her bailiwick. "The way to abolish an urban ghetto," she told me, "is not to drive the Negroes out but to pull whites in. Let's erect important city institutions in Harlem, put up industrial and office buildings, diversify the area in such a way as to make it as essential as any other to the total operations of the city." A few days before I saw her, Mrs. Motley had been nominated by President Johnson to become the first Negro woman to occupy a federal judgeship. Perhaps her greatest legacy as Manhattan's borough president may be a blueprint for a new Harlem that will one day emerge from the drawing board.

A new emphasis on economics, decent living conditions and political power is discernible in many quarters of the movement. Dr. Martin Luther King, who for more than ten years worked to desegregate parks, buses, bus terminals and restaurants, is today more interested in getting out the Negro vote and in improving Negro slums.

A similar switch has occurred in CORE and SNICK, so long identified with sit-ins and Freedom Rides in behalf of the integration of public accommodations. The switch cannot entirely be accounted for by the legal victories obtained in the field of public accommodations; *de facto,* this battle has been far from won in many parts of the South, no matter what the law says.

I spoke to Elizabeth Sutherland, head of the New York office of SNICK. "We're in politics now," she said. To SNICK, politics isn't quite what it is to a politician; rather, it consists of an abiding faith in the ability of the poor and uneducated to govern themselves, and in an untiring search for ways to inspire them to do so. Two years ago, working alongside CORE and other groups, SNICK helped to create the Mississippi Freedom

Democratic Party, designed to pressure the state's regular Democratic party into accepting genuine integration. Today, according to Miss Sutherland, it is seeking to build in Alabama what amounts to an independent all-Negro Black Panther Party—in practice, if not in principle, a Jim Crow party in reverse.

"The BPP won't elect a president in 1968," said Miss Sutherland, "or even a governor. But there are many counties where the Negro vote can outnumber the whites. Negroes will have a chance to elect decent county officials, including sheriffs, and to win representation on county agricultural committees, which are extremely important to farmers and sharecroppers."

I have already noted the remarkable growth of color consciousness among organizations originally dedicated to the idea of the color-blind society. In SNICK and CORE, this phenomenon has affected even their interior organization. A writer friendly to SNICK notes that many of its Negro staff members are demanding that their organization be "black-led, black-controlled and black-dominated." James Farmer, for many years head of CORE, tells of how he avoided a racial floor fight in his organization by persuading a white coworker—"a brilliant and dedicated man," according to Mr. Farmer—not to run against a Negro for CORE's national chairmanship. In his recent book, *Freedom—When?*, he speaks of a "mood ebony" that has overtaken many Negro civil rights workers, and explains it as a result of the Negroes' desire to get out, at long last, from under white leadership. And speaking for CORE, he adds bluntly: "We want outside help, not outside advice."

Is integration really furthered by driving whites into subordinate positions in civil rights organizations? It almost seems a contradiction in terms. On the other hand, there are Negroes— and whites too—who are convinced that the black man must stand on his own feet before he will have the strength to stand as an equal alongside the white.

SNICK, especially, is an abrasive force in the civil rights movement. Although nonviolent, it is revolutionary, at least in theory; it is contemptuous of the middle-class main stream of American life. But it also realizes that neither the temper of the country nor the nature of its own organization is conducive to revolution. It is so determinedly democratic that it frowns upon leadership, even its own; and whoever heard of revolution without revolutionary discipline? "I admit the anomaly," said Miss Sutherland. "Here we are, dedicated to the demechanization of society, to the elevation of the worth of the individual, trying to build political parties and trade unions—which are nothing if they are not machines."

But anomalies will not stop the militants of CORE and SNICK and the N.A.A.C.P. And in the end their greatest monument is not likely to be revolution, or even new and ground-breaking legislation; their monument will be people in motion—especially the black poor of the South who for so long have been thought crushed beyond all possibility of movement. And it will not diminish the achievement if the motion proves to be, as is most likely, in less revolutionary directions than SNICK, at least, would like.

For more than threescore years the N.A.A.C.P., oldest, largest and in many ways most influential organization in its field, has been the weather vane, more or less, of the civil rights movement. I presented John A. Morsell, associate director, with a long list of questions on the past and on the immediate future of his organization and of the movement.

Employment of Negroes? "Better, but not good enough. Something should be done to get labor to revise its attitudes toward Negroes, particularly in the building trades."

Progress in school integration? "Good in the border states, spotty in the North and nil to token in the Deep South."

Voting? "Principally a problem of educating the low-income groups, especially in the South."

Housing? "The most difficult of all problems, showing the least progress."

Does the movement seek more law or better enforcement of existing law? "Both, with perhaps the greater emphasis on enforcement. But obviously the wanton killing of civil rights workers in the South must be made a federal crime—the crime of murder—and we must figure out a way to select fair juries. On housing, the executive branch of the government has the power, if it is willing to use it, to stop major lines of credit to anyone who wants to build segregated housing."

Have street demonstrations outlived their usefulness? "Through repetition they have lost some effect. But they can still be useful when the goal is clear and relevant. Boycotts are especially effective in local situations, but only where one is certain that there is sufficient support. You don't get a merchant to hire Negroes just by waving a placard in front of a TV camera."

Has the civil rights movement gained or lost support among whites recently? "I've no doubt riots alienate whites. But I suppose the biggest factor is the tendency of people to think that a problem is solved when a law is passed." Did Dr. Morsell agree with those who say that the civil rights movement has placed too much reliance on liberal whites who cannot be relied upon in times of crisis? "There are plenty of Negroes who can't be relied upon in times of crisis. We need more support from liberal whites, not less."

We talked of the future. Dr. Morsell gave no indication of any drastic change in N.A.A.C.P. strategy. "There will be shifts in emphasis as occasion requires," he said. "Jobs, housing, the vote, education—these are primary concerns for the whole movement, as well as for ourselves. We will continue to use the tactics that have served us well in the past. Of course, it is important for us to involve as large a segment of the Negro masses as possible. We haven't been altogether remiss in that respect."

There is a solidity, a reasonableness, a conservatism, about the N.A.A.C.P., as there is about the National Urban League, that is reassuring to the solid and reasonable middle-class visitor. But are these the qualities the Negro American community as a whole is looking for in its leaders? It depends, I think, on how resistant the white majority in this country will prove to the further progress demanded by the Negro.

A clear indication of this is found in the attitude of the Urban League, which has always been the most conservative of the civil rights bodies and the most deeply rooted in middle-class mores. Today Whitney M. Young, Jr., the league's executive director, warns:

"We are not free of the possibility of riots this summer. The ingredients that precipitated past riots are still here, and among Negroes there is more impatience, a greater anger. They are upset that along about every spring there's a great flurry of activity to produce something for the summer to 'keep it cool.' But it appears to them that the powers-that-be are more interested in peace and order than they are in the promotion of justice and equal opportunity."

Other Negro leaders phrase their warnings more militantly. A Negro friend who is a CORE activist in the Boston area told me: "You whites have the answer to violence, not us. Will whites stop killing civil rights workers? Will white cops start treating Negroes as human beings? Will white employers give us a decent break on decent jobs? Will something meaningful be done about Negro schools and slums? Give me your answers and I'll tell you whether the riots in Watts can be put down as past history or as a model for history to come."

These questions, welling up as they do from the Negro's profound sense of frustration, have a point. I quote a paragraph from the preface of a collection of essays entitled *What the Negro Wants:* "Race relations in the United States are more strained than they have been in many years. Negroes are disturbed by the continued denial of what they consider to be their legitimate aspirations and by slow, grudging grant of a few concessions. White Americans express alarm at what they call the excessive insistence by Negroes upon a too rapid change in the *status quo.* Serious riots have broken out in both Northern and Southern cities. . . ."

This was written not last year, nor the year before, but in 1944 —22 years ago. Will the time ever come for the Negro when the more things change, the more they *won't* remain the same? The answer, say the Negroes, is up to the white Americans; the crisis is theirs, not the civil rights movement's.

If there is no crisis in the civil rights movement, there is undeniably much soul-searching. Should the movement now concentrate on housing? Schools? Jobs? Political action? Should the race problem be considered as something unique, or simply as another facet of the great social ills of our time: poverty, ignorance, alienation, the chaos of our exploding cities? There is even debate on whether integration is the goal or merely the means to a goal. Should Negroes seek a place in the melting pot or should they insist on remaining Negroes, equal as citizens but deliberately nourishing their own cultural heritage? Jimmy Brown, the great Negro football player, has said that he doesn't want to live among whites but demands the right to do so if he chooses. Is it, then, not integration that the Negro should seek but *the right to freedom of choice?*

Most of these questions the Negro must answer for himself; he must establish his own identity. But it is natural for me, as a member of the white majority, to hope that whatever his goals, the Negro will be patient and reasonable in pressing for them. *Were I a Negro, however, I am certain that I would not always have the patience to be reasonable, or always have reason to be patient.* Between the attitudes of white man and black lies an abyss that good will alone cannot bridge. But there is evidence that law, properly enforced, can furnish the bridge. *Law changes attitudes,* according to Paul B. Sheatsley, of the National Opinion Research Center at the University of Chicago. In 1956, when the school desegregation decision was only two years old, not more than 12 per cent of Southern parents favored school desegregation. By 1963 the figure had climbed to 30 per cent. Today it is better than 50 per cent.

Speaking not as a civil rights polemicist but as a social scientist dedicated to the analysis of statistical tables, Mr. Sheatsley says flatly: "The mass of white Americans are engaged in the painful task of adjusting to an integrated society. It will not be easy for most, but one cannot at this date doubt the basic commitment. In their hearts they know that the American Negro is right." Then when, the Negro asks, will so many whites stop acting as if he were wrong?

BIBLIOGRAPHY

Books

Ajayi, J. F. A. *Christian Missions in Nigeria, 1841–1891.* London, 1965.

Anene, J. C. *Africa in the Nineteenth and Twentieth Centuries.* London, 1966.

—— *Southern Nigeria in Transition, 1885–1906.* Cambridge, England, 1965.

Aptheker, Herbert, ed. *A Documentary History of the Negro People in the United States.* (2 vols.) New York, 1951.

Baldwin, James. *Go Tell It on the Mountain.* New York, 1953.

Bancroft, Frederic. *Slave-Trading in the Old South.* Baltimore, 1931.

Barraclough, Geoffrey. *An Introduction to Contemporary History.* (rev. ed.) New York, 1966.

Beard, Charles and Mary R. *The Rise of American Civilization,* vol. 2. New York, 1927.

Bone, Robert. *The Negro Novel in America.* New Haven, 1965.

Boorstin, Daniel. *The Americans: The Colonial Experience.* Chicago, 1958.

Bovill, E. W., *Caravans of the Old Sahara.* London, 1933.

—— *The Golden Trade of the Moors.* London, 1958.

Boxer, Charles R. *Race Relations in the Portuguese Colonial Empire, 1415–1825.* London, 1963.

Broderick, Francis L. *W. E. B. Du Bois: Negro Leader in a Time of Crisis.* Stanford, 1959.

Brown, Claude. *Manchild in the Promised Land.* New York, 1966.

Brown, William Wells. *The Negro in the American Rebellion, 1867.* Boston, 1867.

Bruchey, Stuart. *Cotton and the Growth of the American Economy, 1790–1860.* New York, 1967.

Chesnutt, Charles. *The Marrow of Tradition.* Boston, 1901.

Clapperton, Hugh. *Journal of Second Expedition into the Interior of Africa from the Bight of Benin to Sokoto.* London, 1829.

Clark, Kenneth B. *Dark Ghetto.* New York, 1965.

—— *Prejudice and Your Child.* Boston, 1963.

Cornish, Dudley T. *The Sable Arm: Negro Troops in the Union Army, 1861–1865.* New York, 1956.

Coulter, E. M. *The South During Reconstruction, 1865–77.* Louisiana, 1947.

Craven, Avery. *The Coming of the Civil War.* Chicago, 1942.

—— *The Repressible Conflict.* Baton Rouge, 1939.

Cronon, E. David. *Black Moses: The Story of Marcus Garvey and the Universal Negro Improvement Association.* Madison, 1955.

Curtin, Philip D. *African History.* New York, 1964.

—— *The Image of Africa, British Ideas and Action, 1780–1850.* Madison, 1964.

Davidson, Basil. *The African Past.* Boston, 1964.

—— *The Lost Cities of Africa.* Boston, 1959.

—— *Black Mother.* London, 1961.

Davis, David B. *The Problem of Slavery in Western Culture.* New York, 1966.

Degler, Carl. *Out of Our Past: The Forces That Shaped Modern America.* New York, 1959.

Dike, K. O. *Trade and Politics in the Niger Delta, 1830–1855.* Oxford, 1956.

Donald, David. *Lincoln Reconsidered: Essays on the Civil War Era.* New York, 1956.

Donnan, Elizabeth. *Documents Illustrative of the History of the Slave Trade to America.* (4 vols.) Washington, D.C., 1930.

Douglass, Frederick. *The Life and Times of Frederick Douglass.* Hartford, 1881.

Drake, St. Clair and Horace R. Cayton. *Black Metropolis.* London, 1946.

Duberman, Martin. *The Antislavery Vanguard.* Princeton, 1965.

Du Bois, W. E. B. *Black Reconstruction in America.* New York, 1935.

—— *Dusk of Dawn: An Essay Toward an Autobiography of a Race Concept.* New York, 1940.

—— *The Souls of Black Folk.* Chicago, 1903.

Dunbar, Paul Laurence. *The Sport of the Gods.* New York, 1902.

Elkins, Stanley M. *Slavery: A Problem in American Institutional and Intellectual Life.* Chicago, 1959.

Essien-Udom, E. U. *Black Nationalism.* Chicago, 1962.

Fanon, Frantz. *The Wretched of the Earth.* New York, 1965.

Foner, Philip S. *The Life and Writings of Frederick Douglass.* (4 vols.) New York, 1950–55.

Franklin, John Hope. *The Emancipation Proclamation.* New York, 1963.

—— *From Slavery to Freedom: A History of American Negroes.* New York, 1967.

—— *The Militant South, 1800–1861.* Cambridge, England, 1956.

—— *Reconstruction After the Civil War.* Chicago, 1961.

Frazier, E. F. *Black Bourgeoisie.* New York, 1955.

—— *The Free Negro Family: A Study of Family Origins Before the Civil War.* Nashville, 1932.

—— *The Negro Family in the United States.* Chicago, 1949.

Freyre, Gilberto. *The Masters and the Slaves.* New York, 1946.

Gara, Larry. *The Liberty Line: The Legend of the Underground Railroad.* Louisville, 1961.

Garvey, Amy Jacques, ed. *Philosophy and Opinions of Marcus Garvey of Africa for the Africans.* New York, 1923.

Gossett, Thomas F. *Race: The History of An Idea in America.* Dallas, 1963.

Gray, L. C. *History of Agriculture in the Southern United States to 1860.* Washington, D.C., 1933.

Harris, Marvin. *Patterns of Race in the Americas.* New York, 1964.

Herskovits, Melville J. *Myth of the Negro Past.* New York, 1941.

Hodgkin, Thomas. *Nigerian Perspectives.* New York, 1960.

Hofstadter, Richard. *The American Political Tradition.* New York, 1948.

Hopkins, Pauline. *Lillian Simmons.* Boston, 1915.

Isaacs, Harold R. *The New World of Negro Americans.* New York, 1963.

Jensen, Merrill. *The New Nation.* New York, 1950.

Johnson, James Weldon. *Along This Way.* New York, 1935.

—— *Black Manhattan.* New York, 1930.

King, Martin Luther. *Strength to Love.* New York, 1963.

—— *Stride Toward Freedom.* New York, 1958.

—— *Why We Can't Wait.* New York, 1964.

Klein, Herbert S. *Slavery in the Americas.* Chicago, 1966.

Lewis, Anthony. *Gideon's Trumpet.* New York, 1964.

—— *Portrait of a Decade.* New York, 1964.

Lincoln, C. Eric. *The Black Muslims in America.* Boston, 1961.

—— *My Face Is Black.* Boston, 1964.

Litwack, Leon F. *North of Slavery, the Negro in the Free States, 1790–1860.* Chicago, 1961.

Logan, Rayford. *The Negro in American Life and Thought: The Nadir, 1877–1901.* New York, 1954.

Lynd, Staughton. *Antifederalism in Dutchess County.* New York, 1962.

—— ed. *Nonviolence in America.* New York, 1965.

Malcolm X. *Autobiography of Malcolm X.* New York, 1965.

McColley, Robert. *Slavery and Jeffersonian Virginia.* Urbana, Illinois, 1964.

McKay, Claude. *Selected Poems of Claude McKay.* New York, 1917.

McPherson, James M. *The Negro's Civil War: How American Negroes Felt and Acted During the War for the Union.* New York, 1965.

—— *The Struggle for Equality: Abolitionists and the Negro in the Civil War and Reconstruction.* Princeton, 1964.

Meier, August. *Negro Thought in America, 1880–1915.* Ann Arbor, 1963.

—— and Broderick, Francis L., eds. *Negro Protest Thought in the Twentieth Century.* Indiana, 1965.

—— and Rudwick, Eliott M., *From Plantation to Ghetto.* New York, 1966.

Mitchell, Margaret. *Gone With the Wind,* 4th ed. New York, 1938.

Morison, Samuel Eliot and Henry Steele Commager. *The Growth of the American Republic.* New York, 1950.

Myrdal, Gunnar. *An American Dilemma.* New York, 1944.

Nell, William C. *The Colored Patriots of the American Revolution.* Boston, 1855.

Nevins, Allan, ed. *America Through British Eyes,* revised and enlarged edition. New York, 1948.

—— *Ordeal of the Union.* New York, 1947.

Nkrumah, Kwame. *Autobiography of Kwame Nkrumah.* Edinburgh, 1957.

Nordholt, Schulte. *The People That Walk in Darkness.* New York, 1960.

North, Douglass C. *The Economic Growth of the United States.* New York, 1966.

Oliver, Roland. *The Dawn of African History.* New York, 1961.

Omer-Cooper, J. D. *The Zulu Aftermath.* Illinois, 1966.

Osofsky, Gilbert. *Harlem: The Making of a Ghetto.* New York, 1966.

Palmer, H. R. *Sudanese Memoirs.* Lagos, 1928.

Pease, William and Jane. *The Antislavery Argument.* Indiana, 1965.

Phillips, U. B. *American Negro Slavery.* New York, 1918.

—— *The Course of the South to Secession.* New York, 1939.

Quarles, Benjamin. *Frederick Douglass.* Washington, D.C., 1948.

—— *The Negro in the American Revolution.* Chapel Hill, 1961.

—— *The Negro in the Civil War.* Boston, 1953.

—— *Lincoln and the Negro.* New York, 1962.

Randall, James G. and Donald, David. *Civil War and Reconstruction*, 2nd ed. Boston, 1961.

Record, Wilson. *Race and Radicalism: The NAACP and the Communist Party in Conflict*. New York, 1964.

Reddick, Lawrence. *Crusader Without Violence: Martin Luther King, Jr.* New York, 1959.

Redding, Saunders. *Lonesome Road: The Story of the Negro in America*. New York, 1958.

Rose, Arnold M., ed. *Assuring Freedom to the Free*. Detroit, 1964.

Rotberg, Robert I. *Political History of Tropical Africa*. New York, 1965.

Schlesinger, Jr., Arthur M. *The Age of Jackson*. Boston, 1945.

—— *The Age of Roosevelt*. (3 vols.) Boston, 1959.

—— *A Thousand Days*. Boston, 1965.

Shepperson, George and Price, Thomas. *Independent African, John Chilembwe and the Origins, Settling and Significance of the Nyasaland Native Uprising of 1915*. Edinburgh, 1958.

Shugg, Roger W. *Origins of the Class Struggles in Louisiana*. Baton Rouge, 1939.

Simkins, Francis and Woody, Robert H. *South Carolina During Reconstruction*. Chapel Hill, 1932.

Stampp, Kenneth M. *The Era of Reconstruction*. New York, 1965.

—— *The Peculiar Institution*. New York, 1956.

Stanton, William R. *The Leopard's Spots: Scientific Attitudes Toward Race in America, 1815–1859*. Chicago, 1960.

Tannenbaum, Frank. *Slave and Citizen*. New York, 1946.

Taylor, A. A. *The Negro in South Carolina During the Reconstruction*. Washington, D.C., 1924.

—— *The Negro in Tennessee, 1865–1880*. Washington, D.C., 1941.

—— *The Negro in the Reconstruction of Virginia*. Washington, D.C., 1926.

Taylor, Joe Gray. *Negro Slavery in Louisiana*. Baton Rouge, 1963.

Tindall, George B. *South Carolina Negroes, 1877–1900*. Columbia, 1952.

Turner, Frederick Jackson. *The United States, 1830–1850*. New York, 1935.

Vansina, Jan. *Kingdoms of the Savanna*. Madison, 1965.

Verlinden, Charles. *L'Esclavage dans l'Europe Médiévale*. Brugge, De Tempel, 1955.

Wade, Richard C. *Slavery in the Cities: The South, 1820–1860*. New York, 1964.

Washington, Booker T. *Up From Slavery*. New York, 1901.

Wharton, Vernon L. *The Negro in Mississippi, 1865–1890*. Chapel Hill, 1942.

Williams, George Washington. *The History of the Negro Troops in the War of the Rebellion*. New York, 1888.

Williamson, Joel. *After Slavery, The Negro in South Carolina During Reconstruction, 1861–1877*. Chapel Hill, 1965.

Wilson, Joseph T. *The Black Phalanx: The History of the Negro Soldiers of the United States*. Hartford, 1888.

Wilson, Monica. *Reaction to Conquest*. London, 1936.

Wolfson, Freda. *Pageant of Ghana*. New York, 1958.

Woodson, Carter G. *A Century of Negro Migration*. Washington, D.C., 1918.

Woodward, C. Vann. *The Burden of Southern History*. Baton Rouge, 1960.

—— *Origins of the New South, 1877–1913*. Baton Rouge, 1951.

—— *Reunion and Reaction*. New York, 1951.

—— *The Strange Career of Jim Crow*. New York, 1955.

—— *Tom Watson, Agrarian Rebel*. New York, 1938.

Woodward, W. E. *Meet General Grant*. New York, 1928.

Wright, Richard. *Black Boy*. New York, 1944.

—— *Native Son*. New York, 1940.

Periodicals

Berger, Morroe. "The Black Muslims," *Horizon*. January, 1964.

Bernstein, Victor H. "Why Negroes Are Still Angry," *Redbook*. July, 1966.

Bond, Horace Mann. "Social and Economic Forces in Alabama Reconstruction," *Journal of Negro History*. July, 1938.

Cantor, Milton. "The Image of the Negro in Colonial Literature," *New England Quarterly*. December, 1963.

Degler, Carl. "Slavery and the Genesis of American Race Prejudice," *Comparative Studies in Society and History*, II. October, 1959.

Donald, David. "The Scalawag in Mississippi Reconstruction," *Journal of Southern History*, X. November, 1944.

Drimmer, Melvin. "Redirection in the Study of Slavery," *Phylon*, XXV. Fall, 1965.

Du Bois, W. E. B. "The African Roots of War," *Atlantic Monthly*. May, 1915.

—— "Reconstruction and Its Benefits," *American Historical Review*, XV. July, 1910.

Franklin, John Hope. "Pioneer Negro Historians," *Negro Digest*. February, 1966.

Goveia, Elsa. "Comment on 'Anglicanism, Catholicism and the Negro Slave,'" *Comparative Studies in Society and History*, VII. April, 1966.

Handlin, Oscar and Mary. "Origins of the Southern Labor System," *William and Mary Quarterly*, VII. April, 1950.

Jordan, Winthrop D. "Modern Tensions and the Origins of American Slavery," *Journal of Southern History*, XXVIII. February, 1962.

—— "The Influence of the West Indies on the Origins of New England Slavery," *William and Mary Quarterly*, XVIII. April, 1961.

Klein, Herbert S. "Anglicanism, Catholicism and the Negro Slave," *Comparative Studies in Society and History*, VII. April, 1966.

Lynd, Staughton. "On Turner, Beard and Slavery," *Journal of Negro History*, SLVIII. October, 1963.

—— "Slavery and the Founding Fathers." This paper was read at the meeting of the AHA in Washington, D.C., December, 1964.

Macrae, D. G. Review of *Slavery* by Stanley Elkins, *British Journal of Sociology*, XI. September, 1960.

Owsley, Frank L. "The Fundamental Cause of the Civil War: Egocentric Sectionalism," *Journal of Southern History*, VII. February, 1941.

Reddick, Lawrence. "A New Interpretation for Negro History," *Journal of Negro History*, XXII. January, 1937.

Rodney, Walter. "African Slavery and Other Forms of Social Oppression on the Upper Guinea Coast in the Context of the Atlantic Slave Trade," *Journal of African History*, VII. 1966.

Schlesinger, Jr., Arthur M. "The Causes of the Civil War: A Note on Historical Sentimentalism," *Partisan Review*, XVI. October, 1949.

Shepperson, George. "Notes on Negro American Influences on the Emergence of African Nationalism," *Journal of African History*, I. 1960.

Sio, Arnold A. "Interpretations of Slavery: The Slave Status in the Americas," *Comparative Studies in Society and History*, VII. April, 1965.

Stampp, Kenneth M. "The Historian and Southern Negro Slavery," *American Historical Review*, LVII. April, 1952.

Stone, I. F. "The Pilgrimage of Malcolm X," *New York Review of Books*, V. November 11, 1965.

Trevor-Roper, Hugh. "The Rise of Christian Europe," *The Listener*. November 28, 1963.

Woodson, Carter G. Review, *Mississippi Valley Historical Review*, V. March, 1919.

Woodward, C. Vann. "The Political Legacy of Reconstruction," *The Journal of Negro Education*, XXVI. Summer, 1957.

INDEX